Racial and Ethnic Groups

FIFTEENTH EDITION

Richard T. Schaefer
DePaul University

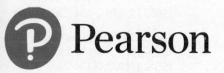
Pearson

330 Hudson Street, NY, NY 10013

Portfolio Manager: Jeff Marshall
Development Editor: Steven Rigolosi
Marketing Manager: Jeremy Intal
Program Manager: Erin Bosco
Project Coordination, Text Design, and Electronic Page Makeup: Integra-Chicago

Cover Designer: Jennifer Hart Design
Cover Photo: John Lund/Getty Images
Manufacturing Buyer: Mary Ann Gloriande
Printer/Binder: LSC Communications, Inc.
Cover Printer: Phoenix Color/Hagerstown

Library of Congress Cataloging-in-Publication Data

Names: Schaefer, Richard T., author.
Title: Racial and ethnic groups / Richard T. Schaefer.
Description: 15th edition. | Hoboken, N.J. : Pearson Higher Education, 2019.
  Identifiers: LCCN 2017029686 (print) | LCCN 2017030879 (ebook) |
  ISBN 9780134736525 (Revel) | ISBN 9780134732855 (hardcover) |
  ISBN 9780134736730 (softcover)
Subjects: LCSH: Minorities—United States. | United States—Ethnic relations.
  | United States--Race relations. | Prejudices—United States.
Classification: LCC E184.A1 (ebook) | LCC E184.A1 S3 2019 (print) | DDC
  305.800973—dc23
LC record available at https://lccn.loc.gov/2017029686

1 17

Rental Edition:
ISBN 10:   0-134-73285-5
ISBN 13: 978-0-134-73285-5

Revel Access Code:
ISBN 10:   0-134-73652-4
ISBN 13: 978-0-134-73652-5

Books á la Carte Edition:
ISBN 10:   0-134-73662-1
ISBN 13: 978-0-134-73662-4

Instructor's Review Copy:
ISBN 10:   0-134-73673-7
ISBN 13: 978-0-134-73673-0

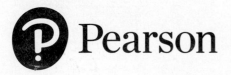

www.pearsonhighered.com

To my grandchildren, Matilda and Reuben,
may they grow to flourish
in our multicultural society

Brief Contents

Contents

Part II Ethnic and Religious Sources of Conflict

4 Immigration   78

5 Ethnicity, Whiteness, and Religion   103

Part III Major Racial and Ethnic Minority Groups in the United States

6 Native Americans: The First Americans   132

Part IV   Other Patterns of Dominance

15   Women: The Oppressed Majority   322

16   Beyond the United States:
The Comparative Perspective   344

17   Overcoming Exclusion   364

Features

Speaking Out

- "Problem of the Color Line," by W. E. B. Du Bois (Chapter 1)
- "What Can I Do at Work?" by Southern Poverty Law Center (Chapter 2)
- "The Conversation We're *Not* Having When We Talk About Affirmative Action," by Gail Christopher (Chapter 3)
- "My Parents Were Deported," by Diane Guerrero (Chapter 4)
- "The Next Americans," by Tomás Jiménez (Chapter 5)
- "Kinship in Modern Times," by Vi Waln (Chapter 6)
- "Olympic Athletes Who Took a Stand," by David Davis (Chapter 7)
- "Black Picket Fences," by Mary Pattillo (Chapter 8)
- "Reconciling Two Identities," by Rosie Molinary (Chapter 9)
- "Puerto Ricans Cannot Be Silenced," by Luis Gutierrez (Chapter 10)
- "May America Be True to Her Dream," by Nihad Awad (Chapter 11)
- "Recognizing Native Hawaiians," by Daniel Akaka (Chapter 12)
- "Statement on Liang Decision," Japanese American Citizens League (Chapter 13)
- "The Neighborhood as a Moral Obstacle Course," by Iddo Tavory (Chapter 14)
- "What Do Women and Men Want?" by Kathleen Gerson (Chapter 15)
- "Africa, It Is Ours!" by Nelson Mandela (Chapter 16)
- "My Journey into the Deaf World," by Erik Olin Wright (Chapter 17)

Relations Across Boundaries

- The Hopi and Navajo Peoples (Chapter 6)
- African Americans and the American Indians (Chapter 7)
- Immigrant Mexicans and U.S.-Born Mexicans (Chapter 10)
- Muslim, Arab, and Jewish Americans (Chapter 11)
- Black and Korean Americans (Chapter 12)

A Global View

- The Roma: A Thousand Years of Discrimination (Chapter 3)
- Immigration and South Africa (Chapter 4)
- Australia's Aboriginal People (Chapter 6)
- France Noire: Black France (Chapter 7)
- The Salvadoran Connection (Chapter 9)
- Muslims in France (Chapter 11)
- Argentina's Jewish Community (Chapter 14)
- Gender Inequality in Japan (Chapter 15)

Research Focus

- Multiracial Identity (Chapter 1)
- Virtual Prejudice and Anti-Prejudice (Chapter 2)
- The Sharing Economy—Another Way to Discriminate (Chapter 3)
- The Hispanic Dairyland (Chapter 4)
- Immigrants: Yesterday and Today (Chapter 5)
- Economic Impact of Casino Gambling (Chapter 6)
- Sundown Towns, USA (Chapter 7)
- Acting White (Chapter 8)
- English-Language Acquisition (Chapter 9)
- Mexican Hometown Associations (Chapter 10)
- Self-Identifying as "Arab American" (Chapter 11)
- Arranged Marriages in America (Chapter 12)
- Tiger Mothers (Chapter 13)
- Intermarriage: The Final Step to Assimilation? (Chapter 14)
- Men Doing Women's Work (Chapter 15)
- Intergroup Contact and South Africa (Chapter 16)
- The Three Maxes (Chapter 17)

Preface

The first two decades of the twenty-first century have witnessed significant social changes. The Latino population in the United States is now larger than the African American population, with the Asian Pacific American population growing faster than either. Meanwhile, White non-Hispanic youth have become a numerical minority when compared to other racial and ethnic groups. Alongside these demographic changes, a series of events have underscored the diversity of the American people.

People cheered on May 1, 2011, upon hearing that Osama bin Laden had been found and killed. However, many American Indian people were troubled to learn that the military had assigned the code name "Geronimo" to the infamous terrorist. The Chiricahua Apache of New Mexico were particularly disturbed to learn that their freedom fighter's name was used in this manner.

Barack Obama, the son of an immigrant, became the first African American president, but Mr. Obama also recognizes other aspects of his ethnicity. On an official state visit to Ireland while president, he made a side trip to the village of Moneygall in County Offaly. His great-great-grandfather Falmouth Kearney, a shoemaker's son, came to the United States from County Offaly in 1850.

Race and ethnicity are an important part of the national landscape and the national agenda. Forty years ago, when writing the first edition of this book, I noted that race is not a static phenomenon. Although race is always a part of the social reality, specific aspects of race and ethnicity change. In the first edition, I noted the presence of a new immigrant group, the Vietnamese, and described the early efforts to define affirmative action. Today, in an increasingly diverse society, we seek to describe the growing presence of Salvadorans, Haitians, Nigerians, Tongans, Somalis, Hmong, and Arab Americans in the United States.

Specific issues may change over time, but they continue to play out against a backdrop of discrimination that is rooted in the social structure and changing composition of the population as influenced by immigration and reproduction patterns. In addition, the breakup of the Soviet Union and changes in Middle Eastern governments have made ethnic, language, and religious divisions even more significant sources of antagonism between and within nations. The old ideological debates about communism and capitalism have been replaced by emotional divisions over religious dogma and cultural traditions.

New to the Fifteenth Edition

The fifteenth edition of *Racial and Ethnic Groups* continues to take full advantage of the most recent data releases from the U.S. Census Bureau through the annual American Community Survey (ACS). The ACS allows each new edition of the text to include updated information (without the ACS, data would be updated only once a decade, based on the results of the ten-year census). Thanks to the ACS, readers will find updated and revised tables, figures, maps, and Internet sources throughout the fifteenth edition. As one example of the thorough updating, we note that over 25 percent of the 1,560 references are new to this edition.

Learning Objectives appear at the beginning of each chapter; these objectives correspond with the numbered **Summary of Learning Objectives** at the end of each chapter. Each Learning Objective corresponds to a major heading in the text, providing students with a built-in road map and study plan for each chapter.

Relevant scholarly findings in a variety of disciplines, including economics, anthropology, social psychology, and communication sciences, are incorporated throughout the book. A **Speaking Out** feature appears in every chapter. These selections provide firsthand commentaries on race and ethnicity in America, helping us appreciate racial and ethnic groups' responses to prejudice and other challenges. The Speaking Out features include excerpts written or spoken by highly regarded members of racial and ethnic groups, including W. E. B. DuBois, Mary Pattillo, Tomás R. Jiménez, and Nelson Mandela.

New **Key Terms** in the fifteenth edition include *blood quantum, casual Islamophobia, colorism, daughter effect, eugenics, intersectionality, microaggressions, sanctuary cities,* and *sharing economy*. Instructors who have taught from earlier editions of this book will see an increased effort to reintroduce key terms throughout the book in an effort to make them a part of the reader's working vocabulary.

Along with the Speaking Out feature, the **Research Focus** and **Global View** boxes offer new insights into the ever-changing nature of race and ethnicity. Twelve of these features are new to the fifteenth edition.

The fifteenth edition adds a new feature, **Relations Across Boundaries**, which describe the interactions between racial, ethnic, and religious groups. This new feature helps readers understand that social relationships in the United States are not necessarily defined and dominated by

White Americans. The Relations Across Boundaries feature is intended to create a dialogue between the student reader and the material in this book.

The **Spectrum of Intergroup Relations** appears in sixteen of the chapters. The Spectrum at the end of the final chapter serves as a summary of the observations made throughout the textbook.

The fifteenth edition includes entirely new sections on contemporary issues related to refugees, the sharing economy and discrimination, ongoing discussions of policy changes for the "DREAMers," and environmental justice and the water system of Flint, Michigan.

Chapter-by-Chapter Changes

As with all previous editions, every line, every source, and every number has been checked for its currency. The goal of *Racial and Ethnic Groups* has always been to provide the most current information possible to document patterns in intergroup relations both in the United States and abroad. The following list details the major changes in each chapter.

Chapter 1, Exploring Race and Ethnicity

- New opening examples
- Latest American Community Survey 2014–2015 data update all statistics in the chapter
- Expulsion example of Muslim and Nepali-speaking Bhutanese; also noted in their resettling in Manchester, New Hampshire, in chapter opening example
- 2014 report on trends in school segregation
- Resistance example added of #BlackLivesMatter movement
- Intersectionality coverage moved forward from Chapter 15 and expanded to include language spoken and critiques of this approach to social inequality
- Key Terms added: *colorism, eugenics, Eurocentrism, intersectionality*

Chapter 2, Prejudice

- New figure on the rise of hate groups
- Latest census data update all income and wealth statistics
- White privilege illustrated by recent study of bus drivers granting or not granting free bus rides
- Latest reports on racial profiling in traffic stops and New York City ending surveillance program in Muslim neighborhoods

- Recent data on minority representation on television and in motion pictures
- New Speaking Out feature: "What Can I Do at Work?" by Southern Poverty Law Center
- Updated figure on foreign-born workers
- Key Term added: *microaggressions*

Chapter 3, Discrimination

- New material on restricting voting rights through banning ex-felons and requiring photo ID
- Latest data on income and wealth by race, ethnicity, and gender
- Research Focus feature: The Sharing Economy— Another Way to Discriminate
- The water supply in Flint, Michigan, as an example of the need for environmental justice
- 2016 *Fisher v. University of Texas at Austin* Supreme Court decision
- Impact of the Great Recession on Black home ownership
- Key Term added: *sharing economy*

Chapter 4, Immigration

- New opener describing immigration in three towns
- Two figures and map on immigration updated through 2015
- New Speaking Out feature: "My Parents Were Deported," by Diane Guerrero
- Proposed "DREAMers" policy outlined
- Updated table on immigration benefits and concerns
- New cartoon on immigration reform
- Expanded section on refugees
- Table on refugees updated to 2015 and contrasted with 2005
- Specific suggestions on how one can help refugees
- Key Term added: *sanctuary city*

Chapter 5, Ethnicity, Whiteness, and Religion

- Chapter title rephrased to reflect emphasis on concept of Whiteness
- Initial section "Unpacking Ethnicity" reorganized
- New table on religious groups and political party affiliations
- Impact of recent immigration on Roman Catholicism and Protestantism in the United States
- New section on company exemptions within discussion of the courts and religion

Chapter 6, Native Americans: The First Americans

- Opener includes controversy over Navajo president election
- Table of major tribal languages updated
- New cartoon on indigenous people welcoming Europeans
- Table on largest American Indian groupings
- Snapshot table of major social indicators updated
- Role of blood quantum in American Indian identity
- New Speaking Out feature: "Kinship in Modern Times," by Vi Waln
- New Research Focus feature: Economic Impact of Casino Gambling
- New cartoon on casino gambling
- New Relations Across Boundaries feature: Hopi and Navajo Peoples
- Continuing environmental controversy of the Dakota Access Pipeline
- Key Term added: *blood quantum*

Chapter 7, African Americans

- LaCrosse, Wisconsin, as a sundown town in chapter opener
- Virginia city confronts on Martin Luther King, Jr. Day observance of General Lee's and General Jackson's birthdays
- Updating to 2015 of U.S. map of proportion of African Americans and figure on religious composition
- Similarity between Black Power and #BlackLivesMatter movements
- New Relations Across Boundaries feature: African Americans and American Indians
- New Speaking Out feature: "Olympic Athletes Who Took a Stand," by David Davis

Chapter 8, African Americans Today

- New Speaking Out feature: "Black Picket Fences," by Mary Pattillo
- Research Focus: "Acting White" within new section "The School Environment"
- New figure comparing Black and White educational levels
- "Criminal Justice" section now includes references to "incarceration nation" and #BlackLivesMatter

- Study documenting drops in 911 calls following violent police–Black suspect encounters
- Updated data in figures on family composition and voter turnout
- Updated figure of Black–White voter turnout comparison over time
- Efforts to weaken the Voting Rights Act
- Key Term *color-blind racism* revisited to describe voting restrictions

Chapter 9, Latinos: Growth and Diversity

- Table on most common surnames in the United States
- Issue of Afro-Latinos and colorism
- "Education" section now includes historical perspective, school segregation, and tracking
- Updated figure comparing Hispanics versus White non-Hispanics going to college
- Updated map on Latino population by state
- Mobilization of Latinos over immigration issues 2006–2007 and 2016–2017
- New cartoon on U.S.–Cuba relations
- Religious affiliations of Hispanics versus total population
- New Speaking Out feature: "Reconciling Two Identities," by Rosie Molinary
- Key Terms revisited: *colorism* and *de jure segregation*

Chapter 10, Mexican Americans and Puerto Ricans

- Reorganized to improve flow from historical to contemporary material
- Lynching of Mexican Americans, 1848–1920
- Elaboration of ethnic paradox in healthcare
- Economic collapse in contemporary Puerto Rico
- Table statistically comparing United States and Puerto Rico
- New Research Focus feature on Mexican hometown associations
- New Relations Across Boundaries feature: Immigrant Mexicans and U.S.-Born Mexican Americans
- New cartoon on congressional indifference toward Puerto Rico's economic problems
- Key Terms revisited: *colorism* and *ethnic paradox*

Chapter 11, Muslim and Arab Americans: Diverse Minorities

- Chapter opener describing Muslims in Bellevue, Washington
- Section distinguishing the terms *Middle Eastern, Muslim,* and *Arab*
- World map updated to show Middle East countries
- U.S. map updated to show most recent data on Arab American population
- 2016 Muslim political party preferences
- 2016–2017 proposals on Muslim immigration
- Figure on Arab American household income data
- New Relations Across Boundaries feature on Muslim, Arab, and Jewish Americans
- New Speaking Out feature: "May America Be True to Her Dream," by Nihad Awad
- Muslim Americans adjusting to college in the United States
- Key Term added: *casual Islamophobia*; revisited: *ethnocentrism, nativism,* and *xenophobia*

Chapter 12, Asian Pacific Americans: An Array of Nationalities

- Chapter reworked to clarify differences among Asian Pacific Americans (APAs)
- Significance of H-IB visas for APAs
- Table listing Asian Pacific American groups
- Updated figure and maps on Asian Pacific Americans
- Given increased hostility, United States being reconsidered as a favorable destination by people in India
- New Relations Across Boundaries feature: Black and Korean Americans
- Review of studies on arranged versus love-based marriages
- Updated figure on APAs in Hawai'i
- Key Terms revisited: *affirmative action, brain drain, color-blind racism, marginality*

Chapter 13, Chinese Americans and Japanese Americans

- Research on the accuracy of the Tiger Mother model among Asian Americans
- Role of color-blind racism in acceptance of model-minority myth
- New Speaking Out feature: "Statement on Liang Decision," by Japanese American Citizens League

- Emergence of Chinese outside of old Chinatowns
- Closer look at the "No, No" internees
- Four factors explaining persistence of anti–Asian American prejudice
- Speaking Out: "Anti-Bullying," by Mike Honda
- Key Terms revisited: *familism, microaggression, principle of third-generation interest, xenophobia*

Chapter 14, Jewish Americans: The Quest to Maintain Identity

- Efforts by temples to recruit Jews
- National and world maps of Jewish population updated to 2017
- Figure on anti-Semitic incidents updated with 2016 report
- Section titled "Case Study: Daily Life of the Orthodox"
- New Speaking Out feature: "The Neighborhood as a Moral Obstacle Course," by Iddo Tavory
- Key Term revisited: *familism*

Chapter 15, Women: The Oppressed Majority

- Data on women CEOs and high earners in S&P 500 in chapter opener
- All tables and figures updated
- Research Focus: Men Doing Women's Work
- Issue of race in the feminist movement and the 2017 Women's March
- Updated figure on women's labor-force participation in selected countries
- Updated figure on ratio of women's to men's earnings in selected occupations
- Updated figure on income by sex, holding education constant
- Update figure on Labor Department data on allocation of housework between men and women
- Key Terms reintroduced: *blaming the victim, glass escalator, intersectionality*
- Key Term added: *daughter effect*

Chapter 16, Beyond the United States: The Comparative Perspective

- Updated table comparing four nations
- Canadian First Nations protest of pipelines
- Unlikelihood of the two-state solution for Israel and Palestine

- Trevor Noah and apartheid
- Key Term revisited: *colorism*

Chapter 17: Overcoming Exclusion

- Updated figures: Actual and Projected Growth of the Elderly Population and Changes in Minority School Population through 2022
- AARP position on 2017 healthcare reform proposals
- Revision of list of famous people with disabilities
- Updated look at LGBT people in television
- Results of 2013 national survey on gays and lesbians
- Issues facing transgender people
- Key Term revisited: *microaggression*

Complete Coverage in Four Parts

Any constructive discussion of racial and ethnic minorities must do more than merely describe events. Part I, "Perspectives on Racial and Ethnic Groups," includes the relevant theories and operational definitions that ground the study of race and ethnic relations in the social sciences. Specifically, the text presents the functionalist, conflict, and labeling theories of sociology in relation to the study of race and ethnicity. It examines the relationship between subordinate groups and the study of stratification. The text also introduces reference group theory from psychology. The extensive treatment of prejudice and discrimination covers anti-White prejudice as well as the more familiar topic of bigotry aimed at subordinate groups. Discrimination is analyzed from an economic perspective, including the latest efforts to document discrimination in environmental issues (such as the location of toxic waste facilities) and the move to dismantle affirmative action. Part I also discusses the important topics of intersectionality and the matrix of domination.

In Part II, "Ethnic and Religious Sources of Conflict," we examine some often-ignored sources of intergroup conflict in the United States: specifically, White ethnic groups and religious minorities. Diversity in the United States is readily apparent when we look at the ethnic and religious groups that have resulted from waves of immigration. Refugees, now primarily from the Middle East and Central America, also continue to raise major issues.

All students need to be familiar with the past to understand present forms of discrimination and subordination. Part III, "Major Racial and Ethnic Minority Groups in the United States," explains both the history and the contemporary status of Native Americans, African Americans, Latinos, Arab and Muslim Americans, Asian Pacific Americans, and Jews in the United States. Social institutions such as education, economy, family, housing, the criminal justice system, healthcare, and politics are discussed with respect to each of the subordinate groups. Institutional discrimination, rather than individual action, is often the source of conflict between the subordinate and dominant elements in the United States.

Part IV, "Other Patterns of Dominance," includes topics related to American racial and ethnic relations. The text recognizes, as Gunnar Myrdal and Helen Mayer Hacker have recognized, that social and institutional relationships between women and men resemble those between Blacks and Whites. Therefore, this book considers women as a subordinate group. Key topics of debate when the first edition of *Racial and Ethnic Groups* was published almost 30 years ago, including equal rights for women and abortion, show no sign of resolution.

Perhaps we can best comprehend intergroup conflict in the United States by comparing it with the ethnic hostilities in other nations. The similarities and differences between the United States and other societies are striking. In Part IV, the text examines the tensions in Mexico, Brazil, Israel, Palestine, and South Africa to document further the diversity of intergroup conflict.

The final chapter highlights other excluded groups: the aged, people with disabilities, gay men, lesbians, bisexual people, and transgender people. This chapter also includes a concluding section that ties together the forces of dominance and subordination and the persistence of inequality that are the subject of this book.

Features to Aid Students

Several features are included in the text to facilitate student learning. **Learning Objectives** at the start of each chapter provide a road map for previewing and mastering chapter content, and an introductory section alerts students to important issues and topics to be addressed in the chapter. Periodically throughout the book, the **Spectrum of Intergroup Relations,** first presented in Chapter 1, is repeated to reinforce major concepts while addressing the unique social circumstances of individual racial and ethnic groups.

Each chapter ends with a **Conclusion** and a **Summary of Learning Objectives. Key Terms** are highlighted in boldface when they are introduced and are listed again at the end of each chapter. This edition also includes Review Questions and Critical Thinking Questions at the end of each chapter. The **Review Questions** test students on their understanding of the chapter's major points; the **Critical Thinking Questions** encourage students to think more deeply about some of the major issues raised in the chapter. An extensive illustration program, which includes maps and political cartoons, expands the text discussion and provokes thought. An end-of-book **Glossary** provides definitions of Key Terms.

Revel™

Revel is an interactive learning environment that deeply engages students and prepares them for class. Media and assessment integrated directly within the authors' narrative lets students read, explore interactive content, and practice in one continuous learning path. Thanks to the dynamic reading experience in Revel, students come to class prepared to discuss, apply, and learn from instructors and from each other.

Learn more about Revel
http://www.pearson.com/revel

Ancillary Materials

This book is accompanied by an extensive learning package to enhance the experience of instructors and students.

INSTRUCTOR'S MANUAL AND TEST BANK Each chapter in the Instructor's Manual offers a variety of resources: Chapter Summary, Chapter Outline, Learning Objectives, Critical Thinking Questions, Activities for Classroom Participation, Key Terms, Suggested Readings, and Suggested Films. Designed to make your lectures more effective and to save preparation time, this extensive resource gathers useful activities and strategies for teaching your course.

Also included in this manual is a test bank offering multiple-choice, true/false, fill-in-the-blank, and/or essay questions for each chapter. The Instructor's Manual and Test Bank are available to adopters at www.pearsonhighered.com/irc.

MYTEST This computerized software allows instructors to create their own exams, to edit any or all of the existing test questions, and to add new questions. Other special features of MyTest include random generation of test questions, creation of alternate versions of the same test, scrambling question sequence, and test preview before printing.

For easy access, this software is available at www.pearson-highered.com/irc.

POWERPOINT PRESENTATIONS The PowerPoint presentations are informed by instructional and design theory. You have the option in every chapter of choosing from Lecture and Illustration (figures, maps, and images) PowerPoints. The Lecture PowerPoint slides follow the chapter outline and feature images from the textbook integrated with the text. They are available to adopters via www.pearsonhighered.com.

Acknowledgments

The fifteenth edition was improved by the suggestions of:

Tonja Conerly, San Jacinto College – South

Catherine Felton, Central Piedmont Community College

Rebecca Hornung, Carthage College

Lori Lundell, Purdue University

Andrea L. Moore, Sacramento State University

Alicia M. Raia-Hawrylak, Rutgers University

I would also like to thank my publishers at Pearson, Billy Grieco and Jeff Marshall, for assisting in the production of this fifteenth edition. Development Editor Steven Rigolosi has drawn on his experience to strengthen this book further and adapt the manuscript to the many digital formats that are available now to the reader. My appreciation also extends to Editor-in-Chief Dickson Musslewhite for his encouragement and support for my textbooks on race and ethnicity.

The truly exciting challenge of writing and researching has always been for me an enriching experience, mostly because of the supportive home I share with my wife, Sandy. She knows so well my appreciation and gratitude, now as in the past and in the future.

Richard T. Schaefer
schaeferrt@aol.com

About the Author

Richard T. Schaefer grew up in Chicago at a time when neighborhoods were going through transitions in ethnic and racial composition. He found himself increasingly intrigued by what was happening, how people were reacting, and how these changes were affecting neighborhoods and people's jobs. In high school, he took a course in sociology. His interest in social issues caused him to gravitate to more sociology courses at Northwestern University, where he eventually received a B.A. in sociology.

"Originally as an undergraduate I thought I would go on to law school and become a lawyer. But after taking a few sociology courses, I found myself wanting to learn more about what sociologists studied and was fascinated by the kinds of questions they raised," Dr. Schaefer says. "Perhaps most fascinating and, to me, relevant to the 1960s was the intersection of race, gender, and social class." This interest led him to obtain his M.A. and Ph.D. in sociology from the University of Chicago. Dr. Schaefer's continuing interest in race relations led him to write his master's thesis on the membership of the Ku Klux Klan and his doctoral thesis on racial prejudice and race relations in Great Britain.

Dr. Schaefer went on to become a professor of sociology. He has taught sociology and courses on multiculturalism for 30 years. He has been invited to give special presentations on racial and ethnic diversity to students and faculty in Illinois, Indiana, Missouri, North Carolina, Ohio, and Texas.

Dr. Schaefer is the author of *Racial and Ethnic Diversity in the USA* (Pearson, 2014) and *Race and Ethnicity in the United States*, ninth edition (Pearson, 2019). He is the general editor of the three-volume *Encyclopedia of Race, Ethnicity, and Society* (2008). He is also the author of the thirteenth edition of *Sociology: A Brief Introduction* (2019), the fourth edition of *Sociology: A Modular Approach* (2015), and the seventh edition of *Sociology Matters* (2018). He coauthored with William Zellner the ninth edition of *Extraordinary Groups* (2015). Schaefer's books have been translated into Chinese, Japanese, Portuguese, and Spanish, as well as adapted for use in Canadian colleges. His articles and book reviews have appeared in many journals, including *American Journal of Sociology, Phylon: A Review of Race and Culture, Contemporary Sociology, Sociology and Social Research, Sociological Quarterly*, and *Teaching Sociology*. He served as president of the Midwest Sociological Society from 1994 to 1995. In recognition of his achievements in undergraduate teaching, he was named Vincent de Paul Professor of Sociology in 2004.

Chapter 1
Exploring Race and Ethnicity

Nature Collection/Alamy Stock Photo

Learning Objectives

1.1 Explain how people are placed in groups.

1.2 Explain the social construction of race.

1.3 Describe how sociology helps us understand race and ethnicity.

1.4 Explain how subordinate groups are created.

1.5 Summarize the consequences of subordinate-group status.

1.6 Describe how resistance and change occur in racial and ethnic relations.

1.7 Define and describe intersectionality.

"Please pass the momos." That's not something you hear very often, unless you're in Bhutan, a small Asian country tucked in the Himalayas—or in Manchester, New Hampshire. In that New England state capital, one finds a growing population of Bhutanese who love their momos—steamed dumplings filled with pork or chicken, which substitutes for the yak or water buffalo meat used back in Bhutan. This refugee group and their children in Manchester are followers of Hinduism and speakers of Nepali. They were forced out of Bhutan in the 1990s by the Buddhist-controlled monarchy.

It was not a quick journey. Most of the over 100,000 Bhutanese refugees spent 20 years in refugee camps before being relocated, with the majority coming to the United States in 2008, just in time for the Great Recession. Initial adjustment in Manchester was challenging, and the reception by locals was not always warm. Within just three years, the 2,000 new arrivals had higher employment rates, higher high-school graduation rates, and lower welfare rates than long-term residents in this city of 110,000. On a rundown street, the Himalayan General Store sells cracked corn, mango pickles, flattened rice, and bags of shiny black kalonji seeds. These Bhutanese Americans will never be the same, and neither will Manchester.

St. Paul, the capital of Minnesota, would seem an unlikely place for racial strife—after all, isn't Minnesota supposed to be the home of liberals and easygoing, friendly people? Yet, in 2016, Philando Castile, a 32-year old African American school nutritionist, was shot dead in his car by a police officer named Jeronimo Yanez, a 28-year-old Mexican American. Castile's death came after he told the officer he was licensed to carry a weapon and was carrying one in his pants pocket. Castile's girlfriend, who was a passenger in the car, along with their four-year-old daughter, recorded much of the incident. Eventually the officer was charged with manslaughter, but not before many protest marches, some of which came close to the governor's mansion. During the period of protests, many were surprised to learn that neighborhood and school segregation in St. Paul have escalated over the past 20 years. Rates of Black incarceration were among the highest in the nation. The number of African Americans living in high-poverty areas in St. Paul increased by 50 percent from 2000 to 2012.

Trying to make sense of the divide and calm frantic people, African American artist Jeremiah Ellison stepped in. The night after the shooting, he mobilized community residents to create murals on the side of an abandoned warehouse to honor the slain Castile. Deciding to become even more involved in finding solutions, he decided to run for city council in 2017. He grew up in a politically aware household—his father is U.S. Congressman Keith Ellison, the first Muslim to be elected to the House of Representatives.

Hamdi Ulukaya is a Turkish immigrant of Kurdish descent. He arrived in the United States in 1994 and started to make and sell feta cheese based on a family recipe. In 2005, using a Small Business Administration loan, he took over a shuttered yogurt plant in upstate New York and transformed and expanded it into the company now known as Chobani. The company employs 2,000 people and has annual sales of $1.5 billion. It is estimated that Ulukaya, the CEO, is worth close to $2 billion.

At a time when many people in the United States were growing suspicious of Muslims—especially Muslim immigrants—Ulukaya decided that he and his company would facilitate immigrant resettlement. His company actively recruits refugees and offers them English-language classes, along with translators in 11 languages. Despite strong criticism from anti-immigrant activists, Ulukaya has held to his position, pointing to the success of the immigrants working for him. Ulukaya joined Bill Gates and other wealthy people in 2015 by signing the Giving Pledge, which commits them to giving away at least half their money to philanthropic causes (Gelles 2016; Halpern and McKibben 2014; Rhee 2016).

Households upended, suspicion of newcomers, starting over in a new land, violence, community action, hard work, and economic success for immigrants are all aspects of race and ethnicity in the United States today.

Hamdi Ulukaya has made a name for himself both as a successful businessman (he is the founder and CEO of Chobani yogurt) and for being an outspoken supporter of immigrants and refugees.

Diane Bondareff/Invision/AP Images

One aspect of the struggle for equality is the continuing effort to identify strategies and services to assist minorities in their struggle to overcome prejudice and discrimination. Among the beneficiaries of programs aimed at racial and ethnic minorities are White Americans, many of whom are far from affluent and have also experienced challenges in their lives.

The election and reelection of the nation's first African American president, Barack Obama (who incidentally carried three states of the former Confederacy), presents the temptation to declare that racial inequality is a thing of the past or that racism in the United States is limited to a few troublemakers. Progress has been made, and expressions of explicit racism are rarely tolerated, yet challenges remain for immigrants of any color and for racial, ethnic, and religious minorities (Massey 2011).

The United States is a diverse nation and is becoming even more so, as Table 1.1 shows. In 2015, approximately 41 percent (more than one-third) of the U.S. population were racial minorities or Hispanic.

Table 1.1 Racial and Ethnic Groups in the United States, 2015

Classification	Number in Thousands	Percentage of Total Population
RACIAL GROUPS		
Whites (non-Hispanic)	188,568	58.7
Blacks/African Americans	40,695	12.7
Native Americans, Alaskan Natives	2,597	0.8
Asian Pacific Americans	21,118	7.0
Chinese	4,761	1.5
Asian Indians	3,982	1.2
Filipinos	3,899	1.2
Vietnamese	1,980	0.6
Koreans	1,822	0.6
Japanese	1,411	0.2
Pacific Islanders, Native Hawaiians	555	0.1
Other Asian Americans	2,708	0.5
Arab Americans	1,963	0.6
Two or more races	9,982	3.1
ETHNIC GROUPS		
White ancestry	144,960	
Germans	45,526	14.2
Irish	32,713	10.2
English	23,959	7.5
Italians	17,070	5.3
Poles	9,231	2.9
Scottish and Scots-Irish	8,492	2.6
French	7,969	2.5
Jews	7,200	1.8
Hispanics (or Latinos)	56,496	17.6
Mexican Americans	35,797	11.1
Puerto Ricans	5,373	1.7
Salvadorans	2,172	0.7
Cubans	2,107	0.7
Dominicans	1,873	0.6
Guatemalans	1,378	0.4
Colombians	1,082	0.3
Other Hispanics	6,764	2.1
TOTAL (ALL GROUPS)	321,419	

Note: Arab American population excluded from White total. All data are for 2015. Percentages do not total 100 percent, and when subcategories are added, they do not match totals in major categories because of overlap between groups (e.g., Polish American Jews or people of mixed ancestry such as Irish and Italian). Only the seven largest White ancestry groups listed.

SOURCE: American Community Survey 2016a: Tables B02001, B02018, B03001, B03001, B04006; Steinhardt Social Research Institute 2016.

As Figure 1.1 shows, between 2014 and 2060, the Black, Hispanic (or Latino), Asian Pacific Americans, and Native American population is expected to increase to about 56 percent of the U.S. population. This trend toward "majority-minority" became particularly noticeable in 2011, when Latino and non-White babies outnumbered White newborns for the first time in the United States (Bureau of the Census 2012d).

Figure 1.1 U.S. Population by Race and Ethnicity, 2014 and 2060 (Projected)

According to projections by the Census Bureau, the proportion of U.S. residents who are White non-Hispanics will decrease significantly by the year 2060. By contrast, the proportion of both Hispanic Americans and Asian Pacific Americans will rise significantly.

SOURCE: Author estimates based on U.S. Census data in Colby and Ortman, 2015:9.

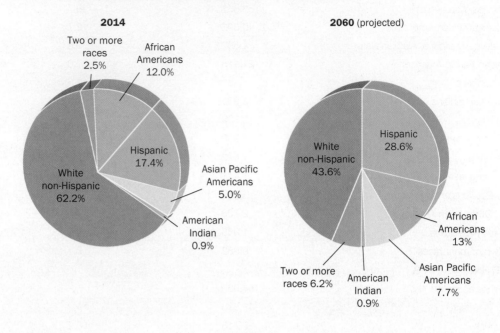

How Are We Grouped?

1.1 **Explain how people are placed in groups.**

In every society, not all groups are treated or viewed equally. Identifying a subordinate group or a minority in a society seems to be a simple task. In the United States, the groups readily identified as minorities—Blacks and Native Americans, for example—are outnumbered by non-Blacks and non-Native Americans. However, having minority status is not necessarily a result of being outnumbered. A social minority need not be a mathematical one. A **minority group** is a subordinate group whose members have significantly less control or power over their own lives than do the members of a dominant or majority group. In sociology, *minority* means the same as *subordinate*, and *dominant* is used interchangeably with *majority*.

Confronted with evidence that a particular minority in the United States is subordinate to the majority, some people respond, "Why not? After all, this is a democracy, so the majority rules." However, the subordination of a minority group involves more than its inability to rule over society. A member of a subordinate or minority group experiences a narrowing of life's opportunities—for success, education, wealth, the pursuit of happiness—that goes beyond any personal shortcoming he or she may have. A minority group does not share in proportion to its numbers what a given society, such as the United States, defines as valuable.

Being superior in numbers does not guarantee a group has control over its destiny or ensure majority status. In 1920, the majority of people in Mississippi and South Carolina were African Americans. Yet African Americans did not have as much control over their lives—let alone control of the states in which they lived—as did Whites. Throughout the United States today are counties or neighborhoods in which the majority of people are African American, Native American, or Hispanic, but White Americans are the dominant force. Nationally, 50.7 percent of the population is female, but men still dominate positions of authority and wealth well beyond their numbers.

A minority or subordinate group has five characteristics: unequal treatment, distinguishing physical or cultural traits, involuntary membership, awareness of subordination, and in-group marriage (Wagley and Harris 1958):

1. Members of a minority experience unequal treatment and have less power over their lives than members of a dominant group have over theirs. Prejudice, discrimination, segregation, and even extermination create this social inequality.

2. Members of a minority group share physical or cultural characteristics such as skin color or language that distinguish them from the dominant group. Each society has its own arbitrary standard for determining which characteristics are most important in defining dominant and minority groups.

3. Membership in a dominant or minority group is not voluntary: People are born into the group. A person does not choose to be African American or White.

4. Minority-group members have a strong sense of group solidarity. William Graham Sumner, writing in 1906, noted that people make distinctions between members of their own group (the in-group) and everyone else (the out-group). When a group is the object of long-term prejudice and discrimination, the feeling of "us versus them" often becomes intense.

5. Members of a minority generally marry others from the same group. A member of a dominant group often is unwilling to join a supposedly inferior minority by marrying one of its members. In addition, the minority group's sense of solidarity encourages marriage within the group and discourages marriage to outsiders.

Although "minority" status is not about numbers, there is no denying that the White American majority is diminishing in size relative to the growing diversity of racial and ethnic groups, as Figure 1.2 illustrates.

Figure 1.2 Minority Population by County

In four states (California, Hawai'i, New Mexico, and Texas) and the District of Columbia, as well as in about one out of every nine counties, minorities constitute the numerical majority.

SOURCE: Data from Jones-Puthoff, 2013, slide 5.

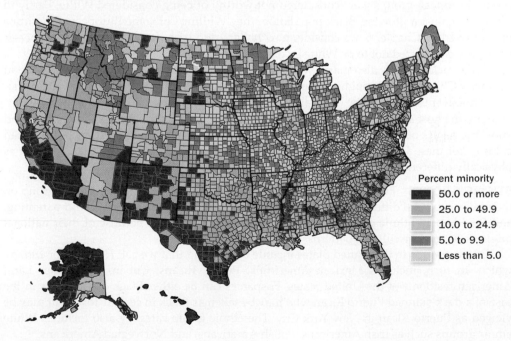

Percent minority
- 50.0 or more
- 25.0 to 49.9
- 10.0 to 24.9
- 5.0 to 9.9
- Less than 5.0

Using available population projections, which are heavily influenced by estimating future immigration patterns, the White population will be outnumbered by other racial groups and Hispanics by 2044. The move to a more diverse nation—one in which no group is the numerical minority—will have social impact in everything from marriage patterns to housing, politics, health care delivery, and education (Colby and Ortman 2015:13).

Types of Minority Groups

There are four types of minority or subordinate groups. All four, except where noted, have the five properties previously outlined. The four criteria for classifying minority groups are race, ethnicity, religion, and gender.

RACIAL GROUPS   The term **racial group** is reserved for minorities and the corresponding majorities that are socially set apart because of obvious physical differences. Notice the two crucial words in the definition: *obvious* and *physical*. What is obvious? Hair color? Shape of an earlobe? Presence of body hair? To whom are these differences obvious, and why? Each society defines what it finds obvious.

In the United States, skin color is one obvious difference. People in the United States have learned informally that skin color is important. We will return periodically in this book to the social importance that people attach to skin color. **Colorism** is the ranking or judging of individuals based on skin tone. In the United States, a binary categorization is often invoked of "Black" or "White," in which White people are usually advantaged. However, even within same-race categories, judgments are often made about people as being lighter or darker (Banton 2012; Norwood 2014).

Other societies use skin color as a standard but may have a more elaborate system of classification. In Brazil, where hostility between races is less prevalent than it is in the United States, numerous categories identify people on the basis of skin color or tone. In the United States, a person is Black or White. In Brazil, a variety of terms such as *cafuso, mazombo, preto,* and *escuro* are used to describe various combinations of skin color, facial features, and hair texture.

The designation of a racial group emphasizes physical differences such as skin tone, as opposed to cultural distinctions. In the United States, minority races include Blacks, Native Americans (or American Indians), Japanese Americans, Chinese Americans, Arab Americans, Filipinos, Hawaiians, and other Asian peoples. The issue of race and racial differences has been an important one, not only in the United States but also throughout the entire sphere of European influence. We should not forget that Whites are a race, too. As we consider in Chapter 4, who is White has been subject to change over history; at one time, certain European groups were considered not worthy of being considered White. Partly to compete against a growing Black population, the "Whiting" of some European Americans has occurred. In Chapter 5, we consider how Italians and Irish, for all intents and purposes, were once considered not to be White by others.

Some racial groups also may have unique cultural traditions, as we can readily see in the many Chinatowns throughout the United States. For racial groups, however, the physical distinctiveness and not the cultural differences generally prove to be the barrier to acceptance by the host society. For example, Chinese Americans who are faithful Protestants and know the names of all the members of the Baseball Hall of Fame may be bearers of American culture. Yet these Chinese Americans are still part of a minority because they are seen as physically different.

ETHNIC GROUPS   Ethnic minority groups are differentiated from the dominant group on the basis of cultural differences such as language, attitudes toward marriage and parenting, and food habits. **Ethnic groups** are groups set apart from others because of their national origin or distinctive cultural patterns.

Ethnic groups in the United States include a grouping that we call *Hispanics* or *Latinos,* which, in turn, includes Mexican Americans, Puerto Ricans, Cubans, and other Latin American residents of the United States. Hispanics can be either Black or White, as in the case of a dark-skinned Puerto Rican who may be taken as Black in central Texas but may be viewed as Puerto Rican in New York City. The ethnic group category also includes White ethnic groups such as Irish Americans, Polish Americans, and Norwegian Americans.

The cultural traits that make groups distinctive usually originate from their homelands or, for Jews, from a long history of being segregated and prohibited from becoming a part of a host society. In the United States, an immigrant group may maintain distinctive cultural practices through associations, clubs, and worship. Ethnic enclaves such as a Little Haiti or a Greektown in urban areas also perpetuate cultural distinctiveness.

Ethnicity and race have been long recognized as important sources of differentiation. More than a century ago, African American sociologist W. E. B. Du Bois, addressing an audience at a world antislavery convention in London in 1900, called attention to the overwhelming importance of the color line throughout the world. The Speaking Out feature reprints remarks by Du Bois, who was the first Black person to receive a doctorate from Harvard and later helped to organize the National Association for the Advancement of Colored People (NAACP). Du Bois's observations give us a historic perspective on the struggle for equality. We can look ahead, knowing how far we have come and speculating on how much farther we have to go.

We also should appreciate the context of Du Bois's insights. He spoke of his "color-line" prediction in light of then-contemporary U.S. occupation of the Philippines and the relationship of "darker to lighter races" worldwide. So today, he would see race matters not only in the sporadic hate crimes we hear about but also in global conflicts (Roediger 2009).

RELIGIOUS GROUPS   Association with a religion other than the dominant faith is the third basis for minority-group status. In the United States, Protestants, as a group, outnumber members of all other religions. Roman Catholics form the largest minority religion. For people who are not a part of the Christian tradition, such as followers of Islam, allegiance

Speaking Out

The Problem of the Color Line

W. E. B. Du Bois

In the metropolis of the modern world, in this the closing year of the nineteenth century, there has been assembled a congress of men and women of African blood, to deliberate solemnly upon the present situation and outlook of the darker races of mankind. The problem of the twentieth century is the problem of the color line, the question as to how far differences of race—which show themselves chiefly in the color of the skin and the texture of the hair—will hereafter be made the basis of denying to over half the world the right of sharing to their utmost ability the opportunities and privileges of modern civilization....

To be sure, the darker races are today the least advanced in culture according to European standards. This has not, however, always been the case in the past, and certainly the world's history, both ancient and modern, has given many instances of no despicable ability and capacity among the blackest races of men.

In any case, the modern world must remember that in this age when the ends of the world are being brought so near together, the millions of black men in Africa, America, and Islands of the Sea, not to speak of the brown and yellow myriads elsewhere, are bound to have a great influence upon the world in the future, by reason of sheer numbers and physical contact.

W. E. B. Du Bois

MPI/Archive Photos/Getty Images

If now the world of culture bends itself towards giving Negroes and other dark men the largest and broadest opportunity for education and self-development, then this contact and influence is bound to have a beneficial effect upon the world and hasten human progress. But if, by reason of carelessness, prejudice, greed, and injustice, the black world is to be exploited and ravished and degraded, the results must be deplorable, if not fatal—not simply to them, but to the high ideals of justice, freedom and culture which a thousand years of Christian civilization have held before Europe....

Let the world take no backward step in that slow but sure progress which has successively refused to let the spirit of class, of caste, of privilege, or of birth, debar from life, liberty, and the pursuit of happiness a striving human soul.

Let not color or race be a feature of distinction between White and Black men, regardless of worth or ability....

Thus we appeal with boldness and confidence to the Great Powers of the civilized world, trusting in the wide spirit of humanity, and the deep sense of justice of our age, for a generous recognition of the righteousness of our cause.

Source: Du Bois 1900 [1969a]: 20–21, 23.

ASSIMILATION.

HETEROGENEOUS.

DIVERSITY.

COALESCE.

I WISH YOU PEOPLE WOULD SPEAK A LANGUAGE I COULD UNDERSTAND.

GROWING HISPANIC POPULATION

CHANGE

Jeff Parker/Cagle Cartoons

CAGLECARTOONS.COM

The changing landscape of the United States is hard to miss, but not all people equally embrace it.

to their faith often is misunderstood and used to stigmatize them. This stigmatization became especially widespread and legitimated by government action in the aftermath of the attacks of September 11, 2001.

Religious minorities include groups such as the Church of Jesus Christ of Latter-day Saints (the Mormons), Jehovah's Witnesses, Amish, and Buddhists. Cults or sects associated with practices such as animal sacrifice, doomsday prophecies, demon worship, or the use of snakes in a ritualistic fashion also constitute religious minorities. Jews are excluded from this category and placed among ethnic groups. Culture is a more important defining trait for Jewish people worldwide than is religious doctrine. Jewish Americans share a cultural tradition that goes beyond theology. In this sense, it is appropriate to view them as an ethnic group rather than as members of a religious faith.

GENDER GROUPS   Gender is another attribute that creates dominant and subordinate groups. Men are the social majority; women, although numerous, are relegated to the position of the social minority. Women are considered a minority even though they do not exhibit all the characteristics outlined earlier (e.g., there is little in-group marriage). Women encounter prejudice and discrimination and are physically distinguishable from men. Group membership is involuntary, and many women have developed a sense of sisterhood.

Women who are members of racial and ethnic minorities face special challenges to achieving equality. They suffer from greater inequality because they belong to two separate minority groups: a racial or ethnic group plus a subordinate gender group.

OTHER SUBORDINATE GROUPS   This book focuses on groups that meet a set of criteria for subordinate status. People encounter prejudice or are excluded from full participation in society for many reasons. Racial, ethnic, religious, and gender barriers are the main ones, but there are others. Age, disability status, physical appearance, and sexual identity are among the factors that are used to subordinate groups of people.

The Social Construction of Race

1.2   Explain the social construction of race.

We see people all around us—some of whom may look quite different from us. Do these differences matter? The simple answer is no, but because so many people have for so long acted as if differences in physical characteristics, geographic origin, and shared culture do matter, distinct groups have been created in people's minds. Race has many meanings for many people. Often these meanings are inaccurate and based on theories that scientists discarded generations ago. As we will see, race is a socially constructed concept (Young 2003).

Biological Meaning

The term *race* as applied to human beings lacks any scientific basis. Distinctive physical characteristics for groups of human beings cannot be identified in the same way that scientists distinguish one animal species from another. The idea of **biological race** is based on the mistaken notion of a genetically isolated human group.

ABSENCE OF PURE RACES   Even past proponents of the belief that sharp scientific divisions exist among humans had endless debates over what the world's races were. Given people's frequent migration, exploration, and invasions, pure genetic types have not existed for some time, if they ever did. There are no mutually exclusive races. Skin tone among African Americans varies tremendously, as it does among White Americans. There is even an overlapping of dark-skinned Whites and light-skinned African Americans. If we grouped people by genetic resistance to malaria and by fingerprint patterns, then Norwegians and many African groups would be the same race. If we grouped people by lactose intolerance, some Africans, Asians, and southern Europeans would belong to one group, and West Africans and northern Europeans would belong to another (Leehotz 1995; Shanklin 1994).

Biologically, no pure, distinct races exist. Despite this scientific fact, people at different times have advocated **eugenics**, the belief that human genetic quality can be improved by selective breeding. Eugenics has taken many forms, including sterilizing people with mental illnesses, banning interracial marriages, and, as in the Holocaust, attempting to exterminate entire groups of people judged to be inferior.

Research as a part of the Human Genome Project mapping human deoxyribonucleic acid (DNA) has served to confirm genetic diversity only, with differences *within* traditionally regarded racial groups (e.g., Black Africans) much greater than those *between* groups (e.g., between Black Africans and Europeans). Contemporary studies of DNA on a global basis have determined that about 90 percent of human genetic variation is within "local populations," such as within the French or within the Afghan people. The remaining 10 percent of total human variation is what we think of today as constituting races and accounts for skin tone, hair texture, and nose shape (Cohen 2016; Feldman 2010).

It is no surprise that the question of whether races have different innate levels of intelligence has led to some of the most explosive controversies (Bamshad and Olson 2003; El-Haj 2007).

INTELLIGENCE TESTS Typically, intelligence is measured as an **intelligence quotient (IQ)**, which is the ratio of a person's mental age to his or her chronological age, multiplied by 100, with 100 representing average intelligence and higher scores representing greater intelligence. It should be noted that there is little consensus over just what intelligence is, other than as defined by such IQ tests. Intelligence tests are adjusted for a person's age so that 10-year-olds take a different test than 20-year-olds. Although research shows that certain learning strategies can improve a person's IQ, generally IQ remains stable as one ages.

A great deal of debate rages over the accuracy of IQ tests. Are they biased toward people who come to the tests with knowledge similar to that of the test writers? Skeptics argue that questions in IQ tests do not truly measure intellectual potential. The question of cultural bias in tests remains a concern. The most recent research shows that differences in intelligence scores between Blacks and Whites are almost eliminated when adjustments are made for social and economic characteristics (Lindsey 2013).

Back in 1994, an 845-page book unleashed another national debate on the issue of IQ. The research efforts of psychologist Richard J. Herrnstein and social scientist Charles Murray, published in *The Bell Curve* (1994), concluded that 60 percent of IQ is inheritable and that racial groups offer a convenient means to generalize about differences in intelligence. Unlike most other proponents of the race–IQ link, the authors offered policy suggestions that included ending welfare to discourage births among low-IQ poor women and changing immigration laws so that the average IQ in the United States is not diminished. Herrnstein and Murray even made generalizations about IQ levels among Asians and Hispanics—two groups that often intermarry—in the United States. In spite of *The Bell Curve* "research," it is not possible to generalize about absolute differences between groups, such as Latinos versus Whites, when almost half of Latinos in the United States marry non-Hispanics.

More than a decade later, the mere mention of the "bell curve" still signals a belief in a racial hierarchy, with Whites toward the top and Blacks near the bottom. The research presented then and repeated today points to the difficulty in definitions: What is intelligence, and

what constitutes a racial group, given generations (and sometimes centuries) of intermarriage? How can we speak of definitive inherited racial differences if there have been intermarriages between people of every color? Furthermore, as people on both sides of the debate have noted, regardless of the findings, we would still want to strive to maximize the talents of each individual. All research shows that the differences within a group are much greater than any alleged differences between group averages.

Why does such IQ research occasionally reemerge when it is clear that the data are subject to different interpretations? The argument that "we" are superior to "them" is appealing to the dominant group. It justifies receiving opportunities that are denied to others. We can anticipate that the debate over IQ and the allegations of significant group differences will continue. Policymakers need to acknowledge the difficulty in treating race as a biologically significant characteristic.

Race as a Social Construction

If race does not distinguish humans from one another biologically, then why does it seem to be so important? It is important because of the social meaning people have attached to it. The 1950 (UNESCO) Statement on Race maintains that race is not a biological phenomenon (Montagu 1972:118).

Race is a social construction that benefits the oppressor, who defines which groups of people are privileged and which groups are not. The acceptance of race in a society as a legitimate category allows racial hierarchies to emerge to the benefit of the dominant "races." For example, inner-city drive-by shootings, which are mostly carried out by people of color, are viewed as a race-specific problem to be remedied by local officials cleaning up troubled neighborhoods. Yet school shootings, which are largely carried out by Whites, are viewed as a societal concern and placed on the national agenda.

People could speculate that if human groups have obvious physical differences, then they could also have corresponding mental or personality differences. No one disagrees that people differ in temperament, potential to learn, and sense of humor, among other characteristics. In its social sense, race implies that groups that differ physically also bear distinctive emotional and mental abilities or disabilities. These beliefs are based on the notion that humankind can be divided into distinct groups. We have already seen the difficulties associated with pigeonholing people into racial categories. Despite these difficulties, belief in the inheritance of behavior patterns and in an association between physical and cultural traits is widespread. When this belief is coupled with the belief that certain groups or races are inherently superior to others, the result is racism. **Racism** is a doctrine of racial supremacy that sees one race as superior to another (Bash 2001; Bonilla-Silva 1996).

We disproved the biological significance of race in the previous section. In modern, complex industrial societies, we find little adaptive usefulness in the presence or absence of prominent chins, the epicanthic eye fold associated with eastern and central Asian peoples, or the comparative amount of melanin in the skin. It is of little importance that people are genetically different; what is important is that they approach one another with dissimilar perspectives. It is in the social setting that race is decisive. Race is significant because people have given it significance.

Race definitions are crystallized through what Michael Omi and Howard Winant (2015) called **racial formation**, a sociohistorical process by which racial categories are created, inhabited, transformed, and destroyed. Those in power define groups of people in a way that depends on a racist social structure. As in the United States, these definitions can become systematic and embedded in many aspects of society for a significant length of time. No one escapes the extent and frequency to which we are subjected to racial formation. The creation of the reservation system for Native Americans in the late 1800s is an example of racial formation. The federal American Indian policy treated previously distinctive tribes as a single group.

With rising immigration from Latin America in the latter part of the twentieth century, the fluid nature of racial formation is evident. As if it happened in one day, people in the United States have spoken about the Latin Americanization of the United States or stated that the biracial order of Black and White has been replaced with a *triracial* order of Black,

White, and Hispanic. Yet even this assertion is overly simplistic given the presence of tribal groups and growing numbers of Asian Pacific Americans. We examine the social context of the changing nature of diversity to understand how scholars have sought to generalize about intergroup relations in the United States and elsewhere (Bonilla-Silva and Dietrich 2011; Biagas Jr. and Bianchi 2015).

In the southern United States, the social construction of race was known as the "one-drop rule." This tradition stipulated that if a person had even a single drop of "Black blood," that person was defined and viewed as Black. In Chapter 6, we discuss "blood quantum," a similar concept used by some contemporary Native American tribes. Today, children of biracial or multiracial marriages try to build their own identities in a country that seems intent on placing them in a single, traditional category—a topic we examine next.

Biracial and Multiracial Identity: Who Am I?

People are now more willing to accept and advance identities that do not fit neatly into mutually exclusive categories. That is, increasing numbers of people are identifying themselves as biracial or multiracial or, at the very least, explicitly viewing themselves as reflecting a diverse racial and ethnic identity. Barack Obama is perhaps the most visible person with a biracial background. President Obama has explicitly stated he sees himself as a Black man, although his mother was White and his White grandparents largely raised him. In 2010, he chose to check the "Black, African American, or Negro" box on his household's census form. Obviously, *biracial* does not mean *biracial identity*.

The diversity of the United States today has made it more difficult for many people to place themselves on the country's traditional and inflexible racial and ethnic landscape. This difficulty reminds us that racial formation continues to take place. As we have seen, the racial and ethnic landscape is constructed not naturally but socially and, therefore, is subject to change and different interpretations. Although our focus is on the United States, almost every nation faces the same challenges.

The United States tracks people by race and ethnicity for myriad reasons, ranging from attempting to improve the status of oppressed groups to diversifying classrooms. But how can we measure the growing number of people whose ancestry is mixed by anyone's definition? In the Research Focus feature, we consider how the U.S. Bureau of the Census deals with this issue.

Besides the increasing respect for biracial identity and multiracial identity, group names undergo change as well. Within little more than a generation during the twentieth century, labels that were applied to subordinate groups changed from *Negroes* to *Blacks* to *African Americans*, from *American Indians* to *Native Americans* or *Native Peoples*. However, more Native Americans prefer the use of their tribal name, such as *Seminole*, instead of a collective label. The old 1950s statistical term of "people with a Spanish surname" has long been discarded, but there is disagreement over a new term: *Latino* or *Hispanic*. Like Native Americans, Hispanic Americans avoid such global terms and prefer their native names, such as *Puerto Ricans* or *Cubans*. People of Mexican ancestry indicate preferences for a variety of names, such as *Mexican American, Chicano*, or simply *Mexican*.

In the United States and other multiracial, multiethnic societies, **panethnicity**, the development of solidarity among related ethnic subgroups, has emerged. The coalition of tribal groups as Native Americans or American Indians to confront outside forces, notably the federal government, is one example of panethnicity. Hispanics or Latinos and Asian Americans are other examples of panethnicity. Although it is rarely recognized by the dominant society, the very terms *Black* and *African American* represent the descendants of many different ethnic or tribal groups, such as African groups of Fulani and Yoruba, as well as Afro Caribbeans (Brown and Jones 2015).

Is panethnicity a convenient label for "outsiders" or a term that reflects a mutual identity? Certainly, many people outside the group are unable or unwilling to recognize ethnic differences and prefer umbrella terms such as *Asian Americans*. For some small groups, combining with others is emerging as a useful way to make themselves heard, but there is always a fear that their own distinctive culture will become submerged. Although many Hispanics share the Spanish language and many are united by Roman Catholicism, only one in four native-born people of Mexican, Puerto Rican, or Cuban descent prefers a panethnic label to nationality or

Research Focus

Multiracial Identity

Approaching Census 2000, a movement began among those who were frustrated by government questionnaires that forced them to identify themselves by only one race. Take the case of Stacey Davis in New Orleans. The young woman's mother is Thai and her father is Creole, a blend of Black, French, and German. People often think Stacey is a Latina, Filipina, or Hawaiian. Officially, she has been "White" all her life because she looks White. Census 2000 for the first time gave people the option to check off one or more racial groups. (However, "biracial" or "multiracial" was not an option.) In other words, Census 2000 was the first time the U.S. government officially recognized different social constructions of racial identity—for example, that a person could be Asian American *and* White.

Most people did select one racial category in Census 2000 and again in 2010. Overall, approximately 9 million people, or 2.9 percent of the total population, selected two or more racial groups in 2010. As Figure 1.3 shows, White and African American was the most common multiple identity, with about 1.8 million people selecting that response. As a group, American Indians were the most likely to select a second category, and Whites were the least likely—further evidence that race is socially defined.

The possible real size of the multiracial population is significantly larger. A 2015 research report found that when one considers the background of grandparents and parents, the size of the U.S. multiracial population is closer to 7 percent, not 2.9 percent.

Complicating the situation is the fact that the Census asks people separately whether they are Hispanic or non-Hispanic. So a Hispanic person can be any race. In the 2010 Census, 94 percent of Hispanics indicated they were one race, but

6 percent indicated two or more races; this proportion was twice as high as it was among non-Hispanics. Therefore, Latinos are more likely than non-Hispanics to indicate a multiracial ancestry.

Changes in measuring race and ethnicity are not necessarily over. For Census 2020, bureau officials are considering adding categories for people of Middle Eastern, North African, or Asian descent. "Hispanic" may even be added as a "race category" along with White, African American, Asian, American Indian/Alaska Native, and Pacific Islander.

Regardless of government definitions, we know that some people do change their racial identity over time, choosing to self-identify as something different. This fluidity in individual self-definition could increase if the nation as a whole appears to be more accepting of biracial and multiracial categories.

The Census Bureau's decision does not necessarily resolve the frustration of hundreds of thousands of people, such as Stacey Davis, who daily face people trying to place them in some convenient racial or ethnic category. However, it does underscore the complexity of social construction and trying to apply arbitrary definitions to the diversity of the human population. A symbol of this social construction of race can be seen in Barack Obama, born of a White woman and a Black immigrant from Kenya. Although he has always identified himself as a Black man, it is worth noting that he was born in Hawai'i, a state in which 23.6 percent of people see themselves as more than one race, compared to the national average of 2.9 percent.

Sources: DaCosta 2007; Humes, Jones, and Ramirez 2011: 2–11; Pew Research Center 2015; Saperstein and Penner 2012; Saulny 2011; Welch 2011; Williams 2005.

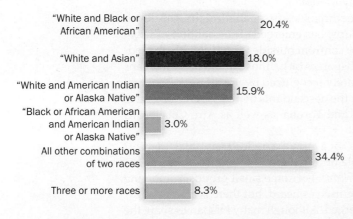

Figure 1.3 Multiple-Race Choices in Census 2010

This figure shows the percentage distribution of the 9 million people who chose two or more races (out of the total U.S. population of 309 million).

SOURCE: Data from Humes, Jones, and Ramirez 2011:10.

ethnic identity. Yet the growth of a variety of panethnic associations among many groups, including Hispanics, continues into the twenty-first century (Espiritu 1992; Mora 2014).

Another challenge to identity is **marginality**: the status of being between two cultures, as in the case of a person whose mother is a Jew and whose father a Christian. A century ago, Du Bois (1903) spoke eloquently of the "double consciousness" that Black Americans feel—being citizens of the United States but viewed as something quite apart from the dominant social groups in society. Incomplete assimilation by immigrants also results in marginality. Although a Filipina woman migrating to the United States may take on the characteristics of her new host society, she may not be fully accepted and may, therefore, feel neither Filipina nor American. Marginalized individuals often encounter social situations in which their identities are sources of tension, especially when the expression of multiple identities is not accepted, and they find themselves being perceived differently in different environments, with varying expectations (Park 1928; Stonequist 1937; Townsend, Markos, and Bergsieker 2009).

Yet another type marginality is that experienced by children of biracial or multiracial parental backgrounds and children adopted by parents of a different racial or ethnic background. For these children or adolescents, developing their racial or ethnic identity requires them to negotiate society's desire to put labels on them (Fryer et al. 2012).

As we seek to understand diversity in the United States, we must be mindful that ethnic and racial labels are just that: labels that have been socially constructed. Yet these social constructs can have a powerful impact, whether they are self-applied or applied by others.

Sociology and the Study of Race and Ethnicity

1.3   Describe how sociology helps us understand race and ethnicity.

Before proceeding further with our study of racial and ethnic groups, let us consider several sociological perspectives that provide insight into dominant–subordinate relationships. **Sociology** is the systematic study of social behavior and human groups, so it is well suited to enlarging our understanding of intergroup relations. The study of race relations has a long, valuable history in sociology. Admittedly, it has not always been progressive; indeed, at times it has reflected the prejudices of society. In some instances, sociology scholars who are members of racial, ethnic, and religious minorities, as well as women, have not been permitted to make the contributions they are capable of making to the field.

Stratification by Class and Gender

That some members have unequal amounts of wealth, prestige, or power is a characteristic of all societies. Sociologists observe that entire groups may be assigned less or more of what a society values. The hierarchy that emerges is called stratification. **Stratification** is the structured ranking of entire groups of people that perpetuates unequal rewards and power in a society.

Much discussion of stratification identifies the **class**, or social ranking, of people who share similar wealth, according to sociologist Max Weber's classic definition. Mobility from one class to another is not easy to achieve. Movement into classes of greater wealth may be particularly difficult for subordinate-group members faced with lifelong prejudice and discrimination (Banton 2008; Gerth and Mills 1958).

Recall that the first property of subordinate-group standing is unequal treatment by the dominant group in the form of prejudice, discrimination, and segregation. Stratification is intertwined with the subordination of racial, ethnic, religious, and gender groups. Race has implications for the way people are treated; so does class. One also must add the effects of race and class together. For example, being poor and Black is not the same as being either one by itself. A wealthy Mexican American is not the same as an affluent Anglo American or Mexican Americans as a group.

Public discussion of issues such as housing or public assistance often is disguised as a discussion of class issues, when, in fact, the issues are based primarily on race. Similarly, some topics such as the poorest of the poor or the working poor are addressed in terms of race when the class component should be explicit. Nonetheless, the link between race and class in society is abundantly clear (Winant 2004).

Another stratification factor that we need to consider is gender. How different is the situation for women as contrasted with men? Returning again to the first property of minority groups—unequal treatment and less control—women do not receive the same treatment as men. Whether the issue is jobs or poverty, education or crime, women typically have more difficult experiences. In addition, the situations women face in areas such as health care and welfare raise different concerns than they do for men. Just as we need to consider the role of social class to understand race and ethnicity better, we also need to consider the role of gender.

Theoretical Perspectives

Sociologists view society in different ways. Some see the world as a stable and ongoing entity. They note the endurance of a Chinatown, the general sameness of male–female roles over time, and other common aspects of intergroup relations. Other sociologists see society as composed of many groups in conflict, competing for scarce resources. Within this conflict, some people or even entire groups may be labeled or stigmatized in a way that blocks their access to what a society values. We examine three theoretical perspectives that are widely used by sociologists today: the functionalist, conflict, and labeling perspectives.

FUNCTIONALIST PERSPECTIVE   In the view of a functionalist, a society is like a living organism in which each part contributes to the survival of the whole. The **functionalist perspective** emphasizes how the parts of society are structured to maintain its stability. According to this approach, if an aspect of social life does not contribute to a society's stability or survival, then it will not be passed on from one generation to the next.

It seems reasonable to assume that bigotry between races offers no such positive function, and so we ask: Why does it persist? Although agreeing that racial hostility is hardly to be admired, the functionalist would point out that it serves some positive functions from the perspective of the racists. We can identify five functions that racial beliefs have for the dominant group:

1. Racist ideologies such as the belief in the inherent inferiority of entire groups of people provide a moral justification for maintaining a society that routinely deprives a group of its rights and privileges.

2. Racist beliefs discourage subordinate people from attempting to question their lowly status and why they must perform "the dirty work"; to do so is to question the very foundation of the society.

3. Racial ideologies not only justify existing practices but also serve as a rallying point for social movements, as seen in the rise of the Nazi party or present-day Aryan movements.

4. Racist myths encourage support for the existing order. Some argue that if there were any major societal change, the subordinate group would suffer even greater poverty, and the dominant group would suffer lower living standards.

5. Racist beliefs relieve the dominant group of the responsibility to address the economic and educational problems faced by subordinate groups.

As a result, racial ideology grows when a value system (e.g., that underlying a colonial empire or slavery) is being threatened (Levin and Nolan 2011:115–145; Nash 1962).

Prejudice and discrimination also cause definite dysfunctions. **Dysfunctions** are elements of society that may disrupt a social system or decrease its stability. Racism is dysfunctional to a society, including to its dominant group, in six ways:

1. A society that practices discrimination fails to use the resources of all individuals. Discrimination limits the search for talent and leadership to the dominant group.

2. Discrimination aggravates social problems such as poverty, delinquency, and crime, and it places the financial burden of alleviating these problems on the dominant group.

3. Society must invest a good deal of time and money to defend the barriers that prevent the full participation of all members.

4. Racial prejudice and discrimination undercut goodwill and friendly diplomatic relations between nations. They also negatively affect efforts to increase global trade.

5. Social change is inhibited because change may assist a subordinate group.

6. Discrimination promotes disrespect for law enforcement and for the peaceful settlement of disputes.

That racism has costs for the dominant group as well as for the subordinate group reminds us that intergroup conflict is exceedingly complex (Bowser and Hunt 1996; Feagin, Vera, and Batur 2000; Rose 1951).

CONFLICT PERSPECTIVE   In contrast to the functionalists' emphasis on stability, conflict sociologists see the social world as being in continual struggle. The **conflict perspective** assumes that the social structure is best understood in terms of conflict or tension between competing groups. The result of this conflict is significant economic disparity and structural inequality in education, the labor market, housing, and health care. Specifically, society is in a struggle between the privileged (the dominant group) and the exploited (the subordinate group). Such conflicts need not be physically violent and may take the form of immigration restrictions, real-estate practices, or disputes over cuts in the federal budget.

The conflict model is often used today to examine race and ethnicity because it readily accounts for the presence of tension between competing groups. According to the conflict perspective, competition takes place between groups with unequal amounts of economic and political power. The minorities are exploited or, at best, ignored by the dominant group. The conflict perspective is more radical and activist than functionalism because conflict theorists emphasize social change and the redistribution of resources.

Those who follow the conflict approach to race and ethnicity have remarked repeatedly that the subordinate group is criticized for its low status. That the dominant group is responsible for subordination is often ignored. William Ryan (1976) calls this phenomenon **blaming the victim**: portraying the problems of racial and ethnic minorities as their fault rather than recognizing society's responsibility.

Conflict theorists consider the costs that come with residential segregation. Besides the more obvious cost of reducing housing options, racial and social class isolation reduces for people (including Whites) all available options in schools, retail shopping, and medical care. People, however, can travel to access services and businesses, and it is more likely that racial and ethnic minorities will have to make that sometimes costly and time-consuming trip.

LABELING THEORY   Related to the conflict perspective and its concern over blaming the victim is **labeling theory**, a concept introduced by sociologist Howard Becker to explain why certain people are viewed as deviant while others engaging in the same behavior are not. Students of crime and deviance have relied heavily on labeling theory. According to labeling theory, a youth who misbehaves may be considered and treated as a delinquent (deviant) if he or she comes from the "wrong kind of family." Another youth from a middle-class family who commits the same misbehavior might be given another chance before being punished.

The labeling perspective directs our attention to the role that negative stereotypes play in race and ethnicity. The image that prejudiced

From the conflict perspective, the emphasis should not be primarily on the attributes of the individual (i.e., blaming the victim) but on structural factors such as the labor market, affordable housing, and availability of programs to assist people with addiction or mental-health issues.

Q-Images/Alamy Stock Photo

people maintain of a group toward which they hold ill feelings is called a stereotype. **Stereotypes** are unreliable generalizations about all members of a group that do not take individual differences into account. The warrior image of Native American (American Indian) people is perpetuated by the frequent use of tribal names or even names such as "Indians" and "Redskins" for sports teams. This labeling is not limited to racial and ethnic groups, however. For instance, age can be used to exclude a person from an activity in which he or she is qualified to engage. Groups are subjected to stereotypes and discrimination in such a way that their treatment resembles that of social minorities. Social prejudice as a result of stereotyping exists toward ex-convicts, gamblers, alcoholics, transgender people, lesbians, gay men, prostitutes, people with AIDS, and people with disabilities, to name a few.

The labeling approach points out that stereotypes, when applied by people in power, can have negative consequences for people or groups. A crucial aspect of the relationship between dominant and subordinate groups is the prerogative of the dominant group to define society's values. U.S. sociologist William I. Thomas (1923), an early critic of racial and gender discrimination, saw that the "definition of the situation" could mold the personality of the individual. In other words, Thomas observed that people respond not only to the objective features of a situation (or person) but also to the meaning these features have for them. So, for example, a lone walker seeing a young Black man walking toward him may perceive the situation differently than if the oncoming person is an older woman. Sociologist Elijah Anderson (2011) has long seen passersby scrutinize him and other African American males more closely and suspiciously than they would women or White males. In other words, people can create false images, definitions, or stereotypes that have real social consequences.

In certain situations, we may respond to negative stereotypes and act on them, with the result that false definitions become accurate. This result is known as a **self-fulfilling prophecy**. A person described as having particular characteristics begins to display the very traits attributed to him or her. Thus, a child who is praised for being a natural comic may focus on learning to become funny to gain approval and attention. In other words, dominant-group definitions of minority groups may have a self-validating effect.

Self-fulfilling prophecies can be devastating for minority groups. For example, as Figure 1.4 shows, the subordinate-group individual may attend a poorly financed school that leaves him or her unequipped to perform jobs that offer high status and pay. He or she then gets a low-paying job and must settle for a much lower standard of living. The rationale of the

Figure 1.4 Self-Fulfilling Prophecy

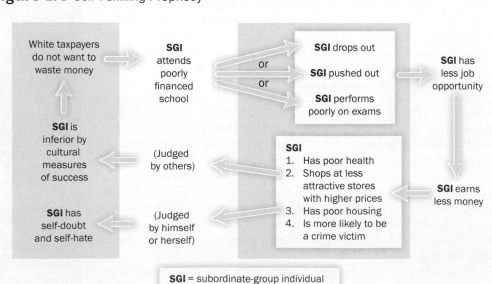

dominant society is that these minority people lack the ability to perform in more important and lucrative positions. Training to become scientists, executives, or physicians is denied to many subordinate-group individuals (SGIs), who are then locked into society's inferior jobs. As a result, the false definition of the self-fulfilling prophecy becomes real. The subordinate group becomes inferior because it was defined at the start as inferior and was, therefore, prevented from achieving the levels attained by the majority.

Because of this vicious circle, talented SGIs may come to see the fields of entertainment and professional sports as their only hope for achieving wealth and fame. Thus, it is no accident that successive waves of Irish, Jewish, Italian, African American, and Hispanic performers and athletes have made their mark on culture in the United States. Unfortunately, these very successes may convince the dominant group that its original stereotypes were valid—that these are the only areas of society in which subordinate-group members can excel. Furthermore, athletics and the arts are highly competitive areas. For every LeBron James and Jennifer Lopez who makes it, many, many more SGIs will end up disappointed.

The Creation of Subordinate-Group Status

1.4   Explain how subordinate groups are created.

Three situations are likely to lead to the formation of a relationship between a subordinate group and the dominant group. A subordinate group can emerge through migration, annexation, and/or colonialism.

Migration

People who emigrate to a new country often find themselves a minority in that new country. Cultural or physical traits or religious affiliation may set the immigrant apart from the dominant group. Immigration from Europe, Asia, and Latin America has been a powerful force in shaping the fabric of life in the United States. **Migration** is the general term used to describe any transfer of population. **Emigration** (by emigrants) means leaving a country to settle in another country. **Immigration** (by immigrants) denotes coming into the new country. As an example, from Vietnam's perspective, the "boat people" were emigrants from Vietnam to the United States, but in the United States they were counted as U.S. immigrants.

Although some people migrate because they want to, leaving one's home country is not always voluntary. Millions have been transported as slaves against their will. Conflict and war have displaced people throughout human history. The twentieth century saw huge population movements caused by two world wars; revolutions in Spain, Hungary, and Cuba; the partition of British India; conflicts in Southeast Asia, Korea, and Central America; and confrontations between Arabs and Israelis. Involuntary migration guarantees a subordinate role for the migrating group. Although enslavement has a long history, all industrialized societies today prohibit slavery. Of course, many contemporary societies, including the United States, bear the legacy of slavery.

In all types of movement, even when a U.S. family moves from Ohio to Florida, but especially regarding emigration, two sets of forces operate: push factors and pull factors. *Push factors* discourage a person from remaining where he or she lives. Religious persecution and economic factors such as dissatisfaction with employment opportunities are common push factors. *Pull factors* encourage a person to move to a new location. Pull factors that attract an immigrant to a particular country include a better standard of living, friends and relatives who have already emigrated, and a promised job.

Migration has taken on new significance in the twenty-first century partly because of **globalization**, or the worldwide integration of government policies, cultures, social movements, and financial markets through trade and the exchange of ideas. The increased movement of people and money across borders has made the distinction between temporary and permanent migration less meaningful. Even after they have relocated, people maintain global linkages to their former country and with a global economy (Richmond 2002).

Annexation

Nations, particularly during wars or as a result of war, incorporate or attach land through the process of **annexation**. This new land is contiguous to the nation's existing border, as in the German annexation of Austria and Czechoslovakia in 1938 and 1939 and in the U.S. Louisiana Purchase of 1803. The Treaty of Guadalupe Hidalgo, which ended the Mexican-American War in 1848, gave the United States California, Utah, Nevada, most of New Mexico, and parts of Arizona, Wyoming, and Colorado. The indigenous peoples in some of this huge territory were dominant in their society one day, only to become minority-group members the next.

When annexation occurs, the dominant power generally suppresses the language and culture of the minority. Such was the practice of Russia with the Ukrainians and Poles, and of Prussia with the Poles. Minorities often try to maintain their cultural integrity despite annexation. In the twentieth century, Poles inhabited an area divided into territories ruled by three countries but maintained their own culture across political boundaries.

Colonialism

Colonialism has been the most common way for one group of people to dominate another. **Colonialism** is the maintenance of political, social, economic, and cultural dominance over people by a foreign power for an extended period (Bell 1991). Colonialism is rule by outsiders, but unlike annexation, it does not involve actual incorporation into the dominant people's nation. The long-standing control that was exercised by the British Empire over much of North America, parts of Africa, and India is an example of colonial domination (Figure 1.5).

Figure 1.5 World Colonial Empires (1900)

Events of the nineteenth century increased European dominance over the world. By 1900, most independent African nations had disappeared, and the major European powers and Japan took advantage of China's internal weakness to gain both trading ports and economic concessions.

SOURCE: DIVINE, ROBERT A.; BREEN, T. H.; WILLIAMS, R. HAL; GROSS, ARIELA, J.; BRANDS, H. W., AMERICA: PAST AND PRESENT, 10th Ed., © 2013, p. 506. Reprinted and Electronically reproduced by permission of Pearson Education, Inc., Upper Saddle River, New Jersey.

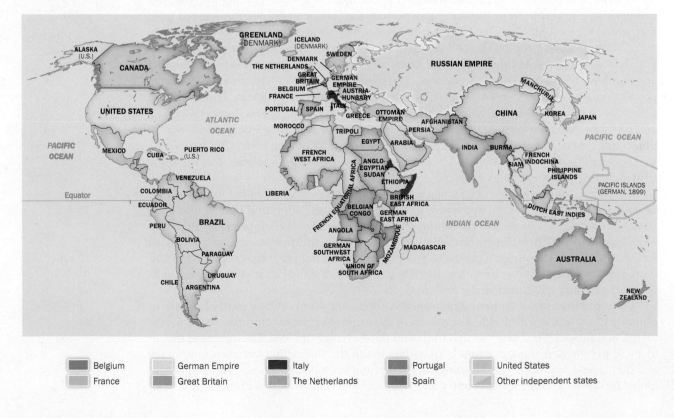

Figure 1.6 Spectrum of Intergroup Relations

EXPULSION	SEGREGATION	ASSIMILATION

INCREASINGLY UNACCEPTABLE — MORE TOLERABLE

EXTERMINATION	SECESSION	FUSION	PLURALISM
or genocide	or partitioning	or amalgamation or melting pot	or multiculturalism

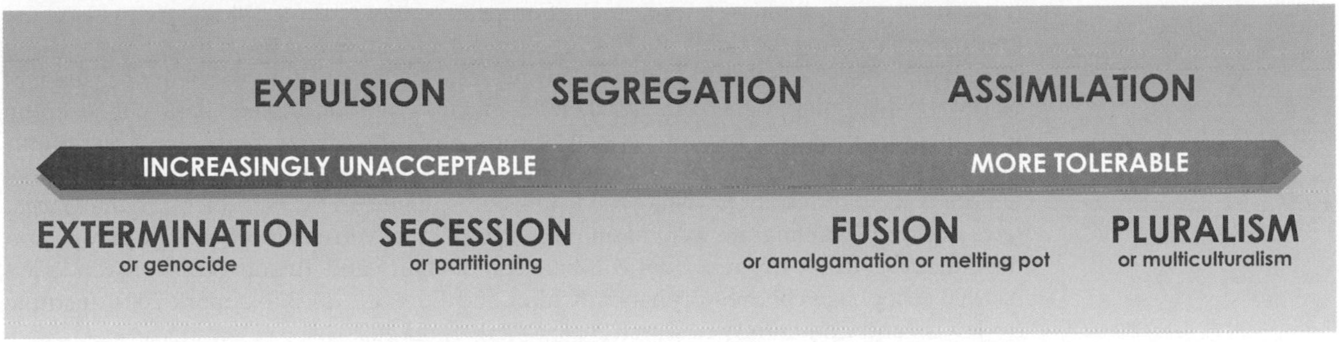

Societies gain power over a foreign land through military strength, sophisticated political organization, and investment capital. The extent of power may also vary according to the dominant group's scope of settlement in the colonial land. Relations between the colonizing nation and the colonized people are similar to those between a dominant group and exploited subordinate groups. Colonial subjects generally are limited to menial jobs and the wages from their labor. The natural resources of their land benefit the members of the ruling class.

By the 1980s, colonialism, in the sense of political rule, had become largely a phenomenon of the past, yet industrial countries of North America and Europe still dominated the world economically and politically. Drawing on the conflict perspective, sociologist Immanuel Wallerstein (1974) described today's global economic system as very similar to the economic system that prevailed at the height of colonialism. Wallerstein advanced the **world systems theory**, which views the global economic system as divided between nations that control wealth and those that provide natural resources and labor. The limited economic resources available in developing nations worsen many of the ethnic, racial, and religious conflicts noted at the beginning of this chapter. In addition, the presence of massive inequality between nations only serves to encourage immigration generally and, more specifically, the movement of many of the most skilled workers from developing nations to the industrial nations.

The Spectrum of Intergroup Status

Relationships between and among racial, ethnic, and religious groups, as well as other dominate-subordinate relationships, are not static. These relations change over time, sometimes in one's own lifetime. To illustrate this idea, we can use the Spectrum of Intergroup Relations in Figure 1.6. These relationships can be viewed along a continuum from those largely unacceptable to the subordinate group (such as extermination and expulsion) to those that are more tolerated (such as assimilation and pluralism).

The Consequences of Subordinate-Group Status

1.5   Summarize the consequences of subordinate-group status.

A group with subordinate status faces several consequences. These differ in their degree of harshness, ranging from physical annihilation to absorption into the dominant group. In this section, we examine seven consequences of subordinate-group status: extermination, expulsion, secession, segregation, fusion, assimilation, and pluralism.

Extermination

The most extreme way to deal with a subordinate group is to eliminate it. **Genocide** is the deliberate, systematic killing of an entire people or nation. This term is often used in reference to the Holocaust, Nazi Germany's extermination of 12 million European Jews and other ethnic minorities during World War II. The **Holocaust** was the state-sponsored systematic persecution and annihilation of European Jews by Nazi Germany and its collaborators. The move to eliminate Jews from the European continent started slowly, with Germany gradually restricting the rights of Jews: for example, by preventing them from voting, living outside the Jewish ghetto, and owning businesses. Much anti-Semitic cruelty was evident before the beginning of the war. *Kristallnacht*, or the "Night of Broken Glass," in Berlin on November 9, 1938, was a turning point toward genocide. Ninety Berlin Jews were murdered, hundreds of homes and synagogues were set on fire or ransacked, and thousands of windows were broken in Jewish-owned stores. Despite the obvious intolerance they faced, Jews desiring to immigrate were often turned back by government officials in Europe and the Americas. In 1994, a genocidal war between the Hutu and Tutsi people in Rwanda left 300,000 school-age children orphaned (Chirot and Edwards 2003; Naimark 2004; Institute for Jewish and Community Research 2008; DellaPergola 2007).

The term **ethnic cleansing** refers to the forced deportation of people, accompanied by systematic violence, including death. The term was introduced in 1992 when ethnic Serbs instituted a policy intended to "cleanse"—eliminate—Muslims from parts of Bosnia.

Genocide also appropriately describes White policies toward Native Americans in the nineteenth century. In 1800, the American Indian population in the United States was approximately 600,000; by 1850, it had been reduced to 250,000 through warfare with the U.S. Army, disease, and forced relocation to inhospitable environments, all of which led to the death of many Native Americans.

In 2008, the Australian government officially apologized for its past brutality toward and neglect of its native people, the Aboriginal population. The government's policies led to a quarter of Aboriginal children, the so-called lost generation, being taken from their families and placed in orphanages or foster homes, or being put up for adoption by White Australians, until the policies were finally abandoned in 1969 (Johnston 2008).

Expulsion

Dominant groups may choose to force a specific subordinate group to leave certain areas or even vacate a country. Expulsion, therefore, is another extreme consequence of minority-group status. European colonial powers in North America and eventually the U.S. government itself drove almost all Native Americans off their tribal lands and into unfamiliar territory.

In the 1990s, the monarchy in Bhutan, which was sympathetic to Buddhists, expelled 107,000 Nepali-speaking Hindus from the southern part of the country. Languishing for nearly 20 years in refugee camps, they eventually were resettled. Some went to Australia or Canada, but the majority (approximately 70,000) came to the United States to communities like Manchester, New Hampshire, as described at the beginning of this chapter.

More recently, beginning in 2009, France expelled over 10,000 ethnic Roma (Gypsies), forcing them to return to their home countries of Bulgaria and Romania. This expulsion appeared to violate the European Union's (EU) ban against targeting ethnic groups, as well as the EU's policy of "freedom of movement." In 2011, the EU withdrew its threat of legal action against France when the government said it would no longer expel Roma in particular but only those living in "illegal camps," which many observers see as a technicality that allows France to get around long-standing human-rights policies.

Stigmatizing and expelling minority groups are not actions of the distant past. Here, police in Paris round up Roma (Gypsies) for subsequent expulsion from the country.

Marc Greiner/Maxppp/ZUMApress/Newscom

Secession

A group ceases to be a subordinate group when it secedes to form a new nation or moves to an already-established nation, where it becomes dominant. After Great Britain withdrew from Palestine, Jewish people achieved a dominant position in 1948, attracting Jews from throughout the world to the new state of Israel. Similarly, Pakistan was created in 1947 during the Indian partition. The predominantly Muslim areas in the north became Pakistan, making India predominantly Hindu.

Throughout the twentieth century, minorities repudiated dominant customs, and they continue to do so. For example, the Estonian, Latvian, Lithuanian, and Armenian peoples, not content to be merely tolerated by the majority, all seceded to form independent states after the demise of the Soviet Union in 1991. In 1999, ethnic Albanians fought bitterly for their cultural and political recognition in the Kosovo region of Yugoslavia.

Some African Americans have called for secession. Suggestions dating back to the early 1700s supported the return of Blacks to Africa as a solution to racial problems. The American Colonization Society suggested resettling Blacks in Liberia, but proposals were also advanced to establish settlements in other areas. Territorial separatism and the emigrationist ideology were recurrent and interrelated themes among African Americans from the late nineteenth century well into the 1980s. The Black Muslims, or Nation of Islam, once expressed the desire for complete separation in their own state or territory within the modern borders of the United States.

Segregation

Segregation is the physical separation of two groups in residence, workplace, and social functions. Generally, the dominant group imposes segregation on a subordinate group. Segregation is rarely complete, however. Intergroup contact inevitably occurs even in the most segregated societies.

Sociologists Douglas Massey and Nancy Denton wrote *American Apartheid* (1993), which described segregation in U.S. cities on the basis of 1990 census data. The title of their book was meant to indicate that segregation in U.S. neighborhoods resembled **apartheid**, the rigid government-imposed racial segregation that prevailed for so long in the Republic of South Africa.

Analysis of census data shows continuing segregation in the United States despite the country's racial and ethnic diversity. Scholars use a *segregation index* to measure separation. This index ranges from 0 (complete integration) to 100 (complete segregation), where the value indicates the percentage of the minority group that needs to move for the minority group to be distributed exactly like Whites. Thus a segregation index of 60 for Blacks–Whites would mean that 60 percent of all African Americans would have to move to have the same residential pattern as Whites.

Table 1.2 lists the most segregated metropolitan areas with large African American, Latino, and Asian American populations. Blacks and Whites are most separated from each other in Milwaukee/Waukesha/West Allis. The Los Angeles/Long Beach/Anaheim metropolitan area finds Whites and Latinos most living apart, and the Edison/New Brunswick, New Jersey, area is where Asians and Whites are most segregated from each other. Typically half to three-quarters of the people would have to move to achieve even distribution throughout the city and surrounding suburbs.

Over the past 40 years, Black–White segregation has declined modestly. Hispanic–White segregation, while lower, has not grown over the last 40 years. Asian–White segregation is even a bit lower but also has been mostly unchanged. Even when we consider social class, the patterns of minority segregation persist. Despite the occasional multiracial neighborhood, segregation prevails (Massey 2016; Rugh and Massey 2014).

This focus on metropolitan areas should not cause us to ignore the continuing legally sanctioned segregation of Native Americans on reservations. Although the majority of our nation's first inhabitants live outside these tribal areas, the reservations play a prominent role in the identity of Native Americans. Although it is easier to maintain tribal identity on the reservation, economic and educational opportunities are more limited in these areas, which are segregated from the rest of society.

A particularly troubling pattern has been the emergence of **resegregation**, or the physical separation of racial and ethnic groups reappearing after a period of relative integration. Resegregation has occurred in neighborhoods and schools after a transitional period of desegregation. For example, in 1954, only one in 100,000 Black students attended a majority White school in the South. Thanks to the civil rights movement and a series of civil rights measures,

Table 1.2 Segregated Metro America

BLACK–WHITE

1. Milwaukee/Waukesha/West Allis	81.0
2. New York/Newark/Jersey City	77.0
3. Chicago/Naperville/Elgin	76.0
4. Detroit/Warren/Dearborn	74.0
5. Cleveland/Elyria	73.0
6. Buffalo/Cheektowaga/Niagara Falls	73.0
7. St. Louis	72.0
8. Los Angeles/Long Beach/Anaheim	68.0

HISPANIC–WHITE

1. Los Angeles/Long Beach/Anaheim	61.0
2. New York/Newark/Jersey City	61.0
3. Providence/Warwick, RI	60.0
4. Boston/Cambridge/Newton, MA	60.0
5. Hartford/West Hartford/East Hartford, CT	58.0
6. Milwaukee/Waukesha/West Ellis	57.0
7. Miami/Ft. Lauderdale/West Palm Beach	56.0
8. Chicago/Naperville/Elgin	56.0

ASIAN–WHITE

1. Edison/New Brunswick, NJ	53.7
2. New York/White Plains	49.5
3. Houston	48.7
4. Los Angeles/Long Beach	47.6
5. Boston	47.4
6. Sacramento, CA	46.8
7. San Francisco	46.7
8. Warren/Farmington Hills, MI	46.3

Note: The higher the value, the more segregated the metropolitan area. Data are 2011–2015 except for Asian–White data, which are for 2010.

SOURCE: Frey 2016; Logan and Stults 2011.

by 1968, Black student attendance in White-majority schools rose to 23 percent and then to 47 percent by 1988. The latest analysis, however, shows continuing racial isolation. A 2014 report documents that nationwide, school segregation prevails. As the minority population has grown, such as in the suburbs recently, segregation has soared (Orfield and Frankenberg 2014).

Given segregation patterns, many Whites in the United States have limited contact with people of other racial and ethnic backgrounds. One study of 100 affluent powerful White men looked at their experiences, past and present, and determined that they had lived in a "White bubble"—their neighborhoods, schools, elite colleges, and workplaces were overwhelmingly White. The continuing pattern of segregation in the United States means our diverse population grows up in very different nations. For many urban Blacks and Latinos, segregation in neighborhoods with limited job opportunities is a social fact (Bonilla-Silva and Embrick 2007; Feagin and O'Brien 2003; Massey 2012).

Segregation by race, ethnicity, religion, tribal or clan affiliation, and sometimes even language grouping occurs throughout the world. The most dramatic government-engineered segregation in recent history was in South Africa. In 1948, Great Britain granted South Africa its independence, and the National Party, dominated by a White minority, assumed control of the government. The rule of White supremacy, well under way as the custom in the colonial period, became more and more formalized into law. To deal with the multiracial population, the Whites devised a policy called apartheid to ensure their dominance. *Apartheid* (in Afrikaans, the language of the White Afrikaners, it means *separation* or *apartness*) came to mean a policy of separate development, euphemistically called *multinational development* by the government. Black South Africans were relegated to impoverished urban townships or rural areas, and their mobility within the country was strictly regulated. Events took a significant turn in 1990, when the South African prime minister legalized once-banned Black organizations and freed Nelson Mandela, leader of the African National Congress (ANC), after 27 years of imprisonment. Soon afterward, Mandela became head of the government, and a half-century of apartheid came to an end.

Fusion

Fusion occurs when a minority and a majority group combine to form a new group. This combining can be expressed as $A + B + C \rightarrow D$, where A, B, and C represent the groups present in a society and D signifies the result, an ethnocultural–racial group that shares some of the characteristics of each initial group. Mexican people are an example of fusion, originating as they do from the mixing of Spanish and indigenous Indian cultures. Theoretically, fusion does not entail intermarriage, but it is very similar to **amalgamation**, the process by which a dominant group and a subordinate group combine through intermarriage into a new people. In everyday speech, the words *fusion* and *amalgamation* are rarely used, but the concept is expressed in the notion of a human **melting pot** in which diverse racial or ethnic groups form a new creation, a new cultural entity (Newman 1973).

The analogy of the cauldron, the "melting pot," was first used to describe the United States by the French observer Crèvecoeur in 1782. The phrase dates back to the Middle Ages, when alchemists attempted to change less-valuable metals into gold and silver. Similarly, the idea of the human melting pot implied that the new group would represent only the best qualities and attributes of the different cultures contributing to it. The belief in the United States as a melting pot became widespread in the early twentieth century. This belief suggested that the United States had an almost divine mission to destroy artificial divisions and create a single kind of human. However, the dominant group had indicated its unwillingness to welcome such groups as Native Americans, Blacks, Hispanics, Jews, Asians, and Irish Catholics into the melting pot. It is a mistake to think of the United States as an ethnic melting pot. Although superficial signs of fusion are present, as in a cuisine that includes sauerkraut and spaghetti, most contributions of subordinate groups are ignored (Gleason 1980).

Marriage patterns indicate the resistance to fusion. People are unwilling, in varying degrees, to marry outside their own ethnic, religious, and racial groups. Until relatively recently, interracial marriage was outlawed in much of the United States. At the time that President Barack Obama's White mother and Black father were married in Hawai'i, their union would have been illegal in 22 other states. Surveys show that 20 to 50 percent of various White ethnic groups report single ancestry. When White ethnics do cross boundaries, they tend to marry within their religion and social class. For example, Italians are more likely to marry Irish, who are also Catholic, than they are to marry Protestant Swedes.

Although it may seem that interracial matches are everywhere, there is only modest evidence of a fusion of races in the United States. Nonetheless, racial intermarriage has been increasing. In 1980, there were 651,000 interracial marriages, but by 2010, there were 5.4 million. By 2015, about 10 percent of people married someone of a different race or ethnicity. Among unmarried couples, the number rises to 14 percent and among same-sex couples to 15 percent.

Among couples in which at least one member is Hispanic, marriages with a non-Hispanic partner account for 28 percent. Taken together, all interracial and Hispanic–non-Hispanic marriages account for 10 percent of married opposite-sex couples today. But this number includes people who have been married for decades. Among new couples, about 17 percent of marriages are between people of different races or between Hispanics and non-Hispanics (Bialik 2017; Bureau of the Census 2010a: Table 60; Lofquist et al. 2012).

While still not typical, more couples are crossing racial and ethnic boundaries in the United States today than in any previous generation. Clearly, this trend will increase the potential for their children to identify as biracial or multiracial rather than in a single category.

Sirtravelalot/Shutterstock

One aspect of assimilation is immigrants' attempt to learn the language of the host society, as shown in this adult bilingual education class.

Assimilation

Assimilation is the process by which a subordinate individual or group takes on the characteristics of the dominant group and is eventually accepted as part of that group. Assimilation is a majority ideology in which A + B + C → A. The majority (A) dominates in such a way that the minorities (B and C) become indistinguishable from the dominant group. Assimilation dictates conformity to the dominant group, regardless of how many racial, ethnic, or religious groups are involved (Newman 1973:53).

To be complete, assimilation must entail an active effort by the minority-group individual to shed all distinguishing actions and beliefs and the unqualified acceptance of that individual by the dominant society. In the United States, dominant White society encourages assimilation. The assimilation perspective tends to devalue alien culture and to treasure the dominant. For example, assimilation assumes that whatever is admirable among Blacks was adapted from Whites and that whatever is bad is inherently Black. The assimilation solution to Black–White conflict has been typically defined as the development of a consensus around White American values.

Assimilation is very difficult. The person being assimilated must forsake his or her cultural tradition to become part of a different, often antagonistic culture. However, cross-border movement is often preceded by adjustments and awareness of the culture that awaits the immigrant. Furthermore, the dominant group, White Americans in this case, totally defines what is an acceptable level of assimilation (Schachter 2016, Skrentny 2008).

Assimilation does not occur at the same pace for all groups or for all individuals in the same group. Typically, the assimilation process is not completed by the first generation—the new arrivals. Assimilation is not a smooth process (Warner and Srole 1945) and tends to take longer under the following conditions:

- The differences between the minority and the majority are large.
- The majority is not receptive, or the minority retains its own culture.
- The minority group arrives over a short period of time.
- The minority-group residents are concentrated rather than dispersed.
- The arrival is recent, and the homeland is accessible.

Segmented assimilation describes the outcome of immigrants and their descendants moving into different classes of the host society. It emphasizes that there is not a single, uniform lifestyle in the United States and that much assimilation is into the working or even lower classes. For a very small number of people, such as high-level and elite engineers and other professionals, the movement might be into the higher reaches of class divisions. However, for many, assimilation may be into a lower class than that enjoyed in their home country and may represent downward mobility even while assimilation progresses (Haller, Portes, and Lynch 2011).

Many people view assimilation as unfair or even dictatorial. However, most members of the dominant group believe it is reasonable that subordinate people shed their distinctive cultural traditions. In public discussions today, assimilation is the ideology of the dominant group in forcing people how to act. Consequently, the social institutions in the United States—the educational system, economy, government, religion, and medical establishment—all push toward assimilation, with only occasional references to the pluralist approach, which we discuss next.

The Pluralist Perspective

Thus far, we have concentrated on how subordinate groups cease to exist (removal) or take on the characteristics of the dominant group (assimilation). The alternative to these relationships between the majority and the minority is pluralism. **Pluralism** implies that various groups in a society have mutual respect for one another's culture, a respect that allows minorities to express their own culture without suffering prejudice or discrimination. Whereas the assimilationist or integrationist seeks the elimination of ethnic boundaries, the pluralist believes in maintaining many of them.

There are limits to cultural freedom. A Romanian immigrant to the United States cannot expect to avoid learning English and still move up the occupational ladder. To survive, a society must have a consensus among its members on basic ideals, values, and beliefs. Nevertheless, there is still plenty of room for variety. Earlier, fusion was described as $A + B + C \rightarrow D$ and assimilation as $A + B + C \rightarrow A$. Using this same scheme, we can think of pluralism as $A + B + C \rightarrow A + B + C$, with groups coexisting in one society (Manning 1995; Newman 1973; Simpson 1995).

In the United States, cultural pluralism is more an ideal than a reality. Although there are instances of cultural pluralism—in the various ethnic neighborhoods in major cities, for instance—the general progression has been for subordinate groups to assimilate. Yet as the minority becomes the numerical majority, the ability to live one's identity becomes a bit easier. African Americans, Hispanics, American Indians, and Asian Pacific Americans already outnumber Whites in most of the largest U.S. cities. The trend is toward even greater diversity. Nonetheless, the cost of cultural integrity throughout the nation's history has been high. The various Native American tribes have succeeded to a large extent in maintaining their heritage, but the price has been bare subsistence on federal reservations.

The United States is experiencing a reemergence of ethnic identification by groups that had previously expressed little interest in their heritage. Groups that make up the dominant majority also are reasserting their ethnic heritages. Various nationality groups are rekindling interest in almost-forgotten languages, customs, festivals, and traditions. In some instances, this expression of the past has taken the form of a protest against exclusion from the dominant society. For example, some Chinese youths chastise their elders for forgetting the old ways and accepting White American influence and control.

The most visible expression of pluralism is language use. As of 2015, more than one in every five people in the United States (21.5 percent) over age five spoke a language other than English at home (American Community Survey 2016a: Table B16001).

Facilitating a diverse and changing society affects just about every aspect of that society. Yet another nod to pluralism, although not nearly so obvious to the general population as language, are the changes within the funeral industry. Where Christian and Jewish funeral practices once dominated, funeral home professionals are now being trained to accommodate a variety of practices. Latinos often expect 24-hour viewing of their deceased, whereas Muslims may wish to participate in washing the deceased before burial in a grave pointing toward Mecca. Hindu and Buddhist requests to participate in cremation are now being respected (Brulliard 2006).

Resistance and Change

1.6 **Describe how resistance and change occur in racial and ethnic relations.**

By virtue of wielding power and influence, the dominant group may define the terms by which all members of society operate. This power is particularly evident in a slave society, but even in contemporary industrialized nations, the dominant group has a disproportionate role in shaping immigration policy, school curricula, and media content.

Subordinate groups do not merely accept the definitions and ideology proposed by the dominant group. A continuing theme in dominant–subordinate relations is the minority group's challenge to its subordination. Resistance by subordinate groups is well documented as they seek to promote change that will bring them more rights and privileges, if not true equality. Often, traditional notions of racial formation are overcome not only

Octavio Jones/ZUMA Press Inc/Alamy Stock Photo

Through recent efforts of collective action, African Americans and others sympathetic to the #BlackLivesMatter campaign have drawn attention to violence against Black youth, as in this demonstration in Tampa in 2016.

through panethnicity but also because Black people, along with Latinos and sympathetic Whites, join in the resistance to subordination (Moulder 1996; Winant 2004).

Resistance can be seen in efforts by racial and ethnic groups to maintain their identity through newspapers and organizations and in today's technological age through cable television stations, blogs, and Internet sites. Resistance manifests itself in social movements such as the civil rights movement, the feminist movement, and gay rights efforts. The passage of such legislation as the Age Discrimination Act or the Americans with Disabilities Act marks the success of oppressed groups in lobbying on their own behalf.

Resistance efforts may begin with small actions. For example, residents of an American Indian reservation may question why a toxic waste dump is to be located on their land. Although the dump may bring in money, the reservation's residents question the wisdom of such a move. Their concerns lead to further investigations of the extent to which American Indian lands are used disproportionately as containment areas for dangerous materials. This action in turn leads to a broader investigation of the ways in which minority-group people often find their neighborhoods "hosting" dumps and incinerators. These local efforts eventually lead the Environmental Protection Agency to monitor the disproportionate placement of toxic facilities in or near racial and ethnic minority communities.

Social media platforms provide a new vehicle for resistance and change. For example, the 2013 acquittal of a man who shot to death Trayvon Martin, an unarmed African American youth, mobilized Blacks and other groups concerned about violence against Black youth. A national survey at the time showed that only 9 percent of African Americans were "satisfied" with the verdict, compared to 25 percent of Hispanics and 49 percent of Whites. Some 60 percent of Whites felt that race was got more attention than it deserved in news coverage of the story.

People throughout the United States organized to call attention to the perceived indiscriminate shooting deaths of Black youths. An activist movement using the hashtag #BlackLivesMatter surfaced and continued to gain strength with each ensuing incident that seemingly showed that a Black life did not matter to a law-enforcement officer. One such incident was the death of Phil Castile in St. Paul, Minnesota, described at the beginning of this chapter (Pew Research Center for the People and the Press 2013).

Change has occurred. At the beginning of the twentieth century, lynching of Blacks was practiced in many parts of the country. At the beginning of the twenty-first century, laws punishing hate crimes are increasingly common and cover a variety of stigmatized groups. Although this social progress should not be ignored, the nation still must focus concern on the significant social inequalities that remain.

An even more basic form of resistance is to question societal values. In this book, we avoid using the term *American* to describe people of the United States because geographically, Brazilians, Canadians, and El Salvadorans are Americans as well. It is easy to overlook how members of the dominant group and social institutions have shaped our understanding of history. African American studies scholar Molefi Kete Asante (2007, 2008, 2015) has called for an **Afrocentric perspective** that emphasizes the customs of African cultures and how they have pervaded the history, culture, and behavior of Blacks in the United States and around the world. Afrocentrism seeks to balance **Eurocentrism** and works toward a multiculturalist or pluralist orientation in which no viewpoint is suppressed. The Afrocentric approach could become part of our school curriculum, which has not adequately acknowledged the importance of this heritage (King and Swartz 2015).

The Afrocentric perspective has attracted much attention in education. Opponents view it as a separatist view of history and culture that distorts both past and present. Its supporters counter that African peoples everywhere can come to full self-determination only when they are able to overthrow the dominance of White or Eurocentric intellectual interpretations (Conyers 2004).

The remarkable efforts by members of racial and ethnic minorities working with supportive White Americans beginning in the 1950s through the early 1970s successfully targeted overt racist symbols, as well as racist and sexist actions. Today's targets are more intractable and tend to emerge from institutional discrimination. Sociologist Douglas Massey (2011) argued that a central goal must be to reform the criminal justice system by demanding repeal of the following: the three-strikes law, mandatory minimum sentencing, and harsher penalties for crack than for powdered cocaine. Such targets are quite different from laws that prevented Blacks and women from serving on juries.

Intersectionality

1.7   Define and describe intersectionality.

Race and ethnicity, as well as other social identifiers, are important and define relationships of power (or lack of power). Yet they do not exist in isolation. Rather, they coexist with religion, gender, age, disability status, and sexual identity (among other identities). **Intersectionality** refers to the overlapping and interdependent system of advantage and disadvantage that positions people in society on the basis of race, class, gender, and other characteristics (Collins and Bilge 2016; Crenshaw 1989).

Awareness of intersectionality grew as female scholars noted that an emphasis on race could ignore other related processes of domination. For example, many women experience social inequality not only because of their gender but also because of their race and ethnicity. These citizens face a double or triple subordinate status based on their intersecting identities. A disproportionate share of this low-status group also is poor. African American feminist Patricia Hill Collins (2000, 2013:232–234) views intersectionality as creating a *matrix of domination* (Figure 1.7). Whites dominate non-Whites, men dominate women, and the affluent dominate the poor—race, class, and gender are interconnected.

Gender, race, and social class are not the only systems of oppression, but they do profoundly affect women and people of color in the United States. Other forms of categorization and stigmatization can also be included in this matrix. If we turn to the global stage, we can add citizenship status and being perceived as a "colonial subject" even long after colonialism has ended.

Figure 1.7 Intersectionality and the Matrix of Domination

Intersectionality illustrates how several social factors—including gender, social class, language spoken, and race and ethnicity—intersect and overlap to create a cumulative impact on a person's social standing.

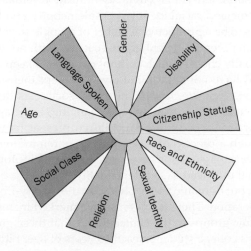

Critics argue that intersectionality is all about people who are obsessed with "identity politics" and who form alliances based on allegedly shared social groupings. Yet intersectionality is not so much about the identities themselves but rather how society uses and abuses these identities to exclude and privilege different groups. Addressing exclusion and acknowledging privilege are not easy; they require change (Crenshaw 2015).

Feminists have addressed themselves to the needs of minority women, but the oppression of these women because of their sex is overshadowed by the subordinate status that White men and White women impose on them because of their race or ethnicity. The question for the Latina (Hispanic woman), African American woman, Asian Pacific American woman, Native American woman, and so on appears to be whether she should unify with her brothers against racism or challenge them for their sexism. The answer is that society cannot afford to let up on the effort to eradicate sexism, racism, and the other forces that create social inequality.

Conclusion

One hundred years ago, sociologist and activist W. E. B. Du Bois took another famed Black activist, Booker T. Washington, to task for saying that the races could best work together apart, like fingers on a hand. Du Bois felt that Black people had to be a part of all social institutions and not create their own. With an African American having been elected and re-elected to the presidency of the United States, Whites, African Americans, and other groups continue to debate what form society should take. Should we seek to bring everyone together into an integrated whole? Or do we strive to maintain as much of our group identities as possible while working as cooperatively as necessary?

In considering the inequalities present today, as we do in the chapters that follow, it is easy to forget how much change has taken place and how much progress has been made. Much of the resistance to prejudice and discrimination in the past, either to slavery or to women's prohibition from voting, came from the members of the dominant group. The indignities still experienced by subordinate groups continue to be resisted as subordinate groups and their allies in the dominant group seek further change.

In this chapter, we have attempted to organize our approach to subordinate–dominant relations in the United States. We observed that subordinate groups do not necessarily contain fewer members than the dominant group. Subordinate groups are classified into racial, ethnic, religious, and gender groups. Biological differences of race are not supported by scientific data. Yet as the continuing debate over standardized tests demonstrates, attempts to establish a biological meaning of race have not been swept entirely into the dustbin of history. The social meaning attached to physical differences remains very significant. The dominant group has defined racial differences in such a way as to encourage or discourage the progress of certain groups.

Subordinate-group members' reactions include the seeking of an alternative avenue to acceptance and success: "Why should we give up what we are, to be accepted by them?" In response to this question, individual ethnic identification remains strong. As a result of this maintenance of ethnic and racial identity, complementary and occasionally competing images of what it means to be a productive member of a single society persist. Pluralism describes a society in which several different groups coexist, with no dominant or subordinate groups. People individually choose which cultural patterns to keep and which to let go.

Subordinate groups have not and do not always accept their second-class status passively. They may protest, organize, revolt, and resist society as defined by the dominant group. Patterns of race and ethnic relations are changing, not stagnant. Indicative of the changing landscape, biracial and multiracial children present us with new definitions of identity emerging through a process of racial formation, reminding us that race is socially constructed. In addition, we assume or have placed upon us multiple social identities that intersect in a manner that may lead to social inequality.

Society is not static, but dynamic and evolving. In the twenty-first century, we are facing new challenges to cooperation. There has been such a marked increase in the population of minority racial and ethnic groups in the United States that these groups will be in the majority well before today's college students reach 40 years of age. Little wonder that scholars are now talking about "super-diversity" and considering whether past notions of race and ethnicity are passé (Bobo 2013).

Continuing immigration and the explosive growth of the Hispanic population—which has more than doubled since 1990—fuels this growth. Latinos are now such a significant portion of the U.S. population that the Spanish-language Telemundo network has introduced English-language subtitles to ensure that its Latino viewers can fully comprehend its programming.

Barack Obama's presidency was a significant period in U.S. history. The fact that he was the first African American (and also the first non-White man) to serve as president demonstrates how much progress the United States has achieved with regard to race relations. It also underscores how long it has taken to make this progress and how much more needs to be accomplished before the United States can truly be "a more perfect union," as stated in the Constitution.

Yet the issues are exceedingly complex. The #BlackLivesMatter movement has brought attention to wrongful deaths of African Americans at the hands of law enforcement and to the needs of the less powerful to be heard. As African American writer Ralph Ellison wrote, "I am invisible, understand, simply because people refuse to see me." Black filmmaker Spike Lee supports the movement but believes we must also talk about the "self-inflicted genocide" of Black-on-Black crime (Smith 2015).

The problems are complex, as are the solutions, but this reality should not freeze us into inaction. The two significant forces that are absent in a truly pluralistic society are prejudice and discrimination. In an assimilation society, prejudice disparages out-group differences, and discrimination financially rewards those who shed their past. In the next two chapters, we explore the nature of prejudice and discrimination in the United States.

Summary of Learning Objectives

1.1 Explain how people are placed in groups.

1. When sociologists define a minority group, they are concerned primarily with the economic and political power, or powerlessness, of the group.

2. A racial group is set apart from others primarily by physical characteristics; an ethnic group is set apart primarily by national origin or cultural patterns.

1.2 Explain the social construction of race.

3. People cannot be sorted into distinct racial groups, so race is best viewed as a social construct that is subject to different interpretations over time.

4. A small but still significant number of people in the United States—more than 9 million— readily see themselves as having a biracial or multiracial identity.

1.3 Describe how sociology helps us understand race and ethnicity.

5. The study of race and ethnicity in the United States often considers the role played by class and gender.

6. We can use three sociological schools of thought to gain insight into racial and ethnic groups and their relationships to the dominant society: the functionalist perspective, the conflict perspective, and labeling theory.

1.4 Explain how subordinate groups are created.

7. Subordinate-group status has emerged through migration, annexation, and colonialism.

8. The Spectrum of Intergroup Relations illustrates the patterns between racial and ethnic groups ranging from those that are extremely harsh to those that are more tolerated.

1.5 Summarize the consequences of subordinate-group status.

9. The social consequences of subordinate-group status include extermination, expulsion, secession, segregation, fusion, assimilation, and pluralism.

1.6 Describe how resistance and change occur in racial and ethnic relations.

10. Racial, ethnic, and other minorities maintain a long history of resisting efforts to restrict their rights.

1.7 Define and describe intersectionality.

11. The intersectionality of overlapping identities plays a role in placing a person in a society's hierarchy.

Key Terms

Review Questions

1. What are the characteristics of subordinate and minority groups?

2. Distinguish between racial groups and ethnic groups.

3. How do biracial and multiracial categories call into question traditional groupings in the United States?

4. How do the conflict, functionalist, and labeling approaches apply to the social construction of race?

5. How do subordinate groups emerge?

6. Characterize the range of intergroup relations from those that are most tolerated to those that are most unacceptable to minority groups. Provide a brief definition of each point along the spectrum of intergroup relations.

7. What roles do subordinate groups play in their own destiny?

8. What is meant by "intersectionality"?

Critical Thinking

1. How do the concepts of "biracial" and "multiracial" relate to W. E. B. Du Bois's notion of a "color line"?

2. How diverse is your town or city? Can you see evidence that some group is being subordinated? What social construction of categories do you see that may be different in your community compared to elsewhere?

3. Select a racial or ethnic group and apply the Spectrum of Intergroup Relations. Can you provide an example today or in the past where each relationship occurs?

4. Identify some protest and resistance efforts by subordinated groups in your area. Have they been successful? Even though some people say they favor equality, why may they be uncomfortable with such efforts? How can people unconnected with such efforts either help or hinder such protests?

5. How does intersectionality enhance our understanding of race and ethnicity?

Chapter 2
Prejudice

Timothy Jacobsen/AP Images

Learning Objectives

2.1 Differentiate between prejudice and discrimination.

2.2 Explain White privilege.

2.3 Summarize the theories of prejudice.

2.4 Define and explain stereotyping.

2.5 Understand color-blind racism.

2.6 Discuss how members of subordinate groups respond to prejudice.

2.7 Explain the ways prejudice can be reduced.

Finding a job with a living wage can be a challenge. Government funds to help the jobless get by while they look for work or training opportunities are limited. So, imagine you are in charge of allocating government assistance, and you want the money to be effective.

A recent study gave a nationwide sample of 1,000 participants the choice to extend $1,500 of assistance to applicants—some with an excellent work ethic, others with a poor work ethic—based on a completed questionnaire. Study participants also had the alternative not to spend the money and thereby help to reduce the state's budget deficit—another very real challenge. Oh, and the study participants received another piece of information besides the assessment of the person's work ethic: the applicants' names—either Laurie and Latoya or Emily and Keisha.

The results of the study were clear. Not surprisingly, hard workers were given more assistance than those judged to be low-quality workers. Faced with a "lazy" recipient, the hypothetical decision-makers were more likely to use the money to offset the budget deficit. However, what seemed to make the real difference was the name on the application. Hardworking Emily was given ten times as much money as hardworking Keisha. Similarly, lazy Laurie received much more than lazy Latoya. In fact, money allocated to the lazy applicant with the White-sounding name came close to what the hardworking Black could expect to be awarded.

In summary, Keisha and Latoya were not evaluated as positively as Emily and Laurie, and the applicants with Black-sounding names were more likely to have assistance withheld (DeSante 2013).

Prejudice is so prevalent that it is tempting to consider it inevitable or, even more broadly, part of human nature. Such a view ignores its variability from individual to individual and from society to society. Not everyone punished Keisha and rewarded Emily. People learn prejudice as children before they exhibit it as adults. Therefore, prejudice is a social phenomenon, an acquired characteristic. A truly pluralistic society would lack unfavorable distinctions caused by prejudicial attitudes toward and among racial and ethnic groups.

Holding ill feelings based on a person's race or ethnicity is cause for concern because the United States is so increasingly diverse. Figure 2.1 shows the increase in minority presence in the first decade of the twenty-first century. Many counties far removed from urban centers, as well as areas with historically large Black and Latino populations, saw minority population increases between 2000 and 2010. The likelihood that prejudices will be expressed, dealt with, or hidden increases and becomes a nationwide phenomenon as more and more communities experience majority-minority interaction.

Ill feeling among groups of different races, ethnicities, or cultures may result from **ethnocentrism**, the tendency to believe that one's culture and way of life are superior to all others. The ethnocentric person judges other groups and other cultures by the standards of his or her own group. This attitude makes it quite easy for people to view other cultures as inferior. Within the United States, we see a woman wearing a veil and may regard her as strange and backward, yet we are baffled when other societies think U.S. women in short skirts are dressed inappropriately. Ethnocentrism and other expressions of prejudice are often voiced, and such expressions sometimes become the motivation for criminal acts.

A very troubling part of contemporary life in the United States and elsewhere is the rise of organized hate groups. Research indicates a fluctuating but larger number of hate groups than a decade ago (Figure 2.2). The Internet and social media platforms give these groups visibility far beyond their numbers. Hate groups include

Figure 2.1 Change in Minority Population by County, 2000–2010

The minority population has grown across the United States, even in many areas that previously had few racial and ethnic minorities.

SOURCE: Data from Humes, Jones, and Ramirez 2011:21.

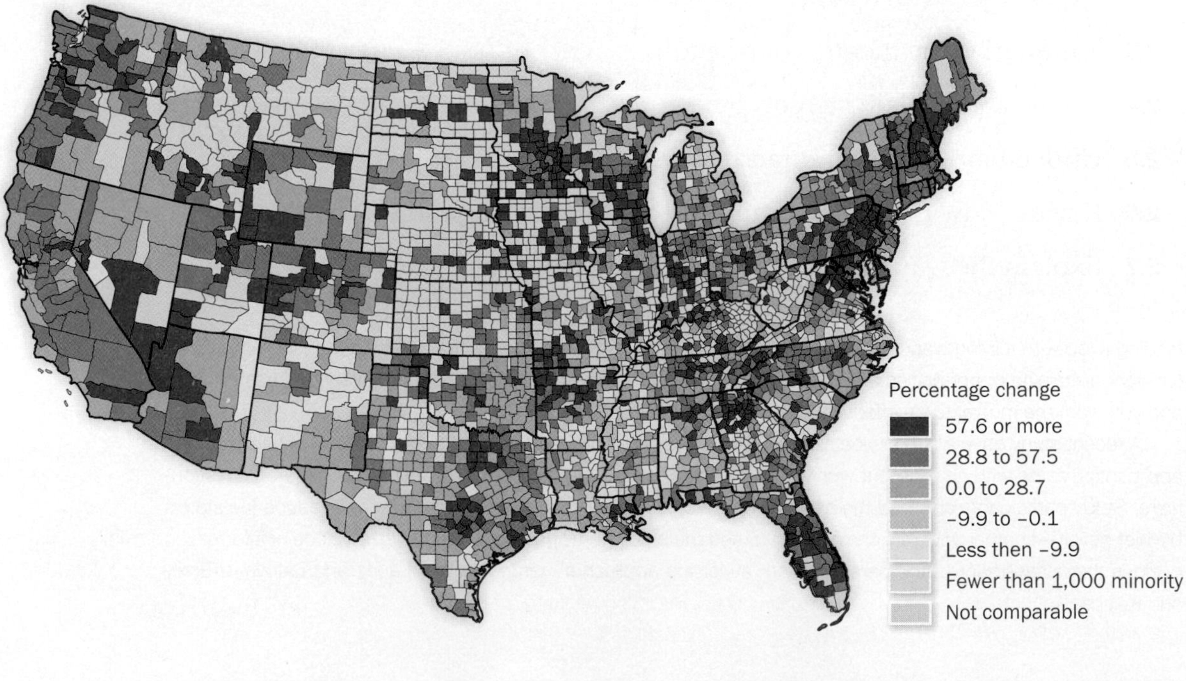

Percentage change

- 57.6 or more
- 28.8 to 57.5
- 0.0 to 28.7
- −9.9 to −0.1
- Less then −9.9
- Fewer than 1,000 minority
- Not comparable

Figure 2.2 Active Hate Groups, 1999–2016

The number of hate and extremist groups has fluctuated over the past 15 years but has remained at well over 750 for several years.

SOURCE: Data from Southern Poverty Law Center 2017.

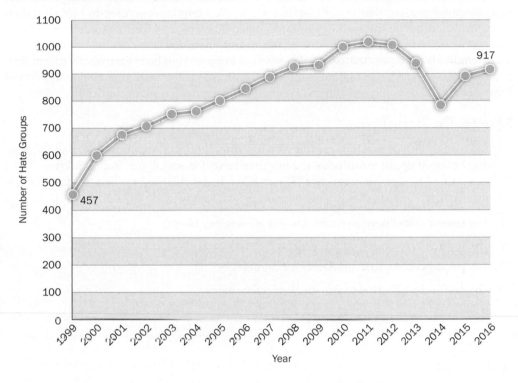

White supremacists, neo-Confederates, and neo-Nazis, as well as anti-White, anti-Jewish Black supremacist minority groups. Collectively, these hate groups target Muslims, immigrants, racial and ethnic groups, and the lesbian, gay, bisexual, and transgender (LGBT) community (Potok 2016; Wines and Saul 2015).

Prejudice and Discrimination

2.1 Differentiate between prejudice and discrimination.

Prejudice and discrimination are related concepts but are not the same. **Prejudice** is a negative attitude toward an entire category of people. The important components in this definition are *attitude* and *entire category*. Prejudice involves attitudes, thoughts, and beliefs—not actions. Prejudice often is expressed using **ethnophaulisms**, or ethnic slurs, which include derisive nicknames such as *honky, gook,* and *wetback.* Ethnophaulisms also include speaking to or about members of a particular group in a condescending way, such as saying, "José does well in school for a Mexican American" or referring to a middle-aged woman as "one of the girls."

A prejudiced belief leads to categorical rejection. Prejudice does not mean you dislike someone because you find his or her behavior objectionable; rather, it means you dislike an entire racial or ethnic group, even if you have had little or no contact with that group. A college student is not prejudiced because he requests a room change after three weeks of enduring his roommate's sleeping all day, playing loud music all night, and piling garbage on his desk. However, he is displaying prejudice if he requests a change after arriving at school and learning that his new roommate is of a specific nationality.

Even short-lived expressions of prejudice can be very hostile. **Microaggressions** are the commonplace daily verbal indignities that members of a minority group experience—for example, calling on a Latina classmate or coworker to comment on immigration policy, or telling a prospective Black job candidate, "I believe the most qualified person should get the job. Regardless of race." Microaggressions can be intentional or unintentional, and the perpetrator is often unaware of the insult (Sue 2010).

Prejudice is a belief or attitude; discrimination is action. **Discrimination** is the denial of opportunities and equal rights to individuals and groups as a result of prejudice or for other arbitrary reasons. Unlike prejudice, discrimination involves *behavior* that excludes members of a group from certain rights, opportunities, or privileges. Like prejudice, it is categorical, with a few rare exceptions. If an employer refuses to hire an illiterate Italian American as a computer analyst, that is not discrimination. If an employer refuses to hire all Italian Americans because he thinks they are incompetent and makes no effort to determine if an Italian American applicant is qualified, that is discrimination.

Prejudice is a complicated aspect of human behavior and has been extensively researched. For a sample of some fascinating research on prejudice, consider the Research Focus, "Virtual Prejudice and Anti-Prejudice," which explores online expressions of prejudice.

Merton's Typology

Prejudice does not necessarily coincide with discriminatory behavior. In exploring the relationship between negative attitudes and negative behavior, sociologist Robert Merton (1949, 1976) identified four major categories (Figure 2.3). The label added to each of Merton's categories may more readily identify the type of person described:

1. The unprejudiced nondiscriminator—or all-weather liberal
2. The unprejudiced discriminator—or reluctant liberal
3. The prejudiced nondiscriminator—or timid bigot
4. The prejudiced discriminator—or all-weather bigot

Research Focus

Virtual Prejudice and Anti-Prejudice

Increasingly larger portions of our daily lives are spent not directly talking with or seeing other people but rather online, in front of our phones, iPads, and computers. Sometimes we indirectly communicate with friends through social media, but many Americans also spend a large amount of time in some virtual world (such as Second Life) separated from reality. What impact can online activities have on reinforcing or undercutting prejudice?

Researchers have looked at video games and found that minorities are vastly underrepresented, and when they do appear it is usually as thugs or athletes. In addition, White players are more likely to recall Black characters as violent and aggressive.

Nonetheless, virtual society can seek to have a positive impact on race and ethnic relations. User-generated video sites (such as YouTube) abound with videos reflecting favorable representations of racial and ethnic groups. For example, one study found that images of American Indians tend to evoke positive responses in online comments. However, viewers seemed most positive when videos were historical rather than dealing with present-day situations. And if ill treatment toward contemporary Native Americans was central to the video, negative comments began to escalate.

The complexity of online representations and prejudice is highlighted in a May 2013 Cheerios advertisement. In the 30-second spot, a White mom tells her biracial daughter that Cheerios is heart-healthy. The six-year-old then scampers into the next room, spilling Cheerios on her Black father's chest while he is napping on the living-room couch. The comments were 10–1 favorable toward the biracial household, but General Mills was forced to disable the comment section because of all the racist remarks that were posted.

Researchers of online prejudice admit the depth of hostility is difficult to assess because many commercial venues and news outlets monitor comments (often at considerable expense) and selectively delete offensive comments, thus giving the casual online user an inaccurate view of how the general public is responding to racially charged topics. It also appears that many who wish to express racist views are retreating to Web sites where such rhetoric will not be challenged. As in everyday life, one cannot assume that the absence of overt prejudice means tolerance.

In the United States, with its historical support and constitutional safeguards for freedom of speech, the government is largely uninvolved in trying to limit online bigotry. However, this is not true everywhere. Germany limits anti-Semitic or pro-Nazi sentiments, and German lawmakers demanded in 2016 that Facebook do more to monitor and censor online hate speech.

Sources: Burgess et al. 2011; Hughley and Daniels 2013; Kenji America 2013; Kopacz and Lawton 2013; Nudd 2013; Scott and Eddy 2016.

Figure 2.3 Prejudice and Discrimination

As Robert Merton's typology shows, prejudice and discrimination are related but are not the same.

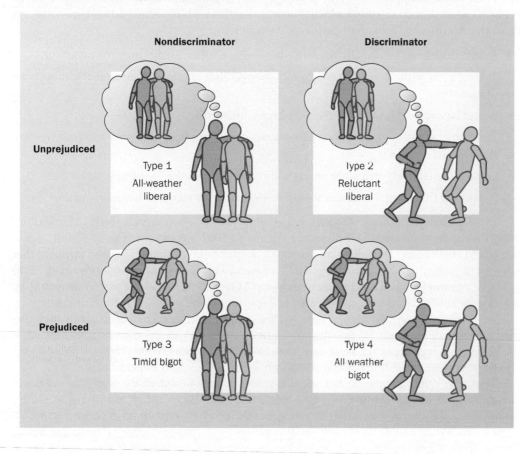

As the term is used in types 1 and 2, *liberals* are committed to equality among people. The all-weather liberal believes in equality and practices it. Merton was quick to observe that all-weather liberals may be far removed from any real contact with subordinate groups such as African Americans or women. Furthermore, such people may be content with their own behavior and do little to change it. The reluctant liberal is not completely committed to equality between groups. Social pressure may cause such a person to discriminate. For example, fear of losing employees may lead a manager to avoid promoting women to supervisory capacities. Equal-opportunity legislation may be the best way to influence a reluctant liberal.

Types 3 and 4 do not believe in equal treatment for racial and ethnic groups, but they vary in their willingness to act. The timid bigot, type 3, will not discriminate if discrimination costs money or reduces profits, or if peers or the government apply pressure against engaging in discrimination. The all-weather bigot acts without hesitation on the prejudiced beliefs he or she holds.

White Privilege

2.2 Explain White privilege.

Being White is not the same as being Black or Latino. Being White in the United States may not ensure success and wealth, but it does limit encounters with intolerance.

White privilege refers to the rights or immunities granted as a particular benefit or favor for being White. This advantage exists unconsciously and is often invisible to the White people who enjoy it (Ferber 2008). Returning to the research described at the beginning of the chapter, we saw how easily Emily and Laurie were privileged over Latoya and Keisha in being awarded government assistance.

Scholar Peggy McIntosh of the Wellesley College Center for Research on Women looked at the privilege that comes from being White and the added privilege of being male. The other side of racial oppression is the privilege enjoyed by dominant groups. Being White or being successful in establishing a White identity carries with it distinct advantages. Among those that McIntosh (1988) identified were the following:

- Being considered financially reliable when using checks, credit cards, or cash

- Taking a job without having coworkers suspect that employment came about because of race

- Never having to speak for all the people of your race

- Watching television or reading a newspaper and seeing people of your own race widely represented

- Speaking effectively in a large group without being called a credit to your race

- Assuming that if legal or medical help is needed, your race will not work against you

Privilege being automatically extended to White people is not an exclusively U.S. phenomenon. Researchers in Australia conducted more than 1,500 observations of young adults, some White and some Black. The young adults boarded a public bus and tried to use a fare card that was out of money to reach a bus stop a mile or two away. In every case, the rider said, "I do not have any money, but I need to get to that stop." Overall, 72 percent of the White would-be riders were allowed to ride free, compared to 36 percent of the people of color. Curiously, even Black bus drivers extended the privilege to Whites, though they were a bit more likely to extend the same opportunity (to ride the bus for free) to Blacks. However, we do not know what the bus drivers were thinking. Were they more likely to view non-White riders with suspicion? Did they consider the White passengers more honest? (Mujcic and Frijters 2013)

Typically, White people do not see themselves as privileged in the way many African Americans and Latinos see themselves as disadvantaged. When asked to comment on their "Whiteness," they are unaware that they go about their daily lives without experiencing microaggressions. White people most likely see themselves as devoid of ethnicity ("no longer Irish," for example), stigmatized as racist, and victims of reverse discrimination. In short, many White people are unaware of the White privilege that informs their lives.

Theories of Prejudice

2.3   Summarize the theories of prejudice.

Prejudice is learned. Friends, relatives, newspapers, books, movies, television, and the Internet all teach it. Awareness of the differences among people that society judges to be important begins at an early age. Several theories have been advanced to explain the rejection of certain groups in a society. We examine four theoretical explanations. The first two, scapegoating and the authoritarian personality, are psychological and emphasize why a particular person harbors ill feelings toward a specific racial or ethnic group. The second two, exploitation theory and the normative approach, are sociological and view prejudice in the context of our interaction in a larger society.

Scapegoating Theory

People use some expressions of prejudice to blame others and to refuse to accept responsibility. **Scapegoating theory** says that prejudiced people believe they are society's victims.

The term *scapegoat* comes from a biblical injunction in which God told the Hebrews to send a goat into the wilderness to symbolically carry away the people's sins.

White privilege in action: A recent study showed that bus drivers in Australia were twice as likely to allow Whites to board a bus even though they could not pay the fare.

sammy/Alamy Stock Photo

Similarly, the theory of scapegoating suggests that rather than accepting guilt for some personal failure, a prejudiced person transfers the blame for failure to a vulnerable group.

In the major tragic twentieth-century example, Adolf Hitler used the Jews as scapegoats for all German social and economic ills in the 1930s. This scapegoating led to the passage of laws restricting Jewish life in pre–World War II Germany and eventually escalated into the mass extermination of Europe's Jews. Scapegoating of Jews persists today. A national survey in 2009 showed that one out of four people in the United States blame "the Jews" for the financial crisis that launched the Great Recession that began in 2008. **Anti-Semitism**—anti-Jewish prejudice and discrimination—remains a very real phenomenon (Malhotra and Margalit 2009).

Today in the United States, both legal and illegal immigrants often are blamed for "real" Americans' failure to secure jobs or desirable housing. The immigrant becomes the scapegoat for one's own lack of skills, planning, or motivation. It is so much easier to blame someone else.

Authoritarian Personality Theory

Prejudice may be influenced by one's upbringing and the lessons taught—and learned—early in life. Several efforts have been made to detail the prejudiced personality, but the most comprehensive effort culminated in a book titled *The Authoritarian Personality* (Adorno et al. 1950). Using a variety of tests and relying on more than 2,000 respondents ranging from middle-class Whites to inmates of San Quentin State Prison (in California), the authors claimed they had isolated the characteristics of the authoritarian personality.

In Adorno and colleagues' view, the **authoritarian personality** has basic characteristics that make him or her likely to be prejudiced. The authoritarian personality adheres to conventional values, practices uncritical acceptance of authority, and is concerned with power and toughness. The authoritarian personality is also characterized by aggressiveness toward people who do not conform to conventional norms or obey authority. According to the researchers, this personality type develops from the experience of harsh discipline in early childhood. A child with an authoritarian upbringing is obedient to authority figures and then later treats others as he or she had been raised to treat them.

This study has been widely criticized, but the very existence of such wide criticism indicates the study's influence. Critics have attacked the study's equation of authoritarianism with right-wing politics (because liberals also can be rigid); its failure to recognize that prejudice is more closely related to other individual traits, such as social class, than to authoritarianism as it was defined; the research methods used; and the emphasis on extreme racial prejudice rather than on more common expressions of hostility.

Despite these concerns about the study, which was completed more than 60 years ago, annual conferences continue to draw attention to how authoritarian attitudes contribute to racism, sexism, and even torture (Kinloch 1974; O'Neill 2008).

Exploitation Theory

Racial prejudice is often used to justify keeping a group in a subordinate economic position. Conflict theorists, in particular, stress the role of racial and ethnic hostility as a way for the dominant group to keep its status and power intact. Indeed, even the less affluent White working class uses prejudice to minimize competition from upwardly mobile minorities.

This **exploitation theory** is part of the Marxist tradition in sociological thought. Nineteenth-century philosopher Karl Marx emphasized exploitation of the lower class as an integral part of capitalism. Similarly, the exploitation or conflict approach explains how racism can stigmatize a group as inferior to justify the exploitation of that group. As developed by Oliver Cox (1942), exploitation theory saw prejudice against Blacks as an extension of the inequality faced by the entire lower class.

The exploitation theory of prejudice is persuasive. Japanese Americans were the object of little prejudice until they began to enter occupations that brought them into competition with Whites. The movement to keep Chinese out of the United States became strongest during the late nineteenth century, when Chinese immigrants and Whites fought over

Table 2.1 Theories of Prejudice

No single explanation of why prejudice exists is satisfactory, but several approaches taken together offer insight.

Theory	Explanation	Example
Scapegoating	People blame others for their own failures.	An unsuccessful applicant assumes that a minority member or a woman got "his" job.
Authoritarian Personality	Authoritarian parents lead their children to develop intolerance.	A rigid person dislikes people who are different.
Exploitation Theory	People use others unfairly for economic advantage.	A minority member is hired at a lower wage level.
Normative Approach	Peer and social influences encourage tolerance or intolerance.	A person from an intolerant household is more likely to be openly prejudiced.

dwindling numbers of jobs. Both the enslavement of African Americans and the forced westward movement of Native Americans were economically motivated to a significant degree.

Normative Approach

Although personality factors are important contributors to prejudice, normative or situational factors also play a role. The **normative approach** takes the view that prejudice is influenced by societal norms and situations that encourage or discourage the tolerance of minorities.

Analysis reveals how societal influences shape a climate for tolerance or intolerance. Societies develop social norms that dictate not only what foods are desirable (or forbidden) but also what racial and ethnic groups are to be favored (or despised). Social forces operate in a society to encourage or discourage tolerance. The force may be widespread, such as the pressure on White Southerners to oppose racial equality even when slavery or segregation was the norm, which would seem to make concerns about equality irrelevant. The influence of social norms may be limited, such as when one man finds himself becoming more sexist as he competes with three women for a position in a prestigious law firm.

The four approaches to prejudice, summarized in Table 2.1, are not mutually exclusive. Social circumstances provide cues regarding the attitudes that a person should adopt; personality determines the extent to which people follow social cues and the likelihood that they will encourage others to do the same. Societal norms may promote or deter tolerance; personality traits suggest the degree to which a person will conform to norms of intolerance. To understand prejudice, we must use all four approaches together.

Stereotypes

2.4 Define and explain stereotyping.

On Christmas Day 2001, Arab American Walied Shater boarded an American Airlines flight from Baltimore to Dallas carrying a gun. The cockpit crew refused to let him fly, fearing that Shater would take over the plane and use it as a weapon of mass destruction. However, Shater carried documentation identifying him as a Secret Service agent, and calls to Washington, D.C., confirmed that he was flying to join a presidential protection force at President George W. Bush's ranch in Texas. Nevertheless, the crew could not get past the stereotype of Arab American men posing a lethal threat (Leavitt 2002).

What Are Stereotypes?

In Chapter 1, we saw that stereotypes play a powerful role in how people come to view dominant and subordinate groups. **Stereotypes** are unreliable generalizations about all members of a group and do not take individual differences into account. Numerous scientific studies have been conducted on these exaggerated images. This research has shown people's willingness to assign positive and negative traits to entire groups of people, which are then applied to particular individuals. Stereotyping causes people to view Blacks as superstitious, Whites as uncaring, and Jews as shrewd. Over the past 80 years of research, social scientists have found that people have become less willing to express such views openly, but prejudice persists (Quillian 2006).

If stereotypes are exaggerated generalizations, then why are they so widely held, and why are some traits assigned more often than others? Evidence for traits may arise out of real conditions. For example, more Puerto Ricans live in poverty than Whites, so the prejudiced mind associates Puerto Ricans with laziness. According to the New Testament, some Jews were responsible for the crucifixion of Jesus, so to the prejudiced mind, all Jews are Christ killers. Some activists in the women's movement are lesbians, so all feminists are seen as lesbians. From a kernel of fact, faulty generalization creates a stereotype.

Labeling individuals with negative stereotypes has strong implications for the self-fulfilling prophecy (discussed in Chapter 1). Studies show that people are all too aware of the negative images others have of them. When asked to estimate the prevalence of hard-core racism among Whites, one in four Blacks agrees that more than half of White people "personally share the attitudes of groups like the Ku Klux Klan toward Blacks." Only one Black in ten says "only a few" White people hold such views. Stereotypes not only influence how people feel about themselves but also affect how people interact with others. If people feel that others hold incorrect, disparaging attitudes toward them, then harmonious relations become increasingly unlikely (Sigelman and Tuch 1997).

Although explicit expressions of stereotypes are becoming less common, it is much too soon to write the obituary of racial and ethnic stereotypes. In addition, stereotyping is not limited to racial and ethnic groups. Other groups are subjected to stereotyping. Probably the most common stereotypes in daily life and the mass media are sexist stereotypes. **Sexism** is the ideology that one sex (male) is superior to the other (female). Images and descriptions of women and even girls often reinforce sexism. **Homophobia**, the fear of and prejudice toward homosexuals, is present in every facet of life: the family, organized religion, the workplace, and the mass media. Like the myths and stereotypes of race and gender, those about homosexuality keep gay men and lesbians oppressed as a group and may also prevent sympathetic members of the dominant group, the heterosexual community, from supporting them. We next consider the use of stereotypes in the contemporary practice of racial profiling.

Stereotyping in Action: Racial Profiling

In recent years, the government has given its attention to a social phenomenon with a long history: racial profiling. According to the Department of Justice, **racial profiling** is any police-initiated action based on race, ethnicity, or national origin rather than the person's behavior. Generally, profiling occurs when law-enforcement officers, including customs officials, airport security, and police, assume that people fitting certain descriptions are likely to be engaged in an illegal activity.

Racial profiling has become a more visible part of the national discussion in recent years. Two developments have been especially important. First is the #BlackLivesMatter (BLM) movement, which emerged to call attention to the shooting deaths of African Americans, especially men, usually by police officers. BLM organized in 2013 after a neighborhood watch coordinator in Florida, George Zimmerman, shot and killed Trayvon Martin, an unarmed Black 17-year old. Zimmerman's acquittal was broadly viewed as a miscarriage of justice. Defensively, some counter the phrase "Black lives matter" with "All lives matter" and call attention to the dangerous position in which police officers often find themselves on a daily basis. However, cameras on bystanders' smartphones and mounted on the dashboards of police vehicles have led to a video record of law-enforcement encounters with African American civilians that many interpret as an excessive, and sometimes lethal, show of force. Not surprisingly, a 2015 national survey showed that only 8 percent of African Americans, compared to 42 percent of Whites, felt that Whites and Blacks have the same chance of receiving fair treatment from the police.

Second are the strident calls for greater scrutiny of Muslims, including Muslim Americans, in the wake of terrorist episodes by Islamic extremists. Notably, then–presidential candidate Donald Trump in 2015 called for a ban on all Muslims entering the United States pending thorough background checks. A national survey of all likely voters at the time showed that over one-third supported Trump's proposal. However, this singling out of people on the basis of their religion received strong condemnation from other political leaders. The broad level of support nonetheless underscores the persistent temptation to use profiling, whether racial or religious, as a shortcut to maintaining public safety (McCormick 2015; Marist Poll 2015: Question 7F).

Racial profiling persists despite overwhelming evidence that it is not effective in identifying potential troublemakers. Whites are more likely to be found with drugs in the areas in which minority group members are disproportionately targeted. A federal study made public in 2005 found little difference nationwide in the likelihood of being stopped by law-enforcement officers on the basis of one's race or nationality, but African Americans were twice as likely as Whites to have their vehicles searched, and Latinos were five times more likely than Whites. In addition, a 2015 study considering the states with the most accurate data tracking "stop and frisk" encounters found that African American drivers were much more likely to be stopped but, except in Rhode Island, were always less likely than Whites to have contraband such as drugs or firearms.

A similar pattern emerged in the likelihood of force being used against drivers: It was three times more likely for Latinos and Blacks than for White drivers. A study of New York City police officers describing some 4.43 million stops between 2004 and mid-2012 found that Blacks and Latinos accounted for 83 percent of people who were stopped and frisked, and a related study found that Whites were 50 percent more likely to be carrying weapons (Center for Constitutional Rights 2011; Apuzzo and Goldstein 2014; Herbert 2010; LaFraniere and Lehren 2015; Tomaskovic-Devey and Warren 2009).

Back in the 1990s, increased attention to racial profiling led not only to special reports and commissions but also to talk of legislating against it. Enacting such legislation proved difficult. The U.S. Supreme Court in *Whren v. United States* (1996) upheld the constitutionality of using a minor traffic infraction as an excuse to stop and search a vehicle and its passengers. Nonetheless, states and other government units are discussing policies and training that would discourage racial profiling. At the same time, most law-enforcement agencies reject the idea of compiling racial data on traffic stops, arguing that it would be a waste of money and staff time.

Efforts to stop racial profiling came to an abrupt end after the September 11, 2001, terrorist attacks on the United States. Suspicions about Muslims and Arabs in the United States became widespread. Foreign students from Arab countries were summoned for special questioning. Legal immigrants identified as Arab or Muslim were scrutinized for any illegal activity and were prosecuted for routine immigration violations that were ignored for people of other ethnic backgrounds and religious faiths.

Calls to end profiling resumed after the Trayvon Martin case. Around the same time, the New York Police Department abandoned its program "The Demographic Unit," which dispatched officers to Muslim neighborhoods to eavesdrop on residents on the street and in mosques and to create detailed files on Muslim Americans (Apuzzo and Goldstein 2014).

The majority of people in the United States think that ethnic and religious profiling should be permitted to maintain national security. In 2010, 53 percent of Americans favored "ethnic and religious profiling," even for U.S. citizens, and wanted Arab Americans to undergo more intensive security checks before boarding planes in the United States (Zogby 2010).

Color-Blind Racism

2.5 Understand color-blind racism.

Over the past three generations, nationwide surveys have consistently shown growing support by Whites for integration, interracial dating, and members of minority groups attaining political office, including president of the United States. How can we reconcile the results of these surveys when thousands of hate crimes occur annually?

Allen Creative/Steve Allen/Alamy Stock Photo

Color-blind racism refers to the use of race-neutral principles to defend the racially unequal status quo. For example, color-blind racism may entail believing that "no discrimination for college admission" should exist—despite the fact that the disparity in educational experiences means that formal college admissions criteria will privilege White high-school graduates. Color-blind racism has also been called *laissez-faire racism, postracialism,* or *aversive racism,* but the common theme is that racial discrimination is a thing of the past. Notions of racial inferiority are rarely expressed despite the fact that proceeding color-blind into the future will perpetuate inequality.

Prejudice or commemoration? In 2015, the Supreme Court upheld Texas's refusal to allow the Confederate flag on a specialty license plate in honor of the Sons of Confederate Veterans. Eight states continue to offer a license plate similar to the rejected Texas sample plate shown here.

An important aspect of color-blind racism is the recognition that race is rarely invoked in public debates on social issues. Instead, people emphasize lower social class, lack of citizenship, or immigration status; these descriptions serve as proxies for race. Furthermore, the emphasis is on individuals failing rather than on recognizing patterns of groups being disadvantaged. Together, these aspects of color-blind racism lead many White people to declare that they are not racist and do not know anyone who is racist. They also lead to the mistaken conclusion that more progress has been made toward racial and ethnic equality and tolerance than has really taken place.

When we survey White attitudes toward African Americans, three conclusions are inescapable. First, attitudes are subject to change; during periods of dramatic social upheaval, dramatic shifts can occur within one generation. Second, less progress was made in the late twentieth century and early twenty-first century than was made in the relatively brief period of the 1950s and 1960s. Third, the pursuit of a color-blind agenda has created lower levels of support for policies that could reduce racial inequality if implemented.

Economically less-successful groups such as African Americans and Latinos have been associated with negative traits to the point that issues such as urban decay, homelessness, welfare, and crime are viewed as race issues even though race is rarely mentioned explicitly. In addition to making it harder to solve difficult social problems, this discourse is another instance of blaming the victim (defined in Chapter 1). These perceptions come at a time when the government's willingness to address domestic ills is limited by increasing opposition to new taxes and continuing commitments to fight terrorism here and abroad. The color line remains, even if more people are unwilling to accept its divisive impact on everyone's lives (Bonilla-Silva 2006; Bonilla-Silva and Embrick with Seamster 2011; Mueller 2017; Omi and Winant 2015:257).

The Mood of the Oppressed

2.6   Discuss how members of subordinate groups respond to prejudice.

Sociologist W. E. B. Du Bois relates an experience from his youth in a largely White community in Massachusetts. He tells how, on one occasion, the boys and girls were exchanging cards, and everyone was having a lot of fun. One girl, a newcomer, refused his card as soon as she saw that Du Bois was Black. He wrote:

> Then it dawned upon me with a certain suddenness that I was different from others...shut out from their world by a vast veil. I had therefore no desire to tear down that veil, to creep through; I held all beyond it in common contempt and lived above it in a region of blue sky and great wandering shadows. (1903:2)

In using the image of a veil, Du Bois describes how members of subordinate groups learn they are being treated differently. In his case and that of many others, the result is a feeling of contempt toward all Whites that continues for a lifetime.

Opinion pollsters have been interested in White attitudes on racial issues longer than they have measured the views of subordinate groups. This neglect of minority attitudes reflects, in part, the bias of the White researchers. It also stems from the contention that the dominant group is more important to study because it is in a better position to act on its beliefs.

The results of a nationwide survey conducted in the United States offer insight into sharply different views on the state of race relations today (Figure 2.4). Latinos, African Americans, and Asian Americans all have strong reservations about the state of race relations in the United States. They are skeptical about the level of equal opportunity and perceive a lot of discrimination. It is interesting to note that Hispanics and Asian Americans, overwhelmingly immigrants, are more likely to believe they will succeed if they work hard. And the majority of all three groups had a positive outlook for the next ten years (New America Media 2007; Preston 2007).

We have focused so far on what comes to mind when we think about prejudice: one group hating another group. But there is another form of prejudice that has been proposed in the past: A group may come to hate itself. Members of groups held in low esteem by society may, as a result, either hate themselves or have low self-esteem, as many social scientists once believed. Research literature of the 1940s through the 1960s emphasized the low self-esteem of minorities. Usually, the subjects were African Americans, but the argument has been generalized to include any subordinate racial, ethnic, or nationality group.

This view of group self-hatred is no longer accepted. We should not assume that minority status influences personality traits in either a good or a bad way. First, such assumptions may create a stereotype. We cannot describe a Black personality any more accurately than we can a White personality. Second, the characteristics of minority-group members are not

Figure 2.4 What Is the State of Race Relations? Three Views
Note: Answers mean respondent chose "very important problem" or "strongly agree" regarding the statements listed. Based on 1,105 interviews in August–September 2007, with bilingual questioners used as necessary.

SOURCE: Data from New America Media 2007: 6, 12, 14, 24, 26.

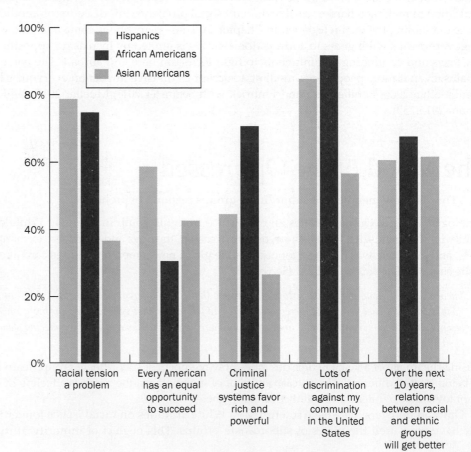

entirely the result of subordinate racial status; they also are influenced by low incomes, poor neighborhoods, and other factors. Third, many studies of personality imply that certain values are normal or preferable, but the values chosen are those of dominant groups.

If assessments of a subordinate group's self-regard are so prone to misjudgments, then why has the belief in low self-esteem been so widely held? Much of the research rests on studies with preschool-age Black children who were asked to express their preferences for dolls with different facial colors. Indeed, one such study by psychologists Kenneth and Mamie Clark was cited in the arguments before the U.S. Supreme Court in the landmark 1954 case *Brown v. Board of Education*, which led to desegregation in public schools. The Clarks' study showed that Black children preferred White dolls, a finding that suggested the children had developed a negative self-image. Although subsequent doll studies have sometimes shown Black children's preference for white-faced dolls, other social scientists contend that this preference shows a realization of what most commercially sold dolls look like rather than low self-esteem (Bloom 1971; Powell-Hopson and Hopson 1988).

Because African American children, as well as the children of other subordinate groups, realistically see that Whites have more power and resources and, therefore, rate them higher does not mean that the children feel inferior. However, children who experience overt discrimination are more likely to display feelings of distress and anxiety later in life. Other studies show that when the self-images of middle-class or affluent African Americans are measured, their feelings of self-esteem are more positive than those of comparable Whites (Coker et al. 2009; Gray-Little and Hafdahl 2000).

Mike Nelson/EPA/Newscom

How do children develop an image of themselves? Toys and playthings have an important role, and many children of racial and ethnic minorities find it difficult to find dolls that look like them. In 2005, a new doll was released: Fulla—an Arab who reflects modesty, piety, and respect, yet underneath her traditional garb she wears chic clothes that a Muslim woman might wear in private.

Intergroup Hostility

Prejudice is as diverse as the nation's population. It exists not only between dominant and subordinate peoples but also among specific subordinate groups. Unfortunately, until recently, little research existed on this subject except for a few social distance scales (discussed later in this chapter) administered to racial and ethnic minorities.

Do different groups get along with one another? Although this question often is framed in terms of the relationships between White Americans and other racial and ethnic groups, we should recognize that prejudice exists among minority groups. In a national survey, people were asked whether they could generally get along with members of other groups. In Figure 2.5, we can see that Whites felt they had the most difficulty getting along with Hispanics. We also see the different views that Blacks, Latinos, Asian Americans, and American Indians hold toward other groups.

It is curious that some minority groups get along better with Whites than with other minority groups.

TRUE!　　　　　　　　　*by Daryl Cagle*

Source: *Wichita Eagle* quoting *Nat'l Conference of Christians and Jews* survey.

Daryl Cagle/CartoonStock.com

*Asian Americans feel they have the **most in common** with Whites, who feel this about Blacks, who feel this about Hispanics. Hispanics feel they have the **least in common** with Blacks, who feel this about Whites who feel this about Asians.*

Figure 2.5 Do We Get Along?

The bars represent the percentage of each group—Whites, Blacks, Hispanics, Asians, and American Indians—that says how well each group gets along with other groups ("Don't Knows" excluded).[1]

[1]Sample size for American Indians is very small and subject to large sample variance.
Note: The wording of the question was: "We hear a lot these days about how various groups in society get along with each other. I'm going to mention several groups and ask whether you think they generally get along with each other or generally do not get along with each other." So, in the "Asked of White Respondents" graph, Whites are asked how Whites get along with each ethnic group; in the "Asked of Black Respondents" graph, Blacks are asked how Blacks get along with each ethnic group, and so on.

SOURCE: Smith, Tom W. 2006:65. Taking America's Pulse III. Intergroup Relations in Contemporary America. Chicago: National Opinion Research Center, University of Chicago. Reprinted by permission of the author.

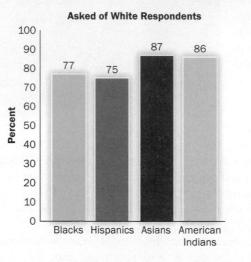

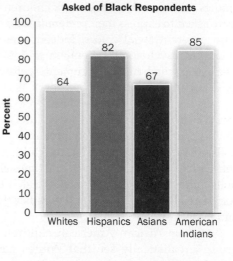

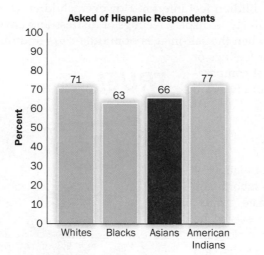

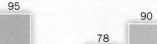
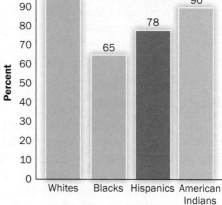

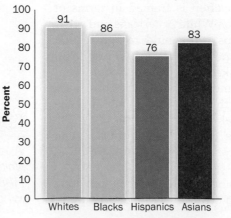

Why would that be? Often, low-income people compete daily with other low-income people and do not readily see the larger societal forces that contribute to their low status. The survey results reveal that many Hispanics are more likely to believe Asian Americans are getting in their way than the White Americans who are the real decision makers in their community.

Research into hostility among marginalized groups has begun to focus on how recent immigrants fit into a complicated picture of multidirectional prejudice. Immigrants themselves bring with them their culture, which includes its own distinctive brand of prejudice that many immigrants then harbor in their new home. Many of the new immigrants to the United States are Black people who have come from either Africa or the Caribbean. They harbor and receive a unique mixture of acceptance and avoidance by U.S.-born Black Americans and display mixed attitudes toward U.S.-born Blacks (Roth and Kim 2013; Waters, Kasinitz, and Asad 2014).

Intergroup hostility sometimes becomes violent. Ethnic and racial tensions among African Americans, Latinos, and immigrants may manifest themselves in hate crimes. Violence can surface in neighborhoods where people compete for scarce resources such as jobs and housing. Gangs become organized along racial lines, much like private clubs "downtown." In recent years, Los Angeles has been particularly concerned about rival Black and Hispanic gangs. Conflict theorists see gang violence as resulting from larger structural forces, but for the average person in such areas, life itself becomes more of a challenge as a result of gang activity (Archibold 2007).

Reducing Prejudice

2.7 Explain the ways prejudice can be reduced.

Focusing on how to eliminate prejudice involves an explicit value judgment: Prejudice is wrong and causes problems for those who are prejudiced and for their victims. As individuals, we can act to stop prejudice. Table 2.2 summarizes ten ways to fight prejudice. The important thing to remember is not to ignore prejudice when you witness it.

The obvious way to eliminate prejudice is to eliminate its causes: the desire to exploit, the sense of being threatened, the need to blame others for one's own failure. Individuals might use personal therapy to help them eliminate these causes, but therapy, even if it works for every individual, is not a solution for an entire society in which prejudice is a part of everyday life.

The answer appears to rest with programs directed at society as a whole. Prejudice is attacked indirectly when discrimination is attacked. Despite prevailing beliefs to the contrary, we *can* legislate against prejudice: Legal statutes and decisions do affect attitudes. In the past, people firmly believed that laws could not overcome norms, especially racist norms. Recent history, especially after the civil rights movement began in 1954, has challenged that once-common belief. Laws and court rulings have mandated equal treatment of Blacks, and Whites have led people to reevaluate their beliefs about what is right and wrong. The increasing tolerance by Whites during the civil rights era from 1954 to 1965 supports this conclusion.

Much research has determined how to change negative attitudes toward groups of people. The most encouraging findings point to education, mass media, intergroup contact, and workplace training programs.

Education

Research on education and prejudice considers two key areas: (1) special programs aimed at promoting mutual respect and (2) the general effect of formal schooling on expressions of bigotry.

Most research studies show that well-constructed school programs have a positive effect on reducing prejudice, at least temporarily. The reduction is rarely as much as one might want,

---

Table 2.2 Ways to Fight Prejudice

1. *Act.* Do something. In the face of hatred, apathy will be taken as acceptance, even by the victims of prejudice themselves.
2. *Unite.* Call a friend or coworker. Organize a group of like-thinking friends from your school, place of worship, or club. Create a coalition that is diverse and includes the young, the old, law-enforcement representatives, and the media.
3. *Support the victims.* Victims of hate crimes are especially vulnerable. Let them know you care in person, or by e-mail or text message. If you or someone you know is a victim of a hate crime, report it to the police or campus authorities.
4. *Do your homework.* If you suspect a hate crime has been committed, do your research to document it.
5. *Create an alternative.* Never attend a rally where hate is a part of the agenda. Find another outlet for your frustration, whatever the cause.
6. *Speak up.* You, too, have First Amendment rights. Denounce the hatred, the cruel jokes. If you see a news organization misrepresenting a group, speak up.
7. *Lobby leaders.* Persuade policymakers, business leaders, community leaders, and executives of media outlets to take a stand against hate.
8. *Look long term.* Participate in or organize events such as annual parades or cultural fairs to celebrate diversity and harmony. Supplement it with a Web site that can be a 24/7 resource.
9. *Teach acceptance.* Prejudice is learned, and parents and teachers can influence the content of a school's curriculum. In a first-grade class in Seattle, children paint self-portraits, mixing colors to match their skin tone.
10. *Dig deeper.* Look into the issues that divide us—social inequality, immigration, and sexual orientation. Work against prejudice. Dig deep inside yourself to identify the prejudices and stereotypes you may embrace. Find out what is happening and act!

SOURCE: Southern Poverty Law Center 2010; Willoughby 2004.

---

however. The difficulty is that a single program is insufficient to change lifelong habits, especially if little is done to reinforce the program's message once it ends. Persuasion to respect other groups does not operate in a clear field because, in their ordinary environments, people are still subjected to situations that promote prejudicial feelings. Children and adults are encouraged to laugh at Polish jokes and cheer for a team named the *Redskins*. Peers may discourage Black adolescents from befriending a White youth. All of these realities undermine the effectiveness of prejudice-reduction programs (Allport 1979).

Studies document that increased formal education, regardless of content, is associated with racial tolerance. Research data show that highly educated people are more likely to indicate respect and liking for groups different from themselves. Why might more education have this effect? It might promote a broader outlook and make a person less likely to endorse myths that sustain racial prejudice. Formal education teaches the importance of qualifying statements such as "even though they have lower test scores, you need to remember the neighborhoods from which they come." Education introduces the learner to the almost infinite diversity of social groups and the need to question and reject rigid categorizations. Colleges increasingly require students to complete a course that explores diversity or multiculturalism. Another explanation is that education does not reduce intolerance but instead makes people more careful about revealing it. Formal education may simply instruct people in the appropriate responses. Whatever the mechanism, the continued trend toward a better-educated population in the United States will likely contribute to a reduction in overt prejudice.

However, college education may not reduce prejudice uniformly. For example, some White students might believe that minority students did not earn their admission into college but rather were admitted based on affirmative action programs. Students may feel threatened as they watch large groups of people of different racial and cultural backgrounds congregating and forming their own groups. Therefore, some aspects of the college experience may foster "we" versus "they" attitudes (Schaefer 1986, 1996).

Mass Media

The mass media may work to reduce prejudice. Television, radio, motion pictures, newspapers, magazines, and the Internet present only a portion of real life, but what effect do they have on prejudice if the content is racist or antiracist, sexist or antisexist? We can reach only a tentative answer to this question, but overall the evidence points to a measurable effect.

Today, over 56 percent of all youth less than 14 years of age in the United States are children of color, but only recently have we seen television reflect their race or cultural heritage. By the 2016–2017 television season, diversity on broadcast television had improved, with 20 percent of the 595 series regular characters played by African Americans, although they were disproportionately male (62 percent). Asian Pacific Americans have gradually grown in prominence on programs such as *The Big Bang Theory*, *Master of None*, and *The Mindy Project*, perhaps spurred on by the success of the 2005 motion picture *Slumdog Millionaire*.

We still do not see across-the-board diversity in the mass media, however. Less than 5 percent of regular series characters were identified as gay, lesbian, or transgender—although this number is significantly higher than it was a few years earlier. Cable networks are improving representation of previously ignored segments of the nation's diversity, including the LGBT community (Amazon's *Transparent*), multiracial casts (AMC's *The Walking Dead* and Netflix's *Orange Is the New Black*), and Latinos (USA's *Queen of the South*). Other cable outlets such as HBO and the Hallmark Channel are more uneven in their representation of diversity. Niche cable networks now target specific groups; BET, OWN, and TV One focus on African Americans, and El Rey focuses on English-speaking Latinos.

Muslims and Arabs have become the new villains of choice in visual media, which threatens to reinforce prejudicial beliefs. In past generations, Arabs and Muslims were shown in mystical ways (as in the Aladdin mythology), but increasingly they have become the perennial bad guys, and another common character is the suffering Muslim woman waiting to be rescued (Matar 2015; Soltas and Stephens-Davidowitz 2015).

It is easy to focus merely on the visual content of the mass media but more difficult to assess the representation of racial and ethnic minority groups behind the scenes, especially in the important policymaking roles. Behind the camera, minority representation in television is low, with only 19 percent of directors and 13 percent of writers being Black, Hispanic, or Asian Pacific American (Blas 2016; GLAAD 2016; Keveney 2016; Ryan 2016; Thakore 2014).

Motion pictures are even less diverse in their representations than television. Less than 29 percent of speaking characters were female during the period 2007 to 2015. Most *Star Wars* fans can easily name all the women who spoke more than a dozen lines in the eight movies released so far—there are just four such female characters. Only 3.4 percent of directors, 10.8 percent of writers, and about one-quarter of top film executives are female. On the big screen, about one in four speaking roles are by a minority actor compared to minorities' 40 percent share of the population (Smith, Choueiti, and Pieper 2016).

Reality or unscripted television programs have dominated prime-time television for the past few years. Because these shows are popular with consumers and relatively inexpensive to produce, broadcast and cable networks have launched shows that feature everyday people or C-list celebrities in some type of competition. While these unscripted shows have been routinely criticized on artistic grounds, they do represent the diversity of the population. They are a significant exception to television dominated by White actors and actresses.

In one area of unscripted television, the color line remains in place. Reality shows that promote creation of romantic partnerships such as *The Bachelor* and *The Bachelorette* do so in an overwhelming all-White dating gallery—at least that has been the case for all seasons through 2016—except for one African American male most remembered for his anti-gay comments (C. Kelly 2016).

Intergroup Contact: Avoidance Versus Friendship

Is prejudice reduced or intensified when people cross racial and ethnic boundaries in their friendships? To answer this question, researchers and theorists have followed two parallel paths of inquiry: social distance and the contact hypothesis.

THE SOCIAL DISTANCE SCALE Robert Park and Ernest Burgess (1921:440) first defined **social distance** as the tendency to approach or withdraw from a racial group. Emory Bogardus (1968) created a scale to measure social distance empirically. His social distance scale, often called the **Bogardus scale**, is now widely used.

The Bogardus scale asks people how willing they would be to interact with various racial and ethnic groups in specific social situations. The situations describe different degrees of social contact or social distance. For example, people are asked whether they would be willing to work alongside, be a neighbor to, or be related

"I'm here at the Academy Awards, otherwise known as the White People's Choice Awards." So began comedian Chris Rock's opening monologue of the 2016 Oscar ceremony, acknowledging that once again only White performers were nominated in all acting categories. This underrepresentation of minority groups led to the #OscarsSo-White movement. In 2017, two African American actors won Oscars, and *Moonlight* became the first-ever movie with an all-Black cast to win the Best Picture Oscar.

Xinhua/Alamy Stock Photo

by marriage to someone of a different group. Over the 70-year period in which the tests were administered, certain patterns emerged. In the top third of the hierarchy are White Americans and northern Europeans. Held at greater social distance are eastern and southern Europeans, and generally near the bottom are racial minorities (Bogardus 1968; Song 1991; Wark and Galliher 2007).

Generally, even the respondents who had friends of different racial and ethnic origins were more likely to show greater social distance—that is, they were less likely to have been in each other's homes, shared fewer activities, and were less likely to talk about their problems with each other. This social distance is unlikely to promote mutual understanding.

EQUAL STATUS CONTACT   Many research studies have confirmed the **contact hypothesis**, which states that intergroup contact between people of equal status in harmonious circumstances causes them to become less prejudiced and to abandon previously held stereotypes. The importance of *equal status* in interaction cannot be stressed enough. If a Puerto Rican is mistreated by his employer, little interracial harmony is promoted. Similarly, the situation in which contact occurs must be pleasant, making a positive evaluation likely for both individuals. Contact between two nurses, one Black and the other White, who are competing for one vacancy as a supervisor may lead to greater racial hostility. In contrast, being employed together in a harmonious workplace or living in the same neighborhood would work against harboring stereotypes or prejudices (Krysan, Farley, and Couper 2008; Schaefer 1976).

The key factor in reducing hostility, in addition to equal-status contact, is the presence of a common goal. If people are in competition, contact may heighten tension, as already noted.

Segregation in schools, neighborhoods, and the workplace undercuts the impact of the contact hypothesis. If there is no positive contact, then how can we expect a decrease in prejudice? National surveys show prejudice directed toward Muslim Americans, but social contact bridges that prejudice. In a 2006 survey, 50 percent of people who were not acquainted with a Muslim favored special identification for Muslim Americans, but only 24 percent of those who knew a Muslim embraced that same view. Similarly, people who are personally familiar with Muslims are more than one-third less likely to endorse special security checks for Muslims and are less nervous when they share an airplane with Muslim men. Although negative views are common toward Muslim Americans today, such views are much less likely to be held by people who have had intergroup contact (Saad 2006; Zafar and Ross 2015).

As African Americans and other subordinate groups slowly gain access to better-paying jobs with more responsibility, the contact hypothesis takes on greater significance. Usually, the availability of equal-status interaction is taken for granted; yet in everyday life, intergroup contact does not conform to the equal-status ideal of the contact hypothesis.

We often are unaware of all the social situations that allow us to meet people of different ethnic and racial backgrounds. Such interactions may increase understanding.

Furthermore, as we have seen, in a highly segregated society such as the United States, contact tends to be brief and superficial, especially between Whites and minorities. Yet there are encouraging signs. For example, more heterosexuals report having a close family member or friend who is gay or lesbian. Recent studies show that the contact hypothesis is working toward lowering prejudice toward members of the LGBT community (Lytle and Levy 2015).

AVOIDANCE VIA THE INTERNET The Internet, smartphones, and social media are often heralded as transforming social behavior, allowing us to network globally. While electronic media do make commu-

nication easier, they do not necessarily increase contact among groups. Avoiding racial, ethnic, and religious minorities online is just another way of doing what previous generations did without the Internet.

Take dating, for example. In the past, many avoided people who looked different at social occasions. Internet daters have a new tool for such avoidance. Studies document that people who use Internet dating services typically use filters or respond to background questions to exclude contact with people different from themselves. While many daters use such filters, Whites are least open to dating racial and ethnic groups different from themselves, African Americans are most open, and Latinos and Asian Americans are somewhere between the two extremes (Robnett and Feliciano 2011).

Sometimes the avoidance is not necessarily initiated by people but by the technology itself. In an increasingly wired world, we are actually less likely to benefit from intergroup contacts and friendships. Facebook, Classmates.com, and LinkedIn allow us to reach out to those who are different from ourselves—or do they? The search engines we use to navigate the Internet are personalized. For example, Google uses as many as 57 sources of information, including a person's location and past searches, to make calculated guesses about the sites a person might like to visit. Google searches have been personalized in this way since 2009. Keep in mind that Google accounts for 82 percent of global Internet searches and captures 98 percent of mobile-phone searches. In 2012, Google carried the process one step further by collecting information from the Web sites that people "friend" or "like" through social media, and then using that information to direct their Web searches.

Although Google's approach may at first sound personalized and convenient, critics charge that it can trap users in their own worlds by routing them ever more narrowly in the same direction. In his book *The Filter Bubble,* online political activist Eli Pariser (2011a, 2011b) contends that search-engine filters enclose us in a kind of "invisible bubble" or "walled garden" that limits what we see to what we are already familiar with. Thus, we are not likely to discover people, places, and ideas that are outside our comfort zone. Secure in our online bubble, which we may not even realize is there, we have little interaction with people different from ourselves (Katz 2012; Zittrain 2008).

What is wrong with that? Given a choice, most of us go only to restaurants whose food we enjoy and read and listen to only those books and radio programs we know we like. Yet, wasn't the Internet supposed to open new vistas to us? If we are investigating a major news event, shouldn't we all see the same information when we search for it? Pariser describes what happened when two friends searched for the term "BP" in the spring of 2010, during the Deepwater Horizon oil rig's accidental discharge of crude oil into the Gulf of Mexico. Using the same browser, the two friends got very different results. One saw links to information about the oil spill; the other saw links to information about BP's CEO, intended for investors.

Corporate Response: Diversity Training

Prejudice carries a cost. This cost is not only to the victim but also to any organization that allows prejudice to interfere with its functioning. Workplace hostility can lead to lost productivity and even staff attrition. Furthermore, if left unchecked, an organization—whether it is a corporation, government agency, or nonprofit enterprise—can develop a reputation for having a "chilly climate." If a business has a reputation for being unfriendly to people of color or to women, qualified people are discouraged from applying for jobs there, and potential clients might seek products or services elsewhere.

How do you battle prejudice in the workplace? The Speaking Out feature "What Can I Do at Work?" offers some suggestions from the Southern Poverty Law Center, a well-known anti-prejudice organization.

In an effort to improve workplace relations, most organizations have initiated some form of diversity training. These programs are aimed at eliminating circumstances and relationships that cause groups to receive fewer rewards, resources, or opportunities. Typically, programs aim to reduce ill treatment based on race, gender, and ethnicity. In addition, diversity training may deal with (in descending order of frequency) age, disability, religion, language, citizenship status, marital status, and parental status (Society for Human Resource Management 2010, 2011).

Speaking Out

What Can I Do at Work?

The workplace is, for some, the only place they experience diversity. For those who live in segregated neighborhoods, attend segregated houses of worship, or take part in segregated hobbies or activities, work becomes the only place they interact with people of varied and diverse backgrounds. It often is, for these people, a testing ground.

The workplace often offers built-in grievance procedures, tied to policies or laws, which can be used to respond to some forms of everyday bigotry. You need not file a lawsuit to have such a policy be effective; many roundtable participants spoke of invoking such policies when speaking up, saying the mere mention carries weight.

Power, too, comes into play at the workplace. The dynamic of an employee speaking to a supervisor is very different than that of a supervisor speaking to an employee. Likewise, an executive's tacit acceptance of bigoted remarks can create an atmosphere where bias thrives—just as one powerfully placed comment from that executive can curb everyday bigotry in significant ways. Who sets the tone at your office? And what leverage do you have with that person? If you lack leverage, who has it? And might that person be an ally?

What Can I Do About Casual Comments?

"Have You Had Diction Lessons?"

An African American businesswoman in the South writes: "I was speaking with a white coworker when, midway through the conversation, she smiled and said, 'You speak so clearly. Have you had diction lessons?'—like for an African American to speak clearly, we'd have to have diction lessons."

A manager writes: "One of my employees constantly makes 'jokes' about people being 'bipolar' or 'going postal' or being 'off their meds.' I happen to know that one of our other employees—within earshot of these comments—is on medication for depression. How can I stop the bad behavior without revealing proprietary information?"

One coworker asks another if she wants to go out for lunch. "We're going to get Ping-Pong chicken," she says, faking a vaguely Asian accent.

An Italian American woman's coworker makes daily comments about her heritage. "Are you in the Mafia?" "Are you related to the Godfather?" There are only six colleagues in the office, and the Italian American woman doesn't know whether—or how—to respond

Speaking Up

Core-value statements and other policies sitting on dusty shelves don't establish an office's culture; casual interactions do. Whether you're a staffer, a manager, or an executive, there's a role for you to play in setting a respectful and unbiased tone in the office. Consider these actions:

- **Interrupt early.** Workplace culture largely is determined by what is or isn't allowed to occur. If people are lax in responding to bigotry, then bigotry prevails. Speak up early and often in order to build a more inclusive environment.

- **Use—or establish—policies.** Call upon existing—too often forgotten or ignored—policies to address bigoted language or behavior. Work with your personnel director or human resources department to create new policies and procedures, as needed. Also ask your company to provide anti-bias training.

- **Go up the ladder.** If behavior persists, take your complaints up the management ladder. Find allies in upper management, and call on them to help create and maintain an office environment free of bias and bigotry.

- **Band together.** Like-minded colleagues also may form an alliance and then ask the colleague or supervisor to change his or her tone or behavior.

What Can I Do About Workplace Humor?

"Please Don't Tell It"

A man mentions to a colleague that he is originally from West Virginia. The colleague laughs and says she knows some "jokes" about people from West Virginia.

She begins to tell one, and it's clear that the "joke" will have an offensive punch line.

The man holds up his hand and says, "Don't tell it. Please don't tell it."

She laughs, perhaps thinking he's joking himself, and tells not one but three "jokes," each with an increasingly bigoted punch line.

The man, at a loss for words, simply sits down when she is done.

Don't laugh. Meet a bigoted "joke" with silence, and maybe a raised eyebrow. Use body language to communicate your distaste for bigoted "humor."

Speaking Up

Humor can enliven the workplace, provide people relief from routine tasks, and help foster team spirit. When humor goes sour, however, the work culture suffers and collegiality can be harmed or damaged. When faced with bigoted "jokes" in the office, try this:

- **Interrupt the laughter.** "Why does everyone think that's funny?" Tell your coworkers why the "joke" offends you, that it feels demeaning and prejudicial. And don't hesitate to interrupt a "joke" with as many additional "no" messages as needed.

- **Set a "not in my workspace" rule.** Prohibit bigotry in your cubicle, your office, or whatever other boundaries define your workspace. Be firm, and get others to join in. Allies can be invaluable in helping to curb bigoted remarks and behavior at the workplace.

Provide alternate humor. Learn and share jokes that don't rely on bias, bigotry, or stereotypes as the root of their humor.

Source: Southern Poverty Law Center, At www.splcenter.org under Publications. Speak Up. Responding to Everyday Bigotry. January 25, 2015, pp. 36-38, 40-42. Used with permission.

It is difficult to make broad generalization about the effectiveness of diversity-training programs because they vary so much between organizations. At one extreme are short presentations that seem to have little support from management. People file into the room, feeling that the training is something they need to get through quickly. Such training is unlikely to be effective and may be counterproductive because it heightens social tensions. At the other end of the continuum is a diversity-training program that is integrated into initial job training, reinforced periodically, and presented as part of the organization's overall mission, with full support from all levels of management. In such businesses, diversity is a core value, and management demands a high degree of commitment from all employees.

Remarkably, the adoption of diversity programs in organizations remains slow more than three decades after the diversity-management paradigm was first widely viewed as good for business (only 10 to 30 percent of businesses have such a program). Even inexpensive steps are not widely adopted. Unfortunately, corporations with lower representation of women and minorities are less likely to embrace diversity programs.

Research into different corporate policies has found two that are particularly effective. Diversity task forces that bring together people from different departments to brainstorm about opening up hiring opportunities appear to eventually increase the diversity in upper management. A second successful policy is the presence of diversity mentoring programs designed for aspiring women and minorities, as well as White men, to help them achieve their career goals. Unfortunately, research suggests that if White men perceive African Americans as the primary organizers of such efforts, the programs can actually have a negative impact.

As Figure 2.6 shows, the workforce is becoming more diverse, and management is taking notice. An increasing proportion of the workforce is foreign-born, and the numbers of U.S.-born African Americans, Latinos, and Asian Pacific Americans also are growing. Growing research in business and the social sciences documents that diversity is an asset in bringing about creative changes. The benefits of workplace diversity are especially true at management levels, where leadership teams can develop innovative solutions and creative ideas. However, it is troubling to note that organizations that have the least diverse leadership are also less likely to adopt any kind of diversity program (DiTomaso, Post, and Parks-Yancy 2007; Dobbin and Kalev 2013; Dobbin, Kalev, and Kelly 2007; Dobbin, Kim, and Kalev 2011; Gose 2013; Kalev, Dobbin, and Kelly 2006).

It is not in an organization's best interests if employees start to create barriers based on, for example, racial lines. Earlier, we learned that equal-status contact can reduce hostility. However, in the workplace, people compete for promotions, desirable work assignments, and better office space, to name just a few sources of friction. When done well, diversity training removes ill feelings among workers, which often reflect the prejudices present in larger society.

To have a lasting impact, diversity training should not be separated from other aspects of the organization. For example, even the most inspired program will have little effect on prejudice if the organization promotes a sexist or ethnically offensive image in its advertising. The University of North Dakota launched an initiative in 2001 to become one of the top institutions for Native Americans in the nation. Yet at almost the same time, the administration reaffirmed its commitment, despite tribal objections, to have the "Fighting Sioux" as its mascot for athletic teams. In 2005, the National Collegiate Athletic Association began to review logos and mascots that could be considered insulting to Native Americans. Finally, 68 percent of the state's voters voted to abandon the logo. In short, it does little good to

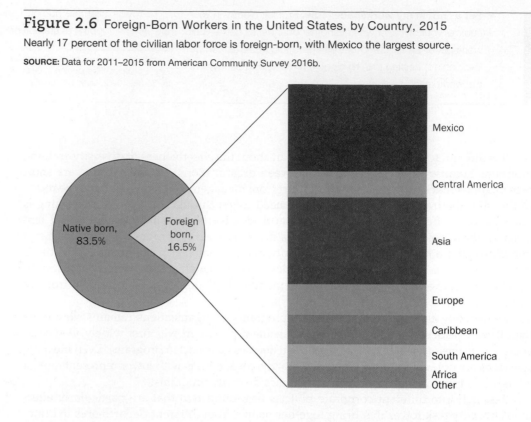

Figure 2.6 Foreign-Born Workers in the United States, by Country, 2015

Nearly 17 percent of the civilian labor force is foreign-born, with Mexico the largest source.

SOURCE: Data for 2011–2015 from American Community Survey 2016b.

offer diversity training if an organization's overt actions propel it in the opposite direction (Kolowich 2015).

Despite the challenges of confronting and eliminating prejudice, an organization with a comprehensive, management-supported program of diversity training can go a long way toward reducing prejudice in the workplace. For the program to be successful, the rest of the organization must also support mutual respect.

Conclusion

This chapter has examined theories of prejudice and measurements of its extent. Prejudice has a long history in the United States. Whispering campaigns suggested that presidents Martin Van Buren and William McKinley were secretly working with the Pope. This whispering emerged into a national debate when John F. Kennedy became the first Roman Catholic to become president. Much more recently, in 2015, 29 percent of Americans believed President Obama to be a Muslim, and only 39 percent believed him to be Christian or Protestant (Barrett 2016).

Are some minority groups now finally being respected? People cheered on May 1, 2011, on hearing that Osama bin Laden had been found and killed. However, the American Indian people were troubled to learn that the military had assigned the code name "Geronimo" to the operation to capture the terrorist. The Chiricahua Apache of New Mexico were particularly disturbed to learn that the name of their freedom fighter was associated with a global terrorist. In response, the U.S. Defense Department said no disrespect was meant to Native Americans. Of course, one can imagine that the operation never would have been named "Operation Lafayette" or "Operation Jefferson" (Dally 2011).

Several theories try to explain why prejudice exists. Theories for prejudice include two that tend to be psychological (scapegoating and authoritarian personality) and emphasize why a particular person harbors ill feelings toward minority groups. Others (exploitation theory and the normative approach) view prejudice in the context of our interaction in a larger society.

Surveys conducted in the United States over the past 60 years point to a reduction of prejudice as measured by the willingness to express stereotypes or maintain social distance. Survey data also show that African Americans, Latinos, Asian Pacific Americans, and American Indians do not necessarily feel comfortable with one another. They have adopted attitudes toward other oppressed groups similar to those held by many White Americans.

The absence of widespread public expression of prejudice does not mean prejudice itself is absent. Recent prejudice aimed at Hispanics, Asian Pacific Americans, and large recent immigrant groups such as Arab Americans and Muslim Americans is well documented. Issues such as immigration and affirmative action reemerge and cause bitter resentment. Furthermore, ill feelings exist between subordinate groups in schools, on the streets, and in the workplace. Color-blind racism allows one to appear to be tolerant while allowing racial and ethnic inequality to persist.

Equal-status contact may reduce hostility between groups. However, in a highly segregated society defined by inequality, such opportunities are not typical. The mass media can help reduce discrimination, but they have not done enough and may even intensify ill feelings by promoting stereotypical images, such as Arab Americans as terrorists or convenience-store clerks, or Latinos as gang members.

Even though we can be encouraged by the techniques available to reduce intergroup hostility, sizable segments of the population still do not want to live in integrated neighborhoods, do not want to work for or be led by someone of a different race, and object to the idea of their relatives marrying outside their own group. People (including minorities) still harbor stereotypes of racial and ethnic minorities.

Reducing prejudice is important because it can lead to support for policy change. There are steps we can take as individuals to confront prejudice and overcome hatred. The ultimate objective is to improve the social condition of oppressed groups in the United States. To consider this challenge, we turn to discrimination in Chapter 3. Discrimination's costs are high to both dominant and subordinate groups. With this fact in mind, we examine some techniques for reducing discrimination.

Summary of Learning Objectives

2.1 **Differentiate between prejudice and discrimination.**

1. Prejudice consists of negative attitudes, and discrimination consists of negative behavior toward a group.

2.2 **Explain White privilege.**

2. White privilege refers to the rights or immunities granted as a particular benefit or favor for being White. Typically unconsciously, White people accept privilege automatically extended to them in everyday life.

2.3 **Summarize the theories of prejudice.**

3. Among explanations for prejudice are the theories of scapegoating, authoritarian personality, exploitation theory, and the normative approach.

2.4 **Define and explain stereotyping.**

4. Stereotypes present the content or images that prejudiced people hold and become accepted as reality.

2.5 **Understand color-blind racism.**

5. Although evidence indicates that the public expression of prejudice has declined, ample evidence exists that people are expressing race-neutral principles (color-blind racism) that perpetuate inequality in society.

2.6 **Discuss how members of subordinate groups respond to prejudice.**

6. Typically, members of minority groups have a significantly more negative view of social inequality than Whites, but the majority of Blacks, Latinos, and Asian Pacific Americans believe matters will improve over the next ten years. There is also persistent intergroup hostility among the minorities themselves; this hostility may turn violent.

2.7 **Explain the ways prejudice can be reduced.**

7. Various techniques are used to reduce prejudice, including educational programs, positive portrayals and inclusion in mass media, friendly intergroup contact, and corporate diversity-training programs.

Key Terms

anti-Semitism, *page 37*
authoritarian personality, *page 37*
Bogardus scale, *page 47*
color-blind racism, *page 41*
contact hypothesis, *page 48*
discrimination, *page 34*
ethnocentrism, *page 32*

ethnophaulism, *page 33*
exploitation theory, *page 37*
homophobia, *page 39*
microaggressions, *page 33*
normative approach, *page 38*
prejudice, *page 33*
racial profiling, *page 39*

scapegoating theory, *page 36*
sexism, *page 39*
social distance, *page 47*
stereotypes, *page 38*
White privilege, *page 35*

Review Questions

1. How are prejudice and discrimination both related and unrelated to each other?

2. If White people are privileged, how do we explain the presence of poverty among Whites?

3. How do theories of prejudice relate to different expressions of prejudice?

4. What is the impact of stereotypes on how we interact with others?

5. How is color-blind racism expressed?

6. What is intergroup hostility?

7. Describe efforts to reduce prejudice through education and the mass media.

8. Explain the role of intergroup contact in reducing prejudice.

Critical Thinking

1. It is said that prejudice is an attitude and discrimination is an action. Can you think of some examples from your experience that draw out people's prejudice toward and discrimination against others?

2. What privileges do you have that you do not give much thought to? Are they in any way related to race, ethnicity, religion, gender, sexuality, or social class?

3. Identify stereotypes associated with a group of people such as older adults or people with physical disabilities.

4. Consider the television programs you watch the most. In terms of race and ethnicity, how well do these programs reflect the diversity of the U.S. population?

5. In what ways do you think interactions over the Internet are promoting prejudice and discrimination? Conversely, do you think the Internet and social media can be used as tools to reduce prejudice and discrimination? If so, how?

Chapter 3
Discrimination

Jim West/Alamy Stock Photo

⌄ Learning Objectives

3.1 Distinguish between relative and absolute deprivation.

3.2 Define hate crimes.

3.3 Summarize how institutions discriminate.

3.4 Describe the effects of discrimination and the efforts to reduce or eliminate it.

3.5 Explain and discuss environmental justice.

3.6 Explain affirmative action and the legal debate surrounding it.

3.7 Explain the glass ceiling in the workplace.

"I didn't get the job" is a frequent complaint that soon leads to reasons "I" did not get the job for which "I" applied. Sometimes people think they didn't get the job because of their race. Is discrimination common in hiring practices?

A dramatic confirmation of discrimination in hiring came with research begun by sociologist Devah Pager in 2003. She sent White, Black, and Latino men out as trained "testers" in Milwaukee and New York City to look for entry-level jobs that required no experience or special training. Each tester was in his twenties and was college educated, but all of them presented themselves as having only a high-school diploma, and each had a similar job history.

The experiences with potential employers were vastly different. Why? Besides having different racial and ethnic backgrounds, some testers indicated in the job application that they had served 18 months in jail for a felony conviction (possession of cocaine with intent to distribute). So what happened when Black Americans applied?

- Black male applicant, jail time: 5 percent received a callback
- Black male applicant, NO jail time: 14 percent received a callback

Clearly, past felons had a harder time continuing through the employment process. What about when White people made the same queries?

- White male applicant, jail time: 17 percent received a callback
- White male applicant, NO jail time: 34 percent received a callback

Once again, applicants with past jail time were less likely to receive a callback. Yet a White job applicant with a jail record received more callbacks for further consideration than did a Black man with no criminal record. Whiteness has a privilege even when it comes to jail time; race, it seems, was more of a concern to potential employers than a criminal background. It is no surprise that an analysis of labor patterns after release from prison finds that wages grow 21 percent more slowly for Black ex-inmates than for White ex-inmates. In another study, Pager documented that Latino job applicants were at a disadvantage similar to that of the African American testers (Pager 2003; Pager, Western, and Bonikowski 2009; Pager and Western 2012).

"I expected there to be an effect of race, but I did not expect it to swamp the results as it did," Pager told an interviewer. Her finding was especially significant because one in three African American men and one in six Hispanic men are expected to serve time in prison during their lifetime compared to one in 17 White men (Greenhouse 2012; Kroeger 2004).

Pager's research, which was widely publicized, eventually contributed to a change in public policy. In his 2004 State of the Union address, and specifically referring to Pager's work, President George W. Bush announced a $300 million monitoring program for ex-convicts who are attempting to reintegrate into society.

Discrimination has a long history, right up to and including the present, of taking its toll on people. **Discrimination** is the denial of opportunities and equal rights to individuals and groups because of prejudice or other arbitrary reasons. In this chapter, we examine the many faces of discrimination, its many victims, and the many ways scholars have documented its presence today in the United States. We examine not only discrimination in housing but also look at differential treatment in employment opportunities, wages, voting, vulnerability to environmental hazards, and even access to membership in private clubs.

Relative versus Absolute Deprivation

3.1   Distinguish between relative and absolute deprivation.

People in the United States find it difficult to see discrimination as a widespread phenomenon. "After all," it is often said, "these minorities drive cars, hold jobs, own their homes, and even go to college." But discrimination does exist in the United States, as it does abroad, where its victims include a broad array of groups. In the Global View feature, we consider how the Roma (or Gypsies) have been victimized.

To understand discrimination in modern industrialized societies such as the United States, we must begin by distinguishing between relative and absolute deprivation.

Conflict theorists have correctly observed that it is not absolute, unchanging standards that determine deprivation and oppression. Although minority groups may be viewed as having adequate or even good incomes, housing, health care, and educational opportunities, their position relative to some other group provides evidence of discrimination.

Relative deprivation is the conscious experience of a negative discrepancy between legitimate expectations and present actualities. After settling in the United States, immigrants often enjoy better material comforts and more political freedom than was possible in the countries they left. If they compare themselves with most other people in the United States, however, they will feel deprived because, although their standards have improved, the immigrants still perceive that they are deprived in relation to other groups.

Absolute deprivation, in contrast, implies a fixed standard based on a minimum level of subsistence, often determined by the government. Discrimination does not necessarily mean absolute deprivation. A Japanese American who is promoted to a management position may still be a victim of discrimination if he or she had been passed over for years because of corporate reluctance to place an Asian American in a highly visible position.

A Global View

The Roma: A Thousand Years of Discrimination

The Roma people (also referred to as Gypsies) are members of a minority group numbering 12 million to 15 million who are dispersed over many countries. The people originated in India, but most Roma now live in Europe, with perhaps as many as 1 million in North America. They continue to be characterized by a nomadic lifestyle, often in response to prejudice and discrimination. Certain common activities, such as fortune telling, traveling together in large caravans, and arranged marriages, often create hostile responses to their arrival in communities. Although the Roma speak their own distinctive language, they have usually adopted the religion of their home region, such as Roman Catholic, Orthodox Christian, or Muslim.

The Roma are the largest ethnic minority in the European Union and are the object of that organization's efforts to address their poor housing, low levels of formal schooling, and high levels of unemployment. Progress is evident in a decline in racially motivated murders of Roma since the early 1990s. Historically, Roma had been subjected to expulsion, but large numbers died in the Holocaust as a part of Hitler's racial purification efforts. In reference to this genocide, a mayor in France responded to complaints about Roma in his area by saying, "Maybe Hitler didn't kill enough of them" (Corbet 2013).

Gypsies themselves have begun to work through established channels to confront discrimination. Simply being Roma makes many authorities assume a child is ill prepared for schooling, as in the Czech Republic, where the majority of children in special schools for the learning disabled are Roma. The Roma brought legal action to stop this practice. In a case compared to the 1954 U.S. *Brown v. Board of Education* decision (which desegregated public schools), the European Court of Human Rights ruled in 2007 in *D. H. and Others v. Czech Republic* that the Czech practice was discriminatory, with Gypsy children receiving inappropriate school placements and substandard education. Actions taken by the Czech Republic to reduce discrimination in 2011 were greeted with muted enthusiasm, with many Roma seeing little change.

In 2013, the stigmatization of the Roma came into sharp focus in Europe as a result of incidents in more than one European country in which onlookers and officials looked at fair-haired, blue-eyed children with Roma adults and assumed that the children had been kidnapped. After the children were taken into protective custody, DNA testing proved the allegations groundless. Clearly, even today the Roma people continue to be victimized.

Sources: Bilefsky 2013; Bourmont 2017; European Roma Rights Centre 2008, 2012; Hacek 2008; Schaefer and Zellner 2015.

Dissatisfaction is likely to arise from feelings of relative deprivation. However, the members of a society who feel most frustrated and disgruntled by the social and economic conditions of their lives are not necessarily worse off in an objective sense. Social scientists have long recognized that the most significant factor in deprivation is how people perceive their situations. As Karl Marx pointed out, the misery of the workers is important in reflecting their oppressed state, but so is their position relative to the ruling class. In 1847, Marx wrote, "Although the enjoyment of the workers has risen, the social satisfaction that they have has fallen in comparison with the increased enjoyment of the capitalist" (Marx and Engels 1955:94).

Marx's assertion explains why the groups or individuals who are most vocal and best organized against discrimination are not necessarily in the worst economic and social situation. However, they are likely to be those who most strongly perceive that, relative to others, they are not receiving their fair share. Resistance to perceived discrimination, rather than the actual amount of absolute discrimination, is the key.

Hate Crimes

3.2 Define hate crimes.

Although prejudice certainly is not new in the United States, it is receiving increased attention as it manifests itself in hate crimes in neighborhoods, at meetings, and on college campuses. The Hate Crime Statistics Act, which became law in 1990, directs the Department of Justice to gather data on hate or bias crimes.

What Are Hate Crimes?

The government elevates an ordinary crime to the status of **hate crime** when offenders choose a victim because of some characteristic—for example, race, ethnicity, religion, sexual orientation, or disability—and provide evidence that hatred prompted them to commit the crime. Hate crimes are sometimes called *bias crimes*.

The Hate Crime Statistics Act created a national mandate to identify such crimes, whereas previously only 12 states had monitored hate crimes. The act has since been amended to include disabilities—physical and mental—as well as sexual orientation as factors that can be considered a basis for hate crimes.

In 2016, law enforcement agencies released hate crime data submitted by police agencies. Even though many hate crimes are not reported (less than one in seven participating agencies reported an incident), a staggering number of offenses that come to law agencies' attention were motivated by hate. While most incidents receive relatively little attention, some grab the headlines and dominate news sites for days. Such was the case in 2015 when a 21-year-old self-described White supremacist walked into a prayer service at a Black church in Charleston, South Carolina, and killed nine people and wounded three others.

Official reports noted more than 5,800 hate crimes and bias-motivated incidents in 2015. As Table 3.1 indicates, race, ethnicity, and ancestry were the apparent motivation for the bias in approximately 57 percent of the reports, and religion and sexual orientation accounted for 18 to 22 percent each. Vandalism against property and intimidation were the most common crimes, but among the more than 4,400 crimes directed against people, 58 percent involved assault, rape, or murder.

The vast majority of hate crimes are committed by members of the dominant group against those who are, relatively speaking, powerless. Only one in five bias incidents based on race are anti-White. Hate crimes, except for those that are most horrific, generally receive little media attention, and anti-White incidents probably receive even less. Hostility based on race knows no boundaries (Witt 2007).

The official reports of hate or bias crimes appear to be only the tip of the iceberg. Government-commissioned surveys conducted over a national cross-section indicate that 192,000 people annually report they have been victims of hate crimes, but only half reported those crimes to the police. Of these, only one out of ten are confirmed as hate crimes, according to the victims. In short, a considerable amount of racial hostility in this country becomes violent (Harlow 2005; Perry 2003).

National legislation and publicity have made *hate crime* a meaningful term, and we are beginning to recognize the victimization associated with such incidents. A current proposal would make a violent crime a federal crime if it is motivated by racial or religious bias. Although passage is uncertain, the serious consideration of the proposal indicates a willingness to consider a major expansion of federal jurisdiction. Currently, federal law prohibits crimes motivated by race, color, religion, or national origin only if they violate a federally guaranteed right such as voting.

Victimized groups do more than experience and observe hate crimes and other acts of prejudice. Watchdog organizations play an important role in documenting bias-motivated violence; such groups include the Anti-Defamation League, the National Institute Against Prejudice and Violence, the Southern Poverty Law Center, and the National Gay and Lesbian Task Force.

To further their agenda, established hate groups have even set up propaganda sites online, thus creating opportunities for previously unknown haters and hate groups to promote themselves. However, hate crime legislation does not affect such outlets because of legal questions involving freedom of speech. More recently, enterprising bigots have begun to use directories to target their attacks through instant messages, in much the same way as they placed harassing telephone calls in the past. Even more creative and subtle are people who have constructed Web sites to attract people who are surfing for information on Martin Luther King, Jr., only to find a site that looks educational but savagely discredits the civil rights activist. A close inspection reveals that a White-supremacist organization hosts the site (Davis 2008; Simon Wiesenthal Center 2008; Working 2007).

Figure 3.1 Distribution of Reported Hate Crimes

SOURCE: Incidents reported for 2015 by Federal Bureau of Investigation 2016a.

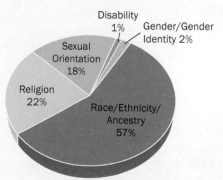

Why Do Hate Crimes Carry Harsher Penalties?

Frequently, one hears of hate crimes being questioned or disputed. After all, the skeptics ask, is not hate involved in every assault or act of vandalism? While many non–hate crimes may be motivated by hatred toward an individual or organization, a hate or bias crime toward a minority is intended to carry a message well beyond the individual victim. When a person is assaulted because he is gay or she is a lesbian, the act is meant to terrorize all gay men and lesbians. Vandalizing a mosque or synagogue is meant to warn all Muslims or Jews that they are not wanted and that their religious faith is considered inferior.

In many respects, today's hate crimes are like the terrorist efforts of the Ku Klux Klan generations ago. Targets may be randomly selected, but the group being terrorized is carefully chosen. In many jurisdictions, having a crime officially classified as a hate crime can increase the punishment. For example, a misdemeanor like vandalism can be increased to a felony. A felony that is a hate crime can carry a greater prison sentence. These sanctions were upheld by the U.S. Supreme Court in the 1993 decision *Mitchell v. Wisconsin*, which recognized that greater harm may be done by hate-motivated crimes (Blazak 2011).

Institutional Discrimination

3.3 Summarize how institutions discriminate.

Individuals practice discrimination in one-on-one encounters, and institutions practice discrimination through their daily operations. Indeed, a consensus is growing today that institutional discrimination is more significant than acts committed by prejudiced individuals.

Social scientists are particularly concerned with how patterns of employment, education, criminal justice, housing, health care, and government operations maintain the social significance of race and ethnicity. **Institutional discrimination** is the denial of opportunities and equal rights to individuals and groups that results from the normal operations of a society.

Civil rights activist Stokely Carmichael and political scientist Charles Hamilton are credited with introducing the concept of institutional racism. *Individual discrimination* refers to overt acts of individual Whites against individual Blacks; Carmichael and Hamilton reserved the term *institutional racism* for covert acts committed collectively against an entire group. From this perspective, discrimination can take place without an individual intending to deprive others of privileges and even without the individual being aware that others are being deprived (Ture and Hamilton 1992).

How can discrimination be widespread and unconscious at the same time? A few documented examples of institutional discrimination follow:

1. Standards for assessing credit risks work against African Americans and Hispanics who seek to establish businesses because many lack conventional credit references. Businesses in low-income areas where these groups often reside also have much higher insurance costs.

2. IQ testing favors middle-class children, especially White middle-class children, because of the types of questions included on the test.

3. The entire criminal justice system, from the patrol officer to the judge and jury, is dominated by Whites who find it difficult to understand life in poverty-stricken areas.

4. Hiring practices often require several years' experience at jobs only recently opened to members of subordinate groups.

5. Many jobs automatically eliminate people with felony records or past drug offenses, a practice that disproportionately reduces employment opportunities for people of color.

Institutional discrimination is so systemic that it takes on the pattern of what has been termed "woodwork racism" in that racist outcomes become so widespread that African

Americans, Latinos, Asian Pacific Americans, and others endure them as a part of everyday life (Feagin and McKinney 2003).

At the beginning of this chapter, we noted how employers routinely pass over job applicants who are felons. To casual observers, this decision may seem reasonable; however, Black and Latino job applicants are more likely to be passed over than Whites. This is a form of institutional discrimination. Recognizing this problem, the Equal Opportunity Commission ruled in 2012 that while employers may consider criminal records, a policy that excludes all applicants with a conviction could violate employment discrimination laws because of this differential impact. This does not mean employers must hire ex-felons, only that blanket exclusions are to be avoided (Greenhouse 2012).

Despite this positive step, concern is growing over another potential example of institutional discrimination in two areas of voting requirements. First are state laws that bar citizens with past felony convictions from voting. The laws vary from state to state, but some states, including Florida, Iowa, and Virginia, have lifetime bans that are more likely to affect potential African American voters. In fact, in seven states (Alabama, Florida, Kentucky, Mississippi, Tennessee, Virginia, and Wyoming) these laws effectively prevent at least 15 percent of African Americans from voting (Lai and Lee 2016).

Second are laws that require ID to vote, sometimes requiring an officially issued photo ID, ostensibly to prevent voter fraud. However, there is little evidence that people have been impersonating eligible voters at the polls. Figure 3.2 summarizes voter ID requirements in the United States.

Courts have been reluctant to uphold such laws, contending that it is not easy for all eligible voters to obtain such a government-provided ID card. These laws disproportionately disenfranchise members of minority groups, including the elderly, simply because they do not have a driver's license. National surveys have found that 25 percent of African Americans and 16 percent of Latino citizens do not have a valid government-issued photo ID, compared

Figure 3.2 Voter ID Requirements in the United States

NOTE: Data as of June 5, 2017.

SOURCE: Data from National Conference of State Legislatures 2017.

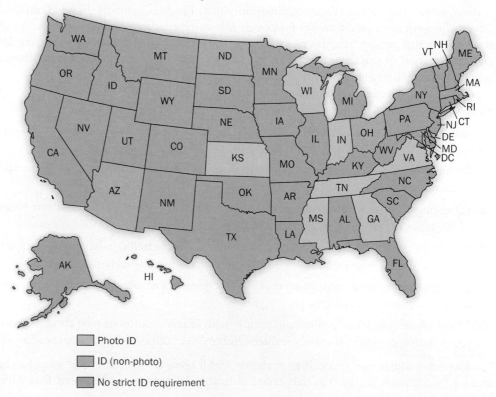

- Photo ID
- ID (non-photo)
- No strict ID requirement

to only 8 percent of White citizens. So, court decisions aside, what we have is another case of institutional discrimination: Through the normal operation of voting regulations, equal rights are more likely to be denied to people of color (Brennan Center 2006, 2013; Dade 2012b).

In other situations, even apparently neutral institutional standards can lead to discriminatory effects. African American students at a Midwestern state university protested a policy under which fraternities and sororities that wanted to use campus facilities for a dance were required to post a security deposit to cover possible damage. The Black students complained that this policy had a discriminatory impact on minority student organizations. Campus police countered that the university's policy applied to all student groups interested in using these facilities. However, because almost all White fraternities and sororities at the school had their own houses, which they used for dances, the policy affected only African American and other subordinate groups' organizations.

Institutional discrimination continuously imposes more hindrances on and awards fewer benefits to certain racial and ethnic groups than it does to others. This is the underlying and painful context of American intergroup relations.

Discrimination Today

3.4 Describe the effects of discrimination and the efforts to reduce or eliminate it.

Discrimination continues to be widespread in the United States. It sometimes results from prejudices held by individuals, but more significantly, it is also found in institutional discrimination. We will look first at measuring discrimination in terms of income and then at efforts that are being made to eliminate or at least reduce it.

Discrimination Hits the Wallet

How much discrimination exists? As in measuring prejudice, challenges arise when trying to quantify discrimination. Measuring prejudice is hampered by the difficulties in assessing attitudes and by the need to take many factors into account. It is further limited by the initial challenge of identifying different treatment. A second difficulty of measuring discrimination is assigning a cost to the discrimination.

An important measure of economic well-being for any household is its annual income and the wealth it has to draw upon in cases of emergency. **Income** refers to salaries, wages, and other money received over a specific period of time; **wealth** is a more inclusive term that encompasses all of a person's material assets, including land and other types of property. Wealth is a measure of what a household owns minus what it owes. We first consider income and then look at wealth later in this chapter.

We can make some tentative conclusions about discrimination by examining income and wealth data. Figure 3.3 uses income data to show the vast income disparity between African Americans and Whites and also between men and women. Figure 3.3 encompasses all full-time workers. White men, with a median income of $60,508, earn about one-third more than Black men and almost twice what Hispanic women earn in wages. The "median" income is the number that splits the group in half—so half of all White men earn more than $60,508 annually, and half earn less.

Yet Asian American men are at the top and edge out White males by $4,000 a year. Why do Asian American men earn so much if race usually serves as a barrier? A significant number of Asian American men with advanced educations have high-earning jobs, which brings up their median income. However, as we will see, given their high levels of schooling, their incomes should be even higher. The economic picture is not entirely positive for Asian Americans, however. Some Asian American groups, such as Laotians and Vietnamese, have high levels of poverty.

Clearly, regardless of race or ethnicity, men outpace women in annual income. The disparity between the incomes of Black women and White men has remained unchanged over the more than 50 years during which such data have been tabulated. It illustrates yet another instance of the greater inequality experienced by minority women.

Figure 3.3 Median Income by Race, Ethnicity, and Gender

Income gaps remain significant, with Hispanic and Native American women needing to work two years in order to earn what Asian American and White men earn in one year.

NOTE: Data released in 2016 for income earned in 2015. Median income is from all sources and is limited to year-round, full-time workers at least 25 years old (American Indian data for 16 years or older). Data for White men and women are for non-Hispanics.

SOURCE: American Community Survey 2016a; American Social and Economic Supplement 2016.

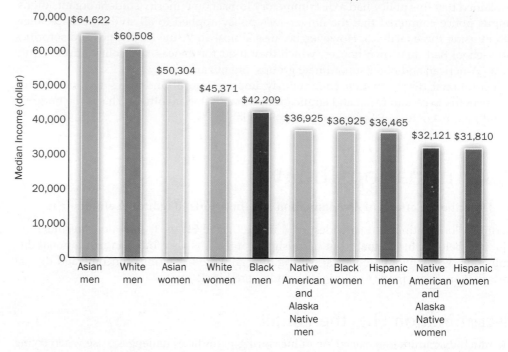

Are these differences entirely the result of discrimination in employment? No. Individuals within the four groups are not equally prepared to compete for high-paying jobs. Past discrimination is a significant factor in a person's current social position. Taxpayers, predominantly White, were unwilling to subsidize the public education of African Americans and Hispanics at the same levels as White pupils. Even as more money has been invested in schools attended by minority groups, today's schools show the continuing results of this uneven spending pattern from the past.

Table 3.1 compares the median income of different groups holding education constant, which means that we can compare Blacks and Whites and men and women with approximately the same amount of formal schooling. More education means more income, but the disparity remains. The gap between races does narrow somewhat as education increases. However, both African Americans and women lag behind their more affluent (White, male) counterparts. The contrast remains dramatic: Women with a master's degree have a median income of $62,379, which means they earn about $9,000 *less* than men who complete only a bachelor's degree.

Thinking over the long term, a woman with a bachelor's degree will work full-time three years to earn $173,000. The typical man can work a little more than 29 months, take over seven months off without pay, and still exceed the woman's earnings. Women, regardless of race, pay at every point. They are often hired at lower starting salaries in jobs comparable to those held by men. Salary increases come more slowly. And by their 30s, they rarely recover from even short maternity leaves.

Note what happens to Asian American households. Asian American families often match similarly educated White families in annual income, but typically there are more earners in their household collectively earning that money than in White family households.

This is the picture today, but is it getting better? According to a Census Bureau report, the answer is no. During the early years of the twenty-first century, Blacks were more likely

Table 3.1 Median Income by Race, Ethnicity, and Sex, Holding Education Constant

Even at the very highest levels of schooling, the income gap remains between Whites and Blacks. Education also has little apparent effect on narrowing the income gap between male and female workers (income values in dollars).

	Race or Ethnicity				Sex	
	White Families	Black Families	Asian Families	Hispanic Families	Male	Female
Total	81,531	39,689	91,780	48,359	52,305	41,679
High School						
Nongraduate	36,308	22,211	44,464	34,708	32,143	22,670
Graduate	60,328	36,790	51,687	44,515	41,569	31,249
College						
Associate degree	79,783	53,183	79,269	68,897	52,072	40,186
Bachelor's degree	105,017	81,455	104,884	88,020	71,385	57,681
Master's degree	122,576	92,344	135,972	104,864	86,738	62,379
Professional degree	164,066	127,250	197,355	122,628	131,189	82,473

NOTE: Data released in 2016 for income earned in 2015. Figures are median income from all sources except capital gains. Included are public-assistance payments, dividends, pensions, and unemployment compensation. Incomes are for all workers 25 years of age and older with earnings. High-school graduates include those with GEDs. Data for Whites are for White non-Hispanics. Family data for Black professional degree-holders' families are author's estimate.

SOURCE: Bureau of Census 2016i: Tables FINC01-4, 6, 8, 9, P-24.

to stay poor than Whites, and those African Americans in the top rung of income were more likely to fall out of that income bracket than their White counterparts among the wealthy. The inequality is dramatic, and the trend is not diminishing (Hisnanick and Giefer 2011).

With education held constant in Table 3.1, can we conclude that the remaining gap is caused by discrimination? Not necessarily. Table 3.1 uses only the amount of schooling, not its quality. Racial minorities are more likely to attend inadequately financed schools. Some efforts have been made to eliminate disparities between school districts, but they have had little success.

How do we explain sex discrimination? Although women usually are not segregated from men in most occupations, educational institutions encourage talented women to enter fields that pay less (nursing or elementary education) than other occupations that require similar amounts of training. Even when women do enter the same occupations as men, the earnings disparity persists. Even controlling for age, a study of census data showed that female physicians and surgeons earned 69 percent of what their male counterparts did. Looking at broad ranges of occupations, researchers in the past few years have attributed between one-quarter and one-third of the wage gap to discrimination rather than to personal choices, skill preparation, and formal schooling (Reskin 2012; Weinberg 2004).

Eliminating Discrimination

Two main agents of social change work to reduce discrimination: (1) voluntary associations organized to solve racial and ethnic problems and (2) the federal government, including the courts. The two are closely related: Most efforts initiated by the government were urged by associations or organizations that represent minority groups. Resistance to social inequality by subordinate groups has been the key to change. Rarely has any government on its own initiative sought to end discrimination based on such criteria as race, ethnicity, and gender.

All racial and ethnic groups of any size are represented by private organizations that are, to some degree, trying to end discrimination. Some groups originated in the first half of the twentieth century, but most have been founded since World War II or have become significant forces in bringing about change only since then. These include church organizations, fraternal social groups, minor political parties, and legal defense funds, as well as more militant organizations operating under the scrutiny of law-enforcement agencies. The purposes, membership, successes, and failures of these resistance organizations dedicated to eliminating discrimination are discussed throughout this book.

The judiciary, charged with interpreting laws and the U.S. Constitution, has a much longer history of involvement in the rights of racial, ethnic, and religious minorities. However, its early decisions protected the rights of the dominant group, as in the 1857 U.S. Supreme Court *Dred Scott* decision, which ruled that slaves remained slaves even when living or traveling in states where slavery was illegal. Not until the 1940s did the Supreme Court revise earlier decisions and begin to grant African Americans the same rights as those held by Whites. The 1954 *Brown v. Board of Education* decision, which stated that "separate but equal" facilities—including schools—were unconstitutional, heralded a new era in which courts began to decide that distinguishing between races in order to segregate was inherently unconstitutional.

The most important legislative effort to eradicate discrimination was the Civil Rights Act of 1964. This act led to the establishment of the Equal Employment Opportunity Commission (EEOC), which has the power to investigate complaints against employers and to recommend action to the Department of Justice (DOJ). If the DOJ sues and the court finds discrimination, then the court can order appropriate compensation to the injured parties. The original act covered employment practices of all businesses with more than 25 employees and nearly all employment agencies and labor unions. A 1972 amendment broadened the coverage to employers with as few as 15 employees.

In addition to establishing the EEOC, the Civil Rights Act of 1964 prohibited discrimination in public accommodations—hotels, motels, restaurants, gas stations, and amusement parks. Publicly owned facilities such as parks, stadiums, and swimming pools were also prohibited from discriminating. Another important provision forbade discrimination in all federally supported programs and institutions, including hospitals, colleges, and road construction projects.

The Civil Rights Act of 1964 was not perfect. Since 1964, several acts and amendments to the original act have been added to cover the many areas of discrimination it left untouched, such as criminal justice and housing. Even in areas singled out for enforcement, discrimination still occurs. Federal agencies charged with enforcement complain that they are underfunded or are denied wholehearted support by the White House. Also, regardless of how much the EEOC may want to act in a particular case, the person who alleges discrimination has to pursue the complaint over a long time that is marked by lengthy periods of inaction. Despite these efforts, devastating forms of discrimination persist. African Americans, Latinos, and others fall victim to **redlining**, the pattern of discrimination against people trying to buy homes in minority and racially changing neighborhoods. The term comes from the early practice of bankers marking a red line on a map to indicate areas or neighborhoods in which it would not make loans.

In the wake of the U.S. Great Recession that began in 2007, researchers looked at the differential impact of home-loan practices and found that redlining has continued. Controlling for a variety of personal financial factors and home values, the researchers analyzed mortgage records in Baltimore, Maryland, and found that Black neighborhood residents paid 5 to 11 percent more in monthly mortgage payments. In addition, the federal government levied a $22 million fine on Hudson City Savings Bank, the nation's seventh-largest bank, which had purposefully avoided building branches in Black and Latino neighborhoods in Buffalo, Milwaukee, Providence, Rochester, and St. Louis; the bank's goal was to avoid offering home loans to local residents. This was not an isolated case; other banks were also fined. As we shall see when we discuss environmental justice later in this chapter, redlining continues to shape contemporary issues (Rugh, Albright, and Massey 2015; Swarns 2015).

Although civil rights laws often have established rights for other minorities, the Supreme Court made them explicit in two 1987 decisions involving groups other than African Americans. In the first of the two cases, an Iraqi American professor asserted that he had been denied tenure because of his Arab origins; in the second, a Jewish congregation brought suit for damages in response to the defacement of its synagogue with derogatory symbols. The Supreme Court ruled unanimously that, in effect, any member of an ethnic minority might sue under federal prohibitions against discrimination. These decisions paved the way for almost all racial and ethnic groups to invoke the Civil Rights Act of 1964 (Taylor 1987).

A setback in antidiscrimination lawsuits came in the 2007 *Ledbetter v. Goodyear Tire and Rubber Co.* ruling, when the Supreme Court told Lilly Ledbetter, in effect, that she was "too late." Ledbetter had been a supervisor for many years at the Gadsden, Alabama, Goodyear Tire Rubber plant when she realized that she was being paid $6,500 less per year than the lowest-paid male supervisor. The Court ruled that she must sue within 180 days of the initial discriminatory paycheck even though it had taken years before she even knew of the differential payment. Given the usual secrecy about salaries in workplaces, this ruling made it difficult for victims of pay discrimination to bring their cases to the courts. Two years later, Congress enacted the Lilly Ledbetter Fair Pay Act, which gives victims more time to file a lawsuit.

Nonetheless, proving discrimination continues to be difficult. Many discriminatory practices, such as those that are a part of institutional discrimination, are seldom subject to legal action. The inability of the Civil Rights Act, similar legislation, and court decisions to end discrimination does not result entirely from poor financial and political support, although it does play a role. The number of federal employees assigned to investigate and prosecute bias cases is insufficient. As we see in Research Focus titled "The Sharing Economy—Another Way to Discriminate," new ways of obtaining services online have created new opportunities to discriminate.

Lilly Ledbetter's failed lawsuit showed the difficulty in documenting what seemed to be obvious gender pay discrimination.

Research Focus

The Sharing Economy—Another Way to Discriminate

In the twenty-first century, a new marketplace has blossomed in the United States and other industrial countries—the sharing economy. The **sharing economy** refers to online economic transactions that place buyers and sellers in direct peer-to-peer contact with no change in the ownership of goods and services. Purchases can range from car rides to short-term living or vacation accommodations. While many consumers applaud these services' ease of use and lower prices compared to conventional businesses, this burgeoning business model is not without its problems.

One concern is that old-fashioned discrimination is emerging in these new markets. For example, Airbnb, which allows people to list their homes for rent online, is a vehicle for allowing people to discriminate based on race, gender, religion, or sexual identity. A 2016 study found that requests from guests with distinctively African American names are 16 percent less likely to get accommodations through Airbnb than people with distinctively White names.

A more subtle and disturbing type of bias is reported by minority users of the sharing economy who successfully secure accommodations, but then encounter neighbors who are surprised to see "different people" on the premises and then call security firms or law enforcement, who immediately show up to investigate the renters.

Researchers at MIT, Stanford, and the University of Washington have found that Black people often have to wait longer to get a ride using services such as Uber and Lyft. Uber drivers are also far more likely to cancel rides for Black customers than for White customers. Representatives from both Uber and Lyft have said that their companies have strong nondiscrimination guidelines for their drivers. In fact, they offer a counterargument: Unlike many taxi companies, Uber and Lyft are available to people living in underserved areas that taxis have historically neglected. These areas' residents are now able to access convenient, affordable rides. Yet some drivers still avoid customers whose online profiles indicate they are not White.

In yet another aspect of discrimination in the new online marketplaces, it was revealed that advertisers on Facebook were using "affinities" that users had created either explicitly or through their online browsing habits. These affinities give advertisers the ability to make reasonable assumptions about the Facebook account holder's race or ethnicity. As a result, some advertisers have avoided making real-estate offers and housing opportunities accessible to "undesirable" Facebook members.

How do operators of sharing and social media platforms respond to these bias reports? Typically, they point to company policies that prohibit discrimination and harassment. Yet sometimes the very electronic tools that make these outlets user friendly, such as noting your preferences, may also serve to facilitate bias.

Uber encountered even more criticism when it used a pricing policy that undercut foreign-born taxi drivers who stopped going to international airports as a form of protest when a presidential travel ban from several predominantly Muslim countries was introduced in January 2017. Simultaneously, the Uber CEO was one of the few high-tech CEOs who agreed to meet with President Trump and serve on an economic advisory board. In response, 200,000 customers deleted their Uber accounts. In the wake of these developments, Uber changed its pricing policy, and the CEO resigned from the board, citing a "perception-reality gap" as the reason.

(Continued)

Admittedly, Silicon Valley is vulnerable to accusations of being out of touch with the diversity of the United States because its owners and policymakers are overwhelmingly White or Asian American men. As bias charges came to light, Airbnb and Uber both quickly moved to hire civil rights attorneys as well as diversity specialists to address discrimination in the sharing economy. In response to advertisers' ability to screen out people based on their "affinity," Facebook now requires its advertisers not to engage in discriminatory advertising on its site.

Clearly, as online options continue to multiply and evolve, society will have to remain vigilant that old-fashioned discrimination is not evolving right along with it.

Sources: Angwin and Parris Jr. 2016; Edelman, Luca, and Svirsky 2017; Glusac 2016; Guo 2016; Guynn 2016, 2017; Isaac 2017; Maheshwari and Isaac 2016.

Wealth Inequality: Discrimination's Legacy

Discrimination that has occurred in the past carries into the present and future. African Americans and other minority groups have had less opportunity to accumulate assets such as homes, land, and savings that can insulate them—and later, their children—from economic setbacks.

As noted earlier, *wealth* is a measure of what a household owns minus what it owes. It is a more inclusive term than *income* and encompasses all of a person's material assets, including land, stocks, and other types of property. Wealth allows one to live better; even modest assets provide insurance against the effects of job layoffs, natural disasters, and long-term illness, and they allow individuals to borrow money at much lower interest rates. Wealth allows children to graduate from college with little or no debt. This simple fact reminds us that for many people, wealth is not always related to assets but also can be measured by indebtedness.

Income disparities among groups are even greater when wealth is considered. Households headed by Whites have considerably higher wealth than those headed by Blacks. As Figure 3.4 shows, the median wealth of all White households in 2013 was $141,000, about 13 times that of Black households. The wealth gap between Black households and White households has widened since 1983 because Whites as a group have accumulated

---

Figure 3.4 Racial and Ethnic Wealth Gap, 1977–2013

By 2013, the typical White household had accumulated about 13 times as much wealth as African American households, and about 10 times as much wealth as Hispanic households.

NOTE: White households are those where both householders are White non-Hispanic or Black non-Hispanic.

SOURCE: Data from Pew Research Center (Kochhar and Fry 2014) analysis of data from the Federal Reserve's Survey of Consumer Finances public-use data.

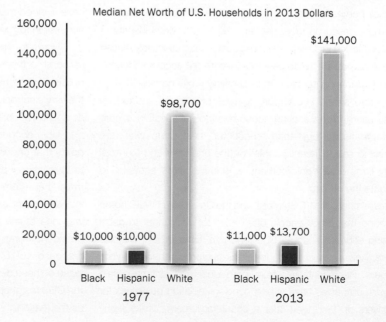

Median Net Worth of U.S. Households in 2013 Dollars

more assets, while Black households' assets have barely grown. The gap between White and Latino households has followed a similar pattern.

The racial and ethnic differences in median net worth are driven in part by differences in home ownership. White householders have consistently higher rates of home ownership than racial and ethnic minorities. For instance, 72 percent of White householders own their own home, compared with 43 percent of Black householders. Today, 45 percent of Hispanic householders are homeowners, while the Asian American homeownership rate is 49 percent (Pew Research Center 2016).

Environmental Justice

3.5   Explain and discuss environmental justice.

Discrimination takes many forms; it can reach far beyond the labor market. Take the example of Flint, Michigan, a city two-thirds Black or Hispanic. This city of over 100,000 was facing hard times due to the closing of automobile factories; the city budget was stretched beyond its limits. Seeking to save money, the bankrupt city government (now taken over by the state of Michigan) chose in 2014 to get its water from the Flint River, which was cheaper than buying treated water as it had for 50 years from Detroit, which acquired its water from Lake Huron. The new water source was found to cause aging pipes to leach lead at unsafe levels into the water supply, permanently jeopardizing brain development in young children.

It took all too long for Michigan to address the problem and begin distributing bottled water to the entire city. Ironically, at about the same time, the state had approved a tax subsidy for a private beverage company to access a pure water aquifer in the northern part of the state to bottle water for commercial use throughout the Midwest. A state government report observed that decades of institutional discrimination, including redlining, created the social environment that allowed the actions of the past few years to be literally toxic (Eligon 2016; Michigan Civil Rights Commission 2017).

The conflict perspective sees the Flint case as one in which pollution harms minority groups disproportionately. **Environmental justice** refers to efforts to ensure that hazardous substances are controlled so that all communities receive protection, regardless of race or socioeconomic circumstance. After the Environmental Protection Agency (EPA) and other organizations documented discrimination in the location of hazardous waste sites, an executive order was issued in 1994 that requires all federal agencies to ensure that low-income and minority communities have access to better information about their environment and have an opportunity to participate in shaping government policies that affect their communities' health. Initial efforts to implement the policy have met widespread opposition, including criticism from some proponents of economic development who argue that the guidelines unnecessarily delay or altogether block new industrial sites.

A national study of households in 2014 found that most people do not reside near industrial hazards that lead to health problems or impair child development. However, those who do live near toxic sites are much more likely to be African Americans. Race is a key factor here even when controlling for income. Black families are more likely to live near toxic sites than White families with similar incomes. The same national study also found that, over time, Whites are more likely to move away from toxic communities than their Black neighbors (Pais, Crowder, and Downey 2014).

Issues of environmental justice are not limited to metropolitan areas. Another continuing problem is abuse of Native American reservation land. Many American Indian leaders are concerned that tribal lands are too often

Bankrupt Flint, Michigan, a predominantly Black and Hispanic city of more than 100,000, decided to acquire a cheaper water supply that ended up polluting its residents' drinking water with dangerous levels of lead.

regarded as toxic waste dumping grounds that go to the highest bidder. However, the economic devastation faced by some tribes in isolated areas has led one tribe in Utah to offer its reservation as a depot for discarded nuclear waste (Jefferies 2007).

As with other aspects of discrimination, experts disagree about environmental issues and their impact on minority groups. There is controversy within the scientific community over the potential hazards, and there is even some disagreement within the subordinate communities being affected, as some observers question the wisdom of an executive order that may slow economic development in areas that desperately need employment opportunities. Other observers counter that such businesses typically employ only a few unskilled workers and make the environment less livable for those left behind. Despite these different viewpoints, environmental justice is an excellent example of resistance and change in the 1990s that the civil rights workers of the 1950s could not have foreseen.

Affirmative Action

3.6   Explain affirmative action and the legal debate surrounding it.

Affirmative action is the positive effort to recruit subordinate-group members, including women, for jobs, promotions, and educational opportunities. The phrase *affirmative action* first appeared in an executive order issued by President John F. Kennedy in 1961. The order called for contractors to "take affirmative action to ensure that applicants are employed, and that employees are treated during employment, without regard to their race, creed, color, or national origin." However, at that time, no enforcement procedures were specified. Six years later, the order was amended to prohibit discrimination on the basis of sex, but affirmative action was still defined vaguely.

Today, affirmative action has become a catchall term for racial-preference programs and goals. It also has become a lightning rod for opposition to any programs that suggest special consideration of women or racial minorities.

Affirmative action seeks to diversify the workplace and other organizational settings.

"Oh, you'll love working here. Nobody treats you any differently just because of your age, race, or gender."

Loren Fishman/CartoonStock.com

Affirmative Action Explained

Affirmative action has been an important tool for reducing institutional discrimination. Whereas earlier efforts were aimed at preventing individual acts of discrimination, federal measures under the "affirmative action" heading have been aimed at procedures that deny equal opportunities, even if they are not intended to be overtly discriminatory.

Affirmative action has been aimed at institutional discrimination in all of the following areas:

- Height and weight requirements that are unnecessarily geared to the physical proportions of White men without regard to the actual characteristics needed to perform the job and that therefore exclude women and some minorities

- Seniority rules, when applied to jobs historically held only by White men, that make more recently hired minorities and women more subject to layoff—the "last hired, first fired" employee—and less eligible for advancement

- Nepotism-based membership policies of some unions that exclude those who are not relatives of members who, because of past employment practices, are usually White

- Restrictive employment leave policies, coupled with prohibitions on part-time work or denials of fringe benefits to part-time workers, that make it difficult for the heads of single-parent families, most of whom are women, to get and keep jobs and also meet their family's needs

- Rules requiring that only English be spoken at the workplace, even when not a business necessity, which result in discriminatory employment practices toward people whose primary language is not English

- Standardized academic tests or criteria geared to the cultural and educational norms of the middle class or White men when these are not relevant predictors of successful job performance

- Preferences shown by law and medical schools in admitting children of wealthy and influential alumni, most of whom are White

- Credit policies of banks and lending institutions that deny mortgages and loans in minority neighborhoods or that deny credit to married women and others who have previously been denied the opportunity to build good credit histories in their own names

Employers also have been cautioned against asking leading questions in interviews, such as "Did you know you would be the first Black to supervise all Whites in that factory?" or "Does your husband mind you working on weekends?" Furthermore, the lack of minority-group or female employees may in itself provide evidence for a case of unlawful exclusion (Commission on Civil Rights 1981; see also Bohmer and Oka 2007).

The Legal Debate

How far can an employer go in encouraging women and minorities to apply for a job before it becomes unlawful discrimination against White men? Since the late 1970s, several bitterly debated cases on this difficult aspect of affirmative action have reached the U.S. Supreme Court. Table 3.2 summarizes the most significant cases.

In the 1978 *Bakke* case (*Regents of the University of California v. Bakke*), by a narrow 5–4 vote, the Supreme Court ordered the medical school of the University of California at Davis to admit Allan Bakke, a qualified White engineer who had originally been denied admission solely on the basis of his race. The justices ruled that the school had violated Bakke's constitutional rights by establishing a fixed quota system for minority students. However, the Court added that it was constitutional for universities to adopt flexible admission programs that use race as one factor in making decisions.

Colleges and universities responded with new policies designed to meet the *Bakke* ruling while broadening opportunities for traditionally underrepresented minority students.

Table 3.2 Key Decisions on Affirmative Action

In a series of split and often very close decisions, the Supreme Court has expressed a variety of reservations regarding affirmative action in specific situations.

Year	Favorable (+) or Unfavorable (−) to Affirmative Action	Case	Vote	Ruling
1971	+	Griggs v. Duke Power Co.	9–0	Private employers must provide a remedy where minorities were denied opportunities, even if unintentional
1978	−	Regents of the University of California v. Bakke	5–4	Prohibited holding a specific number of places for minorities in college admissions
1979	+	United Steelworkers of America v. Weber	5–2	Okay for unions to favor minorities in special training programs
1984	−	Firefighters Local Union No. 1784 (Memphis, TN) v. Stotts	6–1	Seniority means recently hired minorities may be laid off first in staff reductions
1986	+	International Association of Firefighters v. City of Cleveland	6–3	May promote minorities over more-senior Whites
1986	+	New York City v. Sheet Metal	5–4	Approved specific quota of minority workers for union
1987	+	United States v. Paradise	5–4	Endorsed quotas for promotions of state troopers
1987	+	Johnson v. Transportation Agency, Santa Clara, CA	6–3	Approved preference in hiring for minorities and women over better-qualified men and Whites
1989	−	Richmond v. Croson Company	6–3	Ruled a 30 percent set-aside program for minority contractors unconstitutional
1989	−	Martin v. Wilks	5–4	Ruled Whites may bring reverse discrimination claims against Court-approved affirmative action plans
1990	+	Metro Broadcasting v. FCC	5–4	Supported federal programs aimed at increasing minority ownership of broadcast licenses
1995	−	Adarand Constructors Inc. v. Peña	5–4	Benefits based on race are constitutional only if narrowly defined to accomplish a compelling interest
1996	−	Texas v. Hopwood	*	Let stand a lower court decision covering Louisiana, Mississippi, and Texas that race could not be used in college admissions
2003	+	Grutter v. Bollinger	5–4	Race can be a limited factor in admissions at the University of Michigan Law School
2003	−	Gratz v. Bollinger	6–3	Cannot use a strict formula awarding advantage based on race for admissions to the University of Michigan
2009	−	Ricci v. DeStefano	5–4	May not disregard a promotion test because Blacks failed to qualify for advancement
2016	+	Fisher v. University of Texas at Austin	4–3	Rejected a challenge to race-conscious college education programs

*U.S. Court of Appeals Fifth Circuit decision.

The Supreme Court heard arguments in *Fisher v. University of Texas at Austin* arguing that a White woman, Abigail Fisher, missed out on automatic admission under a Texas provision that extended admissions to the top 10 percent of a high school's graduating class. While she was not in the top 10 percent at her school, she contended that non-Whites who did not have comparable academic preparation were admitted and that the top 10 percent provision leaves any further racial consideration unnecessary. In 2016, the Court rejected a lower court's decision challenging this "top 10 percent" admissions policy at the University of Texas at Austin. The ruling did not have any direct impact on any other institution's policies, although other schools probably will re-examine their procedures in light of the *Fisher* decision. Given the long history of legal actions, further challenges to affirmative action can be expected.

So what has happened to minority enrollment in higher education? Because the African American and Latino college-age population is increasing, analysis is difficult. However, in states such as California, Florida, Michigan, and Texas, which have been barred from using race explicitly in admissions, Black and Latino enrollment has dropped. Sometimes schools have approached minority enrollments in a manner similar to that used during the affirmative action period, often by implementing new admissions criteria, but often these non-race-specific criteria have been challenged by the opponents of affirmative action (Hoover 2013).

Has affirmative action truly helped to alleviate employment inequality on the basis of race and gender? This question is difficult to answer, given the complexity of the labor market and the fact that other antidiscrimination measures are in place, but it does appear that affirmative action has had a significant impact in the sectors where it has been applied. Sociologist Barbara Reskin (2012) reviewed available studies looking at workforce composition in terms of race and gender in light of affirmative action policies. She found that gains in minority employment could be attributed to affirmative action policies, both in firms mandated to follow affirmative action guidelines and those that adopted them voluntarily. There is also evidence that some earnings gains can be attributed to affirmative action. Economists M. V. Lee Badgett and Heidi Hartmann (1995), reviewing 26 other research studies, came to similar conclusions: Affirmative action and other federal compliance programs have had a modest impact, but it is difficult to assess their true efficacy, given larger economic changes such as recessions and the rapid increase of women in the paid labor force.

Scholars of the debate over affirmative action in higher education acknowledge that many issues need to be addressed beyond its legal ramifications. In the Speaking Out feature, W. K. Kellogg Foundation Vice President Gail Christopher makes the case for this broader perspective. She discusses the *Fisher* court case noted above, indicating how important the judiciary has become in defining affirmative action. (Christopher wrote this piece before the court made its decision.)

Reverse Discrimination

In addition to academics and researchers, the public—particularly Whites but also some affluent African Americans and Hispanics—have questioned the wisdom of affirmative action. Particularly strident are the charges of **reverse discrimination**: that government actions cause better-qualified White men to be bypassed in favor of women and minority men. *Reverse discrimination* is an emotional term, because it conjures up the notion that somehow women and minorities will subject White men in the United States to the same treatment received by minorities during the past three centuries. Such cases are not unknown, but they are uncommon.

Increasingly, critics of affirmative action call for color-blind policies that would end affirmative action and, they argue, allow all people to be judged fairly. However, would color-blind policies end institutional practices that favor Whites? For example, according to the latest data, 40 percent of applicants who are children of Harvard alumni, who are almost all White, are admitted to the university, compared to 11 percent of nonalumni children.

By contrast, at the competitive California Institute of Technology, which specifically does not use legacy preferences, only 1.5 percent of students are children of alumni. Ironically, studies show that students who are children of alumni are far more likely than either minority students or athletes to run into academic trouble (Kahlenberg 2010; Massey and Mooney 2007; Pincus 2003, 2008).

Supporters of affirmative action contend that as long as businesses rely on informal social networks, personal recommendations, and family ties to make hiring decisions, White men will have a distinct advantage built on generations of being in positions of power. Furthermore, an end to affirmative action would also mean an end to the many programs that give advantages to certain businesses, homeowners, veterans, and farmers. Most of these preference holders are White.

Speaking Out

The Conversation We're *Not* Having When We Talk About Affirmative Action

Gail Christopher

An affirmative action case now before the U.S. Supreme Court provides renewed proof of the urgent need for communities across the country to engage openly in developing deeper understanding about the issue of racism.

Before the successes of the civil rights movement, discrimination against people of color was easy to spot in the United States. Today, many Americans find racist beliefs and attitudes abhorrent, and there's no question that we have made great progress as a country in addressing overt and legalized racism. But these changes in our laws and culture do not mean that racial bias is a thing of the past. . . .

Before the court recesses at the end of June, it will issue a decision in *Fisher v. University of Texas at Austin*. At immediate stake in the case is the university's policy of considering race as one factor among many in its admissions. Even with the policy, the school's student body is not representative of the state's high school graduates. Striking it down would further harm efforts to create diversity in Texas' flagship public university.

If the university prevails, it will be partly a result of the court's recognition of the compelling educational benefits that all students receive when they are part of a diverse student body. These benefits are undeniable and well-documented. For example, when students from different walks of life come together in the classroom, they are able to challenge each other to think critically about their own worldviews.

But a focus on the educational benefits of diversity puts aside the fact that students of color still confront, and must overcome, hidden racial biases in order to succeed in school and in life. That's why a deeper understanding about racism is necessary. As Ronald Brownstein so capably emphasized in a recent *National Journal* story, the state of race in America has changed dramatically since the last time the Supreme Court considered the issue of affirmative action.

Racial bias can manifest itself in far more subtle ways today, and sometimes in far more overt ways. . . . (W)e have witnessed the racist reactions to a simple television commercial that leads with a child of an interracial relationship, and shows both parents. The flood of racist comments to the YouTube page led General Mills to remove the comments section for that video.

And we know that two-thirds of broadcast media about Muslims portrays them as extremists. School teachers may have

Gail Christopher

Cliff Owen/W. K. Kellogg Foundation/AP Images

lower expectations for Hispanic or black students than they have for white students. Doctors may diagnose and treat black patients differently from white patients, even when they present the same symptoms. Mortgage lenders may be more likely to steer homebuyers of color to subprime loans even when they qualify for lower-cost prime loans. . . .

These biases abound in other realms, from art to commerce to the justice system, exacting a toll on the health of people of color, which has an impact upon the future viability of the nation. The point is that they are not necessarily—or even typically—conscious decisions on the part of the teachers, doctors, and lenders. . . .

We must expand the narrative by laying bare the hidden racial biases that act as obstacles in the paths of young people of color who want to go to college. A broader narrative would help us understand the abilities and grit that minority applicants required in order to put themselves on the path to college despite these obstacles. It would move all of us beyond a constrained idea of what prepares students for college success.

African Americans comprise 12 percent of the working-age population in the U.S., yet only 5 percent of doctors and dentists and 3 percent of architects are Black, proportions that have not changed in over two decades.

If we fail to finally open the doors of opportunity to all students in the U.S., regardless of skin color, then we all lose. By the middle of this century, the Census Bureau tells us, the U.S. population will be majority minority. Our ability to compete in the global economy demands that we prepare students from every background for success in college and careers. Our nation's long struggle for equality demands that our campuses come to look more like our communities.

If nothing else, the Supreme Court's impending decision will give us a reason to address the nation's unique legacy of racism and its continuing impact, even in the twenty-first century. Let's not miss that chance.

Source: Christopher, Gail. 2013. The Conversation We're Not Having About Affirmative Action. The Huffington Post. (June 6). Accessible at http://www.huffingtonpost.com/dr-gail-christopher/the-conversation-were-nothaving_b_3398540.html. Used with permission.

Affirmative action is not just a federal issue. It has also emerged as an increasingly important issue in state and national political campaigns. As noted earlier, in 2003, the Supreme Court reviewed the admission policies at the University of Michigan, which may favor racial minorities (see Table 3.2). In 2006, Michigan citizens voted, by a 58 percent margin, to restrict all their state universities from using affirmative action in their admissions policies.

Generally, at the state and local level, discussions have focused on the use of quotas in hiring practices. Supporters of affirmative action argue that hiring goals establish "floors" for minority inclusion but do not exclude truly qualified candidates from any group. Opponents insist that these "targets" are, in fact, quotas that lead to reverse discrimination (Lewin 2006; Mack 1996). California was a battleground for this controversial issue. The California Civil Rights Initiative (Proposition 209) was placed on the ballot in 1996 as a referendum to amend the state constitution and prohibit any programs that give preference to women and minorities for college admission, employment, promotion, or government contracts. Overall, 54 percent of the voters backed the proposition.

In 2009, the Supreme Court ruled 5–4 in the *Ricci v. DeStefano* case in favor of White firefighters. Many observers felt this outcome recognized reverse racism. In 2003, in New Haven, Connecticut, firefighters took an examination to identify possible candidates for promotions, but no African Americans taking the test qualified for advancement. Rather than select all White (including one Hispanic) firefighters, the city threw out the test results. The qualifying firefighters sued, claiming that they were victims of discrimination, and the Supreme Court eventually concurred.

The Glass Ceiling

3.7 Explain the glass ceiling in the workplace.

We have discussed racial and ethnic groups primarily as if they have uniformly failed to keep pace with Whites. Although this general conclusion is accurate, tens of thousands of people of color have matched and even exceeded Whites in terms of income. For example, in 2015, more than 181,000 Black households and over 253,000 Hispanic households earned more than $250,000 (Bureau of the Census 2016i:Table FINC-07). What can we say about financially better-off members of subordinate groups in the United States?

Prejudice does not necessarily end with wealth. Black newspaper columnist De Wayne Wickham (1993) wrote of the subtle racism he had experienced. He heard a White clerk in a supermarket ask a White customer whether she knew the price of an item the computer would not scan; when the problem occurred while the clerk was ringing up Wickham's groceries, she called for a price check. Affluent subordinate-group members routinely report being blocked as they move toward the first-class section aboard airplanes or seek service in upscale stores. Another journalist, Ellis Cose (1993), has called these insults the "soul-destroying slights to affluent minorities" that lead to the "rage of a privileged class."

Discrimination persists for even educated and qualified people from the most privileged family backgrounds. As subordinate-group members are able to compete successfully, they sometimes encounter attitudinal or organizational bias that prevents them from reaching their full potential. They have confronted what has come to be called the **glass ceiling**. This term refers to the barrier that blocks the promotion of qualified workers because of gender or minority-group membership (Figure 3.5). Often, people entering nontraditional areas of employment become marginalized and are made to feel uncomfortable, much like the situation of immigrants who feel like they are part of two cultures, as we discussed in Chapter 1.

There are many reasons for the existence of glass ceilings. It may be that one Black or one woman vice president is regarded as enough, so the second potential minority candidate faces an obstacle to upward movement through the organization. Decision-makers may be concerned that their customers will not trust them if they have too many people of color in top management, or they may worry that a talented woman could become overwhelmed with her duties as a mother and wife and thus perform poorly in a high-level job.

Figure 3.5 Glass Ceilings and Glass Walls

Women and minority men are moving up in corporations, but they encounter glass ceilings that block entry to top positions. In addition, they face glass walls that block lateral moves to areas from which executives are promoted. These barriers contribute to women and minority men not moving into the highest-level decision-making positions in the nation's major corporations.

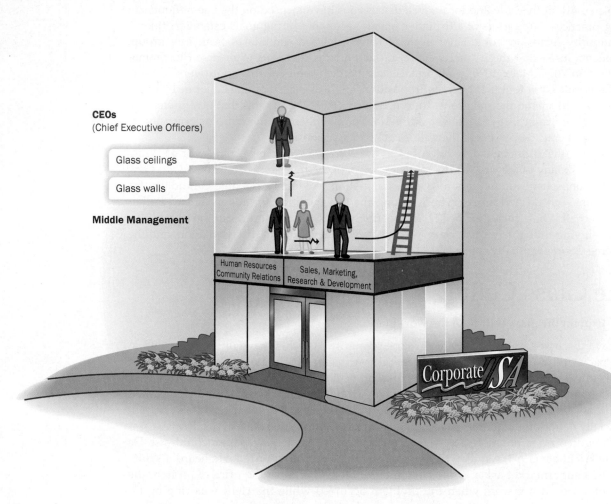

Concern about women and minorities climbing a broken ladder led to the formation in 1991 of the Glass Ceiling Commission, with the U.S. secretary of labor chairing the 21-member group. Initially, it regarded the following as glass ceiling barriers:

- Lack of management commitment to establishing systems, policies, and practices for achieving workplace diversity and upward mobility

- Pay inequities for work of equal or comparable value

- Sex-, race-, and ethnicity-based stereotyping and harassment

- Unfair recruitment practices

- Lack of family-friendly workplace policies

- "Parent-track" policies that discourage parental leave

- Limited opportunities for advancement to decision-making positions

The significant underrepresentation of women and minority men in managerial positions results in large part from the presence of glass ceilings. Sociologist Max Weber wrote more than a century ago that the privileged class monopolizes the purchase of high-priced consumer goods and wields the power to grant or withhold opportunity from others. To

Figure 3.6 Spectrum of Intergroup Relations: Discrimination

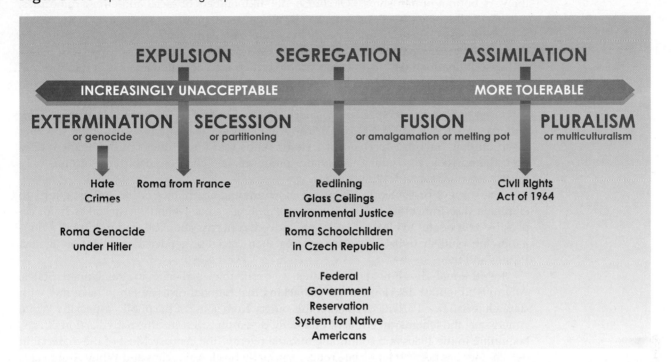

grasp just how White and male the membership of this elite group is, consider the following: 84 percent of the people who serve on the boards of directors of Standard & Poor's listing of the 1,500 largest corporations are men. Among Fortune 500 corporations, just 3 percent of the boards of directors are Hispanic, and 70 percent of the boards did not have a single Latino (Hispanic Association on Corporate Responsibility 2013; Orsagh 2016; Weber 1947).

Catalyst, a nonprofit research organization, conducted interviews in 1992 and again in 2001 with senior and middle managers from larger corporations. The study found that even before glass ceilings are encountered, women and racial and ethnic minorities face **glass walls** that keep them from moving laterally. Specifically, the study found that women tend to be placed in staff or support positions in areas such as public relations and human resources and are often directed away from jobs in core areas such as marketing, production, and sales. Women are assigned to and therefore trapped in jobs that reflect their stereotypical helping nature, and they encounter glass walls that cut off access to jobs that might lead to broader experience and advancement (Bjerk 2008; Catalyst 2001; Lopez 1992).

Researchers have documented a differential impact of the glass ceiling on White males. It appears that men who enter traditionally female occupations are more likely to rise to the top. Male elementary teachers become principals, and male nurses become supervisors. The **glass escalator** refers to the White male advantage experienced in occupations dominated by women. Whereas women may become tokens when they enter traditionally male occupations, men are more likely to be advantaged when they move out of sex-typical jobs. In summary, women and minority men confront a glass ceiling that limits upward mobility and glass walls that reduce their ability to move into fast-track jobs leading to the highest reaches of the corporate executive suite. Meanwhile, White men who choose to enter female-dominated occupations are often rewarded with promotions and positions of responsibility coveted by their fellow female workers (Budig 2002; Cognard-Black 2004).

Figure 3.6 summarizes the spectrum of intergroup relations discussed in this chapter.

Conclusion

What is it like to experience discrimination over and over again? Not just an occasional slight or a possible instance of discrimination, but constantly being treated differently because of your race, ethnicity, or gender? W. E. B. Du Bois (1903:9) wrote in his classic *The*

Souls of Black Folks, "To be a poor man is hard, but to be a poor race in a land of dollars is the very bottom of hardships." Of course, not all members of racial and ethnic minorities, much less all women, are poor, but virtually all can recall instances where they were treated as second-class citizens, not necessarily by White men, but even by members of their own group or by other women.

Discrimination takes its toll, and people can be discriminated against in the informal economy or when looking for a job on the Internet. Even members of minority groups who are not today overtly discriminated against continue to fall victim to past discrimination.

From the conflict perspective, it is not surprising to find the widespread presence of an underclass. Derrick Bell (1994), an African American law professor, has made the sobering assertion that "racism is permanent." He contends that the attitudes of dominant Whites prevail, and society is willing to advance programs on behalf of subordinate groups only when they coincide with White needs.

The surveys presented in Chapter 2 show gradual acceptance of the earliest efforts to eliminate discrimination, but that support is failing as color-blind racism takes hold, especially as it relates to affirmative action. Indeed, concerns about alleged reverse discrimination are as likely to be voiced as concerns about racial or gender discrimination against Whites and men.

Institutional discrimination remains a formidable challenge in the United States. Attempts to reduce discrimination by attacking institutional discrimination have met with staunch resistance. Partly as a result of this outcry from some of the public, especially White Americans, the federal government gradually de-emphasized its affirmative action efforts, beginning in the 1980s and continuing into the twenty-first century. Most of the material in this chapter has been about racial groups, especially Black Americans and White Americans. It would be easy to see intergroup hostility as a racial phenomenon, but that would be incorrect. Throughout the history of the United States, relations between some White groups have also been characterized by resentment and violence. The next two chapters examine the ongoing legacy of immigration and the nature and relations of White ethnic groups.

Summary of Learning Objectives

3.1 Distinguish between relative and absolute deprivation.

1. Discrimination is likely to result in a feeling of relative deprivation, not necessarily absolute deprivation.

3.2 Define hate crimes.

2. A hate crime occurs when offenders are motivated to choose a victim because of some characteristic, such as race, ethnicity, religion, sexual orientation, or disability. Hate crimes are caused by hostility that culminates in a criminal offense.

3.3 Summarize how institutions discriminate.

3. Institutional discrimination results from the normal operations of a society.

4. Discrimination in hiring has been documented through job-testing experiments.

3.4 Describe the effects of discrimination and the efforts to reduce or eliminate it.

5. Inequality continues to be apparent in the analysis of annual incomes (controlling for the amount of education attained) and wealth.

6. The Civil Rights Act of 1964 is a key piece of legislation seeking to reduce or eliminate discrimination. Presidential executive orders, legislative acts, and judicial decisions have all played a part in reducing discrimination.

3.5 Explain and discuss environmental justice.

7. Environmental justice refers to the efforts to ensure that hazardous substances are controlled so that all communities receive protection regardless of race or socioeconomic circumstance.

3.6 Explain affirmative action and the legal debate surrounding it.

8. For over 60 years, affirmative action as a remedy to inequality has been a hotly contested issue, with its critics contending that it amounts to reverse discrimination.

3.7 Explain the glass ceiling in the workplace.

9. Upwardly mobile professional women and minority men may encounter a glass ceiling and be thwarted in their professional efforts by glass walls.

Key Terms

absolute deprivation, *page 56*
affirmative action, *page 68*
discrimination, *page 56*
environmental justice, *page 67*
glass ceiling, *page 73*

glass escalator, *page 75*
glass walls, *page 75*
hate crime, *page 58*
income, *page 61*
institutional discrimination, *page 59*

redlining, *page 64*
relative deprivation, *page 56*
reverse discrimination, *page 71*
sharing economy, *page 65*
wealth, *page 61*

Review Questions

1. Why might people feel disadvantaged even though their incomes are rising and their housing circumstances have improved?

2. How do hate crimes differ from other types of felony crimes?

3. Why does institutional discrimination sometimes seem less objectionable than individual discrimination?

4. How do national income data point to discrimination?

5. What is the wealth disparity among racial and ethnic groups, and what is the trend in this disparity?

6. Explain how the concept of environmental justice relates to understanding racial and ethnic groups.

7. Why does affirmative action remain controversial even though inequality persists?

8. Define and provide an example of reverse discrimination.

9. Distinguish among glass ceilings, glass walls, and glass escalators. How do they differ from more obvious forms of employment discrimination?

Critical Thinking

1. What are the purposes of hate crimes? Do you think they serve those purposes?

2. Discrimination can take many forms. Select a case of discrimination that you think almost everyone would agree is wrong. Then describe another incident in which the alleged discrimination was subtler. Who is likely to condemn and who is likely to overlook such situations?

3. Discuss the social implications of wealth disparity between racial and ethnic groups on social mobility.

4. Resistance is a continuing theme of intergroup race relations. Discrimination implies the oppression of a group, but how can discrimination also unify the oppressed group to resist such unequal treatment?

How can acceptance or integration weaken the sense of solidarity within a group?

5. Voluntary associations such as the National Association for the Advancement of Colored People (NAACP) and government units such as the courts have been important vehicles for bringing about a measure of social justice. In what ways can the private sector—corporations and businesses—also work to end discrimination?

Chapter 4
Immigration

David Grossman/Alamy Stock Photo

∨ Learning Objectives

4.1 Summarize the general patterns of immigration to the United States.

4.2 Describe how restrictionist sentiment has increased in the past 100 years.

4.3 Identify the concerns about immigration policy today.

4.4 Discuss the scope of and issues related to illegal immigration.

4.5 Outline the process of naturalization.

4.6 Explain the connection between globalization and immigration.

4.7 Describe the United States' policies toward refugees.

The 2016 presidential campaign saw candidates addressing immigration policy in vastly different ways. Some proudly posed next to immigrant workers who had revitalized long-shuttered businesses, while others trekked to the U.S.–Mexico border to make the case for increased surveillance and even the building of a wall between the two countries.

Well before that campaign season, immigration had profoundly shaped the United States, and it continues to do so today. For example, in South Orange, New Jersey, a small group of Haitian immigrants can be found every day in the public library, where they study together in their quest to become nurses. When, in 1996, the city became a stop on a direct commuter line into Manhattan, many immigrant households relocated from New York City to take advantage of the more affordable housing in the New Jersey suburbs. Now nearly a third of the library's patrons speak a language other than English at home. Over three-quarters of the public school students are immigrants, mostly illegal, or the children of illegal immigrants.

Also consider rural Garden City, Kansas, a city of 30,000 that coincidentally has a replica of the Statue of Liberty donated by the Boy Scouts in 1950. At the time the statue was donated, Garden City had virtually no foreign-born residents. Today, three-quarters of the public schools' students are immigrants or the children of immigrants. The overseas residents were first attracted to Garden City by new jobs at a beef processing plant, and the economic expansion that followed was fueled by the availability of workers. Eventually, the unemployment rate dropped well below the national average. Today, Garden City residents include immigrants from Burma (Myanmar), Laos, Somalia, and Vietnam, as well as Latin American countries. The relative calm of Garden City was marred when the FBI uncovered a plot by three men from neighboring communities to bomb a housing complex that is home to many Somali Americans. The city's police chief responded that the plot was not just an attack on a specific group but also an attack on "our community."

Clarkston, Georgia, outside of Atlanta, is not an immigrant destination but rather a refugee haven. The town has accepted and helped to resettle more than 60,000 refugees since 1983. At that time, Clarkston embraced a short-lived federal refugee-resettlement program because more of its housing was becoming vacant as residents moved to more affluent communities. Four out of five refugee families became self-sufficient with six months of arriving. However, challenges do exist, especially in educating the refugee children and bringing them up to state educational norms. Now home to 150 nationality groups, Clarkston has come to rely on refugees as a source of economic progress.

American communities (large and small) across the continent are home to immigrants and refugees. While criticism continues about many aspects of immigration policy, which we will consider in this chapter, 53 percent of the public in 2017 indicated they were satisfied with the level of immigration into the United States, and another 5 percent favored more immigrants (Aust 2016; Gates 2017; Gomez 2014; Jonsson 2016a; Toppo and Overberg 2014).

The world is now a global network. The core and periphery countries, described in world systems theory (see Chapter 1), link not only commercial goods but also families and workers across political borders. Social forces that cause people to emigrate are complex. Scholars of immigration often point to *push factors* and *pull factors*. For example, economic difficulties, religious or ethnic persecution, and political unrest may *push* individuals from their homelands. The *pull* factors may be perceptions of a better life in another country or a desire to reunite families or join a community of fellow nationals already established abroad. Immigration into the United States, in particular, has been facilitated by cheap ocean transportation and by other countries' removal of restrictions on emigration.

A potent factor contributing to immigration anywhere in the world is chain immigration. **Chain immigration** refers to a process by which an immigrant sponsors several other immigrants who, upon their arrival, may sponsor still more immigrants. Laws that favor would-be immigrants who already have relatives or someone who can vouch for them financially in the receiving country may facilitate this sponsorship. But probably the most important aspect of chain immigration is that immigrants anticipate knowing someone who can help them adjust to their new surroundings and find a new job, a place to live, and even the kinds of foods that are familiar to them.

muratart/Shutterstock

Garden City, Kansas, a rural community of 30,000, has attracted immigrants from many countries and built a replica of the Statue of Liberty outside the county court house.

Patterns of Immigration to the United States

4.1   Summarize the general patterns of immigration to the United States.

Immigration to the United States has three unmistakable patterns: (1) the number of immigrants has fluctuated dramatically over time, largely because of government policy changes; (2) settlement has not been uniform across the country but centered in certain regions and cities; and (3) the immigrants' countries of origin have changed over time. First, we look at the historical picture of immigrant numbers.

Figure 4.1 Legal Immigration to the United States, 1820–2020

Through the 1950s, immigration to the United States was largely from Europe and Canada. However, since the 1960s, immigration has largely been from Asia and Latin America.

SOURCE: Office of Immigration Statistics 2016 and author's estimates for projection out to 2020.

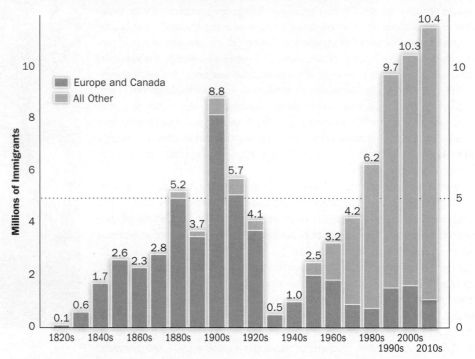

Vast numbers of immigrants have come to the United States. Figure 4.1 indicates the high but fluctuating number of immigrants who arrived during every decade from the 1820s through the beginning of the twenty-first century. The United States received the largest number of legal immigrants during the first decade of the 2000s; that number likely will be surpassed in the second decade of the 2000s. However, the country's population was much smaller in the period from 1900 through 1910, so the numerical impact was even greater then.

Immigrants to the United States have not always received a friendly reception. Open bloodshed, restrictive laws, and the eventual return of almost one-third of immigrants and their children to their home countries attest to some Americans' uneasy feelings toward strangers who want to settle among them. Generally, surveys show immigrants perceiving some ambivalence, and occasionally outright intolerance, from some native-born Americans they encounter.

Before considering the sweep of past immigration policies, let us consider today's immigrant population. About 14 percent of the nation's people are foreign-born—the highest level since the 1920s. As recently as 1979, this proportion was just 4.7 percent. By global comparisons, the foreign-born population in the United States is large but not unusual. Whereas most industrial countries have a foreign-born population of around 6–11 percent, Canada's foreign-born population is 20 percent, and Australia's is 28 percent (Porter 2015).

As noted earlier, immigrants have not settled evenly across the nation. As Figure 4.2 shows, four states—California, New York, Florida, and New Jersey—account for 45 percent of the nation's total foreign-born population but less than 28 percent of the nation's total overall population.

The source regions of immigrants have changed. First, settlers came from Europe, then Latin America, and now, increasingly, Asia. Europeans were the dominant immigrant group through the 1950s. The majority of today's 41.7 million foreign-born people are from Latin America rather than Europe. Primarily, they are from Central America and, more specifically, Mexico (although Mexico is sometimes considered a part of North America). By contrast, Europeans, who dominated the early settlement of the United States, now account for

Figure 4.2 Foreign-Born Population in the United States

SOURCE: Data from American Community Survey 2016a: R0501.

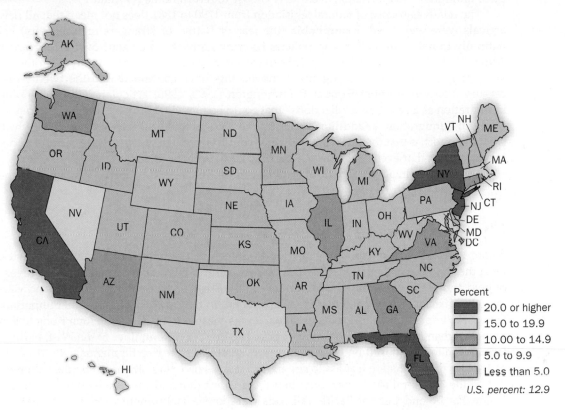

Percent

- 20.0 or higher
- 15.0 to 19.9
- 10.00 to 14.9
- 5.0 to 9.9
- Less than 5.0

U.S. percent: 12.9

fewer than one in seven of the foreign-born today. The changing patterns of immigration have continued into the twenty-first century. Beginning in 2010, the annual immigration from Asia exceeded the level of annual immigration from Latin America for the first time.

The Early Immigrants

Settlers, the first immigrants to the Western Hemisphere, soon followed the European explorers of North America. The Spanish founded St. Augustine, Florida, in 1565, and the English founded Jamestown, Virginia, in 1607. Protestants from England emerged from the colonial period as the dominant force numerically, politically, and socially. The English accounted for 60 percent of the 3 million White Americans in 1790. Although exact statistics are lacking for the early years of the United States, the English were soon outnumbered by other nationalities— particularly Scotch-Irish and Germans—as their numbers swelled. However, the English colonists maintained their dominant position.

Throughout American history, immigration policy has been politically controversial. The U.S. Declaration of Independence criticized the policies of King George III of England for obstructing immigration to the colonies. Toward the end of the nineteenth century, the American republic itself was criticized for enacting immigration restrictions. In the beginning, however, the country encouraged immigration. Legislation initially fixed the residence requirement for naturalization at five years, although briefly, under the Alien Act of 1798, it was 14 years, and so-called dangerous people could be expelled. Other than this brief period of harshness, immigration was unregulated through most of the 1800s, and naturalization was easily available. Until 1870, naturalization was limited to "free white persons" (Calavita 2007).

Although some people hold the mistaken belief that concern about immigration is a relatively new phenomenon, some people also assume that immigrants to the United States rarely reconsider their decision to come to a new country. Analysis of available records, beginning in the early 1900s, suggests that about 35 percent of all immigrants to the

United States eventually migrate back to their home country. The proportion varies, with the figures for some countries being much higher, but the overall pattern is clear: About one in three immigrants to this nation eventually choose to return home (Wyman 1993).

The relative absence of federal legislation from 1790 to 1881 does not mean that all new arrivals were welcomed. **Xenophobia** (the fear or hatred of strangers or foreigners) led naturally to **nativism** (beliefs and policies favoring native-born citizens over immigrants). Although the term *nativism* has largely been used to describe nineteenth-century sentiments, anti-immigration views and organized movements have continued into the twenty-first century. Political scientist Samuel P. Huntington (1993, 1996) articulated the continuing immigration as a "clash of civilizations" that could be remedied only by significantly reducing legal immigration, in addition to closing the borders to illegal arrivals. His view, which enjoys support, is that the fundamental world conflicts of the new century are cultural rather than ideological or even economic (Citrin et al. 2007; Schaefer 2008b).

The most dramatic outbreak of nativism in the nineteenth century was aimed at the Chinese.

The Anti-Chinese Movement

Before 1851, official records show that only 46 Chinese had immigrated to the United States. Over the next 30 years, more than 200,000 Chinese came to this country, lured by the discovery of gold and the opening of job opportunities in the West. Overcrowding, drought, and warfare in China also encouraged them to take a chance in the United States. Another important factor was improved oceanic transportation; it was cheaper to travel from Hong Kong to San Francisco than from Chicago to San Francisco. The frontier communities of the West, particularly in California, looked on the Chinese as a valuable resource to fill manual jobs. As early as 1854, so many Chinese wanted to emigrate that ships had difficulty handling the volume.

In the 1860s, railroad work provided the greatest demand for Chinese labor until the Union Pacific and Central Pacific railroads were joined at Promontory Summit, Utah, in 1869. Union Pacific relied primarily on Irish laborers, but 90 percent of Central Pacific's labor force was Chinese because Whites generally refused to do the backbreaking work over the Western terrain.

With the dangerous railroad work largely completed, people began to rethink the wisdom of encouraging Chinese to immigrate to do the work no one else would do. Reflecting their xenophobia, White settlers found the Chinese immigrants, their customs, and religion difficult to understand. Indeed, few people tried to understand these immigrants from Asia. Although they'd had no firsthand contact with Chinese Americans, Easterners and legislators soon jumped on the anti-Chinese bandwagon as they read sensationalized accounts of the new arrivals' lifestyles.

Even before the Chinese immigrated, stereotypes of them and their customs were prevalent. American traders returning from China, European diplomats, and Protestant missionaries consistently emphasized the exotic and sinister aspects of life in China. **Sinophobes**, people who fear anything associated with China, subscribed to the racist theory developed during the slavery controversy that non-Europeans were subhuman. Americans also were becoming more conscious of biological inheritance and disease, so it was not hard to conjure up fears of alien genes and germs. The only real challenge the anti-Chinese movement faced was convincing people that the negative consequences of unrestricted Chinese immigration outweighed any possible economic gain. Earlier, racial prejudice was subordinated to industrial dependence on Chinese labor for the work that Whites shunned, but acceptance of the Chinese was short-lived. The fear of the "yellow peril" overwhelmed any desire to know more about Asian peoples and their customs (Takaki 1998).

Chinese workers, such as these pictured in 1844, played a major role in building railroads in the West.

Bettmann/Getty Images

Employers were glad to pay the Chinese low wages, but non-Chinese laborers began directing their resentment against the Chinese rather than against their compatriots' willingness to exploit the Chinese. Only a generation earlier, the same concerns were expressed about the Irish, but with the Chinese, the hostility reached new heights because of another factor.

Although many arguments were voiced, racial fears motivated the anti-Chinese movement. Race was the critical issue. The labor-market fears were largely unfounded, and most advocates of restrictions knew that. There was no possibility of the Chinese immigrating in numbers that would match those of Europeans at that time, so it is difficult to find any explanation other than racism for their fears (Winant 1994).

From the sociological perspective of conflict theory, we can explain how the Chinese immigrants were welcomed only when their labor was necessary to fuel growth in the United States. When that labor was no longer necessary, the welcome mat for the immigrants was withdrawn. Furthermore, as conflict theorists point out, restrictions were not applied evenly: Americans focused on a specific nationality (the Chinese) to reduce the number of foreign workers in the nation. Because decision-making at that time rested in the hands of the descendants of European immigrants, the steps taken were most likely to be directed against the least powerful: immigrants from China, who, unlike Europeans seeking entry, had few allies among legislators and other policymakers.

In 1882, Congress enacted the Chinese Exclusion Act, which outlawed Chinese immigration for ten years. It also explicitly denied naturalization rights to the Chinese in the United States; that is, they were not allowed to become citizens. There was little debate in Congress, and discussion concentrated on how to best handle suspending Chinese immigration. No allowance was made for wives and children to be reunited with their husbands and fathers in the United States. Only brief visits of Chinese government officials, teachers, tourists, and merchants were exempted.

In 1892, Congress extended the Exclusion Act for another ten years and added that Chinese laborers had to obtain certificates of residence within a year or face deportation. After the turn of the century, the Exclusion Act was extended again. In 2012, Congress unanimously passed a resolution apologizing for the passage of the Chinese Exclusion Act. This marked only the fourth official apology in the past 25 years—the other three were for slavery, the internment of Japanese Americans during World War II, and mistreatment of native Hawaiians and the overthrow of their rule of the islands (Nahm 2012).

Restrictionist Sentiment Increases

4.2   Describe how restrictionist sentiment has increased in the past 100 years.

As Congress closed the door to Chinese immigration, the debate on restricting immigration turned in new directions. Prodded by growing anti-Japanese feelings, the United States entered into the so-called gentlemen's agreement, which was completed in 1908. Japan agreed to halt further immigration to the United States, and the United States agreed to end discrimination against the Japanese who had already arrived. The immigration ended, but anti-Japanese feelings continued. Americans were growing uneasy that the "new immigrants" would overwhelm the culture established by the "old immigrants." The earlier immigrants, if not Anglo-Saxon, were from similar groups such as the Scandinavians, the Swiss, and the French Huguenots. These people were more experienced in democratic political practices and had a greater affinity with the dominant Anglo-Saxon culture. By the end of the nineteenth century, however, more and more immigrants were neither English-speaking nor Protestant and came from dramatically different cultures.

The National Origin System

Beginning in 1921, a series of measures was enacted that marked a new era in American immigration policy. Whatever the legal language, the measures were drawn up to block the growing immigration from southern Europe (from Italy and Greece, for example) and also

Although it was not opened until 1892, New York Harbor's Ellis Island—the country's first federal immigration facility—quickly became the symbol of all migrant streams to the United States. By the time it closed in late 1954, it had processed 17 million immigrants. Today, their descendants number over 100 million Americans.

to block all Asian immigrants by establishing a zero quota for them.

To understand the effect of the national origin system on immigration, it is necessary to clarify the quota system. Quotas were deliberately weighted to favor immigration from northern Europe. Because of the ethnic composition of the United States in 1920, the quotas placed severe restrictions on immigration from the rest of Europe and from other parts of the world. Immigration from the Western Hemisphere (i.e., Canada, Mexico, Central and South America, and the Caribbean) continued unrestricted. The quota for each nation was set at 3 percent of the number of people descended from each nationality recorded in the 1920 census. Once the statistical manipulations were completed, almost 70 percent of the quota for the Eastern Hemisphere went to just three countries: Great Britain, Ireland, and Germany.

The absurdities of the system soon became obvious, but it was nevertheless continued. British immigration had fallen sharply, so most of its quota of 65,000 went unfilled. However, the openings could not be transferred, even though countries such as Italy (with a quota of only 6,000) had 200,000 people who wanted to immigrate to the United States. However one rationalizes the purpose behind the act, the result was obvious: Any English person, regardless of skill and whether related to anyone already in the United States, could enter the country more easily than, say, a Greek doctor whose children were American citizens. The quota for Greece was 305, with the backlog of people wanting to come to the United States reaching 100,000.

By the end of the 1920s, annual immigration had dropped to one-fourth of its pre–World War I level. The worldwide economic depression of the 1930s decreased immigration still further. A brief upsurge in immigration just before World War II reflected the flight of Europeans from the oppression of expanding Nazi Germany. The war virtually ended transatlantic immigration. The era of the great European migration to the United States had been legislated out of existence.

The Immigration and Nationality Act

The national origin system was abandoned with the passage of the 1965 Immigration and Nationality Act (also called the Hart-Cellar Act), signed into law by President Lyndon B. Johnson at the foot of the Statue of Liberty. The primary goals of the act were to reunite families and to protect the American labor market. The act also initiated restrictions on immigration from Latin America. After the act, immigration increased by one-third, but the act's influence was primarily on the composition rather than the size of immigration. The sources of immigrants now included Italy, Greece, Portugal, Mexico, the Philippines, the West Indies, and South America.

The lasting effect is apparent when we compare the changing sources of immigration over the past 200 years, as shown in Figure 4.3. The most recent period shows that Asian Pacific and Latin American immigrants combined to account for 83 percent of the people who were permitted entry. This contrasts sharply with early immigration (1820–1940), which was dominated by arrivals from Europe.

The nature of immigration laws is exceedingly complex and is subjected to frequent, often minor, adjustments. From 2005 to 2015, between 990,000 and 1,270,000 people were

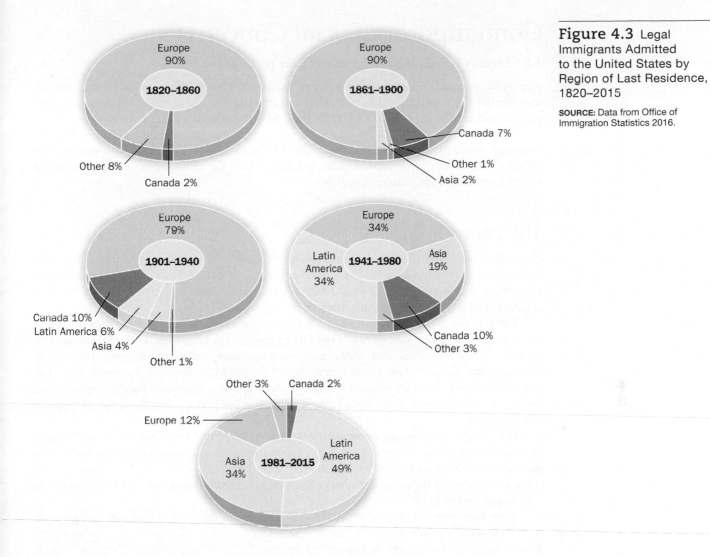

Figure 4.3 Legal Immigrants Admitted to the United States by Region of Last Residence, 1820–2015

SOURCE: Data from Office of Immigration Statistics 2016.

legally admitted to the United States each year. In 2015, people were admitted for the following reasons:

- Relatives of citizens 55%
- Relatives of legal residents 10%
- Employment-based 14%
- Refugees/people seeking political asylum 14%
- Diversity (lottery among applications from nations historically sending few immigrants) 4%
- Other 3%

Overall, two-thirds of immigrants come to join their families, one-seventh because of skills needed in the United States, and another one-seventh because of special refugee status. However, it would be a mistake to think family reunions are easy to accomplish. Because there are limits on how many people can enter legally each year for any one country, backlogs exist for such nations as China, India, Mexico, and the Philippines. So, for example, as of 2016, there was a 23-year backlog for adult children from the Philippines to join their American citizen parents. Similarly, there was a 21-year backlog for the Mexican married children of American citizens to join their parents (Aptekar 2016; Office of Immigration Statistics 2016: Table 6).

Contemporary Social Concerns

4.3 Identify the concerns about immigration policy today.

Although current U.S. immigration policies are less restrictive than those of other nations, they are the subject of great debate. Table 4.1 summarizes the benefits and concerns regarding immigration to the United States. We now consider six continuing criticisms relating to U.S. immigration policy: the brain drain, population growth, mixed-status families, English-language acquisition, economic impact, and illegal immigration. All six, but particularly illegal immigration, have provoked heated debates on the national level and continuing efforts to resolve them with new policies.

The Brain Drain

How often have you identified your science or mathematics teacher or your physician as someone who was not born in the United States? This nation has clearly benefited from attracting human resources from throughout the world, but this phenomenon has had negative effects on the immigrants' nations of origin.

Brain drain is the immigration to the United States of skilled workers, professionals, and technicians who are desperately needed by their home countries. In the mid-twentieth century, many scientists and other professionals from industrial nations, principally Germany and Great Britain, came to the United States. More recently, the brain drain has pulled emigrants from developing nations, including India, Pakistan, the Philippines, and several African nations. They are eligible for H-1B visas that qualify them for permanent work permits.

The H-1B visa program began in 1990. Currently, 65,000 foreigners with at a least a bachelor's degree and a specialized skill receive the H-1B visa. Another 20,000 such visas go to foreign nationals with advanced degrees from U.S. universities. In these cases, people come to the United States on a student visa, secure a degree (say, in engineering), and then may apply for the H-1B.

More than one out of four physicians (27 percent) in the United States is foreign-born and plays a critical role in serving areas with too few doctors. Thousands of doctors have sought to enter the United States, pulled by the economic opportunity. Persons born in India, the Philippines, and China account for the largest groups of foreign-born physicians. The pay differential is so great that, beginning in 2004, when foreign physicians were no longer favored with entry to the United States, physicians in the Philippines retrained as nurses so that they could immigrate to the United States where, employed as nurses, they would make four times what they would earn as doctors in the Philippines. By 2010, one-third of the foreign-born workers employed as registered nurses were born in the Philippines (McCabe 2012; *New York Times* 2005).

Table 4.1 Immigration Benefits and Concerns

Potential Benefits	Areas of Concern
Provide needed skills	Drain needed resources from home country
Pay taxes	Send money home
May come with substantial capital to start business	Less-skilled immigrants compete with already disadvantaged residents
Maintain growth of consumer market	Population growth
Diversify the population	Language differences
Maintain ties with countries throughout the world	May include people with destructive tendencies, such as terrorists and other criminals
Offset relatively low birth rate among U.S.-born nationals	Illegal immigration

Many foreign students say they plan to return home. Fortunately for the United States, many do not, instead continuing to make their talents available in the United States. One study showed that the majority of foreign students receiving their doctorates in the sciences and engineering remained here four years later. Critics note, however, that this foreign supply means that the United States overlooks its own minority scholars. Currently, for every African American and Latino student who receives a doctorate, a foreign citizen receives the same degree in the United States. More encouragement must be given to African Americans and Latinos to enter high-tech career paths.

Conflict theorists see the current brain drain as yet another symptom of the unequal distribution of world resources. In their view, it is ironic that the United States gives foreign aid to improve the technical resources of African and Asian countries while maintaining an immigration policy that encourages professionals in such nations to migrate to our shores. These countries have unacceptable public-health conditions and need native scientists, educators, technicians, and other professionals. In addition, by relying on foreign talent, the United States is not encouraging native members of subordinate groups to enter these desirable fields of employment (Collier 2013).

The H-1B visa program became a part of the controversy over efforts to institute new immigration policies in 2017, which even included a travel ban from certain predominantly Muslim countries. Most heads of tech firms, generally known for being silent on political controversies, condemned these efforts, or at the very least said they did not support measures that either directly or indirectly reduced the flow of desired workers and their relatives and friends. Also relevant is the fact that many successful start-up tech firms were founded or are operated by recent immigrants (Sorkin 2017).

Population Growth

The United States, like a few other industrialized nations, continues to accept large numbers of permanent immigrants and refugees. Although such immigration has increased since the passage of the 1965 Immigration and Nationality Act, the nation's birth rate has decreased. Consequently, the contribution of immigration to population growth has become more significant. As citizen "baby boomers" (Americans born during the post–World War II baby boom) age, the country has increasingly depended on the younger population fueled by immigration.

Immigration, legal and illegal, accounted for 55 percent of the nation's growth from 1965 to 2015. Looking further ahead, consider the following estimates:

- 2055 U.S. population with NO future immigration   338 million
- 2055 U.S. population with immigration continuing at current levels   441 million

These projections compare to a population of 325 million in 2017.

To some observers, the United States is already overpopulated. Environmentalists have weighed in on the immigration issue, questioning immigration's possible negative impact on the nation's natural resources. We consider that aspect of the immigration debate later in this chapter. Thus far, the majority of environmentalists have indicated a desire to keep a neutral position rather than enter the politically charged immigration debate (Lopez, Passel, and Rohal 2015).

The patterns of uneven settlement by immigrants in the United States are expected to continue, so future immigrants' impact on population growth will be felt much more in certain areas, for example, in California and New York rather than in Wyoming or West Virginia.

Although immigration and population growth may be viewed as national concerns, their impact is localized in certain areas, such as Southern California and large urban centers nationwide.

Mixed-Status Families

Little is simple when it comes to immigration. This is particularly true regarding the challenge of the estimated 9 million people living in mixed-status families. **Mixed status** refers to families in which one or more members are citizens and one or more are noncitizens. This situation becomes especially problematic when the noncitizens are illegal or undocumented immigrants.

The problem of mixed status emerges on two levels. On the macro level, when policy debates are made about issues that seem clear to many people—such as whether illegal immigrants should be allowed to attend state colleges or whether illegal immigrants should be immediately deported—the complicating factor of mixed-status families quickly emerges. On the micro level, the daily toll on members of mixed-status households is considerable. Often, the legal resident or even the U.S. citizen in a household finds daily life limited for fear of revealing the undocumented status of a parent, brother, sister, son, or daughter.

About three-quarters of illegal immigrants' children were born in the United States and thus are citizens. This means that perhaps half of all adult illegal immigrants have a citizen in their immediate family. This proportion has grown in recent years. Therefore, some of the issues facing illegal immigrants, whom we discuss later, also affect the citizens in their families; these citizens avoid calling attention to themselves for fear of revealing their mother or father's illegal status. Immigration issues aside, one can only begin to imagine the additional pressure this fear places on families beyond the usual stresses of balancing work and home, school, and children moving through adolescence to adulthood (Gonzales 2011; Gonzalez 2009; Passel and Cohn 2009; Pew Hispanic Center 2011b).

Imagine that you are a U.S. citizen, born here, and that you are unable to prevent both of your parents from being deported. Such was the case for Diane Guerrero, who is better known for her work in television than for her volunteer work with the Immigrant Legal Resource Center, a nonprofit group that advances immigrants' rights. In the Speaking Out box, "My Parents Were Deported," she recounts her family's situation.

A sensitive aspect of mixed-status households is the young people who are in the United States illegally but came here at such a young age that they have no experience in their "home nation," often not understanding the language and culture of the nation to which they could potentially be deported. One solution suggested for children over 15 years old is the DREAM Act: Development, Relief, and Education for Alien Minors. This act would offer a path to legal resident status for high-school graduates despite being in the country illegally. During his administration, President Barack Obama issued an executive order sparing the 750,000 "Dreamers" from deportation; however, executive orders can be reversed by the next administration. At his final press conference as president, Obama (2017) noted the threat to U.S. core values of any attempt to "round up kids … and send them someplace else when they love this country." The issues facing mixed-status families continue to remain a challenge to policymakers.

Language Barriers

For many people in the United States, the most visible signs of immigration are non-English speakers, businesses with foreign-language storefronts, and even familiar stores assuring potential customers that their employees speak Spanish, Polish, Chinese, or another foreign language. Non-English speakers cluster in certain states, but bilingualism attracts nationwide passions. The release in 2006 of "Nuestro Himno," the Spanish-language version of "The Star-Spangled Banner," led to a strong reaction, with 69 percent of people saying it was appropriate to be sung only in English. Yet at least one congressman who decried the Spanish version sang the anthem himself in English with incorrect lyrics (Carroll 2006; Koch 2006).

About 21 percent of the population speaks a language other than English at home, as Figure 4.4 shows. Indeed, 39 different languages are spoken at home by at least 90,000

Speaking Out

My Parents Were Deported

Diane Guerrero

In *Orange Is the New Black*, I play Maritza Ramos, a tough Latina from the 'hood. In *Jane the Virgin*, I play Lina, Jane's best friend and a funny know-it-all who is quick to offer advice.

I love both parts, but they're fiction. My real story is this: I am the citizen daughter of immigrant parents who were deported when I was 14. My older brother was also deported.

My parents came here from Colombia during a time of great instability there. Escaping a dire economic situation at home, they moved to New Jersey, where they had friends and family, seeking a better life, and then moved to Boston after I was born.

Throughout my childhood I watched my parents try to become legal but to no avail. They lost their money to people they believed to be attorneys, but who ultimately never helped. That meant my childhood was haunted by the fear that they would be deported. If I didn't see anyone when I walked in the door after school, I panicked.

And then one day, my fears were realized. I came home from school to an empty house. Lights were on and dinner had been started, but my family wasn't there. Neighbors broke the news that my parents had been taken away by immigration officers, and just like that, my stable family life was over.

Not a single person at any level of government took any note of me. No one checked to see if I had a place to live or food to eat, and at 14, I found myself basically on my own.

While awaiting deportation proceedings, my parents remained in detention near Boston, so I could visit them. They would have liked to fight deportation, but without a lawyer and in an immigration system that rarely gives judges the discretion to allow families to stay together, they never had a chance. Finally, they agreed for me to continue my education at Boston Arts Academy, a performing arts high school, and the parents of friends graciously took me in.

Insecure about being a nuisance and losing my invitation to stay, I worked a variety of jobs in retail and at coffee shops all through high school. And though I was surrounded by people who cared about me, part of me ached with every accomplishment, because my parents weren't there to share my joy.

Diane Guerrero

Robin Platzer/Twin Images/ZUMA Press/Newscom

My family and I worked hard to keep our relationships strong, but too-short phone calls and the annual summer visits I made to Colombia didn't suffice. They missed many important events in my life, including my singing recitals—they watched my senior recital on a tape I sent them instead of from the audience. And they missed my prom, my college application process, and my graduations from high school and college.

My story is all too common. Every day, children who are U.S. citizens are separated from their families as a result of immigration policies that need fixing.

I consider myself lucky because things turned out better for me than for most, including some of my own family members. When my brother was deported, his daughter was just a toddler. She still had her mother, but in a single-parent household, she faced a lot of challenges. My niece made the wrong friends and bad choices. Today, she is serving time in jail, living the reality that I act out on screen. I don't believe her life would have turned out this way if her father and my parents had been here to guide and support her.

I realize the issues are complicated. But it's not just in the interest of immigrants to fix the system: It's in the interest of all Americans. Children who grow up separated from their families often end up in foster care, or worse, in the juvenile justice system, despite having parents who love them and would like to be able to care for them.

I don't believe it reflects our values as a country to separate children and parents in this way. Nor does it reflect our values to hold people in detention without access to good legal representation or a fair shot in a court of law. . . . Keeping families together is a core American value.

Congress needs to provide a permanent, fair legislative solution, but in the meantime families are being destroyed every day, and the president should do everything in his power to provide the broadest relief possible now. Not one more family should be separated by deportation.

Source: Guererro, Diane, Op-Ed, "'Orange is the New Black' actress: My parents were deported." Los Angeles Times. November 15, 2014. Used with permission.

residents. Spanish accounts for 62 percent of the foreign-language speakers at home. As of 2013, about half of the 61 million people speaking a foreign language at home spoke English less than "very well." Since 1980, the largest growth has been in speakers of Spanish, Chinese,

Figure 4.4 Ten Languages Most Frequently Spoken at Home, Other Than English and Spanish, 2013

Of 291 million people over five years of age, 231 million only speak English at home, 38 million speak Spanish, and about 22 million speak some other language.

SOURCE: Data for 2009–2013 in Bureau of the Census 2015a.

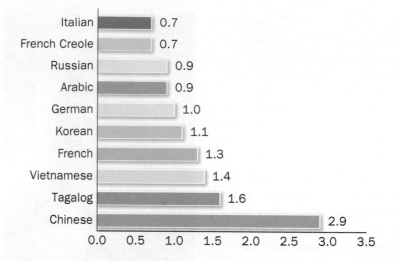

Korean, Vietnamese, Tagalog (the language of the Philippines), Russian, and Farsi (the language of Iran). The largest decreases have all been in European-based languages such as Italian, Greek, German, Yiddish, and Polish (Ryan 2013).

Until the past 40 years, a conscious effort was made to devalue Spanish and other languages and to discourage the use of foreign languages in schools. In the case of Spanish, this practice was built on a pattern of segregating Hispanic schoolchildren from Anglos. In the recent past in the Southwest, Mexican Americans were assigned to Mexican schools to keep Anglo schools all White. These Mexican schools, created through explicit school segregation resulting from residential segregation, were substantially underfunded compared with the Anglo public schools. Legal action against such schools dates back to 1945, but it was not until 1970 that the U.S. Supreme Court ruled, in *Cisneros v. Corpus Christi Independent School District*, that segregation of Mexican Americans was unconstitutional. Appeals delayed implementation of that decision, and not until September 1975 was the plan forcibly overturned in Corpus Christi, Texas (Commission on Civil Rights 1976).

Is it essential that English be the sole language of instruction in schools in the United States? **Bilingualism** is the use of two or more languages in places of work or educational facilities, and it accords each language equal legitimacy. Thus, a program of **bilingual education** may instruct children in their native language (for example, Spanish) while gradually introducing them to the language of the dominant society (English). If such a program also is bicultural, it will teach children about the culture of both linguistic groups. Bilingual education allows students to learn academic material in their own language while they learn a second language. Proponents believe that, ideally, bilingual education programs should also allow English-speaking pupils to become bilingual, but generally these programs are directed only at making non-English speakers proficient in more than one language.

Do bilingual programs help children learn English? It is difficult to reach firm conclusions on the effectiveness of bilingual programs in general because they vary so widely in their approach. The programs differ in the length of the transition to English and how long they allow students to remain in bilingual classrooms. A major study analyzed more than three decades of research, combining 17 different studies, and found that bilingual education programs produce higher levels of student achievement in reading. The most successful are paired bilingual programs—those offering ongoing instruction in a native language and English at different times of the day (Callahan and Gándara 2014; Slavin and Cheung 2003; Soltero 2008).

Attacks on bilingualism in voting and education have taken several forms and have even broadened to question the appropriateness of U.S. residents using any language other than English. Federal policy has become more restrictive. Local schools have been given more authority to determine appropriate methods of instruction; they also have been forced to provide more of their own funding for bilingual education. Adding to the difficulty is that increasingly, school districts outside the central city in suburbs and rural agricultural areas face the challenge of serving non-English-speaking schoolchildren.

In the United States, as of 2017, 32 states have made English their official language. Repeated efforts have been made to introduce a constitutional amendment declaring English as the nation's official language. Even such an action would not completely outlaw bilingual or multilingual government services. It would, however, require that such services be called for specifically, as in the Voting Rights Act of 1965, which requires voting information to be available in multiple languages (U.S. English 2017).

The Economic Impact

There is much public and scholarly debate about the economic effects of immigration, both legal and illegal. Varied, conflicting conclusions have resulted from research ranging from case studies of Korean immigrants' dominance among New York City greengrocers to mobility studies charting the progress of all immigrants and their children. The confusion results in part from the different methods of analysis. For example, the studies do not always include political refugees, who generally are less prepared than other refugees to become assimilated. Sometimes, the research focuses only on economic effects, such as whether people are employed or are on welfare; in other cases, it also considers cultural factors, such as knowledge of English.

Perhaps the most significant factor in determining the economic impact of immigration is whether a study examines the national impact of immigration or only its effects on a local area. Overall, we can conclude from the research that immigrants adapt well and are assets to the national economy. In some local areas, heavy immigration may drain a community's resources. However, it can also revitalize a local economy. Marginally employed workers, most of whom are either themselves immigrants or are African Americans, often experience a negative impact as a result of new arrivals. With or without immigration, competition for low-paying jobs in the United States is high, and those who gain the most from this competition are the employers and the consumers who want to keep wages and prices down (Peri 2014).

The impact of immigration on African Americans deserves special attention. Given that African Americans are a large minority and many continue to be in the underclass, many people, including some Blacks themselves, perceive immigrants as advancing at the expense of the African American community. There is evidence that in the very lowest paid jobs—for example, workers in chicken-processing plants—wages have dropped with the availability of unskilled immigrants to perform them, and Blacks have left these jobs for good. Many of these African Americans do not necessarily move to better or even equivalent jobs. This pattern is repeated in other relatively low-paying, undesirable employment sectors, so Blacks are not alone in being affected; but, given the lack of other job opportunities, the impact on Blacks is longer lasting (Peri 2014).

There is no one portrait, or even a dozen portraits, of the typical situation that describes the economic role of immigrants in the United States. Similarly, there are many explanations for why unauthorized immigration persists. In the Research Focus, we show that labor on Wisconsin dairy farms has been dominated by Latino workers, many of them undocumented.

About 70 percent of illegal immigrant workers pay taxes of one type or another. Many of them do not file to receive refunds or benefits to which they are entitled. For example, the Social Security Administration estimates that nearly 2 million illegal immigrants annually contribute $10 billion into the retirement trust fund and only receive about $1 billion in benefits. This is a net $9 billion cash flow into Social Security, which is a positive effect on this

Research Focus

The Hispanic Dairyland

Dairyland Wisconsin invokes images of rolling hills and pastures, black and white Holstein cows, and roadside shops selling cheese. But now an indispensable part of this portrayal is the important role played by Latino workers.

Since the beginning of the twenty-first century, immigrant workers, almost entirely Hispanic and largely Mexican, have constituted the majority of laborers on large dairy farms. Overall, at least 40 percent of all hired dairy employees on the more than 14,000 dairy farms in Wisconsin are Hispanic. Latinos working in agriculture is not new—nationally, they accounted in 2012 for 24 percent of all employed persons in animal and crop production—but their rapid presence in dairy farming is a twenty-first-century phenomenon. Dairy farmers turned to immigrant workers when they found it difficult to locate "reliable" U.S.-born workers, to use their often-expressed criterion. Dairy farms have also grown larger, requiring additional milking shifts and more workhands.

As one typical dairy farmer with 150 cows said in 2009:

> So as our last two children entered high school, and I realized that soon I would have no family labor to rely on, we moved our farm to all hired labor. I have not been able to hire an American citizen since 1997. I have tried! The way I see it, if we didn't have Hispanics to rely on for a workforce, I don't believe I could continue farming. (Harrison, Lloyd, and O'Kane 2009:2–3)

The important role that Latinos now play on dairy farms is not limited to the Midwest but extends to states like California, Texas, New York, and Vermont, which also used to depend on local workers.

The use of immigrant labor on dairy farms is an example of **occupational segregation**, or the concentration of one particular group of people to a particular job. In this case, we see occupational segregation with respect to Latinos, largely male, to the more manual labor on these farms. They are not involved in caring for the herd, distributing the product, or maintaining equipment, much less owning the farm. They are limited to the "milking parlors," which are the large barns where cows are milked. The Latinos work as "milkers" (hooking the cows to hoses), "pushers" (getting the cows in and out of the parlors), or "cleaners" (scraping manure from the parlors). Cows are milked two to three times a day, every day, so the labor demand is continuous.

Such low-level jobs are now often described as "Mexican" work, regardless of the nationality of the laborer, even though little more than a decade or two ago, all of these jobs were done by family members or local workers. So associated are Latinos with this hard labor that farm operators now speak of the U.S.-born workers as being too weak to do the immigrant labor. Hispanic laborers are so well regarded for working the long hours at tough work that when a worker seems reluctant to do it, he or she is derisively referred to as being "Americanized," a reference to the local people unwilling to labor in the milk parlors. Indeed, occupational segregation has become so well defined that Latinos are now seen as "suited" to the job and unsatisfactory for more-skilled and higher-paying work on the farm. For the workers, their success as milkers has led to chain migration to the area through family and friendship networks as more and more workers are needed.

Even though Hispanic laborers may work for several years on the same farm, there is little interest in training them to do more highly skilled labor. The farm owners recognize that many of these workers may be illegal and do not wish to "invest" in their future. The workers rarely complain, fearing that their illegal status or that of their friends and family members may be disclosed. Given that they labor in rural areas doing work that no one else wants to do, there is little incentive to investigate their legal status, and dairy farms are rarely investigated.

Dairy farms represent a very small aspect of Latino life in the United States, but for dairy farmers, Latinos are extremely important. Therefore, through agriculture lobbying organizations, farm operators and owners are well heard on any immigration bill that may jeopardize their continuing access to their "reliable," if illegal, workforce.

Sources: Department of Agriculture 2010; Campion 2013, Dorschner 2013; Harrison and Lloyd 2012; Jordan 2009; Kohli 2013.

significant federal government program. Supporters of immigration reform also point to increased tax revenue and even more net financial benefits to all local governments if illegal immigrants move toward legal residency (Campbell 2016; Bruinius 2017).

Social science studies generally contradict many of the negative stereotypes about the economic impact of immigration. A variety of recent studies found that immigrants are a net economic gain for the population in times of economic boom as well as in periods of recession. But despite national gains, in some areas and for some groups, immigration may be an economic burden or create unwanted competition for jobs (Kochhar 2006).

Table 4.2 Immigrant Adaptation to the United States

Less Encouraging Signs	Positive Signs
• Although immigrants have lower divorce rates and are less likely to form single-parent households than natives, their rates equal or exceed these rates by the second generation.	• Immigrant families and, more broadly, noncitizen households are more likely to be on public assistance, but their time on public assistance is shorter and they receive fewer benefits than other groups. This generalization is true even when considering special restrictions that may apply to noncitizens.
• Children in immigrant families tend to be healthier than U.S.-born children, but the advantage declines.	• Second-generation immigrants (i.e., children of immigrants) are overall doing as well as or better than White non-Hispanic natives in educational attainment, labor-force participation, wages, and household income.
• Immigrant children attend schools that are disproportionately attended by other poor children and students with limited English proficiency, so they are ethnically, economically, and linguistically isolated.	• Immigrants overwhelmingly (65 percent) continue to see learning English as an ethical obligation of all immigrants.

What about the immigrants themselves? Considering contemporary immigrants as a group, we can draw the following conclusions, summarized in Table 4.2. They represent a mix of successes and challenges to adaptation. These positive trends diverge among specific immigrant groups, with Asian immigrants doing better than European immigrants, who do better than Latino immigrants (Capps, Leighton, and Fix 2002; Farkas 2003; Myers, Pitkin, and Park 2004; Zimmerman 2008).

One economic aspect of immigration that has received increasing attention is the role of **remittances**, the monies that immigrants send back to their countries of origin. The amounts are significant and measure in the hundreds of millions of dollars flowing from the United States to other countries, where they provide substantial support for families and even venture capital for new businesses. Although some observers express concern over this outflow of money, others counter that it probably represents a small price to pay for the human capital that the United States is able to use in the form of the immigrants themselves.

Immigrants in the United States send about $56 billion to their countries of origin annually, and worldwide remittances bring about $582 billion to all the world's countries, easily surpassing all other forms of foreign aid. This cash inflow is integral to the economies of many nations, but it can also fluctuate dramatically during times of economic stress. With the Great Recession beginning in 2008, it was clear that low-skilled immigrants (legal or illegal) took the hardest hit, and as a result, remittances immediately declined (Connor 2016; World Bank Group 2016).

Illegal Immigration

4.4 Discuss the scope of and issues related to illegal immigration.

The most bitterly debated aspect of U.S. immigration policy has been the control of illegal or undocumented immigrants. These immigrants and their families usually come to the United States in search of higher-paying jobs than their home countries can provide. While some people contend there are differences in the terms *illegal, undocumented,* and *unauthorized,* we use the terms interchangeably to refer to people who entered the country without the proper documents, as well as people who entered legally as students or tourists but then remained illegally.

Because by definition illegal immigrants are in the country illegally, the exact number of these undocumented or unauthorized workers is subject to estimates and disputes. Based on the best available information in early 2017, about 11.3 million illegal or unauthorized immigrants live in the United States. This compares with about 3.5 million in 1990 and a peak of 12.2 million in 2007. With employment opportunities drying up during the Great Recession beginning in 2008, significantly fewer people tried to enter illegally, and many unauthorized immigrants returned to their countries (Krogstad 2016).

The public has tied illegal immigrants—and even legal immigrants—to almost every social problem in the nation. They are the scapegoats for unemployment; they are labeled "drug runners" and, especially since September 11, 2001, "terrorists." Arrest, detention, and deportation of illegal immigrants has greatly increased. Their vital economic and cultural contributions to the United States are generally overlooked, as they have been for more than 100 years. Considering illegal immigration from the immigrant's perspective, the possibility of apprehension and punishment does not pose a significant deterrent. However, the decision to enter the country illegally is affected by their assessment of the employment possibilities in the home country and the dangers of border crossing.

Illegal immigration poses significant costs for *aliens*—that is, foreign-born noncitizens— and for other citizens. Civil rights advocates have expressed concern that the procedures used to apprehend and deport people are discriminatory and deprive many aliens of their legal rights. American citizens of Hispanic or Asian origin, some of whom were born in the United States, may be greeted with prejudice and distrust, as if their names automatically imply that they are in the country illegally. In 2017, immigration officials held up the re-entry into the United States of Muhammad Ali, Jr., son of the famous boxer and a U.S.-born citizen. The officials felt he had a suspicious-sounding name, and Ali, Jr., told them he was Muslim when they asked about his religion. Furthermore, citizens and legal residents of the United States may be unable to find work because employers wrongly believe that their documents are forged.

Congress approved the Immigration Reform and Control Act of 1986 (IRCA) after debating it for nearly a decade. The act marked a historic change in immigration policy compared with earlier laws, which are summarized in Table 4.3. Amnesty was granted to 2.7 million illegal immigrants who could document that they had established long-term residency in the United States. Under the IRCA, hiring illegal aliens became illegal, and employers became subject to fines and even prison sentences. Annually, about 400,000 people are deported—increasingly at the border; these people are typically not guilty of any offense other than illegal entry. Farther from the border, deportation has been more limited to those committing crimes, but what constitutes a serious enough crime has been subject to change and periodic review (Thompson and Cohen 2014; Bruinius 2017).

Many illegal immigrants continue to live in fear and in hiding, subject to even more severe harassment and discrimination than before. From a conflict perspective, these immigrants, who are primarily poor and Hispanic or Asian, are firmly lodged at the bottom of the nation's social and economic hierarchies. However, from a functionalist perspective, employers, by paying low wages, are able to produce goods and services that are profitable for industry and more affordable to consumers. Despite the poor working conditions often experienced by illegal immigrants, they continue to come because it is still in their best economic interest to work here in disadvantaged positions rather than to seek wage labor unsuccessfully in their home countries.

Table 4.3 Major Immigration Policies

Policy	Target Group	Impact
Chinese Exclusion Act, 1882	Chinese	Effectively ended all Chinese immigration for more than 60 years
National origin system, 1921	Southern Europeans	Reduced overall immigration and significantly reduced likely immigration from Greece and Italy
Immigration and Nationality Act, 1965 (Hart-Cellar Act)	Western Hemisphere and the less skilled	Facilitated entry of skilled workers and relatives of U.S. residents
Immigration Reform and Control Act, 1986 (IRCA)	Illegal immigrants	Modest reduction of illegal immigration

As the nation became polarized over illegal immigration, some cities decided to become **sanctuary cities** where local law-enforcement officers do not actively hand over illegal immigrants to federal enforcement agents. The "cities" are sometimes entire counties or metropolitan areas, and they include Los Angeles, Denver, Dallas, Chicago, New Orleans, New York City, and Boston. Some border states have even become "sanctuary states." They include New Mexico, California, and North Dakota.

Typically, an illegal immigrant may be arrested for an offense unrelated to citizenship, such as a driving offense, and authorities move forward with disciplining the person based on the offense. However, in sanctuary areas, no further action is taken on the person's illegal status, nor is it brought directly to the attention of federal authorities. Courts have generally ruled that cooperation with federal immigration authorities is voluntary (Cameron 2017).

Border security continues to be a hot-button topic, with "Build a wall" the rallying cry for advocates of increased security.

David R. Frazier Photolibrary, Inc./Alamy Stock Photo

Illegal aliens or undocumented workers are not necessarily transient. One estimate indicates that 66 percent have been here for at least ten years. Many have established homes, families, and networks with relatives and friends in the United States whose legal status might differ from theirs. These are the mixed-status households noted earlier. For the most part, their lives are not much different from those of legal residents, except when they seek services that require documentation proving citizenship status (Krogstad 2016).

The public often thinks in terms of controlling illegal immigration through greater surveillance at the border. After the terrorist attacks of September 11, 2001, greater control of border traffic took on a new sense of urgency, even though almost all of the hijackers had entered the United States legally. It also is very difficult to secure the vast boundaries that mark the United States on land and sea. The cost of the federal government's attempt to police the nation's borders and locate illegal immigrants is sizable.

Numerous civil rights groups and migrant advocacy organizations have expressed alarm regarding people who cross into the United States illegally and perish in the attempt. We will revisit this aspect of immigration in Chapter 9.

So what is the future of immigration reform? It is unlikely to be resolved in any satisfying way because the issues are complex and are wrapped up in economic interests, humanitarian concerns, party politics, constitutional rights, and even foreign policy. Alongside immigration policy is the question of how the nation should accommodate people escaping political and religious persecution.

When it comes to issues of race and ethnicity, South Africa usually evokes past images of *apartheid* and the struggle to overcome generations of racial separation—both important topics that we will consider in Chapter 16. However, in the Global View feature, we consider South Africa's contemporary challenge of dealing with immigration.

Naturalization: The Path to Citizenship

4.5 Outline the process of naturalization.

In **naturalization**, citizenship is conferred on a foreign-born person. The process for achieving citizenship has been outlined by Congress. Naturalization extends to foreigners the same benefits given to native-born U.S. citizens. Naturalized citizens, however, cannot serve as the U.S. president.

Until the 1970s, most people who were naturalized had been born in Europe. Reflecting changing patterns of immigration, Asia and Latin America are now the largest sources of new citizens. In fact, the number of naturalized citizens from Mexico has come close to matching those from all of Europe. In recent years, the number of new citizens going through the naturalization process has been close to 1 million a year (Baker 2009).

A Global View

Immigration and South Africa

With over 52 million people, the Republic of South Africa is not rich by global standards, but its economy is very attractive to most of the African continent. For example, South Africa has a gross national income per person of $12,830, compared to $1,700 in neighboring Zimbabwe. Even when South Africa was ruled by a White-supremacist government, Black Africans from throughout the continent came to the country, fleeing violence and poverty in their home countries, and often went to work mining coal and diamonds. In the post-apartheid era, the numbers of immigrants, legal and illegal, have skyrocketed. Today, South Africa's government is caught between compassion toward those seeking entry and the economy's growing inability to absorb those who seek work and shelter.

In 2008, the world took notice as riots broke out among poor South Africans taking out their rage on even more impoverished foreigners. The growing xenophobia took the government—which advocates racial harmony—by surprise as it tried to quell violence among Black Africans divided by citizenship status and nationality. In a matter of months in early 2008, some 32,000 immigrants had been driven from their homes, with attackers seizing all of their belongings. Some immigrants returned to their home countries—including Burundi, Ethiopia, Ghana, Malawi, Mozambique, and Zimbabwe—but most settled temporarily in camps.

South Africa, with limited government resources, deported over 310,000 immigrants in 2007–2008, a number nearly comparable to that of the United States (which has six times the population). However, estimates of the total number of illegal immigrants in South Africa range from 3 million to 5 million—a much higher proportion than estimated in the United States.

The scapegoating of immigrants, or "border jumpers" as they often are called in South Africa, is not unique to this nation. The tension between South Africans and foreigners has led to concerns over continuing xenophobia with threats toward foreign-owned shops. For the global community that still relishes Nelson Mandela's peaceful ascent to power, South Africa has been a reminder of immigration's challenge throughout the world.

Sources: Dixon 2007; Forced Migration Studies Programme 2010; Kaneda and Bietsch 2016; Koser 2008; Nevin 2008; Onishi 2015; Roodt 2008; South African Institute of Race Relations 2011.

To become a naturalized U.S. citizen, a person must meet the following general conditions:

- be 18 years of age;
- have continually resided in the United States for at least five years (three years for the spouses of U.S. citizens);
- have good moral character as determined by the absence of conviction for selected criminal offenses;
- be able to read, write, speak, and understand words of ordinary usage in the English language; and
- pass a test in U.S. government and history administered orally in English.

Table 4.4 lists some of the questions that immigrants must answer on the citizenship test. This is a sample of the actual questions used; those seeking citizenship must get six out of ten correct to pass. If a person fails, he or she can immediately retake the test with different questions. After failing a second time, typically the person must wait 90 days to retake the test. As of 2013, the fee for applying for citizenship is $725, compared with $95 in 1998.

Although we often picture the United States as having a very insular, nativistic attitude toward foreigners living here, the country has a rather liberal policy toward people maintaining citizenship in their countries of origin. Although most countries do not allow people to maintain dual (or even multiple) citizenships, the United States does not forbid it. Dual citizenship is most common when a person goes through naturalization after already being a citizen of another country or is a U.S.-born citizen and goes through the process of becoming a citizen of another country—for example, after marrying a foreigner (Department of State 2013).

The continuing debate about immigration reform often includes calls for some type of "amnesty" or pathway to citizenship for illegal immigrants. Proposals vary, but requirements

Table 4.4 So You Want to Be a Citizen?

Try these sample questions from the naturalization test (answers below).
1. What do the stripes on the flag represent?
2. How many amendments are there to the Constitution?
3. Who is the chief justice of the Supreme Court?
4. Who was president during World War I?
5. What do we call the first 10 amendments to the Constitution?
6. What are two rights in the Declaration of Independence?
7. Name one right or freedom from the First Amendment.
8. When was the Constitution written?

Answers:
(1) The first 13 states; (2) 27; (3) John Roberts; (4) Woodrow Wilson; (5) Bill of Rights; (6) life, liberty, and the pursuit of happiness; (7) the rights are freedom of speech, religion, assembly, and press, and freedom to petition the government; (8) 1787.

SOURCE: Department of Homeland Security 2017.

usually include proof of long-term residence in the United States, absence of criminal activity, and willingness to accept a waiting period before actual citizenship can occur. Critics of such proposals question the wisdom of "rewarding illegals" but also argue that legal residency for illegal immigrants makes it more likely that their relatives will also apply for legal residency. Current policy, as earlier noted, has created long waiting periods for those abroad trying to join their relatives, but surveys also show that, as in 1986 when some type of amnesty was offered, not all qualified illegal immigrants will seek legal status. For example, in recent years only 46 percent of Hispanic immigrants eligible to naturalize have chosen to become citizens, compared with 71 percent of non-Hispanic immigrants. Difficulties with the English language and the costs of application serve as barriers to the path to citizenship (Lopez and Gonzalez-Barrera 2013).

The Global Economy and Immigration

4.6 Explain the connection between globalization and immigration.

Immigration is defined by political boundaries that bring the movement of people crossing borders to the attention of government authorities. Within the borders of the United States, people may move their residence, but they are not immigrating. For residents in the member nations of the European Union, free movement of people within the union is also protected.

Yet, increasingly, people recognize the need to think beyond national borders and national identity. As noted in Chapter 1, **globalization** is the worldwide integration of government policies, cultures, social movements, and financial markets through trade, movement of people, and the exchange of ideas. In this era of globalization, immigrants are less likely to think of themselves as residents of only one country. For generations, immigrants have used foreign-language newspapers to keep up to date with events in their home countries. Today, cable channels carry news and variety programs from their home countries, and the Internet offers immediate access to the homeland and kinfolk thousands of miles away.

Although it helps in bringing the world together, globalization has also highlighted the dramatic economic inequalities between nations. Today, people in North America, Europe, and Japan consume 32 times more resources than the billions of people in developing nations. Thanks to tourism, media, and other aspects of globalization, the people of less-affluent countries are aware of such affluent lifestyles and, of course, often aspire to enjoy them (Diamond 2003).

Transnationals are immigrants who sustain multiple social relationships that link their societies of origin and settlement. Immigrants from the Dominican Republic, for example, not only identify themselves with Americans but also maintain very close ties to their

Caribbean homeland. They return for visits, send remittances, and host extended stays of relatives and friends. Back in the Dominican Republic, villages reflect these close ties, as shown in billboards promoting special long-distance services to the United States and by the presence of household appliances sent by relatives. The volume of remittances worldwide is easily the most reliable source of foreign money going to poor countries, far outstripping government-sponsored foreign-aid programs.

The presence of transnationals in a country is an example of pluralism. Because transnationals move back and forth, it is not unusual for different generations of the same family to find themselves residing in different countries at any given moment. The recognition that many immigrants sustain multiple relationships, including homeland connections as transnationals, serves to amend the assimilationist view, which appears to gloss over this aspect of immigrants' daily lives in the their new homes (Waldinger 2015).

The growing number of transnationals, as well as immigration in general, directly reflects the world systems analysis we considered in Chapter 1. Transnationals are not new, but the ability to communicate and transfer resources makes the immigration experience today different from that of the nineteenth (and most of the twentieth) century. The sharp contrast between the industrial "have" nations and the developing "have-not" nations only encourages movement across borders. The industrial "haves" gain benefits from such movement even when they seem to discourage it. The back-and-forth movement also serves to increase globalization and helps to create informal social networks between people who seek a better life and those already enjoying increased prosperity.

The transnationals themselves maintain a multithreaded relationship between friends and relatives in the United Sates, their home country, and perhaps other countries where relatives and friends have resettled. Besides the economic impact of remittances described earlier, scholars are increasingly giving attention to "social remittances" that include ideas, social norms, and practices (religious and secular) throughout this global social network (Levitt and Jaworsky 2007).

Refugees

4.7 Describe the United States' policies toward refugees.

Refugees are people who live outside their country of citizenship for fear of political or religious persecution. Approximately 20 million refugees exist worldwide, enough to populate an entire "nation." That nation of refugees would be larger than the Netherlands or Guatemala. The United States has touted itself as a haven for political refugees. However, political refugees have not always received an unqualified welcome.

Policies

The United States resettles between 50,000 and 73,000 refugees annually. Following 9/11, resettlement procedures have become much more cumbersome, and it is much more difficult for foreigners to acquire refugee status and gain entry to the United States. Most refugees receive that designation overseas by the United Nations (UN) and go through medical screening, retinal screening, DNA sampling, and background checks. Other refugees are approved without UN referral because they are close relatives of those already successfully resettled. In either situation, those headed to the United States go through additional security screening undertaken by the Department of State and the Department of Homeland Security.

The United States, insulated by distance from wars and famines overseas, has been able to be selective about which and how many refugees are welcomed. From the arrival of refugees uprooted by World War II through the 1980s, the United States allowed three groups of refugees to enter in numbers greater than regulations would ordinarily permit: Hungarians, Cubans, and Southeast Asians.

Refugees are granted the right to enter a country while they are still residing abroad. **Asylees** are foreigners who have already entered the United States and seek protection because of persecution or a well-founded fear of persecution in their home country.

This persecution may be based on the individual's race, religion, nationality, membership in a particular social group, or political opinion. Asylees are eligible to adjust to lawful permanent resident status after one year of continuous presence in the United States. Asylum is granted to about 10,000 people annually.

Because asylees, by definition, are already here, they are either granted legal entry or returned to their home country. The practice of deporting people who are fleeing poverty has been the subject of criticism. The United States has a long tradition of facilitating the arrival of people leaving Communist nations, including, until 2017, people seeking asylum from Cuba. Mexicans who are refugees from poverty and Haitians running from despotic rule are not similarly welcomed. The plight of Haitians is of particular concern.

Haitians began fleeing their country, often on small boats, in the 1980s. The U.S. Coast Guard intercepted many Haitians at sea, saving some of these boat people from death in their rickety and overcrowded wooden vessels. The Haitians said they feared detentions, torture, and execution if they remained in Haiti. Yet at the time the government viewed most Haitian exiles as economic migrants rather than as political refugees, and thus opposed granting them asylum and permission to enter the United States. Once apprehended, the Haitians were returned to Haiti. In 1993, the U.S. Supreme Court, by an 8–1 vote, upheld the government's right to intercept Haitian refugees at sea and return them to their homeland without asylum hearings.

The devastating 2010 earthquake in Haiti made the government reconsider this policy. At the time, tens of thousands of Haitians in the United States were subject to deportation. A moratorium on deportation was imposed, only to be lifted in 2016 over the objection of social service agencies and members of the Haitian American community. Despite continuing obstacles, the Haitian American community exhibits pride in those who have succeeded. In fact, the initial earthquake refugees tended to come from the Haitian middle class or higher. Some even expressed annoyance at the quality of the public schools their children attended in America compared to the private ones in Haiti (Buchanan, Albert, and Beaulieu 2010; Semple 2016; Winerip 2011).

Concerns About the Refugee Program

Public concerns about admitting refugees have been noted at both extremes. On one side are those who lobby vigorously in favor of allowing more refugees to enter from a particular country that has been especially hard hit by some type of crisis. On the other side are those who feel we do too much already for noncitizens or who believe that U.S. national security is threatened by allowing people to migrate to the United States from the world's trouble spots.

The U.S. government is officially committed to accepting refugees from other nations—but how many and from where is always subject change. Table 4.5 lists the major sources of refugees. Changing political situations and changing policy priorities here and abroad can alter this mix. Because of unrest in the Middle East and North Africa, the United States accepted, in just a four-month period from October 2016 through January 2017, over 4,000 refugees each from Iraq, Syria, and Somalia (Department of State 2017).

Table 4.5 Top Sources of Refugees, 2005 and 2015

2005		2015	
1. Somalia	10,405	Burma (Myanmar)	18,356
2. Laos	8,517	Iraq	12,676
3. Cuba	6,361	Somalia	8,858
4. Russia	5,982	Dem. Rep. of Congo	7,876
5. Liberia	4,289	Bhutan	5,775
Total of All Countries:	53,813		69,920

SOURCE: Jefferys 2006:2; Mossaad 2016:3.

According to the United Nations treaty on refugees, which the U.S. government ratified in 1968, countries are obliged to refrain from forcibly returning people to territories where their lives or liberty might be endangered. However, it is not always clear whether a person is fleeing for his or her personal safety or to escape poverty. Although people in the latter category deserve humane treatment, they do not meet the official definition of refugees and are subject to deportation.

To place the U.S. refugee program in perspective, while in absolute number we may seem to accept large numbers, the United States ranks 47th among 170 countries in terms of wealth and 75th in terms of population. Many other much smaller and poorer nations have received much larger numbers of refugees, with Lebanon, Pakistan, and Turkey hosting more than 1 million refugees each (Martin and Yankay 2013; United Nations High Commission on Refugees 2015, 2016).

While the nation may rethink its refugee policy, people generally view refugees as genuinely deserving of assistance. We might help them by:

- Steering money and goods to individual refugees through crowdfunding sites online
- Donating money directly to refugee and resettlement agencies
- Donating money directly to local organizations working with refugees
- Volunteering time to assist refugees through tutoring, accompanying them to get driver's licenses, and so forth
- Hosting a dinner or serving as an escort for a shopping trip
- Directly sponsoring a refugee family for their first year (This option is not available in the United States but is available to people in Canada and other nations.)
- Advocating at the national or local level for an appropriate refugee policy

These suggestions address the refugee needs in the United States, but most refugee households spend many months or even years in overseas resettlement camps, which offer yet another area of possible assistance (Bernard 2015, 2017; Lieber 2017).

Refugee status has also been generated by environmental factors. Famine, typhoons, rising sea levels, expanding deserts, chronic water shortages, and earthquakes lead to cross-border migration. **Environmental refugees** are people forced to leave their communities because of natural disasters or the effects of climate change and global warming. Overwhelmingly, this forced environmental migration is by vulnerable poor people to developing countries ill suited to accept the arrivals. Despite the exception granted temporarily to Haitian environmental refugees, the United States has no ongoing policy of granting entry to those displaced by environmental factors (Hunter, Luna, and Norton 2015).

In 2017, following through on campaign promises, President Donald Trump cited national security concerns when he issued an executive order instituting an indefinite ban on Syrian refugees and a 120-day ban on refugees from the rest of the world. The administration also indicated that once immigration resumed, the number of refugees allowed into the country would be cut in half from the levels shown in Table 4.5. At the time, most people in national surveys indicated opposition to these steps, but a significant minority, about one-third, approved of President Trump's actions. In a matter of days, courts overruled the bans, but the expectation of a significant reduction in the approval process for new refugees looms (Newport 2017).

Figure 4.5 shows the spectrum of intergroup relations with respect to the concepts discussed in this chapter.

Conclusion

The immigrant presence in the United States can often be heard on the streets and in the workplace as people speak in different languages. Witness the debates of policymakers or among school board members. These debates are not new. The United States has, throughout its history, seen intense debate over the nation's policies that bring immigrants and refugees to the country. In a sense, this debate reflects the deep value conflicts in the U.S. culture and

Figure 4.5 Spectrum of Intergroup Relations: Immigration

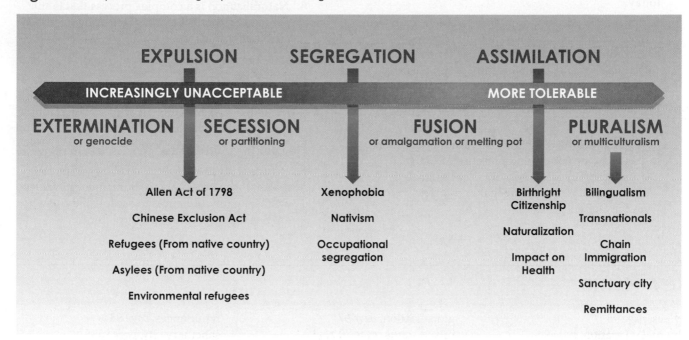

parallels the "American dilemma" identified by Swedish social economist Gunnar Myrdal (1944). One strand of our culture—epitomized by the words "Give us your tired, your poor, your huddled masses" on the Statue of Liberty—has emphasized egalitarian principles and a desire to help people in their time of need.

At the same time, however, hostility to potential immigrants and refugees—the Chinese in the 1880s, European Jews in the 1930s and 1940s, Mexicans and Muslims today—reflects not only racial, ethnic, and religious prejudice but also a desire to maintain the dominant culture of the in-group by keeping out those viewed as outsiders. The conflict between these cultural values is central to the American dilemma of the twenty-first century.

The current debate about immigration is highly charged and emotional. Some people see it in economic terms, while others see the new arrivals as a challenge to the very culture of our society. For many, the general perception is that immigration presents a problem rather than a promise for the future.

Today's concern about immigrants follows generations of people coming to settle in the United States. This immigration in the past produced a very diverse country in terms of both nationality and religion, even before the immigration of the past 60 years. Therefore, the majority of Americans today are not descended from the English, and Protestants account for fewer than half of all worshipers. This diversity of religious and ethnic groups is examined in Chapter 5.

Summary of Learning Objectives

4.1 Summarize the general patterns of immigration to the United States.

1. Immigration to the United States has changed over time from unrestricted to restricted, with the primary sending nations now in Latin America and Asia rather than in Europe.

2. Immigration began being regulated by the United States in the nineteenth century; the first

significant restriction was the Chinese Exclusion Act in 1882.

4.2 Describe how restrictionist sentiment has increased in the past 100 years.

3. Beginning in 1921, the national origins system favored northern and western European immigrants. Not until 1965 were quotas by nation largely lifted.

4.3 **Identify the concerns about immigration policy today.**

    4. The issues affecting immigration policy today include the brain drain, population growth, mixed-status households, English-language acquisition, and economic impact, as well as debates over illegal immigration.

4.4 **Discuss the scope of and issues related to illegal immigration.**

    5. Often more of a concern than legal immigration has been the continuing presence of a large number of illegal immigrants. It is estimated that about 11.1 million illegal immigrants live in the United States.

4.5 **Outline the process of naturalization.**

    6. Naturalization is a complex process that is still pursued by those abroad as well as by unauthorized immigrants.

4.6 **Explain the connection between globalization and immigration.**

    7. The worldwide integration of societies has been facilitated by transnationals who sustain multiple social relationships across borders.

4.7 **Describe the United States' policies toward refugees.**

    8. Refugees present a special challenge to policymakers, who must balance humanitarian values against an unwillingness to accept all those who are fleeing poverty and political unrest.

Key Terms

asylees, *page 98*

bilingual education, *page 90*

bilingualism, *page 90*

brain drain, *page 86*

chain immigration, *page 79*

environmental refugees, *page 100*

globalization, *page 97*

mixed status, *page 88*

nativism, *page 82*

naturalization, *page 95*

occupational segregation, *page 92*

refugees, *page 98*

remittances, *page 93*

sanctuary city, *page 95*

sinophobes, *page 82*

transnationals, *page 97*

xenophobia, *page 82*

Review Questions

1. How would you describe the general patterns of immigration to the United States over the past two centuries?

2. What were the social and economic issues when public opinion mounted against Chinese immigration to the United States in the nineteenth century?

3. How did restrictionist immigration policies develop in the twentieth century?

4. What are the contemporary social concerns about legal immigration today? Briefly describe each.

5. What are the main issues surrounding illegal immigration?

6. How can one become a naturalized citizen in the United States?

7. How is globalization furthered by immigration?

8. What principles appear to guide U.S. refugee policy?

Critical Thinking

1. What are the functions and dysfunctions of immigration?

2. Ultimately, what do you think is the major concern people have about contemporary immigration to the United States: the numbers of immigrants, their legal status, or their nationality and religion?

3. What challenge does the presence of people in the United States speaking languages other than English present for them? For schools? For the workplace? For you?

4. What is your family's immigrant root story? Consider how your ancestors arrived in the United States and also how other immigrant groups have shaped your family's past.

Chapter 5
Ethnicity, Whiteness, and Religion

Stacy Walsh Rosenstock/Alamy Stock Photo

∨ Learning Objectives

5.1 Understand what is meant by ethnicity, including Whiteness.

5.2 Describe the German American experience.

5.3 Identify the major periods of Irish American immigration.

5.4 Explain the Italian American experience.

5.5 Describe the Polish American immigration story.

5.6 Define and explain religious pluralism.

5.7 Understand court rulings on religion.

Once China and the United States established diplomatic relations in 1868, Chinese were allowed to legally immigrate to the United States. Most settled in California, but some made their way to New York City and settled around Mott Street just south of Canal Street. Italians began immigrating in large numbers around the same time, settling in several areas, including along Mulberry Street, one street over from Mott but north of Canal. For 150 years, Italian and Chinese Americans lived in adjoining densely populated neighborhoods.

The changing nature of ethnicity in America's cities was underscored when the 2010 census showed not a single Italian-born person living in New York City's Little Italy. While some people of Italian descent resided there, one was much more likely to find Chinese-born people than people of any other nationality.

By 1940, both Little Italy and Chinatown were tourist destinations. A decade later, few Italians immigrated, and those already in Little Italy began to move out. Over the following decades, the Chinese community and its Chinatown expanded, and by 1980, the Chinese population in New York's Chinatown had surpassed that of San Francisco.

The character of Little Italy (see photo to the left) changed. In 1950, half of the residents were Italian American, with 20 percent of them born in Italy. By 2000, the neighborhood was only 6 percent Italian American, with very few born in Italy. By 2010, the proportion of Italian Americans had edged down to 5 percent, with not a single Italian-born resident. While the area along Mulberry Street remains a powerful symbol to ethnic Italians, today it is defined not as a place to live but by two elements. One is food, as represented by 50 or so restaurants and cafés, as well as an occasional bakery. The other is religion.

Going to church? The Zion English Lutheran Church established in 1801 became in 1853 the Church of the Transfiguration, as the Catholic Church took over the facility to serve the poor Irish. By 1891, it served the Italian neighborhood, but a couple of generations later, Chinese Catholics began to attend, and now its congregation is almost entirely Chinese. Masses are offered in English, Mandarin, and Cantonese.

Looking for the Chinese American Planning Council? Its offices are in Little Italy. Looking for the Museum of Chinese in America? Little Italy. By 2010, the 38-block area of Little Italy and Chinatown were listed as a single historic district on the National Register of Historic Places. So is it "Arrivederci, Little Italy"?

Not yet. Near the Church of the Transfiguration, the annual 11-day festival of San Gennaro takes over several blocks and honors the patron saint of Naples—the point of origin for many of the early Italian immigrants. The festival's climactic parade runs on both Mott Street and Mulberry Street, where most of the residents are Chinese. Some of these Chinese are Catholic, but others follow the Protestant, Buddhist, or Daoist faiths.

Yes, the Italian Americans express concern over the visible Chinese American presence, but often they work with their ethnic neighbors to maintain an Italian presence. What really worries the Italians and even the much more numerous Chinese Americans about losing their ethnic neighborhood and religious institutions is the encroachment of boutiques, fancy little restaurants prepared to pay higher rents, and the dreaded arrival of a Starbucks. There is no negotiating the maintenance of ethnic ties with these agents of social change, so the Italian and Chinese Americans work together. For example, the two groups organized the annual Marco Polo Day, which honors the explorer from Venice who journeyed in the thirteenth century through Central Asia to China (Guest 2003; Krase 2006; National Park Service 2009; Roberts 2011; Tonelli 2004; Two Bridges 2017).

It's May—are you ready for the National Day of Prayer? Congress formalized this observance in 1952. While 89 percent of people in the United States believe there is a God who answers prayers, the increasing diversity of believers makes even the practice of praying increasingly contentious. Some more ecumenical prayers (those with no reference to Jesus Christ, for example, or even to a supreme being) affront many. Specific Biblical, Talmudic, or Qur'anic references have limited appeal across a nation tolerant of so many faiths. So are we too religious or not religious enough (Newport 2016)?

One person's religious or ethnic experience is unlikely to be identical to the next person's; it is this type of diversity that we consider in this chapter. Also, with this diversity we consider how one goes about "fitting in" to a new society. First we will consider the social canvas against which this diversity is painted—Whiteness.

Unpacking Ethnicity

5.1 Understand what is meant by ethnicity, including Whiteness.

Race and ethnicity are discussed all the time in everyday speech, but, as we have seen, they are exceedingly complex terms. Race is socially constructed, as we learned in Chapter 1. Sometimes we seem to define race in a clear-cut manner. A descendant of a Pilgrim is White, for example. But sometimes race is more ambiguous: Children of an African American and Vietnamese American union are biracial, mixed, or whatever they come to be seen as by others. Our recognition that race is socially constructed has sparked a renewed interest in what it means to be White in the United States.

It has also generated interest in what we mean by *ethnicity*. Can we really see "European Americans" as a distinct, identifiable group? Probably not, but we do have ways to differentiate one group from another, often by using nationality terms like "German Americans" (even though Germany as we know it dates back only to about the 1830s). Two aspects of the White race and their ethnic divisions are useful to consider: the historical creation of Whiteness and how contemporary White people may reflect this identity.

Studying Whiteness

When English immigrants established themselves as the political founders of the United States, they also came to define what it meant to be White. Other groups that today are regarded as White—such as Irish, Germans, Norwegians, or Swedes—were not always considered White in the eyes of the English. Differences in language and religious worship, as well as past allegiance to a European king other than the English monarch, meant these groups were seen not so much as Whites in the Western Hemisphere but more as nationals of their home country who happened to reside in North America.

The old distrust in Europe, where, for example, the English viewed the Irish as socially and culturally inferior, continued on this side of the Atlantic Ocean. Writing from England, Karl Marx reported that the average English worker looked down on the Irish the way poor Whites in the U.S. South looked down on Black people (Ignatiev 1994, 1995; Roediger 1994).

As European immigrants and their descendants assimilated to the English and distanced themselves from other oppressed groups such as American Indians and African Americans, they came to be viewed as White rather than as part of a particular "alien" culture. Writer Noel Ignatiev (1994:84), contrasting being White with being Polish, argues, "Whiteness is nothing but an expression of race privilege." This strong statement argues that being White, as opposed to being Black or Asian, is characterized by being a member of the dominant group. Although it may often be invisible, Whiteness is aggressively embraced and defended (Giroux 1997).

In general, White people do not think of themselves as a race or have a conscious racial identity. A White racial identity emerges only when filling out a form asking for self-designation of race or when Whites are culturally or socially surrounded by people who are not White.

However, "Whiteness" is sometimes viewed negatively. One study examined teachers at a predominantly Latino and Black school with a White minority student population. Teachers viewed White students (who would seem to be "privileged") more negatively than poor minority students if the White students came from a lower-class background ("trailer trash") (Morris 2005).

Many immigrants who were not "White on arrival" had to "become White" in a process long forgotten by today's White Americans. The long-documented transparent racial divide that engulfed the South during slavery let us ignore how Whiteness was constructed.

Therefore, contemporary White Americans give little thought to "being White." Consequently, there is little interest in studying "Whiteness" or "being White" except that being White is "not being Black." Unlike non-Whites, who are much more likely to take orders from Whites and who see Whites as leading figures in the mass media, Whites are in the position of not being reminded of their Whiteness.

Unlike racial minorities, Whites usually downplay the importance of their racial identity, although they are willing to receive the advantages that come from being White. Advocating a "color-blind" or "race-neutral" outlook permits the privilege of Whiteness to prevail (Bonilla-Silva 2002; Feagin and Cobas 2008; Yancey 2003).

New scholarly interest seeks to study Whiteness, but not from the vantage point of a White supremacist. Rather, focusing on White people as a race or on what it means to be White today goes beyond any definition that implies superiority over non-Whites. It also is recognized that "being White" is not the same experience for all Whites, any more than "being Asian American" or "being Black" is the same for all Asian Americans or all Blacks. Ignatiev observes that studying Whiteness is a necessary stage in the desired "abolition of whiteness"—just as, in Marxist analysis, class-consciousness is a necessary stage in the desired abolition of class. By confronting and understanding Whiteness, society grasps the all-encompassing power held by the socially constructed White race (Lewis 2004; McKinney 2003; Roediger 2006).

White privilege, introduced in Chapter 2, refers to the rights granted as a benefit or favor of being White and can be an element of Whiteness. Although some Whites consciously minimize the exercise of this privilege, it is difficult to ignore White privilege when a White person is more likely than not to see national leaders, celebrities, and role models who also are White. For every Barack Obama and Jesse Jackson, there are hundreds of movers and shakers who are White. For example, many White people champion the cause of the HBCUs (historically Black colleges and universities), conveniently ignoring that those schools exist because of thousands of HWCUs (historically White colleges and universities) (Bonilla-Silva 2012).

Being White may mean you experience privilege, but it does not necessarily mean that White people are comfortable in "owning" this privilege. In 2017, the public high school in the affluent town of Westport, Connecticut (which is over 90 percent White) asked its students to reflect on the role of White privilege in their lives. The students were largely fine with this assignment of a 1,000-word essay; for example, one senior felt the discussion was important "because on a daily basis, we really aren't exposed to much diversity within our town." Yet the community as a whole was less comfortable with the topic, even though Westport could generally be viewed as liberal, having just voted by a factor of 2–1 for Hillary Clinton over Donald Trump. Some residents indicated their belief that "[saying there is] white privilege was just as racist as saying there is black privilege." Others felt that having the high school discuss the topic would suggest to outsiders that Westport was throwing up "barricades" to others. In short: Whiteness is a sensitive topic.

The people of Westport may not have been comforted when the 2017 winning essay, "The Colors of Privilege," was announced. In his essay, a fifteen-year-old African American sophomore wrote about his experience of moving to Westport from New York City with his family six years earlier. He recounted a series of slights he had experienced. For example, at track practice, some of his White friends were discussing the challenge of getting into their preferred college. Out of nowhere, one said, "Chet, you don't have this problem because you're black." The essayist recalled being stunned and mumbling something instead of firing back, "Your parents are third-generation Princeton and your father runs a hedge fund and yet you think my ride is free?" The second-prize winner, a White student, wrote of recognizing White privilege when seeing how his adopted brother from Ethiopia was treated (Brennan 2017; Melia 2017; Victor 2017).

When race is articulated or emphasized for Whites, it is more likely to be seen as threatening to Whites than as allowing them to embrace their own race or national roots with pride. Behavioral economists Michael Norton and Samuel Sommers (2011) found that Whites view race as a zero-sum game—that is, decreases in bias against African Americans over the past 60 years are associated with increases in what they perceive as bias against Whites. While Norton and Sommers see anti-Black bias as more prevalent today than anti-White feeling in society, their analysis shows that, in the minds of the White respondents, the two biases are coming closer together. In contrast, Black respondents in the study also saw a marked decline in anti-Black bias during the same period but perceived only a modest increase in anti-White feelings. While Norton and Sommers' research deals only with perception of reality, it does suggest that race, and not just that of non-Whites, influences one's perception of society.

Rediscovering Ethnicity

Robert Park (1950:205), a prominent early sociologist, wrote in 1913, "A Pole, Lithuanian, or Norwegian cannot be distinguished, in the second generation, from an American, born of native parents." At one time, sociologists saw the end of ethnicity as nearly a foregone conclusion. W. Lloyd Warner and Leo Srole (1945) wrote in their often-cited *Yankee City* series that the future of ethnic groups seemed to be limited in the United States and that they would be quickly absorbed. Oscar Handlin's *The Uprooted* (1951) told of the destruction of immigrant values and their replacement by American culture. Although Handlin was among the pioneers in investigating ethnicity, assimilation was the dominant theme in his work.

Many writers have shown an almost fervent hope that ethnicity will vanish. For some time, sociologists treated the persistence of ethnicity as dysfunctional because it meant continuing old values that interfered with the allegedly superior new values. For example, holding onto one's language delayed entry into the larger labor market and the upward social mobility it afforded. Ethnicity was expected to disappear, not only because of assimilation but also because aspirations to higher social class and status demanded that it vanish. It was assumed that one could not be ethnic and middle class, much less affluent.

THE PRINCIPLE OF THIRD-GENERATION INTEREST   Historian Marcus Hansen's (1952) **principle of third-generation interest** was an early exception to the assimilationist approach to White ethnic groups. Simply stated, Hansen maintained that in the third generation—the grandchildren of the original immigrants—ethnic interest and awareness would increase. According to Hansen, "What the son wishes to forget, the grandson wishes to remember."

Hansen's principle has been tested several times since it was first put forth. John Goering (1971), in interviewing Irish and Italian Catholics, found that ethnicity was more important to members of the third generation than to the immigrants themselves. Similarly, Mary Waters (1990)—in her interviews with White ethnics living in suburban areas of San Jose, California, and Philadelphia, Pennsylvania—observed that many grandchildren wanted to study their ancestors' language, even though it would be a foreign language to them. They also expressed interest in learning more of their ethnic group's history and a desire to visit their homeland. However, it would be incorrect to assume that White ethnics are expressing or even aware of their ethnicity in very dramatic ways. Old European ethnicity is becoming more and more invisible except in largely ceremonial ways (explored later in this chapter) (Gans 2014).

Like Whites of European descent, many members of third and successive generations of Asian and Latin American immigrants are showing renewed interest in their native languages. The very languages they avoided or even scorned themselves as children, they now want to learn as young adults. "Heritage language" programs have become increasingly common. Even when the descendants may easily communicate in their native language in everyday life, they often lack the language tools necessary for more sophisticated vocabulary or to read their grandparents' language easily (Nawa 2011).

THE ETHNIC PARADOX   While many nearly assimilated Whites are rediscovering their ethnicity (i.e., the principle of third-generation interest), others are at least publicly acknowledging their ethnicity from time to time (i.e., symbolic ethnicity, discussed below). Yet research confirms that preserving elements of one's ethnicity may advance economic success and further societal acceptance.

The term **ethnic paradox** refers to the maintenance of one's ethnic ties in a manner that can assist with assimilation into the larger society. Immigrant youth and adults who maintain their ethnicity tend to have more success as indicated by health measures, educational attainment, and lower incidence of behavioral problems such as delinquency and truancy. We will revisit ethnic paradox in Chapter 9 when we consider how Mexican immigrants and their children tend to be healthier as a group than the successive generations in the United States.

Researchers typically measure ethnic maintenance by facility in the mother language (not just conversational or "street" use) and living with others of the same ethnic background. These clear ethnic ties are not an automatic recipe for success. For example, residing with co-ethnics can lead to exploitation in neighborhoods where people steer those of their own ethnicity into dead-end, poor-paying, and even unhealthy working conditions. Yet for many ethnics, enclaves offer a refuge, sort of a halfway house, between two different cultures. Language maintenance is often critical to being literate and comfortable with English (Desmond and Kubrin 2009).

In the Speaking Out feature, sociologist Tomás Jiménez from Stanford University considers the role of new arrivals in shaping the U.S. national identity and how immigrants manage life in a new society.

SYMBOLIC ETHNICITY   Observers comment on both the evidence of assimilation and the signs of ethnic identity that support a pluralistic view of society. How can both exist simultaneously?

First, the visible evidence of **symbolic ethnicity** might lead us to exaggerate the persistence of ethnic ties among White Americans. According to sociologist Herbert Gans (1979, 2014), ethnicity today increasingly involves symbols of ethnicity, such as eating ethnic food, acknowledging ceremonial holidays such as St. Patrick's Day, and supporting specific

Speaking Out

The Next Americans

Tomás Jiménez

How immigrants and their descendants see themselves will change over time, and they will simultaneously transform many aspects of what it means to be an American. This is undoubtedly an uncomfortable process, fraught with tension between newcomers and established Americans that can occasionally become explosive. But the real issue is whether the United States can provide opportunities for upward mobility so that immigrants can, in turn, fortify what is most essential to our nation's identity.

History is instructive on whether immigrants will create a messy patchwork of ethnicities in the United States. About a century ago, a tide of southern and eastern European immigrants arriving on our shores raised fears similar to those we hear today. Then, as now, Americans worried that the newcomers were destroying American identity. Many were certain that Catholic immigrants would help the pope rule the United States from Rome, and that immigrants from southern Europe would contaminate the American gene pool.

None of this came to pass, of course. The pope has no political say in American affairs, the United States is still a capitalist democracy, and there is nothing wrong with the American gene pool. The fact that these fears never materialized is often cited as proof that European-origin immigrants and their descendants successfully assimilated into an American societal monolith.

However, as sociologists Richard Alba and Victor Nee point out, much of the American identity, as we know it today, was shaped by previous waves of immigrants. For instance, they note that the Christian tradition of the Christmas tree and the leisure Sunday made their way into the American mainstream because German immigrants and their descendants brought these traditions with them. Where religion was concerned, Protestantism was the clear marker of the nonsecular mainstream. But because of the assimilation of millions of Jews and Catholics, we today commonly refer to an American "Judeo-Christian tradition," a far more encompassing notion of American religious identity than the one envisioned in the past....

Even in Los Angeles County, where 36 percent of the population is foreign-born and more than half speak a language other than English at home, English is not losing out in the long run. According to a recent study by social scientists Rubén Rumbaut, Douglas Massey, and Frank Bean, published in the *Population and Development Review,* the use of non-English languages virtually disappears among

Tomás Jiménez

Photo by Randy Michaud

nearly all U.S.-born children of immigrants in the country. Spanish shows more staying power among the U.S.-born children and grandchildren of Mexican immigrants, which is not surprising given that the size of the Spanish-speaking population provides near-ubiquitous access to the language. But the survival of Spanish among U.S.-born descendants of Mexican immigrants does not come at the expense of their ability to speak English and, more strikingly, English overwhelms Spanish-language use among the grandchildren of these immigrants.

An equally telling sign of how much immigrants and their children are becoming "American" is how different they have become from those in their ethnic homelands. Virtually all of today's immigrants stay connected to their countries of origin. They send money to family members who remain behind. Relatively inexpensive air, rail, and bus travel and the availability of cheap telecommunication and e-mail enable them to stay in constant contact, and dual citizenship allows their political voices to be heard from abroad. These enduring ties might lead to the conclusion that continuity between here and there threatens loyalty to the Stars and Stripes.

But ask any immigrant or their children about a recent visit to their country of origin, and they are likely to tell you how American they felt. The family and friends they visit quickly recognize the prodigal children's tastes for American styles, their American accents, and their declining cultural familiarity with life in the ethnic homeland—all telltale signs that they've Americanized. As sociologist David Fitzgerald puts it, their assimilation into American society entails a good deal of "dissimilation" from the countries the immigrants left behind.

American identity is absorbing something quite significant from immigrants and being changed by them. Language, food, entertainment, and holiday traditions are palpable aspects of American culture on which immigrants today, as in the past, are leaving their mark. Our everyday lexicon is sprinkled with Spanish words. We are now just as likely to grab a burrito as a burger. Hip-hop is tinged with South Asian rhythms. And Chinese New Year and Cinco de Mayo are taking their places alongside St. Patrick's Day as widely celebrated American ethnic holidays.

Source: Jiménez, Tomás R. 2007. The Next Americans. *Los Angeles Times* (May 27): M1, M7. Used with permission.

political issues or issues confronting the old country. One example was the push in 1998 by Irish Americans to convince state legislatures to make it compulsory that public schools teach about the Irish potato famine—a significant factor in Irish immigration to the United States. This symbolic ethnicity may be more visible, but it does not interfere with what people do, read, or say, or even whom they befriend or marry. By one analysis, only an estimated 7 percent of White non-Hispanics self-express a significant sense of ethnicity (Scully 2012; Torkelson and Hartmann 2010).

The ethnicity of the twenty-first century, as embraced by English-speaking Whites, is largely symbolic. It does not include active involvement in ethnic activities or participation in ethnic-related organizations. In fact, sizable proportions of White ethnics have gained large-scale entry into almost all clubs, cliques, and fraternal groups. Such acceptance is a key indicator of assimilation. Ethnicity has become increasingly peripheral to the lives of the ethnic groups' members. Although today's White ethnics may not relinquish their ethnic identity entirely, other identities become more important.

Second, the ethnicity that exists may be more a result of living in the United States than of importing practices from the past or the old country. Many so-called ethnic foods or celebrations, for example, began in the United States. The persistence of ethnic consciousness, then, may not depend on foreign birth, a distinctive language, and a unique way of life. Instead, it may reflect the experiences in the United States of a unique group that developed a cultural tradition distinct from that of the mainstream. For example, in Poland, the *szlachta*, or landed gentry, rarely mixed socially with the peasant class. In the United States, however, even with those associations still fresh, *szlachta* and peasants interacted together in social organizations as they settled in concentrated communities segregated physically and socially from other communities (Lopata 1994; Winter 2008).

Third, maintaining ethnicity can be a critical step toward successful assimilation. This ethnic paradox facilitates full entry into the dominant culture. The ethnic community may give its members not only a useful financial boost but also the psychological strength and positive self-esteem that will allow them to compete effectively in a larger society. Thus, we may witness people participating actively in their ethnic enclave while trying to cross the bridge into the wider community (Lal 1995).

Therefore, ethnicity provides continuity with the past in the form of an effective or emotional tie. The significance of this sense of belonging cannot be emphasized enough. Whether reinforced by distinctive behavior or by what Milton Gordon (1964) called a sense of *peoplehood*, ethnicity is an effective, functional source of cohesion. Proximity to fellow ethnics is not necessary for a person to maintain social cohesion and in-group identity. Fraternal organizations or sports-related groups can preserve associations between ethnics who are separated geographically. Members of ethnic groups may even maintain feelings of in-group solidarity after leaving ethnic communities in the central cities for the suburban fringe.

We will now consider four of the many White ethnic groups—German, Irish, Italian, and Polish Americans—that have expressed and to different degrees continue to express their ethnic identity in the United States today.

The German Americans

5.2 Describe the German American experience.

Germany is the largest single source of ancestry of people in the United States today, even exceeding the continents of Africa or Asia. Yet except in a few big-city neighborhood enclaves, the explicit presence of German culture seems largely relegated to bratwurst, pretzels, and Kris Kringle.

Settlement Patterns

In the late 1700s, the newly formed United States experienced the arrival of a number of religious dissenters (including the Amish) from Germany who were attracted by the proclamation of religious freedom as well as prospects for economic advancement. At the time

Figure 5.1 Immigration from Germany, Ireland, Italy, and Poland
Note: Immigration after 1925 from Northern Ireland is not included. No separate data are included for Poland from 1900 to 1920.

SOURCE: Data from Office of Immigration Statistics 2009: Table 2.

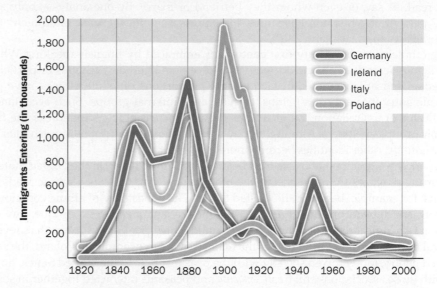

of the American Revolution, immigrants from Germany accounted for about one in eight White residents. German colonial subjects split their loyalty between the revolutionaries and the British, but they were united in their optimistic view of the opportunities the New World would present.

Although Pennsylvania was the center of early settlements, German Americans, like virtually all other Europeans, moved west (to Ohio, Michigan, and beyond), where land was abundant. In many isolated communities, they established churches and parochial schools, and, in some instances, ethnic enclaves that sometimes spoke of creating "New Germanys."

Beginning in the 1830s through 1890, Germans represented at least one-quarter of the immigrants, ensuring their destiny in the settlement of the United States (Figure 5.1). Their major urban presence was in Milwaukee, Chicago, Cleveland, Detroit, and Cincinnati.

Early in the history of America, German immigrant cultural influence was apparent. Although the new United States never voted on making German the national language, publications of the proceedings of the Continental Congress were published in German and English. Yet even in those early years, the fear of foreigners—that is, non-Anglos—prevented Germans from ever getting equal footing with the English.

German Americans, then representing about 10 percent of the population, established bilingual programs in many public schools, but the rise of Germany as a military foe in the twentieth century ended that movement (Harzig 2008; Nelsen 1973).

German Americans in the Twenty-First Century

In 1901, the German-American National Alliance (Deutsche-Amerikanischer National-Bund) was founded to speak for all Germans in the United States—especially urban Protestant middle-class German Americans. As time passed, it sought to commemorate Germans' contributions to the nation's development but also sought to block prohibition against alcohol. With the rise of German military power, many German Americans argued for U.S. neutrality. But these efforts ended quickly, and the organization disbanded after the United States declared war on Germany in 1917.

With World War I and especially the rise of the Nazi era and the war years of the 1930s and 1940s, most German Americans sought to distance themselves from the politics in their homeland. There were anti-German incidents of harassment and intimidation. About 11,000 German Americans (out of 5 million) were interned. Internment refers to World War II-era confinement, within the United States, of people of certain nationalities who by virtue of their national origin were regarded as less trustworthy. However, the scope of German internment did not come close to the internment experienced by Japanese Americans. By comparison, many more German Americans enlisted in the military and played important roles in the war effort (including President Dwight Eisenhower, whose ancestors immigrated to Pennsylvania from Germany in 1741).

Overall, German Americans made the group transition into core society. Indeed, Horace Kallen, who popularized the term *pluralism,* held up German Americans as a success in finding a place in the United States. With the end of wartime tensions, German Americans moved from having multiple identities that included being somewhat marginalized as "Germans" to an identity of "American" and, less explicitly, White (Casey 2015; Russell 2015).

By the latter half of the twentieth century, the animosity toward Germany seemed a part of the distant past. Germany and its people became stalwart friends of the United States, as reflected in statements made by President John F. Kennedy in Berlin in 1963 and President Ronald Reagan in 1987. Both spoke of the U.S. commitment to uniting Germany, and presidential candidate Barack Obama in 2008 spoke in Berlin of a united Europe. When Indian Prime Minister Narendra Modi visited in the United States in 2016, the Indian American community was visibly overjoyed, but when German Chancellor Angela Merkel paid President Donald Trump a state visit in 2017, German America hardly paid notice.

In the past ten years, immigration from Germany, a country of 82 million, has fluctuated between 6,000 and 10,000 annually. The steady immigration for decades placed Germany in the 2000 census as the tenth-largest source of foreign-born residents today, with more than 700,000 (only about 170,000 behind Cuba and Korea). Yet the broad dispersion of these immigrants and their bilingual capability means the numbers are insufficient to create (or re-create) a German cultural presence. Rather, today's German American community is characterized by postwar and historical ties that have long since overshadowed the lingering bitterness of World Wars I and II (Harzig 2008; Office of Immigration Statistics 2016).

Famous German Americans include industrialist John D. Rockefeller, General John Pershing, baseball players Babe Ruth and Lou Gehrig, celebrity Paris Hilton, and actors Sandra Bullock and Katherine Heigl.

Chicago History Museum/Archive Photos/Getty Images

Anti-German sentiment spread in the United States during World War I, escalating dramatically after the United States entered the war in April 1917. A wave of verbal and physical attacks on German Americans was accompanied by a campaign to repress German culture. In this photograph from 1917, a group of children stand in front of an anti-German sign posted in Chicago. As the sign suggests, some people in the United States questioned the loyalty of their German American neighbors.

The Irish Americans

5.3   Identify the major periods of Irish American immigration.

The Irish presence in the United States stretches back to the 1600s and reflects a diversity based on time of entry, settlement area, and religion. Irish Americans have been visible both in a positive way in terms of playing a central role in American life and in a negative way at certain historical periods, being victimized as so many other immigrant groups have been.

Irish Immigration

The Roman Catholics among the early Irish immigrants were a diverse group. Some were members of the privileged classes seeking even greater prosperity. Protestant settlers of all national backgrounds, including those coming from Ireland, were united in their hatred of Catholicism. In most of the colonies, Catholics could not practice their faith openly and either struggled inwardly or converted to Anglicanism (or both). Other Roman Catholics and some Protestants came from Europe as an alternative to prison or after signing articles of indenture and arriving bound to labor for periods of three to five years, and sometimes as long as seven years (Meagher 2005).

The American Revolution (1765–1783) temporarily stopped the flow of immigration, but deteriorating economic conditions in Ireland soon spurred even greater movement to North America. British officials, by making passage to the newly formed republic of the United States expensive, diverted many immigrants to British North America (Canada). Yet the number of Irish immigrants to the United States remained significant and, although still primarily Protestant, drew from a broader spectrum of Ireland both economically and geographically.

Many people mistakenly overlook this early immigration and begin with Irish immigration during the Great Famine (1845–1852). Yet the Irish were the largest group after the English among immigrants during the colonial period. The historical emphasis on the famine immigrants is understandable, given the role that the famine played in Ireland and its impetus for the massive transfer of population from Ireland to the United States.

In 1845, a fungus wiped out the potato crop of Ireland, as well as that of much of western Europe and even coastal America. Potatoes were central to the lives of the Irish, and the devastating starvation did not begin to recede until 1851. Mortality was high, especially among the poor and in the more agricultural areas of the island. To escape starvation and death, some 2 million Irish fled, mostly to England, but then many continued on to the United States. From 1841 through 1890, more than 3.2 million Irish arrived in the United States (Figure 5.1).

These new immigrants fleeing the old country were much more likely to consist of families rather than single men. The arrival of entire households and extended kinship networks increased significantly the rapid formation of Irish social organizations in the United States. This large influx of immigrants led to the creation of ethnic neighborhoods like those described at the beginning of this chapter, complete with parochial schools and parish churches serving as focal points. Fraternal organizations such as the Ancient Order of Hibernians, corner saloons, local political organizations, and Irish nationalist groups seeking the ouster of Britain from Ireland rounded out neighborhood social life in the United States.

Even in the best of times, the lives of the famine Irish would have been challenging in the United States, but they arrived at a very difficult time. Nativist—that is, anti-Catholic and anti-immigrant—movements were already emerging and being embraced by politicians. Antagonism was not limited to harsh words. From 1834 to 1854, mob violence against Catholics across the country led to death, the burning of a Boston convent, the destruction of a Catholic church and the homes of Catholics, and the use of Marines and state militia to bring peace to American cities as far west as St. Louis.

In retrospect, the reception given to the Irish is not difficult to understand. Many immigrated after the potato crop failure and famine in Ireland. They fled not so much to a better life as from almost certain death. The Irish Catholics brought with them a celibate clergy, who struck the New England aristocracy as strange and reawakened old religious hatreds. The Irish were worse than Blacks, according to the dominant Whites, because unlike the slaves and even the freed Blacks, who "knew their place," the Irish did not suffer their mistreatment in silence. Employers balanced minorities by judiciously mixing immigrant groups to prevent unified action by the laborers. For the most part, nativist efforts only led the foreign-born to emphasize their ties to Europe.

Mostly of peasant backgrounds, the arriving Irish were ill prepared to compete successfully for jobs in the city. Their children found it much easier to improve their occupational status over that of their fathers, and they experienced upward mobility in their own lifetimes (Miller 2014: 268–270).

Becoming White

Ireland had a long antislavery tradition, including practices that prohibited Irish trade in English slaves. Some 60,000 Irish signed an address in 1841, petitioning Irish Americans to join the abolitionist movement in the United States. Many Irish Americans already opposed to slavery applauded the appeal, but they were soon drowned out by fellow immigrants who denounced or questioned the petition's authenticity.

The Irish immigrants, subjected to derision and menial jobs, sought to separate themselves from the even lower classes, particularly Black Americans and especially slaves. It was not altogether clear that the Irish were considered "White" during the antebellum (pre–Civil War) period. Irish character was rigidly cast in negative racial typology. Although the shared experiences of oppression could have led Irish Americans to ally with Black Americans, they grasped for Whiteness at the margins of their lives in the United States. Direct competition was not common between the two groups. For example, in 1855, Irish immigrants made up 87 percent of New York City's unskilled laborers, whereas free Blacks accounted for only 3 percent (Greeley 1981; Ignatiev 1995; Roediger 1994).

As Irish immigration continued in the latter part of the nineteenth century until Irish independence in 1921, Irish Americans began to see themselves favorably in comparison to the initial waves of Italian, Polish, and Slovak Roman Catholic immigrants. Irish Americans began to assume more leadership positions in politics and labor unions. Loyalty to the church still played a major role. By 1910, the priesthood was the professional occupation of choice for second-generation Irish American men. Irish women were more likely than their German and English immigrant counterparts to become schoolteachers. In time, Irish Americans' occupational profiles diversified, and they began to experience slow advancement and gradually were welcomed into the White working class as their identity as "White" overcame any status as "immigrant."

For many Irish Americans, a St. Patrick's Day parade is the most visible expression of Irish symbolic ethnicity during the entire year.

With mobility came social class distinctions within Irish America. The immigrants and their children who began to move into the more affluent urban areas were derogatorily referred to as the "lace-curtain Irish." Meanwhile, the lower-class Irish immigrants they left behind were referred to as the "shanty Irish." But as immigration from Ireland slowed and upward mobility quickened, fewer and fewer Irish qualified as the poor cousins of their predecessors. Furthermore, Irish Americans came to play a leadership role in the Roman Catholic Church in the United States. The Irish dominance persisted long after other ethnic groups swelled the ranks of the faithful (Fallows 1979; Lee and Bean 2007; Lee and Casey 2006).

The Contemporary Picture

By 2015, 32.7 million people identified themselves as having Irish ancestry—second only to German ancestry and more than five times the current population of Ireland itself. Massachusetts has the largest concentration of Irish Americans, with 24 percent of the state indicating Irish ancestry.

Irish immigration today is relatively slight, accounting for perhaps one out of 1,000 legal arrivals until 2010, when it climbed to 2,800 because of tough economic times in Ireland. About 122,000 people in the United States today were born in Ireland. Today's Irish American typically enjoys the symbolic ethnicity of food, dance, and music. Gaelic language instruction is limited to fewer than 30 colleges. Visibility as a collective ethnic group is greatest with the annual St. Patrick's Day celebrations, when everyone seems to be Irish, or with the occasional fervent nationalism aimed at curtailing Great Britain's role in Northern Ireland, which is part of the United Kingdom rather than part of the Republic of Ireland. Yet some stereotypes remain concerning excessive drinking, despite available data indicating that alcoholism rates are no higher and are sometimes lower among people of Irish ancestry compared to descendants of other European immigrant groups (Bureau of the Census 2011b; Chazan and Tomson 2011).

St. Patrick's Day celebrations offer an example of how ethnic identity evolves over time. The Feast of St. Patrick has a long history, but public celebrations with parties, concerts, and parades originated in the United States and were then exported to Ireland in the latter part of the twentieth century. Even today, the large Irish American population often defines what authentic Irish is globally. For example, participants in Irish step dancing in the United States have developed such clout in international competitions that they have come to define many aspects of cultural expression, much to the consternation of the Irish in Ireland (Bureau of the Census 2009b; Hassrick 2007).

Well-known Irish Americans can be found in all arenas of American society, including celebrity chef Bobby Flay, songwriter and musician Kurt Cobain, comedian Conan O'Brien, and author Frank McCourt, as well as the political dynasties of the Kennedys in Massachusetts and the Daleys in Chicago. Reflecting growing rates of intermarriage, Irish America also includes singer Mariah Carey (her mother is Irish, her father African American and Venezuelan). Furthermore, on an official state visit to Ireland during his presidency, Barack Obama made a side trip to the village of Moneygall. President Obama's great-great-grandfather Falmouth Kearney, a shoemaker's son, left Moneygall for the United States in 1850.

The Irish were the first immigrant group to encounter prolonged organized resistance. However, strengthened by continued immigration, facility with the English language, strong community and family networks, and familiarity with representative politics, Irish Americans became an integral part of the United States.

The Italian Americans

5.4   Explain the Italian American experience.

Although each European country's immigration to the United States has its own social history, the case of Italians, though not typical of every nationality, offers insight into the White ethnic experience. Italians immigrated even during the colonial period, coming from a highly differentiated homeland, because Italian states were not unified as one nation and escaped foreign domination until 1848.

Early Immigration

Italian Americans played prominent roles during the American Revolution and the early days of the republic. Mass immigration began in the 1880s, peaking in the first 20 years of the twentieth century, when Italians accounted for one-fourth of European immigration (see Figure 5.1).

Italian immigration was concentrated not only in time but also by geography. The majority of the immigrants were landless peasants from rural southern Italy, the Mezzogiorno. Although many people in the United States assume that Italians are a nationality with a single culture, this is not true either culturally or economically. The Italian people recognize multiple geographic divisions within Italy reflecting sharp cultural distinctions. Immigrants brought these divisions with them to the New World.

Many Italians, especially in the early years of mass immigration in the nineteenth century, received their jobs through an ethnic labor contractor, the *padrone*. Similar arrangements have been used by Asian, Hispanic, and Greek immigrants, where the labor contractors, most often immigrants, have mastered sufficient English to mediate for their compatriots. Exploitation was common within the padrone system through kickbacks, provision of inadequate housing, and withholding of wages. By World War I, 90 percent of Italian girls and 99 percent of Italian boys in New York City were leaving school at age 14 to work, but by that time, Italian Americans were sufficiently fluent in English to seek out work on their own, and the padrone system disappeared. Still, by comparison to the Irish, the Italians in the United States were slower to accept formal schooling as essential to success (Sassler 2006).

Along with manual labor, the Catholic Church was a very important part of Italian Americans' lives at that time. Yet they found little comfort in a Catholic Church dominated by an earlier immigrant group: the Irish. The traditions were different; weekly church attendance for Italian Americans was overshadowed by the religious aspects of the *feste* (or festivals) held throughout the year in honor of saints (the Irish viewed the *feste* as practically a form of paganism). These initial adjustment problems were overcome with the establishment of ethnic parishes, a pattern repeated by other non-Irish immigrant groups. Thus, parishes would be staffed by Italian priests, sometimes imported for that purpose. Although the hierarchy of the church adjusted more slowly, Italian Americans were increasingly able to feel at home in their local parish church. Today, more than 70 percent of Italian Americans identify themselves as Roman Catholics (Luconi 2001).

Over the first few generations in the United States, Italian Americans rose up through the social classes largely by acquiring skills in low-skilled occupations rather than acquiring advanced degrees and entering professions. Eventually they began to achieve success in wine and fruit growing and became entrepreneurs of retail outlets in the urban Northeast and Midwest (Llosa 2013).

Constructing Identity

As assimilation proceeded, Italian Americans began to construct a social identity as a nationality group rather than viewing themselves in terms of their native village or province. As Figure 5.2 shows, over time, Italian Americans shed old identities for new ones. As immigration from Italy declined, the descendants' ties became more nationalistic. (This move from local or regional to national identity was followed by the same pattern among Irish and Greek Americans.) In general, early Italian immigrants were not treated well. For example, in turn-of-the-century New Orleans, Italian Americans established special ties with the Black community because both groups were marginalized in Southern society. Gradually, Italian Americans became White and enjoyed all the privileges that came with it. Today, it would be inconceivable to imagine that Italian Americans of New Orleans would reach out to the African American community as their natural allies on social and political issues (Guglielmo and Salerno 2003; Luconi 2001; Steinberg 2007:126).

A controversial aspect of the Italian American experience involves organized crime, as typified by Al Capone (1899–1947). Arriving in the United States poor and uneducated, Italians lived in decaying, crime-ridden neighborhoods. For a small segment of these immigrants, crime was a significant means of upward social mobility. In effect, entering and leading criminal activity was one aspect of assimilation, though not a positive one. Complaints linking ethnicity and crime actually began in colonial times with talk about the criminally inclined Irish and Germans, and they continue with contemporary stereotyping of groups such as Colombian drug dealers and Vietnamese street gangs. The image of Italians as criminals has persisted from Prohibition-era gangsters to the view of Mob families today. It is not at all surprising that Italian Americans have organized groups to counter such negative images.

The fact that Italians often are characterized as criminal, even in the mass media, is an example of **respectable bigotry** toward White ethnics. The persistence of linking Italians, or any other minority group, with crime probably is attributable to attempts to explain a problem by citing a single cause: the presence of perceived undesirables. Many Italian Americans still see their image tied to old stereotypes. A 2001 survey of Italian American teenagers found that 39 percent felt the media presented their ethnic group as criminal or gang members and 34 percent as restaurant workers (Girardelli 2004; IAAMS 2009; National Italian American Foundation 2006; Parrillo 2008).

The immigration of Italians was slowed by the national origins system, described in Chapter 4. As Italian Americans settled permanently, the mutual aid societies that had grown

---

Figure 5.2 Constructing Social Identity Among Italian Immigrants

Over time, Italian Americans moved from seeing themselves in terms of their provincial or village identity to their national identity, at which point they successfully became indistinguishable from other Whites.

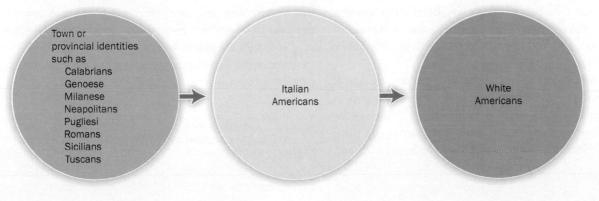

up in the 1920s to provide basic social services began to dissolve. More slowly, Italian Americans came to value education as a means of upward mobility. Even becoming more educated did not ward off prejudice, however. In 1930, for example, President Herbert Hoover rebuked Fiorello La Guardia, then an Italian American member of Congress from New York City, stating that "the Italians are predominantly our murderers and bootleggers" and recommending that La Guardia "go back to where you belong" because "like a lot of other foreign spawn, you do not appreciate this country which supports you and tolerates you" (Baltzell 1964:30).

Although U.S. troops, including 500,000 Italian Americans, battled Italy during World War II, some hatred and sporadic violence emerged against Italian Americans and their property. However, these hate crimes were not limited to actions against individuals. The federal government confined Italian Americans in specific areas of California by virtue of their ethnicity alone, and 10,000 were relocated from coastal areas. In addition, 1,800 Italian Americans who were citizens of Italy were placed in an internment camp in Montana. The internees were eventually freed on Columbus Day 1942 as President Roosevelt lobbied the Italian American community to gain full support for the impending land invasion of Italy (Department of Justice 2001; Fox 1990).

In the Research Focus, we consider how social scientists examine the economic experience of these early Italian immigrants and their children and compare it to the Mexican experience today.

Research Focus

Immigrants: Yesterday and Today

Anyone thinking about the future of today's immigrants might reflect back on the experiences of those who came a century ago. It is widely agreed that, despite difficult times and often harsh treatment by those already here, the immigrants of the late nineteenth and early twentieth century ultimately fared well. Certainly their descendants are doing well today. So can we generalize from this experience to today's immigrants?

Sociologist Joel Perlmann and other scholars have considered the experience of immigrants from southern, central, and eastern Europe who were predominantly low-skilled workers. A significant number of these workers were Italian and Poles. Based on his analysis and that of other sociologists, we find that these early immigrant workers earned typically only between 60 and 88 percent of the wages earned by nonimmigrant Whites in the same occupations.

Contrary to a commonly held belief, these immigrants did not end up in well-paying jobs in manufacturing that led them into the middle class in their own lifetimes. Rather, they remained firmly working class until after World War II. Upward mobility occurred across generations typically, not within the lifetimes of the arriving Italian, Polish, and other southern, central, and eastern European immigrants. In other words, economic parity took about three or four generations, not a decade (as some writers have romantically portrayed it).

With these data as a backdrop, Perlmann looked at contemporary Mexican immigrants. In many ways the deck is stacked against this current immigrant group, which is by far the largest. Unlike their European counterparts of a century ago, many arrivals from Mexico (about 55 percent) labor as illegal immigrants,

which obviously curtails the opportunities available to them and their family members. Today's second-generation Mexicans in the United States are lagging further behind in education compared to the general population than was the comparable generation of the turn-of-the century European immigrants.

The education gap among today's Latinos does not facilitate upward mobility. This situation is particularly challenging given the much greater importance that formal schooling has today for economic success compared to a century ago.

Language acquisition does not appear to be an issue, even given the large concentrations of Spanish-speaking neighborhoods that might seem to work against Hispanics becoming fluent English speakers. Although 23 percent of Hispanic immigrants as a group speak English very well, the percentage of these immigrants who are fluent in English rises to 88 percent among their U.S.-born children and then to 94 percent in the third generation.

It is early to make firm direct comparisons because second-generation Mexican Americans are just coming of age, which means they have less labor-force experience and are just beginning to create their own families. Although the complete entry of today's immigrants into the economy is likely to occur, comparisons to White ethnics suggests that it may take Mexican immigrants longer by at least an additional generation.

Sources: Bean and Stevens 2003; Camarota 2007a; Dickson 2006; Hakimzadeh and Cohn 2007; Katz, Stern, and Fader 2007; Perlmann 2005; Portes 2006; Portes and Rumbaut 2006.

The Contemporary Picture

In politics, Italian Americans have been more successful, at least at the local level, where family and community ties can translate into votes. However, political success did not come easily because many Italian immigrants anticipated returning to their homeland and did not always take neighborhood politics seriously. It was even more difficult for Italian Americans to break into national politics.

Not until 1962 was an Italian American named to a cabinet-level position. Geraldine Ferraro's nomination as the Democratic vice presidential candidate in 1984 was as much an achievement for Italian Americans as it was for women. The opposition to the nomination of Judge Samuel Alito to the Supreme Court in 2006 struck many as bordering on anti–Italian American. Numerous critics used the phrase "Judge Scalito" in obvious reference to the sitting Italian American on the Court, Justice Antonin Scalia (Cornacchia and Nelson 1992).

While as a group, Italian Americans are firmly a part of middle America, they frequently continue to be associated with crime. In 2009, three New Jersey mayors were indicted for corruption, and not all of them were Italian. At the core of the scandal were five Syrian American rabbis, yet newspapers quickly dubbed the situation "New Jersey's 'Italian' Problem." MTV's 2009–2012 successful reality show *Jersey Shore*, which seemed to focus on drinking, hot tubbing, and brawling stars, did not help. Stereotypes and labeling do not go away, and truth is no antidote (McGurn 2009).

There is no lack of famous Italian Americans. They include athlete Joe DiMaggio, politician Rudolph Giuliani, film director Francis Ford Coppola, singers Lady Gaga and Madonna, writer Mario Puzo, actor Leonardo DiCaprio, chef Rachael Ray, and auto racing legend Mario Andretti.

Today, Italian Americans are the seventh-largest immigrant group in the United States. Just how ethnically conscious is the Italian American community? Although the number is declining, 700,000 Americans speak Italian at home; only ten languages are spoken more frequently at home: Spanish, Chinese, Tagalog (Philippines), Vietnamese, Korean, Russian, German, Arabic, Russian, and French Creole. For most of the 17-plus million Italian Americans, however, the language tie to their culture is absent, and, depending on their degree of assimilation, only traces of symbolic ethnicity may remain. As we saw in the chapter opener describing Little Italy in New York City, Italian ethnic enclaves throughout North America are more and more limited to a cluster of Italian restaurants and bakeries. In a later section, we look at the role that language plays for many immigrants and their children (Ryan 2013:3).

The Polish Americans

5.5   Describe the Polish American immigration story.

Immigrants from Poland have had experiences similar to those of the Irish and Italians. They had to overcome economic problems and personal hardships just to make the journey. Once in the United States, they found themselves often assigned to the jobs many citizens had not wanted to do. They had to adjust to a new language and a familiar yet different culture. And always, they were looking back to the family members left behind who either wanted to join them in the United States or never wanted them to leave Poland in the first place.

Like other arrivals, many Poles sought improvement in their lives, a migration that was known as Za Chlebem (For Bread). The Poles who came were, at different times, more likely than many other European immigrants to see themselves as forced immigrants and were often described by, and themselves adopted, the terminology directly reflecting their social roles—exiles, refugees, displaced persons, or émigrés. The primary force for this exodus was Poland's changing political status through most of the nineteenth and twentieth centuries, which was as turbulent as the lives of the new arrivals.

Early Immigration

Polish immigrants were among the settlers at Jamestown, Virginia, in 1608, to help develop the colony's timber industry, but it was the Poles who came later in that century who made a lasting mark. The successful exploits of Polish immigrants such as cavalry officer Casimir Pulaski and military engineer Thaddeus Kosciuszko are still commemorated today in communities with large Polish American populations. As Figure 5.1 shows, it was not until the 1890s that Polish immigration was significant in comparison to some other European arrivals. It is difficult to document the size of this immigration exactly because at various historical periods Poland or parts of the country became part of Austria-Hungary, Germany (Prussia), and the Soviet Union, so that the migrants were not officially coming from a nation called "Poland."

Many of the Polish immigrants had to adjust not only to a new culture but also to a more urban way of life. Sociologists William I. Thomas and Florian Znaniecki, in their classic study *The Polish Peasant in Europe and America* ([1918] 1996), traced the path from rural Poland to urban America. Many of the peasants did not necessarily come directly to the United States but first traveled through other European countries. This pattern is not unique and reminds us that, even today, many immigrants have crossed several countries, sometimes establishing themselves for a period of time before finally settling in the United States (Abbott and Egloff 2008).

Like the Germans, Italians, and Irish, Poles arrived at the large port cities of the East Coast but, unlike the other immigrant groups, they were more likely to settle in cities further inland or work in mines in Pennsylvania. In such areas, they would join kinfolk or acquaintances through the process of chain migration (described in Chapter 4).

The Poles' choice of coal mining as an occupation reflects the continuing tendency of immigrants to work in jobs avoided by most U.S. citizens because they paid little, were dangerous, or both. For example, in September 1897, a group of miners in Lattimer, Pennsylvania, marched to demand safer working conditions and an end to special taxes placed only on foreign-born workers. In the ensuing confrontation with local officials, police officers shot at the protesters, killing 19 people, most of whom were Polish; the others were Lithuanians and Slovaks (Duszak 1997).

Polonia

With growing numbers of Polish immigrants, the emergence of Polonia (meaning Polish communities outside of Poland) became more common in cities throughout the Midwest. Male immigrants who came alone often took shelter through a system of inexpensive boarding houses called *tryzmanie bortnków* (brother keeping), which allowed the new arrival to save money and send it back to Poland to support his family. These funds eventually provided the financial means necessary to bring family members over, adding to the size of Polonia in cities such as Buffalo, Cleveland, Detroit, Milwaukee, Pittsburgh, and, above all, Chicago, where the population of Poles was second only to that in Warsaw, Poland.

Religion has played an important role among Polish immigrants and their descendants. Most of the Polish immigrants who came to the United States before World War I were Roman Catholic. They quickly established their own parishes where new arrivals could feel welcome. Although religious services at that time were in Latin, as they had been in Poland, the many service organizations around the parish, in addition to the Catholic schools, kept the immigrants steeped in the Polish language and the latest happenings back home. Jewish Poles began immigrating during the first part of the twentieth century to escape the growing hostility they felt in Europe, which culminated in the Holocaust. Their numbers swelled greatly until movement from Poland stopped with the invasion of Poland by Germany in 1939; Polish immigration resumed after the war.

Although the Jewish–Catholic distinction may be the most obvious distinguishing factor among Polish Americans, there are other divisions as well. Regional subgroups such as the Kashubes, the Górali, and the Mazurians have often carried great significance with the Polish American community. Some Poles emigrated from areas where German was the language of origin.

As with other immigrant groups, Polish Americans could make use of a rich structure of voluntary self-help associations that were already well established by the 1890s. However, not all organizations smoothly cut across different generations of Polish immigrants. For example, the Poles who came immediately after World War II as political refugees fleeing Soviet domination were quite different in their outlook than the descendants of the economic refugees from the turn of the century. These kinds of tensions in an immigrant community are not unusual, even if they go unnoticed by the casual observer who lumps all immigrants of the same nationality together (Jaroszyn'ska-Kirchmann 2004).

Like many other newcomers, Poles were stigmatized as outsiders and also stereotyped as simple and uncultured—the typical biased view of working-class White ethnics. Their struggles in manual occupations placed them in direct competition with other White ethnics and African Americans, which occasionally led to labor disputes and longer-term tense and emotional rivalries. "Polish jokes" continue to have a remarkable shelf life in casual conversation well into the twenty-first century. Jewish Poles suffer the added indignities of anti-Semitism (Dolan and Stotsky 1997).

Polish American actress Scarlett Johansson reflects the multiple ethnic roots of many Americans today. Though Johansson was born in New York City, her father is a Danish immigrant, and her mother is a U.S.-born Jew whose parents came from Poland and Belarus, then part of the former Soviet Union. She reports celebrating both Hanukkah and Christmas and holds both American and Danish citizenship.

The Contemporary Picture

Today, the number of Polish Americans in the United States is nearly 10 million. Although this number may not seem significant in a country of more than 300 million, we need to recall that today Poland itself has a population of only about 39 million. Polish Americans are a central part of the global Polish community, which has also included Lech Walesa, the Solidarity movement leader who confronted the Soviet Union in the 1980s, and Karol Józef Wojtyla, who became Pope John Paul II in 1978.

Many Polish Americans have retained little of their rich cultural traditions and may barely acknowledge even symbolic ethnicity. Data released in 2013 show about 600,000 whose primary language is Polish—a decline from over 800,000 in 1980. For those still immersed in Polonia, their lives revolve around many of the same religious and social institutions that were the center of Polonia a century ago. For example, 54 Roman Catholic churches in the metropolitan Chicago area still offer Polish-language masses. Although in many of these parishes there may be only one service in Polish serving a declining number of worshippers, a few traditional "Polish" churches still have Polish-speaking priests in residence. Even with the decline in Polish-language service, the Roman Catholic Church actively recruits Polish seminarians, although now English-language training is often emphasized.

In the latter part of the twentieth century, some of the voluntary associations relocated or built satellite centers to serve the outlying Polish American populations. To sustain their activities financially, these social organizations also reached out of the central cities in order to tap into the financial resources of suburban Poles. Increasingly, people of Polish descent also have now made their way into the same social networks populated by German, Irish, Italian, and other ethnic Americans (Bukowczyk 2007; Erdmans 1998, 2006; Lopata 1994; Mocha 1998; Polzin 1973; Shin and Kominski 2010; Stone 2006).

Except for immigrants who fled persecution in their homelands, immigration typically has back-and-forth movement. In the early years of the twenty-first century, there was an identifiable movement of Polish Americans from Polonia to Poland, especially as economic opportunity improved in the home country. One estimate of returnees places it at 50,000 from 2004, when Poland entered the European Union, to 2009. This number is significant in absolute terms but is relatively small given the size of the Polish American community (Fihel and Grabowska-Lusinska 2014; Mastony 2013).

Among the many Polish Americans well known or remembered today are home designer Martha (Kostyra) Stewart, comedian Jack Benny (Benjamin Kubelsky), guitarist Richie Sambora of the rock group Bon Jovi, *Wheel of Fortune* host Pat Sajak, baseball star Stan Musial, football star Mike Ditka, novelist Joseph Conrad (Józef Korzeniowski), singer Bobby Vinton (Stanley Ventula, Jr.), polio vaccine pioneer Albert Sabin, and motion picture director Stanley Kubrick.

WENN Ltd/Alamy Stock Photo

Religious Pluralism

5.6 Define and explain religious pluralism.

Religion plays a fundamental role in society and affects even those who do not practice or even believe in organized religion. **Religion** refers to a unified system of sacred beliefs and practices that encompass elements beyond everyday life that inspire awe, respect, and even fear (Durkheim [1912] 2001).

In popular speech, the term *pluralism* has often been used in the United States to refer explicitly to religion. Although certain faiths are more prominent than others, the United States has a history of greater religious tolerance than most other nations. Today, religious bodies number more than 1,500 in the United States and range from the more than 68 million members of the Roman Catholic Church to sects with fewer than 1,000 adherents. In every region of the country, religion is being expressed in greater variety, whether it be the Latinization of Catholicism and some Christian faiths, the de-Europeanizing of some established Protestant faiths (as with Asian Americans), or the de-Christianizing of the overall religious landscape with Muslims, Buddhists, Hindus, Sikhs, and others. Much of the growth in U.S. religious pluralism is fueled by immigration. For example, the fast-growing Muslim population is 63 percent immigrant (Lipka 2016; Roof 2007).

How do we view the United States in terms of religion? Increasingly, the United States has a non-Christian presence. In 1900, an estimated 96 percent of the nation was Christian; slightly more than 1 percent was nonreligious, and approximately 3 percent held other faiths. In 2014, it was estimated that the nation was 68 percent Christian and another 37 percent are affiliated with non-Christian faiths. The United States has a long Jewish tradition, and Muslims number close to 5 million. A smaller but also growing number of people adhere to such Eastern faiths as Hinduism, Buddhism, Confucianism, and Taoism. Scholars of religious practices have documented the rise of people moving away formal church organizations but note that spirituality remains high and that those who attend services are more devout (McCauley 2015; Pew Research Center 2015a).

Sociologists use the word **denomination** for a large, organized religion that is not linked officially with the state or government. By far, the largest denomination in the United States is Catholicism; yet at least 24 other Christian religious denominations have 1 million or more members (Table 5.1).

At least four non-Christian religious groups in the United States have numbers that are comparable to any of these large denominations: Jews, Muslims, Buddhists, and Hindus. In the United States, each of these denominations numbers more than 1 million members. Within each of these groups are branches or sects that distinguish themselves from one another. For example, the Jewish faith embraces several factions—Orthodox, Conservative, Reconstructionist, and Reform—that are similar in their roots but marked by sharp distinctions. Some Muslims are Sunni and others are Shia. Further divisions are present within these groups, just as among Protestants and, in turn, among Baptists.

The United States has long been described as a Judeo-Christian nation, but with interest in other faiths and continuing immigration. This description, perhaps not accurate to begin with, is certainly not accurate now, partially as a result of the large increase in the number of Muslim Americans.

Islam in the United States has a long history stretching from Muslim Africans who came as slaves into the Muslim community of the present day, which includes immigrants and native-born Americans. President Obama, whose father was a practicing Muslim who lived for years in Indonesia (the country with

Religious diversity characterizes the United States and includes many non-Christian faiths, including Sikhism—a religion that dates from sixteenth-century India and rejects the idea that any single faith has a monopoly on the truth. Here the faithful gather for a Sikh Day parade in New York City.

Table 5.1 Christian Churches with More Than a Million Members

Denomination Name	Inclusive Membership
Roman Catholic Church	68,503,456
Southern Baptist Convention	16,160,088
United Methodist Church	7,774,931
Church of Jesus Christ of Latter-Day Saints	6,058,907
Church of God in Christ	5,499,875
National Baptist Convention, U.S.A., Inc.	5,000,000
Evangelical Lutheran Church in America	4,542,868
National Baptist Convention of America, Inc.	3,500,000
Assemblies of God	2,914,669
Presbyterian Church (U.S.A.)	2,770,730
African Methodist Episcopal Church	2,500,000
National Missionary Baptist Convention of America	2,500,000
Lutheran Church—Missouri Synod (LCMS)	2,312,111
Episcopal Church	2,006,343
Churches of Christ	1,639,495
Greek Orthodox Archdiocese of America	1,500,000
Pentecostal Assemblies of the World, Inc.	1,500,000
African Methodist Episcopal Zion Church	1,400,000
American Baptist Churches in the U.S.A.	1,310,505
Jehovah's Witnesses	1,162,686
United Church of Christ	1,080,199
Church of God (Cleveland, TN)	1,076,254
Christian Churches and Churches of Christ	1,071,616
Seventh-Day Adventist Church	1,043,606
Progressive National Baptist Convention, Inc.	1,010,000

Note: Most recent data as of 2017.

SOURCE: Eileen Lindner (ed.) 2012. *Yearbook of American and Canadian Churches 2011*, Table 2, p. 12. Nashville, TN: Abingdon Press. Reprinted by permission of the National Council of Churches, 2011 Yearbook of American & Canadian Churches.

the largest Muslim population), never sought to hide his roots. However, reflecting the prejudices of many toward non-Christians, Obama stressed his Christian upbringing throughout his presidential campaigns. Indeed, a national survey showed that 55 percent believe the U.S. Constitution establishes the country as a "Christian nation" (Cose 2008; Thomas 2007).

Many faiths have played critical roles in resisting racism and in trying to bring together the nation in the name of racial and ethnic harmony. Broadly defined, faiths represent a variety of ethnic and racial groups. Figure 5.3 considers the interaction of White, Black, and Hispanic races with religions. Muslims, Pentecostals, and Jehovah's Witnesses are much more diverse than Presbyterians or Lutherans. Religion plays an even more central role for Blacks and Latinos than it does for Whites. A national survey indicated that 65 percent of African Americans and 51 percent of Latinos attend a religious service every week, compared to 44 percent of White non-Hispanics (Winseman 2004).

It would be a mistake to focus only on older religious organizations when considering religion's role in society. Local churches that developed into national faiths in the 1990s, such as Calvary Chapel, Vineyard, and Hope Chapel, have a following among Pentecostal believers, who embrace a more charismatic form of worship devoid of traditional ornamentation, with pastors and congregations alike favoring informal attire. New faiths develop with increasing rapidity in what can only be called a very competitive

Figure 5.3 Racial and Ethnic Makeup of Selected Religions in the United States

Note: "Other" includes self-identified mixed races. Evangelical includes Baptist, Lutheran (Missouri and Wisconsin Synods), and Pentecostal, among others. Mainline Protestant includes Methodist, Lutheran (ELCA), Presbyterian, Episcopal, and United Church of Christ, among others, but excludes historically Black churches. Based on a national survey of 35,556 adults conducted in August 2007.

SOURCE: Data from Pew Forum on Religion and Public Life 2008a:120.

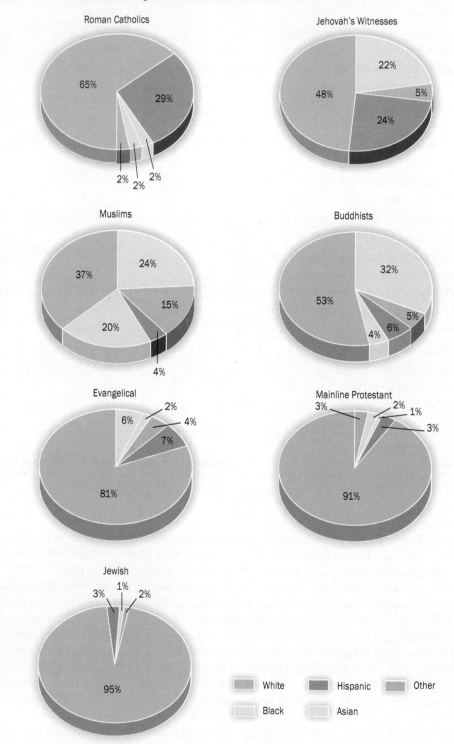

market for individual religious faith. In addition, many people, with or without religious affiliation, become fascinated with spiritual concepts such as angels or become a part of loose-knit fellowships. Religion in the United States is an ever-changing social phenomenon. Other nonmainstream faiths emerge in new arenas, as evidenced by the successful

Table 5.2 Religious Faiths and Politics

Arranged in descending levels of support for the Republican Party

	Republican/Lean Republican	Democrat/Lean Democratic
Mormon	70	19
Evangelical	69	18
United Methodist Church	54	35
Baptist	44	43
Presbyterian	44	47
Roman Catholic	37	44
Jewish	26	64
Muslim	17	62
Buddhist	16	69
Hindu	13	61
African Methodist Episcopal Church	4	92

Notes: Data for 2014. Other possible responses were Independent, Other, No preference, No lean.

SOURCE: Data from Pew Research Center 2015a:188–190.

campaign of Mitt Romney, a Mormon, to win the Republican nomination for president in 2012 or the visible role of celebrities promoting the Church of Scientology (Schaefer and Zellner 2015).

Perhaps not surprisingly, adherents to religious faiths vary dramatically in how they see themselves aligned with the Republican and Democratic political parties, as Table 5.2 shows. While religious faiths typically do not explicitly endorse a party or even specific candidates, they often take positions on social issues that align more with either Republican and Democratic positions.

Despite the sharp divide in political party support, divisive conflicts along religious lines are muted in the United States compared with those in, say, the Middle East. Although not entirely absent, conflicts about religion in the United States seem to be overshadowed by civil religion. **Civil religion** is the religious dimension in the United States that merges public life with sacred beliefs. It also reflects the idea that no single faith is privileged over all others. Indeed, it even encompasses the views of nonbelievers regarding the human condition.

Sociologist Robert Bellah (1967) borrowed the phrase *civil religion* from eighteenth-century French philosopher Jean-Jacques Rousseau to describe a significant phenomenon in the contemporary United States. Civil religion exists alongside established religious faiths, and it embodies a belief system that incorporates all religions but is not associated specifically with any single religion. It is the type of faith to which presidents refer in inaugural speeches and to which American Legion posts and Girl Scout troops swear allegiance. In 1954, Congress added the phrase *under God* to the Pledge of Allegiance as a legislative recognition of religion's significance. Elected officials in the United States, beginning with Ronald Reagan, often conclude even their most straightforward speeches with "God bless the United States of America," which in effect evokes the civil religion of the nation.

Functionalists see civil religion as reinforcing central American values that may be more patriotic than sacred in nature. After major societal upheavals or tragedies, from the 1995 Oklahoma City bombing to the 2001 terrorist attacks and beyond, the mass media often show church services with clergy praying and asking for national healing.

In the following sections, we explore the diversity among the major Christian groups in the United States, such as Roman Catholics and Protestants, as well as how Islam has emerged as a significant religious force in the United States and can no longer be regarded as a marginal faith in terms of the number of followers (Gorski 2010).

Diversity Among Roman Catholics

Social scientists have persistently tended to ignore the diversity within the Roman Catholic Church in the United States. Recent research has not supported the conclusion that Roman Catholics are melding into a single group, following the traditions of the American Irish Catholic model, or even that parishioners are attending English-language churches. Religious behavior has been different for each ethnic group within the Roman Catholic Church. The Irish and French Canadians left societies that were highly competitive both culturally and socially. Their religious involvement in the United States is more relaxed than it was in Ireland and Quebec. However, the influence of life in the United States has increased German and Polish involvement in the Roman Catholic Church, whereas Italians have remained largely inactive. Variations by ethnic background continue to emerge in studies of contemporary religious involvement in the Roman Catholic Church (Eckstrom 2001).

The "ethnic empowerment" of the Roman Catholic Church by European immigration has declined not only as a result of the lower numbers of immigrants from European countries, but also by the next generation losing interest in Catholicism. Move than one in three of the U.S.-born White ethnics have left the Catholic Church since the 1970s (Hout 2016).

So, where does the Roman Catholic Church look for new members? Since the mid-1970s, the Roman Catholic Church in America has received a significant number of new members in immigrants from the Philippines, Southeast Asia, and particularly Latin America. Although these new members have been a stabilizing force offsetting the loss of White ethnics, they have also presented challenges to a church that for generations was dominated by Irish, Italian, and Polish parishes. Perhaps the most prominent subgroup in the Roman Catholic Church is Latinos, who now account for one-third of all Roman Catholic parishioners. Clearly, immigrants are seen as a significant part of the Catholic Church's future in the United States. More than 150 immigration-oriented programs are mounted by the Catholic Church nationwide. Often a program for a patron saint or national feast begins with two national anthems sung—that of the participant's native country and "The Star-Spangled Banner" (Dolan 2013; Goodstein and Steinhauer 2010; Navarro-Rivera, Kosmin, and Keysar 2010).

The Roman Catholic Church, despite its ethnic diversity, has been a powerful force in reducing the ethnic ties of its members, making it a significant assimilating force. The irony here is that so many nineteenth-century Americans heaped abuse on U.S. Catholics for allegedly being un-American and having a dual allegiance. The history of the Catholic Church in the United States may be portrayed as a struggle within the membership between the Americanizers and the anti-Americanizers, with the former ultimately winning. Unlike the various Protestant churches that accommodated immigrants of a single nationality, the Roman Catholic Church had to Americanize a variety of linguistic and ethnic groups. The Catholic Church may have been the most potent assimilating force after the public school system. Comparing the assimilationist goal of the Catholic Church and the current diversity in it leads us to conclude that ethnic diversity has continued in the Roman Catholic Church despite, not because of, this religious institution.

Diversity Among Protestants

Protestantism, like Catholicism, often is portrayed as a monolithic entity. Little attention is given to the doctrinal and attitudinal differences that sharply divide the various denominations in both laity and clergy. However, several studies document the diversity. Unfortunately, many opinion polls and surveys are content to learn only whether a respondent is a Catholic, a Protestant, or a Jew. Digging deeper, Stark and Glock (1968) found sharp differences in religious attitudes within Protestant churches. For example, 99 percent of Southern Baptists had no doubt that Jesus was the divine son of God, as contrasted to only 40 percent of Congregationalists. We can identify four "generic theological camps":

1. *Liberals:* United Church of Christ (Congregationalists) and Episcopalians
2. *Moderates:* Disciples of Christ, Methodists, and Presbyterians
3. *Conservatives:* American Lutherans and American Baptists
4. *Fundamentalists:* Missouri Synod Lutherans, Southern Baptists, and Assembly of God

Figure 5.4 Income and Denominations

Denominations attract different income groups. All groups have both affluent and poor members, yet some denominations have a higher proportion of members with high incomes, while others are comparatively poor.

SOURCE: Based on interviews with a representative sample of 35,000 adults reproduced in the *Pew Forum on Religion and Public Life 2008b*: 78–79, 84–85.

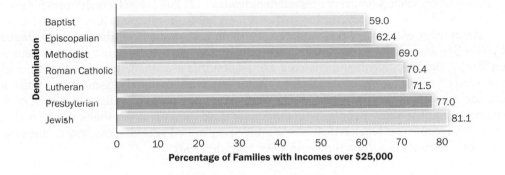

Percentage of Families with Incomes over $25,000

Roman Catholics generally hold religious beliefs similar to those of conservative Protestants, except on essentially Catholic issues such as papal infallibility (the pope's authority in all decisions regarding faith and morals). Whether or not there are four distinct camps is not important: The point is that the familiar practice of contrasting Roman Catholics and Protestants is clearly not productive. Some differences between Roman Catholics and Protestants are inconsequential compared with the differences between Protestant sects.

Secular criteria as well as doctrinal issues may distinguish religious faiths. Research has consistently shown that denominations can be arranged in a hierarchy based on social class. As Figure 5.4 reveals, members of certain faiths, such as Episcopalians, Jews, and Presbyterians, have a higher proportion of affluent members. Members of other faiths, including Baptists, tend to be poorer. Of course, all Protestant groups draw members from each social stratum. Nonetheless, the social significance of these class differences is that religion becomes a mechanism for signaling social mobility. A person who is moving up in wealth and power may seek out a faith associated with a higher social ranking. Figure 5.5 shows similar contrasts in formal schooling.

Protestant faiths have been diversifying, and many of their members have been leaving them for churches that follow strict codes of behavior or fundamentalist interpretations of biblical teachings. This trend is reflected in the gradual decline of the five mainline churches: Baptist, Episcopalian, Lutheran, Methodist, and Presbyterian. As with the Roman Catholic Church, many Protestant faiths have seen their numbers helped by immigrants. Among the countries outside the United States with large Christian populations are China, Mexico, the

Figure 5.5 Education and Denominations

There are sharp differences in the proportion of those with some college education by denomination.

SOURCE: Based on interviews with a representative sample of 35,000 adults and reproduced in the *Pew Forum on Religion and Public Life 2008b*: 78–79, 84–85.

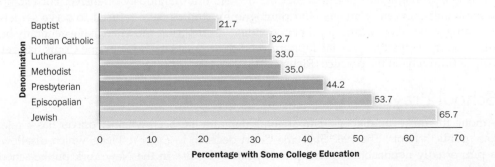

Percentage with Some College Education

Philippines, and Nigeria, which are all significant sources of immigrants to the United States (Brown 2015; Davis, Smith, and Marsden 2007).

Although Protestants may seem to define the civil religion and the accepted dominant orientation, some Christian faiths feel that they, too, experience the discrimination usually associated with non-Christians such as Jews and Muslims. For example, representatives of the liberal and moderate faiths dominate the leadership of the military's chaplain corps. There are 16 Presbyterian soldiers for every Presbyterian chaplain, 121 Full Gospel worshippers for every Full Gospel chaplain, and 339 Muslim soldiers for every Muslim chaplain (Cooperman 2005).

As another example of denominational discrimination, in 1998, the Southern Baptist Convention amended its basic theological statements of beliefs to include a strong statement on family life. The statement included a declaration that a woman should "submit herself graciously" to her husband's leadership. There was widespread criticism of this position outside the Baptist Church, which many Baptists felt was inappropriate and a form of respectable bigotry. Many Baptists wondered why it was acceptable to attack them for their views on social issues when criticism was much more muted against more liberal faiths that are more tolerant of abortion (Bowman 1998; Niebuhr 1998).

Religion and the Courts

5.7 Understand court rulings on religion.

Religious pluralism owes its existence in the United States to the First Amendment declaration that "Congress shall make no law respecting an establishment of religion, or prohibiting the free exercise thereof." The U.S. Supreme Court has consistently interpreted this wording to mean not that government should ignore religion but that it should follow a policy of neutrality to maximize religious freedom. For example, the government may not help religion by financing a new church building, but it also may not obstruct religion by denying a church adequate police and fire protection. We examine five issues that continue to require clarification: company exemptions, school prayer, secessionist minorities and their rituals, creationism (including intelligent design), and the public display of religious (or sacred) symbols.

Company Exemptions

Businesses cannot typically discriminate in their hiring based on a person's religious beliefs, nor can they deny services to people based on their faith. While these laws may seem easy enough to enforce, in recent years the situation has grown more complex.

The effort to offer health insurance to more people led to the passage of the Patient Protection and Affordable Care Act (often called Obamacare), which mandates that more employers provide insurance options. By law, this insurance must include coverage for oral contraceptives, some of which pro-life people regard as bordering on abortion. The Supreme Court in 2014 ruled in favor of businesses being granted exceptions if the law ran contrary to the owner's beliefs. The company that brought the suit, Hobby Lobby, does not require that its 23,000 workers be Christian, but it does seek to create "a positive environment that happens to be based on biblical principles." For example, all its retail outlets are closed on Sundays, but it sells Hanukkah-related merchandise alongside Christmas-themed goods (Liptak 2014).

Another controversy has erupted in which businesses refuse to offer goods and services to people who embrace practices that the owners find religiously offensive. For example, some bakeries, event planners, and photography studios have refused to serve same-sex weddings since they became legal nationwide in 2015. Business owners have generally been unsuccessful in getting judicial support for such actions, but the Supreme Court has yet to rule definitively on the practice (Richey 2016).

School Prayer

Among the most controversial and ongoing disputes has been whether prayer has a role in U.S. public schools. The 1962 Supreme Court decision in *Engel v. Vitale*, which disallowed a purportedly nondenominational prayer drafted for use in the New York public schools, disturbed many people. The prayer was "Almighty God, we acknowledge our dependence upon Thee, and we beg Thy blessings upon us, our parents, our teachers, and our country." Subsequent decisions overturned state laws requiring Bible reading in public schools, laws requiring recitation of the Lord's Prayer, and laws permitting a daily one-minute period of silent meditation or prayer. Despite such judicial pronouncements, children in many public schools in the United States are led in regular prayer recitation or Bible reading. Contrary to what many people believe, religion has not been hounded out of public schools (Yemma 2013).

What about prayers at public gatherings? In 1992, the Supreme Court ruled 5–4 in *Lee v. Weisman* that prayer at a junior high school graduation in Providence, Rhode Island, violated the U.S. Constitution's mandate of separation of church and state. A rabbi had given thanks to God in his invocation. The district court suggested that the invocation would have been acceptable without that reference. The Supreme Court did not agree with the school board that a prayer at a graduation was not coercive. The Court did say in its opinion that it was acceptable for a student speaker voluntarily to say a prayer at such a program (Marshall 2001).

Public schools and even states have mandated a "moment of silence" at the start of the school day in what critics contend is a transparent attempt to get around *Lee v. Weisman.* While legislators clearly intended prayer or religious thoughts when they created these "moments," the courts have to date ruled such policies as constitutional and argued that the policy is secular, rather than sacred. Arkansas in 2013 became the latest state to mandate a minute of silence at the beginning of the school day (ABC Television 2013).

Secessionist Minorities

Several religious groups have been in legal and social conflict with the rest of society. Some can be called **secessionist minorities** in that they reject both assimilation and coexistence in some form of cultural pluralism. The Amish are one such group that comes into conflict with mainstream society because of the Amish beliefs and way of life. The Old Order Amish shun most modern conveniences and maintain a lifestyle dramatically different from that of larger society.

Are there limits to the free exercise of religious rituals by secessionist minorities? Today, tens of thousands of members of Native American religions believe that ingesting the powerful drug peyote is a sacrament and that those who partake of peyote will enter into direct contact with God. In 1990, the Supreme Court ruled that prosecuting people who use illegal drugs as part of a religious ritual is not a violation of the First Amendment guarantee of religious freedom. The case arose because Native Americans were dismissed from their jobs for the religious use of peyote and were then refused unemployment benefits by the state of Oregon's employment division. In 1991, however, Oregon enacted a new law permitting the sacramental use of peyote by Native Americans (*New York Times* 1991).

In another ruling on religious rituals, in 1993 the Supreme Court unanimously overturned a local ordinance in Florida that banned ritual animal sacrifice. The Court held that this law violated the free-exercise rights of adherents of the Santeria religion, in which the sacrifice of animals (including goats, chickens, and other birds) plays a central role. The same year, Congress passed the Religi ous Freedom Restoration Act, which said the government may not enforce laws that "substantially burden" the exercise of religion. Presumably, this legislation gives religious groups more flexibility in practicing their faiths. However, many local and state officials are concerned that the law has led to unintended consequences, such as forcing states to accommodate prisoners' requests for questionable religious activities or to permit a church to expand into a historic district in defiance of local laws (Greenhouse 1996).

The legal acceptance of different faiths has been illustrated in numerous decisions. For example, the courts have allowed Wiccan

After lobbying by Wiccans, the U.S. Department of Veterans Affairs eventually approved the pentacle symbol for use on the cemetery markers of fallen soldiers who self-identify as Witches.

Alex Brandon/AP Images

organizations to enjoy nonprofit status. In addition, the U.S. Department of Veterans Affairs approved of the pentacle symbol for use on national cemetery markers of those fallen soldiers who self-identify as Witches.

Creationism and Intelligent Design

Another area of contention has been whether the biblical account of creation should be or must be presented in school curricula and whether this account should receive the same emphasis as scientific theories. In the famous "monkey trial" of 1925, Tennessee schoolteacher John Scopes was found guilty of teaching the scientific theory of evolution in public schools. Since then, however, Darwin's evolutionary theories have been presented in public schools with little reference to the biblical account in the book of Genesis. People who support the literal interpretation of the Bible, commonly known as **creationists**, have formed various organizations to crusade for the teaching of creationism in U.S. public schools and universities.

In a 1987 Louisiana case, *Edwards v. Aguillard,* the Supreme Court ruled that states may not require the teaching of creationism alongside evolution in public schools if the primary purpose of such legislation is to promote a religious viewpoint. Creationists often seek to influence the choice of textbooks by a local school district or, in states with statewide adoptions by a state board of education; publishers who do not include creationism in their textbooks thus lose the opportunity to sell tens of thousands of textbooks in a particular state or district. The teaching of evolution and creationism has remained a controversial issue in many communities across the United States (Applebome 1996; Rich 2013).

Beginning in the 1980s, those who believe in a divine hand in the creation of life have advanced **intelligent design (ID)**, the idea that life is so complex that it could only have been created by a higher intelligence. Although ID is not explicitly based on the biblical account, many creationists feel comfortable with ID and advocate that it is a more accurate account than Darwinism or, at the very least, that it be taught as an alternative alongside the theory of evolution. In 2005, a federal judge in *Kitzmiller v. Dove Area School District* ended a Pennsylvania school district's intention to require the teaching of ID. In essence, the judge found ID to be "a religious belief" that was only a subtler way of finding God's fingerprints in nature than traditional creationism. Because the issue continues to be hotly debated, future court cases are certain to come (Clemmitt 2005; Goodstein 2005).

Public Displays

Another area of contention has been a battle over public displays that depict symbols of religion or appear to be sacred representations. Can manger scenes be erected on public property? Do people have a right to be protected from large displays such as a cross or a star atop a water tower overlooking an entire town? In a series of decisions in the 1980s and early 1990s, the Supreme Court ruled that tax-supported religious displays on public government property may be successfully challenged but may be permissible if made more secular. Displays that combine a crèche—the Christmas manger scene depicting the birth of Jesus—or the Hanukkah menorah and also include Frosty the Snowman or even Christmas trees have been ruled secular. These decisions have been dubbed "the plastic reindeer rules." In 1995, the Court clarified the issue by stating that privately sponsored religious displays may be allowed on public property if other forms of expression are permitted in the same location.

The issue is far from resolved, because these cases have been decided by close votes. Changes in the Supreme Court's composition in the next few years may lead to different decisions on future cases (Bork 1995; Hirsley 1991; Mauro 1995).

Conclusion

From his cramped basement apartment, Grigore Culian has been producing a biweekly Romanian-language paper called *New York Magazine* since 1997 that provides local news of interest to Romanians in the New York metro area and beyond. There are over 146,000 adults in the United States whose primary language is Romanian. While being a one-person operation is unusual, producing news for a small ethnic community is not. Foreign-language newspapers, radio stations, cable outlets, and video streaming keep ethnic ties alive and go beyond symbolic ethnicity. Media outlets foster a sense of community for hundreds of religious denominations, Christian and non-Christian alike (Lazar 2013).

Considering ethnicity and religion reinforces our understanding of the spectrum of intergroup relations first presented in Chapter 1. The Spectrum of Intergroup Relations (Figure 5.6) shows the rich variety of relationships as defined by people's ethnic and religious identities. The profiles of German, Irish, Italian, and Polish Americans reflect the variety of White ethnic experiences.

Any study of life in the United States, especially one that focuses on dominant and subordinate groups, cannot ignore religion and ethnicity. The two are closely related, as certain religious faiths predominate in certain nationalities. Both religious activity and interest by White ethnics in their heritage continue to be prominent features of contemporary society. People have been and continue to be ridiculed or deprived of opportunities solely because of their ethnic or religious affiliation.

Religion is changing in the United States. As one commercial recognition of this fact, Hallmark created its first greeting card in 2003 for the Muslim holiday Eid-al-fitr, which marks the end of the month-long fast of Ramadan. The issue of the persistence of ethnicity is an intriguing one. Some people may only casually exhibit their ethnicity and practice what has been called symbolic ethnicity. However, can people immerse themselves in their ethnic culture without society punishing them for their desire to be different or to embrace their heritage? The tendency to put down White ethnics through respectable bigotry continues. Despite this intolerance, ethnicity remains a common source of identity for many Americans today. There is also the ethnic paradox, which finds that

Figure 5.6 Spectrum of Intergroup Relations: Ethnicity, Whiteness, and Religion

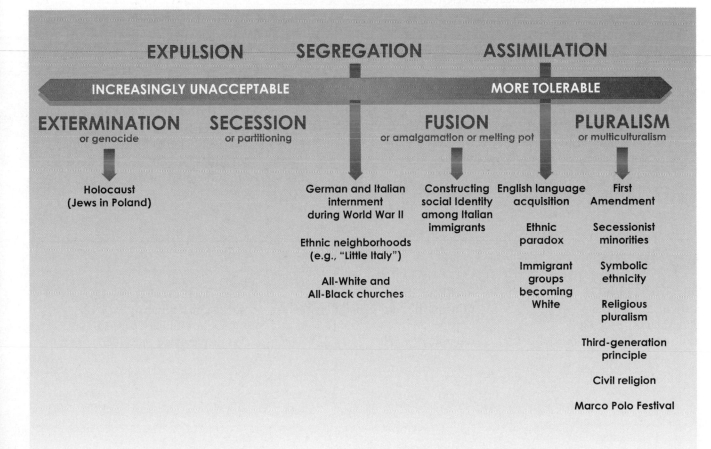

practicing one's ethnic heritage often strengthens people and allows them to move successfully into the larger society.

The issue of religious expression in all its forms also raises a variety of intriguing questions. How can a country that is increasingly populated by diverse and often non-Christian faiths maintain religious tolerance? How might this level of tolerance change in the decades ahead? How will the courts and society resolve the issues of religious freedom? This is a particularly important issue in areas such as company exemptions, school prayer, secessionist minorities, creationism, intelligent design, and public religious displays. Some examination of religious ties is fundamental to completing an accurate picture of a person's social identity.

Summary of Learning Objectives

5.1 Understand what is meant by ethnicity, including Whiteness.

1. While considering race and ethnicity in the United States, we often ignore how White people come to see themselves as a group and in relationship to others. Racial and ethnic groups may achieve "Whiteness" over a period of time.

2. Feelings of ethnicity may be fading among the descendants of Europeans, but they may re-emerge as reflected in either the third-generation principle or, in a more limited fashion, through symbolic ethnicity.

5.2 Describe the German American experience.

3. German Americans are the largest White ethnic group but have been largely incorporated into the core population with little visible distinctive cultural presence apart from food.

5.3 Identify the major periods of Irish American immigration.

4. First regarded very much as "outsiders" and even as not White, people of Irish descent are the second-largest White ethnic group today. The Irish in the United States date back to the colonial period, but a major Irish immigration to the United States took place in the mid-nineteenth century as a result of a potato famine. The twenty-first century saw renewed Irish immigration as a result of economic difficulties in Ireland.

5.4 Explain the Italian American experience.

5. Like the Irish, immigrants from Italy first encountered resistance in the United States but moved up from their lower- and working-class status in the American social hierarchy.

5.5 Describe the Polish American immigration story.

6. Immigration from Poland has created a visible presence of Polonia in several American cities.

5.6 Define and explain religious pluralism.

7. The ethnic diversity of the United States is matched by the many denominations among Christians, as well as the sizable Jewish and Muslim presence.

5.7 Understand court rulings on religion.

8. In its interpretation of the First Amendment, the Supreme Court has tried to preserve religious freedom, but critics have argued that the Court has served to stifle religious expression.

Key Terms

civil religion, *page 123*
creationists, *page 128*
denomination, *page 120*
ethnic paradox, *page 107*

intelligent design, *page 128*
principle of third-generation interest, *page 107*
religion, *page 120*

respectable bigotry, *page 115*
secessionist minority, *page 127*
symbolic ethnicity, *page 107*
White privilege, *page 106*

Review Questions

1. How is Whiteness socially constructed?
2. In what ways can White ethnicity be rediscovered?
3. Explain the impact that World War II had on German Americans both before and after the war.
4. Explain how Irish Americans became "White."
5. How does stereotyping relate to contemporary Italian Americans?

6. What role does Polonia play in the lives of contemporary Polish Americans?
7. How has the non-Christian population been expanding in the United States?
8. How have court rulings affected religious expression?

Critical Thinking

1. In which situations do you see ethnicity becoming more apparent? When does it appear to occur only in response to other people advancing or celebrating their own ethnicity? In these situations, how can ethnic identity be both positive and perhaps counterproductive or even destructive?
2. How do White people you know seem to be aware or unaware of their ethnic roots? Of their Whiteness?

3. Why do you think we are so often reluctant to show our religion to others? Why might people of certain faiths be more hesitant than others?
4. How do religious denominations reflect conservative and liberal positions on social issues? Consider services for the homeless, the need for childcare, the acceptance or rejection of gay men and lesbians, and a woman's right to terminate a pregnancy versus the fetus's right to survive.

Chapter 6
Native Americans: The First Americans

Richard Wong/Alamy Stock Photo

∨ Learning Objectives

6.1 Describe the impact of early treaties and acts of Congress on Native Americans.

6.2 Explain how contemporary federal policies affect Native Americans.

6.3 Discuss the results of Native Americans' collective-action efforts.

6.4 Discuss the macro and micro levels of American Indian identity.

6.5 Summarize the special challenges Native Americans face today with regard to economic development, education, and healthcare.

6.6 Discuss how Native Americans express religion and spirituality.

6.7 Analyze how environmental issues affect Native Americans.

Boozhoo might be the sign that welcomes you at the local coffee shop in this college town. On-campus restroom door signs say *Ikwewag* and *Ininiway*, but fortunately each word is followed by *Women* and *Men*, respectively. No, you're not attending college in a foreign country: You are at Bemidji State University in Bemidji, Minnesota. The town and college have made an effort to make Native Americans, and in particular members of the Ojibwe (or Chippewa) tribe, feel welcome. Using their language also is an effort to keep it alive because fewer than 1,000 people in the United States speak it fluently.

The battle to keep language alive is fought throughout the United States, from Riverton, Wyoming, to Long Island, New York, to the Florida Everglades. Efforts are underway to significantly increase the numbers of the more than 370,000 Native people who currently speak their native language at home.

In Wyoming, Ryan Wilson is teaching the Arapaho language in the Hinono' Eitinino' Oowuu', the Arapaho Language Lodge, because no one under the age of 55 speaks it fluently. The Shinnecock native language on Long Island has not been spoken for nearly 200 years. Drawing on a historical vocabulary list made by Thomas Jefferson during a tribal visit in 1791, linguists are attempting to reintroduce the tribe of 1,700 people to their native language. In Florida, the Miccosukee Indian Schools' efforts to increase the use of the native language are having positive results, as are efforts around the country to increase the low population (only 20.4 percent) of Native people who speak their native language at home.

But there is also controversy among tribal people over how much the schools should invest in language maintenance programs and whether fluency in the language should be a requirement for some jobs. For example, in 2015 the election of the president of the Navajo Nation was plunged into chaos over the requirement that candidates be fluent in the Navajo language. The chief justice of the Navajo Supreme Court retired over the issue of what it means to be fluent. Eventually, the decision was made to allow tribal members to decide as they cast their ballots.

The languages themselves are threatened—easily 70 of the 139 tribal languages in the United States could become extinct within a few years. Table 6.1 lists the ten most commonly spoken languages, although not necessarily spoken fluently, by Native Americans (Frosch 2008; T. Lee 2011; National Congress of American Indians 2012; Pineo and Donovan 2015; Sturtevant and Cattelino 2004).

Although this chapter focuses on the Native American experience in the United States, the pattern of land seizure, subjugation, assimilation, and resistance to domination has been repeated with indigenous people in nations throughout the world, including the tribal people in Mexico, Canada, and throughout Latin America. Hawaiians, another native people who fell under the political, economic, and cultural control of the United States, are considered in Chapter 12. Later in this chapter we also consider the experience of the Aboriginal people of Australia. Indigenous peoples on almost every continent are familiar with the patterns of subjugation and the pressure to assimilate. So widespread is this oppression that the United Nations and its precursor organization, the League of Nations, have repeatedly considered this issue.

The common term *American Indians* tells us more about the Europeans who explored North America than it does about the native people. The label reflects the initial explorers' confusion in believing that they had arrived in "the Indies" of the Asian continent. Thus, reference to the diverse tribal groups as either *American Indians* or *Native Americans* is a result of their forced subordination to the dominant group. Today, most American Indians prefer to identify themselves using their tribal affiliation, such as Cherokee, or affiliations, such as Cheyenne Arapaho, if they have mixed ancestry. To collectively refer to all tribal people in this book, we use *Native Americans* and *American Indians* interchangeably.

Table 6.1 Major Tribal Languages

1. Navajo	166,826
2. Yupik (Alaska)	19,750
3. Dakota (Sioux)	17,855
4. Apache	13,445
5. Keres (Pueblo)	13,190
6. Cherokee	11,465
7. Ojibwa	9,735
8. Choctaw	9,635
9. Zuni	9,615
10. Pima	6,990

SOURCE: Data from Bureau of the Census 2014a.

Figure 6.1 American Indian and Alaska Native Population

SOURCE: Norris, Vines, and Hoeffel 2012: Figure 4 on p. 9.

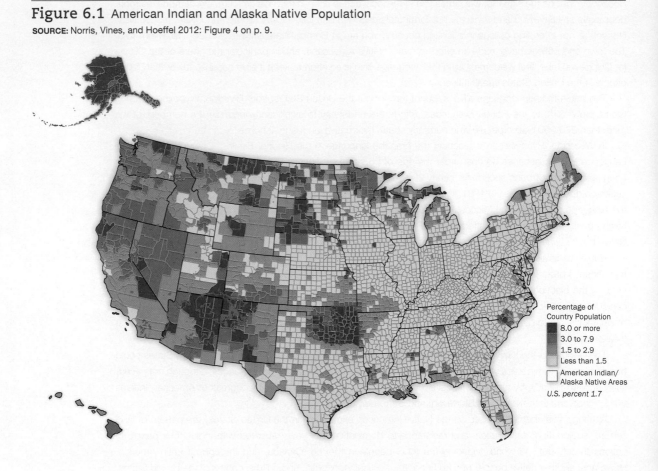

Percentage of
Country Population

■ 8.0 or more
■ 3.0 to 7.9
■ 1.5 to 2.9
□ Less than 1.5
□ American Indian/
Alaska Native Areas

U.S. percent 1.7

An estimated 2.9 million Native Americans and Alaska Natives lived in the United States in 2015. In addition to the 2.9 million people who gave American Indian or Alaska Native as their sole racial identification, another 3.7 million people listed multiple responses that included American Indian. As Figure 6.1 shows, Native Americans are located throughout the United States but are most present in the Southwest, Northwest, northern Great Plains, and Alaska. Twenty-one states have at least 100,000 American Indian and Alaska Natives—Alaska, Arizona, California, Colorado, Florida, Georgia, Illinois, Michigan, Minnesota, New Jersey, New Mexico, New York, North Carolina, Ohio, Oklahoma, Oregon, Pennsylvania, Texas, Virginia, Washington, and Wisconsin (Bureau of the Census 2016n).

European Contacts

6.1 Describe the impact of early treaties and acts of Congress on Native Americans.

Native Americans have been misunderstood and mistreated by their conquerors for centuries. Assuming that he had reached the Indies, Christopher Columbus called the native residents of North America "people of India." The European immigrants who followed Columbus did not understand the native peoples any more than the Native Americans could have anticipated the destruction of their way of life. But the Europeans had superior weaponry, and the diseases they brought wiped out huge numbers of indigenous people throughout the Western Hemisphere.

The first explorers of the Western Hemisphere came long before Columbus and Leif Erikson. The ancestors of today's Native Americans were hunters in search of wild game, including mammoths and long-horned bison. For thousands of years, these people spread through the Western Hemisphere, adapting to its many physical environments. Hundreds of cultures evolved, including the complex societies of the Maya, Inca, and Aztec (Deloria 1995, 2004).

It is beyond the scope of this chapter to describe the many tribal cultures of North America, let alone the ways of life of Native Americans in Central and South America and the islands of the Caribbean. We must appreciate that the term *Indian culture* is a convenient way to gloss over the diversity of cultures, languages, religions, kinship systems, and political organizations that existed—and, in many instances, remain—among the peoples referred to collectively as *Native Americans* or *American Indians*. For example, in the year 1500, an estimated 700 distinct languages were spoken in the area north of Mexico. For simplicity, we refer to these many cultures as *Native American*, but we must be always mindful of the differences this term conceals. Similarly, we refer to non–Native Americans as non-Indians, recognizing in this context that this term encompasses many groups, including Whites, African Americans, and Hispanics in some instances (Schwartz 1994; Swagerty 1983).

The number of Native Americans north of the Rio Grande, estimated at about 10 million in 1500, gradually decreased as their food sources disappeared and they fell victim to diseases, such as measles, smallpox, and influenza, brought by European settlers. By 1800, the Native American population was about 600,000; by 1900, it was fewer than 250,000. This loss of human life can only be described as catastrophic. The United States, which dates back only to 1776, does not bear total responsibility. The pattern of destruction had been well established by the early Spaniards in the Southwest and by the French and English colonists who sought control of the eastern seaboard.

Native Americans did have warfare between tribes. However, their conflicts differed significantly from those of their conquerors. The Europeans launched large campaigns against the tribes, resulting in mass mortality. In contrast, in the Americas, the native tribes limited warfare among themselves to specific campaigns designed for specific purposes, such as recapturing a resource or avenging a loss.

Not all initial contacts sought conquest or led to tragedy. Some missionaries traveled well in advance of settlement in efforts to Christianize Native Americans before they came into contact with less-tolerant Europeans. Fur trappers, vastly outnumbered by Native Americans, were forced to learn the natives' customs, but these trappers established routes of commerce that more and more non-Indians later followed (Glenn 2015; Snipp 1989).

Gradually, the policies directed from Europe toward the indigenous peoples of North America resembled the approach described in the world systems theory. Recall from Chapter 1 that the **world systems theory** takes the view that the global economic system is

"JUST HOW LONG DO YOU ILLEGAL ALIENS PLAN ON STAYING IN OUR COUNTRY?"

Harley Schwadron/CartoonStock.com

divided between nations that control wealth and those that provide natural resources and labor. The indigenous peoples and—more important to the Europeans—the land they occupied were targets of exploitation by Spain, England, France, Portugal, and other nations with experience as colonizers in Africa and Asia (Chase-Dunn and Hall 1998).

Treaties and Warfare

The United States formulated a policy toward Native Americans during the nineteenth century that followed the precedents established during the colonial period. The government policy was not to antagonize the Native Americans unnecessarily. Yet if the needs of tribes interfered with the needs, or even the whims, of non-Indians, then Whites were to have precedence.

Tribes were viewed as separate nations to be dealt with by treaties formed through negotiations with the federal government. Fair-minded as that policy might seem, it was clear from the beginning that the non-Indian government would deal harshly with tribal groups that refused to agree to treaties. Federal relations with the Native Americans were the responsibility of the secretary of war. Consequently, when the Bureau of Indian Affairs (BIA) was created in 1824 to coordinate the government's relationships with the tribes, it was part of the Department of War. The government's primary emphasis was to maintain peace and friendly relations along the frontier. Nevertheless, as settlers moved the frontier westward, they encroached more and more on land that Native Americans had inhabited for centuries.

Table 6.2 summarizes the more significant federal actions of the nineteenth and twentieth centuries, some of which continue in force today.

Table 6.2 Major Federal Policies

Year	Policy	Central Feature
1830	Indian Removal Act	Relocated Eastern tribes westward
1887	Allotment Act	Subdivided tribal lands into individual household plots
1934	Indian Reorganization Act (Wheeler-Howard Act)	Required tribes to develop election-based governments and leaders
1934	Johnson-O'Malley Act	Aided public school districts with Native American enrollments
1946	Indian Claims Commission	Adjudicated litigation by tribes against the federal government
1952	Employment Assistance Program	Relocated reservation people to urban areas for jobs
1953	Termination Act	Closed reservations and their federal services
1971	Alaska Native Settlement Act	Recognized legally the lands of tribal people
1974	Indian Financing Act	Fostered economic development
1975	Indian Self-Determination and Education Assistance Act	Increased involvement by tribal people and governments
1976	Indian Health Care Improvement Act	Provided financial and advisory assistance for healthcare delivery on reservations
1978	Indian Child Welfare Act	Kept Native children with their family and tribes
1988	Indian Gaming Regulatory Act	Allowed states to negotiate gaming (gambling) rights with reservations
1990	Native American Graves Protection and Repatriation Act	Returned Native remains to tribes with authentic claims
1990	Indian Arts and Crafts Act	Monitored authenticity of crafts
1994	American Indian Religious Freedom Act	Sought to protect tribal spirituality, including use of peyote

THE INDIAN REMOVAL ACT (1830)   The Indian Removal Act, passed in 1830, called for the relocation of all Eastern tribes to the west of the Mississippi River. The Indian Removal Act was popular with non–Indians because it opened more land to settlement through annexation of tribal land. Almost all non-Indians felt that the Native Americans had no right to block progress—which was defined as movement by White society. Among the largest groups relocated were the five tribes of the Creek, Choctaw, Chickasaw, Cherokee, and Seminole, who were resettled in what is now Oklahoma. The movement, lasting more than a decade, is called the *Trail of Tears* because the tribes left their ancestral lands under the harshest conditions. Poor planning, corrupt officials, little attention to those ill from a variety of epidemics, inadequate supplies, and the deaths of several thousand Native Americans characterized this forced migration (Hirsch 2009).

The Indian Removal Act disrupted Native American cultures but didn't move the tribes far enough or fast enough to stay out of the path of the ever-advancing non–American Indian settlers. After the Civil War, settlers moved westward at an unprecedented pace. The federal government negotiated with many tribes but primarily enacted legislation that affected them with minimal consultation. The government's first priority was almost always to allow the settlers to live and work, regardless of Native American claims. Along with the military defeat of the tribes, the federal government tried to limit the functions of tribal leaders. If tribal institutions were weakened, it was felt, the Native Americans would assimilate more rapidly.

THE ALLOTMENT ACT (1887)   The Allotment Act of 1887 bypassed tribal leaders and proposed making individual landowners of tribal members. Each family was given as many as 160 acres under the government's assumption that, with land, Native Americans would become more like the White homesteaders who were flooding the not-yet-settled areas of the West.

The effect of the Allotment Act, however, was disastrous. To guarantee that they would remain homesteaders, the act prohibited the Native Americans from selling the land for 25 years. Yet no effort was made to acquaint them with the skills necessary to make the land productive. Many tribes were not accustomed to cultivating land and, if anything, considered such labor undignified, and they received no assistance in adapting to homesteading.

Large parcels of land eventually fell into the possession of non-Indians. For Native Americans who managed to retain the land, the BIA required that, upon the death of the owner, the land be divided equally among all descendants, regardless of tribal inheritance customs. In documented cases, this division resulted in as many as 30 people trying to live off an 80-acre plot of worthless land. By 1934, Native Americans had lost approximately 90 million of the 138 million acres in their possession before the Allotment Act. The land left was generally considered worthless for farming and marginal even for ranching (Blackfeet Reservation Development Fund 2006; Deloria and Lytle 1983).

THE INDIAN REORGANIZATION ACT (1934)   The assumptions behind the Allotment Act and the missionary activities of the nineteenth century were that it was best for Native Americans to assimilate into White society, and that an individual was best considered apart from his or her tribal identity. Gradually, in the twentieth century, government officials began accepting the importance of tribal identity. The Indian Reorganization Act of 1934, also known as the Wheeler-Howard Act, recognized the need to acknowledge, rather than ignore, tribal identity. But assimilation, rather than movement toward a pluralistic society, was still the goal.

Many provisions of the Indian Reorganization Act, including revocation of the Allotment Act, benefited Native Americans. Still, given the legacy of broken treaties, many tribes at first distrusted the new policy. Under the Indian Reorganization Act, tribes could adopt a written constitution and elect a tribal council with a head. This system imposed foreign values and structures. Under it, the elected tribal leader represented an entire reservation, which might include several tribes, some hostile to one another. Furthermore, the leader had to be elected by majority rule, a concept alien to many tribes. Many full-blooded Native Americans resented the provision that mixed-bloods had full voting rights. The Indian Reorganization Act did facilitate tribal dealings with government agencies, but the dictation to Native Americans of certain procedures common to White society and alien to the tribes was another sign of forced assimilation.

As was true of earlier government reforms, the Indian Reorganization Act sought to assimilate Native Americans into the dominant society on the dominant group's terms. In this case, the tribes were absorbed within the political and economic structure of the larger society. Apart from the provision that tribal chairmen were to oversee reservations with several tribes, the Indian Reorganization Act solidified tribal identity. Unlike the Allotment Act, it recognized Native Americans' right to approve or reject some actions taken on their behalf. However, the act still maintained substantial non–Native American control over the reservations. As institutions, the tribal governments owed their existence not to their people but to the BIA. These tribal governments rested at the bottom of a large administrative hierarchy (Cornell 1984; Deloria 1971; McNickle 1973; Washburn 1984; Wax and Buchanan 1975).

In 2000, on the 175th anniversary of the BIA, its director, Kevin Guer, a Pawnee, declared that it was "no occasion for celebration as we express our profound sorrow for what the agency has done in the past." A formal apology followed. The United States is not the only country expressing regret over past actions with its indigenous peoples, as we see in A Global View (Stout 2000).

A Global View

Australia's Aboriginal People

The indigenous people of Australia have continuously inhabited the continent for at least 50,000 years. Today, they number over 600,000 people, constituting about 2.5 percent of the total population. Although this percentage seems small, the legacy of the Aboriginal population is highly visible. The terms *Aboriginal* and *indigenous people* are used here interchangeably.

Aboriginals make up many clans, language groups, and communities with few interconnections except those that are occasionally created through kinship or trade. The cultural practices of these indigenous peoples have historically been very diverse. At the time Europeans arrived, an estimated 600–700 groups spoke 200–250 separate languages as distinct from one another as French is from German. In addition, there were many more dialects of a language that could be more or less understood by indigenous peoples who spoke other languages.

Although Aboriginal belief systems vary in ways that reflect the changing terrain from the Outback to the rainforests, Aboriginals see themselves as having arisen from the land itself and ultimately returning to the land. This set of beliefs is commonly referred to as *Dreaming* or *Dreamtime*; Westerners sometimes view or label this belief system as a cosmology or oral folklore.

As was the case with American Indians, the size of Australia's indigenous population declined dramatically after European settlement and colonialism. The impact of new diseases, some of which were not life-threatening to Europeans, had devastating effects on indigenous communities, which lacked immunity to those diseases. The number of indigenous people also decreased as a result of their mistreatment, the seizure of their land, and the disruption and disintegration of their culture. Many of their distinctive languages disappeared, and no efforts have sought to re-introduce them.

Historically, there was little legal recognition of indigenous people. Not until 1967 were Australian citizenship and voting rights extended to the indigenous people, allowing them access to welfare and unemployment benefits. However, it would be misleading to view Aboriginal people as passive either in colonial days or more contemporary times with respect to their position in Australia. They have taken an active part in efforts to secure their rights.

Reflecting the low regard that White Australians had for the indigenous people, thousands of Aboriginal children were forcibly taken from their families and raised by Whites because it was thought that bringing them into the dominant society's culture was best for the children. The government program affected somewhere between 10 and 30 percent of all Aboriginal children from 1910 to 1970. Finally, in 2008, the Australian government expressed its regret for the "Stolen Generations" and committed to improving the living conditions and future prospects of all Aboriginal people. In 2016, Australia began the process of developing treaties with the Aboriginal people that will give them greater ability to self-govern. The next year, 2017, the first indigenous person was named to the cabinet to oversee healthcare for all people in country—no small undertaking when it comes to the Aboriginal people, who still have a life expectancy ten years shorter than that of White Australians.

Sources: Anderson 2003; Attwood 2003; Australian Bureau of Statistics 2012a, 2012b; The Economist 2017; Innis 2016; Power 2016.

Reservation Life and Federal Policies

6.2   **Explain how contemporary federal policies affect Native Americans.**

Today, more than one-third of Native Americans live on 326 reservations and trust lands in 33 states, which account for a bit more than 2 percent of the land in the United States (Figure 6.2). The reservations play a prominent role in the identities of even those Native Americans who reside far from the tribal lands.

More than any other segment of the population, with the exception of the military, a Native American living on the reservation finds his or her life determined by the federal government. From the condition of the roads to the level of fire protection to the quality of the schools, the federal government, through such agencies as the BIA and the Public Health Service, effectively controls reservation life. Tribes and their leaders are now consulted more than in the past, but ultimate decisions rest in Washington, DC, to a degree that is simply not true for the rest of the civilian population.

The development of reservations created problems that tribes would face for generations. Perhaps the most serious of these problems arose from the federal government's conscious decision to locate tribes that even prior to the arrival of Europeans had been in conflict with one another on the same reservation or adjoining reservations. We consider this situation in more detail in the Relations Across Boundaries feature.

Many of the policies instituted by the BIA in the twentieth century were designed to give tribal people more autonomy, but final control rests with the federal government. Disagreement between the BIA and the tribes, and among Native American groups, has focused on *how* to reduce federal control and subsidies, not on whether they *should be* reduced. The government has taken three steps in this direction since World War II: legal rulings, the Termination Act, and the Employment Assistance Program. We discuss each of these steps in turn.

Figure 6.2 Native American Lands and Communities
SOURCE: Bureau of Indian Affairs 1986: 12–13.

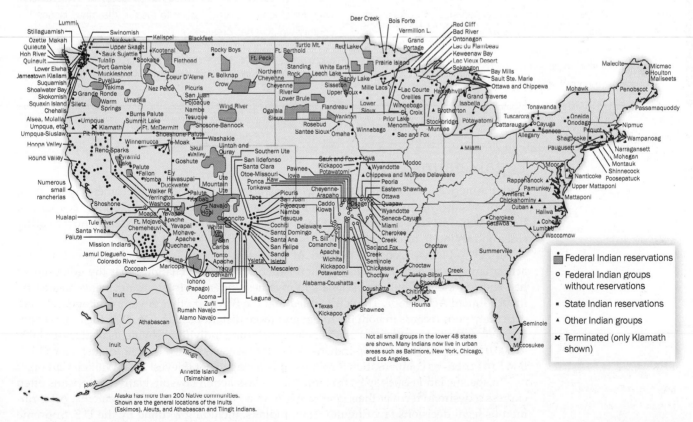

Relations Across Boundaries

The Hopi and Navajo Peoples

American Indian tribes are not all alike and sometimes do not get along, especially if they find themselves competing for scarce resources, whether water (as in the past) or licenses to open gambling casinos (today). However, few tribes have been locked in as long and bitter a conflict as the Hopi and the Navajo.

In the late 1800s, reservation boundaries were carved out for the Navajo and Hopi people, with the federal government creating over 2 million acres as a "joint use area" (JUA) by the two tribes. Initially, mostly the Hopi used the JUA. With the development of ranches and railroads, more Navajos moved into the area with the encouragement of the BIA, which even granted them livestock grazing rights. The BIA pretty much ignored the JUA until non-Indians saw real value in the land.

In 1909, the U.S. Geological Survey conducted a survey in northern Arizona (including the JUA). Its goal was to identify coal deposits that could be used to generate energy for the expanding cities of southern California. Hastily created "tribal councils" under the Indian Reorganization Act consented to the development, and massive mineral excavating facilities were built. Energy efforts expanded in the same area with oil extraction in the 1920s and nuclear power plants in the 1950s. The various energy complexes emit tremendous amounts of pollutants, including sulfur dioxide, nitrogen oxide, carbon dioxide, and mercury, into the air. As a result, the two reservations typically experience air pollution levels ten times worse than those of Los Angeles.

For the past 100 years, disputes have occurred over excavation of land regarded as sacred by the Hopi and whether adequate payments (if any) were made and how they were divided between the two tribes. As the population grew and heavy mineral extraction expanded, the tribal way of life became more and more difficult to sustain. The Navajo-owned cattle livestock competed for grazing land with the Hopi sheep herds. Both tribes saw the elimination of grazing land as destroying their unique culture.

Big corporate energy companies and distant Washington, DC, policymakers were not easy targets for the native people. Instead, the Hopi and Navajo often battled each other in bitter lawsuits and verbal warfare. Complicating the search for a peaceful resolution is the fact that Hopi lands and the JUA are almost entirely surrounded by the Navajo reservation—a tribe that, while poor, is relatively better off than the Hopi.

Numerous plans have been advanced and some even partially carried out to relocate families and to provide financial relief, but the tension remains. As recently as 2016, Arizona Senator John McCain visited the reservations, calling the situation "disgraceful" and the continuing actions of big energy companies a "clear violation of the Constitution and treaties." McCain has long been familiar with the JUA, as he led the effort to enact the 1974 Navajo-Hopi Land Settlement Act to settle the JUA dispute—an act that did not accomplish its goal. Several court judgments and legislative actions later, the issues remain unresolved. Now, on their own initiative, the two tribes have created a "Two Nations, One Voice" commission to work to resolve the many issues the century-old JUA has created.

Sources: Cultural Quarterly Survival 1988; Hopi Tribe 2016; King 2012; Landry 2016; Talbot 2015.

Legal Claims

Native Americans have had a unique relationship with the federal government. In the past, little provision was made for them, as individuals or as tribes, to bring grievances against the government. However, the U.S. Court of Federal Claims and Congress are now hearing cases and trying to resolve disputes.

In 1996, Elouise Cobell, a member of the Blackfeet tribe in Montana, brought a class-action lawsuit on behalf of a half-million American Indians, charging that the government had cheated them of billions of dollars in royalties under the trust arrangements created by the Allotment Act of 1887. The courts ruled that the BIA and other government agencies had extremely poor records in both the recent and more distant past. In late 2009, the federal government agreed to a settlement of $3.4 billion, including individual payments of at least $1,000 to 300,000 individual American Indians. A similar case was settled in 2012 for just over $1 billion to 41 tribes as compensation for similar mismanagement (Hevesi 2011; Williams 2012a).

In specific land issues apart from the *Cobell* class-action lawsuit, Native Americans often express a desire to recover their land rather than accept any financial settlements. After numerous legal decisions favoring the Sioux Indians, including a ruling by the U.S. Supreme Court, Congress finally agreed to pay $106 million for the land that the U.S. government illegally seized in the aftermath of the Battle of the Little Big Horn. The Sioux rejected the money and lobbied Congress for measures, such as the 1987 Black Hills Sioux Nation Act, to return the land to tribal authority. No positive action has yet been taken on these measures. In the meantime, however, the original settlement, the subsequent unaccepted payments, and the accrued interest brought the 2012 total of funds being held for the Sioux to more than $800 million. Despite the desperate need for housing, food, healthcare, and education, the Sioux would prefer to regain the land lost in the 1868 Fort Laramie Treaty and have not accepted payment (Williams 2012b).

The Termination Act (1953)

The Termination Act of 1953 initiated the most controversial government policy toward Native American reservations in the twentieth century. Like many such policies, the act originated with ideas that were meant to benefit Native Americans. In 1947, congressional hearings were held to determine which tribes had the economic resources to be relieved of federal control and assistance. The policy proposed at that time was an admirable attempt to give Native Americans greater autonomy while at the same time reducing federal expenditures, a goal popular among taxpayers.

The services that the tribes received, such as subsidized medical care and college scholarships, were not the result of favoritism. Rather, they fulfilled treaty obligations and therefore should not have been viewed as "special" and deserving to be discontinued. The affected Native Americans therefore viewed the termination as a threat to reduce services rather than a release from arbitrary authority, with greater self-governance coming at a high price.

Unfortunately, the Termination Act as finally passed in 1953 emphasized cost reduction and ignored the tribes' individual needs. Recommendations for a period of tax immunity were dropped. According to the act, federal services such as medical care, schools, and road equipment were supposed to be withdrawn gradually. Instead, when the Termination Act's provisions began to go into effect, federal services were stopped immediately, with minimal coordination between local government agencies and the tribes to determine whether the services could be continued by other means. The effect of the government orders on Native Americans was disastrous, with major economic upheaval in the affected tribes, which could not establish some of the most basic services—such as road repair and fire protection, which the federal government had previously provided. The federal government resumed these services in 1975 with congressional action that signaled the end of another misguided policy intended to benefit tribal peoples (Deloria 1969; Ulrich 2010; Wax and Buchanan 1975).

The Employment Assistance Program

The depressed economic conditions of reservation life might lead us to expect government initiatives to attract business and industry to locate on or near reservations. The government could also provide tax incentives that will eventually pay for themselves. However, such proposals have not been advanced. Rather than take jobs to Native Americans, the federal government decided to lead the more highly motivated American Indians away from the reservation. This policy has further devastated the reservations' economic potential.

In 1952, the BIA began programs to relocate young Native Americans to urban areas. One of these programs, which began after 1962, was called the Employment Assistance Program (EAP). The EAP's primary provision was for relocation of Native Americans, either for individuals or families, at government expense, to urban areas where job opportunities were greater than those on the reservations. The BIA stressed that the EAP was voluntary, but many Native Americans felt compelled to leave the reservations, given the lack of viable economic alternatives available there. The program was not a success for the many Native Americans who found the urban experience unsuitable or unbearable. By 1965, one-fourth to one-third of the people in the EAP had returned to their home reservations. So great was the rate of return that in 1959 the BIA stopped releasing data on the

Figure 6.3 American Indian Poverty Rates, 2007–2011

Note: Data from American Community Survey for 2007–2011 for the 20 cities most populated by American Indian and Alaska Native alone population. White non-Hispanic rate is for the entire nation.
SOURCE: Macartney, Bishaw, and Fontenot 2013:10.

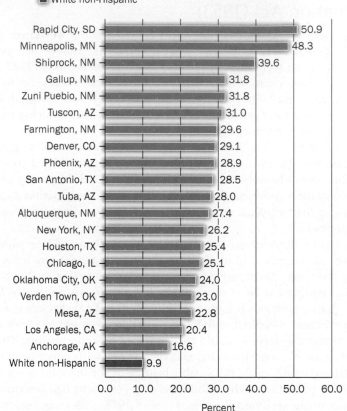

Poverty Rates for the American Indian and Alaska Native Alone Population in the 20 Cities Most Populated by this Group, 2007–2011 ACS

☐ Below poverty: American Indian and Alaska Native Alone
■ White non-Hispanic

City	Percent
Rapid City, SD	50.9
Minneapolis, MN	48.3
Shiprock, NM	39.6
Gallup, NM	31.8
Zuni Puebio, NM	31.8
Tuscon, AZ	31.0
Farmington, NM	29.6
Denver, CO	29.1
Phoenix, AZ	28.9
San Antonio, TX	28.5
Tuba, AZ	28.0
Albuquerque, NM	27.4
New York, NY	26.2
Houston, TX	25.4
Chicago, IL	25.1
Oklahoma City, OK	24.0
Verden Town, OK	23.0
Mesa, AZ	22.8
Los Angeles, CA	20.4
Anchorage, AK	16.6
White non-Hispanic	9.9

Percent: 0.0 10.0 20.0 30.0 40.0 50.0 60.0

Most reservations today have a measure of self-government through an elected tribal council. Pictured is the Navajo tribal council at work.

MATT YORK/AP Images

percentage of returnees, fearing that the information would give too much ammunition to critics of the EAP (Bahr 1972).

Cities have not proven to serve as a simple solution to Native American economic growth. Figure 6.3 shows a Bureau of the Census analysis of recent data. Between 2007 and 2011, White non-Hispanics had an unemployment rate of 9.9 percent, but in each of the 20 cities with the largest Native American population, unemployment levels were higher—ranging from a "low" of 10.6 percent in Anchorage, Alaska, to a high of 50.9 percent in Rapid City, South Dakota. Though these data indicate the desperate employment situation of urban tribal peoples, the Native American employment rate in cities is typically better than on the reservation. Today more than seven of ten Native Americans live in metropolitan areas (Williams 2013).

The movement of Native Americans into urban areas has had many unintended consequences. It has further reduced the labor force on the reservation. Those who leave tend to be better educated, creating the Native American version of the brain drain. Urbanization unquestionably contributed to the development of an intertribal network, or pan-Indian movement, which we describe later in this chapter. The city became the new meeting place of Native Americans, who learned of their common predicament both in the city and on the 325 federally administered reservations. Government agencies also had to develop a policy of continued assistance to nonreservation Native Americans. Despite such efforts, the problems faced by Native Americans in cities persist.

Collective Action

6.3 **Discuss the results of Native Americans' collective-action efforts.**

Native Americans have worked collectively through tribal or reservation government action and across tribal lines. As noted in Chapter 1, the **panethnicity** of solidarity among ethnic subgroups has been reflected in the use of such terms as *Hispanic, Latino*, and *Asian American*. **Pan-Indianism** refers to intertribal social movements in which several tribes, joined by political goals but not by kinship, unite in a common identity. Today, these pan-Indian efforts are most vividly seen in cultural efforts and political protests of government policies (Cornell 1996; Jolivette 2008).

Proponents of these movements see the tribes as captive nations or even colonies. They generally view the federal government as the enemy. Until recently, pan-Indian efforts usually failed to overcome the cultural differences and distrust among tribal groups. However, some efforts to unite have succeeded. The Iroquois made up a six-tribe confederation dating back to the seventeenth century. In the 1880s, the Ghost Dance, a new religious movement incorporated into numerous Native American belief systems, briefly united the Plains tribes, some of which had earlier joined forces to resist the U.S. Army. But these were exceptions. It took nearly 150 years of BIA policies to accomplish a significant level of unification.

The National Congress of American Indians (NCAI), founded in 1944 in Denver, Colorado, was the first national organization representing Native Americans. The NCAI registered itself as a lobby in Washington, DC, hoping to make the Native American perspective heard in the aftermath of the Indian Reorganization Act. Concern about "White people's meddling" is reflected in the NCAI requirement that non-Indian members pay twice as much in dues. The NCAI has had some successes. Early in its history, it played an important role in creating the Indian Claims Commission, and it later pressured the BIA to abandon termination. It is still the most important civil rights organization for Native Americans and uses tactics similar to those of the NAACP (National Association for the Advancement of Colored People), although the problems facing African Americans and Native Americans are legally and constitutionally different.

A later arrival was the more radical American Indian Movement (AIM), which was at one time the most visible pan-Indian group. AIM was founded in 1968 by Clyde Bellecourt (of the White Earth Chippewa) and Dennis Banks (of the Pine Ridge Oglala Sioux), who both lived in Minneapolis at the time. Initially, AIM created a patrol to monitor police actions and document charges of police brutality. Eventually, it promoted programs for alcohol rehabilitation and school reform. By 1972, AIM was nationally known not for its neighborhood-based reforms but for its aggressive confrontations with the BIA and law-enforcement agencies.

Protest Efforts

Fish-ins began in 1964 to protest interference by Washington state officials with Native Americans, who argued that they were fishing in accordance with the 1854 Treaty of Medicine Creek and were therefore not subject to fine or imprisonment, even if they did violate White society's law. The fish-ins had protesters fishing en masse in restricted waterways. This protest was initially hampered by apathy and a lack of unity, but several hundred Native Americans were convinced that civil disobedience was the only way to call attention to their grievances with the government. Legal battles followed, and the U.S. Supreme Court confirmed the treaty rights in 1968. Overall, the fish-ins brought increased public awareness of the deprivations suffered by Native Americans (Bobo and Tuan 2006; D. Johnson 2005).

The fish-ins were only the beginning. After the favorable Supreme Court decision in 1968, other events followed in quick succession. In 1969, members of the San Francisco Indian Center seized Alcatraz Island in San Francisco Bay. The 13-acre island was an abandoned maximum-security federal prison, and the federal government was undecided about how to use it. The Native Americans claimed the "excess property" in exchange for $24 in glass beads and cloth, following the precedent set by the sale of Manhattan more than three centuries earlier. With no federal response and the loss of public interest in the demonstration, the protesters left the island more than a year later. The activists' desire to transform Alcatraz Island into a Native American cultural center did not come to pass. Nonetheless, the event garnered international publicity for the Native American cause. Red Power was born, and Native Americans who sympathized with the BIA were labeled *Uncle Tomahawks* or *apples* (red on the outside, white on the inside).

The most dramatic confrontation between Native Americans and the government happened in what came to be called the Battle of Wounded Knee II. In January 1973, AIM leader Russell Means led an unsuccessful drive to impeach Richard Wilson as tribal chairman of the Oglala Sioux tribe on the Pine Ridge Reservation. In the next month, Means, accompanied by some 300 supporters, started a 70-day occupation of Wounded Knee, South Dakota, site of the infamous cavalry assault in 1890 and now part of the Pine Ridge Reservation. The occupation received tremendous press coverage.

However, the media coverage of the protest did not affect the outcome. Negotiations between AIM and the federal government regarding the occupation brought no positive results. Instead, federal prosecutions were initiated against most participants. AIM leaders Russell Means and Dennis Banks eventually faced prosecution on several felony charges, and both men were imprisoned. By that time, AIM had less visibility as an organization. Russell Means wryly remarked in 1984, "We're not chic now. We're just Indians, and we have to help ourselves" (Hentoff 1984:23; see also Janisch 2008; Nagel 1988, 1996).

Over the past 20 years, AIM activities have decreased as the organization has splintered over dissension on how to prioritize different issues and organizational leadership. Some followers of the AIM tradition have sought to gain clemency for one of its leaders, Leonard Peltier. Imprisoned since 1976, Peltier was given two life sentences for murdering two FBI agents on the embattled Sioux reservation of Pine Ridge, South Dakota. The argument for clemency was supported in two 1992 movie releases: the documentary *Incident at Oglala*, produced by Robert Redford; and the more entertaining but fictionalized *Thunderheart*. To date, clemency appeals to the president to lift the federal sentence have gone unheeded, but this issue remains the rallying point for today's remnants of AIM (Matthiessen 1991; Sandage 2008).

Native American activism remains alive and well, with calls to replace Columbus Day celebrations with Indigenous People's Day and to end the use of American Indian names for sport teams and mascots. The Twitter hashtag #NativeAmericanLivesMatter has emerged to protest police violence. As we will see in the concluding section of this chapter, the environment has been a special focal point of collective action by tribal people (Keane 2015; Lakota People's Law Project 2015).

Powwows offer an opportunity for Native Americans from many tribes to gather for celebrations, competitive dancing and drumming, and selling goods and food.

Robert Brenner/PhotoEdit, Inc.

Solidarity and Powwows

Protest activities have created greater solidarity among Native Americans as they seek solutions to common grievances. Research shows that tribal people born since the collective-action efforts of the 1960s are more likely to reject negative and stereotypical representations of American Indians than those born before the self-determination efforts. Whether through moderate groups such as the NCAI or the more activist AIM chapters, these pan-Indian developments have awakened Whites to Native Americans' grievances and have garnered the grudging acceptance of even the most conservative tribal members, who are more willing to cooperate with government action (Schulz 1998).

Table 6.3 Largest American Indian Groupings

Reservations	
1. Navajo (AZ, NM, UT)	169,321
2. Pine Ridge (SD, NE)	16,906
3. Fort Apache (AZ)	13,014
4. Gila River (AZ)	11,251
5. Osage (OK)	9,920
6. San Carlos (AZ)	9,901
7. Rosebud (SD)	9,809
8. Tohono O'odham (AZ)	9,278
9. Blackfeet (MT)	9,149
10. Flathead (MT)	9,138
Tribes	
1. Navajo	309,584
2. Cherokee	279,935
3. Sioux	124,715
4. Ojibwa/Chippewa	113,377
5. Choctaw	93,501
6. Lumbee	69,600
7. Apache	69,385
8. Pueblo	56,504
9. Iroquois	42,901
10. Creek	41,580
Cities	
1. New York City	111,749
2. Los Angeles	54,236
3. Phoenix	43,724
4. Oklahoma City	36,572
5. Anchorage	36,062
6. Tulsa	35,990
7. Albuquerque	32,571
8. Chicago	26,933
9. Houston	25,521
10. San Antonio	20,137

Note: In terms of tribes, collective South American Indians number 124,715 and Mexican American Indians number 104,170.

SOURCE: 2010 Census in Norris, Vines, and Hoeffel 2012: Tables 4, 6, 7 for Reservations and Cities; American Community Survey 2016b:B02014 for Tribes.

However, the results of collective action have not all been productive, even when viewed from a perspective sympathetic to Native American self-determination. Plains tribes dominate the national organizations, not only politically but also culturally. Styles of dancing, singing, and costuming derived from the Plains tradition are spreading nationwide as common cultural traits. Table 6.3 lists the largest concentrations of Native Americans by reservation, tribe, and city.

The growing visibility of **powwows** became symbolic of Native Americans in the 1990s. The phrase *pau wau* referred to the medicine man or spiritual leader of the Algonquin tribes, but Europeans who watched medicine men dance thought the word referred to entire events. Over the past 100 years, powwows have evolved into gatherings in which Native Americans of many tribes come to dance, sing, play music, and visit.

More recently, they have become organized events featuring competitions and prizes at several thousand locations. The general public sees them as entertainment, but for Native Americans, they are a celebration of their cultures (Eschbach and Applebaum 2000).

American Indian Identity

6.4   Discuss the macro and micro levels of American Indian identity.

Today, American Indian identity occurs on two levels: macro and micro. At the macro level is the recognition of tribes; at the micro level is how individuals view themselves as American Indian and how this perception is recognized.

Sovereignty

Sovereignty in the context of Native Americans refers to tribal self-rule. Supported by every U.S. president since the 1960s, sovereignty is recognition that tribes have vibrant economic and cultural lives. At the same time, numerous legal cases, including many at the Supreme Court level, continue to clarify to what extent a recognized tribe may rule itself and to what degree it is subject to state and federal laws. In 2004, the U.S. Supreme Court ruled 7–2 in *United States v. Lara* that a tribe has the inherent right to prosecute all American Indians, regardless of affiliation, for crimes that occur on the reservation. However, other cases in lower courts continue to chip away at tribal self-government.

This legal relationship can be quite complex. For example, tribal members always pay federal income, Social Security, unemployment, and property taxes, but they do not pay state income tax if they live and work only on the reservation. Whether tribal members on reservations pay sales, gasoline, cigarette, or motor vehicle taxes has been negotiated on a reservation-by-reservation basis in many states.

Focused on the tribal group, sovereignty remains linked to both the actions of the federal government and the actions of individual American Indians. The government ultimately determines which tribes are recognized, and although tribal groups may argue publicly for their recognition, self-declaration carries no legal recognition. This issue is not new, but given the rise of casino gambling (discussed shortly), the determination of what constitutes a sovereign tribe may carry significant economic benefits for the tribe and its members.

A significant step resolving sovereignty was taken in 1971 with the passage of the Alaska Native Claims Settlement Act (ANCSA). The indigenous people gave up their collective claims in exchange for $62.5 million and 44 million acres. In addition, new for-profit corporations owned by Alaska Natives, which included large expanses of land with 12 regional associations and over 200 villages, were established. There was a great deal of debate among the indigenous people but, in the end, this was felt to be the best deal possible given the growing pressure to access valuable natural resources (such as minerals and oil) on the ceded land. Importantly, ANCSA did not include treaties to govern any settlement. However, in the more than 40 years since the passage of ANCSA, economic progress remains uneven, and many issues are unresolved. The act did not address, for example, Native hunting and fishing rights, nor did it address the question of Native government (Native Federation 2013; Huhndorf and Huhndorf 2011).

The federal government takes its gatekeeping role of sovereignty very seriously—the irony of the conquering people determining who are "Indians" in the continental United States is not lost on many tribal activists. In 1978, the Department of the Interior established what it called the *acknowledgment process* to decide whether individual tribes should have a government-to-government relationship with the U.S. federal government. To qualify, the tribe must show that it is a distinct group and trace its continuity since 1900 (Light and Rand 2007).

Individual Identity

Most people reflect on their ancestry to find roots or to self-identify. However, for an individual who perceives himself or herself to be an American Indian, the process is defined by legalistic language. Recognized tribes establish a standard of ancestry, or what is termed **blood quantum**, or the degree of American Indian or Alaska Native blood from a federally recognized tribe.

The blood quantum criterion became increasingly used after the Bureau of Indian Affairs insisted on a Certificate of Degree of Indian or Alaskan Blood to determine whether a particular tribe's members are eligible to receive benefits. Tribes specify the degree of tribal ancestry one needs, which can range from as little as 1/32 up to 5/8. One-quarter is very common among major tribes. Blood quantum is determined totally by biological ancestry, and in fact, the BIA stipulates that the blood quantum of children adopted by Native Americans is based on birth parents alone. Understandably, there is some ambivalence about this procedure because it applies some racial purity measures. Still, tribes see it as an important way to guard against potential "wannabes" (Robertson 2012; Bureau of Indian Affairs 2017; Fitzgerald 2008).

This process may lead some individuals or entire extended families to be disenrolled. For these people, who perceive themselves as worthy of recognition by a tribe but are denied this coveted "enrollment" status, disputes have arisen that are rarely resolved satisfactorily for all parties. This process has occurred for generations but has become more contentious recently for tribes that profit from casino gambling and must determine who is entitled to share in any profits that could be distributed to those on tribal rolls (Russell 2011).

In the Speaking Out feature, journalist Vi Waln, an enrolled member of the Sicangu Lakota Nation of the Rosebud Indian Reservation, describes the challenges of maintaining extended family ties among tribal people and the role that family plays in maintaining identity with one's tribal roots.

Speaking Out

Kinship in Modern Times

Vi Waln

Lakota social systems have always revolved around strong kinship ties. Yet, the ongoing colonization of our people has undermined our sense of relationship to one another. Still, despite all we have faced as Indigenous people, the basic virtue of caring for one's extended family is still alive in contemporary Lakota society.

Vi Waln.

Courtesy of Vi Waln.

September is Kinship Appreciation and Awareness Month in South Dakota. This is a time to recognize the people who care for members of their extended family or others. It's a time to let our grandfathers, grandmothers, aunts, uncles, brothers, sisters, as well as other members of our Tiospaye [extended family], know how much we appreciate their willingness to open their homes to children who need care.

There continues to be a great demand for suitable homes to care for Lakota children. Our reservation communities especially need sober, stable families to open their homes to children who desperately need a place to live. There are many Lakota grandparents who have stepped up to this challenge and are now caring for their own Takoja [grandchildren], as well as other children in need. We appreciate their efforts.

Kinship has always been an essential aspect of Lakota Society. Many Lakota people are aware of the history of our people's willingness to care for the less fortunate tribal citizens, especially children, elders, and others who may need extra help due to a disability. Prior to the coming of the wasicu [White people], there was no such thing as orphans in Lakota society.

Unfortunately, the strength of our Lakota kinship systems has deteriorated over the past 524 years. Today, many Lakota children are taken from their parents by the Department of Social Services and placed in long-term foster care, usually in a non-Indian home. Unfortunately, when our children are placed with or adopted by non-Indian families, they are more likely to grow up without a sense of Lakota identity.

Still, even though our children might be placed in off-reservation homes with non-Indian people, they tend to find their way back to their blood relatives when they reach adulthood. Many Lakota people pray for these children who are lost in the system to return home. But it's very difficult when these relatives who grew up off the reservation try to reestablish ties with their birth families.

For instance, we are well aware of the lateral oppression [marginalized people like tribal members who attack each other] and violence which is so prevalent in most of our reservation communities. For one reason or another, many of our people work very hard at viciously tearing others apart on the reservation. The

(Continued)

crab-in-a-bucket mentality is something everyone living on the reservation has experienced at some point in their life.

Consequently, this dysfunctional behavior makes it difficult for the people who were raised in non-Indian homes to ever experience the sense of kinship that those of us who live on the reservation take for granted. It isn't easy for them to return to their families on the reservation. They often aren't emotionally or mentally prepared to cope with the dysfunctional behavior exhibited by their own relatives.

For instance, relatives who grew up in non-Indian homes off the reservation are often called derogatory names by their own family members. They are often ridiculed or belittled because they were raised by white people. This is conduct unbecoming to Lakota people. This oppressive behavior directed at our own relatives doesn't demonstrate the Lakota value of kinship.

So, even though many of us pray for these lost children to return to their Tiospaye, it often doesn't work out for them. We have to remember that they were not exposed to the lateral oppression that those of us living on the reservation are accustomed to suffering on a daily basis. As a result, many of these relatives who were lost in the social services system as children cannot cope with the treatment they face upon returning to the reservation. Many of them leave again to never return. They would rather stay away then be mistreated by their blood relatives.

We have many Lakota grandparents who are raising their grandchildren, and in some cases, their great-grandchildren. These are the families holding our value of Lakota kinship intact. Also, many of our elders are surviving on a fixed income. They may face many hardships in providing for the basic needs of their grandchildren. It's not fair to our elders when they must step in to raise their abandoned grandchildren. Yet, we rarely hear them complain because they truly understand the importance of Lakota kinship.

Our Lakota grandparents work hard to find ways to provide food, shelter, and clothing for their grandchildren. Grandparents who do not hesitate to take their grandchildren into their homes are being good ancestors. They are determined to help their grandchildren grow up knowing their own Lakota culture. Those children who are fortunate enough to have the support of their extended families are blessed. Even though they may have a hard time, they are still able to have a childhood which allows them to grow up with family.

Many grandparents sacrifice an early retirement in order to provide for their grandchildren. It's not easy to raise children on the reservation today. Alcohol, drugs, violence, peer pressure, and bullying are realities we all live with. Still, many grandparents and other relatives don't give a second thought to opening their home to extended family members in need.

Wopila [Thank You] to the Lakota people who continue to embrace our kinship values. You are the people ensuring Lakota culture stays alive. *Wopila* for your generous efforts to keep our sense of family alive for the unborn generations.

Source: Vi Waln, "Kinship in Modern Times," Lakota Country Times (September 29, 2016). Used with permission.

Native Americans Today

6.5   Summarize the special challenges Native Americans face today with regard to economic development, education, and healthcare.

The United States has taken most of the land originally occupied by or deeded to Native Americans, restricted their movement, unilaterally severed agreements, created a special legal status for them, and, after World War II, attempted to move them again. As a result of these efforts and the generally poor economic conditions of most reservations, substantial numbers of Native Americans live in the nation's most populated urban areas. Table 6.4 provides some broad comparisons between Native Americans and the general population of the 50 states.

How are Native Americans treated today? A very public insult is the continuing use of American Indian names or stereotypical nicknames for athletic teams, including high school teams, college teams, and even professional sports teams in the United States, such as the Washington Redskins. Almost all American Indian organizations, including AIM, have brought attention to these insults and to such spectator practices as the "Tomahawk chop" associated with the Atlanta Braves baseball team.

Many sports fans and college alumni find it difficult to understand why Native Americans take offense at a name such as "Braves" or even "Redskins" if it is meant to represent a team about which they have positive feelings. For Native Americans, however, the use of such names trivializes their past and their presence today; Native American people question why they should be so "honored" if they don't want to be. In response, the National Collegiate Athletic Association (NCAA), which oversees college athletics, has asked colleges to "explain" their use of mascot names, nicknames, team names, or logos such as savages, braves, warriors, chieftains, redmen, and Indians, to name a few. In 2015, the NCAA banned 18 colleges from using "hostile and abusive" names (Sabar 2015; Thomason 2015).

Any discussion of Native American socioeconomic status today must begin with emphasizing the diversity of the people. Besides the variety of tribal heritages already noted,

TABLE 6.4 A Snapshot: Native Americans

	Total Population	Native Americans
Median age	37.8	30.2
Own their houses	63.0%	53.1%
High school graduates	87.1%	82.7%
College graduates	30.6%	19.1%
Speak language at home other than English	21.5%	27.1%
Lack health insurance	9.4%	20.7%
Median household income	$55,775	$38,530
People below poverty level	14.7%	26.6%

SOURCE: Data from Bureau of Census 2016n.

the contemporary Native American population is split between those on and off reservations and those who live in small towns or central cities. Life in these contrasting social environments is quite different, but enough similarities exist to warrant some broad generalizations on the status of Native Americans in the United States.

The sections that follow summarize the status of contemporary Native Americans in economic development, education, and healthcare.

Economic Development

Native Americans are an impoverished people. Even to the most casual observer of a reservation, poverty is evident. Some visitors seem unconcerned, arguing that Native Americans are used to hardship and lived a simple life before the Europeans arrived, making poverty a familiar and traditional way of life. In an absolute sense of dollars earned or quality of housing, Native Americans are not much worse off than the typical American. But in a relative sense that compares their position with that of non-Indians, they are dismally behind on all standards of income and occupational status. Bureau of Indian Affairs (2005) surveys show that overall unemployment is about 50 percent.

Given their lower incomes and higher poverty rates, it is not surprising that many Native Americans are stuck in low-paying occupations. Those who are employed are less likely to be managers, professionals, technicians, salespeople, or administrators. This pattern of low-wage employment is typical of many racial and ethnic minorities in the United States, but Native Americans differ in three areas: their roles in tourism, casino gambling, and government employment.

TOURISM Tourism is an important source of employment for many reservation residents, who either serve the needs of visitors directly or sell souvenirs and craft items. Generally, such enterprises do not achieve the kind of success that improves the tribal economy significantly. Even if they did, sociologist Murray Wax (1971:69) argued, "It requires a special type of person to tolerate exposing himself and his family life to the gaze of tourists, who are often boorish and sometimes offensively condescending in their attitudes." In this sense, tourism might be considered an exploitation of Native peoples.

Tourism represents a complex interaction of the outside world with Native Americans and their culture. Interviews with tourists visiting museums and reservations found that many visitors interpreted their brief experiences to be consistent with their previously held stereotypes of and prejudices toward Native Americans. In addition, some contemporary tourists conscious of the historical context are uncomfortable taking in Native foods and purchasing crafts at tribal settlements despite the reservations' large economic need for such commerce (Laxson 1991; Padget 2004).

Shown here is a poster for *Eclipse*, released in 2010 as a part of the *Twilight* series, which continued with *Breaking Dawn* in 2012. Perhaps one of the strangest effects of the series has been tourists trying to experience the book and movie series by seeking out the Quileute Nation in Washington state. Numbering only 750, this tribe is the subject of the fictionalized account of Native Americans who shape-shift into wolves as enemies of vampires. Tourists receive a hospitable welcome from tribal members, who show off their picturesque rainforest location and a museum exhibit called "The Real Wolves of the Quileute."

Entertainment Pictures/Alamy Stock Photo

Craftwork rarely produces the profits that most Native Americans desire and need. The trading-post business has also taken its toll on Native American cultures. Many non-Indian craft workers have produced the items that tourists want. Creativity and authenticity often are replaced by mechanical duplication of "genuine Indian" curios. Concern and controversy continue to surround art such as paintings and pottery that may not be produced by real Native Americans. In 1935, the federal government began to officially promote tribal arts. The influx of fraudulent crafts was so great that Congress passed the Indian Arts and Crafts Act in 1990, which severely punishes anyone who offers to sell an object as produced by a Native American artisan when it was not. The price of both economic and cultural survival is very high (Indian Arts and Crafts Board 2017).

CASINO GAMBLING   A recent source of significant income and some employment has been the introduction of gambling on reservations. Some forms of gambling, originally part of tribal ceremonies or celebrations, existed long before Europeans arrived in the Western Hemisphere. Today, however, commercial gambling is the only viable source of employment and revenue available to many tribes.

Under the 1988 Indian Gaming Regulatory Act, states must negotiate gambling agreements with reservations and cannot prohibit any gambling already allowed under state law. By 2017, 243 tribal governments in 28 states were operating a variety of gambling operations, including off-track betting, casino tables such as blackjack and roulette, lotteries, sports betting, video games of chance, telephone betting, slot machines, and high-stakes bingo. The gamblers, almost all non–Native Americans, sometimes travel long distances for the opportunity to wager money. The casinos themselves are a form of tribal government enterprise as opposed to private business operations.

In the Research Focus feature, we consider the economic impact of these new gaming operations on Native Americans. Criticism is not hard to find, even among Native Americans, some of whom oppose gambling on moral grounds and because it is marketed in a form that is incompatible with Native American cultures. Similar critiques are leveled at other sources of income for reservations—including online lending businesses and the sale of tobacco and liquor cheaply because state taxes need not be levied. Gambling opponents are concerned about the appearance of compulsive gambling among some tribal members. The majority of the gamblers are not Native Americans, and almost all of the reservation casinos, though owned by the tribes, are operated by non-Indian-owned businesses. Some tribal members feel that the casinos trivialize and cheapen their heritage. The issue of who shares

Jack Corbett/CartoonStock.com

in gambling profits also has led to heated debates in some tribal communities about who is a member of the tribe. In addition, established White gaming interests lobby Congress to restrict the tribes' casinos, which account for about 44 percent of total casino gaming revenue, so they do not compete with nonreservation casinos (Frosch and Zibel 2014; Toensing 2011).

Native Americans' voting clout is very weak, even compared to that of African Americans and Latinos, but their lobbying power has become significant. Casino money fueled the 2006 scandal involving lobbyist Jack Abramoff, who cheated several tribes by pretending to lobby on their behalf. Although many of the political donations Native Americans make are aimed at protecting reservation casinos, tribes' political agendas include obtaining federal grants for education, roads, housing, and other projects. By the 2007–2008 election cycle, tribes with casinos accounted for four of the top donors nationwide (Capriccioso 2011b).

Although income from gambling has not dramatically changed the lifestyle of most Native Americans, it has been a magnet of criticism from outsiders. Critics question the special status afforded to Native Americans and contend that the playing field should be even. Tribal members certainly would endorse this view because most government policies over the past 200 years placed tribes at a major disadvantage. Critics also point to some tribes that made contributions to politicians involved in policies concerning gambling laws. Although some of these contributions may have been illegal, the national media attention was far more intense than was warranted in the messy area of campaign financing. In 2012, tribes made over $3.25 million in contributions to the presidential campaigns—ten times the contributions made just four years earlier. This is another example of how the notion that Native Americans are now playing the White man's game of capitalism "too well" becomes big news (Gold and Tanfani 2012).

Research Focus

Economic Impact of Casino Gambling

While Native American gaming operations are widespread, it should be remembered that not all tribes are involved. Of the 567 federally recognized tribes, only 243 have any gambling operations (not counting charitable bingo operations). However, the economic impact on some reservations has been enormous, and nationwide receipts from reservation casino operations amounted to $28.9 billion in 2014—about 44 percent of all casino gaming revenue in the country.

The few very successful casinos have led to staggering windfalls for particular tribes, but reliance on a single industry can lead to drastic ups and downs, as in the recent Great Recession, when the gaming industry took a major hit. Recently, expansion of gambling outlets, mostly non-tribal, including on the Internet, have led to no growth in receipts on virtually all reservation gaming operations (Meister 2013).

The more typical picture is of moderately successful gambling operations associated with tribes whose social and economic needs are overwhelming. Tribes that have opened casinos have experienced drops in unemployment and increases in household income not seen on nongaming reservations. However, five important factors must be considered:

1. The tribes do pay taxes. They pay $10 billion in gambling-generated taxes and revenue-sharing to local, state, and federal governments. Even after taxes, significant profits exist and can be paid to tribal members or reinvested in collective tribal operations.

2. Nationwide, the economic and social impact of this gambling revenue is limited. The tribes that make substantial revenue from gambling are a small fraction of Native American people. About one-sixth of all gaming facilities account for 70 percent of the total revenue.

3. Even on the reservations that benefit from gambling enterprises, the levels of unemployment are substantially higher and the family income significantly lower than for the nation as a whole.

4. The more successful revenue-generating operations often fund worthwhile projects, ranging from childcare operations serving the reservation to creating museums that publicize the long tribal history, but when revenues slow down, these are the first operations to be reduced or shut down entirely.

5. While gaming generates many jobs, only one about one quarter of jobs are filled by tribal members. In an effort to situate casinos near population centers or interstate highways, some casinos locate well over 100 miles from the tribe.

Gaming may be a legacy of most Native American cultures, but it certainly is not the solution to the continuing economic challenges they face.

Sources: Government Accountability Office 2015; Meister 2016; Robertson 2012; Schlossberg 2014; Williams 2012c.

UNEMPLOYMENT   We have examined sources of economic development such as tourism and legalized gambling, but the dominant feature of reservation life is, nevertheless, unemployment. A government report issued by the Full Employment Action Council opened with the statement that such words as *severe, massive,* and *horrendous* are appropriate to describe unemployment among Native Americans. Official unemployment figures for reservations range from 23 to 90 percent. It is little wonder that census data released in 2010 showed that the poorest county in the nation was wholly on tribal lands: Ziebach County, South Dakota, of the Cheyenne River Reservation, had a 62 percent poverty rate. Two of the other poorest six counties were defined by the Pine Ridge and Rosebud reservations. The other poor counties were either in the devastated Gulf Coast area or defined largely by a prison facility (Joseph 2010).

However, the economic outlook for Native Americans need not be bleak. A single program is not the solution; the diversity of Native Americans and their problems demands a multifaceted approach. The solutions need not be unduly expensive; indeed, because the Native American population is very small compared with the total population, programs with major influence may be financed without significant federal expenditures. Murray Wax (1971) observed that reformers viewing the economically depressed position of Native Americans often seize on education as the key to success. As the next section shows, improving educational programs for Native Americans would be a good place to start.

Education

Government involvement in the education of Native Americans dates as far back as a 1794 treaty with the Oneida Indians. In the 1840s, the federal government and missionary groups combined to start the first school for American Indians. By 1860, the government was operating schools that were free of missionary involvement. Today, laws prohibit federal funds for Native American education from going to sectarian schools. Also, since the passage of the Johnson-O'Malley Act in 1934, the federal government has reimbursed public school districts that include Native American children. The federal government continues to directly fund 185 reservation schools in 23 states (M. Smith 2014).

Federal control of the education of Native American children has had mixed results from the beginning. Several tribes started their own school systems at the beginning of the nineteenth century, financing the schools themselves. The Cherokee tribe developed an extensive school system that taught both English and Cherokee, the latter using an alphabet developed by the famed leader Sequoyah. Literacy for the Cherokees was estimated by the mid-1800s at 90 percent, and they even published a bilingual newspaper. The Creek, Chickasaw, and Seminole also maintained school systems. But by the end of the nineteenth century, all these schools had been closed by federal order. Not until the 1930s did the federal government become committed to ensuring an education for Native American children. Despite the push for educational participation, by 1948, only one-quarter of the children on the Navajo reservation, the nation's largest, were attending school (Pewewardy 1998).

A serious problem in Native American education has been the unusually low level of enrollment. Nationwide, about 15 percent of 16- to 24-year-old Native Americans were high-school dropouts, compared to 6.4 percent among Whites of a similar age. The term *dropout* is misleading because many tribal American schoolchildren have found their educational experience so hostile that they have no choice but to leave. In 2005, the South Dakota Supreme Court ruled that a school serving the Lakota Sioux tribe was routinely calling in the police to deal with the slightest misbehavior. The youth soon developed a juvenile record, leading to what was termed a "school-to-prison pipeline" (Dell'Angela 2005; DeVoe, Darling-Church, and Snyde 2008).

Do Native Americans experience a curriculum that, at the very least, considers the unique aspects of their heritage? It is hoped things have changed since Charles Silberman (1971:173) visited a sixth-grade English class in a school on a Chippewa reservation. The students there were busy writing a composition for Thanksgiving: "Why We Are Happy the Pilgrims Came." Inclusion of Native cultures in the curriculum is uneven at best. Among teachers of eighth-graders attending schools that are at least one-fourth Native American, about one in four reports Native American–focused presentations more than once a month in any subject (DeVoe, Darling-Church, and Snyde 2008).

The assimilationist view argues that to succeed in larger White-dominated society, it is important for Native Americans to start shedding the "old ways" as soon as possible. However, research done in the past ten years has questioned the assimilationist view, concluding that American Indian students can improve their academic performance through educational programs that are less assimilationist and use curricula that build on what the Native American youth learn in their homes and communities.

Representative of this growing body of research is the study completed by sociologist Angela A. A. Willeto among her fellow Navajo tribal people. She studied a random sample of 451 Navajo high school students from 11 different Navajo Nation schools. She examined the impact of the students' orientation toward traditional Navajo culture on their performance. The prevailing view has been that all that is inherently Navajo in a child must be eliminated and replaced with mainstream White society beliefs and lifestyles.

The Navajo tradition was measured by a number of indicators, such as participating in Navajo dances, consulting a medicine man, entering a sweat bath to cleanse oneself spiritually, weaving rugs, living in a traditional hogan (hut), and using the Navajo language. School performance was measured by grades, commitment to school, and aspirations to attend college. Willeto found that the students who lived a more traditional life among the Navajo succeeded in school just as well and were just as committed to success in school and college as high schoolers leading a more assimilated life.

Today, the Navajo Nation's Department of Diné Education promotes embracing the past. For example, in 2012, Barboncito held a competition with students reading an 1868 speech. In his speech, the Navajo leader spoke boldly to General Tecumseh Sherman, whom President Andrew Johnson had dispatched to secure the Navajos' agreement to a treaty. Students were invited to write an essay or prepare a painting that indicated what the speech meant to them in 2012.

These results are important because even many Native Americans themselves accept an assimilationist view. Even within the Navajo Nation, where Navajo language instruction has been mandated in all reservation schools since 1984, many Navajos still equate learning only with the mastery of White society's subject matter (Department of Diné Education 2012; Willeto 1999, 2007).

The picture for Native Americans in higher education is decidedly mixed, with some progress and some promise. Enrollment in college increased steadily from the mid-1970s through the beginning of the twenty-first century, but degree completion, especially the completion of professional degrees, may be declining. The economic and educational backgrounds of Native American students, especially reservation residents, make the prospect of entering a predominantly White college very difficult. Native American students may soon feel isolated and discouraged, particularly if the college does not help them understand the alien world of American-style higher education. Even at campuses with large numbers of Native American students, only a few Native American faculty members or advisors are present to serve as role models.

An encouraging development in higher education in recent years has been the creation of tribally controlled colleges, usually two-year community colleges. The Navajo Community College (now called Diné College), the first such institution, was established in 1968, and by 2017, there were 37 tribal colleges in 14 states, with more than 160,000 residents served. In addition to serving in

The Carlisle Indian School (pictured here in 1901) was a residential school that brought Native Americans from throughout the United States to rural Pennsylvania for three generations. Assimilation was the cornerstone of the curriculum, with the students having their names changed on arrival and being forbidden to display any aspect of their home culture.

Everett Collection Inc/Alamy Stock Photo

some rural areas as the only educational institution for many miles, these colleges also provide services such as counseling and childcare. Tribal colleges enable students to maintain their cultural identity while training them to succeed, which means helping with job placement—a major challenge given the economic situation that most tribal colleges find in their immediate vicinity (American Indian Higher Education Consortium 2017; González 2012).

Healthcare

For Native Americans, *healthcare* is a misnomer, another broken promise in the long line of unmet pledges the government has made. Compared to other groups, Native Americans are more likely to have poorer health and unmet medical needs and to be unable to afford healthcare. They are more likely to have diabetes, trouble hearing, and activity limitations and to have experienced serious psychological distress.

In 1955, amidst criticism even then, the responsibility for healthcare through the Indian Health Service (IHS) transferred from the BIA to the Public Health Service. Although the health of Native Americans has improved markedly in absolute terms since the mid-1960s, their overall health is comparatively far behind all other segments of the population. With the pressure on Native Americans to assimilate in all aspects of their lives, there has been little willingness to recognize their traditions of healing and treating illnesses. Native treatments tend to be noninvasive, with the patient encouraged to contribute actively to the healing benefits and prevent future recurrence. Beginning in the 1990s, a pluralistic effort slowly emerged to recognize alternative forms of medicine, including those practiced by Native Americans. In addition, reservation healthcare workers began to accommodate traditional belief systems as they administered the White culture's medicine (Belluck 2009).

Native American healthcare is very precarious despite the 1976 Indian Health Care Improvement Act. Between 1976 and 2000, the act allowed tribes to recover costs from private health insurance companies, Medicare, and Medicaid; permitted the sharing of facilities with veterans' hospitals; created scholarships for Native Americans to get medical degrees if they returned to serve their tribes; and established community health representatives. The act was allowed to expire in 2000 and was not reauthorized until it was bundled with the Affordable Care Act (ACA or Obamacare). With recent increased attention to reducing ACA coverage, many tribes worry that this linchpin of healthcare will be lost (Collins 2017).

Further contributing to the problems of healthcare and mortality on reservations are often high rates of crime, not all of which is reported. For tribal people along the Mexican–U.S. border, the rising amount and associated violence in the drug trade have only furthered their vulnerability. Poverty and limited job opportunities offer a fertile environment for the growth of youth gangs and drug trafficking. All the issues associated with crime can be found on the nation's reservations. As with other minority communities dealing with poverty, Native Americans strongly support law enforcement but at the same time contend that the very individuals selected to protect them are abusing them. As with efforts for improving healthcare, the isolation and vastness of some of the reservations make them uniquely vulnerable to crime (Eckholm 2010).

Religious and Spiritual Expression

6.6 Discuss how Native Americans express religion and spirituality.

Like other aspects of Native American cultures, religious expression is diverse, reflecting the variety of tribal traditions and the assimilationist pressure of the Europeans. Initially, missionaries and settlers expected Native Americans simply to forsake their traditions for those of European Christianity. Force was sometimes used, as in the repression of the Ghost Dance. Today, many Protestant churches and Roman Catholic parishes with large tribal congregations incorporate customs such as the sacred pipe ceremony, native incenses, sweat lodges, ceremonies affirming care for Earth, and services and hymns in native languages.

Native people typically embrace a broad world of spirituality, whether traditional or reflecting the impact of Europeans. Whereas Christians, Jews, and Muslims adhere to a single deity and often confine spiritual expression to designated sites, traditional American Indian people see considerably more relevance in the whole of the world, including animals, water, and the wind.

After generations of formal and informal pressure on Native Americans to adopt Christian faiths and their rituals, in 1978, Congress enacted the American Indian Religious Freedom Act, which declares that it is the government's policy to "protect and preserve the inherent right of American Indians to believe, express, and practice their traditional religions." However, the act contains no penalties or enforcement mechanisms. For this reason, Hopi leader Vernon Masayesva (1994:93) calls it "the law with no teeth." Therefore, Native Americans have been lobbying to strengthen this 1978 legislation. They are seeking protection for religious worship services for military personnel and incarcerated Native Americans, as well as better access to religious relics, such as eagle feathers, and better safeguards against the exploitation of sacred lands (Deloria 1992; Garroutte 2009).

A major spiritual concern is the stockpiling of Native American relics, including burial remains. Contemporary Native Americans are increasingly seeking the return of their ancestors' remains and artifacts, a demand that alarms museums and archeologists. The Native American Graves Protection and Repatriation Act of 1990 requires an inventory of such collections and provides for the return of materials if a claim can be substantiated. In 2010, the act was revised to cover all Native American remains—even those without identified ties to a tribe (Smith 2011).

In recent years, a specific Native American expression of religion has received significant attention: the ritual use of peyote, which dates back thousands of years. Europeans first noted the Native Americans' sacramental use of peyote in the 1640s. In 1918, the religious use of peyote, a plant that creates mild psychedelic effects, was organized as part of the Native American Church (NAC). At first a Southwest-based religion, since World War II the NAC has spread among northern tribes. The use of the substance is a small part of a long and moving ritual. The exact nature of NAC rituals varies widely. The church maintains the tradition of ritual curing and seeking individual visions. However, practitioners also embrace elements of Christianity, representing a type of religious pluralism of Indian and European identities.

Peyote is a hallucinogen, however, and federal and state governments have been concerned about its use by NAC members. Several states passed laws in the 1920s and 1930s prohibiting the use of peyote. In the 1980s, several court cases involved the prosecution of Native Americans who were using peyote for religious purposes. Finally, in 1994, Congress amended the American Indian Religious Freedom Act to grant Native Americans the right to use, transport, and possess peyote for religious purposes (Martin 2001).

Today's Native Americans are asking that their traditions be recognized as an expression of pluralist rather than assimilationist coexistence. These traditions also are closely tied to religion. Many sites that are sacred to Native Americans, as well as their religious practices, have been under attack. In the next section, we focus on environmental disputes that are anchored in the spiritualism of Native Americans (Kinzer 2000; Mihesuah 2000).

Environment

6.7 Analyze how environmental issues affect Native Americans.

Environmental issues bring together many of the Native American concerns we have previously considered: stereotyping, land rights, environmental justice, economic development, and spiritualism.

First, in some of today's environmental literature, we can find stereotypes of Native peoples as the last defense against the encroachment of "civilization." This image trivializes native cultures, making them into what one author called "New Age savages" (Waller 1996).

Second, many environmental issues are rooted in continuing land disputes arising from treaties and agreements more than a century old (for example, the Navajo-Hopi dispute

Concerns about the environment and worth of ancestral lands spark collective action, as shown here by protesting Native Americans and sympathetic supporters opposing the construction of an oil pipeline near the Standing Rock Sioux reservation.

discussed earlier). Reservations contain a wealth of natural resources and scenic beauty. In the past, Native Americans often lacked the technical knowledge to negotiate beneficial agreements with private corporations—and even when they had this ability, the federal government often stepped in and made the final agreements more beneficial to the non–Native Americans than to the residents of the reservations. The Native peoples have always been rooted in their land. It was their land that was the first source of tension and conflict with the Europeans. At the beginning of the twenty-first century, it is no surprise that land and the natural resources it holds continue to be major concerns.

Third, environmental issues reinforce the tendency to treat the first inhabitants of the Americas as inferior. Native American reservations often lack **environmental justice**—a term we introduced in Chapter 3 to describe efforts to ensure that hazardous substances are controlled so that all communities receive protection regardless of race or socioeconomic circumstances. Reservation representatives often express concern that their lands are used as dumping grounds for hazardous waste (King 2012; Macmillan 2012).

Fourth, environmental concerns by American Indians often are balanced against economic development needs, just as they are in the larger society. On some reservations, authorizing timber companies' access to hardwood forests leads to conflicted feelings among American Indians. However, such arrangements often are the only realistic source of revenue, even if they mean entering into arrangements that more affluent people would never consider. The Skull Valley Goshute tribe of Utah has tried to attract a nuclear waste dump over state government objections. Eventually, the federal government rejected the tribe's plans. Even on the Navajo reservation, a proposed new uranium mine has its supporters—those who consider the promises of royalty payments coupled with alleged safety measures sufficient to offset the past half-century of radiation problems (Pasternak 2010).

Fifth, spiritual needs must be balanced against demands on the environment. For example, numerous sacred sites lie in such public areas as Grand Canyon, Zion, and Canyonlands national parks—sites that, though not publicized, are accessible to outsiders. Tribal groups have sought in vain to restrict entry to such sites. For example, the Standing Rock Sioux tribe, along with sympathetic supporters from throughout (as well as outside of) the Native American community, has protested the 1,200-mile Dakota Access Pipeline (DAPL). The proposed pipeline would transport crude oil from North Dakota shale operations to Illinois. The tribe contends that construction would go through sacred ancestral lands and that pipeline accidents could endanger the fragile watershed. The administration of Barack Obama eventually yielded to the protesters and sought to find a new route, but the Donald Trump administration ordered the DAPL to proceed, leaving another environmental justice issue unresolved (Stand with Standing Rock 2017).

Conclusion

Native Americans have to choose between assimilating to the dominant non-Indian culture and maintaining their identity. In Figure 6.4, we revisit the Spectrum of Intergroup Relations as it relates to Native Americans. Recently, some pluralism has been evident, but the desire to improve themselves economically usually drives Native Americans toward assimilation.

Are Native Americans now receiving respect? The controversy over team names strikes many sports fans and others as "much ado about nothing." But consider closer the case of the NFL team in the nation's capital. The historical derivation of redskin refers not just to skin that is red but also to the nineteenth-century practice of some local governments paying bounties for dead

Figure 6.4 Spectrum of Intergroup Relations: Native Americans

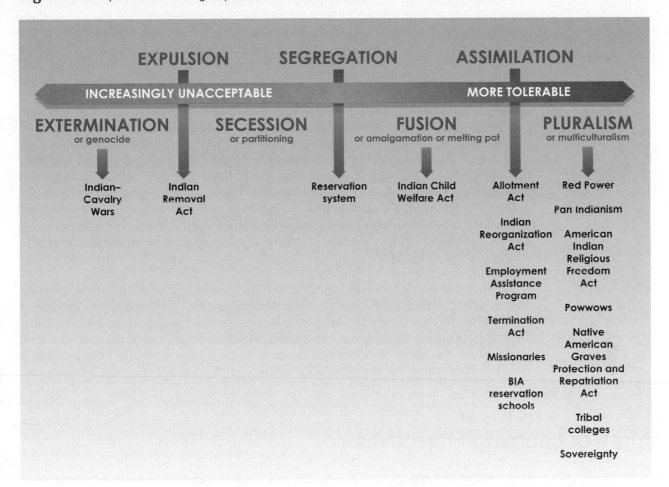

American Indians by requesting the "hunters" to present "redskins." The use of Redskins for Washington's professional team dates back to 1937 and was not intended as a slur. Nonetheless, for many American Indians, including many football fans, it is hateful to see a team so named. Court efforts to remove the offending trademark have apparently failed, with the 2017 Supreme Court ruling 8-0 in a similar case that under the First Amendment even disparaging names can be trademarked. But with the start of every football season, the calls to change the Redskins name are renewed. If they ever again become Super Bowl champions, as they did in 1984, the cries to change will be hard to ignore, but most likely they will be (Belson 2013).

Maintaining one's tribal identity outside a reservation is not easy. One must consciously seek out one's cultural heritage while under pressure to assimilate. Even on a reservation, it is not easy to integrate being Native American with elements of contemporary society. The dominant society needs innovative approaches to facilitate pluralism.

The reservations are economically depressed, but they also are the home of the Native American people spiritually and ideologically, if not always physically. Furthermore, the isolation of reservations means that the frustrations of reservation life and the violent outbursts regarding those frustrations do not alarm large numbers of Whites, as do disturbances in urban centers. Native Americans today, except in motion pictures, are out of sight and out of mind. Since the creation of the BIA in 1824, the federal government has had much greater control over Native Americans than over any other civilian group in the nation. For Native Americans, the federal government and White people are synonymous. However, the typical non-Indian tends to be more sympathetic toward Native Americans than toward African Americans.

Subordinate groups in the United States, including Native Americans, have made tremendous gains and will continue to do so in the years to come. But the rest of the population is not standing still. As Native American income rises, so does White income. As Native American children stay in school longer, so do White children. American Indian healthcare improves, but so does White healthcare. Advances have been made, but the gap remains between the descendants of the first Americans and those of later arrivals.

As the next chapter shows, African Americans have achieved a measure of recognition in Washington, DC, that Native Americans have not. Only 5 percent more numerous than the Black population, Native Americans have a weaker collective voice, even with casino money fueling lobbying efforts. Only a handful of Native Americans have ever served in Congress, and many of the non-Indians representing states with large numbers of Native Americans have emerged as their biggest foes rather than their advocates.

The greatest challenge to and asset of the descendants of the first Americans is their land. More than 120 years after the Allotment Act, Native American people are still seeking what they feel is theirs. The land they still possess, although only a small slice of what they once occupied, is an important asset. It is barren and largely unproductive agriculturally, but some of it is unspoiled and rich in natural resources. It is no wonder that many large businesses, land developers, environmentalists, and casino managers covet Native American land for their own purposes. For Native Americans, the land they still occupy, as well as much of that occupied by other Americans, represents their roots, their homeland.

One Thanksgiving Day, a scholar noted that, according to tradition, at the first Thanksgiving in 1621, the Pilgrims and the Wampanoag ate together. The descendants of these celebrants increasingly sit at distant tables with equally distant thoughts of equality. Today's Native Americans are the "most undernourished, most short-lived, least educated, least healthy." For them, "that long-ago Thanksgiving was not a milestone, not a promise. It was the last full meal" (Dorris 1988:A23).

Summary of Learning Objectives

6.1 Describe the impact of early treaties and acts of Congress on Native Americans.

1. Early European Americans usually did not intend to antagonize the Native peoples unnecessarily, but the needs of the settlers always ruled.

2. Policies created out of warfare and treaties such as the Allotment and Reorganization Acts treated tribal people as inferior to White Europeans.

6.2 Explain how contemporary federal policies affect Native Americans.

3. Reservation life in the first half of the twentieth century was made even more difficult following outcomes in legal claims and the passage of the Termination Act and the Employment Assistance Program. Some of these programs were intended to benefit Native Americans but nonetheless had negative consequences.

6.3 Discuss the results of Native Americans' collective-action efforts.

4. Native Americans have consistently resisted mistreatment through their tribes and reservation organizations and collectively across boundaries through pan-Indian efforts.

6.4 Discuss the macro and micro levels of American Indian identity.

5. American Indians' identity issues emerge today through sovereignty questions at the macro level and self-identification and tribal enrollment at the micro level.

6.5 Summarize the special challenges Native Americans face today with regard to economic development, education, and healthcare.

6. Despite gains over the past couple of generations, Native Americans trail the rest of the country in economic development (including employment), educational levels, and access to quality healthcare.

6.6 Discuss how Native Americans express religion and spirituality.

7. The diversity of American Indian cultures is reflected in religious and spiritual expression. The use of peyote in Native American spiritual practices has been particularly controversial.

6.7 Analyze how environmental issues affect Native Americans.

8. Native Americans have lost much of their historical settlement areas and struggle to achieve environmental justice.

Key Terms

blood quantum, *page 147*
environmental justice, *page 156*
fish-ins, *page 143*

panethnicity, *page 143*
pan-Indianism, *page 143*
powwows, *page 145*

sovereignty, *page 146*
world systems theory, *page 135*

Review Questions

1. How have land rights been a continuing theme in White–Native American relations?

2. What was the motivation behind the Indian Removal Act and the Allotment Act?

3. How have federal government policies influenced reservation life?

4. What steps in the past 50 years have tribal people collectively taken to improve their social situation?

5. How is American Indian identity determined?

6. Do casinos and other gaming outlets represent a positive force for Native American tribes today? Why or why not?

7. How would you describe Native American spirituality today?

8. What is the relationship between Native Americans and the physical environment?

Critical Thinking

1. Consider Independence Day and Thanksgiving Day. How do these national holidays remind Native Americans today of their marginal status?

2. Chronicle how aspects of leisure time, from schoolyard games to Halloween costumes to sports teams, trivialize Native Americans. What experience have you had with such episodes, or what representations have you seen in the mass media?

3. Why do you think that many people in the United States express more benevolent attitudes toward Native Americans than they do toward other subordinate groups such as African Americans and Latinos?

Chapter 7
African Americans

EPG_EuroPhotoGraphics/Shutterstock

∨ Learning Objectives

7.1 Explain the history of slavery in the United States and how it influences life today.

7.2 Summarize the accomplishments of Black leaders in the early twentieth century.

7.3 Discuss the reemergence of Black protests.

7.4 Summarize the key events and outcomes of the civil rights movement.

7.5 Explain how urban areas in the 1960s and 1970s refocused Black–White relations.

7.6 Describe the role of religion in the African American community.

7.7 Examine how recent immigration is adding to the Black community.

The past is always reflected in the present. Back in 1816, Joseph Gee, a landowner from North Carolina, settled along with his 18 slaves in a bend of the Alabama River to establish a large cotton plantation. After the slaves were freed, the Black workers largely remained as sharecroppers and tenant farmers up through the 1930s. People in this Alabama community, now called Gee's Bend, became so impoverished that the Red Cross arrived to prevent them from starving.

Across the river from all-Black Gee's Bend sits the Wilcox county seat, virtually all-White Camden. In 1962, Camden, like several communities in the South, was the site of civil rights protests. Camden was just one example of a sundown town. **Sundown towns** are communities from which non-Whites are systematically excluded from living.

The protesters came from Gee's Bend. They came by ferry, about a ten-minute trip. The people of predominantly White Camden did not like the marchers, so the county closed down the ferry. For over three decades, the ferry remained closed, requiring the 400 residents of all-Black Gee's Bend to drive more than 80 miles each way to get to their jobs, schools, or the hospital. Finally, in 1996, the isolation ended when ferry service was reinstated.

Two residents noted the significance of this event. "This is the first time there has been a concerted effort on the part of Blacks and Whites to do something positive," said Perry Hale, a Black high school teacher. Newspaper publisher Hollis Curl, who is White, remarked, "It's hard for people in other parts of the country to realize what a coming together this has been" (Tyson 1996:4). Relationships between Whites and Blacks in the United States have been marked by many episodes like those along the Alabama River—sometimes those relationships take a step backward, and occasionally they take a step forward.

But daily racism certainly extends far beyond the South. In 2016, La Crosse, Wisconsin, a city with a population of 40,000, apologized for being a sundown town. An official proclamation was passed and was displayed conspicuously in City Hall throughout the holiday season. The people of the city resolved to follow the example of Rev. Martin Luther King, Jr., by examining their own hearts and "seeking to eliminate from our thoughts, words, and actions all racism, prejudice, and discrimination" (La Crosse Office of the Mayor 2016, Vian 2016).

The United States, with more than 41 million Blacks (or African Americans), has the eighth-largest Black population in the world; only Brazil and six countries in Africa have larger Black populations. Despite their large numbers, Blacks in this country have had virtually no role in major national and political decisions and, therefore, captured the world's attention when Barack Obama was elected the first Black president in 2008.

To a significant degree, the history of African Americans is the history of the United States. Black people accompanied the first explorers, and a Black man was one of the first to die in the American Revolution. The enslavement of Africans was responsible for the South's wealth in the nineteenth century and led to the country's most violent domestic strife, the Civil War (1861–1865). After Blacks were freed from slavery, their continued subordination led to sporadic outbreaks of violence in the rural South and throughout urban America. This chapter begins with a brief history of African Americans in the early days of the country and brings us through contemporary times.

The earliest Blacks in what came to be the United States had something less than citizenship, but their experience was only slightly better than slavery. In 1619, 20 Africans arrived in Jamestown, Virginia, as indentured servants. Their children were born free people. Blacks in the British colonies were not the first in the New World, however; some Blacks had accompanied European explorers, perhaps even Columbus. But this information is a historical footnote only. By the 1660s, the British colonies passed laws making Africans slaves for life, forbidding interracial marriages, and making children of slaves bear their mother's status regardless of their father's race. Slavery had begun in North America. More than three and a half centuries later, we still live with its legacy.

Slavery

7.1   Explain the history of slavery in the United States and how it influences life today.

Slavery may seem far removed from the debates over issues that divide Whites and Blacks today. However, contemporary institutional and individual racism, which are central to today's conflicts, have their origins in slavery. Slavery was not merely a single aspect of American society for three centuries; it has been an essential part of life in our country. For nearly half of U.S. history, slavery was not only tolerated but also legally protected by the U.S. Constitution as interpreted by the U.S. Supreme Court.

In sharp contrast to the basic rights and privileges enjoyed by White Americans, Black people in bondage lived under a system of repression and terror. For several

decades, nearly one out five people was Black and enslaved in the United States. Because the institution of slavery was so fundamental to our culture, it continues to influence Black–White relations in the twenty-first century.

Slave Codes

Slavery in the United States rested on five central conditions: slavery was for life, the status was inherited, slaves were considered mere property, slaves were denied rights, and coercion was used to maintain the system (Noel 1972). As slavery developed in colonial America and the United States, so did **slave codes**—laws that defined the low position of slaves in the United States. Although the rules varied from state to state and from time to time and were not always enforced, the most common features of slave codes demonstrate how completely subjugated the Africans were:

1. A slave could not marry or even meet with a free Black.
2. Marriage between slaves was not legally recognized.
3. A slave could not legally buy or sell anything except by special arrangement.
4. A slave could not possess weapons or liquor.
5. A slave could not quarrel with or use abusive language toward Whites.
6. A slave could not possess property (including money) except as allowed by his or her owner.
7. A slave could neither make a will nor inherit anything.
8. A slave could not make a contract or hire himself or herself out.
9. A slave could not leave a plantation without a pass noting his or her destination and time of return.
10. No one, including Whites, was to teach a slave (in some areas, even a free Black) to read or write or to give a slave a book, including the Bible.
11. A slave had to obey established curfews for slaves.
12. A slave could not testify in court except against another slave.

Violations of these rules were dealt with in a variety of ways. Mutilation and branding were not unknown. Imprisonment was rare; most violators were whipped. An owner was largely immune from prosecution for any physical abuse of slaves. Because slaves could not testify in court, a White's actions toward enslaved African Americans were practically above the law (Elkins 1959; Franklin and Higginbotham 2011; Stampp 1956).

Slavery, as enforced through the slave codes, controlled and determined all facets of the lives of enslaved Africans. No exceptions were made for organization of family life and religious worship. Naturally, the Africans had brought their own cultural traditions to America. In Africa, they were accustomed to a closely regulated family life and a rigidly enforced moral code. Slavery rendered it impossible for them to retain family ties in the New World because kinfolk, including their children, were scattered among plantations.

Through the research of W. E. B. Du Bois and many others, we know that slave families had no standing in law. Marriages between slaves were not legally recognized, and masters rarely respected those unions when they sold adults or children. Slave breeding—a deliberate effort to maximize the number of offspring—was practiced with little attention to slaves' emotional needs. The slaveholder, not the parents, decided at what age children would begin working in the fields. The slave family could not offer its children shelter or security, rewards or punishments. The man's only recognized family role was to sire offspring—that is, to be the sex partner of a woman. In fact, slave men often were identified as a slave woman's possession, for example, "Nancy's Tom." Southern law consistently ruled that "the father of a slave is unknown to our law." However, the male slave did occupy an important economic role: Men held almost all managerial positions open to slaves (Du Bois 1970; Dunaway 2003).

Equating Black Africans with slavery reinforced blackness as a race, an inferior race. Recall that **racial formation** is a sociohistorical process by which racial categories are created, inhabited, transformed, and destroyed. The stigmatization of Black Africans during slavery and continuing after its end underscores how people socially construct race. So deeply constructed was this racial formation that it took generations before White people even began to question it (Omi and Winant 2015).

The Attack on Slavery

Although slaves were vulnerable to their owner's wishes, slavery as an institution was vulnerable to outside opinion. For a generation after the American Revolution, restrictions on slaves increased as Southerners accepted slavery as permanent. Slave revolts and antislavery propaganda only accelerated the intensity of oppression the slaves endured. In other words, as slavery was attacked from within and without, conditions for the slaves became harsher, and its defenders became more outspoken in asserting what they saw as its benefits.

Antislavery advocates, or **abolitionists**, included Whites and free Blacks. Many Whites who opposed slavery, such as Abraham Lincoln, did not believe in racial equality. In their minds, even though slavery was a moral evil, racial equality was unimaginable. This inconsistency did not lessen the emotional fervor of the efforts to end slavery. Antislavery societies had been founded even before the American Revolution, but the Constitution dealt the antislavery movement a blow. To appease the South, the framers of the Constitution recognized and legitimized slavery's existence. The Constitution even allowed slavery to increase Southern political power. A slave was counted as three-fifths of a person in determining population representation in the House of Representatives.

Library of Congress Prints and Photographs Division [LC-B811-152-A]

For many generations, Africans were treated by their White slave owners as property, yet they tried to maintain a sense of family life. This 1862 image shows five generations of a family whose members were all born on a plantation in Beaufort, South Carolina.

Abolitionists, both Black and White, continued to speak out against slavery and the harm it was doing not only to the slaves but also to the entire nation, which had become economically dependent on bondage. Frederick Douglass and Sojourner Truth, both freed slaves, became very visible in the fight against slavery through their eloquent speeches and publications. Harriet Tubman, along with other Blacks and sympathetic Whites, developed the Underground Railroad to transport escaping slaves to freedom in the North and Canada (Franklin and Higginbotham 2011).

Slaves from Africa were not the only racial group over whom European settlers extended their domination. The indigenous peoples of North America were also sometimes enslaved and generally regarded as inferior. These conditions created the social context for special relationships between tribal people and the Africans brought across the Atlantic against their will.

Another aspect of Black enslavement was the slaves' own resistance to servitude. Slaves did revolt, and between 40,000 and 100,000 escaped from the South and slavery. However, fugitive slave acts provided for the return of slaves even though they had reached free states. Enslaved Blacks who did not attempt escape, in part because failure often led to death, resisted slavery through such means as passive resistance. Slaves feigned clumsiness or illness; pretended not to understand, see, or hear; ridiculed Whites with a mocking, subtle humor that their owners did not comprehend; and destroyed farm implements and committed similar acts of sabotage. The most dramatic form of resistance was to flee enforced servitude by escaping through the Underground Railroad that linked safe houses and paths to freedom in the North and Canada (Foner 2015).

Slavery's Aftermath

On January 1, 1863, President Lincoln issued the Emancipation Proclamation. The document created hope in slaves in the South, but many Union soldiers resigned rather than participate in a struggle to free slaves. The proclamation freed slaves only in the Confederacy, over which the president had no control. Six months after the surrender of the Confederacy in 1865, abolition became law when the Thirteenth Amendment abolished slavery throughout the nation.

From 1867 to 1877, during the period called Reconstruction, Black–White relations in the South were unlike anything they had ever been. The Reconstruction Act of 1867 put each

Relations Across Boundaries

African Americans and the American Indians

Slaves forcibly brought to the Americas did not just live among European settlers and their descendants but also formed bonds with the Native Americans. The two groups interacted and, in some cases, created shared communities and ways of life. Consider that musical legend Jimi Hendrix often spoke proudly of his Cherokee grandmother.

The nature of Black–Native contact is complex. In early colonial times, Native Americans were enslaved alongside Africans with whom they intermarried. Yet Black Americans often accepted the dominant White construction of society, as evidenced by the famous Buffalo Soldiers, an Army Cavalry regiment composed of African Americans who fought for the Union during the Civil War. From 1866 through the 1890s, the Buffalo Soldiers fought against many western Native American tribes during the Indian Wars. Before the Emancipation Proclamation, tribes sometimes took in runaway slaves, but at the same time tribes in the Southeast modeled themselves after White society and sometimes even kept slaves. For example, the Cherokees were forced to move from the East with their 4,000 slaves to the Indian Territory (Oklahoma). *Freedmen* is the term given to freed slaves and their descendants, and thus *Cherokee Freedmen* refers to contemporary descendants of those slaves. Seminoles also took some slaves, and their descendants are referred to as *Black Seminoles* or *Seminole Freedmen*.

Being Black and Native American, whether in the nineteenth century or the twentieth century, meant navigating very different cultural traditions while sharing a subordinate status and being part of a society whose customs and laws were defined by White America. Prominent among these shared and defining experiences were the forced removal of Blacks from Africa and the forced removals of tribal groups from the eastern United States to further west. Other areas of shared experience are the importance of common practices such as reliance on the extended family, spirituality, folklore, and oral traditions.

A contemporary challenge to harmonious relations has occurred when tribes have tried to identify their members using their standards of blood quantum (see Chapter 6). These rules have led both the Cherokee and Seminole nations to rule that Freedmen are not true members of the tribe. Race, tribal sovereignty, and individual Native American identity collide to create bitter feelings. In addition, these discussions occur in a society defined by White privilege.

These decisions on interpreting blood quantum have led to continuing legal action, and the Bureau of Indian Affairs has suggested that such actions may jeopardize receipt of some federal funds. However, these exclusionary actions are not used by all tribes. For example, the federally recognized Shinnecock Nation of Long Island, New York, is largely biracial.

The historical account of the American Revolution often begins with acknowledging the close Native–Black ties. The first casualty of the Revolution—Crispus Attucks in Boston 1770—was himself the son of an African-born slave and a Natick (or Wampanoag) Native American. Now, almost 250 years later, we are trying to better understand these often-close relationships across the boundaries between African Americans and tribal people.

Sources: Barbery 2013; Meier 2015; Miles 2009, National Museum of the American Indian 2017; Strong 1998.

Southern state under a military governor until a new state constitution could be written, with Blacks participating fully in the process. Whites and Blacks married each other, went to public schools and state universities together, and rode side by side on trains and streetcars. The most conspicuous evidence of the new position of Blacks was their presence in elected office (Du Bois 1969b; Foner 2006).

Nonetheless, discrimination based on racism developed deep roots in the period following the Civil War. Reconstruction failed to truly change the racist social order. Southern states enacted laws meant to keep former slaves and their descendants in a subordinate status. Through these laws, referred to colloquially as **Jim Crow**, segregation became entrenched in the South. The term *Jim Crow* appears to have originated in a dance tune; by the 1890s it was synonymous with segregation and the statutes that kept African Americans in an inferior position.

There was nothing musical about Jim Crow as people took law into their own hands. Between 1877 and 1950, Whites lynched more than 4,000 Black people whom they suspected of wrongdoing—or in some instances just to remind other Black people to "stay in their place." Jim Crow laws gave White people their ultimate authority. In 1896, the U.S. Supreme Court ruled in *Plessy v. Ferguson* that state laws requiring "separate but equal" accommodations for Blacks were a "reasonable" use of state governments' power. Although Jim Crow statutes were eventually overturned, new laws may have a similar impact in the twenty-first century, as we will see in the next section on institutional discrimination (Equal Justice Initiative 2015).

It was in the political sphere that Jim Crow exacted its price soonest. In 1898, the Court's decision in *Williams v. Mississippi* declared constitutional the use of poll taxes, literacy tests, and residential requirements to discourage Blacks from voting. In Louisiana that year, 130,000 Blacks were registered to vote. Eight years later, the number had dropped to only 1,342. When all these measures failed to deprive every African American of the right to vote, White supremacists erected a final obstacle: the **White primary**, which forbade Black voting in election primaries. By the turn of the century, the South had a one-party system, making the primary the significant contest and the general election a mere rubber stamp. Beginning with South Carolina in 1896 and spreading to 12 other states within 20 years, statewide Democratic Party primaries were adopted. The party explicitly excluded Blacks from voting, an exclusion that was constitutional because the party was defined as a private organization that was free to define its own membership qualifications. The White primary brought an end to the political gains of Reconstruction (Lewinson 1965; Woodward 1974).

The United States is not the only country with White people as the socially dominant group and a significant Black population. In the United States, of course, this population grows out of the history of slavery, while as we see in A Global View, it arises out of colonialism in France.

A Global View

France Noire: Black France

Among the ways that subordinate-group status is created are migration and colonialism, as we saw in Chapter 1. Both have played a role in France's contemporary Black population, estimated at 2 million to 5 million out of a population of over 60 million.

Historically, like most European nations, France maintained slavery in its colonies. In the spirit of the French Revolution, slavery was abolished in 1794. Napoleon briefly reintroduced it, but it was definitively abolished in 1834. Racial inequality was seen as incompatible with the French traditions of liberty, equality, and fraternity. Until recently, race was rarely mentioned publicly, and it is still illegal for the French government to collect data about race.

For Black Americans, France has had special appeal. Notable writers and singers from the United States, such as James Baldwin, Josephine Baker, Nina Simone, and Richard Wright, found a welcoming atmosphere in the artistic neighborhoods of Paris. The contemporary Black population in France has its roots in post–World War II immigration from former colonies such as Algeria, Haiti, and other areas in Africa and the Caribbean. Despite the country's tradition of race not being a formal political issue, the French could not ignore injustices and began passing anti-discrimination and anti-racism laws in 1972. A 2007 national survey found that 56 percent of French Blacks had reported discrimination, and over a third felt it was getting worse.

The autumn of 2005 was a turning point as France, and much of the world, was shocked at extended rioting in neighborhoods throughout the country populated by youth of African descent, leading to a national state of emergency. Pre-existing tensions were ignited when two Black youth of Tunisian and Malian descent, thinking they were being chased by police, hid in a power station in suburban Paris, where they were accidentally electrocuted. French-born young people burned thousands of cars, angry about discrimination, poverty, and unemployment. In 2012, the French courts reopened an investigation into whether police failed to come to the aid of the two youths.

Given the high cost of central Paris housing, most immigrants live in high-rise apartment complexes in the outer Paris suburbs or *banlieues*. However, these isolated Black neighborhoods have become stigmatized as "lawless zones" or "outlaw estates," and *banlieues* have developed a reputation as "ghettos." However, the marginal status of the French Blacks is a product of very different racial formation than that of the United States. People of color in France are experiencing a new form of exclusion linked to the modern-day labor market, which provides relatively few opportunities for the employment of unskilled labor. The *banlieue* population is not nearly as segregated as the typical urban Black and Latino neighborhoods in the United States. Also, because housing in the *banlieues* is largely government-controlled, the state plays a much more active role (good and bad) in the lives of Black French people than is typical in the United States.

Today, much of the French Black population feels marginalized. In the national conversation, talk is less about promoting multiculturalism and more about restricting immigration. Underscoring this trend has been the success of the National Front (*Front national*) political party in its cries to deport unemployed immigrants and to halt any immigration from former French colonies of Africa. In spite of and in response to such developments, a more cohesive Black community is emerging in France, with spokespeople, organizations, conferences, and even an annual Black History Month in February with special emphasis on the colonial roots of France's Black citizens.

Sources: Beaman 2015; Browne 2013; *International Herald Tribune* 2007; Keaton, Sharpley-Whiting, and Stoval 2012; Mann 2008; Wacquant, 2007; Winant 2001.

The United States still finds it difficult to come to terms with the power of slavery. Here, we see men dressed as Confederate soldiers in a mock battle at a Civil War reenactment in the Cascade Mountains of Oregon.

The Legacy of Slavery

The legacy of slavery continues more than 150 years after its end in the United States. We can see it in the Capitol and the White House, which were built with slave labor, but we can also see it in the enduring poverty that grips a large proportion of the descendants of slavery.

Insights into slavery and its legacy continue to emerge. For example, historian Craig Steven Wilder (2013), in his book *Ebony and Ivory*, documents the role that the most elite universities played in contributing to slavery. Private colleges readily accepted donations from those who profited from the slave trade or their own plantations, and slaves were used on northern universities and owned by college presidents. Regardless of the abolitionist sentiment at the time, colleges frequently tolerated or even encouraged pro-slavery research and lectures. Even as the Civil War drew near, according to Wilder, the leading American colleges seemed caught in the past.

Serious discussions have taken place for more than 30 years about granting reparations for slavery. **Slavery reparation** refers to the act of making amends for the injustice of slavery. Few people would argue that slavery was wrong and continues to be wrong where it is still practiced in parts of the world. However, what form should reparations take? Since 1989, Congressman John Conyers, a Black Democrat from Detroit, has annually introduced in Congress a bill to acknowledge the "fundamental injustice and inhumanity of slavery" and to call for the creation of a commission to make recommendations for appropriate remedies. This bill has never made it out of committee, but the discussion continues outside the federal government. In 2009, Congress issued a joint resolution apologizing for slavery, but it contained the specific "disclaimer" that nothing in the resolution authorized or supported any claim against the United States (Conyers 2013; Craemer 2015).

The historical and social significance of slavery continues to be marginalized. Hundreds of monuments and memorials commemorating the Confederacy can be found throughout the nation as far north as Montana. While a few have been dismantled (and then only after long debate), others have been erected as recently as 2011. Annually January is marked by the observance of the Martin Luther King, Jr., holiday. But within days of the civil rights leader's birthday are the birthdays of two Confederate generals, Robert E. Lee and Stonewall Jackson. So, in Lexington, Virginia, where the two generals are buried, some townspeople, after annual King Day observances, began on the same day to "flag" the city—standing along streets, some dressed in Civil War costumes, waving Confederate battle flags—more than 150 years after the end of Civil War (Dickerson 2017; Hampson 2017).

The Challenges and Accomplishments of Black Leaders

7.2 Summarize the accomplishments of Black leaders in the early twentieth century.

The institutionalization of White supremacy precipitated different responses from African Americans, just as slavery had. In the late 1800s and early 1900s, several articulate Blacks attempted to lead the first generation of freeborn Black Americans. Most prominent were Booker T. Washington and W. E. B. Du Bois. The personalities and ideas of these two men contrasted. Washington was born a slave in 1856 on a Virginia plantation. He worked in coal mines after emancipation and attended elementary school. Through hard work and driving ambition, Washington became the head of an educational institute for Blacks in Tuskegee, Alabama. Within 15 years, his leadership brought national recognition to the Tuskegee Institute, and he became a national figure. Du Bois, in contrast, was born in 1868 to a free family in Massachusetts. He attended Fisk University and the University of Berlin and became the first Black to receive a doctorate from Harvard. Washington died in 1915, and Du Bois died in self-imposed exile in Africa in 1963.

The Politics of Accommodation

Booker T. Washington's approach to White supremacy is called the *politics of accommodation*. He was willing to forgo social equality until White people saw Blacks as deserving of it. Perhaps his most famous speech was made in Atlanta on September 18, 1895, to an audience that was mostly White and mostly wealthy. Introduced by the governor of Georgia as "a representative of Negro enterprise and Negro civilization," Washington (1900) gave a five-minute speech in which he pledged the continued dedication of Blacks to Whites:

> As we have proved our loyalty to you in the past, in nursing your children, watching by the sick-bed of your mothers and fathers, and often following them with tear-dimmed eyes to their graves, so in the future, in our humble way, we shall stand by you with a devotion that no foreigner can approach, ready to lay down our lives, if need be, in defense of yours. (p. 221)

The speech catapulted Washington into the public forum, and he became the anointed spokesperson for Blacks for the next 20 years. President Grover Cleveland congratulated Washington for the "new hope" he gave Blacks. Washington's essential theme was compromise. Unlike Frederick Douglass, who had demanded the same rights for Blacks as for Whites, Washington asked that Blacks be educated because it would be a wise investment for Whites. He called racial hatred "the great and intricate problem which God has laid at the doors of the South." The Blacks' goal should be economic respectability. Washington's accommodating attitude ensured his popularity with Whites. His recognition by Whites contributed to his large following of Blacks, who were not used to seeing their leaders achieve fame among Whites.

It is easy in retrospect to be critical of Washington and to write him off as simply a product of his times. Booker T. Washington entered the public arena when the more militant proposals of Douglass had been buried. Black politicians were losing political contests and influence. To become influential as a Black, Washington reasoned, required White acceptance. His image as an accommodator allowed him to fight discrimination covertly. He assisted Presidents Roosevelt and Taft in appointing Blacks to patronage positions. Washington's goal was for African Americans eventually to have the same rights and opportunities as Whites. Just as people disagree with leaders today, some Blacks disagreed with the means Washington chose to reach that goal. No African American was more outspoken in his criticism of the politics of accommodation than W. E. B. Du Bois (2011; Norrell 2009).

The Niagara Movement

The rivalry between Washington and Du Bois has been exaggerated. They enjoyed fairly cordial relations for some time. In 1900, Washington recommended Du Bois, at his request, for superintendent of Black schools in Washington, DC. By 1905, however, relations between the two had cooled. Du Bois spoke critically of Washington's influence, arguing that his power was being used to stifle African Americans who spoke out against the politics of accommodation. He also charged that Washington had caused the transfer of funds from academic programs to vocational education. Du Bois's greatest objection to Washington's statements was that they encouraged Whites to place the burden of the Blacks' problems on the Blacks themselves (Du Bois 1903).

As an alternative to Washington's program, Du Bois (1903) advocated the theory of the *talented tenth*, which reflected his atypical educational background. Unlike Washington, Du Bois was not at home with both intellectuals and sharecroppers. Although the very phrase *talented tenth* has an elitist ring, Du Bois argued that these privileged Blacks must serve the other nine-tenths. This argument was also Du Bois's way of criticizing Washington's emphasis on vocational education. Although he did not completely oppose the vocational approach, Du Bois thought education for African Americans should emphasize academics, which would be more likely to improve their position. Drawing on the talented tenth, Du Bois invited 29 Blacks to participate in a strategy session near Niagara Falls in 1905. Out of a series of meetings came several demands that unmistakably placed the responsibility for the problems facing African Americans on the shoulders of Whites.

The Niagara Movement, as it came to be called, was closely monitored by Booker T. Washington. Du Bois encountered difficulty gaining financial support and recruiting prominent people, and Du Bois (1968) himself wrote, "My leadership was solely of ideas. I never was, nor ever will be, personally popular" (p. 303). The movement's legacy was educating a new generation of African Americans in the politics of protest. After 1910, the Niagara Movement ceased to hold annual conventions. In 1909, however, the Niagara Movement leaders founded the National Association for the Advancement of Colored People (NAACP), with White and Black members. It was through the work of the NAACP that the Niagara Movement accomplished most of the goals set forth in 1905. The NAACP also marked the merging of White liberalism and Black militancy, a coalition unknown since the end of the abolition movement and Reconstruction (Rudwick 1957; Morris 2015).

As Du Bois agitated for social change, he continued to conduct groundbreaking research into race relations. He oversaw the Atlanta Sociological Laboratory; its work at the time was generally ignored by the White-dominated academic institutions but is now gradually being rediscovered (Wright 2006).

In 1900, 90 percent of African Americans lived in the South. Blacks moved out of the South and into the West and North, especially the urban areas in those regions, during the post–Civil War period and continued to migrate through the 1950s and 1960s. By the 1980s and 1990s, a return to the South began as job opportunities grew in that part of the country and most vestiges of Jim Crow vanished in what had been the Confederacy states. By 2010, 55 percent of African Americans lived in the South, compared to 33 percent of the rest of the population (Figure 7.1).

A pattern of violence, with Blacks usually the victims, started in the South during Reconstruction and continued into the twentieth century, when it also spread northward. In 1917, a riot in East St. Louis, Illinois, claimed the lives of 39 Blacks and nine

Figure 7.1 Black Population, 2015

Note: 2015 proportion nationally according to the five-year American Community Survey was 12.7 percent.

SOURCE: Bureau of the Census 2016r: Table R0202.

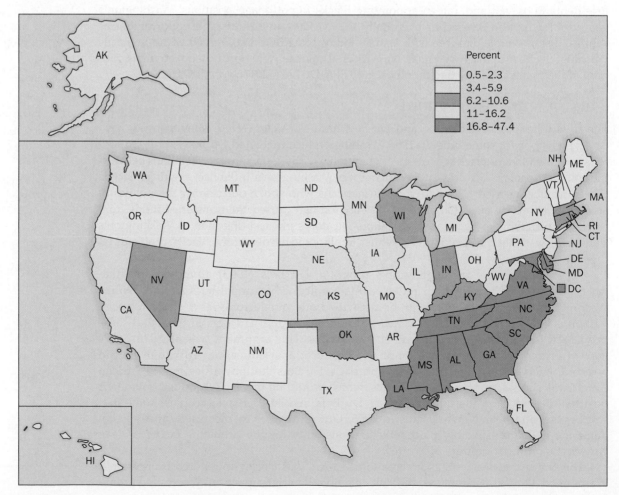

Whites. The several days of violence resulted from White fear of social and economic gains made by Blacks. So much violence occurred in the summer of 1919 that it is commonly called the "red summer." Twenty-six riots broke out throughout the country as White soldiers who returned from World War I feared the new competition that Blacks represented. This period of violence against African Americans also saw a resurgence of the Ku Klux Klan, which at its height had nearly 9 million members (Berlin 2010; Grinspan 2013; Schaefer 1971, 1980).

As documented by historians and sociologists, the South certainly did not have a monopoly on racism. In the Research Focus, we consider in more detail the sundown towns defined at the beginning of this chapter. These towns, which kept Blacks out at night, were found throughout the North beginning in 1890 and continued well into the last quarter of the twentieth century.

Research Focus

Sundown Towns, USA

Sundown towns are communities from which non-Whites are systematically excluded from living. In the United States, they emerged in the late nineteenth century and persisted until the late twentieth century. Sundown towns existed throughout the nation, but more often they were located in northern states that were not pre–Civil War slave states. Although the precise number of sundown towns in the United States is unknown, it is estimated that there were several thousand such towns throughout the nation.

The term *sundown town* comes from signs once posted at the city limits reading "Nigger, Don't Let the Sun Set on YOU." In addition to excluding African Americans, these towns often excluded Chinese Americans, Japanese Americans, Mexican Americans, Jews, and Native Americans—citizens and noncitizens alike. In some cases, the exclusion was official town policy. In other cases, the racist policy was enforced through intimidation. This intimidation could occur in a number of ways, including harassment by law-enforcement officers with the blessing of the local citizens.

Although sundown towns may seem a relic of the distant past, sociologist James Loewen estimates that by 1970, *more than half* of all incorporated communities outside the traditional South excluded African Americans. Many of these communities had no history of Blacks in residence. Such towns persisted even throughout the era of the civil rights movement. The city council of New Market, Iowa, for example, suspended its sundown ordinance for one night in the mid-1980s to allow an interracial band to play at a town festival, but the ordinance went back into effect the next day.

So what is it like today in these communities? Few sundown towns today have significant populations of excluded people. Some towns where colleges are located have benefited from efforts to desegregate their hometown. Such has been the case with initiatives by Lawrence University in Appleton, Wisconsin. What Loewen calls "recovering" sundown towns face continuing challenges to developing good race relations to attract African American families, including biased school curricula and overwhelmingly White teaching staffs. Practices that discourage desegregation persist across the country.

Sources: Loewen 2005, 2017; Loewen and Schaefer 2008.

Reemergence of Black Protests

7.3 Discuss the reemergence of Black protests.

American involvement in World War II signaled improved economic conditions for both Whites and Blacks. Nearly a million African Americans served in the military in rigidly segregated units. Generally, more Blacks participated in the armed services in World War II than in previous military engagements, but efforts by Blacks to contribute to the war effort at home were hampered by discriminatory practices in defense plants.

A. Philip Randolph, president of the Brotherhood of Sleeping Car Porters, threatened to lead 100,000 Blacks in a march on Washington in 1941 to ensure their employment and not have Black workers targeted for dismissal. Randolph's proposed tactic was nonviolent direct action, which he modeled on Mahatma Gandhi's practices in India. Randolph made it clear that he intended the march to be an all-Black event because he saw it as neither necessary nor desirable for Whites to lead Blacks to their own liberation. President Franklin Roosevelt responded to the pressure and agreed to issue an executive order prohibiting

Mike Keefe/Cagle Cartoons

Despite their second-class status until well after World War II, African Americans have contributed to every war effort. Notable were the Tuskegee Airmen, an all-Black unit of pilots who flew during World War II and received numerous decorations for valor. Surviving members continue to gather in celebratory reunions.

discrimination if Randolph would call off the march. The order and the Fair Employment Practices Commission it set up did not fulfill the original promises, but a precedent had been established for federal intervention in job discrimination (Garfinkel 1959).

Racial turmoil during World War II was not limited to threatened marches. Racial disturbances occurred in cities throughout the country, with the worst riot occurring in Detroit in June 1943. In that case, President Roosevelt sent in 6,000 soldiers to quell the violence, which left 25 Blacks and 9 Whites dead. The racial unrest was paralleled by a growth in civil disobedience as a means to achieve Black equality. The Congress of Racial Equality (CORE) was founded in 1942 to fight discrimination with nonviolent direct action. This interracial group used sit-ins to open restaurants to Black patrons in Chicago, Baltimore, and Los Angeles (Grimshaw 1969).

The war years and the postwar period saw several U.S. Supreme Court decisions that suggested the Court was moving away from tolerating racial inequities. The White primary elections endorsed in Jim Crow's formative period were finally challenged in the 1944 *Smith v. Allwright* decision. The effectiveness of the victory was limited; many states simply passed statutes that used new devices to frustrate African American voters.

A particularly repugnant legal device for relegating African Americans to second-class status was the **restrictive covenant**, a private contract entered into by neighborhood property owners stipulating that property could not be sold or rented to certain minority groups, thus ensuring that they could not live in the area. In 1948, the Supreme Court finally declared in *Shelley v. Kramer* that restrictive covenants were not constitutional, although it did not actually attack their discriminatory nature. The victory was in many ways less substantial than it was symbolic of the Supreme Court's new willingness to uphold the rights of Black citizens.

The Democratic administrations of the late 1940s and early 1950s made a number of promises to Black Americans. The party adopted a strong civil rights platform in 1948, but its provisions were not enacted. Once again, union president Randolph threatened Washington, DC, with a march. This time, he insisted that as long as Blacks were subjected to a peacetime draft, the military must be desegregated. President Truman responded by issuing an executive order on July 26, 1948, that desegregated the armed forces. The U.S. Army abolished its quota system in 1950, and training camps for the Korean War were integrated. Desegregation was not complete, however, especially in the reserves and the National Guard, and even today the armed forces face charges of racial favoritism. Whatever its shortcomings, the desegregation order offered African Americans an alternative to segregated civilian life (Moskos and Butler 1996).

The Civil Rights Movement

7.4 Summarize the key events and outcomes of the civil rights movement.

It is difficult to say exactly when a social movement begins or ends. Usually, a movement's ideas or tactics precede the actual mobilization of people and continue long after the movement's driving force has been replaced by new ideals and techniques. This description applies to the civil rights movement and its successor: the continuing struggle for African American freedom. Before 1954, there were some confrontations of White supremacy: the CORE sit-ins of 1942 and efforts to desegregate buses in Baton Rouge, Louisiana, in 1953. The civil rights movement gained momentum with a Supreme Court decision in 1954 that eventually desegregated the public schools, and it ended as a major force in Black America with the civil disorders of 1965 through 1968. However, beginning in 1954, toppling the traditional barriers to full rights for Blacks became the rule, not the exception (Figure 7.2).

Figure 7.2 Major Events of the Civil Rights Movement

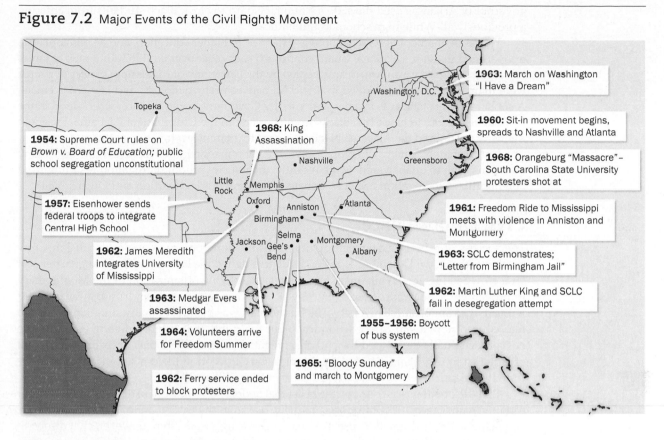

1963: March on Washington "I Have a Dream"

1960: Sit-in movement begins, spreads to Nashville and Atlanta

1954: Supreme Court rules on *Brown v. Board of Education*; public school segregation unconstitutional

1968: King Assassination

1968: Orangeburg "Massacre"– South Carolina State University protesters shot at

1957: Eisenhower sends federal troops to integrate Central High School

1961: Freedom Ride to Mississippi meets with violence in Anniston and Montgomery

1962: James Meredith integrates University of Mississippi

1963: SCLC demonstrates; "Letter from Birmingham Jail"

1963: Medgar Evers assassinated

1962: Martin Luther King and SCLC fail in desegregation attempt

1964: Volunteers arrive for Freedom Summer

1955–1956: Boycott of bus system

1962: Ferry service ended to block protesters

1965: "Bloody Sunday" and march to Montgomery

Map labels: Topeka, Washington, D.C., Nashville, Greensboro, Little Rock, Memphis, Oxford, Anniston, Atlanta, Birmingham, Jackson, Selma, Gee's Bend, Montgomery, Albany

The Struggle to Desegregate Public Schools

For the majority of Black children, public school education meant attending segregated schools. Southern school districts assigned children to school by race rather than by neighborhood, a practice that constituted **de jure segregation**, or segregation that results from children being assigned to schools specifically to maintain racially separate schools. It was this form of legal humiliation that was attacked in the landmark decision of *Linda Brown et al. v. Board of Education of Topeka, Kansas*.

Seven-year-old Linda Brown was not permitted to enroll in the grade school four blocks from her home in Topeka, Kansas. Rather, school board policy dictated that she attend the Black school almost two miles away. This denial led the NAACP Legal Defense and Educational Fund to bring suit on behalf of Linda Brown and 12 other Black children. The NAACP argued that the Fourteenth Amendment was intended to rule out segregation in public schools. Chief Justice Earl Warren of the Supreme Court wrote the unanimous opinion that "in the field of public education the doctrine of 'separate but equal' has no place. Separate educational facilities are inherently unequal."

The freedom that African Americans saw in their grasp at the time of the *Brown* decision amounted to a reaffirmation of American values. What Blacks sought was assimilation into White American society. The motivation for the *Brown* suit did not come merely because Black schools were inferior, although they were. Blacks were assigned to poorly ventilated and dilapidated buildings, with overcrowded classrooms and unqualified teachers. Less money was spent on Black schools than on White schools throughout the South in both rural and metropolitan areas. The issue was not such tangible factors, however, but the intangible effect of not being allowed to go to school with Whites. All-Black schools could not be equal to all-White schools. Even in this victory, Blacks reaffirmed White society and the importance of an integrated educational experience.

The reaction to the *Brown* decision showed the deep-rooted prejudice in the South. Resistance to court-ordered desegregation took many forms. Some people called for impeachment of all the Supreme Court justices. Others petitioned Congress to declare the Fourteenth Amendment unconstitutional. Cities closed schools rather than comply. The governor of Arkansas used the state's National Guard to block Black students from entering a previously all-White high school in Little Rock.

The issue of school desegregation was extended to higher education, and Mississippi state troopers and the state's National Guard confronted each other over the 1962 admission of James Meredith, the first African American accepted by the University of Mississippi. Scores of people were injured and two were killed in this clash between segregationists and law enforcement. A similar defiant stand was taken a year later by Governor George Wallace, who "stood in the schoolhouse door" to block two Blacks from enrolling in the University of Alabama. President Kennedy federalized the Alabama National Guard to guarantee admission of the students.

Unfortunately, *Brown* did not resolve the school segregation controversy, and many questions remain unanswered. More recently, the issue of school segregation resulting from neighborhood segregation has been debated (Pettigrew, 2011; Reardon and Owens 2014).

Civil Disobedience

The success of a yearlong boycott of city buses in Montgomery, Alabama, dealt Jim Crow another setback. On December 1, 1955, Rosa Parks defied the law and refused to give her seat on a crowded bus to a White man. Her defiance led to the organization of the Montgomery Improvement Association, headed by 26-year-old Martin Luther King, Jr., a Baptist minister with a PhD from Boston University. The bus boycott was the first of many situations in which Blacks used nonviolent direct action to obtain the rights that Whites already enjoyed. The boycott eventually demanded the end of segregated seating. The *Brown* decision woke up all of America to racial injustice, but the Montgomery boycott marked a significant shift away from the historical reliance on NAACP court battles (Killian 1975).

Civil disobedience is based on the belief that people have the right to disobey the law under certain circumstances. This tactic was not new. Blacks in the United States had used it before, and Gandhi also had urged its use in India. Under King's leadership, however, civil disobedience became a widely used technique and even gained a measure of acceptability among some prominent Whites. King called attention to manmade laws that were unjust and should not be obeyed because they were not right, not in accordance with God's higher moral code (1963:82).

In disobeying unjust laws, King (1958:101–107) developed this strategy:

- actively but nonviolently resisting evil,

- not seeking to defeat or humiliate opponents but to win their friendship and understanding,

- attacking the forces of evil rather than the people who happen to be doing the evil,

- being willing to accept suffering without retaliating,

- refusing to hate the opponent, and

- acting with the conviction that the universe is on the side of justice.

Martin Luther King, Jr., and Malcolm X were the defining figures of the African American struggle for rights and dignity in the 1960s.

King, like other Blacks before him and since, made it clear that passive acceptance of injustice was intolerable. He hoped that by emphasizing nonviolence, Southern Blacks would display their hostility to racism in a way that would undercut violent reaction by Whites.

Congress had still failed to enact any sweeping federal barrier to discrimination. Following the example of A. Philip Randolph in 1941, Blacks organized the March on Washington for Jobs and Freedom on August 28, 1963. With more than 200,000 people participating, the march was a high point of the civil rights movement. The mass of people, middle-class Whites and Blacks looking to the federal government for support, symbolized the struggle. However, a public opinion poll conducted shortly before the march documented the continuing resentment of the majority of Whites: 63 percent were opposed to the rally (Gallup 1972).

King (1971:351) delivered his famous "I Have a Dream" speech before the large crowd; he looked forward to a time when all Americans would be able to unite together. Just 18 days later, a bomb exploded in a Black church in Birmingham, Alabama, killing four little girls and injuring 20 other people.

Despair increased as the November 1963 election results meant segregationists were successful in their bids for office. Most distressing was the assassination of President Kennedy on November 22. Blacks had found Kennedy to be an appealing president despite his previously mediocre legislative record in the U.S. Senate. His death left doubt as to the direction and pace of future actions on civil rights by the executive branch under President Lyndon Baines Johnson. Two months later, however, the Twenty-Fourth Amendment was ratified, outlawing the poll tax that had long prevented Blacks from voting. The enactment of the Civil Rights Act on July 2, 1964, was hailed as a major victory and provided, at least for a while, what historian John Hope Franklin called "the illusion of equality" (Franklin and Higginbotham 2011).

In the months that followed passage of the Civil Rights Act, the pace of the movement to end racial injustice slowed. The violence continued, however, from the Bedford–Stuyvesant section of Brooklyn to Selma, Alabama. Southern state courts still found White murderers of Blacks innocent, and the accused had to be tried and convicted in federal civil, rather than criminal, court on the charge that by killing a person one violates that person's civil rights. Government records, which did not become public until 1973, revealed a systematic campaign by the FBI, which believed that civil rights groups were subversive. The FBI attempted to infiltrate those groups in an effort to discredit them. It was in such an atmosphere that the Voting Rights Act was passed in August 1965 to overcome legal barriers at the state and local levels that prevented African Americans from exercising the right to vote under the Fifteenth Amendment (Blackstock 1976).

Civil disobedience has not been limited to obvious efforts to change government policies. In the Speaking Out feature, sports columnist David Davis recalls the demonstration at the 1968 Olympics by two African American athletes.

Speaking Out

Olympic Athletes Who Took a Stand

David Davis

When the medals were awarded for the men's 200-meter sprint at the 1968 Olympic Games, *Life* magazine photographer John Dominis was only about 20 feet away from the podium. "I didn't think it was a big news event," Dominis says. "I was expecting a normal ceremony. I hardly noticed what was happening when I was shooting."

Indeed, the ceremony that October 16 "actually passed without much general notice in the packed Olympic Stadium," *New York Times* correspondent Joseph M. Sheehan reported from Mexico City. But by the time Sheehan's observation appeared in print three days later, the event had become front-page news: for politicizing the Games, U.S. Olympic officials, under pressure from the International Olympic Committee, had suspended medalists Tommie Smith and John Carlos and sent them packing.

1968 Summer Olympics in Mexico City

World History Archive / Alamy Stock Photo

Smith and Carlos, winners of the gold and bronze medals, respectively, in the event, had come to the ceremony dressed to protest: wearing black socks and no shoes to symbolize African American poverty, a black glove to express African American strength and unity. (Smith also wore a scarf, and Carlos beads, in memory of lynching victims.) As the national anthem played and an international TV audience watched, each man bowed his head and raised a fist. After the two were banished, images of their gesture entered the iconography of athletic protest.

"It was a polarizing moment because it was seen as an example of black power radicalism," says Doug Hartmann, a University of Minnesota sociologist and the author of *Race, Culture, and the Revolt of the Black Athlete: The 1968 Olympic Protests and Their Aftermath.* "Mainstream America hated what they did."

The United States was already deeply divided over the Vietnam War and the civil rights movement, and the serial traumas of 1968—mounting antiwar protests, the assassinations of Martin Luther King Jr. and Robert F. Kennedy, the beating of protesters during the Democratic National Convention by Chicago police—put those rifts into high relief. Before the Olympics, many African-American athletes had talked of joining a boycott of the Games to protest racial inequities in the United States. But the boycott, organized by sociologist Harry Edwards, never came off. As students at San Jose State University, where Edwards was teaching, Smith and Carlos took part in that conversation. Carlos, born and raised in Harlem, was "an extreme extrovert with a challenging personality," says Edwards, now emeritus professor of sociology at the University of California at Berkeley. Smith, the son of sharecroppers who grew up in rural Texas and California, was "a much softer, private person." When they raised their fists on the medals stand, they were acting on their own.

Among the Games athletes, opinions were divided. Australia's Peter Norman, the winner of the silver medal in the 200-meter sprint, mounted the podium wearing a badge supporting Edwards' organization. Heavyweight boxer George Foreman—who would win a gold medal and wave an American flag in the ring—dismissed the protest, saying, "That's for college kids." The four women runners on the U.S. 400-meter relay team dedicated their victory to the exiled sprinters. A representative of the USSR was quoted as saying, perhaps inevitably, "The Soviet Union never has used the Olympic Games for propaganda purposes."

Smith and Carlos returned home to a wave of opprobrium—they were "black-skinned storm troopers," in the words of Brent Musburger, who would gain fame as a TV sportscaster but was then a columnist for the *Chicago American* newspaper—and anonymous death threats. The pressure, Carlos says, was a factor in his then-wife's suicide in 1977. "One minute everything was sunny and happy, the next minute was chaos and crazy," he says. Smith recalls, "I had no job and no education, and I was married with a 7-month-old son."

Both men played professional football briefly. Then Carlos worked at a series of dead-end jobs before becoming a counselor at Palm Springs High School, where he has been for the past 20 years. Now 63 and remarried, he has four living children (a stepson died in 1998). Smith earned a bachelor's degree in social science from San Jose State in 1969 and a master's in sociology from the Goddard-Cambridge Graduate Program in Social Change in Boston in 1976. After teaching and coaching at Oberlin College in Ohio, he settled in Southern California, where he taught sociology and health and coached track at Santa Monica College. Now 64 and retired, he lives with his third wife, Delois, outside Atlanta. He has nine children and stepchildren.

The two athletes share what Smith calls a "strained and strange" relationship. Carlos says he actually let Smith pass him in 1968 because "Tommie Smith would have never put his fist in the sky had I won that race." Smith, who won the race in a world-record 19.83 seconds, dismisses that claim as nonsense.

But both men insist they have no regrets about 1968. "I went up there as a dignified black man and said: 'What's going on is wrong,'" Carlos says. Their protest, Smith says, "was a cry for freedom and for human rights. We had to be seen because we couldn't be heard.".

Source: Davis, David, Olympic Athletes Who Took a Stand, *Smithsonian Magazine*, August 2008.

Fifty years after the simple gestures made by Tommie Smith and John Carlos, San Francisco 49er quarterback Colin Kaepernick refused to stand for the national anthem as a protest to reported incidents of police brutality and in support of #BlackLivesMatter. As in 1968, public reaction was fierce, both for and against.

The Urban Stage

7.5   Explain how urban areas in the 1960s and 1970s refocused Black–White relations.

Just as the civil rights movement was reaching the attention of the entire nation, the focus and rhetoric shifted very quickly from small-town Dixie to the urban industrial North.

Urban Violence and Oppression

Riots involving Whites and Blacks did not begin in the 1960s. As noted earlier in this chapter, urban violence occurred after World War I and even during World War II, and violence against Blacks in the United States is nearly 350 years old. But the urban riots of the 1960s affected Blacks and Whites in the United States and throughout the world so extensively that they deserve special attention. However, it is important to remember that most violence between Whites and Blacks has not been large-scale collective action but has involved only a small number of people.

The summers of 1963 and 1964 were a prelude to the riots that gripped the country's attention. Although most people knew of the civil rights efforts in the South and legislative victories in Washington, everyone realized that the racial problem was national after several cities outside the South experienced violent disorder. In April 1968, after the assassination of Martin Luther King, Jr., more cities exploded with violence than in all of 1967. Even before the summer of 1968 began, 369 instances of civil disorder had taken place. Communities of all sizes were hit (Oberschall 1968).

As the violence continued and affected many ghettos, a popular explanation was that riot participants were mostly unemployed youths who had criminal records, often involving narcotics, and who were vastly outnumbered by the African Americans who repudiated the looting and arson. This explanation was called the **riff-raff theory** or the **rotten-apple theory** because it discredited the rioters and absolved the barrel of apples (that is, White society) of responsibility. However, research shows that the Black community expressed sympathy toward the rioters and that the rioters were not merely the poor and uneducated but also included middle-class, working-class, and educated residents (Sears and McConahay 1969, 1973; Tomlinson 1969; Turner 1994).

Several alternatives to the riff-raff theory explain why Black violent protest increased in the United States at a time when the nation was seemingly committed to civil rights for all. One explanation stands out: Black frustration with rising expectations in the face of continued deprivation relative to Whites.

The standard of living of African Americans improved remarkably after World War II, and it continued to do so during the civil rights movement. However, White income and occupation levels also improved, so the gap between the groups remained. **Relative deprivation** is the conscious feeling of a negative discrepancy between legitimate expectations and current actualities (Wilson 1973). Recall from Chapter 3 that feelings of relative deprivation often are the basis for perceived discrimination.

At the same time that African Americans were feeling relative deprivation, they also were experiencing growing discontent. **Rising expectations** refers to the increasing sense of frustration that legitimate needs are being blocked. Blacks felt that they had legitimate aspirations to equality, and the civil rights movement reaffirmed that discrimination had blocked upward mobility. As the horizons of African Americans broadened, they were more likely to make comparisons with Whites and feel discontented. The civil rights movement resulted in higher aspirations for Black America, yet for the majority of Blacks, life remained unchanged. Not only were their lives unchanged, but there was also a widespread feeling that the existing social structure held no prospects for improvement (Garner 1996; Sears and McConahay 1970; Thomas and Thomas 1984).

Black Power and #BlackLivesMatter

The riots in the Northern ghettos captured the attention of Whites, and "Black Power" was what they heard. But Black Power was born *not* of Black violence but out of White violence. On June 6, 1966, James Meredith was carrying out a one-person march from Memphis to Jackson, Mississippi, to encourage fellow African Americans to overcome their own fears and vote after the passage of the Voting Rights Act. During that march, an unidentified assailant shot and wounded Meredith. Blacks from throughout the country immediately continued the march. During the march, Stokely Carmichael of the Student Nonviolent Coordinating Committee proclaimed to a cheering Black crowd, "What we need is Black Power." King and others later urged "Freedom Now" as the slogan for the march. A compromise dictated that no slogan would be used, but the mood of Black America said otherwise (King 1967; Lomax 1971).

Today, it is not difficult to understand why the term *Black Power* frightened many Whites. The emergence of the #BlackLivesMatter (BLM) movement in 2013 caused many Whites to feel that BLM served only to worsen the racial divide and that BLM was suggesting that White lives do not matter. It appears very difficult for people who are privileged to accept that any acknowledgment of subjugation does not tacitly mean their position is society is being undermined (Taylor 2016).

By advocating Black Power, Carmichael distanced himself from the assimilationism of King. Carmichael rejected the goal of assimilation into White middle-class society. Instead, he said, Blacks must create new institutions. To succeed in this endeavor, Carmichael argued that Blacks must follow the same path as the Italians, Irish, and other White ethnic groups. "Before a group can enter the open society, it must first close ranks.... Group solidarity is necessary before a group can operate effectively from a bargaining position of strength in a pluralistic society" (Ture and Hamilton 1992:44). Prominent Black leaders opposed the concept; many feared that Whites would retaliate even more violently. King (1967) saw Black Power as a "cry of disappointment" but acknowledged that it had a "positive meaning."

Eventually, Black Power gained wide acceptance among Blacks and even many Whites; it remains to be seen if the same will happen with #BlackLivesMatter. Although it came to be defined differently by nearly every new proponent, support of Black Power generally implied endorsing Black control of the political, economic, and social institutions in Black communities. One reason for its popularity among African Americans was that it gave them a viable option for surviving in a segregated society. It also speaks to positive feelings about Blackness and Black culture, as well as a strong sense of Black pride. The civil rights movement strove to end segregation, but the White response showed how committed White society was to maintaining it. Black Power presented restructuring society as the priority item on the Black agenda (Carmichael and Thelwell 2003).

The Religious Force

7.6   Describe the role of religion in the African American community.

It is not possible to overstate the role religion has played—good and bad—in the social history of African Americans. Historically, Black leaders have emerged from the pulpits to seek out rights on behalf of all Blacks. Churches have served as the basis for community organization in neighborhoods abandoned by businesses and even government. Religion may be a source of antagonism as well.

The Africans who were brought involuntarily to the Western Hemisphere were non-Christian. They were therefore seen as heathens and barbarians. To "civilize" the slaves in the period before the Civil War, Southern slaveholders encouraged and often required their slaves to attend church and embrace Christianity. The Christian churches to which Blacks were introduced in the United States encouraged them to accept their inferior status, and religious teaching equated Whiteness with salvation, presenting Whiteness as an acceptable, even preferred, object of reverence.

Despite being imposed in the past by Whites, the Christian faiths are embraced by most African Americans today. As Figure 7.3 shows, African Americans are overwhelmingly Protestant, with the majority belonging to historically Black churches. Du Bois (1996, 2003) wrote of the importance of the church in the Black community but was also critical that the church failed at times to be more than a social organization stratified by class boundaries.

Black churches continue to be socially involved in their communities, but, like White Americans, more African Americans are becoming unaffiliated with a specific faith. About 18 percent of Black Americans, compared to 24 percent of Whites, indicated in a 2014 survey that they were religiously unaffiliated, atheistic, or agnostic.

Figure 7.3 Religious Profile of African Americans

SOURCE: Data from Pew Research Center 2015b: 72.

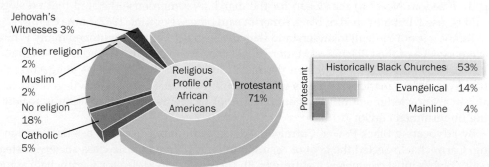

A variety of non-Christian groups have exerted a much greater influence on African Americans than the reported numbers of their followers suggest. For example, the Nation of Islam, which became known as the Black Muslims, has attracted a large number of followers and received a good deal of attention. We look at this group and other groups attracting African American Muslims in greater detail in Chapter 11 when we consider the large Muslim community in the United States.

The New Immigration

7.7   Examine how recent immigration is adding to the Black community.

Improved living conditions for Black people made the United States an attractive destination for Black people, as it had been for generations for people from Europe. Here, Somali women are selling clothes in Minneapolis.

When they think of the upsurge of arrivals in the United States seeking permanent residency, most people imagine immigrants from Latin America and Asia. Yet a substantial flow of immigrants has come from Africa and the Caribbean. This immigration is all the more dramatic because there had been little immigration of Black people to the United States in the 100 years following the Civil War. Obviously, the world's Black population was acutely aware of how people of color had been treated in the United States. Furthermore, restrictive legislation made it difficult for people to emigrate from Africa.

The increase is startling: Only around 800,000 Black American were foreign-born in 1980; that number rose to about 3.8 million by 2013. Overall, most were born in the Caribbean, primarily Jamaica and Haiti, but an increasing proportion were born in Africa.

These new additions to the African American community are a diverse group, including newcomers who first came to study, others who came to join relatives, and some who came as refugees. They and their descendants are often not taking long to make their presence felt. Colin Powell is the son of Jamaican immigrants, and President Barack Obama's father was a Kenyan immigrant.

To many people in the United States, the sheer size of this recent immigrant group has gone unnoticed. This is probably because of the relative concentration of the immigrants in certain urban areas. Nearly 40 percent of Black immigrants live in either the New York City or Miami–Fort Lauderdale metropolitan areas.

These new immigrants experience all the problems of transitioning into a new society experienced by other immigrants. Similarly, many foster ties to home. Compared to other immigrants, Black immigrants are more likely to be legal and to speak English. Yet these Black immigrants are confronted by a society still deeply divided by race. Although they typically were aware of divisions before immigrating, trying to navigate racial formation as it has emerged in the United States often presents daily challenges to these newcomers (Anderson 2015; Berlin 2010; Greer 2013; Waters, Kasinitz, and Asad 2014).

Conclusion

African Americans' move from slavery to freedom took centuries and was opposed every step along the way. An example is the popular publication *The Negro Motorist Green Book*, by Harlem civic leader Victor Green, which began publication in the 1930s and continued into the 1960s. The book offered African American travelers information on where they would be welcomed in diners, hotels, and even private residences. Even decades after slavery ended, Blacks taking road trips found it useful to have guidance to avoid indignities, which ranged from disrespectful service to sundown towns (McGee 2010).

The dramatic events affecting African Americans today have their roots in the forcible bringing of their ancestors to the United States as slaves. In the South, whether as slaves or later as victims of Jim Crow, Blacks were not a real economic threat to any but the poorest Whites, but affluent Whites perceived a potential threat from Blacks. During their entire history in the United States, Blacks have been criticized when they rebelled and praised when

Figure 7.4 Spectrum of Intergroup Relations: African Americans

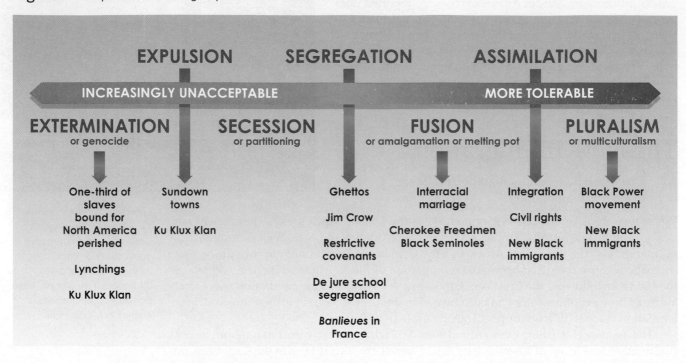

they went along with the system. During the era of slavery, revolts were met with increased suppression; after emancipation, leaders who called for accommodation were applauded.

While slavery was banned in the United States some 150 years ago, it still leaves its mark. The revelation that President Barack Obama is descended from slaves at first glance did not seem newsworthy. But this ancestry was through his White mother, not his Black father. Remember, President Obama's African heritage is through his father, who came to the United States in the twentieth century. His slave roots are from John Punch, a native of Cameroon in Africa. Held in bondage on a plantation near Jamestown in the 1600s, he fathered children with a White woman, among whose descendants are Ann Durham, Obama's White mother (Nicholson 2013:70).

In their efforts to bring about change, Blacks have differed in their willingness to form coalitions with Whites. It is often forgotten just how violent the reaction was to the civil rights effort from White Americans and much of the government. Our annual observance of Martin Luther King, Jr.'s birthday each January tends to be marked by emphasis on "coming together" and "shared values" rather than "resistance" or "we shall overcome." Back in 1961, 61 percent of all Americans disapproved of the protesters. And as for resistance? Eighty-five percent of Whites in 1966 felt mass demonstrations and sit-ins "would hurt the advancement of civil rights" (Izadi 2017).

African Americans who resisted in the days of either slavery or the civil rights movement would have concurred with Du Bois's (1903) comment that a Black person "simply wishes to make it possible to be both a Negro and an American, without being cursed and spit upon by his fellows, without having the door of opportunity closed roughly in his face" (pp. 3–4).

How much progress has been made? That progress covers several hundred years, beginning with slavery and ending with rights recognized constitutionally, but there is still much work to be done. Let us consider Topeka, Kansas, the site of the 1954 *Brown v. Board of Education* case. Linda Brown, one of the original plaintiffs, also was touched by another segregation case. In 1992, the courts held that Oliver Brown, her grandchild, was victimized because the Topeka schools were still segregated, now for reasons of residential segregation. The remedy to separate schools in this Kansas city is still unresolved. Figure 7.4 shows the Spectrum of Intergroup Relations for African Americans, as discussed in this chapter.

Chapter 8 assesses the status of African Americans today. Recall the events chronicled in this chapter as you consider the advances that Blacks have made. These events are a reminder that any progress has followed years—indeed, generations—of struggle by African Americans, often enlisting the support of Whites seeking to end second-class status for African Americans.

Summary of Learning Objectives

7.1 Explain the history of slavery in the United States and how it influences life today.

1. Slavery was a system that defined the people forcibly brought from Africa, identifying them and their descendants as the property of their masters and governed by slave codes. Despite the total restrictiveness of slavery as an institution (slaves had no rights), slaves often tried to resist the system while abolitionists worked to secure the slaves' freedom.

7.2 Summarize the accomplishments of Black leaders in the early twentieth century.

2. Throughout history, many individuals have emerged as leaders within the African American community. Particularly noteworthy were Booker T. Washington and W. E. B. Du Bois. Although they took different approaches, both expressed dissatisfaction with the second-class status of being Black in America.

7.3 Discuss the reemergence of Black protests.

3. An often overlooked period in Black–White relations is the period around World War II when African Americans organized to counter generations of entrenched Jim Crow practices.

7.4 Summarize the key events and outcomes of the civil rights movement.

4. Most White Americans did not voluntarily embrace major social change. It was achieved only in response to years of civil disobedience through the civil rights movement and the example set by Martin Luther King, Jr.

7.5 Explain how urban areas in the 1960s and 1970s refocused Black–White relations.

5. Although many White Americans felt that the civil rights movement had accomplished real change, this illusion was dramatically shattered as urban violence and growing militancy occurred not only in the South, which had been the battleground of the civil rights movement, but also in Northern cities.

7.6 Describe the role of religion in the African American community.

6. Historically, the church has been a major force in the Black community, and it continues to be a major part of the social culture, although more African Americans now say they are unaffiliated with any specific faith.

7.7 Examine how recent immigration is adding to the Black community.

7. A significant recent trend in the long history of Black people in the United States has been the increase in immigration from Africa and the Caribbean.

Key Terms

abolitionists, *page 163*
civil disobedience, *page 172*
de jure segregation, *page 171*
Jim Crow, *page 164*
racial formation, *page 162*

relative deprivation, *page 175*
restrictive covenant, *page 170*
riff-raff theory, *page 174*
rising expectations, *page 175*
rotten apple theory, *page 174*

slave codes, *page 162*
slavery reparation, *page 166*
sundown towns, *page 161*
White primary, *page 165*

Review Questions

1. In what ways were slaves defined as property?

2. How are W. E. B. Du Bois and Booker T. Washington both similar and different in what they sought to accomplish?

3. How did Black Americans respond to injustices during World War II?

4. If civil disobedience is nonviolent, then why has so much violence been associated with it?

5. How did observers of the urban riots tend to dismiss the riots' social importance?

6. Why has religion proved to be a force for both unity and disunity among African Americans?

7. How has the size of the Black community in the United States been increased by recent immigration?

Critical Thinking

1. How much time do you recall spending in school thus far learning about the history of Europe? How about Africa? What do you think this says about the way education is delivered or what we choose to teach and learn?

2. What would you consider the three most important achievements in civil rights for African Americans since 1950? What roles did Whites and Blacks play in making these events happen?

3. Growing numbers of Blacks are immigrating to the United States (especially to the eastern United States) from the Caribbean. What impact might this immigration have on what it means to be Black in the United States? What would the social construction of race say about this development?

Chapter 8
African Americans Today

Cleve Bryant/PhotoEdit Inc.

Learning Objectives

8.1 Describe the major educational issues facing African Americans.

8.2 Understand the economic situation of Black Americans.

8.3 Identify the strengths of and challenges facing African American families.

8.4 Explain the housing situation in the African American community.

8.5 Identify the present concerns about the criminal justice system with respect to African Americans.

8.6 Explain the healthcare dilemma faced by African Americans.

8.7 Describe the current role of African Americans in U.S. politics.

African Americans have made significant progress in many areas, but they have not kept pace with White Americans in many sectors. African Americans have advanced in formal schooling to a remarkable degree, although in most areas, residential patterns have left many public schools predominantly Black or White. Higher education also reflects the legacy of a nation that has operated two schooling systems: one for Blacks and another for Whites. Gains in earning power have barely kept pace with inflation, and the gap between Whites and Blacks has remained largely unchanged. African American families are susceptible to the problems associated with a low-income group that also faces discrimination and prejudice. Housing in many areas remains segregated, despite growing numbers of Blacks in suburban areas. African Americans are more likely than Whites to be victims of crimes and to be arrested for violent crimes. The subordination of Blacks is also apparent in healthcare delivery. African Americans have made substantial gains in elected office but still are underrepresented compared with their numbers in the general population.

This chapter assesses education, economic situation, family life, housing, criminal justice, healthcare, and politics among the nation's African Americans. Some of the advances are remarkable. However, the deprivation of the African American people relative to Whites remains, even if absolute deprivation has softened.

Education

8.1 Describe the major educational issues facing African Americans.

The African American population in the United States has placed special importance on acquiring education, beginning with its emphasis in the homes of slave families even when the formal institution of marriage was prohibited and continuing through the creation of separate schools for Black children because public schools were closed to them by custom or law. Today, long after the passage of the Civil Rights Act (1964) and *Brown v. Board of Education* (1954), education remains a controversial issue. Because racial and ethnic groups generally realize that formal schooling is the key to social mobility, they want to maximize this opportunity for upward mobility and, therefore, want better schooling. White Americans also appreciate the value of formal schooling and do not want to do anything that they perceive will jeopardize their own position.

Several measures document the inadequate education received by African Americans, starting with the quantity of formal education. Blacks as a group have always attained less education than Whites as a group. Despite programs such as Head Start, which are directed at all poor children, White children are still more likely to have formal pre-kindergarten education than are African American children. Older Black children generally drop out of school sooner and, therefore, are less likely to receive high school diplomas and college degrees.

The gap between Whites and Blacks in receiving college degrees has not been reduced in recent years, as Figure 8.1 shows. Presently, about 37 percent of White non-Hispanics age 25 years and over have a bachelor's degree or higher, compared to about 23 percent of African Americans. The proportion of Blacks holding a college degree today is about what it was for Whites in the mid-1980s.

Proposals to improve educational opportunities for African Americans often argue for more funding. Yet there are disagreements over what changes would lead to the best outcome. For example, educators and African Americans in general engage in significant debates over the content of curriculum that is best for minority students. Some schools have developed academic programs that take an Afrocentric perspective and immerse students in African American history and culture. However, a few of these programs have been criticized for ignoring fundamentals. On other occasions, the Afrocentric curriculum has even been viewed as racist against Whites. Debates over a few controversial programs attract a lot of attention, clouding the widespread need to reassess the curriculum for racial and ethnic minorities.

Middle- and upper-class children occasionally face barriers to a high-quality education, but they are more likely than the poor to have a home environment that is favorable to learning. Even African American schoolchildren who stay in school are not guaranteed equal opportunities in life. Many high schools do not prepare students who are interested in college for advanced schooling. The problem is often that schools are failing to meet the needs of students, not that students are failing in school.

The School Environment

Having a formal education for Black Americans is not the same as it is for White Americans. One compelling characteristic is that the two groups are educated largely in isolation from each other, as they are from Latinos.

It has been more than 60 years since the U.S. Supreme Court issued its unanimous ruling in *Brown v. Board of Education of Topeka, Kansas* that separate educational facilities are inherently unequal. What has been the legacy of that decision? Initially, the courts,

Figure 8.1 Educational Attainment of White Americans and Black Americans

Blacks have made tremendous progress in terms of receiving college degrees, but so have Whites. Today's level of college completion among adult African Americans is about the level White Americans reached in the mid-1980s.

Note: Data for adults age 25 and over in 2016. White attainment figures are for White non-Hispanics. Associate degree data include both academic and occupational programs.

SOURCE: Bureau of the Census 2017c: Table 3.

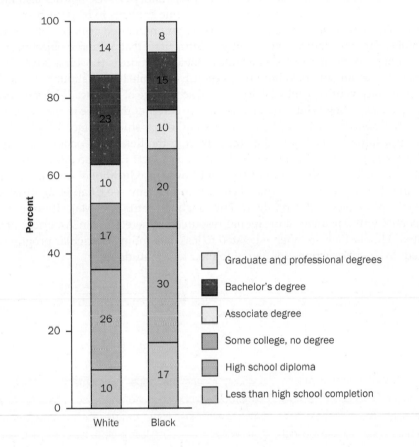

with the support of the federal government, ordered Southern school districts to end racial separation. But as attention turned to larger school districts, especially in the North, the challenge was to have integrated schools even though the neighborhoods were segregated. In addition, some city school districts were predominantly African American and Hispanic and were surrounded by suburban school districts that were predominantly White. This type of school segregation, which results from residential patterns, is called **de facto segregation**.

Initially, courts sought to overcome de facto segregation just as they had de jure school segregation in the *Brown* case. Typically, students were bused within a school district to achieve racial balance, but in a few cases, Black students were bused to predominantly White suburban schools and White children were bused into the city. In 1974, however, the Supreme Court ruled in *Milliken v. Bradley* that it was improper to order Detroit and the suburbs to have a joint metropolitan busing solution. These and other Supreme Court decisions effectively ended initiatives to overcome residential segregation, once again creating racial isolation in the schools. Indeed, even in Topeka, one-third of the schools are segregated.

School segregation has been so enduring that the term **apartheid schools** has been coined to refer to schools that are overwhelmingly (90 percent or more) Black. An analysis released in 2016 by the Civil Rights Project of UCLA documented that 19 percent of the nation's Black students attend an apartheid school, and this proportion rose to more than half in New York, Illinois, and Maryland. If there has been any trend, it is that the typical African American student was less likely to have White classmates in 2016 than in 1988 (Orfield, Ee, Frankenberg, and Siegel-Hawley 2016).

Although studies have shown positive effects of integration, a diverse student population does not guarantee an integrated, equal schooling environment. For example, **tracking** in schools, especially middle and high schools, intensifies segregation at the classroom level. Tracking is the practice of placing students in specific curriculum groups on the basis of test scores and other criteria. It also has the effect of decreasing White–Black classroom interactions because African American children are disproportionately assigned to general classes, and more White children are placed in college-preparatory classes. Studies also indicate that African American students are more likely than White students to be punished for subjective offenses, such as being disrespectful and making an unfounded criticism of the school staff, while Whites are disproportionately guilty of infractions that are more objective, such as defacing school property or possessing a knife or tobacco products (Loveless 2017; Tyson 2013).

One of the commonly held but not necessarily accurate beliefs about the school environment is that Black youth do not wish to take full advantage of their academic ability for fear of being viewed as "acting White" by their peers. We consider this issue in the Research Focus.

So if the notion that the difficulty that some Black students face in school is not due to their opposition to "acting White" (as shown in the Research Focus), why are so many people still advancing this incorrect explanation as a fact? Doing so allows us to blame the student and "Black culture" and not confront how our educational institutions are underperforming. This is another example of **color-blind racism** (see Chapter 2), in which we use race-neutral principles to defend the racially unequal status quo. Majority-minority schools today persist with far fewer educational resources. Where African Americas attend more integrated schools, they are often relegated to less demanding curricular programs and face increased disciplinary actions compared to their fellow students.

Research Focus

Acting White

A common view advanced by some educators is that African Americans, especially young men, do not succeed in school because they do not want to be caught "acting White." That is, they avoid at all costs taking school seriously and do not accept the authority of teachers and administrators. Whatever the accuracy of such a generalization, acting White clearly shifts the responsibility of low school attainment from the school to the individual and, therefore, can be seen as yet another example of blaming the victim. **Acting White** is also associated with speaking proper English or with cultural preferences like listening to rock music rather than hip-hop.

In the context of high achievers, to what extent do Blacks *not* want to act White? Many scholars have noted that individuals' efforts to avoid looking like they want an education has a long history and is hardly exclusive to any one race. Students of all colors may hold back for fear of being accused of being "too hardworking."

Back in the 1950s, one heard disparaging references to "teacher's pet" and "brown nosing." Does popularity come to high school debaters and National Honor Society students, or to cheerleaders and athletes? Academic-oriented students are often viewed as social misfits, nerds, and geeks and are seen as socially inept, even if their skill-building will later make them more economically independent and often more socially desirable. For minority youth, including African Americans, to take school

seriously means they must overcome their White classmates' same desire to be cool and not be seen as a geek. In addition, Black youth must come to embrace a curriculum and respect teachers who are much less likely to look or sound like them.

The acting-White thesis overemphasizes personal responsibility rather than structural features such as quality of schools, curriculum, and teachers. Therefore, it locates the source of Black miseducation—and by implication, the remedy—in the African American household.

Of course, not all Whites act White. To equate acting White with high academic achievement has little empirical or cultural support. Studies comparing attitudes and performance show that Black students have the same attitudes—good and bad—about achievement as their White counterparts. Too often, we tend to view White slackers who give a hard time to the advanced placement kids as "normal," but when low-performing African Americans do the same thing, it becomes a systemic pathology undermining everything good about schools. The research consensus is that the primary stumbling block is not acting White or acting Black but being presented with similar educational opportunities.

Sources: Buck 2011; Covay 2013; Downey 2008; Fordham and Ogbu 1986; Lewis 2013; Ogbu 2004; Tyson 2011.

Higher Education

Higher education for Blacks reflects the same pattern as primary and secondary education. Although strides were made in the period after the civil rights movement, a plateau was reached in the mid-1970s. African Americans are more likely than Whites to be part-time students and to need financial aid, which began to be severely cut in the 1980s. Many are also finding the social climate on predominantly White campuses less than positive. As a result, the historically Black colleges and universities (HBCUs) are once again playing a significant role in educating African Americans. For a century, they were the only real source of college degrees for Blacks. Then, in the 1970s, predominantly White colleges began to recruit African Americans. As of 2017, however, the 100 HBCUs still accounted for about one-fifth of all Black college graduates (Thurgood Marshall College Fund 2017).

As Figure 8.1 shows, although African Americans are more likely today to be college graduates, the upward trend of the 1970s and 1980s has moderated. Several factors account for this reversal in progress:

1. Reductions in financial aid and more reliance on loans, coupled with rising costs, have discouraged African American students who would be the first members of their families to attend college.

2. Pushing for higher standards in educational achievement without providing remedial courses has locked out many minority students.

3. Employment opportunities, though slight for African Americans without some college, have continued to lure young African Americans who must contribute to their family's income and who otherwise might have gone to college.

4. Negative publicity about affirmative action may have discouraged some African Americans from even considering college.

5. Attention to what appears to be a number of racial incidents on predominantly White college campuses has also been a discouraging factor.

Colleges and universities seem uneasy about these problems, though publicly the schools appear committed to addressing them.

There is little question that special challenges face African American students who attend colleges with overwhelmingly White faculty, advisors, coaches, administrators, and student body. The campus culture may be neutral at best, and it is sometimes hostile to members of racial minorities. The high attrition rate of African American students on predominantly White college campuses confirms the need for a positive environment.

The disparity in schooling becomes even more pronounced at the highest levels, and the gap is not closing. Only 8.4 percent of all doctorates awarded in 2015 were to native-born African Americans, more than double the proportion of 3.0 percent in 1990. However, foreign students received twice the number of doctorates of U.S.-born Black Americans (National Center for Education Statistics 2016: Table 324.20).

In summary, the educational picture for Black Americans is uneven—marked progress in absolute terms (Blacks are much better educated than they were a generation ago), but little progress relative to Whites in the gap in educational attainment. Sixty years ago, the major issue appeared to be school desegregation, but the goal was to improve the

Very few African Americans are entering positions that few people of any color reach. Arnold W. Donald was named CEO of Carnival Cruise Lines Corporation in 2013. Before that, he worked for 30 years at Monsanto Company, having received his B.S. from Carleton College and his mechanical engineering degree from Washington University. In 2017, just four other African Americans were heads of Fortune 500 corporations.

James D. Morgan/Getty images

quality of education received by Black schoolchildren. Today, the chief concern of African American parents and most educators is the same—quality education. W. E. B. Du Bois advanced the same point in 1935—what a Black student needs, he said, "is neither segregated schools nor mixed schools. What he needs is Education" (p. 335).

The Economic Picture

8.2 Understand the economic situation of Black Americans.

The general economic picture for African Americans has gradually improved over the past 50 years, but this improvement is modest compared with that of Whites, whose standard of living also has increased. Like their White counterparts, African Americans in the twenty-first century have moved when they can to areas of the nation (such as the South and West) that hold better economic prospects. Figure 8.2 shows the percentage change of Black population by county between 2000 and 2010.

In terms of absolute deprivation, African Americans are much better off today but have not experienced significant improvement with respect to their relative deprivation to Whites on almost all economic indicators. To better understand today's economic reality, we first focus on the Black middle class and then turn to a broader overview of the occupations in which African Americans work.

The Black Middle Class

Many characterizations of the African American community overemphasize the poorest segment of that community. Also overemphasized and exaggerated is how much success African Americans have achieved. Social scientists face the challenge of avoiding a selective, one-sided picture of Black society. The problem is similar to viewing a partially filled glass of water. Does one describe it as half empty and emphasize the need for assistance?

Figure 8.2 Percent Change of Black Population by County: 2000–2010

A larger percentage change in the Black population has occurred in places like Arizona, New Mexico, rural California, and rural parts of the East. Central cities like Los Angeles, Chicago, and Detroit saw declines during the first decade of the twenty-first century.

SOURCE: Data from Jones 2012: Slide 10.

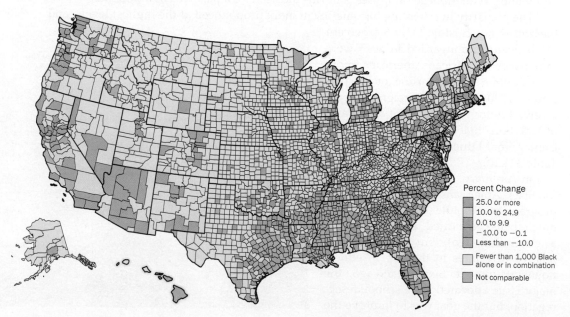

Or does one describe the glass as half full to recognize the group's accomplishments? The most complete description acknowledges both perspectives.

Social scientists have long recognized the importance of class. **Class**, as defined by sociologist Max Weber, refers to people who share a similar level of wealth and income. The significance of class in people's lives is apparent to all—not just in the type of cars one drives or where one goes on vacation but also in the quality of public schools available and the healthcare one receives.

Besides class, two measures are useful for determining the overall economic situation of an individual or household: income and wealth. **Income** refers to salaries, wages, and other money received; **wealth** is a more inclusive term that encompasses all of a person's material assets, including land and other types of property.

A clearly defined African American middle class has emerged. In 2016, about 27 percent of African American households earned more than the median income for White non-Hispanic households of $62,950. Nearly one-third of Blacks, then, are middle class or higher. Nonetheless, as Black income has increased, Blacks' wealth relative to Whites has lagged significantly. Many observers have attempted to describe this Black middle class (Proctor, Semega, and Kollar 2016: Table FINC-03).

Directing attention to the Black middle class requires that we consider the relative importance of race and social class. The degree to which affluent Blacks identify themselves in class terms or racial terms is an important ideological question. W. E. B. Du Bois (1952) argued that when racism decreases, class issues become more important. As Du Bois saw it, exploitation would remain, and many of the same people would continue to be subordinate. Black elites might become economically successful, either as entrepreneurs (Black capitalists) or professionals (Black white-collar workers).

The complexity of the relative influence of race, income, and wealth was apparent in the controversy surrounding the publication of sociologist William J. Wilson's *The Declining Significance of Race* (1980 [2012]). Pointing to the increasing affluence of African Americans, Wilson concluded, "Class has become more important than race in determining Black life-chances in the modern industrial period" (p. 150). The policy implications of his conclusion are that programs must be developed to confront class subordination rather than ethnic and racial discrimination. Wilson did not deny the legacy of discrimination reflected in the disproportionate number of African Americans who are poor, less educated, and living in inadequate and overcrowded housing. However, he pointed to "compelling evidence" that young Blacks were competing successfully with young Whites.

The Speaking Out features offers an excerpt from *Black Picket Fences: Privilege and Peril Among the Black Middle Class*. The author, sociologist Mary Pattillo, wrote about the Groveland neighborhood of Chicago, where she was doing ethnographic research on the precarious nature of maintaining a Black middle-class community.

The Black middle class is better off than poor African Americans, but studies show that in urban areas their surrounding social environment more closely mirrors that of poor Whites than middle-class Whites. This social environment has consequences for housing quality, access to retail and medical providers, and public safety (Reardon, Fox, and Townsend 2015; Sharkey 2014).

Employment

This precarious economic situation for African Americans—the lack of dependable assets—is particularly relevant as we consider their employment picture. Higher unemployment rates for Blacks have persisted since the 1940s, when they were first documented. Even in the best economic times, the Black unemployment rate is significantly higher than it is for Whites. In 2016, as the United States emerged from the Great Recession, the Black unemployment rate stood at 8.1 percent, compared to 4.2 percent for Whites. Considerable evidence exists that Blacks are the first fired as the business cycle weakens.

The employment picture is especially grim for young African American workers. Following the recent recession, for Black youth age 16–19, unemployment at the end of 2016 was 26 percent. The lack of stable employment in early adulthood has lifelong implications (Bureau of Labor Statistics 2017a).

Speaking Out

Black Picket Fences

Mary Pattillo

On a tour of Chicago's neighborhoods, our jumbo coach bus drove through a predominantly African American neighborhood not too far from Groveland. And just as middle class. It was a cold autumn morning, and the tree-lined streets were completely empty. Yet there were conspicuous clues that somebody cared deeply about this neighborhood. Matching lampposts stood like sentries at the edge of each home's neat lot. Welcoming block-club placards on the corners—"Please Drive Slowly"—conveyed a concern for children who might be too engrossed in play to mind the traffic. The occasional candy wrapper or grocery bag on a few lawns did not ruin the overall tidiness. The homes with fresh paint, edged grasses, and decorative screen doors outnumbered the properties of loafers who had ceded victory to the weeds, or refused to sweep the sidewalk.

As we took in the pleasant sights, our learned Chicago tour guide, who was white, reported to our group of sightseers, most of whom were also white. "From looking at it, some you might think this is a predominantly white neighborhood, but actually this neighborhood is all black." He spoke as if he let us in on a little secret.

The guide's comment, dressed in its disclosing tone, initially struck me as narrow-minded, since I had, after all, grown up in a like neighborhood, and was not at all surprised by this find in Chicago. Yet with the near completeness of racial segregation in many large American cities, it would indeed be difficult for many whites to just happen upon a place like Groveland. For the most part—and especially in cities like Chicago, Milwaukee, St. Louis, Newark, Buffalo, Philadelphia, and so on—African Americans live on the "black side of town," and whites on the "white side of town." To a somewhat lesser extent and depending on the city, Hispanic and Asian American groups each year have their "side of town," too.

People's routine patterns ensure that they have little reason or opportunity to see Groveland and neighborhoods like it. The average nonblack citizen's ignorance of these enclaves is bolstered by the common belief in academia that the black middle class actually moved away from black neighborhoods after the 1960s, leaving behind their poorer former neighbors. Recognizing all this, perhaps black middle-class neighborhoods *are* a secret. And the black middle class, while far from a secret, is shrouded in misperception.

Groveland's first generation of residents who entered adulthood in the immediate post–World War II era remember a time of largesse. With their stable jobs and in search of better housing, African American college-educated professionals moved to Groveland. Along with them came customer service representatives, hairdressers, transit employees, and railroad workers. All earned enough to buy a home and perhaps send the children to Catholic school, or take a yearly

Mary Pattillo

Use with the permission of Mary Pattillo.

trip back Down South. They replaced the white residents who were also benefiting from postwar prosperity, and were looking to move to the growing suburbs. Far from integration, the change in Groveland was complete racial turnover. As Groveland's African American residents established their stake in the neighborhood, the statues of Jesus in the old neighborhood churches were painted darker, the restaurants started serving soul food, and the drugstores stocked black hair-care products. In their new, attractive neighborhood, Groveland's first generation began to reap the benefits of the civil rights movement.

The expansion of the black middle class in the 1950s, 1960s, and very early 1970s came to a halt in the last two-and-a-half decades of the twentieth century. The generations that followed Groveland's African American pioneer settlers have found it progressively more difficult to match what their parents amassed in those days of plenty. Executive profit-hoarding, corporate and government downsizing, and global labor markets have pillaged the wallets of the American middle class, both white and black. But with lower incomes and a flimsier financial cushion, African Americans are more susceptible than whites to slipping back down the class ladder.

A contemporary profile of the black middle class reveals that higher-paid professionals and executives do not predominate as they do among the white middle class. Instead, office workers, salespeople, and technical consultants—all lower-middle-class jobs—make up the majority of black middle-class workers. Working-class African Americans, who have been even harder hit by production shifts, are also an integral part of neighborhoods like Groveland.

Linda Brewer, a Groveland resident in her mid-thirties, listed the jobs that anchored her parents' generation. "A lot of these people around here, you know, post office workers, steel mills. They father had two jobs," she reflected. "But them jobs are no longer here. So now they kids are poor." The second generation, of which Linda is a member, struggles to buy homes, or maintain the homes their parents purchased. Along with the third generation of teenagers and young adults, they are somewhat bewildered by the fact that without a college degree, they often have to live with their parents in order to get full consumption and leisure mileage out of their lower-middle-class paychecks. The black middle class is particularly fragile. As Anna Morris [born in Groveland and now raising her own family there] summarized, "I get enough to get by. I don't get any more. I take care of my children. I think we're sort of well-to-do, but who could say. You could go any way any day."

Source: Mary Pattillo-McCoy. 1999. Black Pickett Fences: Privilege and Peril Among the Black Middle Class. University of Chicago Press. Used with permission.

Social scientists have cited many factors to explain why official unemployment rates for young African Americans are so high:

- Many African Americans live in the depressed economy of the central cities.
- Immigrants and illegal aliens present increased competition.
- White middle-class women have entered the labor force.
- Illegal activities whereby youths can make more money are increasingly prevalent.

None of these factors is likely to change soon, so Depression-like levels of unemployment probably will persist (Haynes 2009; Wagmiller Jr. and Lee 2014).

The numbers noted above consider only official unemployment. The federal government counts as unemployed people only those who are actively seeking employment. Therefore, to be officially unemployed, a person must not hold a full-time job, must be registered with a government employment agency, and must be engaged in submitting job applications and seeking interviews. The official unemployment rate leaves out millions of Americans, Black and White, who are effectively unemployed. It does not count people who are so discouraged they have temporarily or permanently given up looking for employment. **Underemployment** (working at a job for which one is overqualified), involuntarily working part-time instead of full-time, or being employed only intermittently further compounds the problem of unemployment.

Although a few African Americans have smashed through the glass ceiling and made it into the top echelons of business or government, more have entered a wider variety of jobs. As Table 8.1 shows, African Americans, who constitute 12.7 percent of the population, are underrepresented in high-status, high-paying occupations. Fortunately, the taboo against putting Blacks in jobs in which they would supervise Whites has weakened, and the percentage of African Americans in professional and managerial occupations has shown remarkable improvement. However, much improvement can still be made.

Family Life

8.3 Identify the strengths of and challenges facing African American families.

In its role as a social institution providing for the socialization of children, the family is crucial to its members' life satisfaction. The family also reflects the influence, positive or negative, of income, housing, education, and other social factors. For African Americans, the family reflects both amazing stability and the legacy of racism and low income across many generations.

Table 8.1 Percentages of African American Employees in Selected Occupations, 1982–2015

Occupation	1982	1995	2015
Lawyers and judges/ Legal occupations	7.2	7.6	6.8
Physicians	2.3	3.6	6.4
Registered nurses	8.2	8.4	12.2
College professors	4.8	6.2	5.1
Librarians	7.2	7.6	8.5
Social workers	16.1	23.7	22.0
Managers	3.9	7.5	7.3
Sales workers	3.8	7.8	12.3
Cashiers	10.0	15.8	17.4
Police	9.3	11.2	13.5

Note: "Lawyer and judges" changed to "Legal occupations" after 1995.

SOURCES: Bureau of the Census 1984: Table 616 on pp. 419–420; 1996: Table 637 on pp. 405–407; and Bureau of Labor Statistics 2016a: Table 11.

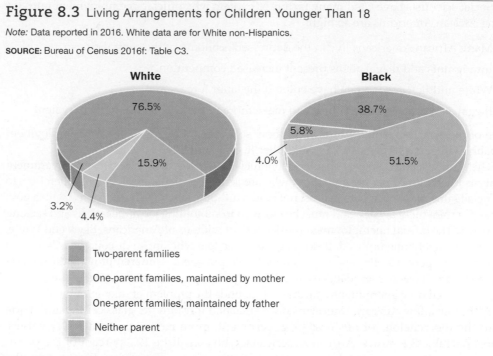

Figure 8.3 Living Arrangements for Children Younger Than 18

Note: Data reported in 2016. White data are for White non-Hispanics.

SOURCE: Bureau of Census 2016f: Table C3.

White

76.5%

15.9%

3.2%

4.4%

Black

38.7%

5.8%

4.0%

51.5%

- ■ Two-parent families
- ■ One-parent families, maintained by mother
- ■ One-parent families, maintained by father
- ■ Neither parent

Challenges to Family Stability

More than one-third of African American children had both a father and a mother present in 2016 (Figure 8.3). Although single-parent African American families are common, they are not universal. In comparison, such single-parent arrangements were also present in about one in five White families. Regardless of race, there has been a remarkable retreat from marriage.

It is just as inaccurate to assume that a single-parent family is necessarily deprived as it is to assume that a two-parent family is always secure and happy. Nevertheless, life in a single-parent family can be extremely stressful for all single parents and their children, not just those who are members of subordinate groups. Because the absent parent is more often the father, the lack of a male presence almost always means the lack of a male income. This monetary impact on a single-parent household cannot be overstated.

For many single African American women living in poverty, having a child is an added burden. However, the tradition of extended family among African Americans eases this burden somewhat. The absence of a husband does not mean that no one shares in childcare: Out-of-wedlock children born to Black mothers often live with their grandparents and form three-generation households.

No single explanation accounts for the rise in single-parent households. Sociologists attribute the rapid expansion in the number of such households primarily to shifts in the economy that have kept Black men, especially in urban areas, out of work. The phenomenon certainly is not limited to African Americans. Increasingly, both White and Black unmarried women bear children. More and more parents, both White and Black, divorce, so even children born into a two-parent family might end up living with only one parent.

Strengths of African American Families

In the midst of ever-increasing single parenting, another picture of African American family life becomes visible: success despite discrimination and economic hardship. Robert Hill (2003), of the National Urban League and Morgan State University, listed the following five strengths of African American families that allow them to function effectively in a hostile (racist) society.

1. *Strong kinship bonds:* Blacks are more likely than Whites to care for children and the elderly in an extended family network.

2. *A strong work orientation:* Poor Blacks are more likely to be working, and poor Black families often include more than one wage earner.

3. *Adaptability of family roles:* In two-parent families, an egalitarian pattern of decision making is the most common. The self-reliance of Black women who are the primary wage earners best illustrates this adaptability.

4. *Strong achievement orientation:* Working-class Blacks indicate a greater desire for their children to attend college than do working-class Whites. A majority of low-income African American children want to attend college.

5. *A strong religious orientation:* Since the time of slavery, Black churches have been the impetus behind many significant grassroots organizations.

Social workers and sociologists have confirmed through social research the strengths that Hill noted first in 1972, despite continuing institutional discrimination, gun violence, drug trafficking, the HIV/AIDS epidemic, and homelessness. In the African American community, these five factors are the sources of family strength (Hill 2003; Hudgins 1992).

Increasingly, social scientists are looking at both the weaknesses and the strengths of African American family life. Expressions of alarm about instability date back to 1965, when the Department of Labor issued the report *The Negro Family: The Case for National Action*. The document, commonly known as the Moynihan Report after its principal author, sociologist Daniel Patrick Moynihan, outlined a "tangle of pathology" with the Black family at its core. More recently, two studies—the Stable Black Families Project and the National Survey of Black Americans—sought to learn how Black families encounter problems and resolve them successfully with internal resources such as those that Hill outlined in his highly regarded work (Coates 2015; Department of Labor 1965).

The most consistently documented strength of African American families is the presence of an extended family household. The most common feature is having grandparents residing in the home. Extended living arrangements are twice as common in Black households as in White ones. These arrangements are recognized as having the important economic benefit of pooling limited economic resources. Because of the generally lower earnings of African American heads of household, income from second, third, and even fourth wage earners is needed to achieve a desired standard of living or, in too many cases, simply to meet daily needs (Haxton and Harknett 2009; Ellis and Simmons 2014).

Housing

8.4 Explain the housing situation in the African American community.

Housing plays a major role in determining the quality of a person's life. For African Americans, as for Whites, housing is the result of personal preferences and income. For most people, housing is critical to their quality of life and often represents their largest single asset. However, African Americans' housing has been restricted through discrimination, which has not been the case for Whites.

Although Black housing has improved—as indicated by statistics on home ownership, new construction, density of living units, and quality as measured by plumbing facilities—African Americans remain behind Whites on all these standards. The quality of Black housing is inferior to that of Whites at all income levels, yet Blacks pay a larger proportion of their income for shelter.

As noted earlier, White children in the United States attend predominantly White schools, Black children attend predominantly Black schools, and Hispanic children attend predominantly Hispanic schools. This school segregation is not only the result of the failure to accept busing but also the effect of residential segregation. In their studies on segregation, Douglas Massey and Nancy Denton (1993) concluded that racial separation "continues to exist because white America has not had the political will or desire to dismantle it" (p. 8). In Chapter 1, we noted the

Zoning laws that may stipulate expensive building materials help keep out the less affluent, who are more likely to be African American.

pervasiveness of residential segregation as reflected in a recent analysis of housing patterns (refer back to Table 1.2). Racial isolation in neighborhoods has improved only modestly over the past two generations.

What factors create residential segregation in the United States? Among the primary factors are the following:

- Because of private prejudice and discrimination, people refuse to sell or rent to people of the "wrong" race, ethnicity, or religion.

- The prejudicial policies of real estate companies steer people to the "correct" neighborhoods.

- Government policies do not effectively enforce anti-bias legislation.

- Public housing policies today, as well as past construction patterns, reinforce the location of housing for the poor in inner-city neighborhoods.

- Policies of banks and other lenders create race-based barriers to financing home purchasing.

The issue of racial-based financing deserves further explanation. In the 1990s, new attention was focused on the persistence of **redlining**, the practice of discriminating against people trying to buy homes in minority and racially changing neighborhoods.

It is important to recall the implications of this discrimination in home financing for the African American community. Earlier in the chapter, we noted the great disparity between Black and White family wealth and its implications for present and future generations. The key factor in this inequality has been the failure of African Americans to accumulate wealth through home buying. The recent subprime housing loan scandal led disproportionately to a foreclosure crisis in the African American community, only increasing the divide in equal housing opportunity (Reid, Bocian, Li, and Quercia 2017).

A dual housing market is part of today's reality, although attacks continue against the remaining legal barriers to fair housing. In theory, **zoning laws** are enacted to ensure that specific standards of housing construction will be satisfied. These regulations can also separate industrial and commercial enterprises from residential areas. However, some zoning laws in suburbs have curbed the development of low- and moderate-income housing that would attract African Americans who want to move out of the central cities.

For years, constructing low-income public housing in the ghetto has furthered racial segregation. The courts have not ruled consistently on this matter in recent years so, as with affirmative action, public officials lack clear guidance. Even if court decisions continue to dismantle exclusionary housing practices, the rapid growth of integrated neighborhoods is unlikely. In the future, African American housing probably will continue to improve and remain primarily in all-Black neighborhoods. This gap is greater than can be explained by differences in social class.

Criminal Justice

8.5 Identify the present concerns about the criminal justice system with respect to African Americans.

A complex, sensitive topic affecting African Americans is their role in criminal justice. It was reported for 2015 that Blacks constitute 4.6 percent of all lawyers, 14 percent of police officers and detectives, 24.7 percent of correctional officers, and 28.8 percent of security guards—but 35 percent of jail and prison inmates (Bureau of Labor Statistics 2016a: Table 11; Carson and Anderson 2016).

Data collected annually in the FBI's Uniform Crime Report show that Blacks account for 26 percent of arrests, even though they represent only about 13 percent of the nation's population. Conflict theorists point out that the higher arrest rate is not surprising for a group that is disproportionately poor and, therefore, much less able to afford private attorneys, who might be able to prevent formal arrests from taking place. Even more significantly, the Uniform Crime Report focuses on index crimes (mainly property crimes), which are the type of crimes most often committed by low-income people.

These numbers are staggering, but as dramatic as they are, it is not unusual to hear exaggerations presented as facts, such as "more Black men are in prison than are in college." The reality is sobering enough—523,000 in prison compared to 2,791,000 in college. About one in 16 White males can expect to go to a state or federal prison during his lifetime, yet for Black males, this lifetime probability is one out of three.

Most (actually 70 percent) of all the violent crimes against Whites are perpetrated by Whites, according to the FBI. In contrast to popular misconceptions about crime, African Americans and the poor are especially likely to be the victims of serious crimes. This fact is documented in **victimization surveys**, which are systematic interviews of ordinary people carried out annually to reveal how much crime occurs. These Department of Justice statistics show that African Americans are 29 percent more likely to be victims of violent crimes than are Whites (Carson and Anderson 2016; Federal Bureau of Investigation 2016b: Table 43; National Center for Education Statistics 2016: Table 306.10; Truman and Morgan 2016).

Image Source / SuperStock

While the number of African American judges is growing, they still are too few in number. For example, in Cook County, Illinois, which includes Chicago, Black criminal court judges account for 21 percent of the total, which seems impressive, but Blacks are the defendants in 72 percent of the cases (Chaney 2009).

Central to the concerns of minorities regarding the criminal justice system is **differential justice**—that is, Whites are dealt with more leniently than are Blacks, whether at the time of investigation, arrest, indictment, conviction, sentencing, incarceration, or parole. Studies demonstrate that police often deal with African American youths more harshly than with White youth. Law is a public social institution and in many ways reproduces the inequality experienced in life (Peterson 2012).

We can see differential justice at work at many levels of the criminal justice system. The #BlackLivesMatter (BLM) campaign, which became a national movement in 2013, arose from the initial encounters that Black people often have with those entrusted to enforce the law. Through cell phone and body-camera videos, people watched case after case of differential treatment as police mortally wounded unarmed Black civilians. Not nearly as public is the fact that Blacks are often three times as likely to be excluded from serving on a jury. The Supreme Court ruled 7–1 in 2016 that Georgia prosecutors in *Foster v. Chatman* had disproportionately barred African Americans from serving on juries in death-penalty cases.

BLM seeks to bring an end to injustice in law enforcement. Regrettably, as inappropriate police actions come to the attention of the general public, civilians are less likely to cooperate. In 2004, off-duty Milwaukee police officers severely beat unarmed Frank Jude, a 17-year old African American, suspecting he had stolen a police badge at a house-warming party they all were attending. No badge was found, and subsequent charges against some of the officers ended in acquittal, although seven were found guilty and given prison sentences. Scholars have found that 911 calls seeking police assistance declined by half for about a year in all Milwaukee neighborhoods but especially all-Black neighborhoods. Similar significant reductions in contacting police were found following law enforcement's violent encounters with Black men that received public attention in New York City in 2006, Milwaukee again in 2007, and Oakland, California, in 2009 (Desmond, Papachristos, and Kirk 2016).

Due to its high level of incarceration, the United States has been termed "an incarceration nation." The United States has the highest prison rate by far, followed by Cuba, Rwanda, Russia, and El Salvador. With Black Americans hardest hit by jail sentences, additional strain is placed on African American communities and households. Sociologist Michelle Alexander has likened the high level of Black incarceration to a "new Jim Crow" where, like generations ago, young African Americans are kept in their place under the threat of expulsion/incarceration (Alexander 2012; Coates 2015; Newman 2016; Prison Policy 2017).

It has also been accepted, albeit reluctantly, that the government cannot be counted on to address inner-city problems. In crimes involving African Americans, legal system scholars have observed **victim discounting**, or the tendency to view crime as less socially significant if the victim is viewed as less worthy. For example, the numerous killings of Black youth going to and from school attract much less attention than, for example, a shooting spree that takes five lives in a suburban school. When a schoolchild walks into a cafeteria or schoolyard with automatic weapons and kills a dozen children and teachers, it is a case of national alarm, as it was in Columbine, Colorado, or Newtown, Connecticut. When children kill each other in drive-by shootings, it is viewed as a local concern, reflecting the need to clean up a dysfunctional neighborhood. Many African Americans note that the main difference between these two situations is not the death toll but who is being killed: middle-class Whites in the schoolyard shootings and Black ghetto youth in the drive-by shootings. A recent analysis of smartphone data coupled with surveys and enforcement records shows that African Americans, even if they are not living in disadvantaged areas, are more likely to be exposed to violence (Browning et al. 2017).

It is most important to remember that crime and victimization cannot be viewed in isolation but must be seen as interconnected with education, employment, the quality of healthcare, and the homes to which one returns at the end of the day. W. E. B. Du Bois noted over a century ago that crime was difficult to address precisely because "it is a phenomenon that stands not alone, but rather as a symptom of countless wrong social conditions" (1996:242).

Healthcare

8.6 Explain the healthcare dilemma faced by African Americans.

In 1996, a shocking study published in a prestigious medical journal revealed that two-thirds of boys in Harlem, a predominantly Black neighborhood in New York City, can expect to die young or in mid-adulthood—that is, before they reach age 65. In fact, they have less chance of surviving even to age 45 than their White counterparts nationwide have of reaching age 65. The medical researchers noted that it is not the stereotyped images of AIDS and violence that explain the staggering difference. Rather, Black men are much more likely to fall victim to unrelenting stress, heart disease, and cancer (Fing, Madhavan, and Alderman 1996).

Morbidity and mortality rates for African Americans as a group (not just Harlem men) are equally distressing. Compared with Whites, Blacks have higher death rates from heart disease, pneumonia, diabetes, and cancer. Whites live significantly longer than Blacks. So, for example, among those born in 2000, at one extreme, a White woman could anticipate living to age 83, while a Black man could expect a lifespan of 74 years—that is, equivalent to what White females who were born in 1935 could reasonably expect (Arias 2015).

Drawing on the conflict perspective, sociologist Howard Waitzkin (1986) suggests that racial tensions contribute to African Americans' medical problems. In his view, the stress resulting from racial prejudice and discrimination helps explain the higher rates of hypertension found among African Americans (and Hispanics) than among Whites. Death resulting from hypertension is twice as common in Blacks as in Whites; it is believed to be a critical factor in Blacks' high mortality rates

A NATIONAL ACADEMY OF SCIENCE'S INSTITUTE OF MEDICINE REPORT FINDS MINORITIES ARE LESS LIKELY TO RECEIVE PROPER MEDICAL CARE THAN WHITES.

from heart disease, kidney disease, and strokes (Cooper, Rotimi, and Ward 1999; Green et al. 2007).

Even when medical care is accessible, numerous studies have documented the reluctance of African Americans to trust the medical establishment. Whether seeking medical care, donating blood, or signing up for organ donation programs, Black Americans are underrepresented. There is good reason: a long history of mistreatment up to the present. Some is the result of explicit discrimination—in the past, Blacks were banned from medical schools, denied access to "White blood" as soldiers in the military until after World War II, and prohibited from joining the American Medical Association (until the 1960s). But the reasons go even deeper than explicit discrimination.

Many people, White as well as Black, are familiar with the notorious Tuskegee syphilis study. In this federal government study, which began in 1932, Black men in Alabama who suffered from syphilis were left untreated so that researchers could observe the progression of the disease. Despite the discovery of effective treatments in 1945, the men were not given any medical assistance until the press uncovered the program in 1972. Such events have caused many African Americans to be particularly suspicious of the medical establishment.

Regrettably, the Tuskegee study was neither an isolated incident nor the first or last abuse of African Americans with respect to healthcare. For generations, the role of medical practitioners with respect to people of color was either to verify their worth as slaves or to determine for their masters whether their property was really sick or just trying to get out of doing slave labor. Professor of Ethics at Harvard Medical School Harriet Washington (2007) coined the term **medical apartheid** to refer to the separate and unequal healthcare system in the United States that continues to characterize healthcare for African Americans as well as Latinos.

A 1991 experiment implanted the now-defunct birth control device Norplant into African American teenagers in Baltimore in a program that was applauded by some observers as a way to "reduce the underclass" (Rosenstiel 1990). From 1992 to 1997, Columbia University undertook a study that sought to determine whether there is a biological or genetic basis that might cause violent behavior to run in families—and all the boys recruited for the study were Black. Researchers had misled the parents, claiming their children were simply coming in for a series of tests and questions when, in fact, they were given potentially risky doses of the same drug found in the controversial Fen-phen weight-loss pill, which was later banned when it was found to cause heart irregularities.

All of these episodes make the Black community's suspicions of medicine fairly understandable—but perhaps most disturbing is the almost complete omission of the Black community from medical consideration with regard to important studies and treatments. Only 1 percent of the nearly 20 million Americans enrolled in biomedical studies or clinical trials are Black. This means that African Americans have often missed out on the latest breakthroughs. For example, virtually no Blacks were included in the original studies of the HIV inhibitor AZT, so when the drug came into widespread use in 1991, the Food and Drug Administration had little evidence of its impact on Blacks and erroneously reported that it was not effective for Black patients (Centers for Disease Control and Prevention 2013).

Related to the healthcare dilemma is the problem of environmental justice (introduced in Chapter 3). Problems associated with toxic pollution and hazardous garbage dumps are more likely to be faced by low-income Black communities than by their affluent counterparts. This disproportionate exposure to environmental hazards can be viewed as part of the complex cycle of discrimination faced by African Americans and other subordinate groups in the United States.

Just how significant is the impact of poorer health on the lives of the nation's less-educated people, less-affluent classes, and subordinate groups? Drawing on a variety of research studies, population specialist Evelyn Kitagawa (1972) estimated the "excess mortality rate" to be 20 percent. In other words, 20 percent more people were dying than otherwise might have because of poor health linked to race and class. Using Kitagawa's model, we can calculate that if every African American in the United States were White and had at least one year of college education, some 57,000 fewer Blacks would have died in 2012 and in each succeeding year (author's estimate based on Bureau of the Census 2011a: Table 1).

Politics

8.7 Describe the current role of African Americans in U.S. politics.

There are 29 million Black voters in the United States (outnumbering Latino voters by 3 million). An African American man has now served two terms as President. Of the 15 cabinet departments, only Defense and Interior have not had an African American director. The number of Black elected officials increased from fewer than 1,500 in 1970 to over 10,500 in 2011 (Bureau of the Census 2016v; Joint Center for Political and Economic Studies 2011).

African Americans take voting seriously. Barack Obama's 2008 electoral victory was impressive and, while not a landslide, his winning margin indicated widespread support among Blacks and non-Blacks alike. Expectedly, at least 93 percent of Blacks backed Obama in 2008. Eight years later, African Americans showed their continuing support for the Democratic nominee, but Hillary Clinton's backing by 88 percent of African Americans was a bit more modest (Connelly 2008; Kreiter 2016).

A major landmark came in 2012, when the proportion of Blacks voting exceeded that of White non-Hispanics for the first time. As Figure 8.4 shows, over 66 percent of eligible African American voters voted, compared to 64 percent of White non-Hispanics. Scholars and others will be watching to see if this increased voter participation is a temporary "Obama effect" or a lasting pattern. In either case, it represents a dramatic change from a half-century ago, when Jim Crow practices prevented millions of Black people from reaching the polls.

However, major challenges confront the continued success of African American politicians. Locally elected Black officials usually find it difficult to make the jump to statewide office. Voters, particularly non-Black voters, have difficulty seeing Black politicians as anything other than representatives of the Black community, and they express concern that African Americans will not represent the views of Whites and other non-Blacks. Another big hurdle is acquiring the money necessary to seek a major office. Current Black Congressman Keith Ellison observes, "As long as minority congressional members represent districts that tend to be lower income, then your funding base is going to be smaller, which will put you at a dollar disadvantage when you want to run for statewide office" (Nicholas and King 2013: A4).

Figure 8.4 Voting Rates in Presidential Elections

In the space of two generations, African American voters have made significant strides. In the past, Jim Crow laws blocked African Americans from voting booths in many parts of the nation. By 2012, the proportion of Blacks turning out to vote for Barack Obama exceeded the proportion of voting Whites in the same presidential election. The sea change was achieved through a combination of hard work on the part of Black Americans themselves, many facets of the civil rights movement, favorable federal and court actions, and finally, in 2008 and 2012, the desire to vote for a Black man for president of the United States. However, 2016 saw a reversal of that trend, with a decline in Black voter turnout.

SOURCE: File 2017.

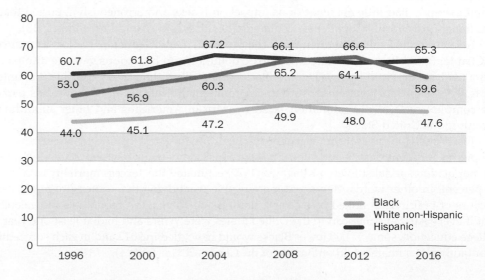

Political gains made by African Americans, as well as Hispanics, have also been placed in jeopardy by legal actions that challenged race-based districts. Boundaries for elective office, ranging from city council positions to the U.S. House of Representatives, have been drawn in such a way as to concentrate enough members of a racial or ethnic group to create a "safe majority" to make it likely that a member of that group will get elected. In Chapter 3, we noted how a growing number of states have pushed to require photo ID, regarded by many as a modern-day example of institutional discrimination, because such measures have a greater negative impact on potential Black voters than on the general electorate.

The changing racial and ethnic landscape can be expected to have an impact on future strategies to elect African Americans to office, but new concerns have arisen over the 1965 Voting Rights Act. In 2013, the Supreme Court's 5–4 decision in *Shelby County v. Holder* invalidated the provisions that require jurisdictions in states with a history of discriminatory voting practices to meet special criteria to ensure that any future changes are fair to all. Affected states felt it was time to stop punishing them for old Jim Crow practices. Voting advocates felt that new, more color-blind racism could undo decades of progress. In addition to the battle over ID requirements, civil rights supporters continue to be concerned over attempts to end same-day voter registration, reduction of the early voting period, and limiting preregistration of 16- and 17 year-olds—all of which are institutional steps that serve to suppress Black voter turnout, even though proponents of such actions deny this intention.

The Black Congressional Caucus (which now has 45 members) gathered in 2017. Collectively, the Caucus is an important political force representing areas in Alabama, California, the District of Columbia, Florida, Georgia, Illinois, Indiana, Louisiana, Maryland, Michigan, Minnesota, Mississippi, Missouri, Nevada, New Jersey, New York, North Carolina, Ohio, Pennsylvania, South Carolina, Texas, the Virgin Islands, Virginia, and Wisconsin.

Conclusion

Maintaining the African American agenda as a part of the larger American agenda continues to be warranted. Twice before in U.S. history, African Americans have received significant attention from the federal government and, to some degree, from the larger White society. The first period extended from the Civil War to the end of Reconstruction. The second period was during the civil rights movement of the 1960s. In both periods, the government acknowledged that race was a major issue, and society made commitments to eliminate inequality. As noted in Chapter 7, Reconstruction was followed by decades of neglect, and on several measures, the position of Blacks deteriorated in the United States. A similar situation was noted after the gains of the civil right movement. Although the 1980s and 1990s were not without their successes, race was clearly not a major social issue on the national agenda. Even inner-city violence grabbed the nation's attention for only a few fleeting moments; in the meantime, color-blind attacks on school integration and affirmative action persisted.

With the election and re-election of Barack Obama, many people summed up his *individual* achievement as "mission accomplished" for the equal opportunity for *all* Black Americans with the rest of society. So is it really necessary to keep talking "race" or the need to address the legacy of slavery, an institution now behind us by about 150 years? The answer is yes.

In the twenty-first century, the issues confronting Black Americans serve to highlight concerns of the entire population. For example, the issue of affordable housing continues to reappear in the headlines, especially in the wake of so many people unable to pay their mortgages in the past decade. While Black renters and homeowners face the additional burden of the legacy of housing discrimination, any significant effort to address poor housing conditions and the high costs of decent family housing would benefit the nation as a whole.

Furthermore, in the past few years, people of all colors and national origins have expressed concern for public safety. So if we were to address the issues of racial profiling and

Figure 8.5 Spectrum of Intergroup Relations: African Americans Today

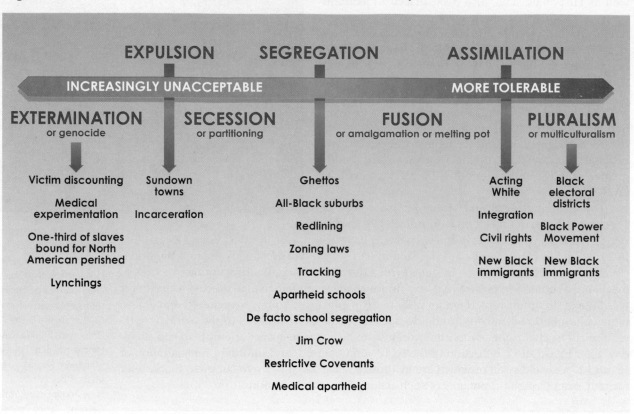

unsafe inner-city neighborhoods, all people would benefit. If stagnating gains in the life expectancy of African Americans and medical apartheid were seriously addressed, the general health of the entire nation would improve. Similarly, and perhaps most dramatically, if the quality of education that Black students receive from preschool through college were to improve, so too would the schooling of all young people.

Black and White Americans have dealt with the continued disparity between the two groups by endorsing several ideologies, as shown in the Spectrum of Intergroup Relations (Figure 8.5). Assimilation was the driving force behind the civil rights movement, which sought to integrate Whites and Blacks into one society. People who rejected contact with the other group endorsed separatism, though, as Chapter 2 showed, neither Whites nor Blacks generally supported separatism. In the late 1960s, the government and various Black organizations began to recognize cultural pluralism as a goal, at least paying lip service to many African Americans' desire to exercise cultural and economic autonomy. Perhaps on no other issue is this desire for control more evident than in the schools.

Substantial gains have been made, but will the momentum continue? Improvement has occurred in a generation inspired to bring about further change. If the resolve to continue toward that goal lessens in the United States, then the picture may become bleaker, and the rate of positive change may continue to decline.

Summary of Learning Objectives

8.1 Describe the major educational issues facing African Americans.

1. African Americans have made gains in all levels of formal schooling but still fall behind the gains made by others.

8.2 Understand the economic situation of Black Americans.

2. Typically, Black Americans are underrepresented in high-wage, high-status occupations and overrepresented in low-wage, low-status occupations. Income and wealth disparities persist between Black Americans and White Americans, with African Americans often unable to accumulate wealth and assets.

8.3 Identify the strengths of and challenges facing African American families.

3. Family life among Black Americans has many strengths, including a strong kinship network. A particular challenge faces Black middle-class households, which may find themselves losing their middle-class status due to changes in the job market and the economy.

8.4 Explain the housing situation in the African American community.

4. While de jure segregation has faded, residential de facto segregation persists.

8.5 Identify the present concerns about the criminal justice system with respect to African Americans.

5. Blacks are more likely to be victims of crime and more likely to be arrested and imprisoned than are Whites. Critics suggest that minorities are subjected to differential justice and victim discounting.

8.6 Explain the healthcare dilemma faced by African Americans.

6. Healthcare statistics reveal significantly higher morbidity and mortality rates for African Americans built on a pattern of healthcare that has been termed medical apartheid.

8.7 Describe the current role of African Americans in U.S. politics.

7. Black Americans have made strides in being elected to office and increasing voter turnout in recent decades, though they still face challenges in being elected to state or national office. Black voter turnout in the 2016 presidential election was lower than in the presidential elections of 2008 and 2012.

Key Terms

acting White, *page 184*
apartheid schools, *page 183*
class, *page 187*
color-bind racism, *page 184*
de facto segregation, *page 183*

differential justice, *page 193*
income, *page 187*
medical apartheid, *page 195*
redlining, *page 192*
tracking, *page 184*

underemployment, *page 189*
victim discounting, *page 194*
victimization surveys, *page 193*
wealth, *page 187*
zoning laws, *page 192*

Review Questions

1. What did the civil rights movement seek to accomplish with respect to education? To what degree have these goals been realized?

2. What challenges face the African American middle class?

3. What are the biggest assets and challenges facing African American families?

4. Describe the impact that residential segregation has on the quality of housing for Black Americans.

5. How would you characterize the experiences of African Americans in the criminal justice system?

6. What is "medical apartheid"?

Critical Thinking

1. Now, more than 50 years after he made his famous "I Have a Dream" speech, how would Martin Luther King, Jr., view the state of Black progress today (if he were still alive)?

2. Specifically review the three paragraphs in King's 1963 speech where he speaks of his "dream." (The speech is available at http://www.archives.gov/press/exhibits/dream-speech.pdf.) King speaks of children in Alabama, working together, and freedom. What dreams might he hold today for the nation's future?

3. What has been the ethnic and racial composition of the neighborhoods you have lived in and the schools you have attended? Consider how the composition of one may have influenced the other. What steps would have been necessary to ensure more diversity?

4. How are the problems in crime, housing, and healthcare interrelated?

Chapter 9
Latinos: Growth and Diversity

RosalreneBetancourt 3/Alamy Stock Photo

⌄ Learning Objectives

9.1 Discuss the characteristics of Latinos, and explain Latino panethnicity.

9.2 Describe the current economic picture for Latinos in the United States.

9.3 Understand Latino patterns of education and English-language attainment.

9.4 Explain the current role of Latinos in U.S. politics.

9.5 Summarize the role of religion in Latino communities.

9.6 Examine and understand the culture of Cuban Americans.

9.7 Describe the diversity among Central and South Americans.

One would not be surprised to hear fellow citizens in Miami, Florida, or El Paso, Texas, speaking Spanish, but what about in a small town in Illinois, Kansas, or Alabama? Change can be unsettling in a small town, and when the change involves increased diversity, the reaction can vary substantially from one community to the next.

Beardstown is an Illinois River town of about 6,000 people. The town's economy is based on the surrounding rich agricultural land. The major employer for over two decades has been a meat-processing plant that offers decent wages for hard, often dangerous work. Immigrants directly from Mexico as well as Mexican Americans from elsewhere were lured to Beardstown by the low cost of living and the jobs that locals did not want. Today, the town, which was founded by Germans, is over a third Hispanic, and its public schools are 50 percent Hispanic. While townspeople say the influx of Hispanic people has kept the local economy alive and culturally vibrant, the area was slow to mount bilingual programs not just for the schools but also for local businesses and public services from the hospital to the city hall.

The U.S. Hispanic rural population is not limited to a small town in Illinois. In Ulysses, Kansas, which is similar in size and ethnic composition to Beardstown, Luz Gonzalez opened The Down-Town Restaurant to serve the area's growing Hispanic population. Initially, she mainly served Mexican food but also found a clientele among long-term residents for diner food. So Gonzalez learned to prepare potato salad and other dishes that were exotic to her.

Despite such success stories, Hispanic workers are not always welcome and do not always feel comfortable in their new surroundings. In Slocomb, Alabama, a town of 2,000 people that bills itself as "Home of the Tomato," many of the local Latino workers who pick green beans, peaches, and strawberries fear seeking healthcare at the local clinic. The staff is friendly enough and speaks Spanish, but on the way there, the workers may face roadblocks as part of immigration crackdowns. Even if the laborers are citizens, they fear exposing relatives and friends who are illegal immigrants.

In many rural areas, the population has declined steadily. Latinos are often filling in the void, whether in Alabama, Illinois, Kansas, or (as we saw in Chapter 4's Research Focus) in America's Dairyland in Wisconsin. By one estimate, more than a third of U.S. rural counties have lost population, but in 86 percent of these, the Hispanic population has increased, which serves to minimize overall population loss.

While increases in the number of Spanish-speaking children is a challenge for schools, without their growing presence, districts would face an almost certain dramatic loss of school funding and massive spending cuts (Beardstown CUSD 15 2017; Costantini 2011; Galewitz 2012; Jordan 2012; Mather and Pollard 2007; Sulzberger 2011; Wisniewski 2012).

What has been termed the "Latinization of America" is evident in the most common last names in the country, as Table 9.1 shows. According to population projections, about one in four people will be of Latin American origin in the United States by 2065, compared to one in five in 2015. Collectively, this group is called *Hispanics* or *Latinos*, two terms that we use interchangeably in this book. Latinos accounted for over half the nation's population growth between 2000 and 2010. Just considering the public schools in larger cities, Latinos account for over 40 percent of first-graders in Chicago, New York City, San Diego, and Phoenix; over 60 percent in Dallas and Houston; over 70 percent in Los Angeles; and over 85 percent in San Antonio (Cohn 2015; Thomás Rivera Policy Institute 2009).

Table 9.1 "Hello. My Name Is…" Most Popular Last Names

1990	2010
1. Smith	1. Smith
2. Johnson	2. Johnson
3. Williams	3. Williams
4. Jones	4. Brown
5. Brown	5. Jones
6. Davis	**6. Garcia**
7. Miller	7. Miller
8. Wilson	8. Davis
9. Moore	**9. Rodriguez**
10. Taylor	**10. Martinez**
11. Anderson	**11. Hernandez**
12. Thomas	**12. Lopez**
13. Jackson	**13. Gonzalez**

SOURCE: Data from Bureau of the Census 2016c.

Figure 9.1 Hispanic Population of the United States by Origin

Note: "Other Hispanic" includes Spanish Americans and Latinos identified as mixed ancestry, as well as other Central and South Americans not otherwise indicated by specific country. All nationalities with more than 1 million are indicated.

SOURCE: Data from American Community Survey 2016b.

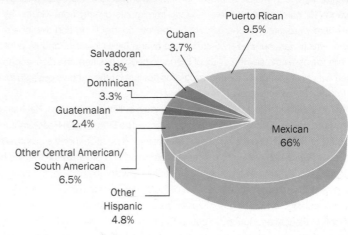

Nearly 36 million Hispanics in the United States (two-thirds) are Mexican Americans, or Chicanos. Figures 9.1 and 9.2 illustrate the diversity of Latinos and their national distribution in the United States. Except for Puerto Ricans, who are U.S. citizens by birth, legal status is a major issue within the Latino community. The specter of people questioning Latinos about their legal status even looms over legal residents. According to a national survey, the majority of Hispanic adults in the United States worry that they, a family member, or a close friend could be deported (Lopez and Gonzalez-Barrera 2013).

Some people regard the increased presence of Latinos in the United States as a growth engine for everything from the arts and music to the economy, while a few see it as the death knell of a great nation. Others compare the Americanization of Latinos to the assimilation of Italian Americans more than century ago. Whatever the perspective, the growth of the Hispanic population is undeniable, and its presence will be felt for generations to come (Leonhardt 2013).

Figure 9.2 Where Most Hispanic Americans Live

Fifty-two percent of the nation's Hispanics live in just three states—California, Florida, and Texas.

SOURCE: Data from American Community Survey 2016b.

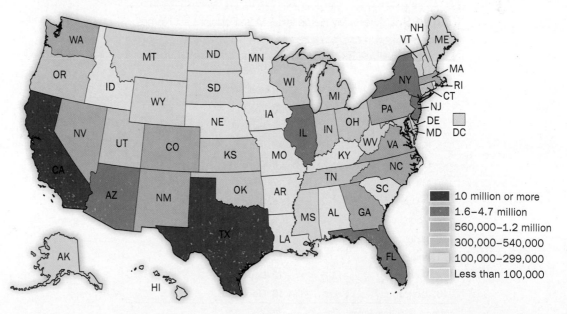

Latino Identity

9.1 Discuss the characteristics of Latinos, and explain Latino panethnicity.

Is there a common identity among Latinos? Is a panethnic Latino identity emerging? Recall that **panethnicity** is the development of solidarity between ethnic subgroups.

At issue are the terms *Hispanic* and *Latino* themselves. Non-Hispanics often give these labels to the diverse group of native-born Latino Americans and immigrants. This labeling reflects the views of the dominant group in grouping all Spanish-speaking people (and sometimes Portuguese-speaking people) under one umbrella, just as the dominant group places quite different American Indian tribes or Asian Pacific Americans into one collective group. However, Hispanics do not share a common historical or cultural identity; definitions of their ethnic identity may lead to heated debates even among those who share the same ethnic heritage. Lumping all Hispanics into one category reflects a lack of understanding of their history and the history of the United States.

Still, the question remains: Are Hispanics or Latinos themselves developing a common identity? While generally two-thirds of Latinos and Hispanics in the United State agree that they share a common culture, that does not mean they feel they share a common ethnic-group name. Overall, about half would prefer to use country of origin to identify themselves, such as *Mexican American*; the balance is split between *Hispanic* or *Latino* and *American*.

Among Hispanic youth age 16–25, only a minority (about 20 percent) prefers to use panethnic names such as *Hispanic* or *Latino*. In Miami, Florida, bumper stickers proclaim *"No soy Hispano, soy Cubano"* (translation: "I am not Hispanic, I am Cuban"). As might be expected, identity preferences vary according to whether one is an immigrant or is U.S.-born of U.S.-born Hispanics. About 72 percent of immigrant youth prefer country of origin compared to 32 percent of grandchildren (Pew Hispanic Center 2009, 2012a).

A professional writer who is proud of her Latino heritage, Rosie Molinary (2017) is the founder of Circle de Luz, a nonprofit that empowers young Latinas in Charlotte, North Carolina. The Speaking Out feature reprints a selection from her book *Hijas Americanas* (*American Daughters*), in which she writes of growing up Latina and navigating her two identities through college.

Speaking Out

Reconciling Two Identities

Rosie Molinary

I never had Latino girlfriends growing up. I only knew two Mexican American girls at my high school. In college, there were two older Cuban American women whose beauty and classiness intimidated the hell out of me.

I have had Latino guy friends. Not boys I dated. Well, one. Almost. They were mostly just friends who understood me and helped me ease into a feeling of home. Two who stand out in my mind are Braulio and Christopher...Braulio was like my immediate family. When Braulio and I first met it seemed as if we had already been together for a lifetime. He came home with me during Thanksgiving and Christmas breaks. He completed our family, and the way he recognized me made me feel more complete. Before Braulio, I had no idea what feeling at home meant, really, because I'd spent so much time feeling like "the other."

Rosie Molinary.

Used with the permission of Rosie Molinary.

Once, on a visit to New York City when I was in college, someone called out to me. "Hey Boricua, over here!" a young man yelled from his apartment stoop. I looked around, wondering whom he was yelling at. Then it dawned on me: He was talking to me. Intimidated, I sped up. Later, I considered why I ran, why the Boricua in me did not march over to that stoop and ask, *"¿Qué quieres?"* ["What do you want?"] But I had grown up in South Carolina. Besides my sister, I was the only Puerto Rican girl most anyone else knew. A counselor in the admissions office assumed I was a Spanish major; she looked at me with a knowing glint in her eye—an obnoxious look that told me she believed that studying Spanish might indeed be the only way I could succeed.

She proceeded to tell me that I'd been granted admission not because I was an academic powerhouse, but because of what I might add to the campus. I felt the weight of needing to act polite, to be good, to play nice. I said nothing. Instead I let her offensive comment hang in the air between us. I walked away from her that day, just as I walked away from that the guy in New York City. I wasn't sure where I fit in or what I was. I was someone who knew what it was like to be seen, but not valued or heard.

I'd also been told plenty of times that I wasn't Puerto Rican enough, or even Puerto Rican at all—despite Spanish being my first language, despite the fact that I had no relatives living in the United States. Once, in a college committee meeting about diversity, a woman I knew well looked right past me as she asked the group why we didn't have any Latinos on the committee. What I came to understand was that sometimes, despite my own reality, I was considered Latina enough to take care of every quota under the sun and other times not Latina enough to fulfill a single one.

Thinking back to that summer afternoon in New York City, I now realize that I hurried away from the guy who yelled at me not because I was scared of him, but because I was scared of what he would find in me. *What if I had stopped and talked to him? What if he told me that I wasn't Puerto Rican enough? What if my own* compadre *chose not to claim me? Where would that leave me in my understanding of myself?*

There I was. Being recognized as Puerto Rican—perhaps for the first time without trying—but the possibility of being denied that I belonged was too much to bear. I've often wondered what would have happened if I had risen up and claimed an identity that was mine for the taking. But it would take a while before I

could finally revel in the joy that the Latina in me had been so easily recognized. . . .

Through college, I struggled with not belonging, with feeling alone. Some of my isolation was just the routine isolation that so many feel during a new stage of life, but most of it was about ethnicity, socioeconomic class, and being so distinctly different looking and different feeling from everyone else on campus. In those years, I wanted desperately to break the barrier I felt between myself and others. I wanted to leave a favorable impression on people, I wanted to matter.

My junior year, my college roommate—a close friend— watched me while I put in my contacts and said, "You would be so exotic looking if you had different colored eyes."

That comment, as much as it mortifies her now that she ever said such a thing, summed up how I felt in college. I was not exotic enough to be considered rare and worthy, and I was just different enough to not be considered.

I remember a letter I wrote that same year. A friend had written me and asked whether I felt I had chosen the right school. My response is still clear in my mind. It wasn't the perfect school for me, I wrote. It wasn't a natural fit, and I didn't always feel comfortable. Only now can I look back and recognize how precocious and accurate that assessment was. Because it was only later that I fell in love with the sense of not belonging, with the idea of not having just one place to call my own. Eventually, I could just be who I set out to be each day. Some people would like it, some people would not, but at the end of the day, I could still meet my own eyes in the mirror.

Source: Molinary 2007: 6–8. Molinary, Rosie. Hijas Americanas: Beauty, Body Image, and Growing Up Latina. Emeryville CA: Seal Press, 2007. Used with permission.

Another tricky issue is how Latinos identify themselves in racial terms now and in the future. In Chapter 1 we noted the importance of **colorism** in the United States—the ranking or judging of individuals based on skin color. Typically, the sharp White–Black divide is absent in Latinos' home countries, where race, if socially constructed, tends to be along a color gradient. A **color gradient** places people along a continuum from light to dark skin color rather than in two or three distinct racial groupings. The presence of color gradients is yet another reminder of the social construction of race. Terms such as *mestizo Hondurans, mulatto Colombians,* or *African Panamanians* reflect this continuum of color gradient.

In the United States, Latinos tend to avoid taking on the label of being "White" or "Black," although lighter-skinned Hispanics generally distinguish themselves from Black Americans. Yet in a 2014 national survey, about one-quarter of U.S. Hispanics considered themselves "Afro-Latino, Afro-Caribbean, or Afro-country of origin." This self-description does not automatically mean they identify themselves as "Black" but rather that they can report themselves as a combination of White, Hispanic, mixed, tribal, or Black. These multiple dimensions of colorism reflect the long colonial history of Latin America during which many peoples—indigenous Americans, Europeans, Asians, and freed and enslaved Africans—mixed together (López and Gonzalez-Barrera 2016; Telles and Paschel 2014).

The Economic Picture

9.2 Describe the current economic picture for Latinos in the United States.

Among the many indicators of how well a group is doing economically in the United States, income is probably the best one. In Figure 9.3, we see a side-by-side picture of the income of Hispanic vs. White non-Hispanic workers as reported by the Census Bureau. The picture is very stark, with the Latino incomes appearing to be the reverse of the White earnings. These data are limited to full-time year-round workers, so they significantly understate the difference. Many more Latino workers are unemployed or work only seasonally and/or part-time.

A study released in 2011 documented the high increase in the Latino poverty rate from 1977 through 2010, except for a brief period of decline during the relative prosperity the nation experienced in the late 1990s. The government has measured poverty for generations, and while Blacks have a higher poverty rate than Whites, the largest group of children below the poverty level had always been Whites. By the second decade of the 2000s, however, Hispanic children as a group far outnumbered White children in poverty. By 2010, 6.1 million Latino children were living in poverty, compared to 5 million White and 4.4 million Black children. Reflecting the low wages that Latinos often receive in the United States, poor Hispanic children are much more likely to have a working parent than poor children in the White or Black communities (Lopez and Velasco 2011).

Income is only one part of the picture. Low levels of wealth—total assets minus debt—are characteristic of Hispanic households. Although they appear, as a group, to have slightly higher levels of wealth than African American households, Hispanic households average less than 12 cents for every dollar in wealth owned by White non-Hispanic households. In the previous chapter we noted the disastrous effect of the Great Recession and the housing foreclosure crisis on African Americans. As a group, Latinos were hit even harder—an effect that will have a lasting impact on wealth accumulation by future generations. The trend is not encouraging, with the Hispanic–non-Hispanic gap growing. In summary, Latinos not only are likely to continue to earn much less annually but also to have fewer financial resources to fall back on (Keister, Vallejo, and Borelli 2014; Kent 2010; Rugh 2015).

Figure 9.3 Hispanic vs. White Earnings

Note: Data for 2010 as tabulated in the Annual Social and Economic Supplement, 2011. Data are only for full-time, year-round workers age 15 and older; earnings are the sum of wage and salary income and self-employment income.

SOURCE: Bureau of the Census 2011e: Table 21.

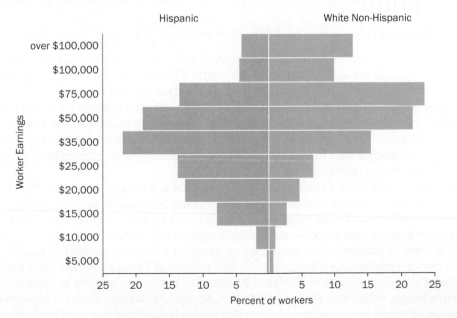

Table 9.2 Hispanic Origin Groups

Group	Poverty Rate	Bachelor's Degree	Proficient in English	Foreign Born
Mexican Americans	27%	9%	64%	36%
Puerto Ricans	27%	16%	82%	1%
Cubans	18%	24%	58%	59%
Salvadorans	20%	7%	46%	62%
Dominicans	26%	15%	55%	57%
Guatemalans	26%	8%	41%	67%

Note: Includes the six largest groups; all reporting at least 1 million in 2010.

SOURCE: Motel, Seth, and Eileen Patten. 2012. The 10 Largest Hispanic Origin Groups: Characteristics, Rankings, Top Counties. Washington DC: Pew Hispanic Center.

Table 9.2 summarizes several key measures, including income, broken down by the six largest Latino groups. The high rate of poverty is very troubling.

By studying the income and poverty trends of Latino households, we can see how much—but also how little—has been accomplished in terms of reducing social inequality among ethnic and racial groups. Although the income of Latinos has gradually increased over the past 30 years, so has White income. The gap in income between the two groups has remained relatively constant. Indeed, the $45,148 income of the typical Latino household in 2015 was about $30,000 less than the income of the White non-Hispanic household (Proctor, Semega, and Kollar 2016).

A growing proportion of poor African Americans find it increasingly difficult to obtain meaningful work. Once employed, studies suggest they hit a "blue-collar ceiling," finding it difficult to move into better-paying jobs with benefits such as insurance and a pension. The same is true of today's poor Latinos, but their situation is much more difficult to predict. On the one hand, as a group, poor Latinos are more geographically mobile than poor African Americans, which increases Latinos' prospects of a brighter future. On the other hand, 54 percent of foreign-born Latinos and 17 percent of native-born Latinos send money abroad to help relatives, which puts a greater strain on supporting themselves in the United States (Fuller, McElmurry, and Koval 2011; Lopez, Livingston, and Kochhar 2009).

Education

9.3   Understand Latino patterns of education and English-language attainment.

Schooling for Latinos has been a challenge—and not just because of language issues. In the past, Hispanic schoolchildren were arbitrarily assigned to create all-Latino schools. This **de jure segregation**—assignment of schoolchildren to maintain separate schools—has a very long history. The Supreme Court finally struck down the practice in *Mendez v. Westminster* in 1947, seven years before the more famous school segregation case *Brown v. Board of Education*. Yet even as desegregated schools are supposed to be the law, tracking within schools maintains a high level of isolation of Latino schoolchildren from their non-Hispanic classmates (Meraji 2014; Ochoa 2013).

Looking at education among contemporary Latinos is a study in contrasts. Progress has been significant, but they are often stigmatized as being more academically challenged than their White and Asian Pacific American peers. Yet, as Figure 9.4 shows, the percentage of Hispanics who leave high school to start college is comparable to that of the general population.

The level of attainment as measured by years of schooling completed beyond high school remains modest. As a group in 2015, 14.8 percent of Latinos 25 years and older have a bachelor's degree, compared to over 34.2 percent of Whites. As we saw in Table 9.2, there is a wide range, with some groups like Cuban Americans having relatively high levels of college completion, but collectively, Latino attainment lags behind that of Whites. More and

Figure 9.4 Latinos Starting College, 1977–2015

Since 2010, the proportion of Latino high school graduates who start college is roughly comparable to that of White non-Hispanic students.

Note: Data are for 18- to 24-year-olds having completed public high school or its equivalency.

SOURCE: Data from National Center for Educational Statistics 2016: Table 347.

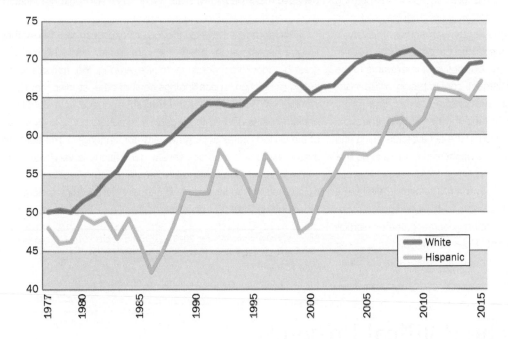

more Latino students are receiving their degrees, but their success in completing college in a timely fashion is lower than that of their White classmates (American Community Survey 2016a: Tables B1500H and B1502L).

A complicating factor in educational attainment is becoming proficient in English. The importance is not lost on Latinos, who have cited language skills more frequently than immigration status, income, education, or skin color as an explanation for discrimination against them. In 2007, 46 percent said it was the biggest cause of discrimination (Hakimzadeh and Cohn 2007).

Therefore, English language acquisition is key to both education and the future economic development of Hispanics, as it is for immigrants from most countries. In the Research Focus, we consider the latest data on immigrants and their descendants' fluency in English.

Research Focus

English-Language Acquisition

Few issues swirling around the everyday life of Latinos in the United States are more heated than fluency in English. Political efforts to declare English the official language of the United States continue, the funding of bilingual programs is constantly in jeopardy, and native English speakers often resent hearing even accented English in the workplace or in public. Ironically, people who proudly see themselves as Latino but do not speak Spanish experience resentment from some Hispanics who feel the English speakers are too assimilated. Arizona Diamondbacks pitcher David Hernandez, a third-generation Mexican American raised in Sacramento, California, told reporters that when he first broke into professional baseball, his many Latin American teammates kept trying to speak Spanish and could not understand why he would not engage them in conversations.

Yet these tensions occur against a backdrop where English-language acquisition is not debated among immigrants as a whole. They see learning English as vital to advancement because those who lack fluency have greater problems in the job market and even have more limited exposure to newer technologies such as the Internet. They also know that speaking with a Spanish accent, much less not speaking English very well or at all, is stigmatized throughout the United States outside of Latino communities.

The reality is that most immigrants and their offspring quickly become fluent in English and abandon their mother tongue. By the second generation after the immigrants' arrival (that is, the immigrants' grandchildren), use of the mother tongue has virtually disappeared.

In surveying adults using both English and Spanish-speaking interviewers in southern metropolitan Los Angeles and San Diego, scholars looked at language retention across a variety of immigrant nationalities. This area is the nation's largest receiver of immigrants, accounting for one out of five of immigrants to the United States, and it has the largest concentration of Spanish-speaking individuals. In such metropolitan areas one might anticipate significant retention of the mother tongue and slow acceptance or use of English. Given all the outlets for listening and reading in Spanish, for example, one might expect there to be little motivation to learn English.

Instead, the researchers found in Southern California a move away from speaking the mother tongue and a move toward English. With each succeeding generation, the proportion speaking the mother tongue drops. Retention of Spanish is higher than is the survival of mother tongue by Asian and European

immigrants. But even among the grandchildren of immigrants from Mexico and other Spanish-speaking countries, at most one in three speak fluent Spanish. Among their children (that is, the immigrants' great-grandchildren), only 5 percent can speak Spanish. "Fluency" in speaking is not a very high standard, because many people who are fluent speakers could not write or read even a simple document in Spanish.

The apparent move toward the use of English over the mother tongue persists even though the immigrants' grandchildren and great-grandchildren continue to live among the nation's large Latino population. These findings confirm other studies that show immigrants' acquisition of the English language in a couple of generations. Based on these data, researchers sometimes speak of the United States as a "graveyard" for languages. The ability to sustain bilingualism across several generations is very limited. In summary, language continues to be a hot-button issue, but largely by the second generation, and certainly by the third generation, proficiency in the language of the host society becomes dominant.

Sources: *The Arizona Republic* 2013; Feagin and Cobas 2014; Fox and Livingston 2007; Hakimzadeh and Cohn 2007; Krogstad 2016a; Rumbaut, Massey, and Bean 2006.

The Political Presence

9.4   Explain the current role of Latinos in U.S. politics.

Until the late twentieth century, Latinos' political activity had been primarily outside conventional electoral politics. In the 1960s, urban Hispanics, especially Mexican Americans, developed activist groups aimed at what were regarded as especially unsympathetic policies of school administrators. About the same time, labor organizer César Chávez crusaded to organize migrant farmworkers. Efforts to organize agricultural laborers date back to the turn of the twentieth century, but Chávez was the first to achieve any success. These laborers had never won collective bargaining rights, partly because their mobility and extreme poverty made it difficult for them to organize into a unified group.

Both major political parties have begun to acknowledge that Latinos are a force in the election process. For Puerto Ricans and Cuban Americans (as discussed later in this chapter), the central issue has been the political future of their respective island homelands. Nonetheless, Republicans and Democrats have sought to gain support among Latinos. This recognition of Latinos by established political parties has come about primarily as a result of the growth of the Hispanic population and also due to policies that have facilitated voting by non-English-speaking voters. As Figure 9.5 shows, eligible Latino voters comprise a significant part of the total potential vote in many parts of the nation.

For a generation, political scholars spoke of the Latino power at the ballot box, but the Hispanic presence at the polls has not always lived up to expectations. The turnout often has been poor because although Hispanics were interested in voting, many were ineligible to vote under the U.S. Constitution. They were noncitizens or, despite bilingual voting information, found that getting properly registered was a challenge.

The situation began to change with the 2010 Congressional elections and especially the 2012 presidential election. In the Obama–Romney race, Latinos nationwide constituted one out of every ten voters, and their numbers were almost double that or even more in the key swing or battleground states of Colorado, Florida, Nevada, and Virginia. In coming years, the potential for an even greater Latino political presence is strong.

Anticipating greater turnout, political parties are advancing more Hispanic candidates. Democrats have been decidedly more successful in garnering the Hispanic vote, with

Figure 9.5 Latinos as a Percent of Eligible Voters

SOURCE: Pew Hispanic Center 2011a, data based on 2008 Census Bureau sample. (c) 2011 Pew Hispanic Center, a Pew Research Center project. Latinos as a Percent of Eligible Voters, By Congressional District. http://pewhispanic.org/docs/?DocID=26

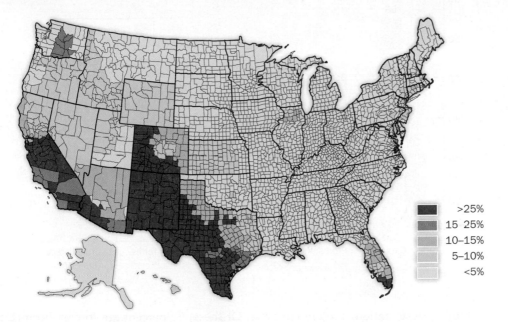

Legend:
- >25%
- 15–25%
- 10–15%
- 5–10%
- <5%

ultimately 71 percent of Latinos backing Democratic candidate Barack Obama in 2012 and 66 percent voting for Hillary Clinton over Donald Trump in 2016. While not all Latinos necessarily support easing immigration regulations, the tone in Republican arguments for strict immigration laws alienates most Latinos. The Democrats promoted policies that would allow those who immigrated illegally as children or even as infants with their parents a path to permanent residency following successful completion of their schooling. However, the Republicans officially oppose such steps and encourage deportation for most illegal immigrants, including immediate deportation upon detection (Krogstad and Lopez 2016).

Like African Americans, Latinos resent that every four years the political movers and shakers rediscover that they exist. Latino community leaders derisively label candidates' fascination with Latino concerns near election time as either *fiesta politics* or *Hispandering*. Between major elections, modest efforts have been made to court their interest except by Latino elected officials; however, this situation may change with increased Latino presence at the ballot box.

The election of Donald Trump created a new sense of urgency for the Latino Victory Fund, the political action committee that works to elect liberal Hispanic political candidates. As the Trump White House dropped the Spanish language translation website, the Fund renewed its efforts to identify viable candidates to work against the plans to curb sanctuary cities, roll back certain civil-rights protections, and detain more illegal immigrants. At the same time, the Victory Fund took some pleasure in witnessing the election of the first Latina to the Senate, Catherine Cortez Masto of Nevada (Davis 2017).

Religion

9.5 **Summarize the role of religion in Latino communities.**

The most important formal organization in the Hispanic community is the church. Most Puerto Ricans and Mexican Americans express a religious preference for the Catholic Church. About 55 percent of Hispanics are Roman Catholic. Figure 9.6 provides more detailed information about Latinos' specific religious affiliations.

Recently, the Roman Catholic Church has become more community oriented, seeking to identify Latino, or at least Spanish-speaking, clergy and staff to serve Latino parishes. The lack of Spanish-speaking priests is compounded because a smaller proportion of men are training for the priesthood, and even fewer of them speak Spanish. Only 6 percent

Figure 9.6 Religious Affiliation of Latinos

SOURCE: Data from Pew Research Center Religion and Public Life 2014: 29.

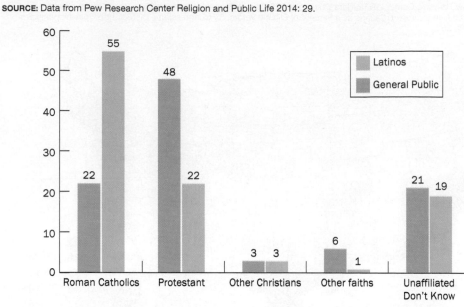

of Catholic priests nationwide are Hispanic. Of these, 80 percent are foreign-born (U.S. Conference of Catholic Bishops 2017).

Not only is the Catholic Church important to Hispanics, but Hispanics also play a significant role in the church. Hispanics account for more than a third of Roman Catholics in the United States. Many interpreted the selection of Pope Francis from Argentina in 2013 as an acknowledgment of the Latin American role in the global Roman Catholic Church. Indeed, the population growth of Mexican Americans and other Hispanics has been responsible for the Catholic Church's continued growth in recent years, while the number of adherents to mainstream Protestant faiths has declined. The Catholic Church is trying to adjust to Hispanics' more expressive manifestation of religious faith, which is reflected in frequent reliance on their own patron saints and the presence of special altars in their homes. Catholic churches in some parts of the United States are even starting to accommodate observances of the Mexican *Día de los Muertos*, or Day of the Dead. Such practices are a tradition from rural Mexico, where religion was followed without trained clergy.

Although Latinos are predominantly Catholic, their membership in Protestant and other Christian faiths is growing. Both first-generation Latinos (that is, the immigrant generation) and the U.S.-born are leaving Catholicism for other Christian faiths or leaving organized religion altogether. However, this pattern is not unique to Hispanic Catholics.

Pentecostalism, a type of evangelical Christianity, is becoming more popular among Hispanics in Latin America and elsewhere. Adherents to Pentecostal faiths hold beliefs similar to those of evangelicals but also believe in the infusion of the Holy Spirit into services and in religious experiences such as faith healing. Pentecostalism and similar faiths are attractive to many Latinos because they offer followers the opportunity to express their religious fervor openly. The membership in any of the churches is small, at least initially, offering a sense of community and often Spanish-speaking leadership. More than one-quarter of Latino Protestants who have left the Roman Catholic Church now identify as Pentecostal. Gradually, the more established faiths are recognizing the desirability of offering Latino parishioners a greater sense of belonging (Masci 2014; Pew Research Center Religion and Public Life 2014).

As noted at the beginning of this discussion, the church is the most important organization for the Latino community. It is more than just about religion. For example, as efforts have been made to restrict immigration or increase deportation efforts, faith-based groups and individual churches have been pivotal in mobilizing protests. Literally millions of Hispanics mobilized first in 2006 and again in 2016 to protest enforcement-oriented steps in immigration reform (Coddou 2016).

Cuban Americans

9.6 **Examine and understand the culture of Cuban Americans.**

Fourth in number only to Mexican Americans, Puerto Ricans, and Salvadorans (who are the subject of a Research Focus later in this chapter), Cuban Americans are a significant ethnic Hispanic minority in the United States. Their presence in this country has a long history, with Cuban settlements in Florida dating back to as early as 1831. These settlements tended to be small, close-knit communities organized around a single enterprise, such as a cigar-manufacturing firm.

Until recently, however, the number of Cuban Americans was very modest. The 1960 census showed that 79,000 people who had been born in Cuba lived in the United States. Fidel Castro's assumption of power after the 1959 Cuban Revolution led to sporadic immigration to the United States and for generations defined the Cuban American political agenda in the United States. By 2015, more than 2.1 million people of Cuban birth or descent lived here.

Immigration

Cuban immigration to the United States since the 1959 revolution has been continuous, but there were three significant influxes of Cuban immigrants through the 1980s. First, the initial exodus of about 200,000 Cubans after Castro's assumption of power lasted about three years. Regular commercial air traffic continued despite the United States' severing of diplomatic relations with Cuba. This first wave stopped with the missile crisis of October 1962, when all legal movement between the two nations was halted.

An agreement between the United States and Cuba in 1965 produced the second wave of immigration through a program of freedom flights—specially arranged charter flights from Havana to Miami. Through this program, more than 340,000 refugees arrived between 1965 and 1973. Despite efforts to encourage these arrivals to disperse into other parts of the United States, most settled in the Miami area (Abrahamson 1996).

The third major migration, the 1980 Mariel boatlift, has been the most controversial. In 1980, more than 124,000 refugees fled Cuba in the "freedom flotilla." In May of that year, a few boats from Cuba began to arrive in Key West, Florida, with people seeking asylum in the United States. President Jimmy Carter (1978:1623), reflecting the nation's hostility toward Cuba's communist government, told the new arrivals and anyone else who might be listening in Cuba that they were welcome "with open arms and an open heart." As the number of arrivals escalated, it became apparent that Fidel Castro had used the invitation as an opportunity to send prison inmates, patients from mental hospitals, and drug addicts. However, the majority of the refugees were neither marginal to the Cuban economy nor social deviants.

Other Cubans soon began to call the refugees of this migration **Marielitos**. The word, which implies that these refugees were undesirable, refers to Mariel, the fishing port west of Havana from which the boats departed and where Cuban authorities herded people into boats. The term *Marielitos* remains a stigma in the media and in Florida. Because of their negative reception by longer-established Cuban immigrants and the group's modest skills and lack of formal education, these immigrants had a great deal of difficulty in adjusting to their new lives in the United States (Masud-Piloto 2008b).

There are some interesting parallels between the freedom flotilla and Irish immigration of more than a century earlier (discussed in Chapter 5). Both represent immigration based on difficult economic conditions and reliance on family ties to make a successful life in the United States. In addition, both groups often received a hostile reaction when they arrived, and both groups were exploited, but in different ways. The Irish were taken advantage of by people who used them for cheap labor, and the Cuban refugees were exploited by both the United States and Cuba for political reasons. One important difference is that dissatisfied Irish immigrants could return to Ireland if they wished, whereas for the Cubans, there was no turning back (Miller 2014).

Unlike the earlier waves of Cuban immigrants, the Marielitos grew up in a country bombarded with anti-American images. Despite these initial problems, most were eventually accepted by the Hispanic community, and many have found employment. Most have applied for permanent resident status. Government assistance to these

The December 2014 renewal of diplomatic relations between the United States and Cuba heralded the possibility of a new era for trade and tourism. It also changed the way that Cubans can seek permanent residency in the United States. Beginning in January 2017, they were no longer granted special status as refugees from a communist government.

Alfredo Martirena/CartoonStock.com

immigrants was limited, but some groups of Cuban Americans in the Miami area provided substantial help. However, for a small core group, adjustment was impossible. The legal status of a few of these detainees (for example, arrivals who were held by the government pending clarification of their refugee or immigrant status) was ambiguous because of alleged offenses committed in Cuba or in the United States (Peréz 2001).

Beginning in 1994, the United States had a *dry foot, wet foot* policy with respect to arrivals from Cuba. Government policy generally allowed Cuban nationals who managed to reach the United States (*dry foot*) to remain, whereas those who were picked up at sea (*wet foot*) were sent back to Cuba. In the aftermath of renewed U.S.–Cuban diplomatic relations, this unique policy ended in January 2017, leaving Cubans desiring to enter the United States permanently to navigate the maze of programs faced by migrants from any other nation.

The Current Picture

Compared with other recent immigrant groups and with the Latino population as a whole, Cuban Americans are doing well. As Table 9.2 shows, Cuban Americans have college completion rates that are significantly higher than those of other Latino groups. In general, Cuban Americans today compare favorably with other Hispanics, although recent arrivals as a group trail behind White Americans.

The presence of Cubans has been felt in urban centers throughout the United States, but most notably in the Miami area. Throughout their various immigration phases, Cubans have been encouraged to move out of southern Florida, but many have returned to Dade County (metropolitan Miami), with its warm climate and proximity to other Cubans and to Cuba itself. According to a 2015 statistical profile, 68 percent of all Cuban Americans lived in Florida, with the majority in the Miami area (Klas 2016).

Probably no ethnic group has had more influence on the fortunes of a city in a short period of time than have the Cubans on Miami. Most people consider the Cubans' economic influence to be positive. With other Latin American immigrants, Cubans have transformed Miami from a quiet resort to a boomtown. To a large degree, they have re-created the Cuba they left behind. Today, the population of Miami is more than 59 percent foreign-born—more than any other U.S. city. Residents like to joke that one of the reasons they like living in Miami is that it is close to the United States (Malone et al. 2003).

All Cuban immigrants have had much to adjust to, and they have not been able to immediately establish the kind of life they sought. Although some of those who fled Cuba were forced to give up their life's savings, the early immigrants of the first wave were generally well educated and had professional or managerial backgrounds, and therefore met with greater economic success than later immigrants. However, regardless of the occupations the immigrants were able to enter, their families had to make tremendous adjustments. Women, who typically did not work outside the home, often had to seek employment. Immigrant parents found their children being exposed to a foreign culture. All the challenges typically faced by immigrant households were complicated by the uncertain fates of those they left behind in Cuba.

The primary adjustment among South Florida's Cuban Americans has been more to one another than

Ethnic enclaves of shopping, restaurants, and places to converse emerge wherever people of the same nationality are concentrated. Pictured here is Little Havana in Miami.

to Whites, African Americans, or other Latinos. The prolonged immigration now stretching across two generations has led to differences between Cuban Americans in terms of ties to Cuba, social class, and age. There is no single Cuban American lifestyle.

The long-range prospects for Cubans in the United States depend on several factors. Of obvious importance are events in Cuba; many exiles have publicly proclaimed their desire to return to Cuba if the communist government is overturned. A powerful force in Miami politics is the Cuban American National Foundation, which takes a strong anti-Castro position. The organization has actively opposed any proposals that the United States develop a more flexible policy toward Cuba. More moderate voices in the Cuban exile community have not been encouraged to speak out. Indeed, sporadic violence has even occurred within the community over U.S.–Cuban relations.

Cuban Americans have selectively accepted Anglo culture. Cuban culture itself has been tenacious; Cuban immigrants do not feel they need to forget Spanish while establishing fluency in English, the way other immigrant children have shunned their linguistic past. Still, a split between the original exiles and their children is evident. Young people are more concerned about the Miami Dolphins football team than they are about what is happening in Havana. They are increasingly open to reestablishing relations with a Raúl Castro–led Cuba (Mazzei 2016).

Central and South Americans

9.7   Describe the diversity among Central and South Americans.

Immigrants who have come from Central and South America are a diverse population that has not been closely studied. Indeed, most government statistics treat its members collectively as "other" and rarely differentiate among them by nationality. As Figure 9.7 shows, there are 20 nations in Latin America, each with its own identity.

For example, people from Chile and Costa Rica have little in common other than their hemisphere of origin and the Spanish language, if that. Some come from indigenous populations, especially in Guatemala and Belize, and have a social identity apart from any national allegiance. Also, not all Central and South Americans have Spanish as their native tongue. For example, Brazilians speak Portuguese, people from French Guyana speak French, and those from Suriname speak Dutch.

One fact that is clear is that immigration from Central and South America has increased dramatically. From 1990 to 2010, the Cuban and Puerto Rican population in the United States increased about 70 percent, compared to 137 percent for Mexican Americans. During the same period, Salvadoran immigrants increased by 192 percent, Guatemalans by 289 percent, and Hondurans by 383 percent (Logan and Turner 2013).

Many of the nations of Central and South America have a complex system of placing people into myriad racial groups. Their experience with a color gradient in their home countries necessitates an adjustment when they experience the Black–White racial formation of the United States.

Added to language diversity and the color gradient are social-class distinctions, religious differences, urban-versus-rural backgrounds, and differences in dialect, even among those who speak the same language. Social relations among Central and South American groups with one another, Latinos in general, and non-Latinos defy generalization. Central and South Americans do not form, nor should they be expected to form, a cohesive group, nor do they naturally form coalitions with Cuban Americans, Mexican Americans, or Puerto Ricans (Orlov and Ueda 1980).

Immigration

Immigration from the various Central and South American nations has been sporadic, influenced by U.S. immigration laws and social forces operating in the home countries. Perceived economic opportunities escalated the northward movement in the 1960s. By 1970, Panamanians and Hondurans represented the largest national groupings, most of them being identified in the census as "nonwhite." By 2010, El Salvador, Guatemala, and Colombia were the top countries of origin, each with at least a million immigrants present.

Figure 9.7 Latin America

Diversity is the name of the game when it comes to Latin America. Central America includes six nations, and South America another 13. Mexico is typically considered part of North America.

Immigration often comes through Mexico, which may serve as a brief stop along the way or represent a point of settlement for six months to three years or even longer.

Since the mid-1970s, increasing numbers of Central and South Americans have fled unrest in their home countries. Most notably, Salvadorans' movement to the United States reached the point recently where they surpassed Cuban Americans as the third-largest Hispanic group in the nation.

Starting in about 1978, war and economic chaos in El Salvador, as well as Nicaragua and Guatemala, prompted many to seek refuge in the United States. The impact of the turmoil cannot be exaggerated. Regarding the total populations of each country, it is estimated that anywhere from 13 percent of Guatemalans to 32 percent of Salvadorans left their respective countries. Not at all a homogeneous group, the immigrants range from Guatemalan Indian peasants to wealthy Nicaraguan exiles. These latest arrivals probably had some economic motivation for migration, but this concern was overshadowed or at least matched by their fear of being killed or hurt if they remained in their home country (Camarillo 1993; Gomez 2015).

In the Global View feature, we look at the close relationship between the people of El Salvador and the United States.

A Global View

The Salvadoran Connection

El Salvador is a Central American country with over 6 million people. Like many other Latin American countries, most Salvadorans are mestizo (mixed Native American and Spanish origin), with maybe one in ten of Spanish ancestry viewing themselves as "White." An even smaller group is indigenous native people who have held onto their native cultures, including distinctive languages.

Political unrest, hurricanes, and volcanic eruptions have propelled people to emigrate in search of better opportunities. Salvadorans immigrated to the United States not so much out of a desire to be a citizen of another country but largely out of fear of remaining in their home country. The everyday violence is difficult to comprehend because El Salvador has a murder rate 15 times that of the United States. Reliance on coffee as an export, which was controlled by a small elite, also limited upward mobility by those who sought to improve their lives.

Early in the twentieth century, emigration to neighboring countries such as Honduras was the goal, but by the 1980s, immigration patterns had expanded to include not only the region but also Canada, Australia, and, in particular, the United States. A 2013 survey in El Salvador showed that 79 percent had a positive view of the United States, compared to only 17 percent who had a negative view. Fully two-thirds report having acquaintances who have moved to find a better life in the United States, and six in ten say they would migrate if they had the means and opportunity to do so.

As of 2015, nearly 2.2 million Salvadorans were in the United States. About two-thirds were born in El Salvador; the balance were born in the United States to Salvadoran immigrants. Economically, they are doing much better than their counterparts back home, but their income is approximately 18 percent less than that of the general U.S. population.

Most people think of assimilation in positive or neutral terms. An immigrant acquires the language of the host society or adjusts his or her attire to "fit in" a bit more. Assimilation means taking on the characteristics of the dominant culture, even though some of those behaviors and traits may actually be negative. Such an instance occurs when some Latinos, including newly arrived Salvadorans, become involved in criminal gangs.

Media coverage in both the United States and El Salvador has drawn attention to some young Salvadorans who have returned home and established gang organizations to which they belonged in the United States. At the other extreme are those who returned and resisted gang membership, only to be killed. Immigration and Customs Enforcement (ICE), part of the U.S. Department of Homeland Security, has cracked down on foreign-born residents involved in criminal activities and quickly deported them. This get-tough policy has led to a deportation-and-return cycle as Salvadoran police report that 90 percent of the gang members return to the United States. Critics of the ICE policy argue that most arrests are for immigration offenses and not criminal actions and that many suspected "associates" are often lumped in with hard-core gang members, which only reinforces gang ties.

In contrast and perhaps more typical of the Salvadoran–U.S. connection is the hamlet of Brentwood on Long Island. The Salvadoran presence is unmistakable in Brentwood's fish stores, markets, and 40 restaurants whose culinary offerings range from Salvadoran *pupusas* to Italian dishes such as chicken francese. In the 1980s, as Salvadorans fled civil war in their home country, they were attracted to the wooded landscape of Long Island and the presence of Spanish-speaking Puerto Ricans. By 2000, the government of El Salvador opened a consulate in this Long Island community.

Like Mexican Americans, the Salvadorans have created hometown clubs or associations that relate to a specific village that receives remittances. **Remittances** are monies that immigrants send to their countries of origin. Among immigrants, Salvadorans have the highest level of remittances: about 17 percent of El Salvador's gross national product, which is the largest proportion of any country except for Haiti. These immigrant-created organizations have specific objectives of improving the quality of life back home so that people are less likely to want or need to leave El Salvador.

Sources: Berger 2008; Cordova 2005; The Economist, 2017c; Hernández-Arias 2008; Migration Policy Institute 2015; Pew Research Global Attitudes Project 2013; Preston 2010; Quirk 2008; Waldinger 2007.

The Current Picture

Two issues have clouded the recent settlement of Central and South Americans. First, many of the arrivals are illegal immigrants. Among those uncovered as undocumented workers, citizens from El Salvador, Guatemala, and Colombia are outnumbered only by Mexican nationals. Second, significant numbers of highly trained and skilled people have left these countries, which are in great need of professional workers. We noted in Chapter 4 how immigration often produces a **brain drain**: immigration to the United States of skilled workers, professionals, and technicians.

The challenges to immigrants from Latin America are reflected in the experience of Colombians, who number more than a half million in the United States. The initial arrivals from this South American nation after World War I were educated middle-class people who quickly assimilated to life in the United States. Rural unrest in Colombia in the 1980s, however, triggered large-scale movement to the United States, where these newer Colombian immigrants had to adapt to a new culture and to urban life. The adaptation of this later group has been much more difficult. Some have found success by catering to other Colombians. For example, enterprising immigrants have opened bodegas (grocery stores) to supply traditional, familiar foodstuffs. Similarly, Colombians have established restaurants, travel agencies, and real-estate firms that serve other Colombians. However, many immigrants are obliged to take menial jobs and to combine the income of several family members to meet the high cost of urban life. Colombians of mixed African descent face racial as well as ethnic and language barriers (Guzmán 2001).

What is likely to be the future of Central and South Americans in the United States? Although much will depend on future immigration, they could assimilate over the course of generations. One less-positive alternative is that they will become trapped with Mexican Americans as a segment of the low-paid labor market for the urban areas where they live. A more encouraging possibility is that they will retain an independent identity, like the Cubans, while also establishing an economic base. For example, nearly 720,000 Dominicans (from the Dominican Republic) settled in the New York City area, where they make up a significant 6 percent of the population. In some neighborhoods, such as Washington Heights, one can easily engage in business, converse, and eat just as if one were in the Dominican Republic. People continue to remain attentive to events in Dominican politics, which often command greater attention than events in the United States. However, within their local neighborhoods, Dominicans are focused on improving employment opportunities and public safety (American Community Survey 2009: Table B03001).

Conclusion

The signals are mixed today, as they have been for the last two hundred years. Progress alternates with setbacks. Moves forward in one Latino group coincide with steps back among other groups. Figure 9.8, the Spectrum of Intergroup Relations, summarizes the experience of Latinos in the United States described throughout this chapter.

Latinos' role in the United States typically began with warfare resulting in the United States annexing territory or as a result of revolutions pushing refugees or immigrants here. In recent times, the Latino role in warfare has been to serve in uniform for the United States. "In World War II, more Latinos won Medals of Honor than any other ethnic group," said Democratic Representative Matthew Martinez, a former U.S. Marine who represented part of Los Angeles. "How much blood do you have to spill before you prove you are a part of something?" (Whitman 1987:49). Many veterans of Iraq and Afghanistan are Latinos who, even though legal residents of the United States, were not in a status that would make citizenship easy. Typically, Congress had to pass a resolution making fallen soldiers citizens after their death, and on rare occasion would facilitate citizenship for a living veteran. Under a new rule, families can now use their deceased as a sponsor for their own residency papers. In the 20 years from 1990 to 2010, the proportion of Latino

Figure 9.8 Spectrum of Intergroup Relations: Latinos

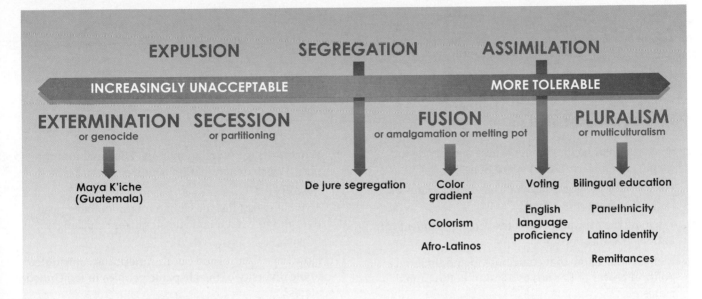

ready-reserve military personnel rose from 5 to 9.3 percent (Bureau of the Census 2011a: Table 514 on p. 337; Jonsson 2005; McKinley 2005).

While considering Latinos in American society, we constantly must also consider the impact of events in their home countries, whether Cuba, El Salvador, or any of the many nations represented. We must also remember the common Spanish refrain "*Si usted no habla inglés puede quedarse rezagado*": "If you don't speak English, you might be left behind."

Summary of Learning Objectives

9.1 Discuss the characteristics of Latinos and explain Latino panethnicity.

1. Latinos do not share a common cultural or single historical identity, yet a panethnic identity emerges in many aspects of life in the United States.

9.2 Describe the current economic picture for Latinos in the United States.

2. Economically, life for Latinos continues to improve—but relative to Whites, the gap has hardly changed over the past two generations.

9.3 Understand Latino patterns of education and English-language attainment.

3. Latinos aspire to further education, but completion of college remains a challenge despite a commitment to becoming fluent in English.

9.4 Explain the current role of Latinos in U.S. politics.

4. A part of the assimilation as well as pluralism among Latinos has been growing involvement in electoral politics, which has been recognized by both the Democratic and Republican parties.

9.5 Summarize the role of religion in Latino communities.

5. Religion is a central focus in the lives of Latinos but is increasingly being defined by denominations outside of Roman Catholicism.

9.6 Examine and understand the culture of Cuban Americans.

6. Cuban Americans are the fourth-largest Hispanic group and continue to be defined, to some extent, by the political relationship between the United States and Cuba. Younger Cuban Americans tend to be more supportive of normalizing relations with Cuba.

9.7 Describe the diversity among Central and South Americans.

7. Many of the nations of Central and South America have been major sources of immigrants to the United States in recent years, with each group having distinctive cultural traditions.

Key Terms

brain drain, *page 216*
color gradient, *page 204*
colorism, *page 204*

de jure segregation, *page 206*
Marielitos, *page 211*
panethnicity, *page 203*

Pentecostalism, *page 210*
remittances, *page 215*

Review Questions

1. What different factors seem to unite and divide the Latino community in the United States?

2. How would you summarize the economic status of Latinos as a group?

3. What are the aspirations and the accomplishments of Latinos in education?

4. Identify the factors that contribute to and limit the political power of Latinos as a group in the United States.

5. What is the role of religion in the Hispanic community? Which denomination is prevalent, and which are growing?

6. To what extent has the Cuban migration been positive, and to what degree do significant challenges remain?

7. How have Central and South Americans contributed to the diversity of the Hispanic peoples in the United States?

Critical Thinking

1. Language and culture are almost inseparable. How do you imagine your life would change if you were not permitted to speak your native language? How would your life be affected if you were expected to speak some language other than your native language?

2. Is a collective, panethnic Latino identity good, or is it counterproductive? Explain.

3. Which social forces propel Latinos toward a single ethnic identity, and which serve to maintain individual nationality groups?

Chapter 10
Mexican Americans and Puerto Ricans

Jack Hollingsworth/Exactostock/SuperStock

Learning Objectives

10.1 Understand the history of Mexican Americans.

10.2 Describe the social circumstances of contemporary Mexican Americans.

10.3 Explain the challenges that Puerto Rico faces.

10.4 Discuss Puerto Rican life and culture today, including the social construction of race.

Citizenship is the basic requirement for receiving one's legal rights and privileges in the United States. However, for Mexican Americans, citizenship has been an ambiguous concept at best. Mexican Americans (or Chicanos) have a long history in the United States that stretches back before the nation was even formed to the early days of European exploration. Santa Fe, New Mexico, was founded more than a decade before the Pilgrims landed at Plymouth Rock. Mexican American people trace their ancestry to the merging of Spanish settlers with the Native Americans of Central America and Mexico. This ancestry dates to the brilliant Mayans and Aztecs, whose civilizations reached their peak about 700 CE and 1500 CE, respectively. However, roots in the land do not guarantee a group any dominance over it. Over several centuries, the Spaniards conquered the land and merged with the

Native Americans to form the Mexican people. In 1821, Mexico obtained its independence, but this independence was short-lived: Domination from the north began less than a generation later.

Today, Mexican Americans are creating their own destiny in the United States while functioning in a society that is often concerned about immigration, both legal and illegal. In the eyes of some, including a few in positions of authority, to be Mexican American is to be suspected of being in the country illegally or, at least, of knowingly harboring illegal aliens. Two-thirds of legal Mexican immigrants have yet to begin the process of becoming naturalized U.S. citizens. Yet annually, about 100,000 become naturalized citizens—the largest number of any country of origin and more than twice that of the next largest sources of naturalized citizens, India and the Philippines (Office of Immigration Statistics 2016).

While the citizenship status of other Latino groups is complicated, it seems clear that Puerto Ricans should have U.S. citizenship. Since a federal act in 1917 clarified the law, a Puerto Rican born on the island is as much a U.S. citizen as someone born in Kansas. However, ambiguities remain. Even Native Americans, who are subject to some unique laws and are exempt from other laws because of past treaties, have a future firmly dominated by the United States. This description does not necessarily fit Puerto Ricans, whose homeland is the last major U.S. colonial territory and, indeed, one of the few colonies remaining in the world. Besides assessing the situation of Puerto Ricans on the mainland, we also need to consider the United States' relationship with Puerto Rico.

The Mexican American Community Emerges

10.1 Understand the history of Mexican Americans.

Wars play a prominent part in any nation's history. The United States was created as a result of the colonies' war with England to win their independence. In the 1800s, the United States acquired significant neighboring territory in two different wars. The legacy of these wars and the resulting annexation created the two largest Hispanic minorities in the United States: Mexican Americans and Puerto Ricans.

A large number of Mexicans became aliens in the United States without ever crossing a border. These people first became Mexican Americans at the conclusion of the Mexican–American War (1846–1848). This two-year war culminated with an 11-month U.S. occupation of the northern part of Mexico. Today, Mexicans visit the Museum of Interventions in Mexico City, which outlines the war and how Mexico permanently gave up half its country. The war is still spoken of today as "the Mutilation" (Weiner 2004).

In the war-ending Treaty of Guadalupe Hidalgo, signed February 2, 1848, Mexico acknowledged the U.S. annexation of Texas. It also ceded California and most of Arizona and New Mexico to the United States for $15 million. In exchange, the United States granted citizenship to the 75,000 Mexican nationals who remained on the annexed land after one year. Along with citizenship, the United States was to guarantee religious freedom, property rights, and cultural integrity—that is, the right to continue Mexican and Spanish cultural traditions and to use the Spanish language.

The Roman Catholic Church has a long history among Mexicans and Mexican Americans. The Mission San Xavier del Bac in Tucson, Arizona, was founded in 1692.

Wild Geese / Fotolia

The Early Mexican American Experience

The beginnings of the Mexican experience in the United States were as varied as the people themselves. Some Mexican Americans were affluent, with large land holdings. Others were poor peasants barely able to survive. Along such rivers as the Rio Grande, commercial towns grew up around the increasing river traffic. In New Mexico and Arizona, many Mexican American people welcomed the protection that the U.S. government offered against several Native American tribes. In California, the gold miners quickly dominated life, and Anglos controlled the newfound wealth. One generalization can be made about the many segments of the Mexican

American population in the nineteenth century: They were regarded as a conquered people. In fact, even before the war, many Whites who traveled into the West were already prejudiced against people of mixed blood (in this instance, against Mexicans). Whenever Mexican American and Anglo interests came into conflict, Anglo interests won.

Lynching was one of the most oppressive aspects of Black–White relations in the United States, but lynchings were not limited to Blacks. The Mexican American community was also victimized. Recent historical scholarship has documented at least 547 lynchings of Mexicans between 1848 and 1928. These lynchings occurred not only in the southwestern United States but also far from the border in Nebraska and Wyoming. The pretext of the alleged crimes and the presence of mobs were not unlike those that led to the lynching of Black people during the Jim Crow era. Lynching of Mexican Americans declined during the second decade of the twentieth century, in no small part as the result of the Mexican government's pressure on the United States (Carrigan and Webb 2013, 2015).

A pattern of second-class treatment for Mexican Americans had emerged well before the twentieth century. Gradually, the Anglo system of property ownership replaced the Hispanic and Native American systems. Mexican Americans who inherited land proved to be no match for Anglo lawyers. Court battles provided no protection for poor Spanish-speaking landowners. Unscrupulous lawyers occasionally defended Mexican Americans successfully, only to demand half the land as their fee. Anglo cattle ranchers gradually pushed out Mexican American ranchers. By 1892, the federal government was granting grazing privileges on public grasslands and forests to anyone *except* Mexican Americans. Effectively, the people who became Mexican *Americans* had become outsiders in their own homeland. The ground was laid for the twentieth-century social structure of the Southwest, an area of growing productivity in which minority groups increased in size but remained largely subordinate.

The Immigration Northward

Nowhere else in the world do two countries with such different standards of living and wage scales share such an open border. Immigration from Mexico is unique in several respects. First, it has been a continuous large-scale movement for most of the past 100 years. The United States did not restrict immigration from Mexico through legislation until 1965. Second, the proximity of Mexico encourages past immigrants to maintain strong cultural and language ties with their homeland through friends and relatives. Return visits to the old country are only one- or two-day bus rides for Mexican Americans, not once-in-a-lifetime voyages, as they were for most European immigrants. The third point of uniqueness is the aura of illegality that has surrounded Mexican immigrants. Throughout the twentieth century, the suspicion in which Anglos have held Mexican Americans has contributed to mutual distrust between the two groups.

The years before World War I (1914–1918) brought large numbers of Mexicans into the expanding agricultural industry of the Southwest. The Mexican revolution of 1909–1922 thrust refugees into the United States, and World War I curtailed the flow of people from Europe, leaving the labor market open to Mexican Americans. After the war, continued political turmoil in Mexico and more prosperity in the Southwest brought still more Mexicans across the border.

Simultaneously, corporations in the United States, led by agribusiness, invested in Mexico in such a way as to maximize their profits but minimize the amount of money remaining in Mexico; leaving the money in Mexico would have provided more jobs for Mexicans. Conflict theorists view this investment as part of the continuing process through which American businesses, with the support and cooperation of affluent Mexicans, have used Mexican people when doing so has been in corporate leaders' best interests. Affluent Mexicans use poor Mexican workers as cheap laborers in their own country, and Americans use them here as cheap laborers or as undocumented workers, and then dismiss them when they are no longer useful (Guerin-Gonzales 1994).

Beginning in the 1930s, the United States embarked on a series of measures aimed specifically at Mexicans. The Great Depression brought pressure on local governments to care for the growing number of unemployed and impoverished. Government officials developed a quick way to reduce welfare rolls and eliminate people seeking jobs: Ship Mexicans back to Mexico. This program of deporting Mexicans in the 1930s was called **repatriation**. As officially stated, the program was constitutional because only illegal aliens were to be repatriated. In reality, Mexicans and even people born in the United States of Mexican background were deported to relieve the economic pressure of the depression. The legal process of fighting a deportation order was overwhelming, especially for a poor Spanish-speaking family. The Anglo community largely ignored this outrage against the civil rights of those deported and showed no interest in helping repatriates ease the transition (Balderrama and Rodriguez 2006).

When the depression ended, Mexican laborers again became attractive to industry. In 1942, when World War II (1939–1945) had depleted the labor pool, the United States and Mexico agreed to a program allowing migration across the border by contracted laborers, or **braceros**. Within a year of the initiation of the bracero program, more than 80,000 Mexican nationals had been brought in; they made up one-eleventh of the farmworkers on the Pacific Coast. The program continued with some interruptions until 1964. It was devised to recruit labor from poor Mexican areas for U.S. farms. In the program, which was supposed to be supervised jointly by Mexico and the United States, minimum standards were to be maintained for transportation, housing, wages, and healthcare of the braceros. Ironically, these safeguards placed the braceros in a better economic situation than Mexican Americans, who often worked alongside the protected Mexican nationals. Mexicans were still regarded as a positive presence by Anglos only when they were useful, and the Mexican American people were merely tolerated.

Like many policies of the past relating to disadvantaged racial and ethnic groups, the legacy of the bracero program lives on. After decades of protests, the Mexican government finally issued checks of $3,500 to former braceros and their descendants. The payments were to resolve disputes over what happened to the money the U.S. government gave to the Mexican government to assist in the braceros' resettlement in Mexico. To say that these payments were "too little, much too late" is an understatement.

Another crackdown on illegal aliens, called either Operation Wetback or Special Force Operation, began in 1954. The term *wetbacks* or **mojados**—derisive slang for Mexicans who enter illegally—refers to those who swim across the Rio Grande to gain entry to the United States. Like other roundups, this effort failed to stop the illegal flow of workers. For several years, some Mexicans were brought in under the bracero program while other Mexicans were being deported. With the end of the bracero program in 1964 and stricter immigration quotas for Mexicans, illegal border crossings increased because legal crossings became more difficult (J. Kim 2008).

More dramatic than the negative influence that continued immigration has had on employment conditions in the Southwest is the effect on the Mexican and Mexican American people themselves. Routinely, the rights of Mexicans, even the rights to which they are entitled as illegal aliens, are ignored. Of the illegal immigrants deported, few have been expelled through formal proceedings. The Mexican American Legal Defense and Education Fund (MALDEF) has repeatedly expressed concern over how the government handles illegal aliens.

Against this backdrop of legal maneuvers is the tie that the Mexican people have to the land, both in today's Mexico and in the parts of the United States that formerly belonged to Mexico. *Assimilation* may be the key word in the history of many immigrant groups, but for Mexican Americans, the key term is **La Raza**, literally *the people* or *the race*. Among many contemporary Mexican Americans, however, the term connotes pride in a pluralistic Spanish, Native American, and Mexican heritage. Mexican Americans cherish their legacy and, as we shall see, strive to regain some of the economic and social glory that once was theirs (Acosta 2015).

Despite the passage of various measures designed to prevent illegal immigration, neither the immigration nor the apprehension of illegal aliens is likely to end. Economic conditions are the major factor. For

Latinos infrequently appear in the mass media in central roles, much less on successful television programs. Although animated, *Dora the Explorer* on Nickelodeon is an exception to this rule; the title character makes an appearance here in the annual Macy's Thanksgiving Day Parade.

Jennifer Mitchell / Splash News / Newscom

example, the prolonged recession beginning in 2008 weakened the U.S. job market and led to a significant decline in individuals seeking to enter the United States from Mexico either legally or illegally. Increased deportations might have contributed to a decline in the number of Mexican Americans in the United States if it were not for U.S.-born children of Mexican ancestry.

In general, the Mexican American community is subject to racial profiling that renders their presence in the United States suspect in the eyes of many Anglos. Mexican Americans will likely continue to be closely scrutinized by law-enforcement officials because their Mexican descent makes them suspect as potential illegal aliens.

In the United States, Mexican Americans have mixed feelings about illegal Mexican immigrants. Many are their kin, and Mexican Americans realize that entry into the United States brings Mexicans better economic opportunities. However, numerous deportations only perpetuate the Anglo stereotype of Mexican and Mexican American alike as surplus labor. Mexican Americans, largely the product of past immigration, find that the continued controversy over illegal immigration places them in the conflicting roles of citizen and relative. Mexican American organizations opposing illegal immigration must confront people to whom they are closely linked by culture and kinship, and they must cooperate with government agencies they deeply distrust.

Chávez and the Farm Laborers

The best-known Hispanic labor leader for economic empowerment was César Chávez (1927–1993), the Mexican American who crusaded to organize migrant farmworkers. Efforts to organize agricultural laborers date back to the turn of the twentieth century, but Chávez was the first to achieve any success. Before Chávez, these laborers had never won collective bargaining rights, partly because their mobility made it difficult for them to organize into a unified group.

In 1962, Chávez, then 35 years old, formed the National Farm Workers Association, later to become the United Farm Workers (UFW). Organizing migrant farmworkers was not easy because they had no savings to pay for organizing or to live on while striking. Growers could rely on an almost limitless supply of Mexican laborers to replace the Mexican Americans and Filipinos who went on strike for higher wages and better working conditions.

Despite initial success, Chávez and the UFW were plagued with continual opposition by agribusiness and many lawmakers. During this time the UFW was also trying to heighten public consciousness about the pesticides used in the fields. Chávez had difficulty fulfilling his objectives. By 2011, union membership had dwindled from a high of 80,000 in 1970 to a reported 5,000. Nevertheless, what he and the UFW accomplished was significant. First, they succeeded in making federal and state governments more aware of the exploitation of migrant laborers. Second, the migrant workers, or at least those organized in California, developed a sense of their own power and worth that will make it extremely difficult for growers to abuse them in the future as they had in the past. Third, working conditions improved. California agricultural workers were paid an average of less than $2 an hour in the mid-1960s. Still, given the lack of regular harvesting work, by 2011 a migrant farmworker's wages for a year rarely topped $12,000,

Labor leader César Chávez advocated a boycott of grapes until workers received better wages and improved working conditions.

Dan Mills/ZUMA Press/Newscom

even though the worker did labor that few White Americans would do for three times that wage.

The struggle continues. At the beginning of the twenty-first century, special-interest groups sponsored efforts to permit more foreign workers, primarily from Mexico and Central America, to enter the United States temporarily at even lower wages. About three-quarters of all farmworkers in the United States are Mexican or Mexican American. The problems of migrant farmworkers are inextricably tied to the lives of both Latinos and Latin Americans (Greenhouse 2015; Matthiessen 2014; Ríos 2011; Wozniacka 2011).

Mexican Americans Today

10.2 Describe the social circumstances of contemporary Mexican Americans.

As we have seen in this chapter and in Chapter 9, Hispanics or Latinos include a broad variety of groups with different experiences historically and different life circumstances today. In this section we consider the contemporary social circumstances of Mexican Americans. But first we consider how Mexican Americans are sometimes on different sides of highly political and emotional issues, such as immigration policy. The Relations Across Boundaries feature considers how racial and ethnic groups are in conflict with one another as well as with the dominant White society.

Relations Across Boundaries

Immigrant Mexicans and U.S.-Born Mexican Americans

Any national survey of attitudes toward immigration reform or border surveillance quickly reveals that Whites hold much more restrictionist attitudes than Latinos, African Americans, and Asian Pacific Americans. Whatever the wording of the question, the results are consistent: Hispanics indicate a preference for immigration reform, anti-deportation policies, more pathways to citizenship, and openness to accepting refugees. However, not all Latinos support these measures, just as all Mexican Americans do not welcome more immigrants.

Mexican Americans consider a number of social issues to be important, and some of these issues—such as the economy and jobs—typically resonate more than any immigration issue. For example, one survey showed that 18 percent of Mexican Americans do not consider immigration an important issue at all. However, Mexican Americans tend to be more pro-immigration than Latinos from other countries, particularly Puerto Ricans, who are, of course, U.S. citizens by birthright. Still, Latinos are typically more in favor of immigration than African Americans, who are more favorably inclined than White Americans. With each passing generation, Hispanic views on the immigration issue more closely mirror White attitudes.

In interviews with Mexican Americans long removed from migration, scholars uncover definite intergenerational differences with newly arrived Mexicans. For example, one third-generation Arizona woman whose grandfather was a bracero said, "We are all of the same culture but you can't expect that because I'm Latina and you are too that I'm going to support you when you

are breaking the law [by entering the United States illegally]" (Vega 2014: 1773).

When it comes to attitudes toward other racial and ethnic groups, Latinos show greater tolerance even when they are in direct competition for jobs and housing with another minority group such as African Americans in places like southern California.

The development of panethnic Latino organizations is relatively recent. Civic and lobbying groups have a long history in the Latino community, but prior to 1970, they reflected the interests of a single nationality group. Over time, given the increase in immigration from a growing number of Latin American countries, coupled with the success of unified national Black civil rights groups, activist groups have emerged to speak collectively for all Hispanics. Even Univision, which has its roots in Texas in the 1950s, moved from a Mexican-oriented programming schedule to a broader panethnic appeal, even to the point of avoiding slang or humor that appealed only to a specific nationality group. However, these developments lead people, especially non-Hispanics, to fail to appreciate the differences among Latinos and that these groups' interests vary—immigration for Mexican Americans, foreign diplomacy for Cuban Americans, and federal control issues for Puerto Ricans.

Sources: Lopez, Passel and Rahal 2015; Mora 2014; Rouse, Wilkinson, and Garand 2010; Telles and Ortiz 2008; Vanetik and Tucker 2015; Vega 2014; Wijeyesinghe and Jackson III 2012.

The Borderlands

"The border is not where the U.S. stops and Mexico begins," said Mayor Betty Flores of Laredo, Texas. "It's where the U.S. blends into Mexico" (Gibbs 2001:42). The term **borderlands** in this book refers to the area of common culture along the border between Mexico and the United States. Though particularly relevant to Mexicans and Mexican Americans, the growing Mexican influence is relevant to the other Latino groups that we discuss. Figure 10.1 offers a representation of and pertinent information about the borderlands.

Legal and illegal emigration from Mexico to the United States, day laborers crossing the border regularly to go to jobs in the United States, the implementation of the North American Free Trade Agreement (NAFTA), and the exchange of media across the border all make the notion of separate Mexican and U.S. cultures obsolete in the borderlands.

Numerous civil rights groups and migrant advocacy organizations have expressed alarm regarding people who cross into the United States illegally and perish in the attempt. Some die in deserts, in isolated canyons, and while concealed in containers or locked in trucks during attempts to smuggle them across the border. Several hundred die annually in the Southwest by seeking ever more dangerous crossing points because border control has increased. Organizations, some affiliated with churches, have sought to offer relief. Even local law enforcement agencies have started to install emergency call boxes in remote areas so desperate border crossers can get assistance (Campoy 2014).

The economic position of the borderlands is complex in terms of both businesses and workers. Very visible on the Mexican side are **maquiladoras**. These foreign-owned operations are exempt from paying Mexican taxes and are not required to provide insurance or benefits for their workers. The labor costs (wages plus benefits) at the maquiladoras are typically $8 to $16 per hour; these wages are very good in comparison to prevailing wage standards in Mexico, making jobs at the maquiladoras very desirable to Mexicans. However, as low as these hourly wages seem to businesspeople in industrial countries, multinational

---

Figure 10.1 The Borderlands

In search of higher wages, undocumented Mexicans often attempt to cross the border illegally, risking their lives in the process. Maquiladoras located just south of the U.S.–Mexican border employ Mexican workers at wages far lower than those earned by U.S. workers. The Mexican workers and Mexican Americans send large amounts of money, called remittances, to assist kinfolk and communities in Mexico. Simultaneously, the U.S. government continues to harden the border, even experimenting with a "virtual fence" where a system of radar towers and ground sensors has been set along a 28-mile stretch of the Arizona–New Mexico desert. Many Americans also support the idea of erecting a longer conventional fence or wall.

SOURCES: Prepared by the author based on Archibold and Preston 2008; Marosi 2007; Office of Immigration Statistics 2016; World DataBank 2017.

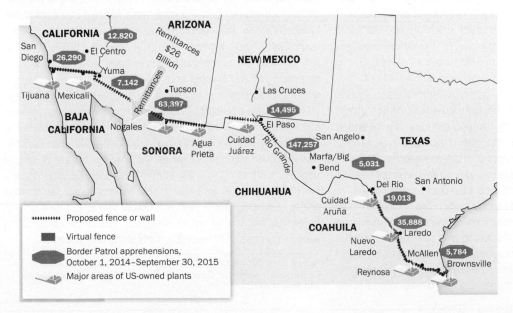

corporations soon found even lower wages in China and the Philippines. More than 75 percent of the new 700,000 maquiladora jobs created by NAFTA were eliminated between 2000 and 2011 (Cañas, Coronado, and Gilmer 2006; Rabinovitch 2011; Ribas-Mateos 2015).

Immigrant workers have a significant economic impact on their home country while they are employed in the United States. Many Mexicans, as well as other Hispanic groups, send some part of their earnings back to family members in their native countries. These **remittances** total an estimated $26 billion annually. Most of the money is spent to pay for food, clothing, and housing, but a growing proportion is being invested to create small businesses.

The close cultural and economic ties to the home country that are found in the borderlands also can be found with other Latino groups. Thus economic and political events in the homeland often continue to play a prominent role in the lives of immigrants and their children, and even grandchildren, in the United States. In recent years, Mexicans have also turned their attention to their other borders as migrants from other Latin American countries enter Mexico, sometimes illegally, to either settle there or move north to the United States.

Whatever the outcome of intensifying fortifications along the U.S.-Mexican border, many people in the borderlands see the region as neither exclusively American nor exclusively Mexican. There is a shared sense of community. In 2016, people living close to both sides of the border in sixteen different areas were asked if the United States should build a wall to secure the border. Many people living in the United States would not be surprised to hear that 86 percent of those living in Mexico close to the Mexican border rejected a wall, but fully 72 percent on the U.S. side did as well. Residents on both sides were more likely to choose to refer to people across the border as "neighbors" rather than economic competitors, exploiters, criminals, or racists (Bilker 2016).

One visible indicator of the extended and continuing immigration, as well as back-and-forth movement between Mexico and the United States, is the emergence of hometown associations, described in the Research Focus feature.

Research Focus

Mexican Hometown Associations

Inland from the borders, *clubes de orundo* or hometown associations (HTAs) have sprung up in northern cities with large settlements of Mexicans. **Hometown associations** consist of members who share a common place of origin. The HTAs typically are nonprofit organizations that maintain close ties to the hometowns in Mexico and engage in development projects back home. It is estimated that there are more than 3,000 HTAs in the United States. The links between the HTAs and the home countries are maintained partially due to the visible presence of **transnationals**—immigrants who sustain multiple social relationships that link their societies of origin and settlement.

HTAs collect money for improvements in hospitals and schools that are beyond the means of the local people back home. Sometimes the HTAs send the money back home in the form of remittances, but the transfer can also take the form of goods or merchandise being sent to relatives. The impact of HTAs has become so strong that some states in Mexico have begun programs whereby they will match funds from HTAs to encourage such public-spirited efforts.

At first glance, the flow of support back to the homeland would seem to be a "win-win" situation, making the Mexican Americans feel better about leaving the homeland and creating an incentive for them to work hard in the United States while providing aid to their old home south of the border. However, tensions sometimes emerge in the local Mexican communities, where stay-at-home residents feel overlooked by local officials, who may appear to favor relatives of Mexican Americans. On a more regional level, the locals with few ties to Mexican Americans may perceive that government allocations or improvements in the infrastructure (such as roads, utilities, and so forth) pass them by. This feeling of neglect has been intensified by Mexico's creation in 2002 of the *Tres por Uno* ("three for one") program. For every peso remitted by migrants, the Mexican federal, state, and municipal governments add 3 pesos each (Global Forum in Migration and Development 2017).

HTAs began as informal, volunteer-driven social organizations, and many still are. In more and more communities, they are now using salaried staff and have even formed federations with other HTAs. They are truly oriented to the immigrant community at large; some HTAs actively mobilized residents in the United States to participate in the 2006–2007 and the 2016–2017 marches and protests over immigration issues. Among the issues of special concern to the HTAs have been President Donald Trump's campaign promises to either block Mexico-bound remittances unless Mexico agrees to pay for a border wall or to create a "wire transmitter fee" that would, in effect, tax remittances, also for the express purpose of increasing security along the border.

Source: Bada 2014; Browne 2017; Duquette-Rury 2016; Portes, Escobar, and Radford 2007; Somerville, Durama, and Terrazas 2008; Vonderlack-Navarro and Sites 2015.

Healthcare

Life chances are people's opportunities to provide themselves with material goods, positive living conditions, and favorable life experiences. Mexican Americans and other minority group members have more limited life chances. Perhaps in no other area does this disadvantage apply so much as in the healthcare system.

Hispanics as a group are locked out of the healthcare system more often than any other racial or ethnic group. Although federal law requires that emergency medical treatment be available to all people, even illegal immigrants, many Hispanics—even those with legal residency but who have relatives here illegally—are wary of seeking medical treatment. About one out of six (16.2 percent) had no health insurance (or other coverage such as Medicaid) for all of 2015, compared with 7.5 percent of White non-Hispanics and 11.1 percent of Blacks and Asian Pacific Americans. Predictably, the uninsured are less likely to have a regular source of medical care. This means that they wait for a crisis before seeking care. Fewer are immunized, and rates of preventable diseases such as lead poisoning are higher. Those without coverage are increasing in number, a circumstance that may reflect a further breakdown in healthcare delivery or may be a result of continuing immigration (Barnett and Vornovitsky 2016).

The healthcare problem facing Mexican Americans and other Hispanic groups is complicated by the lack of Hispanic or Spanish-speaking health professionals. Hispanics account for only 6.4 percent of physicians and 8.6 percent of dentists. One does not need to be administered healthcare by someone in one's own ethnic group, but the paucity of Hispanic professionals increases the likelihood that the group will be underserved (Bureau of Labor Statistics 2016a: Table 11).

Some Mexican Americans and many other Latinos have cultural beliefs that make them less likely to use the medical system. They may interpret their illnesses according to **curanderismo**: Latino folk medicine, a form of holistic healthcare and healing. This orientation influences how one approaches healthcare and even how one defines illness. Most Hispanics probably use folk healers, or *curanderos,* infrequently, but perhaps 20 percent rely on home remedies. Although these are not necessarily without value, especially if a dual system of folk and establishment medicine is followed, reliance on natural medications may be counterproductive. Another aspect of folk beliefs is the identification of folk-defined illnesses such as *susto* (or fright sickness) and *atague* (or fighting attack). Although these complaints, alien by these names to Anglos, often have biological bases, they must be dealt with carefully by sensitive medical professionals who can diagnose and treat illnesses accurately (Belliard and Ramirez-Johnson 2005; Dansie 2004; Lara et al. 2005).

An intriguing aspect of Mexican American health, as well as the health of other immigrants, is that most wellness indicators confirm the ethnic paradox. Recall from Chapter 5 that the **ethnic paradox** refers to the maintenance of one's ethnic ties in a way that can assist with assimilation in society. In terms of health, Mexican immigrants, by continuing to maintain their cultural practices, embrace a healthier lifestyle than their American counterparts. So, while it may benefit them to assimilate into American society, it is the very act of clinging to their home culture that keeps them generally healthier. Among these healthy practices are eating healthier (which makes them less likely to be obese) and being less likely to smoke. These results are all the more remarkable when one considers that these immigrants are less likely to have the same access to healthcare providers as the general population. Regrettably, the paradox is not permanent. As the immigrants assimilate, with each successive generation their health indicators deteriorate relative to White non-Hispanics (Riosmena, Root, Humphrey, Steiner, and Stubbs 2015).

Family Life

The most important organization or social institution among Mexican Americans, or for that matter any group, is the family. The structure of the Mexican American family differs little from that of families in the United States, a statement remarkable in itself, given the impoverished status of a significant number of Mexican Americans.

Latino households are described as laudably more "familistic" than others in the United States. **Familism** means pride and closeness in the family, which results in family obligation and family loyalty coming before individual needs. The family is the primary source of both social interaction and caregiving. Familism has been likened to a thick social network where one's family defines everyday social interaction.

Familism has been viewed as both a positive and a negative influence on individual Mexican Americans and Puerto Ricans. It has been argued that familism has had the negative effect of discouraging youths with a bright future from taking advantage of opportunities that would separate them from their family. Familism is generally regarded as good, however, because an extended family provides emotional strength in times of crisis. Close family ties maintain the mental and social well-being of the elderly. Most Latinos, therefore, see the intact extended family as a norm and as a nurturing unit that provides support throughout a person's lifetime.

U.S. Hispanic families are undergoing transition with the growth of more multigenerational families born in the United States, as well as family members from the homeland. The situation is complicated by the mixed status present in so many Latino extended families (with the obvious exception of Puerto Ricans, for whom U.S. citizenship is automatic). Recall from Chapter 4 that **mixed status** refers to families in which one or more members is a citizen and one or more members is a noncitizen. The situation is especially problematic when the noncitizens are illegal or undocumented immigrants. All the usual pressures within a family become magnified when there is mixed status.

Although immigration makes generalizing about Latinos as a group very difficult at any one point in time, analysis of available data indicates that Hispanic households are taking on more of the characteristics of the larger U.S. society. For example, cohabiting couples with or without children were relatively uncommon among Hispanic groups but now are coming to resemble the pattern of non-Hispanics. Similarly, Mexican-born women now living in the United States are more likely to have married earlier, but later generations of women born in the United States are more likely to marry later. The same is true for Puerto Rican women born on the island, compared with those born on the mainland.

In addition, we begin to see a more individualistic orientation than a collective orientation or familism. The new individualism is more likely to encourage family members to move away from their relatives or, more dramatically, lead to desertion or divorce. Studies with other established, longer-term immigrant groups suggest that family members become more individualistic in their values and behavior over time. People both within and outside the Latino community are interested to see if Hispanics will follow this pattern and whether the familism that has characterized much of the Latino community will fade.

In the future, the greatest factor that may lead to a decline in familism is marriage across ethnic lines. Continuing immigration from Mexico has tended to slow out-group marriage, but during periods of lessened migration, immigrants have been more likely to form unions with different Latino groups or with non-Hispanics (Comeau 2012; Jacobson, England, and Barrus 2008; Landale and Oropesa 2007; Sarkisian, Gerena, and Gerstel 2007; Zambrana 2011).

Puerto Rico: The Island

10.3 Explain the challenges that Puerto Rico faces.

Puerto Ricans' current association with the United States, like that of the Mexican people, began as the result of the outcome of a war. The island of Borinquén, later called Puerto Rico, was claimed by Spain in 1493. The native inhabitants, the Taíno Indians, were significantly reduced in number by conquest, slavery, and genocide. Although for generations the legacy of the Taíno was largely thought to be archaeological, recent DNA tests revealed that more than 60 percent of Puerto Ricans today have a Taíno ancestor. About 20,000 identified themselves as Taíno in the 2010 census (Cockburn 2003:41; Kearns 2011).

Puerto Rico, located about 1,000 miles from Miami (Figure 10.2), has never been the same since Columbus discovered it in 1493. The original inhabitants of the island succumbed

Figure 10.2 Puerto Rico

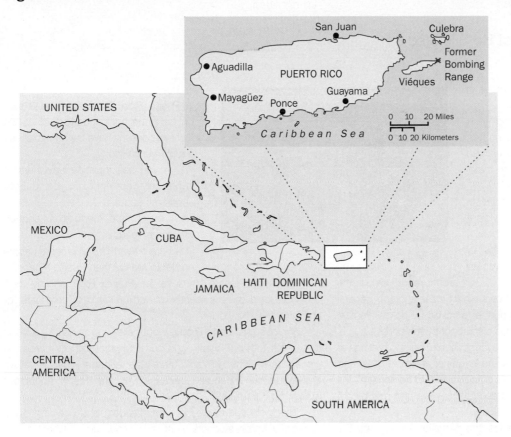

in large proportions to death by disease, tribal warfare, hard labor, unsuccessful rebellions against the Spanish, and fusion with their conquerors.

Among the institutions Spain imported to Puerto Rico was slavery. Although slavery in Puerto Rico was not as harsh as it was in the southern United States, the legacy of the transfer of Africans is present in the appearance of Puerto Ricans today, many of whom are seen by people on the mainland as Black.

Territorial Rule by the United States

After Spain ruled Puerto Rico for four centuries, the United States seized the island in 1898 during the Spanish–American War. Spain relinquished control of Puerto Rico in the Treaty of Paris. Puerto Rico's value for the United States, as it had been for Spain, was mainly its strategic location, which was advantageous for maritime trade.

The beginnings of rule by the United States quickly destroyed any hope that Puerto Ricans—or Boricua, as Puerto Ricans call themselves—had for self-rule. All power was given to officials appointed by the president, and Congress could overrule any act of the island's legislature. Even the spelling was changed briefly to Porto Rico to suit North American pronunciation. English, previously unknown on the island, became the only language permitted in the school systems. The people were colonized—first politically, then culturally, and finally economically (Aran et al. 1973; Christopulos 1974).

The Jones Act of 1917 extended U.S. citizenship to Puerto Ricans, but Puerto Rico remained a colony. This political dependence changed in 1948, when Puerto Rico elected its own governor and became a commonwealth. This status, officially Estado Libre Asociado or Associated Free State, extends to Puerto Rico and its people privileges and rights different from those of people on the mainland. Although Puerto Ricans are U.S. citizens and elect their own governor, they may not vote in presidential elections and have no voting representation in Congress. They are subject to military service, Selective Service registration, and

Speaking Out

Puerto Ricans Cannot Be Silenced

Luis Gutierrez

Two weeks ago, I spoke about a serious problem in Puerto Rico.

The problem is a systemic effort by the ruling party to deny the right of the people to speak freely, to criticize their government openly, and to make their voices heard.

I talked about student protests that had been met with violent resistance by Puerto Rican police. I talked about closed meetings of the legislature, and about efforts to silence the local Bar Association.... [A recent report] details the complaints of students, legislators, the press, and the general public who were beaten and pepper sprayed by police. Female students were treated with gross disrespect by the police.

This was the government's overreaction to demonstrations at the University over budget cuts and layoffs of at least 17,000 and maybe as many as 34,000 public employees. And demonstrations at the Capitol over budget cuts and layoffs were also met by riot police, clubs, and more pepper spray.

The images of police tactics and behavior explain why the Department of Justice is investigating the Puerto Rican police for "excessive force" and "unconstitutional searches."

How could you see these images and not speak out?

And I was hardly the first to speak out about these matters and will not be the last....

And what was the response to my speech defending the right of the Puerto Rican people to be heard?

It was to challenge my right to be heard.... A leading member of the [Puerto Rican] ruling party even said, "Gutierrez was not born

Luis Gutierrez

Scott J. Applewhite/AP Images

in Puerto Rico. His kids weren't born in Puerto Rico. Gutierrez doesn't plan on being buried in Puerto Rico.... So Gutierrez doesn't have the right to speak about Puerto Rico...."

If you see injustice anywhere, it is not only your right but your duty to speak out about it....

I may not be Puerto Rican enough for some people, but I know this: Nowhere on earth will you find a people harder to silence than Puerto Ricans.

You won't locate my love for Puerto Rico on my birth certificate or a driver's license, my children's birth certificate, or any other piece of paper.

My love for Puerto Rico is right here—in my heart—a heart that beats with our history and our language and our heroes. A place where—when I moved there as a teenager—people talked and argued and debated because we care deeply about our island and our future.

That's still true today—and that freedom is still beating in the hearts of university students, workingmen and women, labor leaders, lawyers, and environmentalists and every person who believes in free speech. You will not silence them, and you will not silence me.

Abraham Lincoln, a leader who valued freedom above all else, said: "Those who deny freedom to others deserve it not for themselves."

It's good advice, and I hope Puerto Rican leaders take it.

Source: Spoken by Gutierrez in the House of Representatives, March 2, 2011. Gutierrez 2011.

all federal laws. Puerto Ricans have a homeland that is and at the same time is not a part of the United States.

The commonwealth period that began in 1948 has been significant for Puerto Rico. Change has been dramatic, although it is debatable whether all change has been progress. The popularity of music groups such as Menudo with Ricky Martin and then much more recently Lin-Manuel Miranda, creator of the musicals *Hamilton* and *In the Heights*, shows that Puerto Ricans appeal to the broader culture. Yet despite such success stories, Puerto Rican music is almost never aired on non-Hispanic radio stations.

The Puerto Rican people have vibrant and distinctive cultural traditions, as seen clearly in their folk heroes, holidays, sports, and contemporary literature and drama. However, the dominance of U.S. culture makes it difficult to maintain Puerto Rican culture on the mainland and even on the island itself.

Puerto Rico and its people reflect a phenomenon called **neocolonialism**, which refers to former colonies' continuing dependence on foreign countries. Initially, this term was used to refer to African nations that, even after gaining political independence from Great Britain, France, and other European nations, continued to find their destiny in the hands of the former colonial powers. Although most Puerto Ricans today are staunchly proud of their U.S. citizenship, they also want to have a national identity independent of the United States. This goal has not been easy to achieve and likely will continue to be a challenge.

Since 1902, English has been the island's official language, but Spanish was the language of the people, reaffirming the island's cultural identity independent of the United States. In 1992, however, Puerto Rico established Spanish as an additional official language.

In reality, the language issue is related more to ideology than to substance. Although English is required in primary and secondary schools, and textbooks might be written in English, classes are conducted in Spanish. Indeed, Spanish remains the language of the island; less than 5 percent of the islanders speak only English, and among Spanish-speaking adults, only about another 15 percent speak English "very well" (Bureau of the Census 2016s: Table B16001).

In the Speaking Out feature, Congressman Luis Gutierrez speaks to the U.S. House of Representatives about what he considers abuse of authority by the Puerto Rican government against its residents. It is interesting that this U.S.-born son of Puerto Rican parents defends himself against charges that he is an island "outsider" and thus should not comment on events in Puerto Rico.

The Island Economy

Looking at the statistical snapshot in Table 10.1, we can see the major divide between the island of Puerto Rico and the mainland United States.

The United States' role in Puerto Rico has produced an overall economy that, though strong by Caribbean standards, remains well below that of the poorest areas of the United States. For many years, the federal government exempted U.S. industries locating in Puerto Rico from taxes on profits for at least ten years, but that tax break suddenly ended in 2006, leading to an ongoing recession in Puerto Rico. In the past, when Puerto Rico was attractive to mainland-based corporations, the island's agriculture was largely ignored, a problem that continues today. Furthermore, the mainland businesses sent the profits gained on Puerto Rico back to the mainland instead of reinvesting them in Puerto Rico.

Puerto Rico's economy is now in severe trouble, with a ten-year recession showing no sign of ending. Efforts to raise the wages of Puerto Rican workers only make the island less attractive to labor-intensive businesses—that is, those that employ large numbers of unskilled people. To deal with growing social needs, the Puerto Rican government has spent itself into huge debt that is beyond its ability to pay off. Calls for federal intervention have increased, but as of 2017, lawmakers in Washington, DC, have taken little action. This dire economic situation, in turn, has led to an exodus from the island to the mainland. Indeed, proportionately, the loss of people ranks eighth in the world—a bit less than Estonia but ahead of Serbia, Ukraine, and Romania (Abel and Deitz 2014; Statista 2017; Timiraos 2016).

Puerto Rico is an example of the world systems theory initially presented in Chapter 1. Recall that **world systems theory** sees the global economic system as divided between industrialized nations that control wealth and developing countries that are controlled and

Table 10.1 A Comparison: Puerto Rico and the United States

	United States	Puerto Rico
Population (in millions)	323.1	3.4
Language spoken at home other than English	21%	95%
Median household income	$53,889	$19,355
Poverty rate	13.5%	46.1%

SOURCE: Data from Bureau of the Census 2017b.

exploited. Although Puerto Rico may be better off compared with many other Caribbean nations, it clearly is at the mercy of economic forces in the United States and, to a much lesser extent, other industrial nations. Puerto Rico finds itself caught "in between": Its people have the advantages of U.S. citizenship, but the island plays a peripheral role in the overall economy of the United States.

Issues of Statehood and Self-Rule

Puerto Ricans have consistently argued and fought for independence for most of the 500 years since Columbus landed. They continue to do so in the twenty-first century. The contemporary hybrid commonwealth arrangement is popular with many Puerto Ricans, but some prefer statehood and others call for complete independence from the United States. Table 10.2 summarizes the advantages and the disadvantages of Puerto Rico's current status as a territory or commonwealth and the alternatives of statehood and independence.

The arguments for continued commonwealth status include a perception of special protection from the United States. Among some island residents, the idea of statehood invokes the fear of higher taxes and an erosion of their cultural heritage. Commonwealth supporters argue that independence includes too many unknowns, so they embrace the status quo. Others view statehood as a key to increased economic development and expanded tourism.

Proponents of independence have a long, vocal history of insisting on Puerto Rico's need to regain its cultural and political autonomy. Some supporters of independence have

Table 10.2 Puerto Rico's Future

Continuing Territorial Status (Status Quo)	
Pros	Cons
• Island is under U.S. protection. • Islanders enjoy U.S. citizenship with a distinct national identity. • Residents don't pay federal income taxes (they do pay into Social Security, Medicare, and 32 percent to island tax collectors). • The United States provides federal funds in the sum of $22 billion annually and offers other tax advantages. • Island retains representation in the Miss Universe pageant and Olympic Games.	• United States has ultimate authority over island matters. • Residents cannot vote for president. • Residents who work for any company or organization that is funded by the United States must pay federal income taxes. • Although Puerto Rico has a higher standard of living than other Caribbean islands, it has half the per capita income of the poorest U.S. states. • Island cannot enter into free-trade agreements.
Statehood	
Pros	Cons
• Permanent and guaranteed U.S. citizenship and an end to U.S. colonial rule over the island. • The island would receive federal money to build infrastructure. • The island would be able to enjoy open-market trade with U.S. allies. • The island would acquire five seats in the House of Representatives and two seats in the Senate, enabling the island to have more political clout and the people to vote in presidential elections.	• Possibility of English-only requirements (loss of cultural or national identity). • An increased influx of money could result in extreme inflation, leading to further economic deterioration because of the current muddled economic situation. • Businesses that take advantage of certain tax benefits could leave the island, and future businesses might not consider locating there. • Island would lose representation in international sporting events such as the Olympic Games.
Independence	
Pros	Cons
• Island would retain language and culture. • Island would be able to participate in the global economy. • End of U.S. colonial rule over the island.	• Islanders would lose U.S. citizenship. • Island would lose U.S. protection. • Island would lose federal funds.

SOURCES: Author, based on Let Puerto Rico Decide 2005; Poston and Farris 2012; President's Task Force on Puerto Rico's Status 2005; Williams 2006, 2007.

even been militant. In 1950, nationalists attempted to assassinate President Harry Truman, killing a White House guard in the process. Four years later, another band of nationalists opened fire in the gallery of the U.S. House of Representatives, wounding five members of Congress. Beginning in 1974, a group calling itself the Armed Forces of National Liberation (FALN, for Fuerzas Armadas de Liberación Nacional) took responsibility for more than 100 explosions that continued through 1987. The FALN is not alone; at least four other militant groups advocating independence were active in the 1980s. The island itself is occasionally beset by violent demonstrations, often reacting to U.S. military installations there—a symbol of U.S. control (Santos-Hernández 2008).

The issue of Puerto Rico's political destiny is, in part, ideological. Independence is the easiest way for the island to retain and strengthen its cultural and political identity.

Many Puerto Ricans see their current economic plight as a result of actions taken and not taken by Congress over the last twenty years.

Some nationalists express the desire that an autonomous Puerto Rico develop close political ties with communist Cuba. However, the crucial arguments for and against independence probably are economic. An independent Puerto Rico would no longer be required to use U.S. shipping lines, which are more expensive than those of foreign competitors. However, an independent Puerto Rico might be faced with tariffs (taxes) when trading with its largest current customer, the mainland United States. These tariffs would likely have large negative effects on the Puerto Rican economy. Also, Puerto Rican migration to the mainland could be restricted.

In 2017, Puerto Ricans voted on the island's future status in a nonbinding referendum. The options were statehood, current territorial/commonwealth status, and independence. The ruling government in Puerto Rico at the time firmly backed statehood. Both opposing political parties at the time, one favoring independence and the other continuation of the current commonwealth status, called on Puerto Rican citizens not to vote because the referendum did not guarantee any outcome. With most Puerto Ricans sitting out the referendum, those who did cast a ballot overwhelmingly favored statehood. Regardless of the outcome of any referendum in Puerto Rico, both the U.S. House and Senate would have to approve any change. As it has for over a century, the political future of Puerto Rico remains in doubt (Robles 2017).

Puerto Ricans Today

10.4 Discuss Puerto Rican life and culture today, including the social construction of race.

Being Puerto Rican does not necessarily garner the respect this ethnic identity deserves. Dubbed *Los Borinqueneers* (bohr-ehn-kin-EERS), the all-Puerto Rican 65th Infantry Regiment served in World Wars I and II for the Army. In the Korean War, they saved the 1st Marine Division in 1950 by opening an escape route for them from Chinese troops. It was not until 2014 that the regiment received the Congressional Gold Medal. Fittingly, at the same ceremony, the Gold Medal was also awarded to the all-Japanese American units and Navajo code talkers of World War II, as well as the Tuskegee Airmen, an all-Black squadron of military pilots (Gibson 2014).

The Bridge Between the Island and the Mainland

Despite their U.S. citizenship, immigration officials occasionally challenge Puerto Ricans, who find their papers scrutinized more closely than do other U.S. citizens because other Latin Americans attempt to enter the country posing as Puerto Ricans.

Puerto Ricans came to the mainland in small numbers in the first half of the twentieth century, often encouraged by farm labor contracts similar to those extended to Mexican braceros. During World War II, the government recruited hundreds of Puerto Ricans to work on the railroads, in food-manufacturing plants, and in copper mines on the mainland. But migration has been largely a post–World War II phenomenon. The 1940 census showed fewer than 70,000 Puerto Ricans on the mainland. By 2015, more than 5.3 million Puerto Ricans lived on the mainland, and 3.4 million residents lived on the island.

Among the factors that have contributed to migration are the economic pull away from the underdeveloped and overpopulated island, the absence of legal restrictions against immigration, and relatively cheap air transportation. As the migration continues, the mainland offers the added attraction of a large Puerto Rican community in New York City, which makes adjustment easier for new arrivals.

New York City has a formidable population of over 700,000 Puerto Ricans, but significant changes have taken place. First, Puerto Ricans no longer dominate the Latino scene in New York City, making up only a little more than a third of the city's Hispanic population; within New York City, Puerto Ricans are outnumbered by Dominicans. New York City is now following the pattern of other cities such as Miami, where a single group no longer defines the Latino identity.

Second, Puerto Ricans are now more dispersed throughout the mainland's cities and even in rural areas of the South. Indeed, the Puerto Rican population in New York City declined from nearly 1 million in 1980 to about 720,000 in 2013, but in Florida the Puerto Rican population has grown from under 100,000 to over a million (Day and Madhani 2015; Greene 2014; Krogstad 2015).

Puerto Ricans returning to their native island have become a significant force. Indeed, they now are called **Neoricans**, or *Nuyoricans*, a term the islanders also use for Puerto Ricans in New York. Longtime islanders direct a modest amount of hostility toward these Neoricans, who number near 100,000, or about 2 percent of the population. They usually return from the mainland with more formal schooling, more money, and a better command of English than native Puerto Ricans. It is no surprise that Neoricans compete very well with islanders for jobs and land (Lopez and Velasco 2011).

The Social Construction of Race

The most significant difference between race in Puerto Rico and race on the mainland is that Puerto Rico, like so many other Caribbean societies, has a **color gradient**, a term that describes distinctions based on a continuum of skin color rather than by sharp categorical separations. The presence of a color gradient reflects past (and ongoing) fusion between different groups. Rather than seeing people as either Black or White, Puerto Ricans perceive people as ranging from pale white to very black. Compared to U.S. society as a whole, Puerto Ricans are more sensitive to degrees of difference in skin color and are less likely to pigeonhole a person into one of two racial categories.

The presence of a color gradient rather than two or three racial categories does not necessarily mean less prejudice. Generally, however, societies with a color gradient permit more flexibility, and therefore are less likely to impose specific sanctions against a group of people based on skin color alone. Puerto Rico has not suffered interracial conflict or violence; its people are conscious of different racial heritages. Studies disagree on the amount of prejudice in Puerto Rico, but most agree that **colorism** (the ranking or judging of individuals based on skin tone) does affect Puerto Ricans. There is no question that much of the colorism is thrust upon Puerto Ricans by mainland culture. For example, during the history of *Los Borinqueneers* (the all-Puerto Rican 65th Infantry Regiment), darker-skinned Puerto Ricans were routinely separated and placed in segregated all-Black military units.

Racial identification in Puerto Rico depends a great deal on the attitude of the individual making the judgment. If one thinks highly of a person, then he or she may be seen as a member of a more acceptable racial group. Several terms are used in the color gradient to describe people racially: *blanco* (white), *trigueño* (bronze- or wheat-colored), *moreno* (dark-skinned), and *negro* (black) are a few. Factors such as social class and social position determine race, but on the mainland race is more likely to determine social class. This situation may puzzle people from the mainland, but racial etiquette on the mainland may be just as difficult for Puerto Ricans to comprehend and accept. Puerto Ricans arriving in the United States may find a new identity thrust on them by the dominant society based on their skin color (Denton and Villarrubia 2007; Landale and Oropesa 2002; Loveman and Muniz 2007; Orozco 2016; Roth 2012).

Puerto Rico continues to face new challenges beyond race distinctions. First, with congressional approval in 1994 of NAFTA, Mexico, Canada, and the United States became integrated into a single economic market. The reduction of trade barriers with Mexico, coupled with that nation's lower wages, undercut Puerto Rico's commonwealth advantage. Second, many more island nations now offer sun-seeking tourists from the mainland alternative destinations to Puerto Rico. Cruise ships present another attractive option for tourists. Given the economic problems of the island, it is not surprising that increasing numbers of Puerto Ricans migrate to the mainland.

Conclusion

David Gomez (1971) described Mexican Americans as "strangers in their own land." Puerto Ricans, by contrast, are still struggling to determine the political destiny of their island nation. These struggles make nationality a very real part of the daily lives of Mexican Americans and Puerto Ricans. Can they also preserve their cultures along with a sense of national fervor, or will these be casualties of assimilation?

As we have seen, even when we concentrate on just Mexican Americans or Puerto Ricans out of the larger collective group of Hispanics or Latinos, diversity remains. Mexican Americans are divided among the Hispanos and the descendants of earlier Mexican immigrants, the U.S.-born of Mexican descent, and the more recent arrivals from Mexico. Among the Mexican American immigrants, further distinctions exist between those who are legal and the minority who are illegal. Puerto Ricans can be classified by virtue of residency and the extent to which they identify with the island culture. For many Puerto Ricans, the identity dilemma is never truly resolved: "*No soy de aquí ni de allá*"—"I am not from here nor from there"—is a common refrain (Comas-Díaz et al. 1998).

Economic change is also apparent. Poverty and unemployment rates are high among Mexican Americans and Puerto Ricans, and new arrivals from Mexico and Puerto Rico are particularly likely to enter the lower class, or working class at best, upon arrival in the United States. However, there is a growing middle class within the Hispanic community.

Mexican culture is alive and well in the Mexican American community. Some cultural practices that have become more popular here than in Mexico are being imported back to Mexico, with their distinctive Mexican American flavor. All of this change is occurring in the midst of a reluctance to expand bilingual education and a popular move to make English the official language of the United States. In 1998, Puerto Rico observed its 500th anniversary as a colony: four centuries under Spain and another century under the United States. Its dual status as a colony and as a developing nation has been the defining issue for Puerto Ricans, even those who have migrated to the mainland.

Figure 10.3 shows the spectrum of intergroup relations with respect to Mexican Americans and Puerto Ricans.

Figure 10.3 Spectrum of Intergroup Relations: Mexican Americans and Puerto Ricans

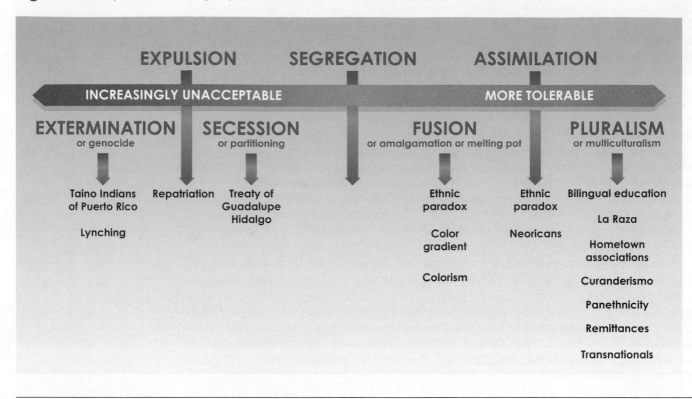

Summary of Learning Objectives

10.1 Understand the history of Mexican Americans.

1. As a result of the 1848 Treaty of Guadalupe Hidalgo, which ended the Mexican–American War, the United States acquired a significant amount of Mexican territory, starting the long history of Latinos in the United States.

2. Federal policies such as repatriation, the bracero program, and Operation Wetback reflect the U.S. attitude toward Mexico and its people as a source of low-wage labor to be encouraged or shut off as dictated by U.S. economic needs.

10.2 Describe the social circumstances of contemporary Mexican Americans.

3. Mexican Americans today have a mixed experience with health delivery and are aided by

the ethnic paradox of new arrivals being relatively healthy compared to later generations. Similarly, the family can provide valuable insulation from the challenges of poverty and prejudice.

10.3 Explain the challenges that Puerto Rico faces.

4. Puerto Ricans have enjoyed U.S. citizenship by birth since 1917, but the island remains a commonwealth of the United States. The future status of Puerto Rico remains the key political issue within the Puerto Rican community.

10.4 Discuss Puerto Rican life and culture today, including the social construction of race.

5. Like much of the rest of the Caribbean and Latin America, Puerto Rico has more of a color gradient in terms of race than the sharp Black–White dichotomy of the mainland.

Key Terms

borderlands, *page 225*
braceros, *page 222*
color gradient, *page 234*
colorism, *page 235*
curanderismo, *page 227*
ethnic paradox, *page 227*
familism, *page 228*

hometown associations, *page 226*
La Raza, *page 222*
life chances, *page 227*
maquiladoras, *page 225*
mixed status, *page 228*
mojados, *page 222*
neocolonialism, *page 230*

Neoricans, *page 234*
remittances, *page 225*
repatriation, *page 222*
transnationals, *page 226*
world systems theory, *page 231*

Review Questions

1. In what respects has Mexico been viewed as both a source of workers and a place to leave unwanted laborers?

2. How does the ethnic paradox relate both to pluralism and assimilation?

3. In what respects are Hispanic families similar to and different from Anglo households?

4. How does the case of Puerto Rico support the notion of race as a social concept?

Critical Thinking

1. Are Mexican Americans assimilated, and are recent Mexican immigrants likely to assimilate over time?

2. What role do the borderlands have in defining Mexican Americans to themselves and to the nation as a whole?

3. Observers often regard the family as a real strength in the Latino community. How can this strength be harnessed to address some of the challenges that Mexican Americans and Puerto Ricans face in the United States?

4. Consider what it means to be patriotic and loyal in terms of being a citizen of the United States. How do the concerns that Puerto Ricans have for the island's future affect those notions of patriotism and loyalty?

Chapter 11
Muslim and Arab Americans: Diverse Minorities

David Grossman/Alamy Stock Photo

∨ Learning Objectives

11.1 Distinguish among Muslim, Arab, and Middle Eastern Americans.

11.2 Describe the Arab American community.

11.3 Describe the Muslim American community.

11.4 Summarize Muslim and Arab immigration to the United States.

11.5 Explain Islamophobia.

11.6 Discuss the contemporary experiences of Arab and Muslim Americans.

What do you find between a Mormon church and a 7-11 convenience store? The question sounds like a setup for a joke, but it describes the reality in Bellevue, Washington. In 2003, the Islamic Center of Eastside, or, as it is also called, the Bellevue Masjid, took over the location formerly occupied by a Korean church. At the Islamic Center, Muslims from Saudi Arabia, Yemen, Egypt, Iraq, Kenya, Sudan, Mali, Pakistan, Bangladesh, Malaysia, China, Canada, and South American countries come together to worship.

Not necessarily Arab or Middle Eastern, they pray together as followers of Islam and deal with their everyday issues. Among the more mundane concerns was insufficient parking, but that problem was remedied by the adjacent Mormon church welcoming them to use its parking lot Monday through Saturday (Muslims come to the mosque four times a day for prayer). The mosque, in turn, offered the Mormons the use its parking lot for the Mormons' Sunday worship overflow.

As with other mosques, incidents have occurred that brought attention from the law—all a part of a national rise in anti-Muslim incidents, first after 9/11 and then again since about 2014 as international concerns over terrorism surfaced. Sporadic vandalism occurred at the Bellevue Masjid and, at times, threatening literature was placed under the windshield wipers of cars at nearby Islamic schools. In 2016, windows were broken at the mosque, and the interior was vandalized a couple of times. In the midst of these events, Community and interfaith groups convened meetings to show support for the Muslim community.

Then, in 2016, a man was arrested for telling people in the parking lot that he was "going to assassinate everyone" at the mosque. In January 2017, an arsonist substantially damaged the mosque. Fortunately, no one was injured, but the building was beyond repair. The neighboring Mormon church immediately offered its facilities to the mosque worshippers until a new mosque can be built. Several themes are present in the tale of the Bellevue Masjid: worshippers from many national and ethnic backgrounds coming together, sporadic vile incidents of hatred, and spontaneous and continuous assistance from others (Mathias 2017; Scigliana 2013).

Muslim and Arab Americans, as well as Middle Eastern Americans, are different groups in the United States. Although the groups overlap, with some Muslim Americans being of Arab ancestry, they are distinct from one another. Most Arab Americans are not Muslim, and most Muslim Americans are not of Arab background. Within each group is significant diversity that can be seen by differences in forms of religious expression, ancestral background, and how recently they arrived in the United States. "Middle Easterner" is yet another identifier that adds to both the confusion and complexity. All these groups have been seen and stereotyped in the West through the lens of orientalism.

Orientalism is the simplistic view of the people and history of the Orient (generally, the region of the Middle East to East Asia), with no recognition of change over time or the diversity within its many cultures. Palestinian American literary scholar Edward Said (1978) stressed how so many people in North America and Europe came to define, categorize, and study the Orient and thereby create a static stereotype of hundreds of millions of people stretched around the globe.

Orientalism is a more specific form of ethnocentrism. Recall that **ethnocentrism** is the tendency to believe that one's culture and way of life are superior to all others. Certainly, European orientalists viewed this "other" mass culture as substandard compared to the European way of life. This stigmatizing became wider with the outbreak of terrorism and, specifically, the events of September 11, 2001. Even without these violent events, it is a challenge for Muslim Americans, Arab Americans, and Middle Eastern Americans to sort out their identities, but nonetheless all three groups function in strong and growing communities in the United States.

Identifying Arab, Muslim, and Middle Eastern Americans

11.1 Distinguish among Muslim, Arab, and Middle Eastern Americans.

The three identifiers "Arab," "Muslim," and "Middle Eastern" are frequently used interchangeably, but each term applies to very different people in the United States.

The U.S. Bureau of the Census is now seriously considering including "Middle Eastern" or "Middle Eastern or North African" as a category to be included in the 2020 census. Historically, the term "Middle East" came into use in twelfth-century Europe to designate the area of British rule between the East (that is, England) and the Near East (India) and Far East (Singapore and Hong Kong).

Although the term *Middle East* is frequently used, it is an ambiguous geographic designation that includes large numbers of people who are neither Muslim nor Arab (such as Israeli Jews). Collectively, in the misguided view of orientalism, Middle Easterners are lumped together and collectively subjected to prejudice and discrimination but are not eligible for supportive efforts such as affirmative action. Nationals and their descendants from these countries are often called "Middle Eastern," but not all scholars (much less the general public) agree on what constitutes the Middle East. Indeed, when the Census Bureau reached

Figure 11.1 Arab, Muslim, and Middle Eastern Countries

Arabs, Muslims, and Middle Easterners are a mix of racial, religious, ethnic, and geographical definitions and social identifiers. The designations in this map reflect the consensus on Arab nations, countries either majority Muslim or approaching majority in this generation, and what constitutes the Middle East and North Africa.

SOURCE: Author, based on *Chambers Book of Facts* 2005; Coogan 2003; Pew Forum on Religion and Public Life 2011; Ramirez 2015.

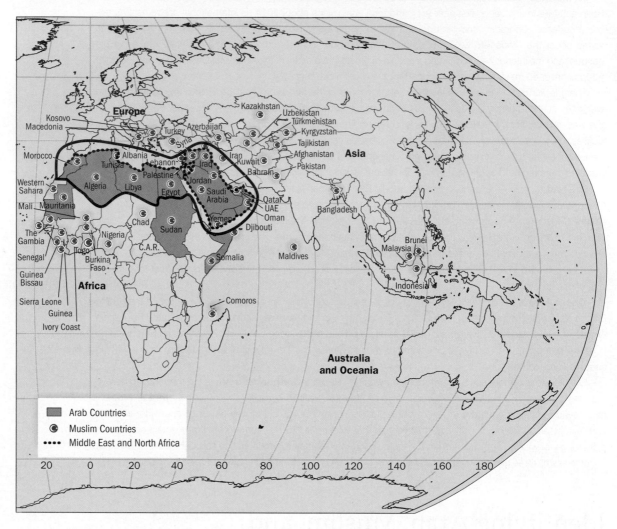

out to experts develop a definition, it found that only one nationality, Lebanese, was universally considered Middle Eastern and that up to 40 nationalities were specified (Ramirez 2015). The map in Figure 11.1 shows the best scholarly consensus on the current definition of the Middle East.

Compared to Arab Americans and Muslim Americans, there are relatively few groups or associations that see themselves as representing Middle Eastern Americans. Similarly, there is little movement in the United States toward developing a common identity around this identifier even though the term is still used to describe people and locations.

We are considering Arab Americans and Muslim Americans together in this chapter for several reasons. First, we need to clarify the distinctions between two groups that are often incorrectly referred to as a single population. Second, we seek to overcome the prism of orientalism through which many contemporary Americans view the Arab and Muslim world. Orientalism discounts and diminishes the diversity of Arabs and Muslims, thereby allowing outsiders to come up with simplistic descriptions and policies. Orientalism has led people to see a sweeping unity among Arab and Muslim societies, leading to an unchanging and a clearly outdated image. We must focus on smaller, culturally consistent groups or countries rather than surrender to the temptation of a single broad generalization.

Figure 11.2 Relationship Between Muslim and Arab Americans

Many Arab Americans are not Muslims, and most Muslim Americans are not Arabs.

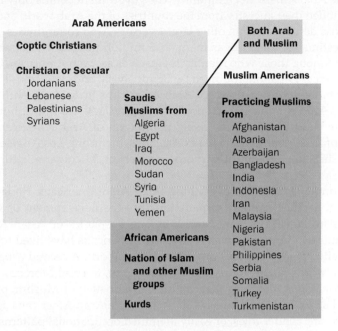

The Arab American and Muslim American communities are among the most rapidly growing subordinate groups in the United States. Westerners often confuse the two groups. Arabs are an ethnic group, while Muslims are a religious group. Typically, Islam is the faith (like Christianity), and a Muslim is a believer of that religion (just as Christians are believers in Christianity). Worldwide, many Arabs (12 million) are not Muslims, and most Muslims (85 percent) are not Arabs (David and Ayouby 2004).

Figure 11.2 illustrates the relationship between ethnic groups and a religion that crosses many nationalities. As we can see, one cannot accurately identify Muslims by nationality alone, and clearly being Arab does not necessarily mean being a follower of Islam.

In the balance of this chapter, we will turn first to Arab Americans and then to Muslim Americans, regularly noting the relationships between the two.

Arab Americans

11.2 Describe the Arab American community.

The term *Arab Americans* refers to the immigrants and their descendants from the countries that now make up the Arab world (see Figure 11.1). As defined by the membership of the Arab League, there are 22 Arab nations: Algeria, Bahrain, Comoros, Djibouti, Egypt, Iraq, Jordan, Kuwait, Lebanon, Libya, Mauritania, Morocco, Oman, Palestine, Qatar, Saudi Arabia, Somalia, Sudan, Syria, Tunisia, United Arab Emirates, and Yemen. Not all people living in these countries are necessarily Arab (for example, the Kurds of Iraq are not Arab), and some Arab Americans may have emigrated from non-Arab countries such as Great Britain or France, where their families have lived for generations.

The Arabic language is the single most unifying force among Arabs, although not all Arabs and certainly not all Arab Americans can read and speak Arabic. As the language evolved over the centuries, people in different parts of the Arab world began to speak with different dialects, using their own choices of vocabulary and pronunciation. Although most Arab Americans are not Muslim, the fact that the Qur'an (or Koran) was originally written in Arabic 1,400 years ago gives the knowledge of Arabic special importance. Many Arabs read the Qur'an in Arabic, just as many Jews read the Torah in Hebrew. In contrast, Christians almost always read the Bible in a translation that is in their native tongue.

Estimates of the size of the Arab American community differ widely. Despite the Census Bureau's efforts to enlist expert assistance, census results are widely thought to severely undercount the Arab American community. The government counts only those individuals who have identified their ancestry from the countries of the Arab world and, therefore, does not include those descended from other large overseas Arab communities.

By some estimates, there are as many as 3 million people with Arab ancestry in the United States. Among those who identify themselves as Arab American, the largest single source of ancestry is Lebanon, followed by Egypt, Syria, and Palestine. These four groups accounted for more than two-thirds of Arab Americans in 2014. As with other racial and ethnic groups, Arab Americans, as shown in Figure 11.3, are not uniformly distributed throughout the United States. This rising population of Arab Americans has led to the development of Arab retail centers in several cities, including Los Angeles, Chicago, New York City, Washington, DC, and Dearborn and Detroit, Michigan (Brittingham and de la Cruz 2005).

Diversity underlies virtually everything about Arab Americans. (In fact, the term *Arab Americans* is yet another example of **panethnicity**—the development of solidarity among subgroups—as in the case of panethnicity among Hispanics or Asian Americans.) First, there are variations in time of arrival. Many Arab Americans have lived for several generations in the United States, whereas others are foreign-born. A second aspect of diversity is point of origin, which ranges from urban Cairo, Egypt, to rural Morocco. Third, there is a rich variety of religious traditions that can include Christian or Muslim, practicing or non-practicing, and so forth. It is impossible to characterize Arab Americans as having a single family type, specific gender roles, or easily identified occupational patterns (Dallo, Ajrouch, and Al-Snih 2008; David 2008).

As with any ethnic or immigrant community, divisions have arisen over who can truly be counted as a member of the community. Sociologist Gary David (2003, 2007) developed the concept of the **deficit model of ethnic identity**. This model states that others view one's

---

Figure 11.3 Arab American Population, 2014

Only 14 states and the District of Columbia have more than one half percent of the population identified as Arab American.

SOURCE: U.S. Bureau of the Census data in American Community Survey 2015b.

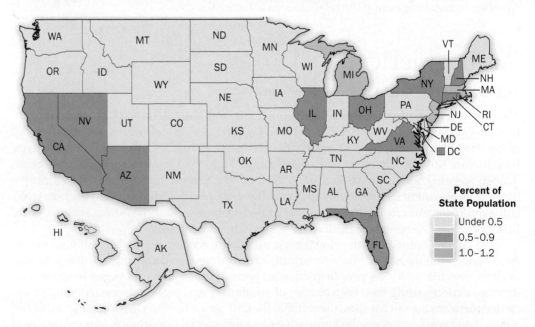

Percent of State Population

- Under 0.5
- 0.5–0.9
- 1.0–1.2

identity by subtracting away characteristics corresponding to some ideal ethnic type. Each factor encompassing a "perfect" ethnic identity missing from a person's background or identity leads others to view the person as more assimilated and less ethnic. Arab Americans are considered "less ethnic" if they are unable to speak Arabic, if they are married to non-Arabs, and if they have never been to the home country.

One Arab American can come to regard another Arab American as either "too American" or "too Arab." Arab American organizations, magazines, and associations may seek to cater to the entire Arab American community, but, more likely, they cater to certain segments based on nationality, religion, and degree of assimilation. Organizations may also be founded by people who gravitated to one another because they share the same sense of what it means to be Arab American. As noted in the Research Focus feature, younger Arab Americans seem more willing to self-identify as Arab American even though they actually may be more assimilated to U.S. culture than their parents.

Research Focus

Self-Identifying as "Arab American"

Racial identity and ethnic identity are important aspects of the immigrant experience. **Blended identity** is a self-image and worldview that combines religious faith, a cultural background based on nationality, and the status of being a resident of the United States. We have already considered how blended identity functions among other ethnic groups, but how might this identity change over time for Arab Americans? An Arab immigrant to the United States does not necessarily go through a process of shedding one identity for another (assimilation). Immigrants and even their children and future generations may hold onto multiple identities.

Consider the example of a Pakistani American. As Figure 11.4 shows, Muslims often find their daily activities defined by their faith, their nationality, and their status as Americans. Younger Muslims especially can move freely among the different identities. In Chicago, Muslim college students perform hip-hop in Arabic with lyrics like "La ilaha ila Allah" ("There is no God but Allah"). In Fremont, California, high-school Muslim girls and some of their non-Muslim girlfriends hold an alternative prom, decked out in silken gowns, dancing to both 50 Cent and Arabic music, and dining on lasagna but pausing at sunset to face Mecca (one of Islam's holiest sites, located in Saudi Arabia) and pray.

Sociologist Kristine Ajrouch and political scientist Amaney Jamal conducted a survey of Arab Americans in the Detroit metropolitan area. Overall in the United States, 80 percent of Arab Americans select "White" on their census forms because the government does not offer "Arab" as an option for race. Yet, when given that option, Ajrouch and Jamal found many chose Arab American as a self-identifier but also considered themselves "White."

Being Arab American does not mean that you do not see yourself as American. Indeed, 94 percent of Arab Americans who

Figure 11.4 Blended Identity of Muslim Americans

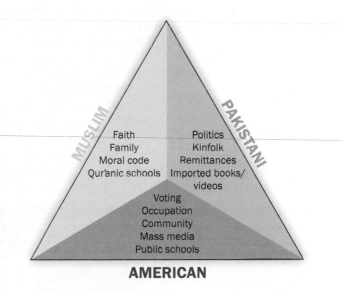

are citizens describe themselves as very or quite proud to be American, compared to 98 percent of the general population.

Interestingly, younger Arab Americans seem more willing to use the label "Arab American." Researchers wonder if the post–9/11 world has given being Arab and/or Muslim American new meaning. Will younger people, as they become adults, embrace "Arab American" in a sense of unity or seek to distance themselves from it due to fear of being marginalized by society?

Sources: Abdulrahim 2009; Ajrouch 2011; Ajrouch and Jamal 2007; de la Cruz and Brittingham 2003.

Muslim Americans

11.3 Describe the Muslim American community.

Islam, with approximately 1.7 billion followers worldwide, is second to Christianity among the world's religions in terms of number of adherents. Put another way, globally, Muslims make up about 24 percent of the world's population, compared to 33 percent for Christians (Pew Templeton 2015).

Although news events and a worldview of orientalism suggest an inherent conflict between Christians and Muslims, the two faiths are similar in many ways. Both are monotheistic (i.e., based on a single deity) and indeed worship the same God. *Allah* is the Arabic word for God and refers to the God of Moses, Jesus, and Muhammad. Both Christianity and Islam include a belief in prophets, an afterlife, and a judgment day. In fact, Islam recognizes Jesus as a prophet, though not as the son of God. Islam reveres both the Old and New Testaments as integral parts of its tradition. Both faiths impose a moral code on believers, which varies from fairly rigid proscriptions for fundamentalists to relatively relaxed guidelines for liberals (Goodstein 2011).

Islam in the United States

Islam is guided by the teachings of the Qur'an (or Koran), which Muslims believe was revealed to the seventh-century prophet Muhammad. The Qur'an includes the collected sayings, or *hadeeth*, and the deeds of Muhammad, which are called *Sunnah*, or the way of the prophet. Muhammad was an orphan who grew up to become a respected businessman who rejected the widespread polytheism of his day and turned to the one god (Allah) as worshipped by the region's Christians and Jews. Muslims believe that the angel Gabriel visited Muhammad and began reciting the word of Allah (the Qur'an). Muslims see Muhammad as the last in a long line of prophets; Abraham, Moses, and Jesus preceded him.

Islam is communal, encompassing all aspects of one's life. Consequently, in countries that are predominantly Muslim, the separation of religion and state is not considered necessary or even desirable. In fact, governments in Muslim countries often reinforce Islamic practices through their laws. Muslims do vary in their interpretation of several traditions, some of which, such as the requirement for women to wear face veils, are disputed.

Certain rituals referred to as the "pillars of wisdom" characterize Islam. Muslims fast during the month of Ramadan, which marks the revelation of the Qur'an to the Prophet

Colleges and employers are increasingly setting aside areas in which Muslims can carry out their daily prayers. Here at MIT in Cambridge, Massachusetts, Muslims gather for afternoon prayers.

Rick Friedman/Corbis Historical/Getty Images

Muhammad; they pray to Allah, facing Mecca, five times a day; they make charitable donations; and they say, where possible, Friday afternoon prayers within their community. They also undertake the **hajj**, the pilgrimage to Mecca, at least once in their lifetime. This city in contemporary Saudi Arabia is home of the House of Allah, or Ka'aba, which was built by Abraham and his son Ishmael. Muslims perform the hajj in accordance with the Qur'an and in the manner prescribed by Muhammad in his Sunnah.

Islamic believers are divided into a variety of faiths and sects, such as Sunnis and Shi'is (or Shiites). These divisions sometimes result in antagonisms between the members, just as there are religious rivalries between Christian denominations. The large majority of Muslims in the United States are Sunni Muslims—literally, those who follow the Sunnah, the way of the prophet. Compared to other Muslims, they tend to be more moderate in their religious orthodoxy. The Shi'is (primarily from Iraq, Iran, and southern Lebanon) are the second-largest group. The two groups differ on who should have been the *caliph,* or ruler, after the death of Muhammad. This disagreement resulted in different understandings of beliefs and practices, concluding in the Sunni and Shi'is worshipping separately from each other. They worship separately even if it means crossing national and linguistic lines to do so—provided there are sufficient numbers of Shi'is to support their own mosque, or *masjid*.

As a part of a larger national study of all religious congregations, regular surveys of mosques in the United States are conducted. The latest report placed the number at over 2,100, with a quarter founded since 2000. A mosque typically counts about 1,200 people participating in some religious observance. Data indicate that about 44 percent of Muslims report going to religious services every week—about the same as reported by Protestants, Jews, and Roman Catholics (Abu Dhabi Gallup 2011; Bagby 2012).

There are many expressions of Islamic faith and even divisions among Sunnis and Shi'is, so to speak of Muslims as either Sunni or Shi'i would be akin to speaking of Christians as either Roman Catholic or Baptist, forgetting that there are other denominations as well as sharp divisions within the Roman Catholic and Baptist faiths. Furthermore, there are Muslim groups unique to the United States; later in this chapter we focus on the largest one—Islam among African Americans.

Verses in the Qur'an prescribe to Muslims **jihad**, or struggle against the enemies of Allah. Typically, Muslims interpret jihad as their internal struggle for spiritual purity. Today, a very visible minority of Muslims in the world use jihad as a pretext to carry out an armed struggle against what they view as the enemies of the Palestinians, such as Israel and the United States. Such interpretations, even if held by a few, cannot be dismissed because Islam is a faith without an established hierarchy; there is no Muslim pope to deliver the one true interpretation, and there is no provision for excommunication. Individual *imams*, leaders or spiritual guides of a mosque, can offer guidance and scholarship, but Islam's authority rests with the scripture and the teachings of the prophet (Belt 2002).

Based on the most recent studies, there are at least 2.6 million and perhaps as many as 3 million Muslims in the United States. About two-thirds are U.S.-born citizens. In terms of ethnic and racial background, estimates still vary widely. Estimates range as follows:

- 20–42 percent African American
- 24–33 percent South Asian (Afghan, Bangladeshi, Indian, and Pakistani)
- 12–32 percent Arab
- 15–22 percent "other" (Bosnian, Iranian, Turkish, and White and Hispanic converts)

There appears to be total agreement that the Muslim population in the United States is growing rapidly through immigration and conversion (Bagby 2012; Grossman 2008; Pew Forum on Religion and Public Life 2011). We consider the relationships among Muslims, Arabs, and Jewish Americans in the Relations Across Boundaries feature.

A majority of U.S. Muslims (56 percent) believe that many religions can lead to eternal life. Most Americans (65 percent), including nearly two-thirds of American Christians (64 percent), share this view. American Muslims seem to be closer to their fellow citizens than their global counterparts are. This "American" attitude is far less common among Muslims: A median of just 18 percent of Muslims worldwide think religions other than Islam can lead to eternal life (Lugo et al. 2013).

Relations Across Boundaries

Muslim, Arab, and Jewish Americans

Over the past 1,400 years, few groups have been so linked in history as Muslims and Jews. Both faiths claim Abraham (Ibrahim in the Muslim tradition) as the founder of their religion, with Judaism tracing its heritage through Abraham's son Isaac and wife Sarah, while Islam traces its heritage through Abraham's son Ishmael. Yet the tensions that have sometimes arisen between Muslims and Jews globally have little to do with religious scripture but rather conflicts over natural resources, such as water and oil, and political control. The continuing struggle of Israel and Palestine (the latter a predominantly Muslim Arab people—described in detail in Chapter 16) is the most recent manifestation of these conflicts. The alliances that countries like the United States, Great Britain, and France have formed with Israel serve to bring the conflict beyond the Middle East.

In the United States today, most scholars and observers concur that American Muslims, Arab Americans, and Jewish Americans see a natural alliance despite continuing disputes back in the Middle East. All feel threatened, whether by anti-Semitic and Islamophobic incidents or a long history of being used as scapegoats in issues facing larger society. Many Jews saw the call by some U.S. politicians in 2016 for a registry or database of all Muslim as all too similar to Nazi Germany's policies regarding Jews beginning in 1933. Furthermore, the current level of public opinion suspicious about or opposed to Muslim immigration into the United States is very similar to the levels of public opposition to Jewish immigration back in 1939.

The mutual concerns have led to the formation of local and even national alliances between Jews and Muslims. Prominent among them is the Muslim-Jewish Advisory Council, founded in 2016. Its co-chairs are two Fortune 500 chief executives: Farooq Kathwari (of furniture company Ethan Allen), who is Muslim, and Stanley Bergman (of medical products distributor Henry Schein), who is Jewish. They seek to take action on hate crimes, noting that the majority of religiously motivated crimes have targeted Jews and that anti-Muslim hate crimes have risen by 67 percent.

During the 2017 U.S. protests against a potential government ban against Muslim immigration, one woman carried a sign that read "Granddaughter of Holocaust survivors standing with refugees, Muslim immigrants." The Hebrew Immigrant Aid Society, first organized to assist Jews fleeing tyranny in Europe, now assists all refugees. Half of the people they assist are Muslim.

Despite these efforts, unity has not been achieved on all fronts. Nation of Islam leader Louis Farrakhan has continually expressed anti-Semitic views ranging from the charge that Jews were responsible for the slave trade to accusing Israel of orchestrating the 9/11 attacks. Studies in Europe show somewhat higher levels of anti-Semitism among Muslims than among non-Muslims, but similar studies have not been completed in the United States to date, although some are underway. In response to more general questions not aimed toward opinions of specific groups, Muslim Americans are less condoning of violence against other people than are Americans with other religious affiliations.

Sources: Anti-Defamation League 2015a, 2015b; Demick 2017; Goldstein 2016; Lawrence 2014; Muslim Jewish Advisory Council 2017; Tharoor 2015.

Black Muslims

African Americans who embrace Islam form a significant segment within the Muslim American community—about 28 percent of all Muslims in the nation. There are about one million Black American Muslims, or about 2 percent of all African Americans, yet they are estimated to account for 90 percent of all converts to Islam in the United States (Pew Research Center 2015).

The history of Black American Islam begins in the seventeenth century, when members of some Muslim tribes were forcibly brought to the American colonies. It is estimated that 10 percent of African slaves were Muslim. Slave owners discouraged anything that linked them culturally to Africa, including their spiritual beliefs. Furthermore, many in the South saw "Christianizing" slaves as part of their mission in civilizing the enslaved people. Enslaved Muslims in the colonies and elsewhere often resisted the pressure to assimilate to the dominant group's faith and maintained their dedication to Islam (Ba-Yunus and Kone 2004; Leonard 2003; McCloud 1995).

It was exceedingly difficult, perhaps even impossible, for a collective Muslim community to survive slavery. Organized Muslim groups within the African American community grew and dispersed in the late nineteenth century and the first half of the twentieth century. Resurgence of Islam among Black Americans often centered around the leadership of charismatic people such as West Indian–born Edward Wilmot Blyden and North Carolinian Noble

Pictorial Parade/Archive Photos/Getty Images

Malcolm X, reflecting his conversion to Islam, made a pilgrimage to the Muslim holy city of Mecca. On this trip in 1964, the year before his assassination in New York City, he also met with area leaders such as Prince Faisal al-Saud of Saudi Arabia.

Drew Ali, who founded the Moorish Science Temple. Typically, followers of the movements dispersed at the death of the central leader; but with each movement, the core of converts to Islam grew within the African American community (Turner 2003).

Like other Muslims, generally African Americans who follow Islam are not tightly organized into a single religious fellowship. However, most today trace their roots either to the teachings of W. Fard Muhammad or, just as significantly, to those who responded against his version of the faith. Little is known of the early years of the immigrant W. Fard Muhammad, who arrived in Detroit around 1930, introducing the teaching of Islam to poor African Americans. He spoke strongly against adultery and alcohol consumption (which are forbidden by Islamic tradition) and smoking and dancing (which are prohibited among some Muslims). However, he also spoke of the natural superiority of Black people, which would cause them to win out in the inevitable struggle between Blacks and Whites—but only if they adopted their "natural religion" and reclaimed their identities as Muslims (Lincoln 1994; Turner 2003).

Malcolm X, originally a member of the Nation of Islam, became a powerful and brilliant voice of Black self-determination in the 1960s. He was an authentic folk hero to his sympathizers then and remains so to many people today, more than a generation after his death. Besides his own followers, he commanded an international audience and is still referred to in a manner befitting a prophet. Indeed, Spike Lee's 1993 movie, based on the *Autobiography of Malcolm X*, introduced him to another generation. Malcolm X was highly critical of the civil rights movement in general and of Martin Luther King, Jr., in particular.

Malcolm X is remembered for his sharp attacks on other Black leaders, for his break with the Nation of Islam, and for his apparent shift to support the formation of coalitions with progressive Whites. He is especially remembered for taking the position that Blacks must resist violence "by any means necessary," which greatly concerned supporters of nonviolent action. By the last year of his life, Malcolm X (by then known as Malik El-Shabazz) had taken on a very different orientation. He created the secular Organization of Afro-American Unity, which was meant to internationalize the civil rights movement. Three assassins ended Malcolm X's life in 1964. "His philosophy can be summarized as pride in Blackness, the necessity of knowing Black history, Black autonomy, Black unity, and self-determination for the Black community" (Pinkney 1975: 213; see also Dyson 1995; Kieh 1995).

In recent years, Minister Louis Farrakhan, despite leading a small proportion of Black Muslims, has been the most visible spokesperson among the various Black Muslim groups. Farrakhan broke with the successors of Elijah Muhammad and named his group Nation of Islam, adopting, along with the name used by the earlier group, the more unorthodox-to-Islam ideas of Elijah Muhammad, such as Black moral superiority. Farrakhan jumped into

the limelight, a   el have given his teachings an anti-Sei

Although   articular—and his anti-
Israeli foreign p   is speeches and writings
reflect the basic   and homosexuality are
condemned. Sel   re endorsed. Farrakhan
is not pessimistic   s. As leader of the 1995
Million Man Ma   nericans nationwide to
register to vote a   96).

Traditionally,   some friction between
the African Amer   dhere to the Nation of
Islam, and immig   may feel that the larger
Islamic communit   ession faced by people
who are Black an   Muslims often assume
incorrectly that all   ck superiority view and do not
follow orthodox M   traditions. It is likely that a single dominating voice of Islam will not
emerge among African Americans. That is not surprising because a pluralistic interpretation
of faith is common to Muslims worldwide, just as it is to Christians and Jews (Hill et al. 2015).

Immigration to the United States

11.4 Summarize Muslim and Arab immigration to the United States.

The history of both Muslims and Arabs in the United States is a long one, but their visibility as a true immigrant presence is more of a twentieth-century phenomenon. As already noted, a significant proportion of African slaves were followers of Islam. Even earlier, Spanish Muslims accompanied explorers and conquistadores to the Americas. In the nineteenth century, contingents of Arabs made dramatic impressions at a series of world's fairs held in Philadelphia, St. Louis, and Chicago, where millions of fairgoers had certainly their first contact with and probably their first awareness of Arab culture. Fairgoers came away with an awareness of cultures previously unknown to them, but probably saw these cultures through the lens of orientalism. Positive reports of the reception of these delegations began to encourage Arabs, particularly those from Syria and Lebanon, to immigrate to the United States. At about the same time, other Arabs immigrated as the result of encouragement from U.S.-funded missionary programs in the Middle East.

Just as immigration of Arabs and, to a lesser extent, practicing Muslims began to number in the thousands each year in the early twentieth century, World War I intervened; and then the restrictive national origin system (see Chapter 4), with its pro-Western and northern European bias, slowed the Arab and Muslim movement to the United States. As with so many other immigrant groups, the pattern was for immigration to be disproportionately male and the destination to be cities of the East Coast. Pressure to assimilate caused many newcomers to try to reduce the differences between themselves and their host country. So, for example, many women ceased to cover their heads—a practice common to both Christian Arab and Muslim women.

The immediate aftermath of 9/11 led to about a 30 percent decline in Arabs and Muslims immigrating to the United States because of their apprehension over the reception they would receive and increased scrutiny of their entry documents by the federal government. The numbers of tourists and students declined nearly by half. However, recently, numbers have begun to rebound. In 2005, more than 40,000 arrivals from Muslim countries sought permanent residency, resulting in the highest annual numbers of Muslim immigrants since 2000. Some new residents even argue they are better off in post–9/11 America because Islamic centers are more organized, and free legal help is more accessible (Elliott 2006).

With U.S. military operations increasing in Muslim-majority countries such as Iraq, Syria, and Afghanistan, refugees increased in the period from 2007 to 2016 to the point that Arabs and Muslims approached half of all refugees who entered the nation. However, refugees make up only one-tenth of all immigrants granted lawful entry. Among non-refugees arriving, Muslims account for only one in ten (Connor 2016a).

During the 2016 presidential campaign, concerns about terrorists from Muslim-majority countries rose as a result of highly publicized and deadly terrorist incidents that occurred in France and Belgium in 2015. Following through on his campaign promises, President Donald Trump issued an executive order banning all people, including refugees and visa holders, from seven Muslim-majority countries. Opponents characterized the ban as a twenty-first century example of **nativism**, a set of beliefs and policies favoring native-born citizens over immigrants. Nativism was first used in the United States in the banning of Chinese immigrants in the 1880s.

The Supreme Court temporarily upheld the ban except for those who had close ties to the United States through family members, employment, college attendance, or pending emergency hospital-care arrangements. While Muslims, as well as Arabs, continue to arrive, the ban enjoyed significant support among the general public. Over 40 percent of respondents in national surveys supported the seven-nation ban, and about the same proportion approved indefinitely ending the Syrian refugee program. Some feel that this support is less a result of concerns about the nation's safety and more an expression of prejudice against Muslims—the subject of the next section (Newport 2017).

Islamophobia

11.5 Explain Islamophobia.

In what ways do prejudice and discrimination manifest themselves with respect to Muslim and Arab Americans? In form and magnitude, they are much like that shown to other subordinate groups. Regrettably, this situation has gone beyond orientalism, in which one sees a group of people as "the other" and as somewhat frightening. **Islamophobia** refers to a range of negative feelings toward Muslims and their religion. Those feelings range from generalized intolerance to hatred. Islamophobia is a more specific, targeted form of **xenophobia**, the fear or hatred of strangers or foreigners.

The current xenophobic expressions against Muslims are strikingly different than earlier expressions of xenophobia because, in the twenty-first century, they have taken on a decidedly patriotic fervor; that is, many people who overtly express anti-Muslim or anti-Arab feelings also believe themselves to be pro-American (Halstead 2008).

Few normalizing or positive images are available. Rarely are Arab and Muslim Americans portrayed in the media as exhibiting normal behavior such as shopping, attending a sporting event, or even eating without the subtext of terrorism lurking in the shadows. Furthermore, the interests of the United States are often depicted either as leaning against the Arabs and Muslims, as in the Israeli–Palestinian violence, or presented as dependent on them, as in the close diplomatic ties the United States maintains with countries such as Saudi Arabia.

The 2016 presidential campaign and the ensuing debate over the seven-country travel ban in 2017 legitimized into the mainstream many broad generalizations about followers of Islam. As a presidential candidate, Donald Trump had argued that the nation was becoming a dumping ground for everyone else's problems, including those of the Middle East. He called for "a total and complete shutdown of Muslims entering the United States until our country's representatives can figure out what is going on." Yet he also expressed concern over the plight of Syria's Christians and indicated that to safeguard the country we need to consider having a "look at the mosques" in the United States. The phrase **casual Islamophobia** describes statements previously regarded as extreme that are now becoming accepted by large portions of the general public. Simply put, aspects of Islamophobia have become acceptable to increasing numbers of people and viewed as a rational global view (Blee 2016; Johnson and Weigel 2015; Kurzman 2016; Selod 2016).

Hate crimes and harassment directed at Arab and Muslim Americans rose sharply after 9/11, compared to the mid-1990s. Hate crimes and harassment have remained high. Incidents have ranged from beatings to vandalism of mosques to organized resistance to Arabic school openings, as described in the chapter opener about Bellevue, Washington. Surveys show that a complex view of Arab and Muslim Americans exists in the United States. For example, surveys since 2001 show that one in four people believe several anti-Muslim stereotypes—for

Speaking Out

May America Be True to Her Dream

Nihad Awad

This Fourth of July weekend, friends and families around the country will gather together to celebrate the freedoms we cherish as Americans, those for which countless generations have struggled and sacrificed so much.

We celebrate our freedom from oppression, freedom to practice our religion, representation in our government, and self-determination.

Yet as recent events targeting African Americans have made abundantly clear, we still have a long way to go to achieve full equality under the flag we will fly high this weekend.

The terror attack on an African Methodist Episcopal Church in Charleston, South Carolina, the abuse of African American teens by a police officer in McKinney, Texas, and police-involved shootings and mistreatment of men, women, and children of color across our nation point to the lingering structural racism in our society. These troubling incidents must be honestly addressed before we can truly be the nation President Abraham Lincoln described as "conceived in Liberty, and dedicated to the proposition that all men are created equal."

While much was accomplished through the civil rights movement during the '50s and '60s, much still remains to be done.

No less corrosive to the American values on which our country was founded is the pervasive hate to which American Muslims have increasingly found themselves subjected.

Recent, and largely unreported, incidents of anti-Muslim hate include a Texas road rage shooting in which the alleged gunman reportedly shouted "Go back to Islam" before firing at and killing the victim, the "execution-style" killings of three young Muslims in Chapel Hill, North Carolina, hate vandalism and threats targeting mosques and Islamic schools nationwide, a planned religiously motivated attack on a Muslim community in New York, and the murder of a Muslim teen in Kansas City who was run down by a vehicle painted with anti-Islam slurs.

In one much-publicized incident, armed anti-Islam protesters recently harassed worshipers at an Arizona mosque; several of

Nihad Awad

Muhammad Hamed/REUTERS/Alamy Stock Photo

those present at the rally displayed Nazi-themed symbols.

Racism and Islamophobia are branches of the same poisonous tree: Both rely on stereotypes and misinformation for their creation and continuation; both harm not only those targeted by bigotry, but also the society that allows hate to fester and pits one group against another.

Despite these terrible incidents, there are some clear signs of hope and optimism, particularly in the outpouring of love for the victims of the deadly shooting in Charleston and in the subsequent almost-universal repudiation of the Confederate flag as a symbol of racism and oppression, one to which CAIR [the Council on American-Islamic Relations] added its voice.

We saw a similar outpouring of support for worshipers at the Arizona mosque assaulted by hate-speech, and even witnessed a neighborhood "love-in" for an Iowa Muslim-American whose house was painted with Islamophobic and threatening graffiti.

The American Muslim community will continue to stand with our fellow Americans of all beliefs and backgrounds as we together struggle to achieve true freedom and equality.

As Dr. Martin Luther King said in his 1965 Independence Day sermon delivered at Ebenezer Baptist Church in Atlanta, Georgia, "Never before in the history of the world have so many racial groups and so many national backgrounds assembled together in one nation. And somehow if we can't solve the problem in America the world can't solve the problem, because America is the world in miniature and the world is America writ large."

He added: "We have a great dream. It started way back in 1776, and God grant that America will be true to her dream."

Amen to that.

Source: Nihad Awad. "May America Be True to Her Dream" July 4, 2015. Blog at www.cair.com; CAIR Address: Council on Islamic-American Relations. Used with permission.

instance, that Islam teaches violence and hatred. Still, by 2012, only 40 percent of people had a favorable image of Islam compared to 41 percent who viewed it unfavorably. Efforts to tap into college students' opinions find greater hostility toward Arabs and Muslims than toward any other racial or ethnic group. Similarly, among adults, 62 percent said in 2014 they were very concerned about the possibility of rising Islamic extremism in the United States (Parrillo and Donoghue 2013; Pew Research Center U. S. Politics and Policy 2014).

In the Speaking Out feature, Nihad Awad, national executive director of the Council on American-Islamic Relations (CAIR), the nation's largest civil rights and advocacy organization, draws parallels on the violence experienced by African Americans and anti-Islam incidents.

Arab Americans and Muslim Americans, like other subordinate groups, have not responded passively to their treatment. Their communities have created organizations to counter negative stereotypes and to offer schools material responding to the labeling that has occurred. Even before 2001, Arab Americans and Muslim Americans were becoming active in both major political parties in the United States. Given the presence of Islamophobia, the position of being Arab or Muslim in the United States grew more complex and contentious in the wake of the events of September 11, 2001, despite the public efforts of many Arabs and Muslims to proclaim their loyalty to the United States. Furthermore, surveys show that Muslim Americans are less likely than Protestants or Roman Catholics to condone small groups targeting and killing civilians or even to suggest such actions are ever justified (David and Jalbert 2008; Lawrence 2014; Pew Forum on Religion and Public Life 2011; Selod and Embrick 2013).

So, given all this unrest, casual Islamophobia, and continuing debates over immigration policy as it relates to overseas Muslims and Arabs, how does this segment of the population go about its everyday life in the United States? We explore that question in the next section.

Contemporary Life in the United States

11.6 Discuss the contemporary experiences of Arab and Muslim Americans.

As already noted, Arab Americans tended to immigrate to urban areas. There they have filled a variety of occupational roles; since the 1965 Immigration and Naturalization Act, immigrants have been filling skilled and professional roles in the United States. Another way in which Arab Americans often find opportunities for upward mobility is by becoming self-employed merchants or entrepreneurs. They typically are financially unable to buy into prosperous businesses or high-end retail stores. Rather, they have tended to become involved in precisely those businesses that privileged Whites have long since left behind or avoided altogether. To some degree, Arabs follow the same pattern as Jewish and Korean immigrant entrepreneurs, operating stores in low-income areas of central cities that major retailers ignore. Opportunities for success are great, but those opportunities also mean that the Arab American merchant faces the challenges of serving a low-income population with few consumer choices and a history of being exploited by outsiders (Cainkar 2006).

According to the Census Bureau analysis of the income of Arab American households (Figure 11.5), people reporting Arab ancestry show a higher income than the general

---

Figure 11.5 Median Household Income of Arab Americans

Note: Based on American Community Survey 2007–2010.

SOURCE: Author created, based on American Community Survey, 2007–2010, Asi and Beaulieu 2013: Figure 2.

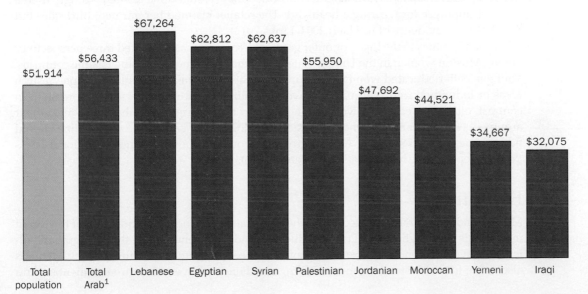

$51,914	$56,433	$67,264	$62,812	$62,637	$55,950	$47,692	$44,521	$34,667	$32,075
Total population	Total Arab[1]	Lebanese	Egyptian	Syrian	Palestinian	Jordanian	Moroccan	Yemeni	Iraqi

population. However, there is a wide range among Arab ancestry groups, ranging from Lebanese Americans who report incomes over 25 percent higher than the general population to those of Yemeni and Iraqi Americans with household incomes 33 percent lower.

Family Life and Gender

As with any people, the family plays a central role in the lives of both Muslim and Arab Americans. Given the diversity within both groups, it is impossible to generalize about typical patterns. Traditionally, Islam permitted men to have multiple wives—a maximum of four. The Qur'an admonished Muslim men to do justice economically and emotionally to their wives, and if they could not, then they should have only one wife. In some non-Islamic countries, this practice of multiple marriages is legal, but it is exceedingly rare for Muslim households in countries where the law is not supportive.

In the United States, for those who are recent immigrants or the children of immigrants, family patterns are more likely to be affected by the traditions of their homeland than by the fact that they are Muslim or Arab. The role of women receives a great deal of attention because their clothing is a conspicuous symbol that some non-Muslims and non-Arabs interpret as repression of women in Arab or Muslim society. There is a full range of views of women among Muslims and Arabs, just as there is among Christians and other religions and ethnicities. However, Islam does stress that women need to be protected and should present themselves modestly in public. This code is operationalized very differently among countries where Muslims dominate, and it varies within Muslim populations in the United States (Haeri 2004).

Sexism and sexist behavior are universal. However, the perception of gender practices in Muslim societies has received special attention in the Western media. Individually, all Muslims, men and women alike, must cover themselves and avoid revealing clothes that are designed to accentuate contours of the body and to emphasize its physical beauty. According to the Qur'an, more revealing garments can be worn in private with one's family or before members of the same sex, so in some Muslim countries, some beaches and public pools are designated for use by men only or by women only.

The prophet Muhammad indicated in his Sunnah that the female body should be covered except for the face, hands, and feet. Hence, traditional Muslim women should wear head coverings. The **hijab** refers to a variety of garments that allow women to follow the guidelines of modest dress. It may include head or face coverings; and it can take the form of a headscarf rather than something that actually covers the face; the latter would be dictated by a cultural tradition, not by Islam. U.S. Muslims select from an array of traditional garments from Muslim countries. These garments include long, loosely tailored coats or a loose black overgarment along with a scarf and perhaps a face veil. U.S. Muslim women are just as apt to wear long skirts or loose pants and overblouses that they may buy at any local retail outlet. While there is general tolerance of wearing a hijab in the United States, this perspective is not universal. In 2013, a federal court ruled that Abercrombie & Fitch wrongly fired a Muslim employee for wearing a headscarf. The retailer claimed her garment hurt sales but could offer no evidence of it (Haeri 2004; Lipka 2013).

When it comes to the hijab, or outer garments, research has identified three perspectives among Muslim women in the United States and other settlements outside Islamic countries. Younger, better-educated women who support wearing the hijab in public draw on Western ideas of individual rights, arguing in favor of veiling as a form of personal expression. In contrast, older, less-educated women who support the wearing of hijab tend to make their arguments without any reference to Western ideology. They cannot see why veiling should be an issue in the first place. A third group of women, of all ages and educational backgrounds, oppose the hijab (Read 2007; Zempi 2016).

Education

Muslim and Arab Americans recognize the importance of education, and many of the recent immigrants have high levels of formal education and have benefited by the immigration policy that gave preference to those having job skills needed to enter the United States. Muslims also value formal instruction in their faith, and there are several hundred elementary and secondary schools, the majority attached to mosques, that offer what has been referred to in other religious contexts as a parochial school education. Increasing numbers of Muslims are turning to home schooling either out of a desire to adhere to their customs in a way that is difficult to do in public schools or out of a concern over the prejudice their children may experience (Brittingham and de la Cruz 2005).

Schools are specific to particular expressions of Islam and specific nationalities, and some schools serve principally Black Muslims. Qur'anic or Sunday schools also coexist, offering specifically religious instruction either to those attending mosque schools or as a supplement for children enrolled in public schools. A major growth industry has emerged in North America that provides curriculum materials and software to serve these schools, which start in preschool and continue through college, including graduate education (Leonard 2003; MacFarquhar 2008).

Children attending public schools encounter the type of adjustment experienced by those of a religious faith different from the dominant one of society. Although public schools are intended to be secular, it is difficult to escape the orientation of many activities to Christmas and Easter or dietary practices that may not conform to the cultural tradition of the children's families. In some school districts with larger Muslim student populations, strides have been made to recognize religious diversity. A few have granted Eid-al-Fitr, the day marking the end of Ramadan, as an official school holiday for all students (Avila 2003; Sataline 2009).

A significant proportion of Muslim American children attend schools that are either all Muslim by explicit design (that is, private schools) or are predominantly Muslim as a result of residential segregation. Therefore, college is often the first time that many Muslim American students mingle with a large number of classmates who either do not understand Muslim practices or are intolerant of Islam. They also find that Christian practices are privileged or at least regarded as the norm.

The college experience for Muslims is further complicated by the Muslim college students themselves differing by their adherence to Muslim cultural practices with respect to drinking, smoking, and dating—all of which are common in a college setting. The prevalence of these activities presents challenges to Muslim college students, especially women, who are trying to advance academically and at the same time be true to their identity as Muslims. Many Muslim college students join a Muslim student organization, either formally defined or informally created, but they may also find the interpretation of Muslim identity as too restrictive or not restrictive enough given their own socialization (Khadour 2016; Mir 2014).

Politics

Muslim and Arab Americans are often politically aware. For those who identify with their homeland, politics may take the form of closely monitoring international events as they affect their home country and perhaps their kinfolk who still live there. Admittedly, because U.S. foreign policy often is tilted against some areas such as Palestine, the concerns that Arab Americans may have about events abroad may not be relieved by statements made and actions taken by U.S. government officials. On a different level, Muslims and Arab Americans

Congressman Keith Ellison, first elected in 2006, was the first Muslim to have served in Congress. Here Rep. Ellison is shown speaking with constituents in Minneapolis.

have gradually become more involved in politics in the United States. In the recent past, the most visible Arab American in politics was consumer advocate Ralph Nader, who tried to open up presidential politics to consider a true alternative to the two-party system.

Within the traditional two-party system, Arab and Muslim Americans tend to be socially conservative. They favor school vouchers, are anti-abortion, and are opposed to gay marriage and civil unions. Yet they tend to vote for Democrats, whom they perceive as being more sensitive to the problems facing Arab and Muslim countries. This tilt away from the Republican Party escalated during the 2016 presidential campaign as the party leader called for a ban on all Muslims entering the United States until security measures could be improved. By 2016, a national survey showed 70 percent of

ZUMA Press Inc/Alamy Stock Photo

A Global View

Muslims in France

Historically, France has not been a destination of immigrants, especially from outside Europe. In the efforts to rebuild France following World War II, workers came to France from its colonies in North Africa; many of them were Muslim. As countries such as Algeria, Morocco, and Tunisia (refer to Figure 11.1) gained their independence in the 1950s and 1960s, immigration to France grew. In 2010, the Muslim population totaled 7.5 percent of the general population of France and today comprises both continuing immigration and the children and grandchildren of immigrants. The Muslim population of France is projected to exceed 10 percent by 2050.

For Muslims born in France, a growing proportion see their status in comparison to other French men and women rather than to their forebears in North Africa, to whom their immigrant parents were more likely to compare their status.

In 1989, the French government banned Muslim girls in public school from wearing headscarves, taking the position that religious symbols have no place in schools. Critics argued that Muslims were being targeted while Christian children continued to wear crosses. In 2004, largely to avoid these concerns, a new law was passed nationwide that forbids any visible sign of religious affiliation, including yarmulkes (skull caps) for Jews, crosses for Christians, headscarves for Muslims, and so on.

In 2011, the wearing of the face veil became illegal in all public places. While this type of covering is uncommon among Muslims in France, this latest prohibition was seen as a further stigmatization of the Muslim community. In the law's first year, 425 women wearing full-face veils were fined ($188 each) and another 66 received warnings. These numbers are quite small; police admit they rarely enforce the law, having no desire to increase tensions. Government officials said the law was merely a security measure to keep people from hiding their faces, but the law also calls for a prison sentence for anyone forcing another person to wear the full-face veil—clearly a measure aimed at Muslims.

Tensions remain. In 2011 and 2015, Muslim extremists attacked the offices of the magazine Charlie Hebdo, which had satirized Muhammad in cartoons (Islam forbids any visual representation Muhammad). November 2015 saw terrorist attacks in Paris leaving 130 dead. These events have led to open support of the larger Muslim community in France but also to renewed calls for surveillance of the Muslim community and an end to open acceptance of immigrants and refugees.

Sources: Chrisafis 2011; Erlanger and Camus 2012; Llana 2015; Mann 2008; Pew Templeton 2015; Woesthoff 2008.

Muslims leaning toward the Democrats compared to only 13 percent toward the Republicans. A 2012 survey showed 75 percent of Arab Americans supporting President Obama for reelection. In 2016, Keith Ellison, an African American Muslim Democrat from Minneapolis, was reelected to his fifth term to the House of Representatives and became a serious contender to head the Democratic National Committee (Council on Islamic–American Relations 2016).

Muslims in the United States often express the view that their faith encourages political participation. They note that as the prophet Muhammad lay on his deathbed, he explicitly refused to name a successor, preferring that the people choose their own leaders. Individual Arabs and Muslims have sought elective office and have been appointed to high-level positions.

Nonetheless, there is a clear distancing between the major political parties and Muslims and Arab Americans. Although there are frequent official welcoming statements of support, close identification (as might be evidenced by routine dinners and convention appearances) are rare. This distancing is a sharp contrast to the ways in which politicians cater to African Americans and Latinos to gain votes. As charges have escalated in the past decade that some organizations and charities in the Arab and Muslim community were financially assisting overseas groups unfriendly to Israel or even supportive of terrorism, U.S. politicians began to take the safe position of refusing campaign money from virtually any group linked to the Muslim or Arab community. Some Muslims were also annoyed by Barack Obama's vociferous denial that he was a Muslim, as his Kenyan-born father had been, as if being a Muslim was akin to being a Communist or, even worse, a terrorist.

Muslim minorities in countries other than the United States also face challenges, as we consider in the Global View feature, "Muslims in France."

News events have fueled anti-Arab, anti-Muslim feeling. The attacks of September 11, 2001, engineered by Arab Muslim terrorists, caused many Americans to associate Arab and Muslim Americans with America's enemy in the war against terrorism. As the economy softened and taxpayers paid for increased security, Arab and Muslim Americans became scapegoats. Subsequent terrorist events, including those carried out by self-radicalized individuals, such as the 2013 Boston Marathon bombing and the 2016 Orlando nightclub shooting, served to keep 9/11 in people's minds.

In light of these ongoing suspicions and growing casual Islamophobia, some citizens have found themselves under special surveillance because of racial profiling at airports and border checkpoints. As noted earlier, **racial profiling** is any police-initiated action based on race, ethnicity, or national origin rather than on a person's behavior. Profiling of Arabs and Muslims became especially intense after September 11, 2001.

In the weeks after 9/11, surveys showed that both Muslim and Arab Americans supported the president's policy of going after terrorists. At the same time, they were fearful that continued military action would hurt how the United States is viewed. In the wake of 9/11, expressions and proof of loyalty were forced on Arab and Muslim Americans.

In an effort to locate domestic terrorists, the U.S. Department of Justice required that all foreign-born Muslim men report to the Bureau of Citizenship and Immigration Services to be photographed, fingerprinted, and interviewed. With very little public notice, 144,513 Muslim men from 25 countries reported during a five-month period ending in 2003. Of those who reported, about 13,000 faced deportation because of violations such as overstaying their visas, and 11 remained in custody because they were suspected terrorists (King 2004; Lewis 2003).

In the period since 9/11, law-enforcement agencies have tried and abandoned as unproductive infiltrating Muslim and Arab American communities and neighborhoods. Yet local agencies and the FBI continue to rely on outreach programs that encourage informants to share information about those who are likely to be radicalized and to plan terrorist attacks. Many in these minority communities see such surveillance activities as necessary but are also uneasy because the mere presence of such programs conveys distrust (Hirsh 2016).

Conclusion

We have seen the diversity within the Native American tribal community and among Latinos. Prejudice, discrimination, and responses of resistance have typified these groups and African Americans' long history in the United States. Now we can see that Arab Americans and Muslim Americans share these experiences. Not very numerous in absolute terms until the latter part of the twentieth century, both Arabs and Muslims have built on a fragmented history in the United States that goes back 200 years. When Muslims were less numerous, it was difficult for them to maintain any sense of communal identity, but as their numbers increased, identifiable groups have emerged.

There is wide diversity among Arab Americans and Muslim Americans in the United States. For the descendants of earlier Arab settlers, their identity as Arabs may be discounted by recent Arab immigrants through a process explained by the deficit model of ethnic identity. For the Muslim community, the divisions within the faith overseas are reproduced in the United States, with the added significant presence of African Americans who have embraced Islam.

World and domestic events of recent years, and especially the early years of the twenty-first century, have created some new challenges for these peoples. In some respects, the continuing conflict between Israel and Palestine has served to create an Arab identity that was largely nonexistent a few generations ago when more strictly nationalistic agendas prevailed. Similarly, the agenda of fundamentalist and militant Muslims has created an "us versus them" mentality that is found both in international organizations and on street corners in the United States.

Pulitzer Prize–winning journalist Andrea Elliott (2011) used the term "Generation 9/11" to refer to American Muslims who have come of age since the attacks on the World Trade Center and the Pentagon. "Will we ever belong?" they ask. Young Muslim and Arab Americans are not the first ethnic or racial group to ask this question in light of a defining moment that causes a large group to be harshly stigmatized (Goodstein 2010; Mir 2014). Figure 11.6 places various concepts related to Muslim and Arab Americans along the Spectrum of Intergroup Relations.

Sporadic terrorist activities—mostly abroad but also in the United States—carried out in the name of Islam have led to the emergence of casual Islamophobia. This lack of true understanding of Arab and Muslim cultures is not totally new but rather is built on the orientalism

Figure 11.6 Spectrum of Intergroup Relations: Muslim and Arab Americans

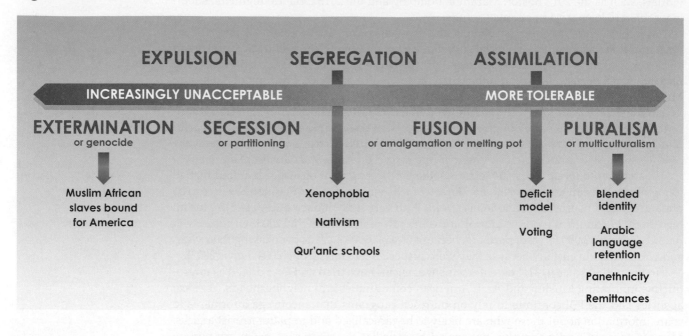

that has its roots in the initial contacts between Europeans and the people of the Middle East and South Asia.

Many Arab and Muslim Americans, like other U.S. citizens, are seeking to define themselves and move ahead in their society. The challenges facing them do seem measurably greater than they were just a few years ago, but their efforts to create bridges are also significant.

Summary of Learning Objectives

11.1 Distinguish among Muslim, Arab, and Middle Eastern Americans.

1. The three identifiers "Arab," "Muslim," and "Middle Eastern" are frequently used interchangeably, but each term applies to very different people in the United States. Although the term *Middle East* is frequently used, it is an ambiguous geographic designation that includes large numbers of people who are neither Muslim nor Arab (such as Israeli Jews). Arabs are an ethnic group, while Muslims are a religious group. One cannot accurately identify Muslims by nationality alone, and being Arab does not necessarily mean being a follower of Islam.

11.2 Describe the Arab American community.

2. Arab Americans (an ethnic group) are a diverse group representing nationalities from Africa, Europe, and Asia, who may or may not be Muslim.

11.3 Describe the Muslim American community.

3. Muslims (a religious group) include converts to the faith as well as immigrants and their descendants, and they may or may not be Arab.

The United States is also home to a significant number of African American Muslims.

11.4 Summarize Muslim and Arab immigration to the United States.

4. Many of the early Muslims in the Americas came as slaves, whereas most Arab Americans have come during the past half-century.

11.5 Explain Islamophobia.

5. Given the presence of Islamophobia, the position of being Arab or Muslim in the United States grew more complex and contentious in the wake of the events of September 11, 2001, despite the public efforts of many Arabs and Muslims to proclaim their loyalty to the United States.

11.6 Discuss the contemporary experiences of Arab and Muslim Americans.

6. Muslims and Arab Americans are diverse groups with differing beliefs regarding family and gender roles; however, both groups embrace education. Politics is becoming of more interest to both the Arab community and the Muslim community; these groups' interests are expanding beyond issues specific to the Middle East.

Key Terms

blended identity, *page 243*
casual Islamophobia, *page 249*
deficit model of ethnic
   identity, *page 242*
ethnocentrism, *page 239*
hajj, *page 245*

hijab, *page 252*
Islamophobia, *page 249*
jihad, *page 245*
nativism, *page 249*
orientalism, *page 239*

panethnicity, *page 242*
racial profiling, *page 255*
xenophobia, *page 249*

Review Questions

1. What are the dimensions of diversity among Arab Americans?

2. How would you characterize the Muslim faith in the United States?

3. How has the immigration of Muslims and Arabs been influenced by U.S. government policies?

4. What is the extent of Islamophobia in your community?

5. Summarize the approaches of Arab and Muslim Americans toward family, education, gender roles, and politics.

Critical Thinking

1. Apply the deficit model of ethnic identity to another group besides Arab Americans.

2. How are the Arab and Muslim communities varied in terms of language, social class, citizenship status, nationality, and religion?

3. Identify groups other than Arab Americans and Muslim Americans that have recently been

subjected to prejudice, perhaps in your own community.

4. What are some characteristics associated with Muslim and Arab Americans that have come to be viewed as negatives, but when practiced by Christian Whites are seen as positives?

Chapter 12
Asian Pacific Americans: An Array of Nationalities

Brand X Pictures/Getty Images

⌄ Learning Objectives

12.1 Summarize the groups that comprise Asian Pacific American communities.

12.2 Explain the model minority image.

12.3 Describe the Asian Indian experience.

12.4 Describe the Filipino American experience.

12.5 Describe the Korean American experience.

12.6 Discuss the Southeast Asian American communities.

12.7 Explain how Hawai'i and its people embody cultural diversity.

If the diversity of racial and ethnic groups is not yet apparent in this book, one need only look at the diversity among those collectively labeled *Asian Pacific Americans* (APAs). Consider Priscilla Chan, who in May 2012 at age 27 was married and had sushi and Mexican food served at the reception. Both her parents, ethnic Chinese from Vietnam who arrived in the United States via refugee camps in the 1970s, worked such long hours in Boston restaurants that her grandmothers, who spoke no English, raised her. Born in the United States, Chan became the first person in her family to go to college, and she graduated from Harvard. She majored in biology and later taught grade school while attending medical school. Of special interest is the fact that she married a non-Asian (Facebook founder Mark Zuckerberg) and thus is an example of the 29 percent of recent Asian American newly-weds who married non-Asians.

One could also look at football in Texas. The phrase "Friday night lights" is synonymous with Texas high school football, but at one school, many of the players were born on the Pacific island of Tonga. As 6-foot-2-inch, 297-pound Trinity High offensive tackle Uatakini Cocker takes the line, he screams, "Mate ma'a Tonga," which means "I will die for Tonga." He is one of 16 Tongan Americans playing for the school. The team plays at a 12,000-seat stadium and has competed in 26 state playoffs. Trinity is located in Euless, which adjoins the Dallas-Fort Worth Airport, where Tongans first started working in the early 1970s. The success among some of these first immigrants initiated a pattern of **chain immigration**, whereby Tongan immigrants sponsor later immigrants. Euless boasts about 4,000 people who were either born in Tonga or are their descendants.

Also Consider "The 100 Years Living Club," a group of elderly immigrants from India who gather at a mall in Fremont, California. These elders may talk about the latest community news, cheap flights to Delhi, or their latest run-ins with their daughters-in-law.

Then there is Vietnamese American Tuan Nguyren, in his mid-fifties, who tends to 80 areas in rural South Carolina, where he oversees 160,000 chickens. His wife lives 50 miles away, where she operates a nail salon. They get together about once a week, and the main topic of conversation is how they are putting their four daughters through college. Making a poultry farm succeed is hard work, and Nguyren has mentored other Vietnamese Americans who have struggled with the effort.

Finally, we could venture to Minot, North Dakota, and dine at Charlie's Main Street Café on chicken fried steak and mashed potatoes. The proprietor is Korean-born Geewon Anderson, who came here via Anchorage and Minneapolis. Ranch dressing and sunny-side-ups were all new to her, but she is already seen as a fixture in a city of 40,000 that is 94 percent White. At night, she relaxes by watching Korean soap operas on satellite television (Brown 2009; Copeland 2011; Eligon 2013; Euless Historical Preservation Committee 2011; Holson and Bilton 2012; Longman 2008; Small 2011).

Immigration to the United States is more than quaint turn-of-the-century black-and-white photos taken at Ellis Island of arrivals from Europe. Immigration, race, and ethnicity are being lived out among people of all ages, and for no collective group is this truer than for Asian Pacific Americans (APAs), who live throughout the United States but are not evenly distributed across the states (Figure 12.1). California has the largest APA population, and Hawai'i has the largest proportion of APAs.

Figure 12.1 Where Most Asian Pacific Americans Live

SOURCE: Based on American Community Survey 2015a: Table PEPSR5H

1.1–6.7 million
500,000–900,000
200,000–499,000
100,000–199,000
Less than 100,000

Overview of Asian Pacific Americans

12.1 **Summarize the groups that comprise Asian Pacific American communities.**

The successive waves of immigrants to the United States from the continent of Asia and many Pacific islands comprise a large number of nationalities and cultures. In addition to the seven specific nationality groups listed in Figure 12.2 are a diverse group of peoples who are collectively referred to as Asian Pacific Americans (APAs) and sometimes as Asian Pacific Islanders.

Besides the different nationalities and cultures represented, another distinguishing dimension is the conditions under which the original immigrants came to the United States. Some were recruited for work that ranged from unskilled labor (such as farmwork) to highly skilled professions, including medicine, engineering, and technology. Others came to the United States as refugees or to escape religious or political oppression. These differences have and will continue to influence the experience in the United States for immigrants and their descendants (Lee and Zhou 2014b).

Diversity

The different groups of Asian Pacific Americans have little in common. They do not share religion, language, or alphabet, and what common history is present usually includes centuries of conflict (for example, between the Chinese and Japanese people). Rather, these peoples are grouped by an expansive geographical location that encompasses eastern and southern Asia and the many islands in the Pacific Ocean. It should be noted that the Russian Federation includes many people who would normally be considered Asian, but because of census classifications based on nation of birth are considered "Russian" and thus fall under the umbrella of immigrants from Europe. The U.S. Bureau of the Census and the Social Security Administration distinguish among 60 APA nationality, ethnic, and tribal groups, as Table 12.1 shows.

A recent survey asked: "Which geographical region has been the largest source of immigrants to the United States in the last few years?"

- 70 percent said "Latin America," but that answer is wrong.

- 13 percent said "Middle East." This answer is also incorrect.

    Only 7 percent gave the correct answer of "Asia" (Lopez, Passel, and Rohal 2015).

Figure 12.2 Asian Pacific Americans

Chinese Americans are the largest group, but Indian, Filipino, and Vietnamese Americans all number over 1 million.

NOTE: Lists all specific groups with more than 750,000 members.
SOURCE: Based on American Community Survey 2015a: B02006, B2016

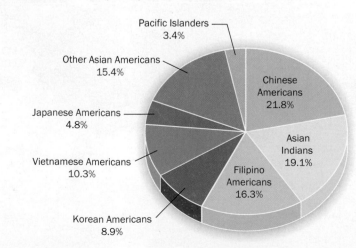

Pacific Islanders 3.4%
Other Asian Americans 15.4%
Japanese Americans 4.8%
Vietnamese Americans 10.3%
Korean Americans 8.9%
Chinese Americans 21.8%
Asian Indians 19.1%
Filipino Americans 16.3%

Table 12.1 Asian Pacific American Groups in the United States

Asian	Pacific Islander
Afghan	Carolinian
Asian Indian	Chuukese
Bangladeshi	Cook Islander
Bhutanese	Fijian
Bruneian	Guamanian or Chamorro
Burmese	I-Kiribati
Cambodian	Kosraean
Celebesian	Maori
Chinese	Mariana Islander
Filipino	Marshallese
Hmong	Melanesian
Indonesian	Micronesian
Iwo Jiman	Native Hawaiian
Japanese	Nauruan
Javanese	New Caledonian
Korean	Niuean
Laotian	Ni-Vanuatu
Malaysian	Palauan
Maldivian	Papua New Guinean
Mongolese	Pohnpeian
Montagnard	Polynesian
Nepalese	Saipanese
Okinawan	Samoan
Pakistani	Solomon Islander
Singaporean	Tahitian
Sri Lankan	Tuvaluan
Taiwanese	Tokelauan
Thai	Tongan
Tibetan	Trukese
Vietnamese	Yapese

NOTE: Groups as enumerated separately in the 2010 census or so designated by the Social Security Administration.

SOURCE: Hixson, Hepler, and Kim 2012:16; Hoeffel, Rastagi, Kim, and Shahid 2012:14; Social Security Administration 2017.

Collectively, in 2014, APAs in the United States numbered about 22 million—a 9 percent increase since 2010. APA immigration has outpaced Latino immigration since the beginning of the twenty-first century. Before 2009, APA immigration exceeded that of all Latinos entering the country. Since 2013, China and India combined have overtaken Mexico as the largest source of immigrants (American Community Survey 2015a; Taylor 2013).

The continued growth of the APA population is not expected to slow anytime soon. The overall population change of the United States between 2014 and 2060 is projected at about 31 percent, but the Asian American population is expected to grow by 128 percent and the Pacific Islander population by 63 percent. These increases are much larger than those of White Americans and greatly surpass projected growth among African Americans and Latinos (Colby and Ortman 2015).

The diversity among APAs leads to some of the same generalizations made about Native Americans. Both groups are a collection of diverse peoples with distinct

Table 12.2 Asian Pacific Origin Groups

Group	Foreign-Born	Bachelor's Degree	Proficient in English	Poverty Rate
Chinese Americans	76	51	52	14
Asian Indians	87	70	76	9
Filipino Americans	69	47	48	6
Vietnamese Americans	84	26	41	15
Korean Americans	78	53	64	15
Japanese Americans	32	46	82	8
General U.S. Population	16	28	90	13

NOTE: Based on 2012 national survey except for poverty rate, which is based on 2010 income.

SOURCE: Pew Social and Demographic Trends 2012: 13, 30, 33, 37, 41, 44, 47, 50.

linguistic, social, and geographic backgrounds. Perhaps the most "shared" trait is that many Americans make little distinction between APAs, just as they fail to see differences among Native Americans.

As Table 12.2 shows, even limiting the analysis to the six largest groups shows quite a range in the proportion of foreign-born people, attainment of a college degree, proficiency in English, and poverty rate.

Despite the large APA population—which already exceeds the total African American population—many APAs feel ignored. They see "race and ethnicity" in America framed as a Black–White issue or, more recently, as a "triracial" issue that includes Hispanics. But where are the Asian Americans in these generalizations about the United States? For example, tens of thousands of Asian Americans, especially Vietnamese Americans, were displaced by Hurricane Katrina in 2005, but they received little media attention. Immigration issues often focus on Latin America, but what about challenges facing Asians who seek legal entry to the United States or the Asian Americans who are already here?

Political Activity and Pan-Asian Identity

For young APAs, life in the United States often is a struggle for identity because their heritage is often devalued by those in positions of influence. Sometimes identity means finding a role in White America; other times, it involves finding a place among Asian Americans collectively and then locating oneself within one's own racial or ethnic community.

Individually, APAs are more likely to identify themselves by their country of origin than by some broader label like "Asian American." A 2012 survey showed that 62 percent prefer using nation of origin (Chinese or Chinese American). Almost equal numbers see themselves as American (14 percent) as Asian or Asian American (19 percent). As time passes between the initial immigrant's arrival and with each successive generation, identification with the nation of origin fades. This trend is also facilitated by intermarriage. Overall, in a three-year period (2008–2010), about 29 percent of APAs married a non-Asian, and another 6 percent married a person from a different Asian group. Interestingly, opinion surveys show that APAs make little distinction between out-marriage to a non-Asian or to an APA from a different country—that, for a Japanese American, marrying a White American or a Chinese American is about the same (Taylor 2013).

Against this backdrop of a search for identity, it is no surprise to see APAs seeking recognition for themselves. Historically, APAs have followed the pattern of other immigrant groups: They bring social organizations, associations, and clubs from the homeland and later develop groups to respond to the special needs identified in the United States.

Rather than being docile, as APAs are often labeled, they have organized in labor unions, played a significant role in campus protests, and been active in immigration rights issues. In the wake of boosted anti-immigrant sentiments after 9/11, APAs staged demonstrations in several cities in an effort to persuade people to become citizens and register to vote. They were once again visible in protests during the controversy over immigration reform in 2015–2016 and strongly opposed any ban on Muslim immigrants (Chang 2007; Ramakrishnan 2016).

The Voting Rights Act requires Asian-language materials in cities and counties where either 5 percent or 10,000 voting-age citizens speak the same native Asian language and have limited English proficiency. Following the release of the 2010 Census, that act now applies to cities in Alaska, California, Hawai'i, Illinois, Massachusetts, Michigan, Nevada, New Jersey, New York, Texas, and Washington (Pratt 2012).

Democrats and Republicans are increasingly regarding APAs as a growing political force in the United States. For some time, the Republicans and Democrats seemed to evenly share the APA electorate. Increasingly, Asian American voters have backed the Democratic Party. In 2012, President Obama received a 73 percent backing from APAs in his bid for re-election. National survey data in 2016 showed that about two-thirds of APAs lean toward the Democrats in general. However, there are differences among APA groups. Asian Indians, Japanese Americans, and Korean Americans are the most pro-Democrat. Cambodian and Vietnamese Americans are pro-Democrat, but they are less enthusiastic about it. Of special note is the potential influence of APA voters in swing states like Nevada, North Carolina, and Virginia (Peters 2016; Ramakrishnan 2016).

Issues like immigration and talk of increased deportations often transcend party politics and unify APAs. So do sporadic issues of violence. Such was the case of New York police officer Peter Liang, who was born in Hong Kong. Liang had been on the job for just a year and a half when he fired his gun in a housing project's darkened stairwell. That shot killed an African American man who just happened to be visiting his girlfriend. Liang was convicted of manslaughter, and thousands of APAs joined in protest over what they saw as "selective justice," pointing to all the White law-enforcement officers who had not been prosecuted for similar on-duty fatal shootings (Bruinius 2016).

Despite the diversity among groups of Asian Americans and Asian Pacific Islanders, they have been treated as a monolithic group for generations. Out of similar experiences have come panethnic identities in which people share a self-image, as do African Americans or Whites of European descent. As noted in Chapter 1, **panethnicity** is the development of solidarity between ethnic subgroups. Are APAs finding a panethnic identity?

It is true that in the United States, extremely different Asian and Pacific Islander nationalities have been lumped together in past discrimination and current stereotypes. The majority of research supports the idea that APAs identify by their own nationality group, but it also indicates that most *sometimes* think of themselves as APA. Some observers contend that a move toward a pan-Asian identity represents a step in assimilation by downplaying cultural differences (Espiritu 1992; Wong et al. 2011).

Pan-Asian identity often serves to solidify and strengthen organizing at the grassroots level when APAs are trying to bring about change in neighborhoods and communities where they are outnumbered and underrepresented in the corridors of political power. From this perspective, pan-Asian unity is necessary and urgent for all Asian groups (Mitra 2008; Okamoto and Gast 2013).

Mark Lynch/CartoonStock.com

Is There a Model Minority?

12.2 **Explain the model minority image.**

"Asian Americans are a success! They achieve! They succeed! They have no protests, no demands. They just do it!" This is the general image that people in the United States often hold of Asian Americans as a group. APAs constitute a **model minority** because, although they have experienced prejudice and discrimination, they seem to have succeeded economically, socially, and educationally without resorting to political or violent confrontations with Whites.

Some observers point to the existence of a model minority as a reaffirmation that anyone can get ahead in the United States. Proponents of the model minority view declare that because Asian Americans have achieved success, they have ceased to be subordinate and are no longer disadvantaged. This labeling is a variation of **blaming the victim**: With Asian Americans, it is praising the victim. Examining aspects of the educational and economic status of Asian Americans allows a more thorough exploration of this view (Ryan 1976).

Educational Levels

Asian Americans, as a group, have impressive school-enrollment rates in comparison to the total population. In 2010, half of Asian Americans 25 years of age or older held bachelor's degrees, compared with 28 percent of the White population. These rates vary among Asian American groups: Asian Indians, Filipino Americans, Korean Americans, Chinese Americans, and Japanese Americans have higher levels of educational achievement than other Asian American groups. In fact, Indian Americans as a group are more likely to have a college degree than Whites. Yet other groups, such as Vietnamese Americans, the Hmong, and Pacific Islanders, including Native Hawaiians, have much lower levels of education than White Americans (Bureau of the Census 2007b, 2011a; Guillermo 2015; Taylor 2013).

However, this encouraging picture regarding some Asian Americans does have some qualifications that question the optimistic model minority view. According to a study of California's state university system, although Asian Americans often are viewed as successful overachievers, they have unrecognized and overlooked needs, and they have experienced discomfort and harassment on campus. As a group, they also lack Asian faculty and staff members to whom they can turn for support. They confront many identity issues and must do a "cultural balancing act" along with all the usual pressures faced by college students. The report noted that an "alarming number" of Asian American students appear to be experiencing intense stress and alienation, problems that have often been "exacerbated by racial harassment" (Ohnuma 1991; Teranishi 2010).

Even the positive stereotype of Asian American students as academic stars or whiz kids can be burdensome to the people so labeled. Asian Americans who do only modestly well in school may face criticism from their parents or teachers for their failure to conform to the whiz kid image. Some Asian American youths disengage from school when faced with these expectations or receive little support for their interest in vocational pursuits or athletics (Lee and Zhou 2014a).

Sippakorn / Shutterstock

While the widely held public perception is that Asian Americans have a fast track to college, many Asian Americans perceive that admissions policies work against them. The culprits, in their view, are:

- limits or quotas limits on the number of Asian Americans at highly selective universities, and

- affirmative action that works against them by failing to consider them as eligible.

Recall that **affirmative action** refers to positive efforts to recruit subordinate group members for jobs, promotions, and educational opportunities.

Asian Americans have been vocal in saying that they are not generally considered in such programs and that in fact they lose places to less-qualified Whites.

Indeed, some activist Asian American groups were conspicuously vocal in their disappointment in the *Fischer* Supreme Court case that ruled against the White plaintiff who felt she was unfairly passed over for admission in Texas. Efforts are underway to force elite institutions like Harvard, Yale, Dartmouth, and Brown to make public their admissions records. While Asian Americans account for 15 percent to 25 percent of Ivy League college enrollment, some argue that the percentage would be even greater if they were treated like White applicants, or even like African American and Latino high school graduates. Many argue that this barrier to advancement continues in the labor market (Asian-American Coalition for Education 2017; Bachelder 2015; The Economist 2014).

Economic Status

APAs account for almost 6 percent of the U.S. population, but they represent fewer than 2 percent of Fortune 500 CEOs and corporate officers. Most of these standouts are immigrants who started up successful technological and information companies. A national survey showed that APAs who are successful in the corporate world must manage themselves so they don't seem "too ambitious" or have "too many ideas." Only 28 percent of Asian Americans feel very comfortable "being themselves" at the workplace, compared to 45 percent of African Americans, 41 percent of Latinos, and 42 percent of White workers (Center for Work-Life Policy 2011; Chin 2016).

Despite the widespread belief that they constitute a model minority, APAs are victims of both prejudice and violence. At issue is what has been termed the "perpetual foreigner" view of APAs. After the terrorist attacks of September 11, 2001, anti-Asian violence increased dramatically for several months in the United States. The first fatality was an Asian Indian American who was shot and killed by a gunman in Mesa, Arizona; the gunman shouted, "I stand for America all the way" (National Asian Pacific American Legal Consortium 2002; Xu and Lee 2013).

This anti–Asian American feeling is built on a long cultural tradition. The term *yellow peril* dates back to the view of Asian immigration, particularly from China, as unwelcome. **Yellow peril** came to refer to the generalized prejudice toward Asian people and their customs. The immigrants were characterized as heathen, morally inferior, drug addicted, savage, or lustful. Although the term was first used around the turn of the twentieth century, this anti-Asian sentiment is very much alive today. Many contemporary Asian Americans find this intolerance very unsettling given their conscientious efforts to extend their education, seek employment, and conform to the norms of society. Hate crimes against APAs persist and have even risen in recent years (Hurh 1994; Lee et al., 2007).

The resentment against APAs is not limited to overt expressions of violence. Like other subordinate groups, APAs are subject to institutional discrimination. As defined in Chapter 3, **institutional discrimination** is the denial of opportunities and equal rights to individuals and groups that results from the normal operations of a society. For example, some APA groups have large families and find themselves subject to zoning laws stipulating the number of people per room, which makes it difficult for family members to live together. Kinfolk are unable to legally take in family members. Whereas we may regard these family members as distant relatives, many Asian cultures view cousins, uncles, and aunts as relatives to whom they have a great deal of familial responsibility.

The marginal status of APAs leaves them vulnerable to both selective and collective oppression. In 1999, news stories implicated Wen Ho Lee, a nuclear physicist at Los Alamos National Laboratory in New Mexico, as a spy for China. Subsequent investigation, during which Lee was imprisoned under very harsh conditions, concluded that the naturalized citizen scientist had indeed downloaded secret files to an unsecured computer, but there was no evidence that the information ever went further.

In the aftermath of the Wen Ho Lee incident, a new form of racial profiling emerged. Recall that **racial profiling** is any police-initiated action that relies on race, ethnicity, or national origin rather than a person's behavior. Despite Lee being found not guilty, Asian Americans were viewed as security risks. A survey found that 32 percent of the people in the United States felt that Chinese Americans are more loyal to China than to the United States. In fact, the same survey showed that 46 percent were concerned about Chinese Americans passing secrets to China. Subsequent studies found that Asian Americans were avoiding top-secret science labs for employment because they became subject to racial profiling at higher security levels (Committee of 100 2001; Department of Energy 2000; Lee with Zia 2006; Wu 2002).

Another misleading sign of the apparent success of APAs is their high incomes as a group. APA family income approaches parity with that of Whites because of their greater achievement than Whites in formal schooling. If we look at specific educational levels, however, Whites earn more than their Asian counterparts of the same age. APAs' average earnings increased by at least $2,300 for each additional year of schooling, whereas Whites gained almost $3,000. APAs as a group have significantly more formal schooling but have lower household family income. We should note that to some degree, some APAs' education is from overseas and, therefore, may be devalued by U.S. employers. Yet, in the end, educational attainment does not pay off as much if one is of Asian descent as it does for White non-Hispanics (Kim and Sakamoto 2010; Zeng and Xie 2004).

So even with all the "tools" to succeed—supportive family, high achievement, and often attending prestigious schools—APAs often hit what has been termed a *bamboo ceiling*. The **bamboo ceiling** refers to the barrier that talented APAs face because of resentment and intolerance directed toward them. The bamboo ceiling is clearly a nod to the term *glass ceiling*, which has historically been used to address barriers that women and minority-group men have faced in the workplace. For example, 11 percent of law firm associates were APAs as of 2014, but only 3 percent of partners were APAs. The presence of the bamboo ceiling reflects the cultural values and social norms that impact Asian professionals' interactions with others and cause others to make negative judgments about them (The Economist 2015b; Hyun 2006, 2009).

Striking contrasts are evident among APAs. For every APA household in 2015 with an annual combined income of $200,000 or more, another household earns fewer than $20,000 a year. Collectively, 11.4 percent of APAs were below the poverty level in 2015 compared to 9.1 percent of White non-Hispanics. Almost every APA group has a higher poverty rate than White non-Hispanics. The lone exception is Filipinos, who tend to live in the relatively high-income states of Hawai'i and California (Proctor, Semega, and Kollar 2016: Table A-1; National CAPACD 2012).

At first, one might be puzzled to see criticism of a positive generalization such as "model minority." Why should the stereotype of adjusting without problems be a disservice to APAs? The answer is that this incorrect view excludes APAs from social programs and conceals unemployment and other social ills. When representatives of Asian groups seek assistance for those in need, people who have accepted the model minority stereotype resent them. This problem is especially troubling given that issues of substance abuse and juvenile delinquency need to be addressed within the APA community.

According to research, the model minority myth seems to be embraced by people who subscribe to **color-blind racism**—the use of race-neutral principles to defend the racially unequal status quo. Individuals who view APAs as uniformly successful are also likely to see discrimination as absent in both school and work; for them, inequality is essentially a thing of the past. They also endorse anti-APA sentiments such as seeing them as perpetual foreigners (Parks and Yoo 2016).

The positive stereotype of the model minority reaffirms the U.S. system of mobility: New immigrants, as well as established subordinate groups, ought to achieve more merely by working within the system. At the same time, viewed from the conflict perspective outlined in Chapter 1, the model minority myth is yet another instance of blaming the victim: If Asian Pacific Americans have succeeded, then Blacks and Latinos must be responsible for their own low status, thus absolving society of any responsibility (Chen 2012; Chou and Feagin 2008; Xu and Lee 2013).

Asian Indians

12.3 Describe the Asian Indian experience.

The second-largest APA group (after Chinese Americans) is composed of immigrants from India and their descendants. This group numbers over 2.8 million. This is quite a change since the arrival of some 6,000 Indians from Asia between 1904 and 1911 to work as farmhands.

Immigration

Like several other Asian immigrant groups, Asian Indians (or East Indians) are recent immigrants. Only 17,000 total came to the United States between 1820 and 1965, with the majority of those arriving before 1917. These pioneers were subjected to some of the same anti-Asian measures that restricted Chinese immigration. For example, the Supreme Court (1923) ruled that Asian Indians could not become naturalized citizens because they were not White and therefore were excluded under the 1917 law that applied to all natives of Asia. This prohibition continued until 1946.

Immigration law in the second half of the twentieth century dropped nationality preferences, although it gave priority to the skilled, so the Asian Indians arriving from the 1960s through the 1980s tended to be urban, educated, and English-speaking. More than twice the proportion of Asian Indians age 25 and older had a college degree, compared with the general U.S. population. These families experienced a smooth transition from life in India to life in the United States. They usually settled in urban areas or near universities or medical centers. Initially, they flocked to the Northeast, but by 1990, California had edged out New York as the state with the largest concentration of Asian Indians. The growth of Silicon Valley's information technology industry further expanded the number of Asian Indian professionals in northern California. Today, more than a quarter of the Indian-born workforce is employed in the tech industry. Half of all skilled workers under the H-1B visa program since 2005 have come from India (Bureau of the Census 2007a; Chakravorty, Kapur, and Singh 2017; Purnell 2017).

Some recent immigrants, sponsored by earlier immigrant relatives, are displaying less facility with English, and the training they have tends to be less easily adapted to the U.S. workplace. They are more likely to work in service industries, usually with members of their extended families. They also often take positions that many Americans reject because of the long hours, the seven-day workweek, and vulnerability to crime. Consequently, Asian Indians are as likely to be cab drivers or managers of motels or convenience stores as they are to be physicians or college professors. Asian Indians see the service industries as transitional jobs to acclimatize them to the United States and to give them the money they need to become more economically self-reliant (Dhingra 2012; Kalita 2003).

Ties to the homeland are most economically apparent in remittances to India, estimated at $71 billion per year. The United States is the second-largest source of remittances to India (after the United Arab Emirates). The money goes to relatives and communities, and it can even be significant enough to build an entire *airport* (toward which 10,000 Indians contributed) (Chakravorty, Kapur, and Singh 2017; The Economist 2015a).

The Current Picture

It is difficult to generalize about Asian Indians because, like all other Asian Americans, they reflect a diverse population in their home country. With more than 1.3 billion people in 2017, India will be the most populous nation in the world by 2025. Diversity governs every area. The Indian government recognizes 18 official languages, each with its own cultural heritage. Some languages can be written in more than one type of script. Hindus are the majority in India and also among the immigrants to the United States, but significant religious minorities include Sikhs, Muslims, Jains, and Zoroastrians.

Religion among Asian Indians presents a diverse picture. About half (51.2 percent) are Hindu, 19 percent are Christian, and 10 percent are Muslim. Among initial immigrants, religious orthodoxy often is stronger than it is in India. Many Asian Indians also recognize local practices, with 73 percent of the Hindus in the United States celebrating Christmas.

Although other Indian traditions are maintained, older immigrants see challenges not only from U.S. culture but also from pop culture from India, which is imported through motion pictures and magazines. The situation is very dynamic as the Asian Indian population navigates the twenty-first century in the United States (Kurien 2004, 2007; Pew Forum on Religion and Public Life 2012).

In the Research Focus, we consider one cultural practice faced by Asian Indians and other immigrant groups that is not a part of American mainstream culture: arranged marriages.

Research Focus

Arranged Marriages in America

In some cultures, the proverbial question is not "Does he or she love me?" but rather "Whom do my parents want me to marry?" An **arranged marriage** occurs when others (often the parents) choose a person's marital partner. Typically, in arranged marriages, the two people in the couple do not even know each other, much less have any mutual romantic interest.

The idea of arranged marriages seems strange to most youth growing up in the U.S. culture that romanticizes finding Mr. or Ms. Right. In an arranged marriage, the bride and groom start off on neutral ground, with no expectations of each other. Understanding develops between them as the relationship matures. The couple selected is assumed to be compatible because they are chosen from very similar social, economic, and cultural backgrounds.

Historically, arranged marriages are not unusual and even today are common in many parts of Asia and Africa. In cultures where arranged marriage is common, young people tend to be socialized to expect and look forward to such unions.

But what happens in cultures that send very different messages? For example, immigrants from India, Pakistan, Bangladesh, and Nigeria may desire that their children enter an arranged union, but their children are growing up in a culture where many of their schoolmates are obsessed with dating as a prelude to marriage and endlessly discuss the latest episodes of *The Bachelor* and *The Bachelorette*.

Are arranged marriages in the United States successful? Several studies (based on small samples) have attempted to answer this question and have come to widely different conclusions. Such studies have reached widely different conclusions. Some studies have found that arranged marriages result in higher marital satisfaction, while other studies find lower marital satisfaction or no difference from love-based marriages.

Studies of young people (in countries such as Canada and the United States) whose parents still cling to the tradition of arranging their children's marriages document the challenges of arranged marriages. Many young people do still embrace their parents' tradition. As one first-year female Princeton student of Asian Indian ancestry put it, "In a lot of ways, it's easier. I don't have pressure to look for a boyfriend" (Herschthal 2004). Young people like her will look to their parents and other relatives to finalize a mate or accept a match with a partner who has been selected in their parents' home country.

In some cases, arranged marriages have been modified to *assisted marriages* in which parents identify a limited number of possible mates based on "bio-data" that screen for caste, family background, and geography. Children get final veto power but rarely head out on their own when seeking a mate. Young men and women may date on their own, but when it comes to marrying, they limit themselves to a very narrow field of eligibles brought to them by their parents.

The combination of arranged and assisted marriages has meant that Asian Indian immigrants have the highest rates of ethnic endogamy (in-group marriage) of any major immigrant group in the United States—about 92 percent in-group marriage, with the majority of Indian American couples including spouses who were both raised in the United States.

Sources: Bellafante 2005; Chakravorty, Kapur, and Singh 2017; Johnson and Bachan 2013; Regan, Lakhanpal, and Anguiano 2012.

Maintaining traditions within the family household is a major challenge for Asian Indian immigrants to the United States. These ties remain strong, and many Asian Indians see themselves as more connected to their relatives 10,000 miles away than Americans are to their kinfolk less than 100 miles away. Parents are concerned about the erosion of traditional family authority. For example, Asian Indian children, dressed like their peers, go to fast-food restaurants and eat hamburgers while out on their own, yet Hindus and many Asian Indian Muslims are vegetarians. Sons do not always feel the responsibility to the family that tradition dictates. Daughters, whose occupation and marriage could, in India, be closely controlled by the family, assert their right to choose work and, in an even more dramatic break from tradition, select their husbands.

Until recently Asian Indians reported little ill treatment. A 2012 survey found that 10 percent regard discrimination as a minor problem, with only 18 percent reporting that they had been treated unfairly because of their national origin. High-profile events have changed that perception as Indian Americans have literally entered the crosshairs of anti–Middle Eastern bigotry. Notably, in 2017, two Asian Indian American engineers were shot (one fatally) by a man drunkenly telling them to "go home." Within two weeks of that incident, another Indian American in Washington State was shot in his driveway by a gunman who shouted, "Go back to your country." These incidents have added to growing insecurity in India among those contemplating going to college or seeking work in the United States. Public disclosures that President Trump's administration was considering significantly cutting back on the H-1B visa program has only fueled these concerns (Barry and Najar 2017; Purnell 2017; Sahgal 2013).

Like other immigrant groups, Asian Indians to varying degrees maintain their cultural traditions. These traditions may represent no more than **symbolic ethnicity**—the emphasis on ethnic food and ethnically associated political causes rather than deeper ties to one's heritage. For Indian Americans, symbolic ethnicity sometimes means attending India cinema ("Bollywood") or musical performances. Another activity growing in popularity is Indian-style dancing. *Bhanga* dancing, a celebratory folk dance once confined to one area of India, has become common not only at Indian American weddings but also at other times. Cities and college teams take part in well-attended "blowouts" (competitions) pitting the best against the best (Chacko and Menon 2013; Chakravorty, Kapur, and Singh 2017).

An international Bhangra music and dance troop performs in Long Beach, California as part of a dance competition produced by Asian Indian students at UCLA. The Bhangra is a kind of folk dance that is performed at the time of crop harvesting in the northern states of India.

Filipino Americans

12.4 Describe the Filipino American experience.

Little has been written about the Filipinos, although they are the third-largest APA group in the United States, after Chinese and Indians. Social science literature considers them Asians for geographic reasons, but physically and culturally, they also reflect centuries of Spanish colonial rule and the more recent U.S. colonial government and occupation.

Immigration Patterns

Immigration from the Philippines has been documented since the eighteenth century; it was relatively small but significant enough to create a "Manila Village" along the Louisiana coast around 1750. Increasing numbers of Filipino immigrants came as American nationals when, in 1899, the United States gained possession of the Philippine Islands at the conclusion of the Spanish–American War. In 1934, the islands gained commonwealth status. The Philippines gained their independence in 1948 and with it lost their unrestricted immigration rights. Despite the close ties that remained, immigration was sharply restricted to only 50–100 people annually until the 1965 Immigration Act lifted these quotas. Before the restrictions were removed, pineapple growers in Hawai'i lobbied successfully to import Filipino workers to the islands.

Besides serving as colonial subjects of the United States, Filipinos played another role in this country. The U.S. military accepted Filipinos for selected positions. In particular, the Navy put Filipino citizens to work in kitchens. Filipino veterans of World War II believed that their U.S. citizenship would be expedited. This expectation proved unfounded; the problem was only partially resolved by a 1994 federal court ruling. However, it was not until a special presidential action in 2009 that Filipino American veterans received compensation to partially acknowledge their service in World War II. Finally, in 2016, Filipino Americans received the medals of valor customarily granted to other soldiers and veterans (NaFFAA 2016; Padilla 2008a; Perry and Simon 2009).

Filipino immigration can be divided into four distinct periods:

1. The first generation, which immigrated in the 1920s, was mostly male and employed in agricultural labor.

2. A second group, which also arrived in the early twentieth century, immigrated to Hawai'i to serve as contract workers on Hawai'i's sugar plantations.

Filipino Americans protest in Washington, DC for full veteran benefits for Filipinos who served in World War II.

3. The post–World War II arrivals included many war veterans and wives of U.S. soldiers.

4. The newest immigrants, who include many professionals (physicians, nurses, and others), arrived under the 1965 Immigration Act. More than 40 percent of Filipino Americans have immigrated since 1990 (Bureau of the Census 2007a; McNamara and Batalova 2015).

As in other Asian groups, the people are diverse. In addition to these stages of immigration, Filipinos can also be defined by various states of immigration (different languages, regions of origin, and religions)—distinctions that sharply separate people in their homeland as well. In the Philippines and among Filipino immigrants to the United States, eight distinct languages with an estimated 200 dialects are spoken. Yet assimilation is underway; a 1995 survey showed that 47 percent of younger Filipino Americans speak only English and do not speak Tagalog, the primary language of the Philippine people (Bonus 2000; Kang 1996; Pido 1986).

The Current Picture

The Filipino population increased dramatically when restrictions on immigration were eased in 1965. About 40 percent of the new arrivals qualified for entry as professional and technical workers, but like Koreans, they have often worked at jobs ranked below those they left in the Philippines. Surprisingly, U.S.-born Filipinos often have less formal schooling and lower job status than the newer arrivals. The U.S.-born come from poorer families that are unable to afford higher education, and they have been relegated to unskilled work, including migrant farmwork. Their poor economic background means that they have little start-up capital for businesses. Therefore, unlike other Asian American groups, Filipinos have not developed small business bases such as retail or service outlets that capitalize on their ethnic culture.

A significant segment of the immigration from the Philippines, however, constitutes a more professional educated class in the area of health professionals. Although a positive human resource for the United States, it has long been a **brain drain** on the medical establishment of the Philippines. Brain drain, as defined in Chapter 4, refers to the immigration of skilled workers, professionals, and technicians who are desperately needed in their home countries. When the United States ceased giving preference to physicians from abroad, doctors in the Philippines began to enter the United States retrained as nurses, which dramatically illustrates the huge income differences between the United States and the Philippines. The recent immigrants also send significant money back as remittances to help members of the extended family (DeSilver 2013; McNamara and Batalova 2015; Zarembro 2004).

Despite their numbers, no significant single national Filipino social organization has formed. There are several explanations. First, Filipinos' strong loyalty to family (*sa pamilya*) and church, particularly the Roman Catholic Church, works against time-consuming efforts to create organizations that include a broad spectrum of the Filipino community. Second, their diversity makes forming ties here problematic. Divisions along regional, religious, and linguistic lines present in the Philippines persist in the United States. Third, although Filipinos have organized many groups, those groups tend to be club-like or fraternal. They do not seek to represent the general Filipino population and, therefore, remain largely invisible to Anglos. Fourth, although Filipinos initially stayed close to events in their homeland, they show every sign of seeking involvement in broader non-Filipino organizations and avoiding group exclusiveness. Three-quarters of Filipino Americans are citizens, which is a larger proportion than for most APA groups (Bonus 2000; Kang 1996; Lau 2006; Posadas 1999; Taylor 2013).

Korean Americans

12.5 Describe the Korean American experience.

Korean Americans, numbering more than 1.4 million, are now the fifth-largest APA group, yet they often are overlooked in studies in favor of groups such as Chinese Americans and Japanese Americans, who have a longer historical tradition in the United States.

In 1948, Sammy Lee, born of Korean immigrants, became the first Asian American to win a gold medal at the Olympics. It was not an easy path to victory because he faced prejudice and discrimination in southern California. He was able to practice in the public pool only one day a week—the day on which the water was immediately drained and refilled. The rest of the time he was forced to dive into a pile of sand.

Historical Background

Today's Korean American community is the result of three waves of immigration. The initial wave of a little more than 7,000 immigrants came to the United States between 1903 and 1910, when laborers migrated to Hawai'i. Under Japanese colonial rule (1910–1945), Korean migration was halted except for a few hundred "picture brides" allowed to join their prospective husbands.

The second wave took place during and after the Korean War (1950–1953), accounting for about 14,000 immigrants from 1951 through 1964. Most of these immigrants were war orphans and wives of American servicemen. Little research has been done on these first two periods of immigration.

The third wave was initiated by the passage of the 1965 Immigration and Nationality Act, which made it much easier for Koreans to immigrate. In the four years before the passage of the act, Koreans accounted for only 7 of every 1,000 immigrants. In the first four years after the act's passage, 38 of every 1,000 immigrants to the United States were Korean. This third wave, which continues today, reflects the admission priorities set up in the 1965 immigration law. These immigrants have been well educated and have arrived in the United States with professional skills. More than 40 percent of Korean Americans have arrived in the United States since 1990, but by 2011 immigration had slowed to a trickle of fewer than 5,000 annually (Bureau of the Census 2007b; Dolnick 2011; Kim and Yoo 2008; Min 2013).

However, many of the most recent immigrants must at least initially settle for positions of lower responsibility than those they held in Korea and must pass through a period of economic adjustment and even disenchantment that can last for several years. These problems document the pain of adjustment: stress, loneliness, alcoholism, family strife, and mental disorders. Korean American immigrants who accompanied their parents to the United States when young now occupy a middle, marginal position between the cultures of Korea and the United States. They have been called the **ilcho-mose**, or "1.5 generation." Today, they are middle-aged, remain bilingual and bicultural, and tend to form the professional class in the Korean American community (Hurh 1998; Kim 2006).

The Current Picture

Today's young Korean Americans (almost all of whose parents come from South Korea, not North Korea) face many of the cultural conflicts common to any initial generation born in a new country. The parents may speak the native tongue, but the signs on the road to opportunity are in the English language, and the road itself runs through U.S. culture. It is very difficult to maintain a sense of Korean culture in the United States; the host society is not particularly helpful. Although the United States fought a war there and U.S. troops remain in South Korea, Korean culture is foreign to most contemporary Americans. In the few studies of attitudes toward Koreans, White Americans respond with vague negative attitudes or simply lump Korean Americans with other Asian groups.

Studies by social scientists indicate that Korean Americans face many problems typical for immigrants, such as difficulties with language—53 percent of Korean Americans report limited English proficiency. In Los Angeles, home to the largest concentration, more than 100 churches have only Korean-language services, and local television stations feature several hours of Korean programs. The Korean immigrants' high level of education should help them cope with the challenge. Although Korean Americans stress conventional Western schooling as a means to success, Korean schools have also been established in major cities. Typically operated on Saturday afternoons, they offer classes in Korean history, customs, music, and language to help students maintain their cultural identity Hurh and Kim 1984; Johnson et al. 2010; Zong and Batalova 2014).

Korean American women commonly participate in the labor force, as do many other Asian American women. About 60 percent of U.S.-born Korean American women and half the Korean American women born abroad work in the labor force. These figures may not seem striking compared with the data for White women, but the cultural differences make the figures more significant. Korean women come here from a family system with established, well-defined marital roles: The woman is expected to serve as homemaker and mother only. Although these roles are carried over to the United States, because of their husbands' struggles to establish themselves, women are pressed to help support their families financially as well.

Many Korean American men begin small service or retail businesses and gradually involve their wives in the business. Wages do not matter because the household mobilizes to make a profitable enterprise out of a marginal business. Under economic pressure, Korean American women must move away from traditional cultural roles. However, the move is only partial; studies show that despite the high rate of participation in the labor force by Korean immigrant wives, first-generation immigrant couples continue in sharply divided gender roles in other aspects of daily living.

Korean American businesses are seldom major operations; most are small. They do benefit from a **kye** (pronounced "kay"), a special form of development capital (or cash) used to subsidize businesses called. Korean Americans pool their money through the kye, an association that grants members money on a rotating basis to allow them to gain access to additional capital. Kyes depend on trust and are not protected by laws or insurance, as bank loans are. Kyes work as follows: Say, for example, that 12 people agree to contribute $500 a year. Then, once a year, one of these individuals receives $6,000. Few records are kept, because the entire system is built on trust and friendship. Rotating credit associations are not unique to Korean Americans; West Indians and Ethiopians have used them in the United States also. Not all Korean business entrepreneurs use the kye, but it does represent a significant source of capital. Ironically, these so-called mom-and-pop entrepreneurs, as they encounter success, feel competitive pressure from national chains that come into their areas after Korean American businesses have created a consumer market (Reckard 2007; Watanabe 2007).

One area of Korean American commerce that has sometimes been tension-filled is reflected in relationships with African Americans, as discussed in the Relations Across Boundaries feature.

Among Korean Americans, the church is the most visible organization holding the group together. Half of the immigrants were affiliated with Christian churches before immigrating. One study of Koreans in Chicago and Los Angeles found that 70 percent were affiliated with Korean ethnic churches, mostly Presbyterian, with small numbers of Catholics and Methodists. Korean ethnic churches are the fastest-growing segment of the Presbyterian and Methodist faiths. The church performs an important function, apart from its religious one, in giving Korean Americans a sense of attachment and a practical way to meet other Korean Americans. The churches are much more than simply sites for religious services; they assume multiple secular roles for the Korean community. As the second generation seeks a church with which to affiliate as adults, they may find the ethnic church and its Korean-language services less attractive, but for now, the fellowship in which Korean Americans participate is both spiritual and ethnic (Min 2013).

Relations Across Boundaries

Black and Korean Americans

In the early 1990s, nationwide attention was focused on the friction between Korean Americans and other subordinate groups, primarily African Americans but also Hispanics. In New York City, Los Angeles, and Chicago, Korean American merchants confronted African Americans who were allegedly robbing them. The African American neighborhood groups sometimes responded with hostility to what they perceived as the disrespect and arrogance of the Korean American entrepreneurs toward their Black customers.

While intergroup contact can lead to less prejudice (as discussed in Chapter 2), the nature of the social interaction between Korean and Black Americans was not conducive to tolerance. On the one hand were the Korean American business owners, who typically lived outside the neighborhood, had limited English proficiency, and were seeking to maximize profits. On the other hand were the African American consumers with limited funds and even more limited opportunities of where to shop.

Why did Korean Americans set up shops in African American neighborhoods? Koreans often settled in urban areas seeking economic opportunities that seemed promising even if the businesses had been vacated by successful earlier immigrant groups and White entrepreneurs. Such friction is not new; earlier generations of Jewish, Italian, and Arab merchants encountered similar hostility from what seemed to be an unlikely source—another oppressed subordinate group.

The conflict was dramatized in Spike Lee's 1989 movie *Do the Right Thing*, in which African Americans and Korean Americans clashed. The situation arose because Korean Americans are the latest immigrant group prepared to cater to the needs of the inner city and, as of 2011, owned 70 percent of small grocery stores in New York City, which had been abandoned by business owners who have moved up the economic ladder. Not long after *Do the Right Thing* appeared in movie houses, the Korean American community in Los Angeles suffered devastating losses in the wake of the 1992 acquittal of police officers accused of beating African American motorist Rodney King. Ensuing riots included the damaging and burning of more than 2,000 Korean-owned businesses, creating a rift that has not yet been overcome.

The Korean–Black conflict is part of the larger economic picture dominated by the White-controlled marketplace of goods and services. Efforts continue to heal the divide, including through a Los Angeles Black–Korean Alliance that after six years dissolved to become a part of the larger Multicultural Collaborative that also embraced Hispanic participation.

Sources: Dhingra and Rodriguez 2014; Dolnick 2011; Hurh 1998; N. Kim 2008; Min 2013; New America Media 2007; New York Times 1992; Roth and Kim 2013; Yamato 2017.

Southeast Asian Americans

12.6 Describe the Southeast Asian American communities.

The people of Southeast Asia—Vietnamese, Cambodians, and Laotians—were part of the former French Indochinese Union. "Southeast Asian" is an umbrella term used for convenience; the peoples of these areas are ethnically and linguistically diverse. Ethnic Laotians constitute only half of the Laotian people, for example; a significant number of Mon-Khmer, Yao, and Hmong form minorities. Numbering nearly 2 million in 2015, Vietnamese Americans are the largest group, with about 10 percent of the total Asian Pacific American population.

The Refugees

The problem of U.S. involvement in Indochina did not end when all U.S. personnel were withdrawn from South Vietnam in 1975. The final tragedy was the reluctant welcome that Americans and people of other nations gave to the refugees from Vietnam, Cambodia, and Laos. One week after the evacuation of Vietnam in April 1975, a Gallup poll reported that 54 percent of Americans were against giving sanctuary to the Asian refugees. Another 36 percent were in favor, and 11 percent were undecided. The primary objection to Vietnamese immigration was that it would further increase unemployment in the United States (Schaefer and Schaefer 1975).

Many Americans offered to house refugees in their homes, but others declared that the United States had too many Asians already and was in danger of losing its "national character." This attitude toward the Indochinese has been characteristic of the feeling that Harvard sociologist David Riesman called the **gook syndrome**. *Gook* is a derogatory term for an Asian, and the syndrome refers to the tendency to stereotype these people in the worst possible light. Riesman believed that the American news media created an unflattering image of the South Vietnamese and their government, leading the American people to believe they were not worth saving (Luce 1975).

The initial 135,000 Vietnamese refugees who fled in 1975 were joined by more than a million running from the later fighting and religious persecution that plagued Indochina. The United States accepted about half of the refugees, some of them the so-called boat people, primarily Vietnamese of ethnic Chinese background, who took to the ocean in overcrowded vessels, hoping that some ship would pick them up and offer sanctuary. Hundreds of thousands were placed in other nations or remained in overcrowded refugee camps administered by the United Nations.

The Current Picture

Like other immigrants, refugees from Vietnam, Laos, and Cambodia face a difficult adjustment. Few expect to return to their homelands for visits, and fewer expect to return permanently. Indeed, Vietnamese Americans are especially upbeat about coming to America, with a 2012 survey showing that 94 percent view opportunities to get ahead in the United States as better than the opportunities in Vietnam. Therefore, many see the United States as their permanent home and the home of their children (Taylor 2013).

Language also is a factor in adjustment by the refugees; a person trained as a manager in Vietnam cannot hold that position in the United States until he or she is fairly fluent in English. The available data indicate that refugees from Vietnam have increased their earnings rapidly, often by working long hours. Partly because Southeast Asians comprise significantly different subgroups, assimilation and acceptance are not likely to occur at the same rate for all.

Although most refugee children spoke no English upon their arrival here, they have done extremely well in school. Studies indicate that immigrant parents place great emphasis on education and are pleased by the prospect of their children going to college—something rare in their homelands. The children do very well with this encouragement. It remains to be seen whether this motivation will decline as members of the next generation look more to their American peers as role models.

In 1995, the United States initiated normal diplomatic relations with Vietnam, which has led to more movement between the nations. Gradually, Vietnamese Americans are returning to visit but generally not to take up permanent residence. **Viet Kieu**, Vietnamese living abroad, are making a return visit—up to 1 million of the 5 million worldwide by 2015. Generational issues are also emerging as time passes. In Vietnamese communities from California to Virginia, splits emerge over a powerful symbol—under what flag to unite a nationality. Merchants, home residents, and college Vietnamese student organizations take a stand when they decide whether to display the yellow-with-red-bars flag of the now-defunct South Vietnam, sometimes called the "heritage flag," or the red-with-yellow-star flag of the current (and Communist) Vietnam (Hung 2015; Tran 2008).

Meanwhile, for the more than 1.5 million Vietnamese Americans, settlement patterns here vary. Little Saigons can be found in major cities in the United States, long after the former South Vietnam capital of Saigon became Ho Chi Min City. Like many other immigrant groups in the second generation, some Vietnamese have moved into suburbs, where residential patterns tend to be rather dispersed, but one can still spot mini-malls with Vietnamese restaurants and grocery stores—some even sporting sloping red-tiled roofs. Other Vietnamese Americans remain in rural areas—for example, the Gulf Coast fishermen who were rendered homeless by Hurricane Katrina in 2005. Perhaps one sign of how settled Vietnamese Americans have become is that some of the same organizations that helped the refugees learn English are now helping younger Vietnamese Americans learn Vietnamese (Van Landingham 2015).

Case Study: A Hmong Community

Wausau (population 39,000) is a community in rural Wisconsin that is best known, perhaps, for the insurance company bearing its name. To sociologists, it is distinctive for its sizable Hmong (pronounced "Mong") population. The Hmong come from rural areas of Laos and Vietnam, where they were recruited to work for the CIA during the Vietnam War (1955–1975). This association made life very difficult for them after the United States pulled out of Vietnam. Hence, many immigrated, and the United States has maintained a relatively open policy to their becoming permanent residents. Wausau finds itself with the greatest percentage of Hmong of any city in Wisconsin. Hmong and a few other Southeast Asians account for 11 percent of the city's population and about 18 percent of its public school students (Christensen 2012).

In the 2008 motion picture *Gran Torino*, Clint Eastwood portrays a bitter retired autoworker who is suspicious of his Hmong neighbors in Detroit but comes to appreciate their willingness to help and their strong family values.

The Hmong, who numbered nearly 300,000 as of 2015, immigrated to the United States from Laos and Vietnam after the end of the U.S. involvement in Vietnam in April 1975. The transition for the Hmong was difficult because they were typically farmers with little formal education. Hmong have tended to form tight-knit groups organized around community leaders. Typically, cultural traditions surrounding marriage and funerals remain strong among Hmong Americans. Some are giving up Hmong traditional worship of spirits for Christian faiths. Perhaps reflecting their entry into mainstream culture, Hmong culture and the challenges faced by the Hmong in the United States were explored in Clint Eastwood's 2008 fictional film *Gran Torino* (Lamborn, Nguyen, and Bocanegra 2013; *Hmong Studies Journal* 2017; Pfeifer 2008a).

Like other refugees from Southeast Asia at the time, the first Hmong came to Wausau at the invitation of religious groups. Others followed as they found the surrounding agricultural lands were places they could find work. The availability of jobs created a pipeline of chain immigration to communities like Wausau. As defined earlier, *chain immigration* refers to migration in which an immigrant sponsors several other immigrants who, on their arrival, may sponsor still more. Even with sponsors or relatives, the Hmong immigrants, who came from a very rural peasant society, faced dramatic adjustment upon their arrival in the industrialized United States (Vang 2010).

Recalls of elected officials are rare in the United States, but in December 1993, opponents of a busing plan to distribute Hmong children among schools organized a special election that led to the removal of five school board members. This election left the Wausau board with a majority who opposed the busing plan that had integrated Asian American youngsters into mostly White elementary schools. By 2016, 19 percent of the school district was Asian American, but neighborhood schools continued to play an important role in Wausau so that among elementary schools, the proportion of Asian American children ranged from less than 4 percent to 40 percent (Wausau School District 2016).

How events will unfold in Wausau is unclear. A 2015 stabbing death of a Hmong 13-year-old was attributed to gang violence between Asian Americans and Blacks and Latinos. However, positive signs are identifiable in Wausau and other centers of Hmong life in the United States. Immigrants and their children are moving into nonagricultural occupations. Enrollment in citizenship classes is growing. Public healthcare programs directed at the Hmong community are widely publicized. The Wausau Area Hmong Mutual Association, funded by a federal grant and the local United Way, offers housing assistance. Although many of these immigrants struggle to make a go of it economically, large numbers have been able to move off public assistance. Older Hmong residents still encounter language barriers and suffer from a lack of formal schooling, but the younger generation is emerging to face some of the same

Figure 12.3 Hawai'i: Racial Composition

SOURCE: Data from American Community Survey 2015a: Tables B02006, B02007, and DP05.

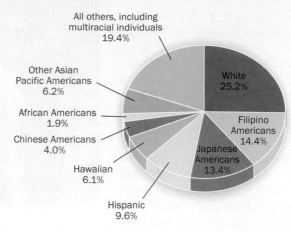

All others, including multiracial individuals 19.4%

Other Asian Pacific Americans 6.2%

African Americans 1.9%

Chinese Americans 4.0%

Hawaiian 6.1%

Hispanic 9.6%

White 25.2%

Filipino Americans 14.4%

Japanese Americans 13.4%

identity and assimilation questions experienced by other APA groups (Dally 2011; Menchaca 2008; Peckham 2002; Uhlig 2015).

Hawai'i and Its People

12.7 **Explain how Hawai'i and its people embody cultural diversity.**

The entire state of Hawai'i appears to be the complete embodiment of cultural diversity. Nevertheless, despite a dramatic blending of different races living together, prejudice, discrimination, and pressure to assimilate are very much present in Hawai'i. As we will see, life on the island is much closer to that in the rest of the country than to the ideal of a pluralistic society. Hawai'i's population is unquestionably diverse, as Figure 12.3 shows.

To grasp contemporary social relationships, we must first understand the historical circumstances that brought the following races together on the islands: the native Hawaiians, also known as the **kanaka maoli** (meaning "real or true people"); the various Asian peoples; and the **Haoles** (pronounced "hah-oh-lehs"), the term often used to refer to Whites in Hawai'i (Ledward 2008, Okamura 2008).

Historical Background

Geographically remote, Hawai'i was initially populated by Polynesian people who had their first contact with Europeans in 1778, when English explorer Captain James Cook arrived. The Hawaiians (who killed Cook) tolerated the subsequent arrival of plantation operators and missionaries. Fortunately, the Hawaiian people were united under a monarchy and received respect from the European immigrants, a respect that developed into a spirit of goodwill. Slavery was never introduced, even during the colonial period, as it was in so many areas of the Western Hemisphere. Nevertheless, the effect of the White arrival on the Hawaiians themselves was disastrous. Civil warfare and disease reduced the number of full-blooded natives to fewer than 30,000 by 1900, and the number is probably well under 10,000 now. Meanwhile, large sugarcane plantations imported laborers from China, Portugal, Japan, and, in the early 1900s, the Philippines, Korea, and Puerto Rico.

In 1893, a revolution encouraged by foreign commercial interests overthrew the monarchy. During the revolution, the United States landed troops, and five years later, Hawai'i was annexed as a territory to the United States. The 1900 Organic Act guaranteed racial equality, but foreign rule dealt a devastating psychological blow to the proud Hawaiian people. American rule had mixed effects on relations between the races. Citizenship laws granted civil rights to all those born on the islands, not just the wealthy Haoles. However, the anti-Asian laws still applied, excluding the Chinese and Japanese from political participation.

The 1941 attack on Pearl Harbor led to greater surveillance of Japanese Americans, with about 2 percent of the population placed in an internment camp near Honolulu similar to the internment camps on the mainland (described in Chapter 13). Yet because of their central role in the economy and other social institutions, island Japanese Americans did not face the extended hostility experienced by their mainland counterparts (Japanese Cultural Center of Japanese Americans in Hawaii 2017).

Cathy Bussewitz/AP Images

The Sovereignty Movement

Hawai'i has achieved some fame for its good race relations. Tourists, who are predominantly White, have come from the mainland and have seen and generally accepted the racial harmony. Admittedly, Waikiki Beach, where large numbers of tourists congregate, is atypical of the islands, but even there, tourists cannot ignore the differences in intergroup relations. If they look closely, they will see that the low-wage workers in the resorts and tourist industry tend to be disproportionately of Asian descent (Adler, Kess, and Adler 2004).

Reflecting the desire to protect lands held as culturally significant by Native Hawaiians, people protest the proposed expansion of the Mauna Kea astronomical observatory on Hawai'i.

One clear indication of the multicultural nature of the islands is the degree of *exogamy*: marrying outside one's own group. The out-group marriage rate varies annually but seems to be stabilizing; about 40 percent of all marriages performed in the state involving residents are exogamous. The rate varies by group, from a low of 37 percent among Haoles to around 63 percent among Chinese Americans and African Americans, with about half of Native Hawaiians outmarrying (Hawaiian State Data Center 2016).

Prejudice and discrimination are not alien to Hawai'i. Attitudinal surveys show definite racial preferences and sensitivity to color differences. Housing surveys taken before the passage of civil rights legislation showed that many people were committed to nondiscrimination, but racial preferences were still present. Certain groups sometimes dominate residential neighborhoods, but there are no racial ghettos. The various racial groups are not distributed uniformly among the islands, but they are clustered rather than sharply segregated.

The **sovereignty movement** is the effort by the indigenous people of Hawai'i, the kanala maoli, to secure a measure of self-government and restoration of their lands. The movement's roots and significance to the people are very similar to the sovereignty efforts by tribal people on the continental United States. The growing sovereignty movement has also sought restoration of—or at least compensation for—the Native Hawaiian land that has been lost to Anglos over the past century. Reaction to the movement has ranged from nonnative Hawaiians who see these efforts as a big, racist land grab to indigenous Hawaiians who see it as just not enough.

The Hawaiian term *kanaka maoli,* meaning "real or true people," is gaining in popularity to reaffirm the indigenous people's special ties to the islands. Sometimes, the Native Hawaiians successfully form alliances with environmental groups that want to halt further commercial development on the islands. In 1996, a Native Hawaiian vote was held, seeking a response to the question, "Shall the Hawaiian people elect delegates to propose a Native Hawaiian government?" The results indicated that 73 percent voting were in favor of such a government structure.

Since the vote, the state Office of Hawaiian Affairs has sought to create a registry of Hawaiians. About 123,000 people, more than halfway to an estimated 200,000 people of significant Hawaiian descent on the islands, have come forward. In 2008, a Native Hawaiian independence group seized the historic royal palace in Honolulu to protest the U.S.-backed overthrow of the Hawaiian government more than a century ago. Although the occupation

Speaking Out

Recognizing Native Hawaiians

Daniel Akaka

[The Native Hawaiian Government Reorganization Act] allows us to take the necessary next step in the reconciliation process. The bill does three things. First, it authorizes an office in the Department of the Interior to serve as a liaison between Native Hawaiians and the United States. Second, it forms an interagency task force chaired by the Departments of Justice and Interior, and composed of officials from federal agencies that administer programs and services impacting Native Hawaiians. Third, it authorizes a process for the reorganization of the Native Hawaiian government for the purposes of a federally recognized government-to-government relationship. Once the Native Hawaiian government is recognized, an inclusive democratic negotiations process representing both Native Hawaiians and non-Native Hawaiians would be established. There are many checks and balances in this process. Any agreements reached would still require the legislative approval of the State and Federal governments.

Opponents have spread misinformation about the bill. Let me be clear on some things that this bill does not do. My bill will not allow for gaming. It does not allow for Hawai'i to secede from the United States. It does not allow for private land to be taken. It does not create a reservation in Hawai'i.

What this bill does do is allow the people of Hawai'i to come together and address issues arising from the overthrow of the Kingdom of Hawai'i more than 118 years ago.

It is time to move forward with this legislation. To date, there have been a total of twelve Congressional hearings, including five

Daniel Akaka

joint hearings in Hawai'i held by the Senate Committee on Indian Affairs and the House Natural Resources Committee. Our colleagues in the House have passed versions of this bill three times. We, however, have never had the opportunity to openly debate this bill on its merits in the Senate. We have a strong bill that is supported by Native communities across the United States, by the State of Hawai'i, and by the Obama Administration.

Last week, I met with officials and community leaders in the state of Hawai'i to share my intention to reintroduce this legislation. I received widespread support. This support was not surprising. A poll conducted by the *Honolulu Advertiser* in May of last year reported that 66 percent of the people of Hawai'i support federal recognition for Native Hawaiians. And 82 percent of Native Hawaiians polled support federal recognition....

I encourage all of my colleagues to stand with me and support this legislation. I welcome any of my colleagues with concerns to speak with me so I can explain how important this bill is for the people of Hawai'i. The people of Hawai'i have waited for far too long. America has a history of righting past wrongs. The United States has federally recognized government-to-government relationships with 565 tribes across our country. It is time to extend this policy to the Native Hawaiians.

Source: Akaka, Daniel. 2011. Native Hawaiian Federal Recognition. Accessed June 1, 2011, at http://Akaka.senate.gov/public/index.cfm?FuseAction=Issues.Home&issues=Akaka%20Bill&content_id=24#Akaka%20Bill.

---

lasted barely a day, the political discontentment felt by many Native Hawaiians persists (Kana'iolowalu 2016; Magin 2008; Okamura 2008).

The sovereignty movement has been stymied on a couple of fronts. First, Congress failed to consider the Native Hawaiian Government Reorganization Act, or the Akaka Bill, named for the late U.S. Senator Daniel Akaka, whose defense of the bill is partially reprinted in the Speaking Out feature. It would have given people of Hawaiian ancestry more say over resources, provided affordable housing, taken steps to preserve culture, and created a means by which they could better express their grievances. Second, the Supreme Court intervened to stop the counting of a 2015 election arranged by the state of Hawai'i to select delegates for a constitutional convention to deal with Native Hawaiian issues. The Court's objection was that voting was limited to only Native Hawaiians (D'Angelo 2015).

Regardless of the outcome of the sovereignty movement, the multiracial character of the islands will not change quickly, but the identity of the Native Hawaiians has already been affected. Although they have a rich cultural heritage, they tend to be very poor and often view the U.S. occupation as the beginning of their cultural and economic downfall.

Still, there are positive developments. *"E Heluuelu Kaqkou"* ("Let's read together"), Nako'hlani Warrington tells her third graders. She has no need to translate because she is

Figure 12.4 Spectrum of Intergroup Relations: Asian Pacific Americans

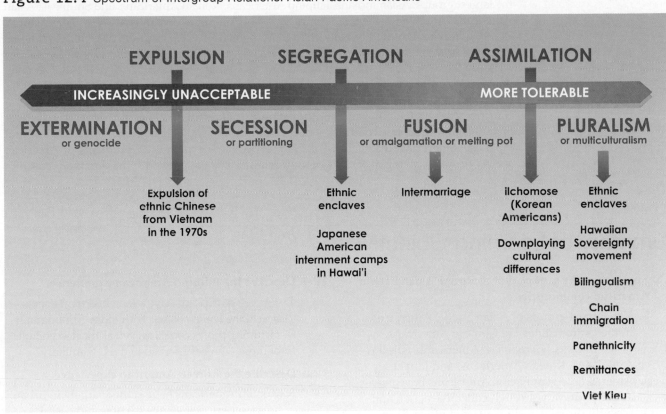

teaching at the public immersion school where all instruction is in the Hawaiian language. Not too long ago, it was assumed that only linguistic scholars would speak Hawaiian, but efforts to revive it in general conversation have resulted in its use well beyond "aloha." In 1983, only 1,500 people were considered native speakers; by 2016, over 18,600 indicated they speak Hawaiian at home. This use of the language goes well beyond symbolic ethnicity. Language perpetuity is being combined with a solid grade school education, and a supportive doctoral program in the Hawaiian language was introduced in 2007 (Hawaiian State Data Center 2016; Kana'iaupuni 2008).

Figure 12.4 shows the Spectrum of Intergroup Relations for Asian Pacific Americans.

Conclusion

Asian Pacific Americans are a rapidly growing group. Despite striking differences between them, they are often viewed as if they arrived all at once and from one culture. Also, they are often characterized as a successful or model minority. However, individual cases of success and some impressive group data suggest that the diverse group of peoples who make up the APA community are not uniformly successful. Indeed, despite high levels of formal schooling, APAs earn far less than Whites with comparable education and continue to be victims of discriminatory employment practices.

The diversity within the APA community belies the similarity suggested by the panethnic label *Asian American*. Chinese and Japanese Americans share a history of several generations in the United States. Filipinos are veterans of a half-century of direct U.S. colonization and a cooperative role with the military. In contrast, Vietnamese, Koreans, and Japanese are associated in a negative way with three wars. Korean Americans come from a nation that still has a major U.S. military presence and a persistent "cold war" mentality. Korean Americans and Chinese Americans have become small-business entrepreneurs. Filipinos, Asian Indians, and Japanese Americans tend to live more broadly throughout the population than other groups of APAs.

Who are the APAs? This chapter has begun to answer that question by focusing on four of the largest groups: Asian Indians, Filipino Americans, Korean Americans, and Southeast Asian Americans. Attention sometimes comes to Asian Americans in unusual ways. For example, 24-year-old Nina Davuluri of New York was crowned Miss America in 2013. Her parents immigrated from India 30 years ago. While many saw this accomplishment as the acceptance of APAs by the mainstream, the announcement was followed by a barrage of tweets disparaging the beauty queen's ethnic heritage and wondering if she was American enough (Sahgal 2013).

Hawai'i is a useful model because of its more harmonious social relationships across racial lines. Although it is not an interracial paradise, Hawai'i does illustrate that, given proper historical and economic conditions, deep, continuing conflict is not inevitable. Chinese and Japanese Americans, the subjects of Chapter 13, have experienced problems in American society despite striving to achieve economic and social equality with the dominant culture.

Summary of Learning Objectives

12.1 Summarize the groups that comprise Asian Pacific American communities.

1. The largest groups of Asian Pacific Americans in the United States are Chinese Americans, Asian Indians, Vietnamese Americans, Filipino Americans, Korean Americans, and Japanese Americans. Asian Pacific Americans have been active politically through collective action and recently through seeking elected office. They embrace their unique identity but sometimes acknowledge their broader pan-Asian identity.

12.2 Explain the model minority image.

2. Often, Asian Americans are labeled as a model minority, which overlooks the many problems they face and serves to minimize the challenges of succeeding despite prejudice and discrimination.

12.3 Describe the Asian Indian experience.

3. Asian Indians are a diverse group culturally and, although most are Hindu, embrace a number of faiths. Many Asian Indians work in the tech industry. This group has a high degree of in-group marriage (endogamy).

12.4 Describe the Filipino American experience.

4. Filipino Americans have a long historical connection to the United States, with today's immigrants including professionals as well as the descendants of those who have served in the U.S. military.

12.5 Describe the Korean American experience.

5. Korean Americans have settled largely in urban areas, where many have become successful entrepreneurs.

12.6 Discuss the Southeast Asian American communities.

6. Southeast Asians' presence in the United States has typically resulted from waves of refugees. They have created significant settlements throughout the United States and often have dispersed throughout the larger population. Southeast Asian communities include Vietnamese, Laotians, and Cambodians.

12.7 Explain how Hawai'i and its people embody cultural diversity.

7. Hawai'i and Native Hawaiians present a different multiracial pattern from that of the mainland, but not one without prejudice and discrimination.

Key Terms

affirmative action, *page 264*
arranged marriage, *page 268*
bamboo ceiling, *page 266*
blaming the victim, *page 264*
brain drain, *page 270*
chain immigration, *page 259*
color-blind racism, *page 266*

gook syndrome, *page 274*
Haoles, *page 276*
ilchomose, *page 271*
institutional discrimination, *page 265*
kanaka maoli, *page 276*
kye, *page 272*
model minority, *page 264*

panethnicity, *page 263*
racial profiling, *page 265*
sovereignty movement, *page 277*
symbolic ethnicity, *page 269*
Viet Kieu, *page 274*
yellow peril, *page 265*

Review Questions

1. How is the model minority image a disservice to both Asian Americans and other subordinate racial and ethnic groups?

2. How successful have Asian Pacific Americans been in organizing themselves politically?

3. Describe the Asian Indian community in the United States.

4. What are some of the defining moments in the Filipino American experience?

5. What generational differences can you identify among Korean Americans?

6. Distinguish among the different Southeast Asian groups in the United States.

7. To what degree do race relations in Hawai'i offer both promise and a dose of reality to the future of race and ethnicity on the mainland?

Critical Thinking

1. What stereotypical images of Asian Pacific Americans can you identify in the contemporary media?

2. Coming of age is difficult for anyone, given the challenges of adolescence in the United States. How is it doubly difficult for the children of immigrants? How do you think the immigrants themselves, such as those from Asia and the Pacific Islands, view this process?

3. *American Indians*, *Hispanics*, and *Asian Pacific Americans* are all convenient terms to refer to diverse groups of people. Do you see these umbrella terms as being more appropriate for one group than for the others?

Chapter 13
Chinese Americans and Japanese Americans

A. Ramey / PhotoEdit, Inc.

∨ Learning Objectives

13.1 Understand the history of the Chinese Americans.

13.2 Describe the present-day circumstances of Chinese Americans.

13.3 Summarize the Japanese American experience through World War II.

13.4 Describe the contemporary Japanese American experience.

13.5 Identify how prejudice and discrimination against Chinese and Japanese Americans persist.

As years and generations pass, how is identity maintained—or is it? And what if you throw a party and few people come? In 2007, Japanese Americans in Los Angeles's Little Tokyo threw a daylong party with Asian hip-hop along with traditional martial arts demonstrations to bring Japanese Americans scattered across southern California together for a day. Debbie Hazama, 35, a homemaker with three children, drove with her husband from the suburbs because she recognizes there are not many Japanese Americans where she lives, and she wants her children "to stay connected."

Three years earlier, the Los Angeles Japanese American Festival was in full swing in mid-July when, during the opening ceremonies, a 24-year-old South Pasadena woman grabbed a heavy mallet and took a swing at a drum, just as she had practiced doing for months. Nicole Miyako Cherry, the daughter of a Japanese American mother and a White American father, had not had much interest in her Japanese roots except for wearing a kimono for Halloween as a youngster. Yet in the past couple of years, she had begun to take interest in all things Japanese, including visiting Japan. Looking to her future as a social work therapist, she says she would like her own children to learn Japanese, go to Japanese festivals, play in Japanese sports leagues, and have Japanese first names (M. Navarro 2004; Watanabe 2007: B13).

Debbie's children and Nicole's experience are examples of the **principle of third-generation interest**, which suggests that ethnic awareness may increase among the grandchildren of immigrants to the United States. Nicole is of mixed ancestral background, so she is obviously making a choice to maintain her Japanese American identity as an important part of her future. But many other Asian Pacific Americans (APAs), particularly recent immigrants, are just trying to survive and accumulate savings for their family here, as well as send remittances to kinfolk in the old country.

Many people in the United States find it difficult to distinguish between Japanese Americans and Chinese Americans physically, culturally, and historically. As we will see in this chapter, the two groups differ in some ways but also share similar patterns in their experiences in the United States.

Chinese Americans: The Early Experience

13.1   **Understand the history of the Chinese Americans.**

China, the most populous country in the world, has been a source of immigrants for centuries. Many nations have a sizable Chinese population whose history can be traced back more than five generations. The United States is one such nation. Even before the great migration from Europe began in the 1880s, more than 100,000 Chinese already lived in the United States. Today, Chinese Americans number more than 3.5 million, as Table 13.1 shows.

Early Settlement Patterns

From its beginning, Chinese immigration has aroused conflicting views among Americans. In one sense, Chinese immigration was welcome because it brought needed hardworking laborers to these shores. At the same time, it was unwelcome because the Chinese also brought an alien culture that the European settlers were unwilling to tolerate. People in the western

Table 13.1 Chinese American and Japanese American Population, 1860–2014

Year	Chinese Americans	Japanese Americans
1860	34,933	—
1880	105,465	148
1900	89,863	24,326
1930	74,954	138,834
1950	117,629	141,768
1960	237,292	464,332
1970	435,062	591,290
1980	806,027	700,747
1990	1,640,000	847,562
2000	2,314,533	796,700
2010	3,347,000	763,000
2014	3,551,337	779,141

NOTE: Data beginning with 1960 include Alaska and Hawai'i.

SOURCE: American Community Survey 2015a: B02006; Barnes and Bennett 2002; Hixson, Hepler, and Kim 2012; Lee 1998:15.

Bettmann/Getty Images

Before and after the Chinese Exclusion Act, settlers attacked Chinese enclaves throughout the West on 183 separate occasions. These immigrants were driven eastward, where they created Chinatowns, some of which are still thriving today. This engraving depicts the Denver riot of 1880, which culminated in one Chinese man being hanged. The lynchers were identified but released the next year. There was no restoration for the damage done by the estimated mob of 3,000 men (Ellis 2004; Pfaelzer 2007).

United States also had a perception of economic competition, and the Chinese newcomers proved to be convenient and powerless scapegoats. As detailed in Chapter 4, the anti-Chinese sentiment led to the passage of the Chinese Exclusion Act in 1882. In many respects we can see how the European settlers viewed the Chinese in the United States in a manner similar to the way that they viewed the Mexican people and Native Americans—as undesirable others.

Even with the repeal of the Exclusion Act in 1943, Chinese immigration was opposed except as a necessity when China became briefly our wartime ally during World War II. Even then, the group that lobbied for repeal, the Citizens' Committee to Repeal Chinese Exclusion, encountered the old racist arguments against Chinese immigration (Glenn 2015; Pfaelzer 2007).

After 1943, Chinese were gradually permitted to enter the United States. In the beginning, the annual limit was 105. Then several thousand Chinese wives of U.S. servicemen were admitted, and college students were later allowed to remain after finishing their education. Not until after the 1965 Immigration Act did Chinese immigrants arrive again in large numbers, almost doubling the Chinese American community. Immigration continues to exert a major influence on the growth of the Chinese American population. It has approached 100,000 annually. The influx was so great in the 1990s that the number of new arrivals in that decade exceeded the total number of Chinese Americans present in 1980.

As the underside of immigration, illegal immigration is also found in the Chinese American community. The lure of perceived better jobs and a better life leads overseas Chinese to seek alternative routes to immigration when laws limit legal migration. The impact of illegal entry in some areas of the country can be significant.

A small but socially significant component of Chinese Americans in the United States are those who have been adopted by American non-Chinese couples. Beginning in 1991, China loosened its adoption laws to address the growing number of children, particularly girls, who were abandoned as a result of the country's one-child policy. This policy strongly encourages couples to have only one child; having more children can impede job promotions and even force a household to accept a smaller dwelling. The numbers of adopted Chinese were small, but over the course of several years, about 7,000 Chinese children were adopted annually. The Chinese government tightened this policy significantly in 2008, reducing the number of annual adoptions. Many of these adoptees, along with their adopting parents, face complex issues of cultural and social identity. Organized efforts now exist to reconnect these children with their roots in China, but for most of their lives, they have been adjusting to being Chinese American in a non-Chinese American family (Department of State 2008; Olemetson 2005).

It is important to appreciate that *Chinese American* is a collective term. There is diversity within this group represented by nationality (China versus Taiwan, for example), language, and region of origin. It is not unusual for a church serving a Chinese American community to have five separate services, each in a different dialect. These divisions can be quite sharply expressed. For example, near the traditional Chinatown of New York City, a small neighborhood has emerged of Chinese from China's Fujian Province. In this area, job postings include annotations in Chinese that translate as "no north," meaning people from the provinces north of Fujian are not welcome. Throughout the United States, some Chinese Americans also divide along pro-China and pro-Taiwan allegiances (Guest 2003; Louie 2004; Sachs 2001).

Chinatowns Today

Chinatowns represent a paradox. The casual observer or tourist sees them as thriving areas of business and amusement, bright in color and lights, exotic in sounds and sights. Behind this facade, however, they have large poor populations and face the problems associated with all slums. Older Chinatowns were often located in deteriorating sections of cities, but increasingly they are springing up in new neighborhoods and even in the suburbs, such as

Monterey Park outside Los Angeles. In the older enclaves, the problems of Chinatowns include the entire range of social ills that affect low-income areas, but some face even greater difficulties because the glitter sometimes conceals the problems from outsiders and even social planners. A unique characteristic of Chinatowns, one that distinguishes them from other ethnic enclaves, is the variety of social organizations they encompass (Liu and Geron 2008).

ORGANIZATIONAL LIFE   The Chinese in the United States have a rich history of organizational membership, much of it carried over from China. Chief among such associations are the clans, or *tsu*; the benevolent associations, or *hui kuan*; and the secret societies, or *tongs*.

The clans, or **tsu**, that operate in Chinatown have their origins in the Chinese practice in which families with common ancestors unite. At first, immigrant Chinese continued to affiliate themselves with those sharing a family name, even if a blood relationship was absent. Social scientists agree that the influence of clans is declining as young Chinese become increasingly acculturated. The clans in the past provided mutual assistance, a function increasingly taken on by government agencies. The strength of the clans, although diminished today, still points to the extended family's important role for Chinese Americans. Social scientists have found parent–child relationships stronger and more harmonious than those among non–Chinese Americans. Just as the clans have become less significant, however, so has the family structure changed. The differences between family life in Chinese and non-Chinese homes are narrowing with each new generation.

The benevolent associations, or **hui kuan** (or *hui guan*), help their members adjust to a new life. Rather than being organized along kinship ties like the clans, hui kuan membership is based on the person's district of origin in China. Besides extending help with adjustment, the *hui kuan* lend money to and settle disputes between their members. They have thereby exercised wide control over their members. In turn, the various *hui kuan* are traditionally part of an unofficial government in each city called the Chinese Six Companies, a name later changed to the Chinese Consolidated Benevolent Association (CCBA). The president of the CCBA is sometimes called the mayor of a Chinatown. The CCBA often protects newly arrived immigrants from the effects of racism. The organization works actively to promote political involvement among Chinese Americans and to support the democracy movement within the People's Republic of China. Some members of the Chinese community have resented, and still resent, the CCBA's authoritarian ways and its attempt to speak as the sole voice of Chinatown.

The Chinese have also organized in **tongs**, or secret societies. The secret societies' membership is determined not by family or locale but by interest. Some have been political, attempting to resolve the dispute over which China (the People's Republic of China or Taiwan) is the legitimate government of their home region, and others have protested the exploitation of Chinese workers. Other *tongs* provide illegal goods and services, such as drugs, gambling, and prostitution. Because they are secret, it is difficult to accurately determine the power of *tongs* today. Most observers concur that their influence has dwindled over the past 70 years and that their functions, even the illegal ones, have been taken over by elements less closely tied to Chinatown.

Some conclusions can be reached about these various social organizations. They serve as pillars of the Chinese American community but are less visible outside the traditional older Chinatowns. Metropolitan Chinese American communities see the increasing significance of nonprofit organizations that work between the ethnic community and the larger society, including the local, state, and federal government (S. Lee 2013; Tong 2000; Zhao 2002; Zhou 2009).

SOCIAL PROBLEMS   It is a myth that Chinese Americans and Chinatowns have no problems. Although overall household income levels ran 20 percent ahead of White non-Hispanics, the poverty of Chinese Americans as a group was 14 percent, compared to only 8.8 percent of Whites. Obviously, many Chinese Americans are doing very well, but a significant group is doing very poorly.

The false impression of Chinese American success grows out of our tendency to stereotype groups as being all one way or another, as well as the Chinese people's tendency to keep their problems within their community. The false image is also reinforced by the desire to maintain tourism. The tourist industry is a double-edged sword. It provides needed jobs, even if some of them pay substandard wages. But it also forces Chinatown to keep its problems quiet and not seek outside assistance, lest tourists hear of social problems and stop coming. Slums do not attract tourists. This parallel between Chinese Americans and Native Americans finds both groups depending on the tourist industry even at the cost of hiding problems (Light et al. 1994).

In the late 1960s, White society became aware that all was not right in the Chinatowns. This awareness grew not because living conditions suddenly deteriorated in Chinese American settlements but because the various community organizations could no longer maintain the facade that hid Chinatowns' social ills. Despite Chinese Americans' remarkable achievements as a group, the inhabitants were suffering by most socioeconomic measures. Poor health, high suicide rates, run-down housing, rising crime rates, poor working conditions, inadequate care for the elderly, and the weak union representation of laborers were a few of the documented problems (Liu and Geron 2008).

Life in Chinatown may seem lively to an outsider, but beyond the neon signs, the picture can be quite different. Chinatown in New York City remained a prime site of sweatshops well into the 1990s. Dozens of women labored over sewing machines, often above restaurants. These small businesses, often in the garment industry, consisted of workers sewing 12 hours a day, six or seven days a week, and earning about $200 weekly—well below minimum wage. The workers, most of whom were women, could be victimized because they were either illegal immigrants who owed labor to the smugglers who brought them into the United States, or they were legal residents unable to find better employment (Finder 1994; Kwong 1994).

The attacks on the World Trade Center in 2001 made the marginal economy of New York's Chinatown even shakier. Although not located near the World Trade Center, Chinatown was close enough to the devastation to feel the drop in customary tourism and a significant decline in shipments to the garment industry. Initially, emergency relief groups ruled out assistance to Chinatown, but within a couple of months, agencies opened up offices in Chinatown. Within two months, 42,000 people in Chinatown had begun receiving relief because 60 percent of businesses had cut staff. Like many other minority neighborhoods, New York City's Chinatown may be economically viable, but it is susceptible to severe economic setbacks that most other areas could withstand much more easily. From 2000 to 2010, Chinatown's population in Manhattan dropped by 9 percent—the first decline ever. Notably, the proportion of foreign-born Chinese also declined (Asian American Federation 2008; J. Lee 2001; Tsui 2011).

Increasingly, Chinese neither live nor work in Chinatowns; most have escaped them or have never experienced their social ills. Nonetheless, Chinatown remains important for many of those who now live outside its borders, although less so than in the past. For many Chinese, movement out of Chinatown is a sign of success. Upon moving out, however, they soon encounter discriminatory real-estate practices and White parents' fears about their children playing with Chinese American youths.

The movement of Chinese Americans out of Chinatowns parallels the movement of White ethnics out of similar enclaves. However, the movement does not necessarily mean transition into an integrated residential area. In some instances, Chinatowns have been re-created in suburbs to serve the continuing influx of Chinese immigrants who seek a smooth transition into American society, as did immigrants a century earlier. The movement out of central-city Chinatowns also signals the upward mobility of Chinese Americans, coupled with their growing acceptance by the rest of the population. This mobility and acceptance are especially evident in the presence of Chinese Americans in managerial and professional occupations.

Despite the problems faced by Chinese immigrants and the constant influx of new arrivals, we should not forget that first and foremost, Chinatowns are communities of people. Originally, in the nineteenth century, they emerged because the Chinese arriving in the United States had no other area in which they were allowed to settle. Today, Chinatowns, whether in central city or in the suburbs, represent cultural decompression chambers for new arrivals and an important symbolic focus for long-term residents. Even among many younger Chinese Americans, these ethnic enclaves serve as a source of identity (Robbins 2015).

Festivals and events serve to gather the members of the Chinese American community, many of whom now live far apart from one another. Shown here is a dragon boat race in Seattle, Washington.

Contemporary Chinese Americans

13.2 Describe the present-day circumstances of Chinese Americans.

Three-quarters of adult Chinese Americans are foreign born, similar to the share among all Asian Pacific Americans but much higher than the 16 percent share among all APA adults. Over two-thirds are U.S. citizens, again comparable to that of all APAs. To gain a better appreciation of their life in the United States today, we will focus on the economic sector first and then turn to family life (Taylor 2013).

Occupational Profile of Chinese Americans

By many benchmarks, Chinese Americans are doing well. As a group, they have higher levels of formal schooling and household income compared to all APAs and even to White non-Hispanics. The Chinese American poverty rate is moderately higher, pointing to the fact that many Chinese Americans are underemployed given their formal levels of education. This fact is confirmed if we take a more detailed look at poverty rates. The poverty rate for native-born and foreign-born Chinese Americans citizens is comparable to the poverty rate among White non-Hispanic citizens. (Department of Labor 2016).

As we might expect, given the high income levels, half of all Chinese Americans serve in management, professional, and related occupations, compared to only a third of the general population. This trend reflects two patterns: first, entrepreneurial development by Chinese Americans who start their own businesses, and second, the immigration of skilled overseas Chinese as well as Chinese students who chose to remain in the United States following the completion of their advanced college degrees (Bureau of the Census 2007a).

The background of the contemporary Chinese American labor force lies in Chinatown. For generations, Chinese Americans were largely barred from working elsewhere. The Chinese Exclusion Act was only one example of discriminatory legislation. Many laws were passed that made it difficult or more expensive for Chinese Americans to enter certain occupations. Whites did not object to Chinese in domestic-service occupations or in the laundry trade because most White men were uninterested in such menial, low-paying work. When given the chance to take better jobs, as they were in wartime, Chinese Americans jumped at the opportunities. Where such opportunities were absent, however, many Chinese Americans sought the relative safety of Chinatown. The tourist industry and the restaurants dependent on it grew out of the need to employ the growing numbers of idle workers in Chinatown.

Chinese-owned businesses continue to be a major source of income for Chinese Americans, but compared to White-owned businesses, they are much smaller and more likely to result from self-investment. They are concentrated in the service sectors, including taxi and limousine providers; personal care services, including beauty and nail salons; food services; and construction (Asian American Foundation 2016).

Family Life

Family life is the major force that shapes all immigrant groups' experience in the United States. Generally, with assimilation, cultural behavior becomes less distinctive. Family life and religious practices are no exceptions. For Chinese Americans, the latest immigration wave has helped preserve some of the old ways, but traditional cultural patterns have undergone change even in the People's Republic of China, so the situation is very fluid.

The contemporary Chinese American family often is indistinguishable from its White counterpart except that the Chinese American family is victimized by prejudice and discrimination. Older Chinese Americans and new arrivals often are dismayed by the more American behavior patterns of Chinese American youths. Change in family life is one of the most difficult cultural changes to accept. Children questioning parental authority, which Americans grudgingly accept, is a painful experience for the tradition-oriented Chinese. The 2011 bestseller *Battle Hymn of the Tiger Mother* by legal scholar Amy Chua touched off heated discussions with its indictment of parents indulging their children and holding up as a model strong parental guidance in children's activities and interests. We look at this controversy more closely in the Research Focus.

Research Focus

Tiger Mothers

It is not often that a memoir sparks a national debate about parenting that extends around the world, but such was the case with a memoir published by a Yale law professor. In 2011, Amy Chua published *Battle Hymn of the Tiger Mother*, in which she recounts how she raised her two American girls, who were teenagers at the time. Her parenting practices followed the child-rearing she experienced from her Chinese parents, who had emigrated from the Philippines and had raised her in Illinois.

The quick takeaway for readers, or even those who never opened the book, was the concept of "Tiger moms"—Chinese American (or maybe all Asian Pacific American) mothers who raise their children in a stern but loving fashion that emphasizes competition for success. The term **tiger mother** has come to refer to a demanding mother who pushes her children to high levels of achievement following practices common in China and other parts of Asia.

Days are filled with music lessons and practice, and handmade greeting cards, but no sleepovers, no television or video games, and no tolerance for any grade but A. Married to a fellow law professor, Chua agreed to raise their children in his Jewish faith (Chua is Roman Catholic) but only if she could be a "Chinese mother." Her book came to be seen as an indictment of the more permissive U.S. child-rearing practices. The *Wall Street Journal* (2011) titled its excerpt from the book "Why Chinese Mothers Are Superior."

Chua does not claim to be a child development specialist and contends that her book is the story of one mother who became frustrated when her second daughter became rebellious at age 13 and chose tennis over piano and violin. Since the ensuing firestorm about the book, Chua has admitted that she has some regrets about the way she raised her daughters, but she continues to defend her strictness and her overall approach as taking the best from "Asian cultures."

So is there really a single method of "Chinese parenting"? Studies of Chinese parenting indicate that there is no one way that most parents rear their children. In addition, Chua's relatively affluent lifestyle allowed her to hire many helpers and access experts while still allowing Chua to work as a full-time professional. Such assistance is well beyond the financial means of most parents. Chua's book also serves to reinforce the model minority stereotype discussed in Chapter 12. There is more emphasis in Asia and among the immigrant households on stressing respect for authority and self-discipline. This approach has its roots in the ethical and philosophical system developed from the teachings of the Chinese philosopher Confucius in the fifth century BCE. Confucian parental goals do stress the importance of perseverance, working hard in school, being obedient, and being sensitive to parents' wishes.

Yet even if it is more common in Asia, this approach is not uniquely Chinese, as Chua admits. For example, NBC journalist Tom Brokaw told Chua that his working-class South Dakotan father was a "Chinese mom." There is also evidence that in China today, especially urban China, parents are becoming more relaxed with their children and growing critical of schools' emphasis on rote memorization.

Perhaps most telling about the notion of "tiger mother" and the ensuing debate is the way it speaks to views of Asia and particularly China as "threats" to America's superpower status. Chua makes explicit reference to the fact that U.S. children are being outperformed on standardized tests by children in other countries and especially in China. So while the concept of the tiger mother offers some insight into the caregiving culture in Asia, it also highlights how Americans see Asian and Asian Pacific Americans.

Sources: Chua 2011, 2016; Paul 2011; Pitt 2013; Russell, Crockett, and Chao 2010; Shah 2012; Wall Street Journal 2011.

The *Tiger Mother* has resonated on two levels. First, Amy Chua has gone public with the fact that she had entered into a legal contract with her daughters when she and her husband bought a Manhattan apartment and allowed their two 20-something daughters to live there. Today, the two young women claim their Mom is now a "hands-off mother" (Chua 2016; *The Week* 2016).

Second, and more importantly, *Battle Hymn of the Tiger Mother* ignited scholarly research into the parenting techniques used by Chinese American parents. The studies have generally noted that there is great variety in parenting styles; the "tiger" approach is one parenting style, but it is not necessarily particularly successful. Generally, Chinese American parents are much more flexible than they are depicted in the best-selling memoir (Cheah, Leung, and Zhou 2013; Jung, Qin, and Park 2013; Kim, Wang, Orozco-Lapray, Shen, and Murtuza 2013).

Close families as depicted in *The Battle Hymn of the Tiger Mother* and confirmed in other studies resonate in many immigrant communities. **Familism** means pride and closeness in the family, which results in family obligations and loyalty coming before individual needs. The Bureau of the Census (2009a: D7) found, for example, that children under 12 in Asian and Hispanic households in the United States were more likely to eat dinner with a parent every day than they were in White or Black households.

Fuse/Corbis/Getty Images

In many Chinese American families, the legacy of China remains. Parental authority, especially the father's, is more absolute, and the extended family is more important than it is in typical White middle-class families. Divorce is rare, and attitudes about sexual behavior tend to be strict because the Chinese generally frown on public expressions of emotion. We noted earlier that Chinese immigrant women in Chinatown often endured a harsh existence. A related problem beginning to surface is domestic violence. Although the available data do not indicate that Asian Pacific American men are any more abusive than men in other groups, their wives, as a rule, are less willing to talk about their plight and to seek help. The nation's first shelter for Asian Pacific American women was established in Los Angeles in 1981, but the problem is increasingly being recognized in more cities (Tong 2000).

Another problem for Chinese Americans is the rise in gang activity since the mid-1970s. Battles between opposing gangs have taken their toll, including the lives of some innocent bystanders. Some scholars trace the gangs to the tongs and thus consider them an aspect, admittedly destructive, of the cultural traditions some groups are trying to maintain. However, a more realistic interpretation is that Chinese American youths from the lower classes are not part of the model minority. Upward mobility is not in their future. Alienated, angry, and with prospects of low-wage work in restaurants and laundries, they turn to gangs such as the Ghost Shadows and Flying Dragons and extort money from Chinese American shopkeepers (Chin 1996; S. Lee 2013; Takaki 1998).

Japanese Americans: The Early Years

13.3 Summarize the Japanese American experience through World War II.

The nineteenth century was a period of sweeping social change for Japan: It brought the end of feudalism and the beginning of rapid urbanization and industrialization. Only a few pioneering Japanese came to the United States before 1885 because Japan prohibited emigration. After 1885, the numbers remained small relative to the great immigration from Europe at the time.

Early Immigration

With little consideration of the specific situation, the American government of the nineteenth century began to apply to Japan the same prohibitions it applied to China. Early feelings of anti-Asian prejudice were directed at the Japanese as well. The Japanese who immigrated into the United States in the 1890s took jobs as laborers at low wages under poor working conditions. Their industriousness in such circumstances made them popular with employers but unpopular with unions and other employees.

Japanese Americans distinguish sharply among themselves according to the number of generations a person's family has been in the United States. Generally, each succeeding generation is more acculturated, and each is successively less likely to know Japanese. The **Issei** (pronounced "EE-say") are the first generation, the immigrants born in Japan. Their children, the **Nisei** ("NEE-say"), are American-born. The third generation, the **Sansei** ("SAHN-say"), must go back to their grandparents to reach their roots in Japan. The **Yonsei** ("YOHN-say") are the fourth generation. Because Japanese immigration is recent, these four terms describe almost the entire contemporary Japanese American population. Some Nisei are sent by their parents to Japan for schooling and to have marriages arranged, after which they return to the United States. Japanese Americans expect such people, called **Kibei** ("keep-bay"), to be less acculturated than other Nisei. These terms sometimes are used loosely, and occasionally Nisei is used to describe all Japanese Americans. However, we use them here as they were intended to differentiate the four generational groups.

The Japanese arrived just as bigotry toward the Chinese had been legislated in the harsh Chinese Exclusion Act of 1882. For a time after the act, powerful business interests on the West Coast welcomed the Issei. The Japanese replaced the dwindling number of Chinese laborers in some industries, especially agriculture. In time, however, anti-Japanese feelings grew out of the anti-Chinese movement. The Whites who disliked the Chinese made the same charges against Japanese Americans. Eventually, a stereotype developed of Japanese Americans as lazy, dishonest, and untrustworthy.

The attack on Japanese Americans concentrated on limiting their ability to earn a living. In 1913, California enacted the Alien Land Act; amendments to the act in 1920 made it even stricter. The act prohibited anyone who was ineligible for citizenship from owning land and limited leases to three years. The anti-Japanese laws permanently influenced the form that Japanese American business enterprise was to take. In California, the land laws drove the Issei into cities. In the cities, however, government and union restrictions prevented large numbers from obtaining the available jobs, leaving self-employment as the only option. Japanese, more than other groups, ran hotels, grocery stores, and other medium-size businesses. Although this specialty limited their opportunities to advance, it did give urban Japanese Americans a marginal position in the expanding economy of the cities (Robinson 2001).

The Wartime Evacuation

Japan's attack on Pearl Harbor on December 7, 1941, brought the United States into World War II and marked a painful tragedy for the Issei and Nisei. Almost immediately, public pressure mounted to "do something" about the Japanese Americans living on the West Coast. Many White Americans feared that if Japan attacked the mainland, Japanese Americans would fight on behalf of Japan, making a successful invasion a real possibility. Pearl Harbor was followed by successful Japanese invasions of one Pacific island after another, and a Japanese submarine actually attacked a California oil tank complex early in 1943.

Rumors mixed with racism rather than facts explain the events that followed. Japanese Americans in Hawai'i were alleged to have cooperated in the attack on Pearl Harbor by using signaling devices to assist the pilots from Japan. Front-page attention was given to pronouncements by the Navy secretary that Japanese Americans held the greatest responsibility for the attack on Pearl Harbor. Newspapers covered in detail FBI arrests of Japanese Americans allegedly engaging in sabotage to assist the attackers. They were accused of poisoning drinking water, cutting patterns in sugarcane fields to form arrows directing enemy pilots to targets, and blocking traffic along highways to the harbor. None of these charges was substantiated, despite thorough investigations. It made no difference. In the 1940s, the treachery of the Japanese Americans was a foregone conclusion regardless of evidence to the contrary (Kashima 2003; Kimura 1988; Lind 1946; ten Broek, Barnhart, and Matson 1954).

EXECUTIVE ORDER 9066 On February 13, 1942, President Franklin Roosevelt signed Executive Order 9066. It defined strategic military areas in the United States and authorized the removal from those areas of any people considered threats to national security. The events

Figure 13.1 Japanese American Internment Camps

Japanese Americans were first ordered to report to assembly centers, from which, after a few weeks or months, they were resettled in internment camps or relocation centers. Ten camps were established in seven states.

SOURCE: Data from National Park Service 2012.

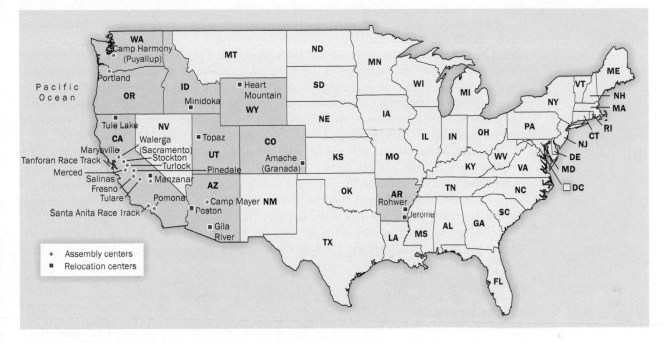

that followed were tragically simple. All people on the West Coast of at least one-eighth Japanese ancestry were taken to assembly centers for transfer to internment camps. These camps are identified in Figure 13.1. Executive Order 9066 covered 90 percent of the 126,000 Japanese Americans on the mainland. Of those evacuated, two-thirds were citizens, and three-fourths were under age 25. Ultimately, 120,000 Japanese Americans were relocated to the camps. Of mainland Japanese Americans, 113,000 were evacuated, but to those were added 219 voluntary residents (White spouses, typically) and, most poignantly of all, the 5,981 who were born in the camps (Robinson 2001; Takaki 1998).

The evacuation order did not arise from any court action. No trials took place. No indictments were issued. Merely having a Japanese great-grandparent was enough to mark a person for involuntary confinement. The evacuation was carried out with little difficulty. For Japanese Americans to have fled or militantly defied the order would only have confirmed the suspicions of their fellow Americans. There was little visible objection initially from the Japanese Americans. The Japanese American Citizens League (JACL), which had been founded by the Nisei as a self-help organization in 1924, even decided not to arrange a court test of the evacuation order. The JACL felt that cooperating with the military might lead to sympathetic consideration later when tensions subsided (Iwamasa 2008b).

Even before reaching the camps, the **evacuees**, as Japanese Americans being forced to resettle came to be called officially, paid a price for their ancestry. They were instructed to carry only personal items. No provision was made for shipping their household goods. The federal government took a few steps to safeguard the belongings they left behind, but the evacuees assumed all risks and agreed to turn over their property for an indeterminate length of time. These Japanese Americans were destroyed economically. Merchants, farmers, and business owners had to sell all their property at any price they could get. Precise figures of the loss in dollars are difficult to obtain, but after the war the Federal Reserve Bank estimated the loss to be $400 million. To place this amount in perspective, in 2010 dollars, the economic damages sustained, excluding personal income, would be more than $3.6 billion (Bureau of the Census 2011a: 473; Commission on Wartime Relocation and Internment of Civilians 1982a, 1982b; Hosokawa 1969; Thomas and Nishimoto 1946).

THE CAMPS   Ten camps were established in seven states. Were they actually concentration camps? Obviously, they were not concentration camps constructed for the murderous purposes of those in Nazi Germany, but such a positive comparison is no compliment to the United States. To refer to them by their official designation as *relocation centers* ignores these facts: The Japanese Americans did not go there voluntarily; they had been charged with no crime; and they could not leave without official approval.

Japanese Americans were able to work at wage labor in the camps. The maximum wage was set at $19 a month, which meant that camp work could not possibly recoup the losses incurred by evacuation. The evacuees had to depend on the government for food and shelter, a situation they had not experienced in prewar civilian life. More devastating than the economic damage of camp life was the psychological damage. Guilty of no crime, the Japanese Americans moved through a monotonous daily routine with no chance of changing the situation. Forced community life, with such shared activities as eating in mess halls, weakened the strong family ties that Japanese Americans, especially the Issei, took so seriously.

Amid the economic and psychological devastation, the camps began to take on some resemblance to U.S. cities of a similar size. High schools were established, complete with cheerleaders and yearbooks. Ironically, Fourth of July parades were held, with camp-organized Boy Scout and Girl Scout troops marching past proud parents. But the barbed wire remained, and the Japanese Americans were asked to prove their loyalty.

A loyalty test was administered in 1943 on a form all evacuees had to fill out: the Application for Leave Clearance. Many of the Japanese Americans were undecided on how to respond to two questions:

> No. 27. *Are you willing to serve in the armed forces of the United States on combat duty, wherever ordered?*
> No. 28. *Will you swear to abide by the laws of the United States and to take no action, which would in any way interfere with the war effort of the United States?* (Daniels 1972:113)

The ambiguity of the questions left many internees confused about how to respond. For example, if Issei said yes to the second question, would they then lose their Japanese citizenship and be left stateless? The Issei would be ending allegiance to Japan but were unable, at the time, to gain U.S. citizenship. Similarly, would Nisei who responded yes be suggesting that they had been supporters of Japan? For these reasons and from a desire to protest their captivity, 6,700 Issei and Nisei answered "no" to the questions and were transferred to the high-security camp at Tule Lake (see Figure 13.1) for the duration of the war (Bigelow 1992; Onishi 2012).

Overwhelmingly, Japanese Americans showed loyalty to the government that had created the camps. In general, security in the camps was not a problem. The U.S. Army, which had overseen the removal of the Japanese Americans, recognized the value of the Japanese Americans as translators in the war ahead. About 6,000 Nisei were recruited to work as interpreters and translators, and by 1943, a special combat unit of 23,000 Nisei volunteers had been created to fight in Europe. The predominantly Nisei unit was unmatched, and it concluded the war as the most decorated of all American units.

Japanese American behavior in the concentration camps can be seen only as reaffirming their loyalty. True, some internees refused to sign an oath, but that was hardly a treasonous act. More typical were the tens of thousands of evacuees who contributed to the U.S. war effort.

A few Japanese Americans resisted the evacuation and internment. Several cases arising out of the evacuation and detention reached the U.S. Supreme Court during the war. Amazingly, the Court upheld lower court decisions such as the 1944 decision in *Korematsu v. United States* on Japanese Americans without raising the constitutionality of the entire plan. Essentially, the Court upheld the idea of an entire race's collective guilt. Finally,

Interned Japanese Americans attempted to recreate social organizations similar to those they had known before being placed in camps. Here a Japanese American Boy Scout troop stands at attention at a Memorial Day ceremony at Manzanar War Relocation Center in California.

nsf/Alamy Stock Photo

after hearing *Mitsuye Endo v. United States*, the Supreme Court ruled, on December 18, 1944, that the detainment was unconstitutional and consequently the defendant (and presumably all evacuees) must be granted freedom. Two weeks later, Japanese Americans were allowed to return to their homes for the first time in three years, and the camps were finally closed in 1946. Each internee was handed $25 and a train ticket (Liptak 2014a; Orenstein 2011).

The immediate postwar climate was not pro–Japanese American. Whites terrorized returning evacuees in attacks similar to those against Blacks a generation earlier. Labor unions called for work stoppages when Japanese Americans reported for work. Fortunately, the most blatant expression of anti-Japanese feeling disappeared rather quickly. Japan stopped being a threat when the atomic bomb blasts destroyed Nagasaki and Hiroshima. For the many evacuees who lost relatives and friends in the bombings, however, it must have been a high price to pay for marginal acceptance (Iwamasa 2008a; Robinson 2001, 2009).

Contemporary Japanese Americans

13.4 Describe the contemporary Japanese American experience.

Until 1960, Japanese Americans were the largest Asian Pacific American group, but they are now outnumbered by the Chinese, Indian, Filipino, and Korean American communities. This change is the result of two key factors: (1) the continuing immigration of these other nationalities, and (2) little movement here from Japan, where people perceive that they enjoy a high standard of living.

Contemporary Japanese Americans tend to have small families and often intermarry, leading to biracial households. Their levels of English proficiency as a group approach those of the nation as a whole. Their home ownership and income levels are higher than the general population, and they have lower poverty rates (Taylor 2013). However, before we consider the economic picture and present-day family life among Japanese Americans in more detail, we must understand how Japanese Americans made the transition from the wartime camps back into mainstream society.

The Evacuation: What Does It Mean?

The social significance of the wartime evacuation has often been treated as a historical anomaly, but in the wake of the stigmatizing of Arab and Muslim Americans after 9/11, the singling out people of Japanese descent almost 70 years ago takes on new meaning. In the heat of the immigration debate of 2016–2017, some elected officials pointed to the national registry of people of Japanese descent and the internment camps as a precedent for how to deal with Muslim Americans as a group. Efforts to formally revoke the 1944 *Korematsu* decision, which ruled internment by virtue of race to be unconstitutional, have failed (Bromwich 2016; Railton 2016).

The evacuation policy cost the U.S. taxpayers a quarter of a billion dollars in construction, transportation, and military expenses. Japanese Americans, as already noted, effectively lost at least several billion dollars. These are only the tangible costs to the nation. The relocation was not justifiable on any security grounds. No verified act of espionage or sabotage by a Japanese American was recorded. So why did the internment happen?

Racism cannot be ignored as an explanation. Japanese Americans were placed in camps, but German Americans and Italian Americans were largely ignored. Many of those whose decisions brought about the evacuation were of German and Italian ancestry. The fact was that the Japanese were expendable. Placing them in camps posed no hardship for the rest of society, and, in fact, other Americans profited by their misfortune. That Japanese Americans were evacuated because they were seen as expendable is evident from the decision not to evacuate Hawai'i's Japanese. In Hawai'i, the Japanese were an integral part of the society; removing them would have destroyed the islands economically (Kimura 1988; Robinson 2009).

Documents recently unearthed show that government officials saw the Japanese Americans collectively as enemy aliens and that it would not be possible to determine loyalty of individual people. Why not? According to the thinking at the time, government leaders felt the "cultural traits" of the Japanese prevented outsiders from telling who was loyal and disloyal (Herzig-Yoshinaga and Lee 2011; Linthicum 2011).

Some people argue that the Japanese lack of resistance made internment possible. This seems a weak effort to transfer guilt—*to blame the victim*. In the 1960s, some Sansei and Yonsei were concerned about the alleged timidity of their parents and grandparents when faced with evacuation orders. However, many evacuees, perhaps even most, may not have really believed what was happening. "It just cannot be that bad," they may have thought. At worst, the evacuees can be accused of being naive. But even if they did see clearly how devastating the order would be, what alternatives were open to them? None.

The Commission on Wartime Relocation and Internment of Civilians in 1981 held hearings on whether additional reparations should be paid to evacuees or their heirs. The final commission recommendation in 1983 was that the government formally apologize and give $20,000 tax-free to each of the approximately 82,000 surviving internees. Congress began hearings in 1986 on the bill authorizing these steps, and President Ronald Reagan signed the Civil Liberties Act of 1988, which authorized the payments. The payments, however, were slow in coming because other federal expenditures had higher priority. Meanwhile, the aging internees were dying at a rate of 200 a month. In 1990, the first checks were finally issued, accompanied by President Bush's letter of apology. Many Japanese Americans were disappointed by and critical of the begrudging nature of the compensation and the length of time it had taken to receive it (Commission on Wartime Relocation and Internment of Civilians 1982a, 1982b; Department of Justice 2000; Haak 1970; Kitano 1976; Robinson 2012; Takezawa 1991).

For 14 years, until 2017, Mike Honda represented in the U. S. House of Representatives the area of California including San Jose and the technology corridor dubbed "Silicon Valley." During World War II, from ages one to almost five, he lived at Camp Amache, a Japanese American internment camp in southeast Colorado (see Figure 13.1). The internment was especially ironic for Honda given his father's service in the U.S. Military Intelligence Service.

Congressman Honda (2014) has observed, "One of the first lessons I learned was that being Japanese carried a negative connotation in America. My parents raised me talking about the injustices of camp, how it was a violation of the Constitution, and how Japanese Americans had been mistreated. I've since followed in their footsteps by advocating for social justice and publicly serving communities that do not have a voice."

Perhaps actor George Takei, of *Star Trek* fame in the role of Lieutenant Sulu, sums up best the wartime legacy of the evacuation of Japanese Americans. As a child, he lived with his parents in the Tule Lake, California, camp (see Figure 13.1). In 1996, on the fiftieth anniversary of the camp's closing and five years before 9/11 would turn the nation's attention elsewhere, he reflected on his arrival at the camp: "America betrayed American ideals at this camp. We must not have national amnesia; we must remember this" (Lin 1996:10).

The Economic Picture

The socioeconomic status of Japanese Americans as a group is different from that of other APAs. Japanese Americans as a group are very well educated and do not have the pockets of poverty found among other APA groups. Also in contrast to other APAs, the Japanese American community is more settled and less affected by new arrivals from the home country.

The camps left a legacy with economic implications; the Japanese American community of the 1950s was very different from that of the 1930s. By the 1950s, Japanese Americans were more widely scattered. In 1940, 89 percent lived on the West Coast. By 1950, only 58 percent of the population had returned to the West Coast. Another difference was that a smaller proportion than before was Issei. The Nisei and later generations accounted for 63 percent of the Japanese population. By moving to places other than the West Coast, Japanese Americans seemed less of a threat than if they had remained concentrated in one geographic region. Furthermore, by dispersing,

Not far from the memory of Japanese Americans is the wartime evacuation experience. *Star Trek*'s George Takei, shown on the right, produced and starred in the Broadway musical, *Allegiance*, to retell his story of growing up in one of the camps.

WENN Ltd/Alamy Stock Photo

Japanese American businesspeople had to develop ties to the larger economy rather than do business mostly with other Japanese Americans. Although ethnic businesses can be valuable initially, those who limit their dealings to those from the same country may limit their economic potential (Oliver and Shapiro 1996: 46).

After the war, some Japanese Americans continued to experience hardship. Some remained on the West Coast and farmed as sharecroppers in a role similar to that of the freed slaves after the Civil War. Sharecropping involved working the land of others, who provided shelter, seeds, and equipment and who also shared any profits at the time of harvest. The Japanese Americans used the practice to gradually get back into farming after being stripped of their land during World War II.

However, perhaps the most dramatic development has been the upward mobility that Japanese Americans collectively and individually have accomplished since the end of World War II. By occupational and academic standards, two indicators of success, Japanese Americans are doing very well. The educational attainment of Japanese Americans as a group, as well as their family earnings, is higher than that of Whites, but caution should be used in interpreting such group data. Obviously, large numbers of APAs, as well as Whites, have little formal schooling and are employed in low-wage jobs. Furthermore, Japanese Americans are concentrated in areas of the United States such as Hawai'i, California, Washington, New York, and Illinois, where wages and the cost of living are far above the national average. Also, the proportion of Japanese American families with multiple wage earners is higher than that of White families. Nevertheless, the overall picture for Japanese Americans is remarkable, especially for a racial minority that had been discriminated against so openly and so recently (Inoue 1989; Kitano 1980; Nishi 1995).

The Japanese American story does not end with another account of oppression and hardship. Today, Japanese Americans have achieved success by almost any standard. However, we must qualify the progress that *Newsweek* (1971) once billed as its "Success Story: Outwhiting the Whites." First, it is easy to forget that several generations of Japanese Americans achieved what they did by overcoming barriers that U.S. society had created, not because they had been welcomed. However, many, perhaps even most, have become acculturated. Nevertheless, successful Japanese Americans still are not wholeheartedly accepted into the dominant group's inner circle of social clubs and fraternal organizations. Second, Japanese Americans today may represent a stronger indictment of society than economically oppressed African Americans, Native Americans, and Hispanics. Whites can use few excuses apart from racism to explain why they continue to look on Japanese Americans as different—as "them."

Family Life

The contradictory pulls of tradition and rapid change that are characteristic of Chinese Americans are also very strong among Japanese Americans today. Surviving Issei see their grandchildren as very nontraditional. Change in family life is one of the most difficult cultural changes for any immigrant to accept in the younger generations.

As cultural traditions fade, the contemporary Japanese American family seems to continue the success story. The divorce rate has been low, although it is probably rising. Similar conclusions apply to crime, delinquency, and reported mental illness. Data on all types of social disorganization show that Japanese Americans have a lower incidence of such behavior than all other minorities; it is also lower than that of Whites. Japanese Americans find it possible to be good Japanese and good Americans simultaneously. Japanese culture demands high ingroup unity, politeness, respect for authority, and duty to community—all traits that are highly acceptable to middle-class Americans. Basically, psychological research has concluded that Japanese Americans share the high-achievement orientation held by many middle-class White Americans. However, one might expect that as Japanese Americans continue to acculturate, the breakdown in traditional Japanese behavior will be accompanied by a rise in social deviance (Nishi 1995).

In the past 40 years, a somewhat different family pattern has emerged in what can almost be regarded as a second Japanese community forming. As Japan's economic engine took off in the latter part of the twentieth century, corporate Japan sought opportunities abroad. Because of its large automobile market, the United States economy became one destination. Top-level executives and their families were relocated to look after these enterprises. These recent immigrants have created a small but significant community of Japanese in the United States. Although they are unlikely to stay, they are creating a presence that is difficult to miss. Several private schools have been established since 1966 in the United States, in which children follow Japanese curriculum and retain their native language and culture. Saturday school is maintained for Japanese American parents whose children attend public school during the week. Although these private academies are removed from the broader culture, they help facilitate the nearby creation of authentic markets and Japanese bookstores. Researchers are interested to see what might be the lasting social implications of these households from Japan (Dolnick and Semple 2011; Lewis 2008; Twohey 2007).

Remnants of Prejudice and Discrimination

13.5   Identify how prejudice and discrimination against Chinese and Japanese Americans persist.

Today, young Japanese Americans and Chinese Americans are very ambivalent about their cultural heritage. The pull to be American is intense, but so are the reminders that in the eyes of many others, Asian Pacific Americans are "they," not "we." Congressman David Wu emigrated from Taiwan in 1961 at age six and became the first person of Chinese descent elected to Congress. In this role, he was invited to a celebration of Asian Pacific American accomplishments at the Department of Energy building but was denied entry. "Profiling was not involved" was the official response, which stated that congressional ID is insufficient to clear security. However, the next day, an Italian American congressman gained entry using the same type of credential (Zhou 2009).

Why does intolerance continue toward Chinese, Japanese, and other APAs? An analysis by the Japanese American Citizens League (2013), noted for its efforts to gain redress for the internment camp survivors, offered four causes:

1. Xenophobia and the visibility of Asian Pacific Americans. **Xenophobia**, the fear or hatred of strangers or outsiders, is certainly present in contemporary society.

2. Economic and international relations that often find the United States at a competitive disadvantage.

3. Media portrayals and public perceptions that continue to perpetuate stereotypes, whether negative or more neutral, like the "model minority" myth.

4. The "Asian Monolith" view, which despite the diversity we have seen among APAs, is still rampant among many White Americans.

All of these factors surface in microaggressions today. As defined in Chapter 2, **microaggressions** are commonplace verbal indignities and continue to be experienced by Asian Pacific Americans.

While misfortune among any racial and ethnic group is a daily occurrence, certain events elevate to the national level. The Speaking Out feature reproduces the Japanese American Citizens League's strong statement in defense of Chinese American police officer Peter Liang, whose conviction for mistakenly killing a civilian was described in Chapter 12. It is significant to note how civil rights groups organized on behalf of one racial or ethnic minority see the strong need to speak up when they identify harm coming to members of other groups.

Chinese Americans and Japanese Americans believe that prejudice and discrimination have decreased in the United States, but subtle reminders remain. Third-generation Japanese Americans, for example, feel insulted when they are told, "You speak English so well." Adopting new tactics, Asian Americans are now trying to fight racist and exclusionary practices (Lem 1976).

Marriage statistics also illustrate the effects of assimilation. At one time, 29 states prohibited or severely regulated marriages between Asians and non-Asians. Today, intermarriage, though not typical, is legal and certainly much more common. The increased intermarriage indicates that Whites are increasingly accepting of Chinese Americans and

Speaking Out

Statement on Liang Decision

The Japanese American Citizens League (JACL), the oldest and largest Asian American civil rights organization, has always stood with those working to create

Japanese American Citizens League

Used with the permission of Japanese American Citizens League.

institutional change. In the case of the tragic death of Akai Gurley, we support justice for Gurley, as well as a fair and just judicial process for former New York police officer Peter Liang. Liang's conviction demonstrates how structural racism can pit communities of color against each other, and only serves to underscore the need for a continued dialogue around the biased treatment of communities of color by the justice system.

In the wake of the conviction of Liang, found guilty of second-degree manslaughter and official misconduct in the death of Gurley, a debate among the Asian American community has spread across the country. While conducting a "vertical patrol" of a public housing complex in Brooklyn in late 2014, Liang accidentally fired his gun in a dark stairwell; the bullet ricocheted off a concrete wall and hit Gurley in the chest. Both Liang and his partner, Shaun Landau, were unable to perform medical procedures on Gurley.

Regardless of how these actions are interpreted, one thing is clear—an innocent man died. It is fair to call into question the training of these officers or the state of the public housing

complex, as symptoms of deeper systemic issues that enabled this tragedy. It is also fair to question the underlying racial implications of this case, as there is no question that Liang, an Asian American, was treated differently from other police officers who have not been held accountable for actions against unarmed men and women of color.

We have seen the struggle for racial equity play out in increasingly numerous violent incidents over the last several years. Instead of fighting within our own community, or against other communities of color, we would remind all those invested in this issue that our outrage at this verdict is not because Liang is being held accountable for his actions—our outrage is at a flawed system that allowed officers in similar situations to not face similar consequences.

There are no winners in a case like this. We must acknowledge that the justice system does not treat everyone equally, that an implicit racial bias disadvantages the majority of those who go through it, and that we must continue having uncomfortable conversations about race to face the reality of the country we live in.

The JACL will continue to work with all who stand together in the fight for racial equity and criminal justice reform.

Source: JJACL Statement on Liang Decision. February 25, 2016 at jal.org. Used with permission.

Japanese Americans. It also suggests that Chinese and Japanese ties to their native cultures are weakening. As happened with the ways of life of European immigrants, the traditional norms are being cast aside for those of the host society. In one sense, these changes make Chinese Americans and Japanese Americans more acceptable and less alien to Whites. But this conclusion points to all the changes in APAs rather than to any recognition of diversity in the United States. As illustrated in the Spectrum of Intergroup Relations (Figure 13.2), intermarriage patterns reflect the fusion of different racial groups; however, compared with examples of assimilation and pluralism, they are a limited social process at present.

The Japanese American community struggles to maintain its cultural identity while also paying homage to those who were interned during World War II. Unfortunately, even as many people see parallels between the collective guilt forced on people of Japanese ancestry during the 1940s and the profiling of Arab and Muslim Americans today, a few are seeking to justify the internment. Textbooks and even a public middle school named after an internee in Washington State have been criticized; critics argue that the subject of Japanese American internment is taught in a biased manner and that arguments in favor of internment being the correct action should also be taught (Malkin 2004; Tizon 2004).

It would be incorrect to interpret assimilation as an absence of protest. Because a sizable segment of the college youth of the 1960s and early 1970s held militant attitudes, and because the Sansei are more heterogeneous than their Nisei and Issei relatives, it was to be expected that some Japanese Americans, especially the Sansei, would become politically active. For example,

Figure 13.2 Spectrum of Intergroup Relations: Chinese Americans and Japanese Americans

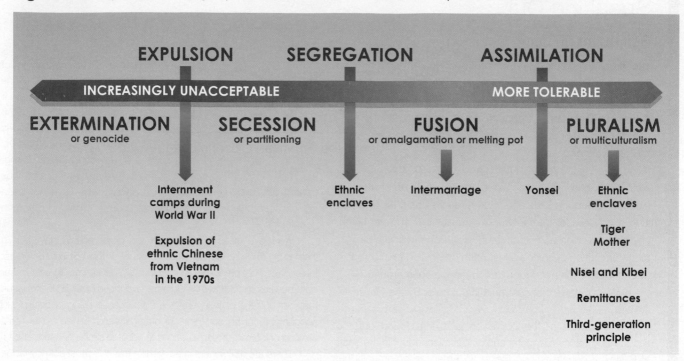

Japanese and other APAs have emerged as activists for environmental concerns ranging from contaminated fish to toxic working conditions, and the targets of Japanese Americans' anger have included the apparent rise in hate crimes in the United States against APAs in the 1990s. They also lobbied for passage of the Civil Rights Restoration Act, which extended reparations to the evacuees. They have engaged in further activism through Hiroshima Day ceremonies that mark the anniversary of the dropping of the first atomic bomb on a major Japanese city during World War II. Also, each February, a group of Japanese American youths makes a pilgrimage to the site of the Tule Lake evacuation camp in a "Lest We Forget" observance. Efforts are also underway to restore other internment sites as historical reminders of what happened. Such protests are modest, but they are a major departure from the silent role played by the Nisei in the years immediately following the closing of the camps (Turkewitz 2016).

Is pluralism developing? The Japanese values that have endured are attitudes, beliefs, and goals shared by and rewarded by the White middle class in America. Japanese Americans of later generations, even those married to non–Japanese Americans, show little evidence of a complete orientation to American culture. All APAs, not only Japanese Americans, are caught in the middle. Any APA is culturally a part of a society that is dominated by a group that excludes him or her because of racial distinctions (Iwasaki and Brown 2014).

Even if Japanese Americans and other APAs wanted to be indistinguishable from all other Americans, society is reluctant to let that happen. Anthropologist Takeyuki Tsuda (2014: 410, 2016) interviewed one fourth-generation Japanese American young woman who recalls being asked at a cocktail party where she was from and responding, "Los Angeles." The fellow partygoer quickly followed up with, "No, where are you originally from?" Still unaware of what was happening, she said "Seattle." When she saw the questioner's puzzled expression, it dawned on her what was happening—she was viewed as a foreigner at that party.

Conclusion

Most White adults are confident that they can distinguish Asians from Europeans. Unfortunately, though, White Americans often cannot tell the different groups of APAs apart based only on their physical appearance—and are not disturbed about their confusion.

However, as we have seen, there are definite differences in the experience of the Chinese and the Japanese in the United States. One obvious difference is in the degree of assimilation. Chinese Americans have maintained their ethnic enclaves more than Japanese Americans have. Chinatowns live on, both as welcomed halfway points for new arrivals and as enclaves where many residents make very low wages. But as we saw at the beginning of Chapter 5, New York City's Chinatown is expanding and has taken over the space formerly referred to as Little Italy. However, there are few Little Tokyos in the United States due to the differences in the cultures of China and Japan. China was almost untouched by European influence, but even by the early 1900s, Japan had already been influenced by the West. Therefore, the Japanese arrived somewhat more assimilated than their Chinese counterparts. The continued migration of Chinese in recent years has also meant that Chinese Americans as a group have been less assimilated than Japanese Americans.

Both groups have achieved some success, but this success has not extended to all members. For Chinese Americans, a notable exception to success can be found in Chinatowns, which, behind the tourist front, are much like other poverty-stricken areas in U.S. cities. Neither Chinese Americans nor Japanese Americans have figured prominently in the executive offices of the nation's largest corporations and financial institutions. Compared with other racial and ethnic groups, APAs have shown little interest in participating in political activity on their own behalf.

However, the success of APAs, especially that of Japanese Americans, belongs to the people themselves, not to U.S. society. First, APAs have been considered successful only because they conform to the dominant society's expectations. Their acceptance as a group does not necessarily indicate growing pluralism in the United States.

Second, the ability of the Nisei, in particular, to recover from the internment camp experience cannot be taken as a precedent for other racial minorities. The Japanese Americans left the camps a skilled group, ambitious to overcome their adversity and placing a cultural emphasis on formal education. They entered a booming economy in which Whites and others could not afford to discriminate even if they wanted to. African Americans after slavery and Hispanic immigrants have entered the economy without skills at a time when the demand for manual labor was limited. Many of them were forced to remain in a marginal economy, whether that of the ghetto, the barrio, or subsistence agriculture. For Japanese Americans, the post–World War II period marked the fortunate coincidence of their having assets and ambition when they could be used to full advantage.

Third, some Whites use the success of APAs to prop up their own prejudice. Bigoted people twist APA success to show that racism cannot possibly play a part in another group's subordination. If the Japanese or Chinese can do it, the illogical reasoning goes, why cannot African Americans? More directly, Japanese Americans' success may serve as a scapegoat for another group's failure ("They advanced at my expense") or as a sign that they are "clannish" or too "ambitious." Regardless of what a group does, a prejudiced eye will always view it as wrong.

As for other racial and ethnic minorities, assimilation seems to be the path most likely to lead to tolerance but not necessarily to acceptance. However, assimilation has a price that is well captured in the Chinese phrase "*Zhancao zhugen*": "To eliminate the weeds, one must pull out their roots." To work for acceptance means to uproot all traces of one's cultural heritage and former identity (Wang 1991).

Summary of Learning Objectives

13.1 Understand the history of the Chinese Americans.

1. Although welcomed for their labor in the nineteenth century, Chinese immigrants quickly came to be viewed as responsible for economic setbacks experienced by the nation, which culminated in the passage of the Chinese Exclusion Act.

13.2 Describe the present-day circumstances of Chinese Americans.

2. Chinatowns are very visible signs of continued growth of the Chinese American population and represent both promise and problems for the immigrants. The family is a central focus in the Chinese community and is critical to the successful adaptation of immigrants to the United States.

13.3 Summarize the Japanese American experience through World War II.

3. Immigrants from Japan, like so many others, were permitted to come when they filled an economic niche but were quickly marginalized socially and legally. The internment of people of Japanese ancestry during World War II is a clear instance of assumed guilt by virtue of race.

13.4 Describe the contemporary Japanese American experience.

4. The prosperity of Japanese Americans as a group reflects their willingness to endure post–World War II marginalization, as well as continued investment in formal schooling for their children. In addition, Japanese Americans' dispersal across the United States helped them form business alliances with non-Japanese-owned companies.

13.5 Identify how prejudice and discrimination against Chinese and Japanese Americans persist.

5. Despite competing effectively in the labor market, or perhaps because of it, Chinese and Japanese Americans continue to experience prejudice and discrimination in the twenty-first century.

Key Terms

evacuees, *page 291*
familism, *page 288*
hui kuan, *page 285*
Issei, *page 290*
Kibei, *page 290*

microaggressions, *page 296*
Nisei, *page 290*
principle of third-
    generation interest, *page 283*
Sansei, *page 290*

tiger mother, *page 288*
tongs, *page 285*
tsu, *page 285*
xenophobia, *page 296*
Yonsei, *page 290*

Review Questions

1. What has been the legacy of the "yellow peril"?

2. In what ways was the placement of Japanese Americans in internment camps unique?

3. In what respects does diversity characterize Chinatowns?

4. How has Japanese American assimilation been blocked in the United States?

5. What are the most significant similarities between the Chinese American and Japanese American experiences? What are the key differences?

Critical Thinking

1. Considering the past as well as the present, are the moves made to restrict or exclude Chinese and Japanese Americans based on economic motives or racist motives?

2. How do we attribute the success of many Asian Pacific Americans despite continuing racism?

3. What events can you imagine that could cause the United States to again identify an ethnic group for confinement in some type of internment camp?

4. What stereotypical images of Chinese Americans and Japanese Americans can you identify in the contemporary media?

Chapter 14
Jewish Americans: The Quest to Maintain Identity

Mark Richards / Photo Edit

Learning Objectives

14.1 Examine whether the Jewish people are considered a race, religion, or ethnic group.

14.2 Summarize the history of Jewish immigration to the United States.

14.3 Describe the extent of anti-Semitism historically and in the present.

14.4 Explain Jewish Americans' economic, educational, and political situation.

14.5 Describe the role of religion among Jewish Americans.

14.6 Explain Jewish identity.

Critical to the Jewish faith is the ability to have a congregation of sufficient size to have a rabbi and to undertake religious obligations such as public prayer. For the many rural congregations and even in some urban areas, finding critical mass can be a challenge. Temple Emanu-El in Dotham, Mississippi, has seen its membership dwindle from 110 in the 1970s to 43 in 2010. In response, it has started to recruit families. Through a program it calls the "Jewish stimulus package," the temple offers families as much as $50,000 to join.

Similarly, in New Orleans, Jewish organizations offered a $1,500 cash incentive to lure Jews back after Hurricane Katrina. Even in New York City, which is home to the largest concentration of Jewish Americans, not all synagogues have enough local households to keep their doors open, so one Jewish center offers $22,500 in rent money to attract Jewish families to its service area in the Bronx.

Picture these images: Swastikas scrawled on classroom walls, desks, lockers, textbooks, and the playground slide. A social studies classroom displaying the country's leader with a swastika drawn on his forehead. Students exchanging Nazi salutes. Germany in the 1930s? No, this was an American middle and high school in 2013. For two years, Jewish students in Pine Bush, New York, complained to the superintendent that so many in the school were exhibiting anti-Semitic behavior that "your expectations for changing inbred prejudice may be a bit unrealistic" (Weiser 2013:A29). As news of this hostile environment spread, the governor of New York directed the New York State Police and the State Division of Human Rights to investigate the situation. Eventually, the district agreed to pay several million dollars to former and current Jewish students who had been taunted by anti-Semitism (Berger 2015; Hu 2012).

The United States has the second-largest Jewish population in the world. This nation's approximately 5.7 million Jews account for 40 percent of the world's Jewish population. Jewish Americans not only represent a significant group in the United States but also play a prominent role in the worldwide Jewish community. The nation with the largest Jewish population, Israel, is the only one in which Jews comprise the majority. Figure 14.1 depicts the worldwide distribution of Jews.

The Jewish people are different from the other subordinate groups we have studied. At least 1,500 years had passed since Jews were the dominant group in any nation until Israel was created in 1948. Even there, Jews are in competition for power. American Jews superficially resemble Asian Pacific Americans in that both groups are largely free from poverty, compared to Chicanos or Puerto Ricans. Unlike those groups, however, the Jewish cultural heritage is not nationalistic in origin. Perhaps the most striking difference is that the history of anti-Jewish prejudice and discrimination (usually called **anti-Semitism**) is nearly as old as relations between Jews and **Gentiles** (non-Jews).

Without question, people in North America and Europe give the countries of the Southern Hemisphere little attention unless they are directly affected. In the Global View feature, we discuss Argentina's Jewish community, which was victimized in 1992 by a deadly attack that is still remembered today.

Figure 14.1 Worldwide Distribution of Jews, 2015

NOTE: Data include all nations with at least 35,000 Jews. Rounded to nearest thousand.

SOURCE: Data from DellaPergola 2015.

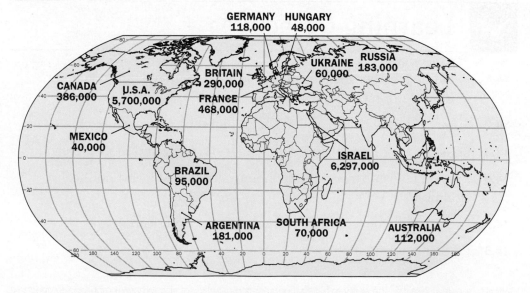

A Global View

Argentina's Jewish Community

Jewish settlements are found throughout the world as a result of the dispersal, or *Diaspora*, from Palestine. Efforts to resettle in Europe often led to local and national actions over several centuries to expel the Jews, so sizable Jewish settlements eventually developed not only in North America but also in Argentina, especially after it obtained its independence from Spain. Argentina currently has the largest Jewish population in Latin America. It is estimated that 181,000 Jews live in Argentina.

The first Jews settled in Argentina shortly after their expulsion from Spain in 1492. Stigmatized, these early settlers often hid their faith from others and soon assimilated with other immigrants from Europe. By the nineteenth century, public vestiges of Jewish worship began to emerge in Argentina. One significant group of Jews from Russia settled in the frontier of Argentina, becoming cowboys or, as they are called there, *gauchos*.

The years after World War II were mixed times for Jews in Argentina because the country's leader, Juan Perón, had been sympathetic to the Nazis and welcomed Hitler's followers to the country. Yet Perón also established early diplomatic relations with Israel, smoothing the way for Israeli Jews who wished to settle in Argentina. Later, human rights abuses during the dictatorship of 1976–1983 were anti-Semitic: Swastikas were carved in people's bodies, and Jews were targeted.

Even more violent was the 1992 bombing of the Israeli embassy (29 dead) and the Jewish center of Asociación Mutual Israelita Argentina (85 dead). The government blamed these events on outside forces, perhaps from Iran, but no convictions have occurred. To this day, the latter remains the largest terrorist act ever to occur on Argentine soil.

In the past three decades, Argentina has taken a consistent pro-Israel position and has cooperated with efforts to locate Nazi war criminals who may still be hiding in Argentina. Argentine Jews have achieved some success in industry but are largely absent in the higher ranks of the military, foreign affairs, and the court system. Visible Jewish buildings have been the targets of attacks, and many synagogues remain tightly guarded. Jewish immigration is now largely a factor of economic conditions. Downturns in the Argentine economy are associated with a migration to Israel and elsewhere, while upswings lead to an influx of immigrants, including Jews. Evidence suggests that the Argentine Jewish population is aging and that total numbers are not growing.

The Jewish community in Argentina resembles that of many other countries. The majority of Jewish youth attend day schools that provide instruction in Judaism and Hebrew. McDonald's has even established its only kosher restaurant outside of Israel. Besides offering a menu conforming to Jews' dietary restrictions, this McDonald's closes for the Sabbath. Buenos Aires, home to the largest urban Jewish population outside of Israel, North America, and Europe, is the center of Jewish life in today's Argentina. It boasts numerous Jewish organizations and one of the world's four remaining daily Yiddish newspapers.

Sources: DellaPergola 2015; Miller 2014; Pew Research Center 2015c; Rosenbloom 2014; Schwartz 2008; Schweimler 2007; Timerman 2002; Weiner 2008.

The Jewish People: Race, Religion, or Ethnic Group?

14.1 **Examine whether the Jewish people are considered a race, religion, or ethnic group.**

Jews are a subordinate group. They fulfill the criteria set forth in Chapter 1:

- Jewish Americans experience unequal treatment from non-Jews in the form of prejudice, discrimination, and segregation.
- Jews share a cultural history that distinguishes them from the dominant group.
- Jews do not choose to be Jewish, in the same way that Whites do not choose to be White and Mexican Americans do not choose to be Mexican American.
- Jews have a strong sense of group solidarity.
- Jewish men and women tend to marry one another rather than marry outside the group.

What are the distinguishing traits for Jewish Americans? Are they physical features, thus making Jews a racial group? Are the distinguishing characteristics matters of faith, suggesting that Jews are best regarded as a religious minority? Or are Jews' chief characteristics cultural and social, making Jews an ethnic group? To answer these questions, we must address the ancient and perennial question: What is a Jew?

The issue of what makes a Jew is not only a scholarly question; in Israel, it figures in policy matters. The Israel Law of Return defines who is a Jew and extends Israeli citizenship to all Jews. Jews are defined as any person who has at least one Jewish grandparent or whose spouse has at least one Jewish grandparent. Currently, Israeli law also recognizes all converts to the faith, but pressure has grown recently to limit citizenship to those whose conversions were performed by Orthodox rabbis. Although this change would have little practical impact, symbolically, this pressure shows the tension and lack of consensus even among Jews over who is a Jew.

The definition of race used here is fairly explicit. The Jewish people are not physically differentiated from non-Jews. True, many people believe they can tell a Jew from a non-Jew, but true distinguishing physical traits are absent. Jews today come from all areas of the world and carry a variety of physical features. Most Jewish Americans are descended from northern and eastern Europeans and have the appearance of Nordic and Alpine people. Many others carry Mediterranean traits that make them indistinguishable from Spanish or Italian Catholics. Many Jews reside in North Africa, and although these Jews are not significantly represented in the United States, many people would view them only as a racial minority: Black. The wide range of variation among Jews makes it inaccurate to speak of a Jewish race in a physical sense (Gittler 1981; Montagu 1972).

To define Jews by religion seems the obvious answer because there are Judaic religious beliefs and rituals. But these beliefs and practices do not distinguish all Jews from non-Jews. To be a Jewish American does not mean that one is affiliated with one of the three Jewish religious groups: Orthodox, Reform, and Conservative. A large segment of adult Jewish Americans (about half) do not participate in religious services or even belong, however tenuously, to a temple or synagogue. They have neither converted to Christianity nor ceased to think of themselves as Jews. Nevertheless, Jewish religious beliefs and the history of religious practices remain significant legacies for all Jews today, however secularized their everyday behavior. In a 2013 national survey, 62 percent of all Jews felt that an "ancestry or culture," much more so than religion, defined what it means to be Jewish (Lugo et al. 2013a).

The trend for some time, especially in the United States, has been toward a condition called **Judaization**, the lessening importance of Judaism as a religion and the substitution of cultural traditions as the ties that bind Jews. Depending on one's definition, Judaization has caused some Jews to become so assimilated in the United States that very traditional Jews no longer consider them acceptable spouses (Gans 1956).

Jewish identity is ethnic. Jews share cultural traits, not physical features or uniform religious beliefs. The level of this cultural identity differs for the individual Jew. Just as some Apaches may be more acculturated than others, the degree of assimilation varies among Jewish people. Some people may base identity on such things as eating traditional Jewish foods, telling Jewish jokes, and wearing the Star of David. For others, this cultural identity may be the sense of a common history of centuries of persecution. For still others, it may be an unimportant identification. They say, "I am a Jew," just as they say, "I am a resident of California."

The question of what constitutes Jewish identity is not easily resolved. The most appropriate explanation of Jewish identity may be the simplest: A Jew in contemporary America is a person who thinks of himself or herself as a Jew. That also means that being a Jew is a choice and, as we discuss later in the chapter, many Jews may not be making that choice (Abrahamson and Pasternak 1998; Himmelfarb 1982).

Immigration of Jews to the United States

14.2 Summarize the history of Jewish immigration to the United States.

As every schoolchild knows, 1492 was the year in which Christopher Columbus reached the Western Hemisphere, exploring on behalf of Spain. That year also marked the expulsion of all Jews from Spain. The resulting exodus was not the first migration of Jews, nor was it the last.

One of the most significant movements among Jews is the one that created history's largest concentration of Jews: the immigration to the United States. The first Jews arrived in 1654 and were of Sephardic origin, meaning that they were originally from Spain and Portugal. These immigrants sought refuge in America after they had been expelled from other European countries, as well as from Brazil.

When the United States gained its independence from Great Britain, only 2,500 Jews lived here. By 1870, the Jewish population had climbed to about 200,000, supplemented mostly by Jews of German origin. They did not immediately merge into the older Jewish American settlements any more than the German Catholics fused immediately with native Catholics. Years passed before the older and newer Jewish settlers' common identity as Jews overcame nationality differences (Dinnerstein 1994; Jaher 1994).

The heaviest migration of Jews to the United States occurred around the end of the nineteenth century and was simultaneous with the great European migration described in Chapter 4. The fact that these groups arrived in the United States at the same time does not mean that the movements of Gentiles and Jews were identical in all respects. One significant difference was that Jews were much more likely to stay in the United States; few returned to Europe. Between 1908 and 1937, one-third of all European immigrants returned to Europe, but only 5 percent of Jewish immigrants did. The legal status of Jews in Europe at the turn of the century had improved since medieval times, but their rights were still revoked from time to time (Sherman 1974).

The immigration acts of the 1920s sharply reduced the influx of Jews, as they did for other European groups. Beginning in about 1933, the Jews arriving in the United States were not merely immigrants; they were also refugees. The tyranny of Germany's Third Reich began to take its toll well before World War II. German and Austrian Jews fled Europe as the impending doom became more evident. Many of the refugees from Nazism in Poland, Hungary, and Ukraine tended to be more religiously orthodox, and they adapted slowly to the ways of the earlier Jewish immigrants, if they adapted at all. The concentration camps, Hitler's speeches, Hitler's decline and fall, the atrocities, the war trials, and the capture of Nazi leaders undoubtedly made all American Jews—natives and refugees, the secular and the orthodox—acutely aware of their Jewishness and the price one may pay for one's ethnicity.

The most distinctive aspect of the Jewish population in the United States today is its concentration in urban areas and in the Northeast. The most recent estimates place more than 44 percent of the Jewish population in the Northeast, compared to 18 percent for the population as a whole (Figure 14.2). Jews are concentrated especially in the metropolitan

Bettman / Corbis

Jewish shoppers, many of them immigrants, crowd Orchard Street in New York City in 1923.

Figure 14.2 Jewish Population Distribution in the United States, 2015

NOTE: The highlighted states have Jewish populations estimated at more than 100,000. Numbers are rounded to the nearest thousand.

SOURCE: Data from Sheskin and Dashefsky 2015.

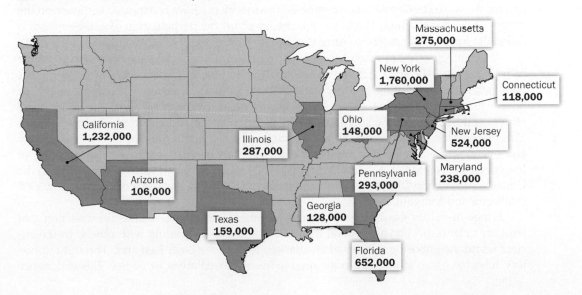

Massachusetts **275,000**

New York **1,760,000**

Connecticut **118,000**

California **1,232,000**

Ohio **148,000**

New Jersey **524,000**

Illinois **287,000**

Maryland **238,000**

Arizona **106,000**

Pennsylvania **293,000**

Georgia **128,000**

Texas **159,000**

Florida **652,000**

areas of New York City, Los Angeles, and South Florida, where altogether they account for 60 percent of the nation's Jewish population.

Anti-Semitism: Past and Present

14.3 Describe the extent of anti-Semitism historically and in the present.

The history of the Jewish people is a history of struggle to overcome centuries of hatred. Several religious observances, such as Passover, Hanukkah, and Purim, commemorate the past sacrifices or conflicts Jews have experienced. Anti-Jewish hostility, or anti-Semitism, has existed since before the beginning of the Christian faith and continues into the present. Scholars have a long history of studying the nature of anti-Semitic thought and action. For example, as long ago as 1899, sociologist Émile Durkheim wrote an essay during what he termed a period of "violent passions" of anti-Semitism sweeping Europe via political decisions (Durkheim 2008 [1899]).

Origins of Anti-Semitism

Many anti-Semites justify their beliefs by pointing to the role of some Jews in the crucifixion of Jesus Christ, although he was also a Jew. For nearly 2,000 years, various Christians have argued that all Jews share in the responsibility of the Jewish elders who condemned Jesus Christ to death. Much anti-Semitism over the ages bears little direct relationship to the crucifixion, however, and has more to do with the persistent stereotype that Jews behave treacherously with members of the larger society in which they live.

A 2004 survey found that 26 percent of Americans felt Jews were "responsible for Christ's death"—a significant increase over a similar survey nine years earlier. At the time of the survey, many Jews felt that Mel Gibson's film *The Passion of the Christ* (2004) reinforced such a view. Indeed, the same survey shows that among those who had seen the film, 36 percent held Jews responsible for the crucifixion (Pew Research Center 2004).

If the stereotype that Jews are obsessed with money is false, how did it originate? Social psychologist Gordon Allport (1979), among others, advanced the **fringe-of-values theory**. Throughout history, Jews have occupied positions economically different from those of Gentiles, often because laws forbade them to farm or practice trades. For centuries, the Christian church prohibited the taking of interest in the repayment of loans, calling it the sin of usury. Consequently, in the minds of Europeans, the sinful practice of money lending was equated with Jews. In reality, most Jews were not moneylenders, and most of those who were did not charge interest. In fact, many usurers were Christians, but because they worked in secret, only the reputation of the Jews was damaged. To make matters worse, the nobles of some European countries used Jews to collect taxes, which only increased the ill feeling against them. To the Gentile, such business practices by the Jews constituted behavior on the fringes of proper conduct. Therefore, this theory about the perpetuation of anti-Semitism is called the *fringe-of-values theory* (American Jewish Committee 1965, 1966a, 1966b; *Time* 1974).

Another relevant approach is **scapegoating theory**, which says that prejudiced people believe they are society's victims. As defined in Chapter 2, scapegoating theory suggests that, rather than accepting guilt for some failure, a person transfers the responsibility for failure to some vulnerable group. In the major tragic twentieth-century example, Adolf Hitler used the Jews as the scapegoat for all German social and economic ills in the 1930s. This premise led to the passage of laws restricting Jewish life in pre–World War II Germany and eventually escalated into the mass extermination of Europe's Jews. Scapegoating of Jews persists even today. A national survey in 2009 showed that one out of four people in the United States blame "the Jews" for the financial crisis that rocked the world starting in 2008 (Malhotra and Margalit 2009).

Fringe-of-values theory is used to explain other stereotypes, such as the assertion that Jews are "clannish," staying among themselves and not associating with others. In the ancient world, neighboring peoples often attacked Jews in the Near East area. Throughout history, Jews have also at times been required to live in closed areas, or *ghettos*. This experience naturally led them to unify and rely on themselves rather than on others. More recently, the stereotype of clannishness has gained support because Jews have been more likely to interact with Jews than with Gentiles. But Gentiles have tended to stay among their own kind, too.

Being critical of others for traits for which you praise members of your own group is an example of **in-group virtues** becoming **out-group vices**. Sociologist Robert Merton (1968) described how proper behavior by one's own group becomes viewed as unacceptable when practiced by outsiders. For Christians to take their faith seriously is commendable; for Jews to withstand secularization is a sign of backwardness. For Gentiles to prefer Gentiles as friends is understandable; for Jews to choose other Jews as friends suggests clannishness. The assertion that Jews are clannish is an exaggeration and also ignores the fact that the dominant group shares the same tendency. It also fails to consider to what extent anti-Semitism has logically encouraged—and indeed, forced—Jews to seek out other Jews as friends and fellow workers (Allport 1979).

The Holocaust

The injustices to the Jewish people continued for centuries. However, it would be a mistake to say that all Gentiles were or are anti-Semitic. History, drama, and other literature record daily, presumably friendly interactions between Jews and Gentiles. At particular times and places, anti-Semitism was an official government policy. In other situations, it was the product of a few bigoted individuals and sporadically became very widespread. Regardless of the scope, anti-Semitism has long been a part of Jewish life, something that Jews have been forced to contend with. By 1870, most legal restrictions aimed at Jews had been abolished in western Europe. Since then, however, Jews have again been used as scapegoats by opportunists who blame them for a nation's problems.

The most infamous of these opportunists was Adolf Hitler, whose "final solution" represented a dramatic example of anti-Semitism at its most deadly; his scapegoating of German Jews for Germany's problems led directly to the Holocaust. The **Holocaust** was the state-sponsored systematic persecution and annihilation of European Jewry by Nazi Germany and its collaborators. The move to eliminate Jews from the European continent started slowly, with Germany gradually restricting the rights of Jews: preventing them from voting, living outside the Jewish ghetto, and owning businesses. Much of the anti-Semitic cruelty was evident before the beginning of the World War II. If there was any doubt, *Kristallnacht,* or the "Night of Broken Glass," in Berlin on November 9, 1938, ended that doubt. Ninety Berlin Jews were murdered, hundreds of homes and synagogues were set on fire or ransacked, and thousands of Jewish store windows were broken.

Despite the obvious intolerance, Jews desiring to immigrate were turned back by government officials in the United States and elsewhere. Just a few months after Kristallnacht, 903 Jewish refugees aboard the ocean liner *St. Louis* were denied entry to Cuba. Efforts to gain entry in the United States, including special appeals to Congress and President Roosevelt, were useless. Ultimately, the ship returned to Germany, and many of the Jews later died in the death camps. Between 1933 and 1945, two-thirds of Europe's total Jewish population was killed. In Poland, Germany, and Austria, 90 percent were murdered. Only 12 percent of the number of Jews who were present in those countries in 1938 are present today (Berger 2010; DellaPergola 2007; Institute for Jewish and Community Research 2008; Wiesel 2006).

Despite the enormity of the tragedy, a small but vocal proportion of the world community are **Holocaust revisionists** who claim that the Holocaust did not happen. A controversial conference in 2006 in Iran brought together revisionists from throughout the world. Debates also continue between those who contend that this part of modern history must be remembered and others, in the United States and Europe, who feel that it is time to put the Holocaust behind us and go on (Fathi 2006).

Despite these attacks on historical reality, the poignant statements by Holocaust survivors such as Elie Wiesel, *The Diary of Anne Frank*, and the release of such films as *Schindler's List* (1993), *Life Is Beautiful* (1998), *The Pianist*

The United States Holocaust Memorial Museum, Washington DC. This picture shows the exhibit "Tower of Faces," which brings visitors face to face with the story of a single small town near the border of Poland and Lithuania, known in Polish as Ejszyszki. In two days in September 1941, the Nazis eradicated almost all of the town's Jews and 900 years of Jewish life in the town. Today, no Jews live there. The hundreds of photographs in "Tower of Faces" represent the once-thriving Jewish life that existed before the Holocaust.

Paul Franklin/Alamy Stock Photo

(2002), *Munich* (2005), *The Reader* (2008), and *Inglorious Basterds* (2009), keep the tragedy of the Holocaust and its legacy in our minds.

Anti-Semitism is definitely not just a historical social phenomenon in Europe. A 2013 survey of Jewish Europeans found that 66 percent believed that anti-Semitism is "a problem" where they live, and 76 percent felt that anti-Jewish bigotry had increased over the past five years. An amazing 40 percent or more of Jews in Belgium, France, and Hungary said they had been considering emigrating for safety reasons. Troubling to many observers is the fact that the recent rise in such perceptions and the rise in accusations against Jews worldwide have excited the anger or disbelief of the non-Jewish masses and non-Jewish elites alike (European Union Agency for Fundamental Rights 2013; Goldberg 2013; Goldhagen 2013).

U.S. Anti-Semitism: Past

Compared with the brutalities the Jews experienced in Europe from the time of the early Christian church to the rule of Hitler, the United States cannot be described as a nation with a history of severe anti-Semitism. Nevertheless, the United States has also had its outbreaks of anti-Semitism, though none have begun to approach the scope or level of that seen in western Europe. An examination of the status of Jewish Americans today indicates the extent of remaining discrimination against Jews. However, contemporary anti-Semitism must be seen in relation to past injustices.

In 1654, the year Jews arrived in colonial America, Peter Stuyvesant, governor of New Amsterdam (the Dutch city later named New York), attempted to expel them from the city. Stuyvesant's efforts failed, but they were the beginning of an unending effort to separate Jews from the rest of the population. Because the pre-1880 immigration of Jews was small, anti-Semitism was little noticed except, of course, by Jews. Most nineteenth-century movements against minorities were targeted at Catholics and Blacks and ignored Jews. In fact, Jews occasionally joined in such movements. By the 1870s, however, signs of a pattern of social discrimination against Jews had appeared. Colleges limited the number of Jewish students or excluded Jews altogether. The first Jewish fraternity was founded in 1898 to compensate for the barring of Jews from campus social organizations. As Jews began to compete for white-collar jobs early in the twentieth century, job discrimination became the rule rather than the exception (Higham 1966; Selzer 1972).

The 1920s and the 1930s were periods of the most virulent and overt anti-Semitism in the United States. In these decades, the myth of an internationally organized Jewry took shape. According to a forged document titled *Protocols of the Learned Elders of Zion*, Jews throughout the world planned to conquer all governments, and the major vehicle for this rise to power was Communism, said by anti-Semites to be a Jewish movement. Absurd though this argument was, some respected Americans accepted the thesis of an international Jewish conspiracy and believed in the authenticity of the *Protocols*.

Henry Ford, founder of the automobile company that bears his name, was responsible for the publication of the *Protocols*. In his later years, Ford expressed regret for his espousal of anti-Semitic causes, but the damage had been done; he had lent an air of respectability to the most exaggerated charges against Jewish people.

It is not clear why Ford, even for a short period of his life, so willingly accepted anti-Semitism. But Ford was not alone. Groups such as the Ku Klux Klan and the German American Bund, as well as radio personalities, preached about the Jewish conspiracy as if it were fact. By the 1930s, these sentiments expressed a fondness for Hitler. Even famed aviator Charles Lindbergh made speeches claiming that Jews were forcing the United States into a war so that Jewish people could profit by wartime production. When the barbarous treatment of the Jews by Nazi Germany was exposed, most Americans were horrified by such events, and people such as Lindbergh were as puzzled as anyone about how some Americans could have been so swept up by the pre–World War II wave of anti-Semitism (Baldwin 2001; Meyers 1943; Selzer 1972).

Historical anti-Semitism is never far below the surface. The discredited *Protocols* was sold online by Walmart through 2004 and described as "genuine" until protests made the large retailer rethink its position. In 2006, a Spanish-language version published in Mexico City enjoyed wide distribution. A 40-part television series based on the *Protocols* produced in 2002 was shown as recently as March 2012 in Egypt (Goldhagen 2013; *Intelligence Report* 2004; Rothstein 2006).

The next section examines anti-Semitic feelings in contemporary America. Several crucial differences between anti-Semitism in Europe and in the United States must be considered. First, and most important, the U.S. government has never promoted anti-Semitism. Unlike its European counterparts, the U.S. government has never embarked on an anti-Semitic program of expulsion or extermination. Second, because anti-Semitism was never institutionalized in the United States as it sometimes has been in Europe, American Jews have not needed to develop a defensive ideology to ensure the survival of their people. A Jewish American can make a largely personal decision about how much to assimilate or how secular to become.

Contemporary Anti-Semitism

Next to social research on anti-Black attitudes and behavior of Whites, anti-Semitism has been the major focus of studies of prejudice by sociologists and psychologists. Jews in the United States expressed little concern about anti-Semitism immediately after World War II. From the late 1960s through the 1990s, however, anti-Semitism again appeared to be a threat in many parts of the world. A 2010 national survey found that 25 percent of Jews felt anti-Semitism was a "very serious problem" and 66 percent felt it was "somewhat of a problem" in the United States. Looking at the statistical data, there is good reason to see this strong concern. More than two-thirds of reported religious hate crimes are perpetrated against Jews. A 2015 multi-nation study found a surge in anti-Semitic incidents worldwide (American Jewish Committee 2010a; Chanes 2007; Hjelmgaard 2015).

INCIDENTS OF ANTI-SEMITISM The Anti-Defamation League (ADL) of B'nai B'rith, founded in 1913, publishes an annual survey of reported anti-Semitic incidents. Although the number has fluctuated, the highest level in the more than 30 years the ADL has been recording such incidents took place in 1994. In 2015, there were more than 550 such incidents. Figure 14.3 shows the fluctuating reported numbers of harassment, threats, and assaults. Some incidents were inspired and carried out by *neo-Nazis* or *skinheads*, groups of young people who champion racist and anti-Semitic ideologies.

In recent years, fewer anti-Semitic incidents have been reported from organized hate groups, but a growing number of anti-Semitic incidents have been reported on college campuses. Anti-Jewish graffiti, anti-Semitic speakers, and swastikas affixed to predominantly

---

Figure 14.3 Anti-Semitic Incidents, 1980–2015

SOURCE: Anti-Defamation League (ADL). 2016. 2015 Audit of Anti-Semitic Incidents. Accessible at http://www.adl.org. Reprinted with permission of the Anti-Defamation League, www.adl.org.

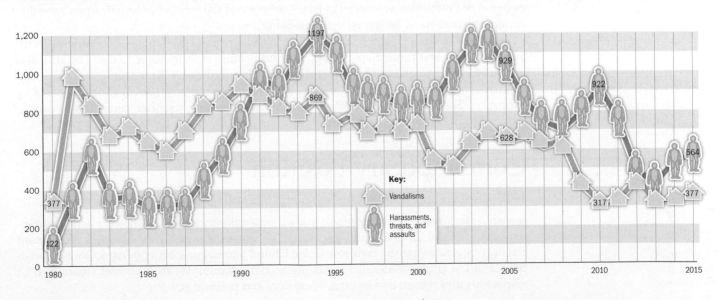

Jewish fraternities are among the documented incidents. Another manifestation of anti-Semitism appears in editorial-style advertisements in college newspapers that argue that the Holocaust never occurred. A chilling development is the growing use of the Internet as a vehicle for anti-Semitism, either delivering such messages or serving as a means of reaching Web sites that spread intolerance (Anti-Defamation League 2016; Gladstone 2016). The rise of social media has allowed the instantaneous transmission of anti-Semitic messages. According to a 2016 study, a staggering 2.6 million anti-Semitic statements were found on Twitter in just one year (Mahler 2016).

AMERICAN JEWS AND ISRAEL   When the Middle East became a major hot spot in international affairs in the 1960s, a revival of 1930s levels of anti-Semitism occurred. Many Jewish Americans expressed concern that because Jews are freer in the United States than they have been in perhaps any other country in their history, they would ignore the struggle of other Jews. Israel's precarious status has proven to be a strong source of identity for Jewish Americans. Major wars in the Middle East in 1967, 1973, and 1991 reminded the world of Israel's vulnerability. Palestinian uprisings in the occupied territories and international recognition of the Palestine Liberation Organization (PLO) in 1988 and 2002 eroded the strong pro-Israel front among the Western powers. Some Jewish Americans have shown their commitment to the Israeli cause by immigrating to Israel.

The majority of Jewish Americans feel the United States should remain active in world affairs, compared to 36 percent of the total U.S. population. However, even among Jews, support of Israel is not uniform. Although not all American Jews agree with Israel's actions, many Jews express support for Israel's struggles by contributing money and trying to influence American opinion and policy to be more favorable to Israel. A survey conducted in 2013 showed that 30 percent of Jewish Americans feel "very attached" to Israel and another 39 percent feel "somewhat attached." But that still leaves nearly a third (31 percent) who feel distant from Israel. One in eight feel that caring about Israel is not an important part of being Jewish. It should also be noted that some people in the Jewish community see Jews who do not totally back Israel as anti-Semitic (American Jewish Committee 2010b; Lugo et al. 2013a).

In the year after the oil embargo (1974), the United Nations General Assembly ignored American and Israeli objections and passed a resolution declaring that "Zionism is a form of racism and racial discrimination." **Zionism**, which initially referred to the old Jewish religious yearning to return to the biblical homeland, has been expressed in the twentieth century in the movement to create a Jewish state in Palestine. Ever since the **Diaspora**, the exile of Jews from Palestine several centuries before Christianity, many Jews have seen the destiny of their people as the establishment of a Jewish state in the Holy Land.

The Zionism resolution, finally repealed by the United Nations in 1991, had no lasting influence and did not change any nation's foreign policy. However, it did increase Jewish fears of reawakened anti-Semitism thinly disguised as attacks on Zionist beliefs. Even the development of agreements between Israel and its Arab neighbors and the international recognition of Palestinian autonomy in Israel did not end the concern of Jewish Americans that continuing anti-Israel feeling reflects anti-Semitism.

An old Yiddish saying, "*Schwer zu sein a Yid*," means "It is tough to be a Jew." Anti-Semitism past and present are related. The old hostilities seem never to die. The atrocities of Nazi Germany have not been forgotten, nor should they be. Racial and ethnic hostility, against any group, unifies the group against its attackers, and Jewish Americans are no exception. The Jewish people of the United States have come together, regardless of nationality, to form a minority group with a high degree of group identity.

Contemporary Position

14.4   Explain Jewish Americans' economic, educational, and political situation.

Jewish Americans have an important role in contemporary America. They are active participants in the fight for civil rights and work on behalf of Israel. These efforts are important but only begin to describe their role in the United States. For a better perspective on Jewish people in the United States, the following sections summarize their current situation with respect to employment and income, education, and political activity.

Table 14.1 Profile of Jews in the United States

	Jewish Americans (%)	All U.S. Residents (%)
INCOME		
Less than $30,000	20	36
More than $150,000	25	38
COLLEGE GRADUATES	58	29
U.S. BORN	86	83
POLITICAL PARTY PREFERENCE		
Democrat/leaning Democrat	70	49
Republican/leaning Republican	22	39
SOCIAL POSITIONS		
Liberal	49	21
Moderate	29	36
Conservative	19	38

SOURCES: Lugo et al. 2013a: 42, 43, 45, 96.

Employment and Income

Discrimination affects all facets of a subordinate group's life. Jews have experienced, and to a limited extent still experience, differential treatment in the American job market. National surveys have shown that most Jews view anti-Semitism as a problem in the United States, although not necessarily in hiring practices. As Table 14.1 shows, through perseverance and emphasis on education, Jewish Americans as a group have overcome barriers to full employment and now enjoy high incomes (American Jewish Committee 2010a; Chiswick 2009).

Using a variety of techniques, social scientists documented declining discrimination more than 20 years ago against Jews in the business world. Sociologist Samuel Klausner interviewed business-school graduates, comparing Jews with Protestants and Catholics who graduated from the same university in the same year. Klausner (1988:33) concluded, "(1) Jewish MBAs are winning positions in the same industries as their Catholic and Protestant classmates; (2) they are rising more rapidly in corporate hierarchies than their Catholic and Protestant colleagues; (3) they are achieving higher salaries than their Catholic and Protestant colleagues." Klausner adds that researchers tested seven indicators of discrimination and in each case failed to find evidence of discrimination against Jewish executives. Interestingly, however, this same study detected substantial discrimination against African Americans and women.

The economic success of the Jewish people as a group obscures the poverty of many individual Jewish families. We reached a similar conclusion in Chapter 12 from income data on Asian Pacific Americans and their image as a model minority. Sociologists largely agree that Jews in 1930 were as likely to be poverty stricken and living in slums as any minority group today. Most have escaped poverty, but what Ann Wolfe (1972) calls "the invisible Jewish poor" remain invisible to the rest of society. Like Chinese Americans, the Jewish poor were not well served by federal experiments to eradicate poverty in the 1960s and 1970s. Although the proportion of the poor among Jews is not as substantial as that among Blacks or Hispanics, it does remind us that not all Jewish families have affluent lifestyles (Gold 1965; Lavender 1977; Levine and Hochbaum 1974).

Education

Jews place great emphasis on education (see Table 14.1). Nearly 60 percent—more than twice the national average—are college graduates. This desire for formal schooling stems, it is argued, from the Judaic religion, which places the rabbi, or teacher, at the center of religious life (Kosmin 2009).

In the United States today, all Jewish congregations emphasize religious instruction more than Protestants typically do. In 2014, it was estimated that the United States had 861 Jewish day schools with 255,000 pupils. Day schools are, in effect, private elementary schools with a substantial proportion of the curriculum devoted to Judaic studies and the learning of Hebrew. The less-religious may attend instruction on Sundays or on weekday afternoons after attending public schools. Most Jews have received some form of formal Jewish education before they reach 30 years of age. The Jewish-sponsored component of higher education is not limited to strict religious instruction such as that found in rabbinical schools. Beginning in 1947, Jews founded graduate schools of medicine, education, social work, and mathematics, along with Brandeis University, which offers both undergraduate and graduate degrees. These institutions are nonsectarian (i.e., admission is not limited to Jews) and are a Jewish-sponsored contribution to higher education (Schick 2014).

The religiously based tradition of lifelong study has left the legacy of a Jewish value system that stresses education. The poverty of Jewish immigrants kept them from devoting years to secular schooling, but they were determined that their children would do better. Despite their high levels of educational attainment, however, some members of the Jewish community express concern about Jewish education. They are disappointed with its highly secularized nature, not only because religious teaching has been limited but also because the Jewish sociocultural experience has been avoided altogether. It may even contribute to Judaization, the lessening importance of Judaism as a religion.

Political Activity

American Jews play a prominent role in politics as both voters and elected officials. Jews as a group are much more likely than the general population to label themselves Democrat (refer to Table 14.1). Jewish voters have backed the Democrat over the Republican presidential candidate for the past 12 presidential elections, with Hillary Clinton receiving 71 percent of the Jewish vote in 2016. The one exception to this pattern of liberalism is gender issues related to the practice of Judaism, particularly among ultraorthodox Jews, whom we consider later in this chapter. Other Jewish religious traditions tend to be very open to egalitarian participation in most aspects of religious ritual, especially when compared to many Christian faiths (Smith and Martínez 2016).

Jews have long been successful in being elected to office—22 Jews served in the House of Representatives and eight in the Senate as of 2017. However, it was not until 1988 that an Orthodox Jew from Connecticut was elected to the U.S. Senate. Joseph Lieberman refrained from campaigning on the Sabbath (Shabbat) each week; his religious views were not an issue. He went on to be named as Al Gore's vice presidential running mate. Even during the campaign, he honored the Sabbath and did not actively campaign on the Sabbath day, even avoiding dialing a telephone to call potential supporters. Many view the positive response to his campaign as a sign of openness to devout Jews as political candidates (Pew Charitable Trust 2000; USA Today 2017).

As in all subordinate groups, the political activity of Jewish Americans has not been limited to conventional electoral politics. The Jewish American community has encompassed a variety of organizations since its beginnings. These groups serve many purposes: some are religious, while others are charitable, political, or educational. No organization, secular or religious, represents all American Jews, but there are more than 300 nationwide Jewish American organizations (Chanes 2008).

Religious Life

14.5 Describe the role of religion among Jewish Americans.

Jewish identity and participation in the Jewish religion are not the same. Many Americans consider themselves Jewish and are considered Jewish by others even though they have never participated in Jewish religious life. The available data indicate that about half of American Jews are affiliated with a synagogue or temple, but only a small proportion consider participation in religious worship as extremely important. Even in Israel, only 30 percent of Jews are religiously observant. Nevertheless, the presence of a religious tradition is an important tie among Jews, even secular Jews (Lugo et al. 2013a).

Judaism embraces several factions or denominations that are similar in their roots but marked by sharp distinctions. No precise data reveal the relative numbers of the three major groups. Part of the problem is the difficulty of placing individuals in the proper group. For example, it is common for a Jew to be a member of an Orthodox congregation but consider him- or herself to be Conservative. The following levels of affiliation are based on a 2013 national survey of Jewish Americans:

- Orthodox—10 percent
- Conservative—18 percent
- Reform—35 percent
- Reconstructionist (and others)—6 percent
- Just Jewish—27 percent
- Don't Know/Atheist/Other—4 percent

Large Orthodox families, conversion to orthodoxy by other Jews, and immigration of traditional Jews to the United States lead to more conservative patterns of religion. Yet many Jewish households are attracted to the moderation of Reform Judaism (Lugo et al. 2013a).

We focus on two forms of Judaism at either end of the continuum: the Orthodox faith, which attempts to uphold a very traditional practice of Judaism; and the Reform faith, which accommodates itself to the secular world. Religious identification is associated with particular generations: Immigrants and older Jews are more likely to be Orthodox, and their grandchildren are more likely to be Reform (*Los Angeles Times* Poll 1998).

The Orthodox Tradition

The unitary Jewish tradition developed in the United States into three sects beginning in the mid-nineteenth century. The differences between Orthodox, Conservative, and Reform Judaism are based on their adherents' varying acceptance of traditional rituals. All three sects embrace a philosophy based on the Torah, the first five books of the Old Testament. The differences developed because some Jews wanted to be less distinguishable from other Americans. Another significant factor in explaining the development of different groups is the absence of a religious elite and bureaucratic hierarchy, which facilitated the breakdown in traditional practices.

Even Orthodox Jews differ in their level of adherence to traditional practices. Among the ultraorthodox are the Hasidic Jews, or Hasidim, who number some 200,000, with half residing chiefly in several neighborhoods in Brooklyn. To the Hasidim, following the multitude of *mitzvahs,* or commandments of behavior, is as important today as it was in the time of Moses. Their spiritual commitment extends well beyond customary Jewish law even as interpreted by Orthodox Jews.

Hasidic Jews wear no garments that mix linen and wool. Men wear a *yarmulke,* or skullcap, constantly, even while sleeping. Attending a secular college is frowned upon. Instead, the men undertake a lifetime of study of the Torah and the accompanying rabbinical literature of the Talmud. Women's education consists of instruction on how to run the home in keeping with Orthodox tradition. Hasidic Jews, who themselves are organized in separate communities, have courts with jurisdiction recognized by the faithful in many matters, especially as they relate to family life.

Orthodox children in New York attend special schools in order to meet minimal New York State educational requirements. Hasidic Jews reflect the devotion to religious study in

Among those Jews in the United States who follow a more Orthodox religious tradition are the Hasidic Jews. Among Hasidic married men as shown here, a round fur hat called a *shtreimel* is worn on the Shabbat (day of Sabbath) and on Jewish holidays.

David Grossman/Alamy Stock Photo

this comment: "Look at Freud, Marx, Einstein—all Jews who made their mark on the non-Jewish world. To me, however, they would have been much better off studying in a yeshiva [a Jewish school]. What a waste of three fine Talmudic minds" (Arden 1975:294). Although devoted to their religion, the Hasidim participate in local elections and politics and are employed in outside occupations. All such activities are influenced by their orthodoxy and a self-reliance rarely duplicated elsewhere in the United States.

Case Study: Daily Life of the Orthodox

Orthodox Jewish life is very demanding, especially in a basically Christian society such as the United States. Rituals that require an Orthodox Jew to constantly reaffirm his or her religious conviction define almost all conduct. Most Americans are familiar with **kashrut**, the laws pertaining to permissible and forbidden foods. When strictly adhered to, kashrut governs not only what foods may be eaten (kosher) but also how the food is prepared, served, and eaten. Besides day-to-day practices, Orthodox Jews have weekly and annual observances.

It is possible to go many hours or days and not think of oneself as "being Presbyterian" or "being Roman Catholic." That is not the case for Orthodox Jews. Sociologist Iddo Tavory conducted an in-depth observational study of a predominantly Jewish community that was just blocks from the bright lights and 24-hour activity of West Hollywood. So how did Orthodox Jews maintain their identity? As we see in the Speaking Out feature, one way was to be careful where they walked.

The attitudes of Orthodox Jews on social issues tend to be conservative. Women may not be rabbis among the Orthodox, although beginning in 2006, women were named to head a congregation in one faction of the faith, but only male members of the congregation could read publicly from the Torah (Goldstein 2010; Lugo et al. 2013a).

Speaking Out

The Neighborhood as a Moral Obstacle Course

The problematic nature of the neighborhood also featured in a joke that Rabbi Chelev-Chittim often made. When not enough people would come to form the ten-man minyan needed for prayer, the rabbi would patiently wait, and then, almost as a matter of course, jokingly threaten that he would "have to go and just pick somebody off Melrose." The humor in these semijokes was partly produced by the juxtaposition of the sacred status of the prayer quorum and the profanity of the sites from which he was threatening to pick the quorum—we have stooped so low, he effectively noted, that our only possible salvation is to turn to profanity.

The question of how to act toward these sites and situations, then, was not as straightforward as that of button-operated crosswalks or the eruv [an urban area enclosed by a wire boundary that symbolically extends the private domain of Jewish households into public areas, permitting activities within it that are normally forbidden in public on the Sabbath]. Of course, if an Orthodox resident was seen standing in line or munching an unkosher "Moe's hotdog," it would indicate that he was rebelling against Orthodoxy, perhaps irreparably. But simply not eating at Moe's did not defuse its danger. The micromanagement of space—questions such as

Iddo Tavory

how to walk by, how to look or avoid looking, whether to ignore the long line of customers or to "look danger in the eye"—was still encountered as an existential dilemma. By developing personal styles of navigating these objects, and learning to read others' actions, residents further positioned themselves.

Indeed, when some Orthodox residents commented on specific moral dangers, others would not necessarily share their view:

After saying my goodbyes to the rabbi, Joe and I walk out of synagogue. I walk down the synagogue stairs toward the exit, as Jonathan Seifeld walks up the stairs, coming back into the synagogue from the street. He stops me and holds me by the shoulders, but also looks at Joe. "When you go out look down, there are things outside that you shouldn't be seeing," he says abruptly. His tone is serious, solemn. Joe and I walk out, our eyes fixed to the ground. I sneak a look from the corner of my eye. Outside, on the sidewalk, the clothes shop next door has put a few manikins, without clothes, in a pile of naked plastic bodies ... As we continue going, Joe sighs, "Really... these are manikins."

Whereas Seifeld saw the manikins as a moral danger, representing human nudity and thus transgressing the edicts and practices of modesty (tsni'yes), Joe took a stance of bemused detachment. To him, the manikins were pieces of plastic, a far cry from a contaminating influence to be avoided. Poking a little fun at Seifeld's presentation of self as a carefully pious Jew, he constituted himself as more sophisticated in his practice, perhaps more "modern." This, of course, did not mean that he was oblivious to the "contamination" of what he saw as transgressive secular spots. On another occasion, walking to a synagogue nearby, Joe would not walk near a cinema that showed "gay movies" and asked me if we could cross the street. In yet other situations, he was vocally critical of the sexualized "secular culture of Melrose" and said he tried to avoid the street when he could. Faced with less fixed questions of morality and danger, different residents constructed different strategies of action, navigating neighborhood space differently. Doing so, they thus developed personal stratifications of moral danger and presentations of self that were not precisely the same across residents.

To continue with the example of walking by Moe's—the hotdog stand next to the synagogue—people acted differently vis-à-vis what most of them saw as impure. Most residents I knew simply ignored Moe's, appearing to treat it as if it did not exist at all. They averted their eyes and looked at the opposite side of the street, concentrated on the pavement, or looked to a distant point on the horizon. Some of them even made it a point to walk through a parking lot between buildings so they wouldn't need to go by it on their way to synagogue.

But not everyone who could avoid it did so. The rabbi in the small synagogue always walked from his house through the main thoroughfares, sometimes even stopping to have a quick glance at the newspaper stand by Moe's and catch the headlines of current events. Since he headed the congregation and was a well-respected Torah scholar, no one in the congregation ever hinted that stopping by Moe's pointed to any impurities of self. It was, rather, a way of holding oneself, a balance he struck between being an urbanite who liked the hustle and bustle of the streets and still noting what he saw as their spiritual poverty. His wife, on the other hand, usually chose to walk a longer route from the synagogue to her house, calling it "the pretty way" and sometimes, facetiously, "the shortcut." And while part of the difference between the ways they navigated between home and synagogue had to do with the enactment of gender—men were more likely in general to be slightly more "daring" than women—it wasn't the only reason. The rabbi and his wife also had different ways of enacting Orthodoxy, and while they were both deeply religious, her stance was more critical of and distanced from the secular world.

Source: Tavory 2016: 131–132

The Reform Tradition

Reform Jews, although deeply committed to the religious faith, have altered many of its rituals. Women and men sit together in Reform congregations, and both sexes participate in the reading of the Torah at services. Women have been ordained as Reform rabbis since 1972. A few Reform congregations have even experimented with observing the Sabbath on Sunday and freely allow their members to drive to attend services (thus violating an Orthodox prohibition against operating machinery on the Sabbath). Circumcision for males is not mandatory. Civil divorce decrees are sufficient and recognized so that a divorce granted by a three-man rabbinical court is not required before remarriage. Reform Jews recognize the children of Jewish men and non-Jewish women as Jews with no need to convert. All these practices are unacceptable to Orthodox Jews.

Conservative Judaism is a compromise between the rigidity of the Orthodox and the extreme modification of the Reform. Because of the middle position, the national organization of Conservatives, the United Synagogue of America, strives to create its own identity and seeks to view its traditions as an appropriate, authentic approach to the faith.

Table 14.2 displays some results of a 2013 national survey on Jewish identification. The three sects here include both members and nonmembers of local congregations. Reform Jews are the least likely of the three groups to participate in religious events, to be involved in the Jewish community, or to participate in predominantly Jewish organizations. Yet in Reform temples, there has been an effort to observe religious occasions such as Rosh Hashanah.

A rabbi blesses a young girl at her Bat Mitzvah in the temple. Jewish children often celebrate a coming-of-age ceremony. According to Jewish law, when Jewish children reach the age of maturity (12 years for girls, 13 years for boys), they become responsible for their actions. At this point, a boy is said to become Bar Mitzvah; a girl is said to become Bat Mitzvah.

Donna Ellen Coleman/Shutterstock

Table 14.2 Jewish Identification by Group

Indices	Orthodox (%)	Conservative (%)	Reform (%)	No Denomination (%)
Very important being Jewish	87	69	43	22
Eating Jewish foods	51	18	9	6
Observance of Jewish law	79	24	11	8
Observance of Christian holidays	6	6	17	28
Member of Jewish organizations	39	27	20	4
Caring about Israel	55	58	42	31

SOURCE: Lugo et al. 2013a: 51, 57, 60.

Like Protestant denominations, Jewish denominations are associated with class, nationality, and other social differences. The Reform Jews are the wealthiest and have the best formal education of the group; the Orthodox are the poorest and least educated in years of formal secular schooling; and the Conservatives occupy a position between the two. A fourth branch of American Judaism, Reconstructionism, an offshoot of the Conservative movement, has only recently developed an autonomous institutional structure with ritual practices similar to those of Reform Jews.

Concerned about the number of followers, some Jewish leaders are trying new tactics to attract or at least not to lose observant Jews. For example, Jews historically have not embarked on recruitment or evangelistic programs to attract new members. Beginning in the late 1970s, Jews, especially Reform Jews, debated the possibility of outreach programs. Least objectionable to Jewish congregations were efforts begun in 1978 aimed at non-Jewish partners and children in mixed marriages. In 1981, the program was broadened to invite conversions by Americans who had no religious connection, but these very modest recruitment drives are still far from resembling those that have been carried out by Protestant denominations for decades (Luo 2006b).

Some Reform leaders are rethinking the requirement that one has to attend three or four years of religious school as a prerequisite to bar or bat mitzvahs. Others are considering dispensing with the youth reading from the Torah in Hebrew—once regarded as a central point of the ceremony. Embracing change is not limited to the more liberal end of the spectrum. Dwindling Orthodox parishes in some parts of the country are offering relocation bonuses to Orthodox families to come join in worship. Many faithful Jews oppose such efforts and argue that practices need to become stricter and less adaptable (Goldstein 2010; Goodstein 2013a; Hu 2012; Luo 2006b).

Jewish Identity

14.6   Explain Jewish Identity.

Ethnic and racial identification can be positive or negative. Awareness of ethnic identity can contribute to a person's self-esteem and give that person a sense of group solidarity with similar people. When a person experiences an identity only as a basis for discrimination or insults, he or she may want to shed that identity in favor of one more acceptable to society. Unfavorable differential treatment can also encourage closer ties between members of the community being discriminated against, as it has for Jews.

Most would judge the diminishing of out-group hostility and the ability of Jews to leave the ghetto as positive developments. However, the improvement in Jewish–Gentile relations also creates a new problem in Jewish social identity. It has become possible for Jews to shed their "Jewishness," or **Yiddishkait**. Many retain their Yiddishkait even in suburbia, where it is more difficult to retain than it is in the ghetto. In the end, however, Jews cannot lose their identity entirely. Jews are still denied total assimilation in the United States no matter how much the individual ceases to think of him- or herself as Jewish.

Social clubs may still refuse membership to Jews, and prospective non-Jewish in-laws may try to interfere with plans to marry (Friedman 1967).

A unique identity issue presents itself to Jewish women, whose religious tradition has placed them in a subordinate position. For example, it was not until 1985 that the first female rabbi of the Conservative tradition was ordained. Jewish feminism has its roots in the women's movement of the 1960s and 1970s, several of whose leaders were Jewish. There have been some changes in **halakha** (Jewish law covering obligations and duties), but it is still difficult for a woman to get a divorce recognized by the Orthodox Jewish tradition. Sima Rabinowicz of upstate New York has been hailed as the Jewish Rosa Parks for her similar bus battle. Rabinowicz refused to give up her seat in the women's section of a Hasidic-owned, publicly subsidized bus to Orthodox men who wanted to pray in private, segregated from women as required by halakha. The courts defended her right to ride as she wished, just as an earlier court had ruled with Rosa Parks in the Birmingham bus boycott. Jewish women contend that they should not be forced to make a choice between their identities as women and as Jews (Baum 1998; Frankel 1995).

We now examine three factors that influence the ethnic identity of Jews in the United States: family, religion, and cultural heritage.

Role of the Family

In general, the family works to socialize children, but for religious Jews it also fulfills a religious commandment. In the past, this compulsion was so strong that the *shadchan* (marriage broker or matchmaker) fulfilled an important function in the Jewish community by ensuring marriage for all eligible people. The emergence of romantic love in modern society made the *shadchan* less acceptable to young Jews, but recent statistics show that Jews are more likely to marry than members of any other group.

Jews have traditionally remained in extended families, intensifying the transmission of Jewish identity. Numerous observers have argued that the Jewish family today no longer maintains its role in identity transmission and that the family is consequently contributing to assimilation. The American Jewish Committee released a report identifying ten problems that are endangering "the family as the main transmission agent of Jewish values, identity, and continuity" (Conver 1976:A2). The following issues are relevant to Jews today:

- More Jews marry later than members of other groups.
- Most organizations of single Jews no longer operate solely for the purpose of matchmaking. These groups are now supportive of singles and the single way of life.
- The divorce rate is rising; there is no presumption of the permanence of marriage and no stigma attached to its failure.
- The birth rate is falling, and childlessness has become socially acceptable.
- Financial success has taken precedence over child raising in importance and for many has become the major goal of the family.
- The intensity of family interaction has decreased, although it continues to be higher than in most other religious and ethnic groups.
- There is less socializing across generation lines, partly as a result of geographic mobility.
- Family members' sense of responsibility to other family members has declined.
- The role of Jewishness is no longer central to the lives of Jews.
- Intermarriage has lessened the involvement of the Jewish partner in Jewish life and the emphasis on Jewish aspects of family life.

Data and sample surveys have verified these trends. Nevertheless, Jewish Americans still have a higher than typical degree of **familism**.

Bill Aron / Science Source

Research Focus

Intermarriage: The Final Step to Assimilation?

Sex and the City's Charlotte York, the quintessential WASP character, descends into a Jewish ritual bath, marking her conversion to Judaism. Although Jewish viewers welcomed this fictional portrayal, is it representative of what happens when Jews take a Gentile spouse today?

As Christianity's influence has grown in Europe and North America, a persistent fear among Jews has been that their children or grandchildren would grow up ignorant of the Torah. Equally undesirable, a descendant might become *apikoros,* an unbeliever who engages in intellectual speculation about the relevance of Judaism. These concerns are growing as Jewish Americans' resistance to marriage outside the Jewish faith declines. In 2005, two-thirds of Jews felt anti-Semitism was the biggest threat to Jewish life, but one out of three saw marriage outside the faith as the largest threat.

Why is intermarriage a social issue rather than a personal dilemma? Intermarriage makes a decrease in the size of the Jewish community in the United States more likely. In marriages that occurred in the 1970s, more than 64 percent of Jews married other Jews. In marriages from 2000 through 2013, that proportion dropped to 42 percent. This trend means that American Jews today are just as likely to marry a Gentile as a Jew. For many, religion is a nonissue—neither parent practices religious rituals. Two-thirds of the children of these Jewish–Gentile marriages are not raised as Jews.

Many Jewish Americans respond that intermarriage is inevitable and that the Jewish community must build on whatever links the intermarried couple may still have with a Jewish ethnic culture. However, studies of households with a Jew who has intermarried show that only 20 to 35 percent of the children are raised Jewish. Similarly, only 15 percent of these families are members of a synagogue.

Sources: American Jewish Committee 2005; Bergman Institute 2011; Chertok, Phillips, and Saxe 2008; Freedman 2003; Lugo et al. 2013a; Sanua 2007; Schwartz 2006; United Jewish Communities 2003.

Familism refers to the pride and closeness in the family that result in placing family obligations and loyalty before individual needs. Jews are more likely than other ethnic or religious groups to be members of a household that interacts regularly with kinfolk. Nonetheless, the trend is away from familism—a trend that could further erode Jewish identity.

Without question, of the ten problems cited by the American Jewish Committee, intermarriage has received the greatest attention from Jewish leaders. Therefore, it has been the subject of significant social research, as the Research Focus details.

Role of Religion

Devotion to Judaism appears to be the clear way to preserve ethnic identity. Yet Jews are divided about how to practice their faith. Many of the Orthodox Jews see Reform Jews as little better than nonbelievers. Even among the Orthodox, some sects, such as the Lubavitchers, try to awaken less-observant Orthodox Jews to their spiritual obligation. Added to these developments is the continuing rise in Jewish out-marriages previously noted. Many Jewish religious rituals are centered in the home rather than in the synagogue, from lighting Sabbath candles to observing dietary laws. Therefore, Jews are far more likely to feel that children cannot be brought up in the faith without family support.

The religious question facing Jews is not so much one of ideology as of observing the commandments of traditional Jewish law. The religious variations among the nearly 6 million Jewish Americans are a product of attempts to accommodate traditional rituals and precepts to life in the dominant society. It is in adhering to such rituals that Jews are most likely to be at odds with the Christian theme advanced in public schools, even if it appears only in holiday parties. Recall that we use the term **marginality** to describe the status of living in two distinct cultures simultaneously. Jews who give some credence to the secular aspects of Christmas celebrations exemplify individuals' accommodating themselves to two cultures—a 2013 national survey indicated that 32 percent of Jews (either currently observant of Judaism or those who were raised Jewish and consider themselves Jewish) had a Christmas tree in their home (Lugo et al. 2013a:80).

Is there a widespread pattern among Jewish Americans of reviving the old ways? Some Jews, especially those secure in their position, have taken up renewed orthodoxy. It is difficult to say whether the sporadic rise of traditionalism among Jews is a significant force or a fringe movement. Novelist Tom Ross at age 67 retook his birth name, Tom Rosenberg. Shortly after coming to the United States, his parents voluntarily anglicized their name. In 2000, Rosenberg reverted to his birth name as a step in reclaiming his roots. Still, at the beginning of the twenty-first century, Jewish leaders in North America and Europe are much more likely to express concern about the increase in the number of secularized Jews than to find reasons to applaud an increase in Yiddishkait (Rosenberg 2000).

Role of Cultural Heritage

For many Jews, religious observance is a very small aspect of their Jewishness. They express their identity instead in a variety of political, cultural, and social activities. For them, acts of worship, fasting, eating permitted foods, and the study of the Torah and the Talmud are irrelevant to being Jewish. Of course, religious Jews find such a position impossible to accept (Liebman 1973).

Many Gentiles mistakenly suppose that a measure of Jewishness is the ability to speak Yiddish. Few people have spoken as many languages as the Jews have through their long history. Yiddish is only one, and it developed in Jewish communities in eastern Europe between the tenth and twelfth centuries. Fluency in Yiddish in the United States has been associated with the immigrant generation and the Orthodox. Sidney Goldstein and Calvin Goldscheider (1968) reported that evidence overwhelmingly supports the conclusion that linguistic assimilation among Jews is almost complete by the third generation. However, in the last generation or two, there has been a slight increase in the use of Hebrew. This change has probably resulted from increased pride in Israel and a greater interaction between that nation and the United States. Other contributing factors are the increase in the use of Hebrew texts in Jewish day schools and in college Jewish studies programs.

Overall, the differences between Jews and Gentiles have declined in the United States. To a large extent, this reduction is a product of generational changes typical of all ethnic groups. The first-generation Mexican American in Los Angeles contrasts sharply with the middle-class White living in suburban Boston. The convergence in culture and identity is much greater between the fourth-generation Mexican American and his or her White counterpart. A similar convergence is occurring among Jews. However, this change does not signal the eventual demise of the Jewish identity. Moreover, Jewish identity is not a single identity, as we can see from the heterogeneity in religious observance, dedication to Jewish and Israeli causes, and participation in Jewish organizations.

Being Jewish comes from the family, the faith, and the culture, but it does not require any one criterion. Jewishness transcends nation, religion, or culture. A sense of peoplehood is present that neither anti-Semitic bigotry nor even an ideal state of fellowship among all religions would destroy. American life may have drastically modified Jewish life in the direction of dominant society values, but it has not eliminated it. Milton Gordon (1964) refers to **peoplehood** as a group with a shared feeling. For Jews, this sense of identity originates from a variety of sources, past and present, both within and without (Goldscheider 2003).

Figure 14.4 shows the Spectrum of Intergroup Relations for Jewish Americans.

Conclusion

Jewish Americans are the product of three waves of immigration originating from three different Jewish communities: the Sephardic, the western European, and the eastern European. They brought different languages and, to some extent, different levels of religious orthodoxy. Today, they have assimilated to form an ethnic group that transcends the initial differences in nationality.

Figure 14.4 Spectrum of Intergroup Relations: Jewish Americans

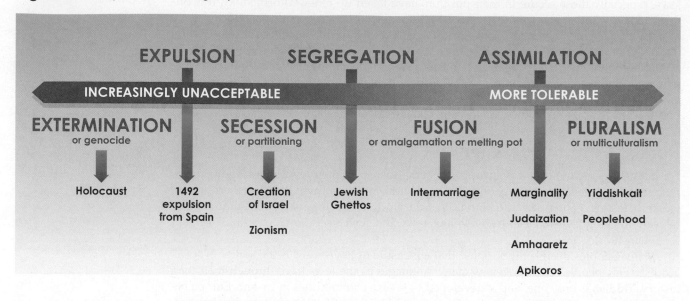

Jews are not a homogeneous group. Among them are the Reform, Conservative, and Orthodox denominations, listed in ascending order of adherence to traditional rituals. Nonreligious Jews make up another group, probably as large as any one segment, and they still see themselves as Jewish.

Jewish identity is reaffirmed from within and outside the Jewish community; however, both sources of affirmation are weaker today. The family, religion, and the vast network of national and community-based organizations strengthen identity. Anti-Semitism outside the Jewish community strengthens the in-group feeling and the perception that survival as a people is threatened.

Today, American Jews face a new challenge: They must maintain their identity in an overwhelmingly Christian society in which discrimination is fading and outbreaks of prejudice are sporadic. Yiddishkait may not so much have decreased as changed. Elements of the Jewish tradition have been shed in part because of modernization and social change. Some of this social change—a decline in anti-Semitic violence and restrictions—is certainly welcome. Although kashrut observance has declined, most Jews care deeply about Israel, and many engage in pro-Israel activities. Commitment has changed with the times, but it has not disappeared (Cohen 1988).

Some members of the Jewish community view the apparent assimilation with alarm and warn against the grave likelihood of the total disappearance of a sizable and identifiable Jewish community in the United States. Others see the changes not as erosion but as an accommodation to a pluralistic, multicultural environment. We are witness to a progressive change in the substance and style of Jewish life. According to this view, Jewish identity, the Orthodox and Conservative traditions notwithstanding, has shed some of its traditional characteristics and has acquired others. The strength of this view comes with the knowledge that doomsayers have been present in the American Jewish community for at least two generations. Only the passage of time will reveal the future of Jewish life in the United States (Finestein 1988; Glazer 1990).

Although discrimination against Jews has gone on for centuries, far more ancient than anti-Semitism and the experience of the Diaspora is the subordinate role of women in societies across the globe. Women were perhaps the first group to be relegated to an inferior role and may be the last to work collectively to achieve equal rights. Our study of women as a subordinate group in Chapter 15 reaffirms the themes in our study of racial and ethnic groups.

Summary of Learning Objectives

14.1 Examine whether the Jewish people are considered a race, religion, or ethnic group.

1. Jews as a group are best considered an ethnic group whose members may or may not be obedient to a Jewish religious tradition.

14.2 Summarize the history of Jewish immigration to the United States.

2. Jewish immigration began in the earliest colonial times and has reflected the ebb and flow of immigration from Europe.

14.3 Describe the extent of anti-Semitism historically and in the present.

3. Anti-Semitism has a long history worldwide, having been institutionalized in many European countries. Although not absent in the United States, it has never been endorsed by government action. The Holocaust is a turning point in modern history and was followed by an influx of Jewish immigrants to the United States. Contemporary anti-Semitism in the United States is frequently documented but is likely to be punctuated by spirited discussions about U.S.–Israel relations.

14.4 Explain Jewish Americans' economic, educational, and political situation.

4. Jewish Americans demonstrate high levels of occupational success built on extensive formal schooling. As a group, they are very politically active.

14.5 Describe the role of religion among Jewish Americans.

5. Religious life is varied among Jews in the United States and is split between nonobservant and observant. Among the latter, a variety of expressions range from very conservative to very liberal adherence to ritual and lifestyle.

14.6 Explain Jewish identity.

6. The acceptance of Jews in the United States has led to high levels of intermarriage, leading many in the Jewish community to lament that Jews are assimilating too quickly and losing their identity.

Key Terms

anti-Semitism, *page 302*
Diaspora, *page 310*
familism, *page 317*
fringe-of-values theory, *page 306*

halakha, *page 317*
Holocaust, *page 307*
Holocaust revisionists, *page 307*
in-group virtues, *page 307*

Judaization, *page 304*
kashrut, *page 314*
marginality, *page 318*
out-group vices, *page 307*
peoplehood, *page 319*

scapegoating theory, *page 306*
Yiddishkait, *page 316*
Zionism, *page 310*

Review Questions

1. Why are the Jewish people most accurately characterized as an ethnic group?

2. What are major patterns of immigration of Jews to the United States?

3. How have the patterns of anti-Semitism changed or remained the same over time?

4. What are the positive and negative aspects of the status of Jewish Americans as a group today?

5. What are the major aspects of Jewish religious life?

6. Why is maintaining Jewish identity so difficult in the United States?

Critical Thinking

1. Most minority groups regard acceptance as a positive outcome. Why do some Jewish Americans feel threatened by being accepted in contemporary Gentile society?

2. How different and similar have the experiences of women in organized religion been compared with those of women in the Jewish faith?

3. How has fusion functioned or not functioned for any other subordinate group when compared with Jews in the United States?

4. Reviewing the Spectrum of Intergroup Relations in Figure 14.4, how do the different entries define and affect Jewish Americans today?

Chapter 15
Women:
The Oppressed Majority

gwimages / Fotolia

Learning Objectives

15.1 Understand gender roles.

15.2 Contrast sociological perspectives on gender.

15.3 Summarize the history of the feminist movement.

15.4 Discuss women's economic situation.

15.5 Describe the experience of women in education.

15.6 Explain gender as it relates to the family.

15.7 Describe women's role in politics.

Women are an oppressed group even though they form the numerical majority. They are a social minority in the United States and throughout Western society. Men dominate in influence, prestige, and wealth. Some women do occupy positions of power, but they are the exceptions, as evidenced by journalistic accounts declaring "she is the first woman" or "the only woman" to hold a specific executive job, such as CEO.

For example, many were taken aback when Twitter became a publicly held company in 2013 and revealed that its board was composed exclusively of men. In some ways, Twitter's revelation should not come as a surprise, as 49 percent of publicly traded information technology businesses have no women on their boards—not even a token member. (That statistic compares to 36 percent of public companies having at least one female board member.)

Many high-tech corporations have not a single female board member, despite having many female consumers and clients. Over one in four corporations have one or no female board members (Catalyst 2016).

In 2014, data revealed that female software developers earn about 10 percent less than their male counterparts. In response, the head of Microsoft speculated on the source of the problem: "Women do not ask for more money from their employers." Social media lit up in response. Many perceived that the male CEO was *offering advice on how to fix women* or **blaming the victim**—portraying the problems of racial and ethnic minorities as the minorities' fault rather than recognizing society's responsibility.

Many people, men and women, find it difficult to conceptualize women as a subordinate group even after hearing about Twitter's all-male board or the head of Microsoft expounding on women's responsibility for the gender pay disparity. Why is it hard to think of women as a subordinate group? After all, not all women live in ghettos. They no longer have to attend inferior schools. They freely interact and live with their alleged oppressors, men. How, then, are they a subordinate group? Let us examine the five properties of a subordinate or minority group introduced in Chapter 1:

1. Women experience unequal treatment. Although they are not segregated by residence, they are victims of prejudice and discrimination.

2. Women have physical and cultural characteristics that distinguish them from the dominant group (men).

3. Membership in the subordinate group is involuntary.

4. Through the rise of contemporary feminism, women have become increasingly aware of their subordinate status and have developed a greater sense of group solidarity.

5. Women are not forced to marry, yet many women feel that their subordinate status is most irrevocably defined within marriage.

In this chapter, the similarities between women and racial and ethnic groups will become apparent (Bates 2017; Guynn 2014; Klinkenborg 2013; Wingfield 2014).

The most common analogy about minorities used in the social sciences is the similarity between the status of African Americans and that of women. Blacks are considered a minority group, but, one asks, how can women as a group be so similar to Blacks? We recognize some similarities in recent history; for example, an entire generation has observed and participated in both the civil rights movement and the women's movement. A background of suffrage campaigns, demonstrations, sit-ins, lengthy court battles, and self-help groups is common to the movements for equal rights for both women and African Americans. But similarities were recognized long before the recent protests against inequality. In *An American Dilemma* (1944), the famous study of race, Gunnar Myrdal observed that women's role in society was parallel to Blacks'. Other observers, such as Helen Mayer Hacker (1951, 1974), later elaborated on the similarities.

What do these groups have in common besides recent protest movements? The negative stereotypes directed at the two groups are quite similar: Both groups have been considered emotional, irresponsible, weak, or inferior. Both are thought to fight subtly against the system: Women allegedly try to outwit men by using feminine wiles, as historically Blacks allegedly outwitted Whites by pretending to be deferential or respectful. To these stereotypes must be added another similarity: Neither women nor African Americans are accepting a subordinate role in society any longer.

Nearly all Whites give lip service to the contention that African Americans are innately equal to Whites, even if they do not wholeheartedly believe it. Blacks and Whites are inherently the same. But men and women are not the same, and they vary most dramatically in their roles in reproduction. Biological differences have contributed to sexism. **Sexism** is the ideology that one sex is superior to the other. Quite different is the view that there are few differences between the sexes. People do not have to be locked into the behavior that accompanies the labels *masculine* and *feminine.* In the United States, people disagree widely as to what implications, if any, the biological differences between the sexes have for social roles. We begin our discussion of women as a subordinate group with this topic.

Gender Roles

15.1 Understand gender roles.

A college man, done with afternoon classes, heads off to get a pedicure and, while the nail polish is drying, sits on a nearby park bench finishing some needlepoint he started. Meanwhile, a college woman walks through the park chewing tobacco and spitting along the path. What is wrong with this picture? We are witnessing the open violation of how men and women are expected to act. So unlikely are these episodes that I have taken them from sociology teachers who specifically ask their students to go out, violate gender expectations, and record how they feel and how people react to their behavior (Nielsen, Walden, and Kunkel 2000: 287).

Gender roles are society's expectations of the "proper" behavior, attitudes, and activities of men and women. Toughness has traditionally been seen in the United States as masculine, desirable only in men, whereas tenderness has been viewed as feminine. A society may require that one sex or the other take the primary responsibility for the socialization of the children, economic support of the family, or religious leadership.

Without question, socialization has a powerful impact on the development of girls and boys in the United States. Indeed, the gender roles first encountered in early childhood often are a factor in defining a child's popularity. Sociologists Patricia Adler and her colleagues (1992) observed elementary school children and found that boys typically achieved high status on the basis of their athletic ability, coolness, toughness, social skills, and success in relationships with girls. By contrast, girls gained popularity based on their parents' economic background and their own physical appearance, social skills, and academic success.

It may be obvious that men and women are conditioned to assume certain roles, but the origin of gender roles as we know them is less clear. Many studies have been done on laboratory animals, such as injecting monkeys and rats with male and female hormones. Primates in their natural surroundings have been closely observed for the presence and characteristics of gender roles. Animal studies do not point to instinctual gender differences similar to the masculine and feminine gender roles observed in humans. Historically, women's work came to be defined as a consequence of the birth process. Men, free of childcare responsibilities, generally became the hunters and foragers for food. Even though women must bear children, men could have cared for the young. Exactly why women were assigned that role in societies is not known.

Women's and men's roles vary across different cultures. Furthermore, we know that acceptable behavior for men and women changes over time in a society. For example, the men in the royal courts of Europe in the late 1700s fulfilled present-day stereotypes of feminine appearance in their display of ornamental dress and personal vanity rather than resembling the men of a century later, although they still engaged in duels and other forms of aggression. The social roles of the sexes have no constants in time or space (Lorber 2005; Taylor, Rupp, and Whittier 2009).

Gender roles can easily be confused with issues concerning human sexuality. We will explore this topic in greater detail in Chapter 17, when we consider how society treats people who are lesbian, gay, bisexual, or transgender. Related to gender roles, but different from them, are two other concepts: gender identity and sexual identity. **Gender identity** refers to how people see themselves as male, female, or something else. This identity can be something different from one's biological sex at birth, although most people develop a gender identity that conforms to their biological identity. **Sexual identity**, also referred to as *sexual orientation*, refers to the self-awareness of being romantically or sexually attracted to a defined group of people. Typically, people become aware of their gender identity at a very young age, but a strong sexual identity may not emerge until well into adolescence.

Sociological Perspectives

15.2 **Contrast sociological perspectives on gender.**

Gender differences are maintained in our culture through the systematic socialization of babies and infants, children, adolescents, and adults. Even though different subcultures and even different families vary in their childrearing practices, we teach our children to be boys and girls, even though men and women are more alike than they are different.

We are bombarded with expectations for our behavior as men and women from many sources simultaneously. Many individual women hold positions involving high levels of responsibility and competence but may not be accorded the same respect as men. Similarly, individual men find the time to get involved with their children's lives only to meet with disbelief and occasional surprise from healthcare and educational systems accustomed to dealing only with mothers. Even when individuals are motivated to stretch the social boundaries of gender, social structure and institutions often impede them. Gender differentiation in our culture is embedded in social institutions: not only the family, but also education, religion, politics, the economy, medicine, and the mass media.

Functionalists maintain that sex differentiation has contributed to overall social stability. Sociologists Talcott Parsons and Robert Bales (1955) argued that to function most efficiently, the family needs adults who will specialize in particular roles. They believed that the arrangement of gender roles with which they were familiar had arisen because marital partners needed a division of labor.

The functionalist view is initially persuasive in explaining the way in which girls and boys are typically brought up in U.S. society. However, it would lead us to expect even girls and women with no interest in children to still become babysitters and mothers. Similarly, boys and men with a caring feeling for children may be "programmed" into careers in the business world. Clearly, such a differentiation between the sexes can have harmful consequences for the person who does not fit into specific roles, while depriving society of the optimal use of many talented people who are confined by sexual labeling. Consequently, the conflict perspective is increasingly convincing in its analysis of the development of gender roles.

Conflict theorists do not deny the presence of a differentiation by sex. In fact, they contend that the relationship between women and men has been one of unequal power, with men being dominant over women. Men may have become powerful in preindustrial times because their size, physical strength, and freedom from childbearing duties allowed them to dominate women physically. In contemporary societies, such considerations are not as important, yet cultural beliefs about the sexes are now long established.

Both functionalists and conflict theorists acknowledge that it is not possible to change gender roles drastically without dramatic revisions in a culture's social structure. Functionalists see potential social disorder, or at least unknown social consequences, if all aspects of traditional sex differentiation are disturbed. Yet for conflict theorists, no social structure is ultimately desirable if it has to be maintained through the oppression of its people.

Applying these perspectives, let's use the Research Focus feature to consider in a very broad sense the research on "men's work" and "women's work" and look specifically at what happens when men do women's work.

The Feminist Movement

15.3 **Summarize the history of the feminist movement.**

Women's struggle for equality, like the struggles of other subordinate groups, has been long and multifaceted. From the very beginning, female activists and sympathetic men who spoke of equal rights for the sexes have been ridiculed and scorned.

In a formal sense, the American feminist movement was born in upstate New York in a town called Seneca Falls in the summer of 1848. On July 19, the first women's rights convention began, attended by Elizabeth Cady Stanton, Lucretia Mott, and other pioneers in the struggle for women's rights. This first wave of feminists, as they are currently known,

Research Focus

Men Doing Women's Work

Social scientists, including sociologists and economists, have explored what happens when men do "women's work" in three key areas.

The first key area is housework. As we will see later in this chapter, women generally do much more housework than men do. The labor that men do around the home tends to be very specific, such as lawn care rather than laundry. This division of labor has traditionally seemed to be very functional for the running of the household, and deviations from the norm are not common. For example, when the husband does the laundry, the mere act is regarded as unusual and often leads to significant praise. Of course, there are exceptions, where men choose to do the laundry or clean the toilets.

The second key area is childcare. As is the case with housework, mothers typically spend many more hours engaged in childcare than fathers do. Again, when the father (rather than the mother) takes time off work to be with a sick child, the man's behavior is considered unusual and is greeted with praise.

The third key area is wage labor, and this topic has been the subject of a growing body of research. As we will see later in this chapter, most occupations are either performed primarily by men (for example, firefighters) or primarily by women (for example, health aides). Some men choose to pursue "women's work," but this choice is more likely when the men had been employed in an occupation for which the demand is dwindling (for example, general welders or coal miners) or when the men are forced to take what is available during times of high unemployment.

What does the research say about men entering jobs typically held by women?

1. Men experience what has been termed the **glass escalator** (see Chapter 3). In these jobs, they are less likely to be laid off than women are, and they are paid more and promoted faster.

2. Men who enter women's jobs are less able to get "men's jobs." These men include racial and ethnic minorities, older job seekers, and people with disabilities.

Conflict theorists believe that this division in the labor force points to work traditionally carried out by women as being less financially rewarded and lower in status. As a result, many policymakers now argue that attention should not be directed solely at improving women's wages in higher-status jobs and that more attention should be paid to the work toward the bottom end of the occupational ladder that men typically avoid.

Sources: Miller 2017a, 2017b; Reskin and Roos 2009; Roos and Stevens 2017.

---

battled ridicule and scorn as they fought for legal and political equality, but they were not afraid to risk controversy on behalf of their cause. In 1872, for example, Susan B. Anthony was arrested for attempting to vote in that year's presidential election.

The Suffrage Movement

The **suffragists** worked for years to get women the right to vote. From the beginning, this reform was judged to be crucial. If women voted, it was felt, other reforms would quickly follow. The struggle took so long that many of the initial advocates of women's suffrage died before victory was achieved. In 1879, an amendment to the Constitution was introduced that would have given women the right to vote. Not until 1919 was it finally passed, and not until the next year was it ratified as the Nineteenth Amendment to the Constitution.

Opposition to giving women the vote came from all directions. Liquor interests and brewers correctly feared that women would assist in passing laws restricting or prohibiting the sale of their products. The South feared the influence that more Black voters (that is, Black women) might have. Southerners had also not forgotten the pivotal role women had played in the abolitionist movement. Despite the opposition, the suffrage movement succeeded in gaining the right to vote for women, a truly remarkable achievement because it had to rely on male legislators.

The Nineteenth Amendment did not automatically lead to other feminist reforms. Women did not typically vote as a bloc and have not been elected to office in proportion to their numbers. The feminist movement as an organized effort that gained national attention faded, regaining prominence only in the 1960s. Nevertheless, the women's movement did not die out completely in the first half of the twentieth century. Many women carried on the struggle in new areas, such as the effort to lift restrictions on birth-control devices (Freeman 1975; Stansell 2010).

The Women's Liberation Movement

Ideologically, the women's movement of the 1960s had its roots in the continuing informal feminist movement that began with the first subordination of women in Western society. Psychologically, it grew in America's kitchens, as women felt unfulfilled and did not know why, and in the labor force, as women were made to feel guilty because they were not at home with their families. In a key achievement, by the 1960s women had attained greater control of when and whether to become pregnant (mostly through the use of contraception).

Suffragists struggled for many years to convince Congress and the states to pass the Nineteenth Amendment to the Constitution. They finally succeeded, and women gained the right to vote beginning in 1920.

Sociologically, several events delayed progress in the mid-1960s. The civil rights movement and the antiwar movement were slow to embrace women's rights. The New Left seemed as sexist as the rest of society in practice, despite its talk of equality. Groups protesting the draft and demonstrating on college campuses generally rejected women as leaders and assigned them traditional duties, such as preparing refreshments and publishing organization newsletters. The core of early feminists often knew one another from participating in other protest or reform groups that had initially been unwilling to accept women's rights as a legitimate goal.

Beginning about 1967, the movement for Black equality was no longer as willing to accept help from sympathetic Whites. As a result, White men moved on to protest the draft, a cause not as crucial to women's lives. Although somewhat involved in the antiwar movement, many White women began to struggle for their own rights, although at first they had to fight alone. Eventually, civil rights groups, the New Left, and most established women's groups endorsed the feminist movement with the zeal of new converts, but initially they resisted the concerns of feminists (Freeman 1973, 1983).

The feminist movement has also brought about a reexamination of men's roles in society. Supporters of "male liberation" want to free men from the constraints of the masculine value system. Boys are socialized to think that they should be invulnerable, fearless, decisive, and even emotionless in some situations. Men are expected to achieve physically and occupationally at some risk to their own values. Failure to take up these traditionally masculine roles and attitudes can mean that a man will be considered less masculine. Male liberation is the logical counterpart of female liberation. If women are to redefine their gender role successfully, men must redefine theirs as workers, husbands, and fathers (Messner 1997; National Organization for Men Against Sexism 2017).

There is beginning to emerge some evidence that men are recognizing the importance of ending discrimination and prejudice against women. Researchers have used the term **daughter effect** to refer the phenomenon of fathers who have daughters being more likely to look after women's interests in general. Researchers have found the daughter effect in legislators and the policies they back. In addition, male CEOs with daughters are less likely to have pay disparity between men and women in their businesses. While the observed relationships are modest, they do suggest that men with firsthand experience of gender discrimination in their own household may work to overcome it in their day jobs (Shufro 2008; Prime 2011).

Since the mid-1960s, the feminist movement has undergone significant change. Betty Friedan, a founder of the National Organization for Women (NOW), argued in the early 1960s that women had to understand the **feminine mystique**, recognizing that society saw them only as their children's mother and their husband's wife. Later, in the 1980s, though not denying that women deserved the same options in life as men, she called for restructuring the "institution of home and wife." Friedan and others began to recognize that many young women are frustrated when time does not permit them to have it all: career, marriage,

OwenDB/Black Star/Newscom

Having three women on the Supreme Court seems impressive, but the number is less impressive when one realizes that only four of the 113 Supreme Court justices who have served through 2017 have been women. Pictured here are Sonia Sotomayor, Ruth Bader Ginsburg, and Elena Kagan. Not pictured is retired justice Sandra Day O'Connor.

and motherhood. Difficult issues remain, and feminists continue to discuss and debate concerns such as the limits that businesses put on careers of women with children, domestic violence, and male bias in medical research (Coontz 2010; Friedan 1963, 1981, 1991).

Feminism Today

Feminism is an ideology whose goal is to establish equal rights for women. Over its long history, writers have spoken of feminism "waxing and waning" as it stressed women's entry into the public life of politics and jobs, then added equality at home, respect for the body, and the environment. Then, in 1998, a cover of *Time* magazine asked "Is Feminism Dead?" The article argued that young women seem to take their improved status for granted and saw their mothers' struggles as no longer relevant.

So, is feminism truly dead? Many feminists resent the question, which may imply that all the concerns facing women have been resolved. A national survey in 2016 show that over two-thirds of women (and one-third of men) identify themselves as a "feminist" or "strong feminist." Younger women (ages 18–34) are more willing to self-label as feminists, but the feminist label is most accepted by women in their fifties.

Today's feminists, especially younger adults, do not seem to rally around a political figure but rather around strong female role models who at times speak out in favor of social causes embraced by feminism. These role models include such celebrities as Jennifer Lawrence, Beyoncé, and Taylor Swift.

Today's feminists argue that they have moved well beyond the early charges that the movement was too obsessed with the concerns of the White middle class and that African American feminists and others were marginalized. Indeed, current polling shows African Americans and Latinos more likely to be self-proclaimed feminists. In Chapter 1, we introduced the concept of intersectionality, which recognizes that gender is just one characteristic that stratifies society and places people in dominant and subordinate categories. **Intersectionality** refers to the overlapping and interdependent system of advantage and disadvantage that positions people in society on the basis of race, class, gender, and other characteristics (Collins 2015; Crenshaw 1989).

A recent case example of intersectionality in action was the 2017 Women's March scheduled the day after President Donald Trump's inauguration. Women dissatisfied by his social positions and the defeat of Democrat challenger Hillary Clinton proposed the pro-women demonstration. Initially, the organizers were all White women, but as preparations continued, the leadership evolved to include African American, Arab American, Latino, and Muslim women. By the time of the march in Washington and cities across the United States, many of the participants had experienced neither White privilege nor the advantages of being a man (Cal and Clement 2016; Stockman 2017).

The Economic Picture

15.4   Discuss women's economic situation.

The labor force has changed in terms of gender over the past 45 years in industrial nations. As Figure 15.1 shows, more and more women are participating in the labor force—that is, either seeking work or already employed.

What about specific jobs? The U.S. Bureau of the Census looked at the earnings of 821 occupations ranging from chief executives to dishwashers, considering individuals' age, education, and work experience. The unmistakable finding was a substantial gap in median earnings between full-time male workers and full-time female workers in the same occupation. As Figure 15.2 shows, in almost every major occupational classification, men earn more. For example, he's an air traffic controller and makes $67,000. She earns $56,000. He's a housekeeper and makes $19,000. She earns $15,000. He's a teacher's assistant and makes $20,000. She earns $15,000 in the same occupation. However, men do not always earn more. The Census Bureau found two occupations out of 821 in which women typically earn about 1 percent more: hazardous materials recovery workers and telecommunications line installers (Weinberg 2004).

Is there less of an earnings gap in high-status occupations? No, there isn't. A 2011 study examined the incomes of female physicians and male physicians. Typically, female

Figure 15.1 Women's Labor Force Participation: International Comparisons

In the United States, as in many other industrial nations, women are increasingly participating in the labor force by either working or by seeking employment.

SOURCE: Developed by author based on data in Department of Labor 2011, 2013c; International Labour Organization 2016.

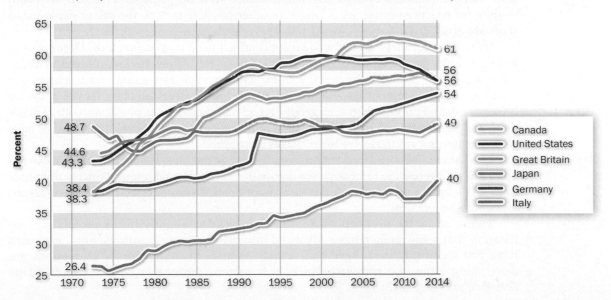

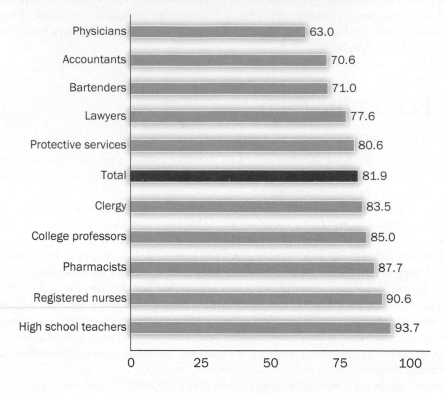

Figure 15.2 Ratio of Women's to Men's Earnings by Occupation

SOURCE: Developed by author based on data in Bureau of Labor Statistics 2016b.

NOTE: Wage data for full-time workers as of February 2017. Protective services include police, detectives, firefighters, correctional officers, and security guards.

Occupation	Value
Physicians	63.0
Accountants	70.6
Bartenders	71.0
Lawyers	77.6
Protective services	80.6
Total	81.9
Clergy	83.5
College professors	85.0
Pharmacists	87.7
Registered nurses	90.6
High school teachers	93.7

physicians' starting salaries were $17,000 a year *lower* than those of their male counterparts. This annual discrepancy has grown with each subsequent survey. The reason is not that women tend to go into lower-paying specialties. That is, women are not more likely to go into pediatrics than heart surgery. Second, even controlling for field, women make less. Well-compensated cardiologists make $228,000 if male, $205,000 if female. Even controlling for practice setting, work hours, or other possible factors, the salary gap persists (LoSasso et al. 2011).

More than any other group, women are confined to certain occupations. **Occupational segregation** by gender reflects the tendency for men and women to be employed in different occupations. Some gender-typed jobs for women, such as nursing and teaching, pay well above the minimum wage and carry moderate prestige. Nevertheless, these jobs are far lower in pay and prestige than such gender-typed male positions as physician, college president, and university professor. When they do enter nontraditional positions, as we have seen, women as a group receive lower wages or salaries.

The data in Table 15.1 present an overall view of the male dominance in high-paying occupations. Among the representative occupations chosen, men unquestionably dominate in those that pay well. Women dominate as receptionists, seamstresses, healthcare workers, and domestic workers.

Trends show the proportions of women increasing slightly in the professions, indicating that some women have advanced into better-paying positions, but these gains have not significantly changed the overall picture. In other words, professions are developing more of a gender balance, but women continue to be at a disadvantage (Wallace and Kay 2012).

Table 15.1 Women as a Percentage of All Workers in Selected Occupations, 1950–2015

Occupation	1950	1980	2015
PROFESSIONAL WORKERS			
Accountants	14.9	36.2	59.7
Engineers	1.2	4.0	13.6
Lawyers	4.1	12.8	34.5
Physicians	6.5	12.9	37.9
Registered nurses	97.8	96.5	89.4
College professors	22.8	33.9	46.5
OTHER OCCUPATIONS			
Carpenters	0.4	1.5	1.8
Protective services (firefighters, police officers, guards)	2.0	9.5	21.3
Retail salespersons	48.9	45.3	49.4
Cashiers	81.7	86.6	72.5
Bookkeepers	77.7	90.5	89.8
Food preparation workers	61.6	66.9	54.5
Private household workers	94.9	97.5	89.3

SOURCE: Developed by author based on data in Bureau of the Census 1951:Tables 218, 1981: Table 675; Bureau of Labor Statistics 2016a: Table 11.

"Look, I agree that you deserve the same salary as your male counterparts, but I have a responsibility to defend the traditional pay structure."

Loren Fishman/CartoonStock.com

Inequality between women and men is a worldwide social phenomenon. In the Global View feature, we look at the gender divide in Japan.

Sources of Discrimination

If we return to the definition of discrimination ("the denial of opportunities and equal rights to individuals and groups because of prejudice or for other arbitrary reasons"), we might ask: Are not men better able to perform some tasks than women, and vice versa? If ability means performance, there certainly are differences. The typical woman can sew better than the typical man, but a man can toss a ball farther than a woman. These are group differences. Certainly, many women out-throw many men, and many men out-sew many women, but society expects women to excel at sewing and men to excel at throwing. The differences in those abilities result from cultural conditioning. Women usually are taught to sew, and men are much less likely to learn that skill. Men are encouraged to participate in sports that require the ability to throw a ball much more than women are. True, as a group men have greater potential for the muscular development needed to throw a ball, but U.S. society encourages men to realize their potential in this area more than it encourages women to pursue athletic skills.

Today's labor market involves much more than throwing a ball and using a needle and thread, but the analogy to these two skills is repeated time and again. Such rationales are used to support sexist practices in all aspects of the workplace. Just as African Americans can suffer from both individual acts of racism and institutional discrimination, women are vulnerable to both sexism and institutional discrimination. Women are subject to direct sexism, such as sexist remarks, and also to differential treatment because of institutional policies.

Removing barriers to equal opportunity would eventually eliminate institutional discrimination. Theoretically, men and women would sew and throw a ball equally well. We

A Global View

Gender Inequality in Japan

Gender inequality is not difficult to document in Japan. With the world's highest literacy rate and high school enrollment rate for women, half of Japanese women quit their jobs upon getting married. Women who do work earn only about 70 percent of men's wages. Only about 9 percent of Japanese managers are women—a ratio that is one of the lowest in the world. Even in developing countries, women are twice as likely to be managers as women in Japan.

It is not hard to understand the contemporary inequality. Until the period after World War II, Japanese women could not vote, and they had little say about where to live compared to their husbands. Japanese women were eventually given the right to vote, but the assumption persisted that they would leave the labor force upon getting married in order to maintain the home and prepare for the inevitable arrival of children.

In 1985, Japan's parliament—at the time, 97 percent men—passed an Equal Employment bill that encourages employers to end sex discrimination in hiring, assignment, and promotion policies. However, feminist organizations were dissatisfied because the law lacked strong sanctions. In a landmark ruling issued in late 1996, a Japanese court for the first time held an employer liable for denying promotions due to sex discrimination.

Has the court's decision made a difference? Labor-force participation has increased, but the increase in women workers has largely been in part-time positions (women account for 70 percent of such workers). Women in full-time positions have moved up the occupational hierarchy a bit, but mainly by delaying marriage or not marrying at all. Once married, college-educated Japanese women, whether they are mothers or not, follow the same path as previous generations, leaving the labor force except perhaps for part-time employment.

Recent recessions and the 2011 tsunami and nuclear power plant disasters notwithstanding, Japanese corporations admit they need a skilled labor force that includes women. Of the total number of managers heading larger departments in Japanese companies, women made up 2.5 percent. In contrast, around 4 percent of corporate managers are women in other developed countries, including the United States and Germany. Research shows that Japanese employers typically exclude women from jobs that provide higher wages.

However, progress has been made in terms of public opinion. In 1987, 43 percent of Japanese adults agreed that married women should stay home, but by 2000 the proportion had dropped to 25 percent. On the political front, Japanese women have made progress but remain vastly underrepresented. In a 2017 study of women in government around the world, Japan ranked 163rd of 194 of the countries studied, with only 9.3 percent of its national legislators being women.

Given the situation, even if it is improving a bit, women in Japan have increasingly begun to start their own businesses. This is a tactic similar to that used by minorities in the United States, who, when blocked at the usual entry points to economic success, literally create their own new entry points. While start-up money is important, aspiring Japanese businesswomen are finding training and mentoring by female entrepreneurs to be invaluable.

Sources: Abe 2011; Aguirre et al. 2012:52–53, Ehara 2005; French 2003; Inter-Parliamentary Union 2017; Kambayashi 2013; Kyodo News 2010; Mun 2010, Raymo and Lim 2011.

say "theoretically" because cultural conditioning would take generations. In some formerly male jobs, such as gas station clerk and attendant, society seems quite willing to accept women. In other occupations, such as president of the United States, it will take longer; many years may pass before full acceptance can be expected in other fields, such as professional contact sports.

Many efforts have been made to eliminate institutional discrimination as it applies to women. The 1964 Civil Rights Act and its enforcement arm, the Equal Employment Opportunity Commission, address cases of sex discrimination. The inclusion of sex bias along with prejudice based on race, color, creed, and national origin was an unexpected last-minute change in the provisions of the landmark 1964 act. However, federal legislation has not removed all discrimination against women in employment. The same explanations presented in Chapter 3 for the lag between the laws and a significant reduction in race discrimination apply to sex discrimination: lack of money to implement the laws, weak enforcement powers, occasionally weak commitment to enforcing the existing laws, and, most importantly, institutional and structural forces that perpetuate inequality.

What should be done to close the gap between the earnings of women and men? As Figure 15.3 shows, women earn more annually with more formal schooling, just like their male counterparts. However, as women continue their education, the wage gap does not narrow and even shows signs of growing. As startling as this gap is, consider what it means over a lifetime. A college-educated woman can expect to make $800,000 less over her work life compared to a college-educated man (National Committee on Pay Equity 2017).

Figure 15.3 Financial Return on Education for Women and Men, 2015

NOTE: See Table 3.1.

SOURCE: Developed by author based on data in Proctor, Semega, and Kollar 2016:PINC-03. Permission Information: Census publications.

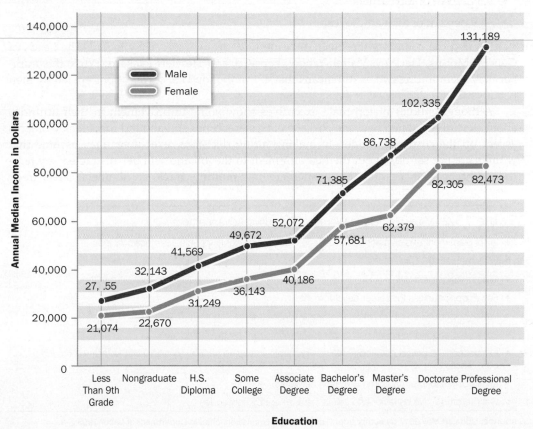

In the 1980s, **pay equity**, or comparable worth, was a controversial solution presented to alleviate the second-class status of working women. It directly attempted to secure equal pay when occupational segregation by gender was particularly pervasive. Pay equity calls for equal pay for different types of work that are judged to be comparable in such factors as employee knowledge, skills, effort, and responsibility.

This doctrine sounds straightforward, but it is not so simple to put into operation. How exactly does one identify jobs of comparable worth? Should a zookeeper be paid more than a childcare worker? Does our society pay zookeepers more because we value caregiving for children less than caregiving for animals? Or do zookeepers earn more than childcare workers because the former tend to be men and the latter are generally women?

Despite some local initiatives, pay equity has not received much support in the United States except from the feminist movement. From a policy perspective, pay equity would have to broaden the 1938 Fair Labor Standards Act and be initiated at the federal level. The Lilly Ledbetter Fair Pay Act (see Chapter 3) still requires an individual or a group to initiate action alleging discrimination to mobilize support. Also, employers can keep salary information secret and even prevent employees from sharing their own wage records. With the government backing away from affirmative action, it is unlikely to launch an initiative on pay equity conditions (National Committee on Pay Equity 2017).

What about women aspiring to crack the glass ceiling? Recall that the **glass ceiling** (see Figure 3.5) refers to the invisible barrier blocking the promotion of a qualified worker because of gender or minority membership. Despite continuing debate over affirmative action, the consensus is that there is little room at the top for women and minorities. The glass ceiling operates so that all applicants may be welcomed by a firm, but when it comes to the powerful or more visible positions, there are limits—generally unstated—on the number of women and people of color welcomed or even tolerated (Table 15.2).

Women are doing better in top management positions than racial minorities, but they still lag far behind men. Consider that in the top 500 companies listed on the S&P (Standard & Poor's) stock index as of March 1, 2017, women accounted for:

- 5.8 percent of all CEOs
- 9.5 percent of top earners
- 44.9 percent of total employees

Among the country's top business leaders, 29 are women. They include the heads of General Motors, Hershey, Mattel, Yahoo!, PepsiCo, and Hewlett-Packard. While this number may seem impressive, it still means that 471 of the top U.S. corporations are led by men (Catalyst 2017a, 2017b).

Although studies of top male executives show some improvement in their attitudes about executive women over the past 40 years, stereotypes still abound that block women's ascent up the corporate ladder. In making hiring decisions, executives may assume that women are not serious about their commitment to the job and will be "distracted" by family and home. They assume that women are on a **mommy track**, an unofficial career track

---

Table 15.2 Major Barriers to Women's Executive Advancement

- Initial placement and clustering in dead-end staff jobs or highly technical professional jobs
- Less mentoring
- Less management training
- Fewer opportunities for career development
- Fewer opportunities for training tailored to the individual
- Lack of rotation to line positions or job assignments that produce revenue
- Less access to critical developmental assignments, including service on highly visible task forces and committees
- Less access to informal communication networks
- Counterproductive behavior and sexual harassment by colleagues

SOURCE: Updated May 2017 by author from Glass Ceiling Commission, cited in Department of Labor 1995:7–8.

that firms use for women who want to divide their attention between work and family. This assumption is false if applied to all women. The idea of the mommy track also implies that corporate men are not interested in maintaining a balance between work and family. Even competitive, upwardly mobile women are not always taken seriously in the workplace (Byker 2016; Carlson, Kacmar, and Whitten 2006; Heilman 2001).

Sexual Harassment

Under evolving legal standards, **sexual harassment** is recognized as any unwanted and unwelcome sexual advances that interfere with a person's ability to perform and enjoy the benefits of a job. Increased national attention was given to sexual harassment in the 1990s and has continued into the present through allegations made against elected officials and high-ranking military officers.

The most obvious example of sexual harassment is the boss who tells an employee, "Put out or get out!" However, the unwelcome advances that constitute sexual harassment may take the form of subtle pressures regarding sexual activity, inappropriate touching, attempted kissing, or sexual assault. Indeed, in the computer age, there is growing concern that sexually harassing messages are being sent anonymously over computer networks through e-mail and mobile phones.

In 1986, in a unanimous decision (*Meritor Savings Bank v. Vinson*), the Supreme Court declared that sexual harassment by a supervisor violates the federal law against sex discrimination in the workplace as outlined in the 1964 Civil Rights Act. If sufficiently severe, harassment is a violation even if the unwelcome sexual demands are not linked to concrete employment benefits such as a raise or promotion. Women's groups hailed the Court's decisiveness in identifying harassment as a form of discrimination. A federal judge subsequently ruled that the public display of photographs of nude and partly nude women at a workplace constitutes sexual harassment. Despite these rulings, it is very difficult legally and emotionally for a person to bring forward a case of sexual harassment (Domino 1995; Roscigno and Schmidt 2007).

Feminization of Poverty

Since World War II, an increasing proportion of the poor in the United States has been women; many of these poor American women are divorced or never-married mothers. This alarming trend has come to be known as the **feminization of poverty**. In 2012, 11.8 percent of all families in the United States lived in poverty, but 30.9 percent of families headed by single mothers did so. Not only are female-headed families much more likely to be poor, but their income deficit relative to being non-poor is much greater than it is in other types of poor families (DeNavas-Walt, Proctor, and Smith 2013:17).

Poor women share many social characteristics with poor men, including low educational attainment, lack of market-relevant job skills, and residence in economically deteriorating areas. However, conflict theorists believe that the higher rates of poverty among women can be traced to two distinct causes: Sex discrimination and sexual harassment on the job place women at a clear disadvantage when seeking upward social mobility.

The burden of supporting a family is especially difficult for single mothers, not only because of low salaries but also because of inadequate child support. The average child-support payment reported in 2016 (for money collected in 2014) for the 46 percent who received the *full* award was a mere $76 per week. This level of support is clearly insufficient for rearing a child in the twenty-first century. In light of

Since the 1970s, "Take Back the Night" protests have occurred on college campuses and elsewhere in dozens of countries to bring attention to date rape and sexual assaults on college campuses. Here we see demonstrators on the campus of the University of Alaska at Fairbanks.

ZUMA Press inc/Alamy Stock Photo

these data, federal and state officials have intensified efforts to track down delinquent spouses and ensure the payment of child support (Grall 2016).

Many feminists feel that the continuing dominance of the political system by men contributes to government indifference to the problems of poor women. As more and more women fall below the official poverty line, policymakers will face growing pressure to combat the feminization of poverty.

Education

15.5   Describe the experience of women in education.

The experience of women in education has been similar to their experience in the labor force: a long history of contribution but in traditionally defined terms. In 1833, Oberlin College became the first institution of higher learning to admit women, two centuries after the first men's college in the United States opened its doors. In 1837, Wellesley became the first women's college. But it would be a mistake to believe that these early experiments brought about equality for women in education: At Oberlin, the women were forbidden to speak in public. Furthermore,

> *Washing the men's clothes, caring for their rooms, serving them at table, listening to their orations, but themselves remaining respectfully silent in public assemblages, the Oberlin "coeds" were being prepared for intelligent motherhood and a properly subservient wifehood. (Flexner 1959:30)*

The early graduates of these schools, despite the emphasis in the curriculum on traditional roles, became the founders of the feminist movement.

Today, research confirms that boys and girls are treated differently in school. In teaching students the values and customs of the larger society, schools in the United States have treated children as if men's education is more important than women's education. Professor of education David Sadker (2016) described this persistence of classroom sexism; his research noted that boys receive more teacher attention than girls, mainly because they call out in class eight times more often. Teachers praise boys more than girls and offer boys more academic assistance. Interestingly, Sadker found that this differential treatment was present in both male and female teachers.

Despite these challenges, in many communities across the nation, girls seem to outdo boys in high school, grabbing a disproportionate share of the leadership positions, from valedictorian to class president to yearbook editor—everything, in short, except captain of the boys' athletic teams. Their numerical advantage seems to be continuing after high school. In the 1980s, girls in the United States became more likely than boys to go to college. Women accounted for more than 56 percent of college students nationwide. And in 2002, for the first time, more women than men in the United States earned doctoral degrees.

Joe Heller / Cagle Cartoons

At all levels of schooling, significant changes also occurred with congressional amendments to the Education Act of 1972 and the Department of Health, Education, and Welfare guidelines developed in 1974 and 1975. Collectively called Title IX provisions, the regulations are designed to eliminate sexist practices from almost all school systems. Schools must make these changes or risk the loss of all federal assistance:

1. Schools must eliminate all sex-segregated classes and extracurricular activities.

2. Schools cannot discriminate by sex in admissions or financial aid and cannot inquire into whether an applicant is married, pregnant, or a parent. Single-sex schools are exempted.

3. Schools must end sexist hiring and promotion practices among faculty members.

4. Although women do not have to be permitted to play on all-men's athletic teams, schools must provide more opportunities for women's sports, both intramural and extramural.

Title IX became one of the more controversial steps ever taken by the federal government to promote and ensure gender equality.

Efforts to bring gender equity to sports have been attacked as excessive. The consequences have not fully been intended. For example, colleges have often cut men's sports rather than build up women's sports. Also, most of the sports with generous college scholarships for women are sports that have not been traditionally attractive to minority women. Yet the number of girls participating in high school athletics has increased from 294,000 in 1972 at the time of the passage of Title IX to over 3.3 million in 2016. Back in 1972, women accounted for just 7 percent of high school athletes; now they account for about 42 percent (National Federation of State High School Associations 2016).

Family Life

15.6 **Explain gender as it relates to the family.**

Our society generally equates work with wages and holds unpaid work in low esteem. Women who do household chores and volunteer work are given little status in U.S. society. Typically, this unrecognized labor is done on top of wage labor in the formal economy. The demands traditionally placed on a mother and homemaker are so extensive that simultaneously pursuing a career is extremely difficult. For women, the family is, according to sociologists Lewis Coser and Rose Laub Coser (1974), a "greedy institution." More recently, other social scientists have also observed the overwhelming burden of the multiple social roles associated with being a mother and working outside the home.

Childcare and Housework

A man can act as a homemaker and caregiver for children, but in the United States, women customarily perform these roles. Studies indicate that men do not even think about their children as much as women do. Sociologist Susan Walzer (1996) was interested in whether there are gender differences in the amount of time that parents spend thinking about the care of their children. Drawing on interviews, Walzer found that mothers are much more involved than fathers in the invisible mental labor associated with taking care of a baby. For example, while involved in work outside the home, mothers are more likely to think about their babies and to feel guilty later if they become so consumed with the demands of their jobs that they fail to think about their babies.

Juggling work and home is an equal opportunity challenge. However, it is mothers who feel the decision most strongly. Among fathers with children under 18, 72 percent prefer to work outside the home, compared to

Tony Freeman / Photo Edit

only 39 percent of similarly situated mothers. There has been little change in these preferences, and differences between moms and dads, over the past 25 years (Saad 2015).

Sociologist Arlie Hochschild has used the term **second shift** to describe the double burden—work outside the home followed by childcare and housework—that many women face and that few men share equitably. As Figure 15.4 shows, this issue has become

Figure 15.4 Chore Wars

Each week, men spend more time in leisure and paid work than women. In households with a child under age six present, men spend about eight hours in childcare a week, and women about 17 hours.

NOTE: Data from American Time Use Survey based on primary or main activities.

SOURCE: Developed by author based on data in Bureau of Labor Statistics 2004: Table 6, 2016b: Tables 1, 8a.

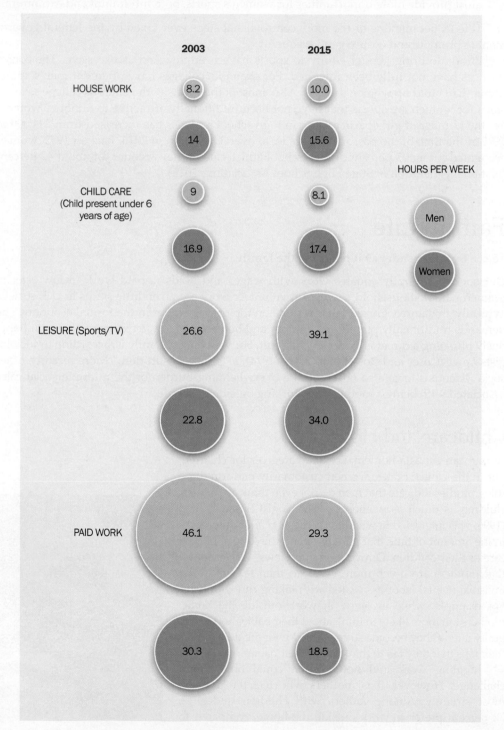

increasingly important as a greater proportion of mothers work outside the home. On the basis of interviews with and observations of 52 couples over an eight-year period, Hochschild reports that the wives (and not their husbands) planned domestic schedules and play dates for children while driving home from the office and then began their second shift (Hochschild 1990, 2016).

Hochschild found that the married couples she studied were fraying at the edges psychologically, and so were their careers and their marriages. The women she spoke with hardly resembled the beautiful young businesswomen pictured in magazine advertisements, dressed in power suits but with frilled blouses, holding briefcases with one arm and happy young children in the other. Instead, many of Hochschild's female subjects talked about being overtired and emotionally drained by the demands of their multiple roles. They were much more intensely torn by the conflicting demands of work outside the home and family life than were their husbands. Hochschild (1990:73) concludes that "if we as a culture come to see the urgent need of meeting the new problems posed by the second shift, and if society and government begin to shape new policies that allow working parents more flexibility, then we will be making some progress toward happier times at home and at work." Many feminists share this view.

There is an economic cost to this second shift. Households do benefit from the free labor of women, but women pay what has been called the **mommy tax**: the lower salaries women receive over their lifetime because they have children. Mothers earn less than men and other women over their lifetime because having children causes them to lose job experience, trade higher wages for the mommy track, and be the victims of discrimination by employers. How high is this mommy tax? Estimates range from 5 to 13 percent of lifetime wages for the first child alone. Having two children lowers earnings 10 to 19 percent. There is no denying that motherhood and the labor market are intertwined. While the mommy tax is not unique to the United States, cross-national comparisons show the mommy tax to be greater in the United States than in countries that have expansive publicly financed childcare systems (Budig and Misra 2010; Coontz 2013).

Family and work continue to present challenges to women and men in the twenty-first century. Sociologist Kathleen Gerson contends in the Speaking Out feature that the workplace is still not adequately meeting the needs of parents.

The Abortion Issue

A particularly controversial subject affecting family life in the United States has been women's desire to have greater control over their bodies, especially their reproduction, through contraceptive devices and the increased availability of abortions. Abortion law reform was one of the demands NOW (the National Organization for Women) made in 1967, and the controversy continues despite many court rulings and the passage of laws at every level of government.

On January 22, 1973, the feminist movement received unexpected assistance from the U.S. Supreme Court in its *Roe v. Wade* decision. By a 7–2 margin, the justices held that the "right to privacy … founded in the Fourteenth Amendment's concept of personal liberty … is broad enough to encompass a woman's decision whether or not to terminate a pregnancy." However, the Court did set certain limits on a woman's right to abortion. During the last three months of pregnancy, the fetus was ruled capable of life outside the womb. Therefore, states were granted the right to prohibit all abortions in the third trimester except those needed to preserve the life, physical health, or mental health of the mother.

The Court's decision in *Roe v. Wade*, though generally applauded by *pro-choice* groups (which support the right to legal abortions), was bitterly condemned by those opposed to abortion. For people who call themselves *pro-life*, abortion is a moral and often a religious issue. In their view, human life begins at the moment of conception rather than when the fetus can stay alive outside the womb. On the basis of this belief, the fetus is a human, not merely a potential life. Termination of this human's life, even before it has left the womb, is viewed as an act of murder. Consequently, anti-abortion activists are alarmed by the more than 1 million legal abortions carried out each year in the United States (Luker 1984).

Speaking Out

What Do Women and Men Want?

Kathleen Gerson

Young workers today grew up in rapidly changing times: They watched women march into the workplace and adults develop a wide range of alternatives to traditional marriage. Now making their own passage to adulthood, these "children of the gender revolution" have inherited a far different world from that of their parents or grandparents. They may enjoy an expanded set of options, but they also face rising uncertainty about whether and how to craft a marriage, rear children, and build a career....

If the realities of time-demanding workplaces and missing supports for caregiving make it difficult for young adults to achieve the sharing, flexible, and more egalitarian relationships most want, then how can we get past this impasse? Clearly, most young women are not likely to answer this question by returning to patterns that fail to speak to either their highest ideals or their greatest fears. To the contrary, they are forming fallback strategies that stress personal autonomy, including the possibility of single parenthood. Men's most common responses to economic pressures and time-demanding jobs stress a different strategy—one that allows for two incomes but preserves men's claim on the most rewarding careers. Women and men are leaning in different directions, and their conflicting responses are fueling a new gender divide. But this schism stems from the intensification of long-simmering work/family dilemmas, not from a decline of laudable values.

Bryan Bedder/Getty Images

Kathleen Gerson

We need to worry less about the family values of a new generation and more about the institutional barriers that make them so difficult to achieve. Most young adults do not wish to turn back the clock, but they do hope to combine the more traditional value of making a lifelong commitment with the more modern value of having a flexible, egalitarian relationship. Rather than trying to change individual values, we need to provide the social supports that will allow young people to overcome work/family conflicts and realize their most cherished aspirations.

Since a mother's earnings and a father's involvement are both integral to the economic and emotional welfare of children (and also desired by most women and men), we can achieve the best family values only by creating flexible workplaces, ensuring equal economic opportunity for women, outlawing discrimination against all parents, and building child-friendly communities with plentiful, affordable, and high-quality childcare. These long-overdue policies will help new generations create the more egalitarian partnerships they desire. Failure to build institutional supports for new social realities will not produce a return to traditional marriage. Instead, following the law of unintended consequences, it will undermine marriage itself.

Source: Gerson 2007: A8, A11.

The early 1990s brought an escalation of violent anti-abortion protests. Finally, a 1994 federal law made it a crime to use force or threats or to obstruct, injure, or interfere with anyone providing or receiving abortions and other reproductive health services. In a 6–3 decision, the Supreme Court upheld the constitutionality of a 36-foot buffer zone that keeps anti-abortion protesters away from a clinic's entrance and parking lot. Abortion remains a disputed issue both in society and in the courts. The law has apparently had some impact, but acts of violence, including murders of clinic workers and physicians, continue.

By 2015, states had passed a vast variety of laws and regulations that limit whether, when, and under what circumstances a woman may obtain an abortion. For example, 19 states require an abortion to be performed in a hospital, rather than a clinic, at some specified point in the pregnancy. Eleven states restrict coverage of abortion in private health insurance plans except when the woman's life is in danger. Seventeen states have mandated counseling before an abortion, and 28 states require a waiting period—usually 24 hours, but in some states 72 hours (Guttmacher Institute 2015).

In terms of social class, the first major restriction on the legal right to terminate a pregnancy affected poor people. In 1976, Congress passed the Hyde Amendment, which banned the use of Medicaid and other federal funds for abortions. The Supreme Court upheld this legislation in 1980. State laws also restrict the use of public funds for abortions. Another obstacle facing the poor is access to abortion providers: In the face of vocal pro-life public sentiment, fewer and fewer hospitals throughout the world are allowing their physicians to perform abortions, except in extreme cases. Only about 13 percent of counties in the United States have even one provider who is able and willing to perform abortions (Blow 2010; Jones et al. 2008).

Political Activity

15.7 Describe women's role in politics.

Women in the United States constitute 53 percent of the voting population and 49 percent of the labor force but only 8 percent of those who hold high government positions. As of the beginning of 2017, Congress included only 104 women (out of 435 members) in the House of Representatives and only 21 women (out of 100 members) in the Senate. Only four states—New Mexico, Oklahoma, Oregon, and Rhode Island—had a female governor at the beginning of 2017. In national elections, women tend to vote less Republican than men do. In the 2008–2016 elections, 54 to 56 percent of women backed either Barack Obama or Hillary Clinton (Tyson and Maniam 2016).

The low number of female officeholders until recently has not resulted from women's inactivity in politics. About the same proportion of eligible women and men vote in presidential elections. The League of Women Voters, founded in 1920, performs a valuable function in educating the electorate of both sexes, publishing newsletters describing candidates' positions and holding debates among candidates. Perhaps women's most visible role in politics until recently has been as unpaid campaign workers—doorbell ringers, telephone callers, newsletter printers, and petition carriers—for male candidates.

Runs for elective office in the 1990s showed women overcoming one of their last barriers to electoral office: attracting campaign funds. Running for office is very expensive, and female candidates have begun to convince backers to invest in their political future. Their success as fundraisers will also contribute to women's acceptance as serious candidates in the future. Overall there has not been a surge in women's political participation, campaign contributions, and volunteering over the past two generations, but rather a slow, steady increase. Elected office is still a man's world, and the time demands of motherhood that sometimes make it difficult to pursue a career also make it difficult to pursue political office (Jardina and Burns 2016).

By considering the intersectionality of different statuses we hold, we recognize how much of our discussion has focused on race and ethnicity coupled with data on poverty, low incomes, and meager wealth. Drawing upon this intersection of identities, we consider in Figure 15.5 what the Spectrum of Intergroup Relations would look for women and men. We recognize that issues of gender domination must be included to fully understand what women of color experience.

Figure 15.5 Spectrum of Intergroup Relations: Women

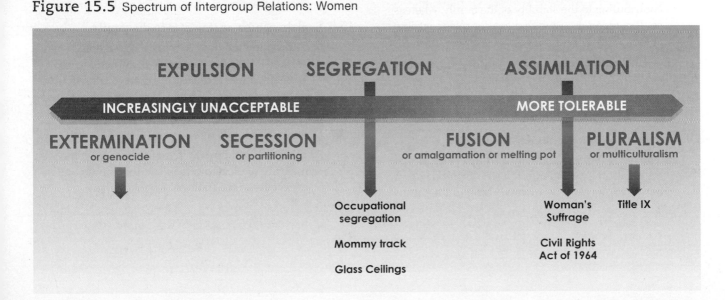

Conclusion

Women and men are expected to perform, or at least to prefer to perform, specific tasks in society. Such expectations cannot be justified by the biological differences between women and men any more than differential treatment based on race can be justified. Psychologists Sandra Bem and Daryl Bem (1970:99) made the following analogy a generation ago that still may apply today:

> *Suppose that a White male college student decided to room with a Black male friend. The typical White student would not blithely assume that his roommate was better suited to handle all domestic chores. Nor should his conscience allow him to do so even in the unlikely event that his roommate said, "No, that's okay. I like doing housework. I'd be happy to do it." We would suspect that the White student would still feel uncomfortable about taking advantage of the fact that his roommate has simply been socialized to be "happy with such an arrangement." But change this hypothetical Black roommate to a female marriage partner, and the student's conscience goes to sleep.*

The feminist movement has awakened women and men to assumptions based on sex and gender. New opportunities for the sexes require the same commitment from individuals and the government as those made to achieve equality between racial and ethnic groups.

Women are systematically disadvantaged in both employment and the family. Gender inequality is a serious problem, just as racial inequality continues to be a significant social challenge. Separate, socially defined roles for men and women are not limited to the United States. Chapter 16 concentrates on the inequality of racial and ethnic groups in societies other than the United States. Just as sexism is not unique to this nation, neither are racism and religious intolerance.

Summary of Learning Objectives

15.1 Understand gender roles.

1. Gender roles are society's expectations of the proper behavior, attitudes, and activities of men and women.

15.2 Contrast sociological perspectives on gender.

2. Functionalists see gender-role differences as contributing to the stability of the family, whereas conflict theorists argue that gender roles contribute to inequality between men and women.

15.3 Summarize the history of the feminist movement.

3. The feminist movement has deep roots in the nineteenth century, and the movement continues to work for parity between men and women.

15.4 Discuss women's economic situation.

4. The labor force is characterized by occupational segregation by gender and a significant pay gap between men and women working in the same occupations. A pattern of increasing poverty among single women has led to the feminization of poverty.

15.5 Describe the experience of women in education.

5. Women have encountered great success in formal schooling. Title IX is helping to eliminate inequities, especially in school athletic programs.

15.6 Explain gender as it relates to the family.

6. Although men have increasingly accepted responsibilities for housework and childcare, women continue to assume more responsibility in the family, leading to a phenomenon referred to as the *second shift.*

15.7 Describe women's role in politics.

7. Despite highly public female politicians, the vast majority of elected officials in the United States, especially at the national level, are men.

Key Terms

blaming the victim, *page 323*

daughter effect, *page 327*

feminine mystique, *page 327*

feminism, *page 328*

feminization of poverty, *page 335*

gender identity, *page 324*

gender roles, *page 324*

glass ceiling, *page 334*

glass escalator, *page 326*

intersectionality, *page 328*

mommy tax, *page 339*

mommy track, *page 334*

occupational segregation, *page 330*

pay equity, *page 334*

second shift, *page 338*

sexism, *page 323*

sexual harassment, *page 335*

sexual identity, *page 324*

suffragists, *page 326*

Review Questions

1. Explain how gender is socially constructed.
2. Briefly summarize the two key sociological approaches (the functionalist perspective and the conflict perspective) to studying women as a minority.
3. How has the focus of the feminist movement changed from the suffragist movement to the present?
4. How do the patterns of women in the workplace differ from those of men?
5. Describe the strides that women have made in formal education over the past several decades.
6. How has the changing role of women in the United States affected the family?

Critical Thinking

1. Women have many characteristics similar to those of minority groups, but what are some differences? For example, women are not segregated from men residentially.
2. How is women's subordinate position different from that of oppressed racial and ethnic groups? How is it similar?
3. In the early 1990s, the phrase *angry white men* was used by some men who viewed themselves as victims of reverse discrimination. In what respect may men now see themselves as victims of reverse discrimination? Do you think these views are justified?
4. How are men and women's roles defined differently when it comes to such concepts as the mommy track, the second shift, and the daughter effect?

Chapter 16
Beyond the United States: The Comparative Perspective

David Brauchli/Sygma/Getty Images

⌄ Learning Objectives

16.1 Summarize the diversity in Mexico.

16.2 Understand Canada's multiculturalism.

16.3 Analyze the degree to which Brazil is a racial paradise.

16.4 Explain the historical and contemporary tensions between Israel and Palestine.

16.5 Explain inequality in the Republic of South Africa.

Confrontations between racial and ethnic groups escalated in frequency and intensity in the twentieth century, and these conflicts have continued into the twenty-first century. In surveying these conflicts, we see two themes emerge: world systems theory and ethnonational conflict. **World systems theory** considers the global economic system as divided between the nations that control wealth and those that provide natural resources and labor. Historically, nations reflect this competition between the "haves" and "have-nots." Whether the laborers are poor Catholics in Ireland or Black Africans, their contribution to the prosperity of the dominant group created the social inequality that continues to exist today (Wallerstein 1974, 2004).

Ethnonational conflict refers to conflicts among ethnic, racial, religious, and linguistic groups within nations. In some areas of the world, ethnonational conflicts are more significant than tension between nations as the source of refugees and even death. Countries in all parts of the world, including the most populous nations, have significant diversity within their borders. Ethnonational conflicts remind us that the processes operating in the United States to deny rights and opportunities to racial and ethnic groups are also at work throughout the world (Connor 1994; Olzak 1998).

The sociological perspective on relations between dominant and subordinate groups treats race and ethnicity as social categories. As social concepts, they can be understood only in the context of the shared meanings attached to them by societies and their members. Although relationships between dominant and subordinate groups vary greatly, there are similarities across societies. Racial and ethnic hostilities arise out of economic needs and demands. These needs and demands may not always be realistic; that is, a group may seek out enemies where none exist or where victory will yield no rewards. Racial and ethnic conflicts are both the results and the precipitators of change in the economic and political sectors (Barclay, Kumar, and Simms 1976; Coser 1956).

Relations between dominant and subordinate groups differ from society to society, as this chapter shows. Intergroup relations in Mexico, Canada, Brazil, Israel, and South Africa are striking in their similarities and contrasts.

Mexico: Diversity South of the Border

16.1 **Summarize the diversity in Mexico.**

Usually in the discussions of racial and ethnic relations, Mexico is considered only as a source of immigrants to the United States. In questions of economic development, Mexico again typically enters the discussion only as it affects the U.S. economy. However, Mexico, a nation of more than 128 million people (in the Western Hemisphere, only Brazil and the United States are more populous), is an exceedingly complex nation (Table 16.1). It is therefore appropriate that we understand Mexico and its issues of inequality better. This understanding will also shed light on the relationship of the Mexican people to the United States.

In the 1520s, Spain overthrew the Aztec Indian tribe that ruled Mexico. Mexico remained a Spanish colony until the 1820s. In 1836, Texas declared its independence from Mexico, and by 1846, Mexico was at war with the United States. As we explained in Chapter 9, the Mexican–American War forced Mexico to surrender more than half of its territory, which now makes up a good deal of the American Southwest. In the 1860s, France sought to turn Mexico into an empire under Prince Maximilian I of Austria but ultimately withdrew after bitter resistance led by a Mexican Indian, Benito Juárez, who later served as the nation's president.

The Mexican Indian People and the Color Gradient

In contemporary Mexico, a major need has been to reassess the relations between the indigenous peoples—the Mexican Indians, many descended from the Mayas—and the government of Mexico. In 1900, the majority of the Mexican population still spoke Indian languages and lived in closed, semi-isolated villages or tribal communities according to ancestral customs. Many of these people were not a part of the growing industrialization in Mexico and were not truly represented in the national legislature. Perhaps the major change for them in the twentieth century was that many intermarried with the descendants of the Europeans, forming a **mestizo** class of people of mixed ancestry. The term *mestizo* is used throughout the Americas to refer to people of mixed European (usually Spanish) and local indigenous ancestry. Mestizos have become increasingly identified with Mexico's growing middle class. They have developed their own distinct culture and, as the descendants of the European settlers are reduced in number and influence, have become the true bearers of the national Mexican sentiment.

Table 16.1 Five-Nation Comparison

Country	Population (in millions)	Gross National Income (GNI) per capita ($) (U.S. = $56,430)	Groups Represented	Current Nation's Formation
Mexico	128.6	$17,150	Mexican Indians, 13%	1823: Independence from Spain
Canada	36.2	$43,970	French speaking, 13% Aboriginal peoples, 4% "Visible" minorities, 16%	1867: Unified as a colony of England 1948: Independence from England
Brazil	206.1	$15,020	White, 48% Pardo (brown, moreno, mulatto), 39% Afro-Brazilians, 8% Asian and indigenous Indians, 1%	1889: Independence from Portugal
Israel	8.1	$34,920	Jews, 76% Arabs, 23%	1948: Independence from British mandate under United Nations
Palestinian Territories	4.0	$5,283 (est.)	Palestinians, 99% Others, 1% (Excluding Jewish settlements)	1999: Israel cedes authority under Oslo Accords
South Africa	55.7	12,830	Black Africans, 79% Whites, 9% Coloureds, 9% Asians, 3%	1948: Independence from England

NOTE: All data for 2010 or most recently available.
SOURCES: Author estimates, based on Bourcier 2012; Canak and Swanson 1998; The Economist 2017b; Kaneda and Bietsch 2016; Minority Rights Group 2017; Statistics Canada 2012; and sources in Table 16.2.

Meanwhile, however, these social changes have left the Mexican Indian people even further behind the rest of the population economically and in terms of educational attainment. Indian cultures have been stereotyped as backward and resistant to progress and modern ways of living. Indeed, the existence of the many Indian cultures was seen in much of the twentieth century as an impediment to the development of a national culture in Mexico (Creighton, Post, and Park 2016).

As noted in Chapter 9, a **color gradient** is the placement of people on a continuum from light to dark skin color rather than in distinct racial groupings by skin color. The color gradient is another example of the social construction of race, in which social class is linked to the social reality (or at least the appearance) of racial purity. In Mexico, an interesting result of the color gradient and a mestizo class is the belief that racism cannot exist in a racially mixed society. This denial of racism does not reflect the social exclusion, discrimination, and prejudice that persist today (Navarrete 2016; Sue 2013).

At the top of this gradient or hierarchy are the *criollos*, the 10 percent of the population who are typically White, well-educated members of the business and intellectual elites with familial roots in Spain. In the middle is the large impoverished mestizo majority, most of whom have brown skin and a mixed racial lineage as a result of intermarriage. At the bottom of the color gradient are the destitute Mexican Indians and a small number of Blacks, some of them the descendants of 200,000 African slaves brought to Mexico. The relatively small Black Mexican community received national attention in 2005 and 2006 following a series of racist events that received media attention. Ironically, although this color gradient is an important part of day-to-day life in Mexico—enough so that some Mexicans use hair dyes, skin lighteners, and blue or green contact lenses to appear more European—nearly all Mexicans are considered part Mexican Indian because of centuries of intermarriage. The view that nearly all Mexicans are part Indian leads to the continuing denial of racism despite the presence of colorism. Recall that **colorism** refers to the ranking or judging of individuals based on skin tone. In Mexico, these judgments lead to negative feelings toward Mexican Indians and Blacks or Afro-Mexicans (Banton 2012; Flores and Telles 2010).

On January 1, 1994, rebels from an armed insurgent group called the Zapatista National Liberation Army seized four towns in the state of Chiapas in southern Mexico. Two thousand lightly armed Mayan Indians and peasants backed the rebels—who had named their organization after Emiliano Zapata, a farmer and leader of the 1910 revolution against a corrupt dictatorship. Zapatista leaders declared that they had turned to armed insurrection to protest economic injustices and discrimination against the region's Indian population. The Mexican government mobilized the army to crush the revolt but was forced to retreat as news organizations broadcast pictures of the confrontation around the world. A ceasefire was declared after only 12 days of fighting, but 196 people had already died. Negotiations between the Mexican government and the Zapatista National Liberation Army collapsed, and there has been sporadic violence ever since.

In response to the crisis, the Mexican legislature enacted the Law on Indian Rights and Culture, which went into effect in 2001. The act allows 62 recognized Indian groups to apply their own customs in resolving conflicts and electing leaders. Unfortunately, state legislatures must give final approval to these arrangements, a requirement that severely limits the rights of large Indian groups whose territories span several states. Tired of waiting for state approval, many indigenous communities in Chiapas have declared self-rule without obtaining official recognition.

Although many factors contributed to the Zapatista revolt, the subordinate status of Mexico's Indian citizens, who account for an estimated 13 percent of the nation's population, was surely important. More than 90 percent of the indigenous population lives in houses without access to sewers, compared with 21 percent of the population as a whole. And whereas just 10 percent of Mexican adults are illiterate, the proportion for Mexican Indians is 44 percent (Minority Rights Group 2017; Stahler-Sholk 2008).

The poverty of Mexican Indians is well documented and in some instances has led to violent protests for social change.

Eduardo Verdugo/AP Images

The Status of Women

Often in the United States we consider our own problems to be so significant that we fail to recognize that many of these social issues exist elsewhere. Gender stratification is an example of an issue we share with almost all other countries, and Mexico is no exception. In 1975, Mexico City was the site of the first United Nations conference on the status of women. Much of the focus was on the situation of women in developing countries; in that regard, Mexico remains typical.

Women in Mexico did not receive the right to vote until 1953. They have made significant progress in that short period in being elected into office, but they have a long way to go. As of 2017, women account for 43 percent of Mexico's national assembly—the eighth highest out of 189 countries—but lack the ultimate decision-making authority in the government and the economic leadership (Inter-Parliamentary Union 2017).

Even when Mexican women work outside the home, they are often denied recognition as active and productive household members, and men are typically viewed as heads of the household in every respect. As one consequence, women find it difficult to obtain credit and technical assistance in many parts of Mexico and to inherit land in rural areas.

Men are preferred over women in the more skilled jobs, and women lose out entirely as factories, even in developing nations such as Mexico, require more complex skills. In 2014, women made up only 38 percent of the paid civilian labor force, compared with about 48 percent in Canada and 47 percent in the United States (Organisation for Economic Co-operation and Development 2016).

In recent decades, Mexican women have begun to address an array of economic, political, and health issues. Often this organizing occurs at the grassroots level and outside traditional government forums. Because women continue to serve as household managers for their families, even when they work outside the home, they have been aware of the consequences of the inadequate public services in low-income urban neighborhoods. As far back as 1973, women in Monterrey, the nation's sixth-largest city, began protesting the continuing disruptions of the city's water supply. At first, individual women made complaints to city officials and the water authority, but subsequently, groups of female activists emerged. They sent delegations to confront politicians, organized protest rallies, and blocked traffic as a means of getting media attention. As a result of their efforts, there have been improvements in Monterrey's water service, although the issue of reliable and safe water remains a concern in Mexico and many developing countries (Bennett 1995; Bennett and Rico 2005).

Mexico is beginning to recognize that the issue of social inequality extends beyond poverty. A national survey found that eight out of ten Mexicans felt it was as important to eliminate discrimination as to eliminate poverty, yet 40 percent said that they did not want to live next to an Indian community, and one-third considered it "normal" for women not to earn as much as men (Thompson 2005).

Canada: Multiculturalism Up North

16.2   Understand Canada's multiculturalism.

Multiculturalism is a fairly recent term in the United States; it is used to refer to diversity. In Canada, it has been adopted as a state policy for more than two decades. Still, many people in the United States see Canada as a homogeneous nation with a smattering of Arctic-type people—merely a cross between the northern mainland United States and Alaska. This is not the social reality.

One of the continuing discussions among Canadians is the need for a cohesive national identity or a sense of common peoplehood. The immense size of the country, much of which is sparsely populated, along with the diversity of its people, have complicated this need.

The First Nations

Like the United States, Canada has had an adversarial relationship with its native peoples. However, the Canadian experience has not been as violent as the U.S. experience. During all three stages of Canadian history—French colonialism, British colonialism, and Canadian nationhood—there was relatively little warfare between Canadian Whites and Canadian Native Americans, at least as compared to the Native American experience in the United States. Nonetheless, similarities remain. Prodded by settlers, colonial governments in Canada (and later Canadian governments) drove the Native Americans from their lands. By the 1830s, Indian reserves were being established that were similar to the reservations in the United States. Tribal members were encouraged to renounce their status and become Canadian citizens. Assimilation was the explicit policy until recently (Champagne 1994; Waldman 1985).

The 1.2 million native peoples of Canada are collectively referred to by the government as the *Aboriginal Peoples* and represent about 4 percent of the population. This population is classified into the following groups:

Like the United States, Brazil, and Mexico, Canada has only recently begun to make amends for past injustices to its First Nations people. Pictured is a settlement of the Nunavut Territory, which has been given special autonomy from the central government of Ottawa.

Ton Koene/Alamy Stock Photo

First Nations or *Status Indians*—The more than 600 tribes or bands officially recognized by the government, numbering about 680,000 in 2006, of whom 40 percent live on Indian reserves (or reservations).

Inuit—The 50,480 people living in the northern part of the country, who in the past were called Eskimos.

Métis (pronounced "may-TEE")—Canadians of mixed Aboriginal ancestry, officially numbering 390,000, many of whom still speak French Métis, a mixed language combining Aboriginal and European words.

Another 35,000 Canadians of mixed native ancestry are counted by the government as First Nations people, but there are perhaps another 600,000 non-status Indians who self-identify as having some Aboriginal ancestry but who are not so considered by the Canadian government (Huteson 2008; Statistics Canada 2012).

The Métis and non-status Indians have historically enjoyed no separate legal recognition, but efforts continue to secure them special rights under the law, such as designated health, education, and welfare programs. The general public does not understand these legal distinctions, so if a Métis or non-status Indian "looks like an Indian," she or he is subjected to the same treatment, discriminatory or otherwise (Indian and Northern Affairs Canada and Canadian Polar Commission 2000).

The Canadian federal constitution of 1982 included a charter of rights that "recognized and affirmed... the existing aboriginal and treaty rights" of the Canadian Native American, Inuit, and Métis peoples. This recognition received the most visibility through the efforts of the Mohawk, one of the tribes of status Indians. At issue were land rights involving some property areas in Quebec that had spiritual significance for the Mohawk. Their protests and militant confrontations reawakened the Canadian people to the concerns of diverse native peoples (Warry 2007).

Some of the contemporary issues facing the First Nations of Canada are very similar to those faced by Native Americans in the United States. Contemporary Canadians are shocked to learn of past mistreatment leading to belated remedies. Exposure of past sexual and physical abuse of thousands of the 150,000 children placed in boarding schools, which existed from 1883 through 1998, led to compensation to former students and an official apology by the government in 2008. Earlier in 2006, as part of a legal settlement, the government set aside $5 billion for payments to surviving students and to document their experiences (The Economist 2015c; Truth and Reconciliation Commission of Canada 2015).

As in the United States, Canadian institutions are reaching out to native people who for generations had been ignored. For example, only 9.8 percent of First Nation people have college degrees, compared to 26.5 percent of the rest of the population. The University of Saskatchewan, located in an area with a large First Nation population, is actively recruiting students and faculty as well as revising its curriculum to be more attractive to the First Nations in a process it refers to as "indigenizing." Detractors criticize such efforts, but many other Canadian colleges are also trying to overcome their colonial past (Porter 2017b).

In another parallel with native peoples of the United States, the First Nations people are demanding control over natural resources. Tribal people also feel that **environmental justice** must be addressed because of the disproportionate pollution they experience. Recall that environmental justice refers to efforts to ensure that hazardous substances are controlled so that all communities receive protection regardless of race or socioeconomic circumstances. First Nations people have protested several oil and natural gas pipelines that have run through their lands, just as some tribal groups have assumed activist positions in the United States (MacDonald and Viera 2015).

The social and economic fate of contemporary Aboriginal peoples reflects many challenges. Only 40 percent graduate from high school, compared to more than 70 percent for the country as a whole. The native peoples of Canada have unemployment rates twice as high as the non-native peoples and an average income one-third lower (Farley 2008; Guly and Farley 2008; Statistics Canada 2012; Warry 2007).

In a positive step, in 1999, Canada created a new territory in response to a native land claim in which the resident Inuit (formerly called *Eskimos*) dominated. Nunavut ("NOO-nah-voot"), meaning "our land," recognizes the territorial rights of the Inuit. Admirable as this event is, observers noted it was easier to grant such economic rights and autonomy to 29,000 people in the isolated expanse of northern Canada than to the Aboriginal peoples of the more populated southern provinces of Canada (Krauss 2006).

The Québécois

Assimilation and domination have been the plight of most minority groups. The French-speaking people of the province of Quebec—the **Québécois**, as they are known—represent a contrasting case. Since the mid-1960s, they have reasserted their identity and captured the attention of the entire nation.

Quebec accounts for about one-fourth of the nation's population and wealth. Reflecting its early settlement by the French, fully 95 percent of the province's population claims to speak French, compared with only 13 percent in the nation as a whole (Statistics Canada 2012).

The Québécois have sought to put French Canadian culture on an equal footing with English Canadian culture in the country as a whole and to dominate in the province. At the very least, this effort has been seen as an irritant outside Quebec and has been viewed with great concern by the English-speaking minority in Quebec.

In the 1960s, the Québécois expressed the feeling that bilingual status was not enough. Even to have French recognized as one of two official languages in a nation dominated by the English-speaking population gave the Québécois second-class status in their view. With some leaders threatening to break completely with Canada and make Quebec an independent nation, Canada made French the official language of the province and the only acceptable language for commercial signs and public transactions. New residents are now required to send their children to French schools. The English-speaking residents felt as if they had been made aliens, even though many of them had roots extending back to the 1700s (Salée 1994).

In 1995, the people of Quebec voted on a referendum: whether they wanted to separate from Canada and form a new nation. The referendum was extremely controversial, given the confusion over how separation would be accomplished and its economic significance. In a very close vote, 50.5 percent of the voters indicated a preference to remain united with Canada. Separatists vowed to keep working for secession and called for another referendum in the future, although surveys show the support for independence has dropped, and the number of separatist candidates elected has declined. Many French-speaking residents now seem to accept the steps that have been taken, but a minority still seeks full control of financial and political policies (Mason 2007; Viera 2014).

Canada is characterized by the presence of two linguistic communities: the Anglophone and the Francophone, with the latter occurring largely in Quebec. Outside of Quebec, Canadians are opposed to separatism; within Quebec, they are divided. Language and cultural issues, therefore, both unify and divide this nation of 36.2 million people.

Immigration and Race

Immigration has also been a significant social force contributing to Canadian multiculturalism. Toronto and Vancouver both have a higher proportion of foreign-born residents than either Los Angeles or New York City. In 2017, Canada admitted about 300,000 immigrants. Canada, proportionately to its population, receives consistently the most immigrants of any nation—three times the rate of the United States. About 20 percent of its population is foreign-born, with an increasing proportion of Asian background rather than European background (Porter 2017a).

Canada also speaks of its **visible minorities**—persons other than Aboriginal or First Nation people whose racial background is non-White. Visible minorities include much of the immigrant population as well as the Black population. In the 2006 census, the visible minority population accounted for 16 percent, compared to less than 5 percent 25 years earlier. The largest visible minority are the Chinese, followed by South Asians collectively, Black Canadians, and Filipinos (Bélanger and Malenfant 2005; Statistics Canada 2012).

People in the United States tend to view Canada's race relations favorably. In part, this view reflects Canada's role as the "promised land" for slaves escaping the U.S. South and crossing the free North to Canada, where they were unlikely to be recaptured. Canadians themselves also foster the view of Canada as a land of positive intergroup relations.

Canadians have long been willing to compare their best social institutions to the worst examples of racism in the United States and to pride themselves on being more virtuous and high-minded. As the United States begins to rethink its refugee policy, Canada has become viewed increasingly as a popular destination by those seeking refuge (Porter, Levin, and Austen 2017).

The social reality, past and present, is quite different. Africans came in 1689 as involuntary immigrants to be enslaved by French colonists. Slavery officially continued until 1833.

It never flourished because the Canadian economy did not need a large labor force, so most slaves worked as domestic servants. Blacks from the United States did flee to Canada before slavery ended, but some fugitive slaves returned after Abraham Lincoln issued the Emancipation Proclamation in 1863. The early Black arrivals in Canada were greeted in a variety of ways. Often they were warmly received as fugitives from slavery, but as their numbers grew in some areas, Canadians became concerned that they would overwhelm the White population (Winks 1971).

The contemporary Black Canadian population, about 2.5 percent of the nation's population, consists of indigenous Afro-Canadians with several generations of roots in Canada, West Indian immigrants and their descendants, and a number of post–World War II immigrants from the United States. Slightly more than half of Canada's Blacks are foreign-born.

Racial issues are barely below the surface. A 2011 study of Toronto's online rental housing market was conducted by sending 5,620 rental inquiries using names that were either typically White or Black or Asian or Muslim or Jewish. Landlords were ten times less willing to rent to the visible minorities as compared to Whites. This was true throughout the city and regardless of the relative affluence of the neighborhood where the apartment was available. Interestingly, the same year that the study was published, the Ontario Human Rights Commission launched programs called "In the Zone" and "Room for Everyone" attempting to end discrimination in housing; the Commission encouraged looking to the United States for best practices to accomplish this goal.

As in the United States, police–Black civilian relations are tense. Concerns are voiced about disproportionate "carding" or street stops of Black Canadians. In Canada, #BlackLivesMatter emerged in 2014 in support of Black Americans but has not turned its attention to perceived injustices in Canada (Hogan and Berry 2011; Levin 2016; Ontario Human Rights Commission 2013; Statistics Canada 2012).

In 1541, Frenchman Jacques Cartier established the first European settlement along the St. Lawrence River, but within a year, he withdrew because of confrontations with the Iroquois. Almost 500 years later, the descendants of the Europeans and Aboriginal peoples are still trying to resolve Canada's identity as issues of ethnicity, race, and language shape the dialogue.

Brazil: Not a Racial Paradise

16.3 Analyze the degree to which Brazil is a racial paradise.

A variety of economic and cultural issues face the indigenous people of Brazil today. To someone who is knowledgeable about race and ethnic relations in the United States, Brazil's patterns of race and ethnic relations may seem familiar. As in the early days of the United States, Europeans overwhelmed the native people as Europe colonized Brazil. Like the United States, Brazil imported Black Africans as slaves to meet the demand for laborers. Even today, Brazil is second only to the United States in the number of people of African descent, excluding nations on the African continent. Another similarity is the treatment of indigenous people. Although the focus here is on Black people and White people in Brazil, another continuing concern is the treatment of Brazil's native peoples as this developing nation continues to industrialize.

The current nature of Brazilian race relations is influenced by the legacy of slavery, as is true of Black–White relations in the United States. However, scholars agree that slavery was not the same in Brazil as it was in the United States, but they disagree on how different it was and how significant these differences were (Elkins 1959; Tannenbaum 1946).

Brazil depended much more than the United States did on the slave trade. Estimates place the total number of slaves imported to Brazil at 4 million—eight times the number brought to the United States. At the height of slavery, however, both nations had approximately the same slave population: 4 million to 4.5 million. Brazil's reliance on African-born slaves meant that typical Brazilian slaves had closer ties to Africa than did their U.S. counterparts. The most significant difference between slavery in the southern United States and in Brazil was the amount of *manumission*—the freeing of slaves. For every 1,000 slaves, 100 were freed annually in Brazil, compared to four per year in the U.S. South.

It would be hasty to assume, however, that Brazilian slave masters were more benevolent. Quite the contrary. Brazil's slave economy was poorer than that of the U.S. South, and so slave owners in Brazil freed slaves into poverty whenever the slaves became crippled, sick, or old. But this custom does not completely explain the presence of the many freed slaves in Brazil. Unlike the situation in the United States, the majority of Brazil's population was composed of Africans and their descendants throughout the nineteenth century. Africans were needed as craft workers, shopkeepers, and boatmen, not just as agricultural workers. Freed slaves filled these needs.

The "Racial Democracy" Illusion

For some time in the twentieth century, Brazil was seen as a "racial democracy" and even a "racial paradise." Indeed, historically the term *race* is rare in Brazil; the term *côr* or *color* is far more common. Historian Carl Degler (1971) identified the **mulatto escape hatch** as the key to the differences in Brazilian and American race relations. In Brazil, the *pardo* (the mixed-race or mulatto) or *moreno* (brown) is recognized as a group separate from either *brancos* (Whites) or *prêtos* (Blacks), whereas in the United States, mulattos are classed with Blacks. Yet this escape hatch is an illusion because mulattos fare only marginally better economically than Black Brazilians or *Afro Brazilians* or *Afro-descendant*, the term increasingly used by college-educated persons and activists in Brazil to refer to the dark end of the Brazilian color gradient. In addition, mulattos do not escape through mobility into the income and status enjoyed by White Brazilians. Labor market analyses demonstrate that Blacks with the highest levels of education and occupation experience the most discrimination in terms of jobs, mobility, and income. In addition, they face a *glass ceiling* that limits their upward mobility (Monk 2016).

Today, the use of dozens of terms to describe oneself along the color gradient (as mentioned earlier with respect to Mexico) is obvious in Brazil because, unlike in the United States, people of mixed ancestry are viewed as an identifiable social group. The 2010 census in Brazil classified 48 percent of the population as White, 39 percent as pardo (mestizo, brown, or mulatto), 8 percent as Afro-Brazilian, and 1 percent as Asian and indigenous Brazilian Indian (see Table 16.1) (Bourcier 2012).

In Brazil, today as in the past, colorism persists. Light skin color enhances status, but the impact is often exaggerated. When Degler advanced the idea of the mulatto escape hatch, he implied that it was a means to success. The most recent income data, controlling for gender, education, and age, indicate that people of mixed ancestry earn 12 percent more than Blacks. Yet Whites earn another 26 percent more than the pardo. Clearly, the major distinction is between Whites and all "people of color" rather than between people of mixed ancestry and Afro-Brazilians (IBGE 2006; Telles 1992, 2004).

The Brazilian Dilemma

Gradually it has come to be recognized that racial prejudice and discrimination do exist in Brazil. A 2000 survey in Rio de Janeiro found that 93 percent of those surveyed believe that racism exists in Brazil, and 74 percent said there was a lot of bias. Yet 87 percent of the respondents said they themselves were not racist (Bailey 2004, 2009b).

During the twentieth century, Brazil changed from a nation that prided itself on its freedom from racial intolerance to a country using its legal system to combat discrimination against people of color. One of the first measures was in 1951 when the Afonso Arinos law was unanimously adopted, prohibiting racial discrimination in public places. Opinion is divided over the effectiveness of the law, which has been of no use in overturning subtle forms of discrimination. Even from

Increasingly, the Brazilian people are recognizing the significant social inequality evident along color lines.

John Maier, Jr./The Image Works

the start, certain civilian careers, such as the diplomatic and military officer ranks, were virtually closed to Blacks. Curiously, the push for the law came from the United States, after a Black American dancer, Katherine Dunham, was denied a room at a São Paulo luxury hotel.

Today, income disparity is significant in Brazil. As Figure 16.1 shows, people of color are disproportionately clustered in the lowest income levels of Brazilian society. Recent analysis indicates that the gap is steadily increasing. Although they are not as disadvantaged as Blacks in South Africa (whom we discuss later in this chapter), the degree of inequality between Whites and people of color is much greater in Brazil than in the United States. The massive government expenditures in support of the 2014 World Cup and the 2016 Olympics only

Figure 16.1 Income Distribution by Race

NOTE: Monthly income for Brazil and the United States in 1996; for South Africa, 1998.

SOURCE: Government agencies as reported in Telles 2004: 108.

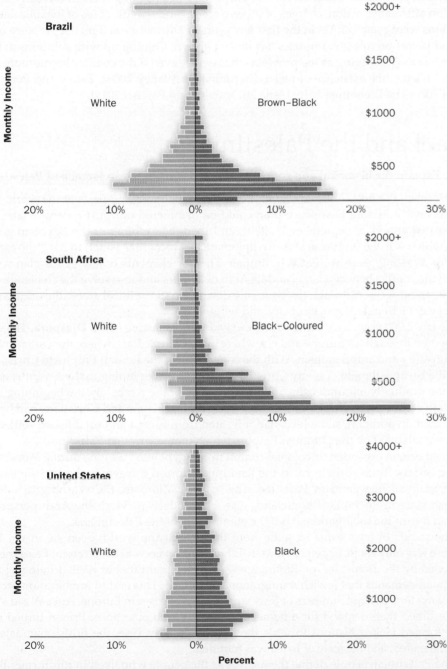

served to underscore the persistence of inequality as they diverted expenditures that might have gone to the poor. Those expenditures also created large public works projects displacing the very poorest Brazilians and offered inadequate provision for new housing (Gradín 2014).

Activism in the United States is often based on the fact societal wealth is so unequal. However, the concentration of income and assets in the hands of a few is much greater in Brazil than it is in the United States. For Afro-Brazilians, even professional status can increase one's social standing only so much. An individual's blackness does not suddenly become invisible simply because he or she has acquired some social standing. The fame achieved by the Black Brazilian soccer player Pelé is a token exception and does not mean that Blacks have it easy or even have a readily available "escape hatch" through professional sports.

A dramatic step was taken to explicitly acknowledge the role of race when Brazil introduced affirmative action measures. Quotas began in 2007, allowing students to indicate their race with their college-entrance applications. Reflecting the color gradient and the lack of clear-cut racial categories, colleges and universities created committees to examine photographs of prospective students for the purpose of determining race. In the early days of Brazilian affirmative action, charges of reverse racism and specific cases of inexplicable classifications were common. Yet in the first few years of affirmative action, the presence of pardos and prêtos on college campuses has indeed grown. Coming up with solutions in Brazil will be just as challenging as the problems themselves even if the country seems more likely to acknowledge the existence of racial discrimination (Bailey 2009a; Bailey and Péria 2010; Daniel 2006; The Economist 2016; Llana 2013; Telles and Paschel 2014).

Israel and the Palestinians

16.4 **Explain the historical and contemporary tensions between Israel and Palestine.**

In 1991, when the first Gulf War ended, hopes were high in many parts of the world that a comprehensive Middle East peace plan could be hammered out. Just a decade later, after the terrorist attacks of September 11, 2001, and then the toppling of the Egyptian government (which was the first Arab state to diplomatically recognize Israel) in 2011, the expectations for a lasting peace were much dimmer. The key elements of any peace plan were to resolve the conflict between Israel and its Arab neighbors and to resolve the challenge of the Palestinian refugees. Although the issues are debated in the political arena, the origins of the conflict can be found in race, ethnicity, and religion.

Nearly 2,000 years ago, the Jews were exiled from Palestine in the **Diaspora**. The exiled Jews settled throughout Europe and elsewhere in the Middle East, where they often encountered hostility and anti-Semitism. With the conversion of the Roman Empire to Christianity, Palestine became the site of many Christian pilgrimages. Beginning in the seventh century, Palestine gradually fell under the Muslim influence of the Arabs. By the beginning of the twentieth century, religious-oriented tourism by both Muslims and Christians had become established. In addition, some Jews had migrated from Russia and established settlements that were tolerated by the Ottoman Empire, which then controlled Palestine.

Great Britain expanded its colonial control from Egypt into Palestine during World War I, driving out the Turks. Britain ruled the land but endorsed the eventual establishment of a Jewish national homeland in Palestine. The spirit of **Zionism**, the yearning to establish a Jewish state in the biblical homeland, was well underway. From the Arab perspective, Zionism meant the subjugation, if not the elimination, of the Palestinians.

Thousands of Jews came to settle from throughout the world; even so, in the 1920s, Palestine was only about 15 percent Jewish. Ethnic tension grew as the Arabs of Palestine were threatened by the Zionist fervor. Rioting grew to such a point that in 1939, Britain yielded to Palestinian demands that Jewish immigration be stopped. This end to immigration occurred at the same time as large numbers of Jews were fleeing Nazism in Europe. After World War II, Jews resumed their demand for a homeland, despite Arab objections. Britain turned to the newly formed United Nations to settle the dispute. In May 1948, the British mandate over Palestine ended, and the state of Israel was founded.

The Palestinian people define themselves as the people who lived in this former British mandate, along with their descendants on their fathers' side. They are viewed as an ethnic group within the larger group of Arabs. They generally speak Arabic, and most of them

(97 percent) are Muslim (mostly Sunni). With a rapid rate of natural increase, the Palestinians have grown in number from 1.4 million at the end of World War II to about 7 million worldwide, including 700,000 in Israel, 2.6 million in the West Bank, and 1.7 million in the Gaza Strip (Central Intelligence Agency 2011; Third World Institute 2007; The Economist 2017b).

Arab–Israeli Conflicts

No sooner had Israel been created than the Arab nations—particularly Egypt, Jordan, Iraq, Syria, and Lebanon—announced their intention to restore control to the Palestinian Arabs, by force if necessary. As hostilities broke out, the Israeli military stepped in to preserve the borders, which no Arab nation agreed to recognize. Some 60 percent of the 1.4 million Arabs fled or were expelled from Israeli territory, becoming refugees in neighboring countries. An uneasy peace followed as Israel attempted to encourage new Jewish immigration. Israel also extended the same services that were available to the Jews, such as education and healthcare, to the non-Jewish Israelis. The new Jewish population continued to grow under the country's Law of Return, which gave every Jew in the world the right to settle permanently as a citizen. The question of Jerusalem remained unsettled, and the city was divided into two separate sections—Israeli Jewish and Jordanian Arab—a division that both sides refused to regard as permanent.

In 1967, Egypt, followed by Syria, responded to Israel's military actions to take surrounding territory in what came to be called the Six-Day War. In the course of defeating the Arab states' military, Israel occupied the Gaza Strip and the West Bank (Figure 16.2). The defeat was all the more bitter for the Arabs as Israeli-held territory expanded.

Figure 16.2 Israeli and Palestinian Lands

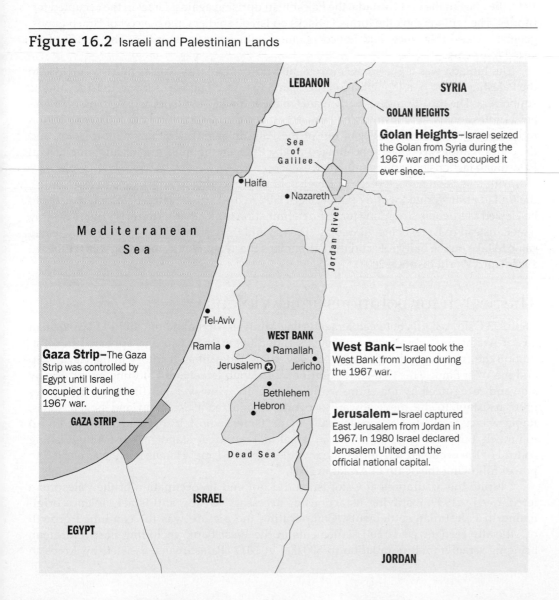

Although our primary attention here is on the Palestinians and the Jews, another significant ethnic issue is present in Israel. Among Israel's Jews, about three-quarters are Israeli-born, and most of the rest are from Europe or North America, but there are significant numbers who have immigrated from Asia and Africa. The Law of Return has brought to Israel Jews of varying cultural backgrounds. European Jews have been the dominant political and economic force, but a significant migration of more religiously observant Jews from North Africa and other parts of the Middle East has created what sociologist Ernest Krausz (1973) called "the two nations."

Almost half of Israeli Jews are secular, with the more religious Jews operating in an almost different social world. Not only are the various Jewish groups culturally diverse, but also there are significant socioeconomic differences: The Europeans generally are more prosperous, better represented in the Knesset (Israel's parliament), and better educated. The secular Jews feel pressure from the more traditional and ultraorthodox Jews, who push for a nation more reflective of Jewish customs and law (Pew Research Center 2016a).

The Intifada

Israel initially regarded the occupied territories as a security zone between Israel and its belligerent neighbors. By the 1980s, however, it was clear that the territories were also serving as the location of new settlements for Jews migrating to Israel, especially from Russia. Palestinians, though enjoying some political and monetary support of Arab nations, saw little likelihood of a successful military effort to eliminate Israel. Therefore, in December 1987, they began the first **Intifada**, the Palestinian uprising against Israel in the occupied territories. The Intifada took the form of attacks on Israeli soldiers, the boycott of Israeli goods, general strikes, resistance, and noncooperation with Israeli authorities. The first Intifada lasted five years.

The Intifada was a grassroots movement whose popularity was as much a surprise to the Palestine Liberation Organization (PLO) and the Arab nations as it was to Israel and its supporters. The broad range of participants in the Intifada—students, workers, union members, professionals, and business leaders—showed the unambiguous Palestinian opposition to occupation. The Intifada began out of the Palestinians' frustrations within Israel, and the confrontations were later encouraged by the PLO, an umbrella organization for several Palestinian factions of varying militancy.

With television news footage of Israeli soldiers appearing to attack defenseless youths, the Intifada transformed world opinion, especially in the United States. Palestinians came to be viewed as a people struggling for self-determination rather than as terrorists out to destroy Israel. Instead of Israel being viewed as "David" and its Arab neighbors as "Goliath," Israel came to take on the bully role and the Palestinians the sympathetic underdog role (Hubbard 1993; Third World Institute 2007).

The Search for Solutions amid Violence

The 1993 Oslo Accords between Israeli Prime Minister Yitzhak Rabin and PLO Chairman Yasser Arafat and subsequent agreements ended the state of war and appeared to set in motion the creation of the first-ever self-governing Palestinian territory in the Gaza Strip and the West Bank. This **two-state solution** envisioned Israel and Palestine living side by side and recognized by the entire world community. However, hardliners on both sides grew resistant to the move toward separate recognized Palestinian and Israeli states. Rabin was assassinated at a peace rally by an Israeli who felt that Israel had given up too much. Succeeding governments in Israel took stronger stands against relinquishing control of the occupied territories. Meanwhile, the anti-Israel Hamas party was elected to power following the death of Arafat in 2004.

Despite the assurances at Oslo, Israel did not end its occupation of the Palestinian territories by 1999, justifying its actions as necessary to stop anti-Israel violence originating in Palestinian settlements. Complicating the picture was the continued growth of officially recognized Israeli settlements in the West Bank, including East Jerusalem, bringing Israel's total population to 500,000 in 2017. Palestinians, assisted by Arabs in other countries, mounted a second Intifada from 2000 through 2004. The second Intifada was precipitated by the Israeli killing of several Palestinians at a Jerusalem mosque. This time, militant Palestinians went outside the occupied territories and targeted civilian sites in Israel through a series of suicide bombings.

Each violent episode brought calls for retaliation by the other side and desperate calls for a ceasefire from outside the region. Israel, despite worldwide denunciation, created a 440-mile "security barrier" of 30-foot-high concrete walls, ditches, and barbed wire to try to protect its Jewish settlers. The barrier served to limit the mobility of peaceful Palestinians trying to access crops, schools, hospitals, and jobs (The Economist 2017b).

The immediate goal is to end the violence, but any lasting peace must address several difficult issues, including the following:

Beginning in 2005, Israel started constructing a 30-foot-high, 440-mile "separation barrier" for security purposes, but the wall also served to keep Palestinians from schools and jobs.

- The status of Jerusalem, Israel's capital, which Muslims view as the third-most-holy city in the world (after Mecca and Medina)

- The future of the Jewish settlements in the West Bank of the Palestinian Authority territories

- The future of Palestinians and other Arabs with Israeli citizenship

- The creation of a truly independent Palestinian national state with strong leadership

- Israel–Palestinian Authority relations, because Palestine's government is controlled by Hamas, which is dedicated to Israel's destruction

- The future of Palestinian refugees elsewhere

Added worries are the uneasy peace between Israel and its Arab neighbors and the sometimes interrelated events in Egypt, Lebanon, Iraq, Iran, and Syria. The complexity of the situation has led some to question the likelihood of a two-state solution and shift discussion to focus on a united country with equal rights for all citizens. But the mere suggestion of a united state does not mean there is any enthusiasm for a united Israeli-Palestinian territory; rather, it points to how little progress has been made toward a two-state reality (Lustick 2013).

The past 65 years have witnessed significant changes: Israel has gone from a land under siege to a nation whose borders are recognized by almost every other nation. Israel has come to terms with the various factions of religious and secular Jews trying to coexist. The Palestinian people have gone from disfranchisement to having territory. Nonetheless, the two-state *solution* is now more likely to be seen as the two-state *illusion* or *delusion*. The current arrangement is extremely fragile.

Republic of South Africa

16.5   Explain inequality in the Republic of South Africa.

In every nation, some racial, ethnic, or religious groups enjoy advantages denied to other groups. Nations differ in the extent of this denial and in whether it is supported by law or by custom. In no other industrial society has the denial been so entrenched in recent law as it has been in the Republic of South Africa.

The Republic of South Africa is different from the rest of Africa because the original African peoples of the area are no longer present. Today, the country is multiracial, as Table 16.2 shows.

The largest group in South Africa is composed of the Black Africans who migrated from the north in the eighteenth century as well as more recent migrations from neighboring African countries over the past 20 years. The Coloured (or Cape Coloureds) (who are of mixed race) and Asian Indians make up the remaining non-Whites. The small White community consists of the English and the Afrikaners, the latter descended from Dutch and other European settlers. As in all other multicultural nations we have considered, colonialism and immigration have left their mark.

Table 16.2 Racial Groups in the Republic of South Africa

	Whites (%)	All Non-Whites (%)	Black Africans (%)	Coloureds (%)	Asian Indians (%)
1904	22	78	67	9	2
1936	21	79	69	8	2
1951	21	79	68	9	3
2010	9	91	79	9	3
2021 (projected)	8	90	80	9	2

SOURCES: Author's estimates, based on Statistics South Africa and Bureau of Market Research in MacFarlane 2006: 8–9; South African Institute of Race Relations 2007: 6, 12; MacFarlane 2008: 2; van den Berghe 1978: 102.

The Legacy of Colonialism

The permanent settlement of South Africa by Europeans began in 1652, when the Dutch East India Company established a colony in Cape Town as a port of call for shipping vessels bound for India. The area was sparsely populated, and the original inhabitants of the Cape of Good Hope, the Hottentots and the Bushmen, were pushed inland like the indigenous peoples of the New World. To fill the need for laborers, the Dutch imported slaves from areas of Africa farther north. Slavery was confined mostly to areas near towns and involved more limited numbers than in the United States. The Boers, semi-nomads descended from the Dutch, did not remain on the coast but trekked inland to establish vast sheep and cattle ranches. The trekkers, as they were known, regularly fought off the Black inhabitants of the interior regions. Sexual relations between Dutch men and slave and Hottentot women were quite common, giving rise to a mulatto group referred to today as Cape Coloureds.

The British entered the scene by acquiring part of South Africa in 1814, at the end of the Napoleonic Wars. The British introduced workers from India as indentured servants on sugar plantations. They had also freed the slaves by 1834, with little compensation to the Dutch slave owners, and had given Blacks almost all political and civil rights. The Boers were not happy with these developments and spent most of the nineteenth century in a violent struggle with the growing number of English colonists. In 1902, the British finally overwhelmed the Boers, leaving bitter memories on both sides. Once in control, however, the British recognized that the superior numbers of the non-Whites were a potential threat to their power, as they had been to the power of the Afrikaners.

The growing non-White population consisted of the Coloureds (the mixed-race population) and the Black tribal groups, collectively called Bantus. The British gave both groups the right to vote but restricted the franchise to people who met certain property qualifications. **Pass laws** were introduced, placing curfews on the Bantus and limiting their geographic movement. These laws, enforced through "reference books" until 1986, were intended to prevent urban areas from becoming overcrowded with job-seeking Black Africans, a familiar occurrence in colonial Africa (Marx 1998; van den Berghe 1965).

Apartheid

In 1948, South Africa was granted its independence from the United Kingdom, and the National Party, dominated by the Afrikaners, assumed control of the government. Under the leadership of this party, the rule of White supremacy, already well underway in the colonial period as custom, became more and more formalized into law. To deal with the multiracial population, the Whites devised a policy called *apartheid* to ensure their dominance. **Apartheid** (in Afrikaans, the language of the Afrikaners, it means "separation" or "apartness") came to mean a policy of separate development, euphemistically called *multinational development* by the government. At the time, these changes were regarded as cosmetic outside South Africa and by most Black South Africans.

The White ruling class was not homogeneous. The English and Afrikaners belonged to different political parties, lived apart, spoke different languages, and worshipped separately, but they shared the belief that some form of apartheid was necessary. Apartheid can perhaps be best understood as a twentieth-century effort to reestablish the master–slave relationship. Blacks could not vote. They could not move throughout the country freely. They were unable to hold jobs unless the government approved. To work at approved jobs, they were forced to live in temporary quarters at great distances from their real homes. Their access to education, healthcare, and social services was severely limited (Wilson 1973).

Events took a significant turn in 1990, when South African Prime Minister F. W. De Klerk legalized 60 banned Black organizations and freed Nelson Mandela (1918–2013), leader of the African National Congress (ANC), after 27 years of imprisonment. Mandela's triumphant remarks after his release appear in the Speaking Out feature.

The next year, de Klerk and Black leaders signed a National Peace Accord, pledging themselves to the establishment of a multiparty democracy and an end to violence. After a series of political defeats, de Klerk called for a referendum in 1992 to allow Whites to vote on ending apartheid. If he failed to receive popular support, he vowed to resign. A record high turnout gave a solid 68.6 percent vote that favored the continued dismantling of legal apartheid and the creation of a new constitution through negotiation. The process toward power sharing ended symbolically when de Klerk and Mandela were jointly awarded the 1993 Nobel Peace Prize (Marx 1998; Ottaway and Taylor 1992; Winant 2001).

South Africa–born comedian and talk show host Trevor Noah (2016) wrote a memoir, *Born a Crime*, in which he describes how he lived in hiding under apartheid because he, as the son of a biracial relationship, was literally a criminal, as were both his parents.

Speaking Out

Africa, It Is Ours!

Nelson Mandela

Amandla! Amandla! i Afrika, mayibuyo! [Power! Power! Africa, it is ours!]

My friends, comrades and fellow South Africans, I greet you all in the name of peace, democracy and freedom for all. I stand here before you no t as a prophet but as a humble servant of you, the people.

Your tireless and heroic sacrifices have made it possible for me to be here today. I therefore place the remaining years of my life in your hands.

On this day of my release, I extend my sincere and warmest gratitude to the millions of my compatriots and those in every corner of the globe who have campaigned tirelessly for my release.

Negotiations on the dismantling of apartheid will have to address the overwhelming demand of our people for a democratic nonracial and unitary South Africa. There must be an end to white monopoly on political power.

And [there must be] a fundamental restructuring of our political and economic systems to ensure that the inequalities of apartheid are addressed and our society thoroughly democratized....

Our struggle has reached a decisive moment. We call on our people to seize this moment so that the process toward democracy is rapid and uninterrupted. We have waited too long for our freedom. We can no longer wait. Now is the time to intensify the struggle on all fronts.

Nelson Mandela

To relax our efforts now would be a mistake which generations to come will not be able to forgive. The sight of freedom looming on the horizon should encourage us to redouble our efforts. It is only through disciplined mass action that our victory can be assured.

We call on our white compatriots to join us in the shaping of a new South Africa. The freedom movement is the political home for you, too. We call on the international community to continue the campaign to isolate the apartheid regime.

To lift sanctions now would be to run the risk of aborting the process toward the complete eradication of apartheid. Our march to freedom is irreversible. We must not allow fear to stand in our way.

Universal suffrage of a common voters' role in a united democratic and nonracial South Africa is the only way to peace and racial harmony.

In conclusion, I wish to go to my own words during my trial in 1964. They are as true today as they were then. I wrote: I have fought against white domination, and I have fought against black domination. I have cherished the idea of a democratic and free society in which all persons live together in harmony and with equal opportunities.

It is an ideal which I hope to live for and to achieve. But if needs be, it is an ideal for which I am prepared to die.

Source: Mandela, Nelson. 1990. Africa, It Is Ours. *New York Times* (February 12): A10. Used with permission of the Nelson Mandela Foundation.

The Era of Reconciliation and Moving On

In April 1994, South Africa held its first universal election. Apartheid had ended. Nelson Mandela's ANC received 62 percent of the vote, giving him a five-year term as president. Mandela enjoyed the advantage of wide personal support throughout the nation. He retired in 1999 when his second term ended. His successors have faced a daunting agenda because of the legacy of apartheid.

A significant step to help South Africa move past apartheid was the creation of the Truth and Reconciliation Commission (TRC). People were allowed to come forward and confess to horrors they had committed under apartheid from 1961 through 1993. If they were judged by the TRC to be truly remorseful, and most were, they were not subject to prosecution. If they failed to confess to all crimes they had committed, they were prosecuted. The stories gripped the country as people learned that actions taken in the name of the Afrikaner government were often worse than anyone had anticipated (Gobodo-Madikizela 2003).

The immediate relief that came with the end of apartheid has given way to greater concerns about the future of all South Africans. Scholars have noted that the "born frees"—the generation coming of age after the dismantling of apartheid—seem to be uninterested in politics (as evidenced by very low voter turnout) and uninvolved in moving social issues forward. In the Research Focus feature, we consider how intergroup contact may affect the views expressed by contemporary South Africans, including this younger generation (Weber 2014).

With the emergence of the new multiracial government in South Africa, we see a country with enormous promise but many challenges that are similar to those of our own

Research Focus

Intergroup Contact and South Africa

There is little question that the Republic of South Africa's recent history has been defined by racism. Every aspect of South African society, from transportation to hospitals to sports, reflects this legacy. So how do White South Africans and Black South Africans get along on a daily basis? They are certainly more likely to meet on an equal-status basis, whether in schools or in the workplace, than they were under apartheid. These conditions would seem to be an ideal opportunity to test the validity of the **contact hypothesis**. Recall that the contact hypothesis draws on the interactionist perspective and holds that intergroup contact between people of equal status in noncompetitive circumstances will reduce prejudice. Can the contact hypothesis hold true in a country with such a long history of intergroup discrimination and conflict supported by the central government?

Since the end of apartheid, surveys have shown that Black Africans are increasingly identifying themselves by the national social identity of "South African" while retaining their own tribal identity. Afrikaans- and English-speaking Whites seem to more increasingly identify with their ethnic group and are less likely to see themselves as South Africans. These observations would not seem to suggest that intergroup contact in the new South Africa can lead to lessening of prejudice. Yet national surveys conducted in the twenty-first century find that contact—especially more regular, intimate contact—leads to more positive feelings among the racial groups in South Africa. Other studies show

increased interaction especially by Whites, as measured by self-reports of having non-White friends or dining with those friends. Contact across racial lines seems to have less positive impact on the attitudes held by Black South Africans. Tests of the contact hypothesis among South African college students show relatively little contact across racial lines, but when it does occur, more positive feelings follow, especially among Whites.

Why do White South Africans seem to be affected more positively by contact? Even if the contemporary contact is harmonious, it occurs within the social context of unequal power position in which "Whiteness" is privileged over "Blackness." Researchers note that given the racist backdrop of today's South Africa, Whites may be quicker to evaluate intergroup contact as equal whereas the long-oppressed Black South Africans are less likely to see themselves as having status equal to that of Whites. Why? Even in today's South Africa, Whites are distinctly more powerful than Blacks. Furthermore, given the magnitude of structural change that South Africa must undergo, it may be especially difficult for Black South Africans to move quickly beyond the apartheid past. Intergroup contact is not a panacea anywhere, including South Africa, but rather one element in moving from an exclusionary society to a more pluralistic one.

Sources: Gibson and Classen 2010; Pettigrew 2010; Tredoux and Finchilescu 2010; Vincent 2008.

multiracial society. Some of the controversial issues facing the ANC-led government are very familiar to citizens in the United States:

Desperate poverty: Despite the growth of a small but conspicuous middle class among Black South Africans, poverty rates stand at 40 percent, compared to 4 percent to 5 percent of White South Africans.

Affirmative action: Race-based employment goals and other preference programs have been proposed, yet critics insist that such efforts constitute reverse apartheid.

Medical care: The nation is trying to confront the duality of private care for the affluent (usually Whites) and government-subsidized care (usually for people of color). AIDS has reached devastating levels, with 13 percent of the population having HIV or AIDS as of 2016.

Crime: Although the government-initiated violence under apartheid has ended, the generations of conflict and years of intertribal attacks have created a climate for crime, illegal gun ownership, and disrespect for law enforcement.

School integration: Multiracial schools are replacing the apartheid system, but for some, the change is occurring too fast or not fast enough.

These issues must be addressed with minimal increases in government spending as the government seeks to reverse deficit spending without an increase in taxes that would frighten away needed foreign investment. As difficult as all these challenges are, perhaps the most difficult is land reform (Dugger 2010; Geddes 2010; South African Institute of Race Relations 2010; Statistics South Africa 2016).

The government has pledged to address the issue of land ownership. Between 1960 and 1990, the government forced Black South Africans from their land and often allowed Whites to settle on it. Beginning in 1994, the government took steps to transfer 30 percent of agricultural land to Black South Africans. Where feasible, the government plans to restore the original inhabitants to their land; where this is not feasible, the government is to make "just and equitable compensation." The magnitude of this land reform issue cannot be overstated. Originally, the goal was to achieve the land transfer by 2004, but by 2012, only 10 percent of the farmland had been transferred. The goal of complete land transfer has now been deferred to 2025. Critics say at the current rate it will take until 2060 to reach the 2004 objective (Kutner and Hermes 2013).

Conclusion

As Figure 16.3 shows, each society, in its own way, illustrates the processes in the Spectrum of Intergroup Relations first introduced in Chapter 1. The examples range from the Holocaust, which precipitated the emergence of Israel, to the efforts to create a multiracial government in South Africa. A study of these five societies, coupled with knowledge of subordinate groups in the United States, provides the background from which to draw some conclusions about patterns of race and ethnic relations in the world today.

By looking beyond our borders, we gain new insights into the social processes that frame and define intergroup relationships. The colonial experience has played a role in all cases we considered in this chapter, but particularly in South Africa. In Mexico and South Africa, which have long histories of multiethnic societies, intergroup sexual relations have been widespread but with different results. Mestizos in Mexico occupy a middle racial group and experience less tension, whereas in South Africa, the Cape Coloureds had freedoms under apartheid that were almost as limited as those of the Black Africans. South Africa enforced de jure segregation, whereas Israeli communities seem to have de facto segregation. Israel's and South Africa's intergroup conflicts have involved the world community. Indigenous people figure in the social landscape of Canada, Brazil, and Mexico. Policies giving preference to previously devalued racial groups are in place in both Brazil and South Africa. Complete assimilation is absent in all five societies considered in this chapter and is unlikely to occur in the near future; the legal and informal barriers to assimilation and pluralism vary for subordinate-group members choosing either option. Looking at the status of women in Mexico reminds us of the worldwide nature of gender stratification and also offers insight into the patterns present in developing nations.

Figure 16.3 Spectrum of Intergroup Relations: Beyond the United States

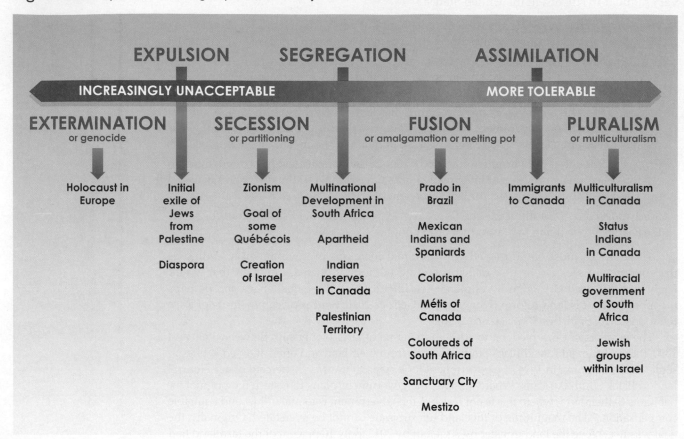

If we add the United States to these societies, the similarities become even more striking. The problems of racial and ethnic adjustment in the United States have dominated our attention, but they parallel past and present experiences in other societies with racial, ethnic, or religious heterogeneity. The U.S. government has been involved in providing educational, financial, and legal support for programs intended to help particular racial or ethnic groups, and it continues to avoid interfering with religious freedom. Bilingual, bicultural programs in schools, autonomy for Native Americans on reservations, and increased participation in decision-making by residents of ghettoes and barrios are all viewed as acceptable goals, although they are not pursued to the extent that many subordinate-group people would like.

The analysis of this chapter has reminded us of the global nature of dominant–subordinate relations along dimensions of race, ethnicity, religion, and gender. In the next chapter, we provide an overview of racial and ethnic relations and explore social inequality along the dimensions of age, disability status, and sexual identity.

Summary of Learning Objectives

16.1 Summarize the diversity in Mexico.

1. Mexico's mosaic of mestizos and native indigenous people creates a diversified society, with segments of the population that feel disadvantaged and ignored. Women are at a social and economic disadvantage in Mexico.

16.2 Understand Canada's multicultural-ism.

2. Canada, with one of the largest proportions of indigenous peoples, continues to develop strategies to promote economic development while preserving cultural traditions. Canada is home to a sizable and growing immigrant community.

3. The sizable French-speaking population within Canada has asked for and receives consideration for its special cultural heritage, which is not fully endorsed by others in the nation.

16.3 Analyze the degree to which Brazil is a racial paradise.

4. Brazil is not a racial paradise, as has sometimes been suggested, but continues to deal with significant disparity among people of color.

16.4 Explain the historical and contemporary tensions between Israel and Palestine.

5. Israel has both a significant Arab population and a diverse Jewish community, among whom there are sharp political and religious differences.

6. Palestinians in the occupied territories are in a difficult economic situation that has been aggravated by the building of a barrier wall between Israel and the Palestinian territories.

16.5 Explain inequality in the Republic of South Africa.

7. The apartheid era in South Africa underscores how race can be a tool for total subjugation of millions of people.

8. The South Africa of the post-apartheid era is marked by reconciliation of the different racial groups, which are facing significant issues involving land, education, health, and public safety.

Key Terms

apartheid, *page 358*
color gradient, *page 346*
colorism, *page 346*
contact hypothesis, *page 360*
Diaspora, *page 354*

environmental justice, *page 349*
ethnonational conflict, *page 345*
Intifada, *page 356*

mestizo, *page 345*
mulatto escape hatch, *page 352*
pass laws, *page 358*
Québécois, *page 349*

two-state solution, *page 356*
visible minorities, *page 350*
world systems theory, *page 345*
Zionism, *page 354*

Review Questions

1. How is color defined in Mexico, and what are the social implications of this definition?

2. On what levels can one speak of an identity issue facing Canada as a nation?

3. What role does race play in Brazilian life?

4. What is the outlook for a two-state solution for Israel and Palestine?

5. To what extent are the problems facing South Africa today the legacy of racial divisions?

Critical Thinking

1. Identify who the native peoples are and what their role has been in each of the societies discussed in this chapter.

2. Social construction of race emphasizes how we create arbitrary definitions of skin color that then have social consequences. Drawing on the societies discussed in this chapter, select one nation and identify how social definitions work in other ways to define group boundaries.

3. Apply the functionalist and conflict approaches of sociology first introduced in Chapter 1 to each of the societies discussed in this chapter.

4. The conflicts outlined in this chapter are examples of ethnonational conflicts, but how have the actions or inactions of the United States contributed to these problems?

Chapter 17
Overcoming Exclusion

shaunl/E+/Getty Images

⌄ Learning Objectives

17.1 Explain how the aged are a social minority.

17.2 Summarize the experience of people with disabilities.

17.3 Identify the equality issues facing the LGBT community.

What metaphor do we use to describe a nation whose racial, ethnic, and religious minorities are on the way to becoming numerical majorities in many cities and, now in the twenty-first century, in several states? For several generations, the image of the melting pot has been used as a convenient description of our culturally diverse nation. The analogy of an alchemist's cauldron was clever, even if a bit ethnocentric. It originated in the Middle Ages, when alchemists used a melting pot to attempt to change less-costly metals into gold and silver.

The Melting Pot was the title of a 1908 play by Israel Zangwill. In the play, a young Russian immigrant to the United States composes a symphony that portrays a nation that serves as a crucible (or pot) where all ethnic and racial groups melt together into a new, superior stock.

The vision of the United States as a melting pot became popular in the first part of the twentieth century, particularly because it suggested that the United States had an almost divinely inspired mission to destroy artificial divisions and create a single humankind. However, the image did not mesh with reality, in which the dominant group (Whites) indicated its unwillingness to welcome Native Americans, African Americans, Hispanics or Latinos, Jews, and Asians (among many others) into the melting pot.

The image of the melting pot is not invoked as often today. Instead, people speak of a *salad bowl* to describe a country that is ethnically diverse. Just as we can distinguish the lettuce from the tomatoes from the peppers in a tossed salad, we can see ethnic restaurants and the persistence of foreign languages in conversations on street corners. The dressing over the ingredients is akin to the shared value system and culture, covering but not hiding the salad's different ingredients.

Yet even the notion of a salad is wilting. Like the image of the melting pot, the image of a salad is static, certainly not indicative of the dynamic changes we see in the United States. It also fails to conjure up the myriad cultural pieces that make up the fabric or mosaic of our diverse nation.

The kaleidoscope offers another familiar and more useful analogy. Patented in 1817 by Scottish scientist Sir David Brewster, the kaleidoscope was a toy and then became a table ornament in the parlors of the rich. Users of this optical device turn a set of mirrors and observe the seemingly endless colors and patterns that are reflected off pieces of glass, tinsel, or beads. The growing popularity of the phrase "people of color" fits well with the idea of the United States as a kaleidoscope. The changing images correspond to the often bewildering array of groups found in our country (Schaefer 1992).

The images created by a kaleidoscope are hard to describe because they change dramatically with little effort. Similarly, in the kaleidoscope of the United States, we find it a challenge to describe the country's dynamic multiracial nature. Yet even as we begin to understand the past, present, and future of the many racial and ethnic groups, we recognize that there are still people other than racial and ethnic minorities who are stigmatized in society. There are many such groups, such as cancer survivors, ex-convicts, marginalized religious groups, obese people, and transgender individuals, to name a few.

We now consider the cases of the aged, people with disabilities, and the LGBT community. This chapter in large part continues the discussion begun in Chapter 1 about the intersections of social factors besides race, class, and gender. Recall that **intersectionality** refers to this overlapping and interdependent system of advantage and disadvantage. It results in the **matrix of domination**, or the cumulative impact of oppression with which many people live (refer to Figure 1.7). As we shall see, being young, free of disabilities, and heterosexual privileges people in many of the same ways that being White does.

The Aged: A Social Minority

17.1 Explain how the aged are a social minority.

Older people in the United States are subject to a paradox. They are a significant segment of the population who, as we shall see, are often viewed with negative stereotypes and are subject to discrimination. Yet they also have successfully organized into a potent collective force that wields significant political clout. Unlike other social groups subjected to differential treatment, this social category will include most of us someday. So, in this one case, the notion of the elderly as "them" will eventually give way to "us."

Older adults share the characteristics of subordinate or minority groups that we introduced in Chapter 1. Specifically:

1. Older adults experience unequal treatment in employment and may face prejudice and discrimination.

2. Older adults share physical characteristics that distinguish them from younger people, and their cultural preferences and leisure activities often differ from those of the rest of society.

3. Membership in this disadvantaged group is involuntary.

4. Older people have a strong sense of group solidarity, as reflected in senior citizen centers, retirement communities, and advocacy organizations.

5. Older people generally are married to others of comparable age.

There is one crucial difference between older people and other subordinate groups, such as racial and ethnic minorities or women: All of us who live long will eventually assume the ascribed status of being an older person (Barron 1953; Wagley and Harris 1958).

Figure 17.1 Actual and Projected Growth of the Elderly Population of the United States, 1960–2060

SOURCES: Author based on Bureau of the Census 2008: Table 2-c, 2012c: Table 3; Colby and Ortman 2015:4; Howden and Meyer 2011: Figure 4.

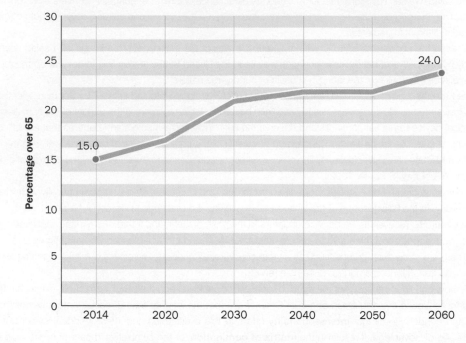

Who Are the Elderly?

As Figure 17.1 shows, an increasing proportion of the population will be composed of older people with each passing decade. This trend is expected to continue well through the twenty-first century as mortality declines and the postwar baby boomers age. Looking over a period of a century, we see the proportion of the population over age 65 increases from less than one in 10 in 1960 to almost one in four by 2060.

Compared with the rest of the population, older adults are more likely to be female, White, and living in certain states. Men generally have higher death rates than women at every age. As a result, elderly women outnumber men by a ratio of three to two. The difference grows with advancing age, so that among the oldest old group (over 100 years), women outnumber men four to one.

About 84 percent of older adults are White non-Hispanic. Although the aged population is growing more racially and ethnically diverse, the higher death rates of racial and ethnic minorities, coupled with immigration to the United States of younger Latinos and Asian Americans, are likely to keep the older population more White than the nation as a whole. Yet the overall pattern of a more diversified population will also be present among our oldest Americans. As Figure 17.2 shows, the population age 65 and over will become increasingly non-White and Latino.

Ageism

Respected gerontologist Bernice Neugarten (1996) observed that negative stereotypes of old age are strongly entrenched in a society that prides itself on being oriented toward youth and the future. In 1968, physician Robert Butler (1990), the founding director of the National Institute on Aging, coined the term **ageism** to refer to prejudice and discrimination against the elderly. Ageism reflects a deep uneasiness among young and middle-aged people about growing old. For many, old age symbolizes disease and death; seeing older adults serves as a reminder that young people too may someday become old and infirm. By contrast, society glorifies youth, seeing it as interchangeable with beauty and the future.

Ageism can be subtle and even well intentioned, as when well-meaning people speak to older people slowly, using simple words. Yet older people are often put off by this behavior, seeing it as patronizing and insincere.

Figure 17.2 Minority Population Age 65 and Older

NOTE: Majority defined here as the population other than White Non-Hispanics.

SOURCE: Bureau of the Census data in Ortman, Velkoff, and Hogan 2014:28.

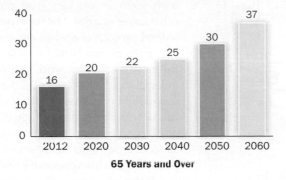

65 Years and Over

When Neugarten first brought attention to age discrimination, she was thinking of attitudes toward people age 55 to 75. With the greater level of health and the expanding lifespan in the United States, this bracket needs to be extended into the 80s and beyond. But do longer lives and better health mean that ageism is gone? In the 2008 presidential election, the age of 72-year-old John McCain became a campaign issue. Criticisms of McCain as "confused" and "losing his bearings" were used, according to some observers, as code for "just too old to be president" (North and Fiske 2013c).

The Research Focus considers some innovative studies that try to pinpoint how young people view the elderly and whether these views have implications for larger society.

Research Focus

The Three Maxes

Three actors, neither ugly nor handsome, step before a video camera and play the same part, "Max." Each wears a checked shirt and identifies himself as from New Jersey and working in a hardware store. One of the actors is 25, another is 45, and the third is 75. This was all a set-up to see if students reacted differently to Max based on his age.

Viewing these "interviews," the students responded differently on whether they liked Max. In one series, the oldest Max indicates that he enjoys the music of Rihanna and Justin Timberlake and sports a Black Eyed Peas T-shirt when he goes out. "Not good, less capable," said the younger evaluators; they would like it better if Max listened to Bing Crosby and wore a Frank Sinatra T-shirt. In another variation, the young participants were told they would actually be interacting with the oldest Max in a community service project. Again, they did not like the Max who was embracing a more youthful culture. Interestingly, evaluators who were in their thirties or older had no problem with the Rihanna-loving Max.

In another variation, the researcher asked undergraduates to offer their opinion of Max, thinking he was to become their partner in a trivia game. In this instance, the video either showed Max as assertive or compliant. Students did not seem to care whether their prospective 25- or 45-year-old teammate was assertive, but the elderly Max received a very negative rating if he was assertive. Male evaluators tended to be harsher raters than women in all the studies, with racial and ethnic differences less significant than age or gender.

These studies point to the belief among younger people that older people should "act their age" and know their place. The kindly "grandfather" and "elder statesman" stereotypes persist. Researchers acknowledge that more work is needed. Little research has been conducted on **microaggressions** experienced by older people. As defined in Chapter 2, microaggressions are the commonplace daily verbal indignities that members of a minority group experience. Microaggressions can be intentional or unintentional, and the perpetrator is often unaware of the insult. For example, would gender make a difference in how the elderly are viewed—a Maxine as well as a Max? That is, would young people be more accepting of a 75-year-old woman sporting a Justin Timberlake T-shirt? How about a more outspoken older woman? Also, the focus here overall is on the plight of older people. Future research should focus on anti-young prejudice and hence discrimination.

The conclusion from these studies is that stereotyping of older people is alive and well among young adults, and these stereotypes may have implications for the lives of senior citizens. As social psychologist Susan Fiske, a co-author of the study, said, "If you want to be an aging gray panther, and speak your mind to your manager, that's fine, but expect consequences" (Winerip 2013: B1).

Sources: North and Fiske 2013a, 2013b; Winerip 2013.

Martha Gradisher/CartoonStock.com

"Of course I can't ask your age during the interview, but see if you remember this song."

The federal Age Discrimination in Employment Act (ADEA), which went into effect in 1968, was passed to protect workers 40 years of age or older from being fired because of their age and replaced with younger workers who presumably would receive lower salaries. The Supreme Court strengthened federal protection against age discrimination in 1996, ruling unanimously that such lawsuits can be successful even if an older worker is replaced by someone older than 40. Consequently, if a firm unfairly fires a 65-year-old employee to make way for a 45-year-old, this act can still constitute age discrimination. Yet, by and large, age discrimination is not viewed as severely as racial or sex discrimination, perhaps because everyone will come to experience it (North and Fiske 2013c).

Research shows that before the enactment of the ADEA, there was evidence of hiring discrimination against older workers, as well as discrimination in promotions and training. Even with the ADEA, age continues to work against many older people, as evidenced by how long it takes them to find employment, the wage decrease they experience when they do become reemployed, and the size of court awards to victims of age discrimination (He et al. 2005).

Although firing workers simply because they are old violates federal law, courts have upheld the right to lay off older workers for economic reasons. Critics contend that later the same firms hire younger, cheaper workers to replace experienced older workers. When economic growth began to slow in 2001 and companies cut back on their workforces, complaints of age bias grew sharply as older workers began to suspect they were bearing a disproportionate share of the layoffs. According to the Equal Employment Opportunity Commission, between 1999 and 2004, complaints of age discrimination rose more than 41 percent. However, evidence of a countertrend has emerged. Some firms have been giving larger raises to older workers to encourage their retirement at the higher salary—a tactic that prompts younger workers to complain of age discrimination (Novelli 2004; Uchitelle 2003).

In contrast to these negative stereotypes present in an ageist society, researchers have found that older workers can be an asset for employers. One study concluded that older workers can be retrained in new technologies, have lower rates of absenteeism than younger employees, and often are more effective salespeople. The study focused on two corporations based in the United States (the hotel chain Days Inns of America and the holding company Travelers Corporation of Hartford) and a British retail chain, all of which have long-term experience in hiring workers age 50 and over. The findings clearly pointed to older workers as good investments. Yet despite such studies, complaints of age bias grew during the economic slowdown beginning in 2001, when companies cut back on their workforces (Equal Employment Opportunity Commission 2001; Telsch 1991: A16).

The courts have made some significant decisions favoring older workers. In 2008, the Supreme Court ruled 7–1 in *Meachan v. Knolls Atomic Power Laboratory* that employers under ADEA had the burden to prove that laying off older workers was based not on age but rather on "some reasonable factor." In this instance, the employer had stated that the older workers were less "flexible" or "retrainable" but failed to present any convincing basis for the layoffs, which affected 31 employees—30 of whom were old enough to be covered by ADEA (Greenhouse 2008).

A degree of conflict is emerging along generational lines that resembles other types of intergroup tension. Although the conflict involves neither violence nor the degree of subjugation found with other dominant–subordinate relations in the United States, a feeling still prevails that jobs and benefits for the elderly come at the expense of younger generations. Younger people are increasingly unhappy about paying Social Security taxes and underwriting the Medicare program, especially because they speculate that they themselves will never receive benefits from these fiscally insecure programs.

Figure 17.3 Poverty Rate Among Older Adults, 1995 and 2016

NOTE: 2015 Data reported in 2016.

SOURCE: Proctor, Semega, and Kollar 2016: Table B-2.

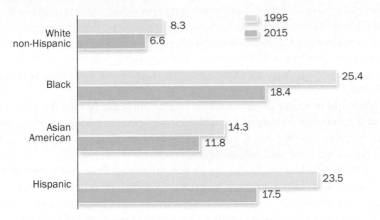

The Economic Picture

The elderly, like the other groups we have considered, do not have a single economic profile. The perception of "elderly" and "poor" as practically synonymous has changed in recent years to a view that the noninstitutionalized elderly are economically better off than the population as a whole. Both views are too simplistic; income varies widely among the aged.

There is significant variation in wealth and poverty among the nation's older people. Some older individuals and couples find themselves poor in part because of fixed pensions and skyrocketing healthcare costs. As Figure 17.3 shows, poverty has declined among the elderly in all racial groups since 1995.

As a group, older people in the United States are neither homogeneous nor poor. The typical older adult enjoys a standard of living that is much higher than at any point in the nation's past. Class differences among the elderly tend to narrow somewhat: Retirees who had middle-class incomes while younger tend to remain better off after retirement than those who had lower incomes, but the financial gap is declining (He et al. 2005).

The decline in poverty rates is welcome. However, advocates of the position that the elderly are receiving too much at the expense of the younger generations point to the rising affluence of the aged as evidence of an unfair economic burden placed on the young and future generations of workers.

As the previously mentioned data indicate, the aged who are most likely to experience poverty are the same people more likely to be poor earlier in their lives: female heads of households and racial and ethnic minorities. Although overall the aged are doing well economically, poverty remains a particularly difficult problem for the thousands of older adults who are impoverished annually by paying for long-term medical care (Quadagno 2014).

Advocacy Efforts by the Elderly

As we have seen with racial, ethnic, and gender groups, efforts to bring about change often require the formation of political organizations and advocacy groups. This is true with older adults and, as we will see later in this chapter, also true for people with disabilities and members of the LGBT community.

The largest organization representing the nation's elderly is the American Association of Retired Persons (AARP), which was founded in 1958 by a retired school principal who was having difficulty obtaining insurance because of age discrimination. Many of AARP's services involve discounts and insurance for its 38 million members (43 percent of Americans age 50 and older). After recognizing that many elderly are still gainfully employed, the organization changed its name to simply AARP. Reflecting its desire to represent older people who are not yet 65, AARP lobbied Congress in 2017 to oppose the repeal of the Affordable Care Act (Obamacare) and the passage of the American Health Care Act, which would reduce Medicare coverage of people age 50–64.

The potential power of AARP is enormous; it represents one out of every four registered voters in the United States. AARP has endorsed voter-registration campaigns, nursing home reforms, and pension reforms. Acknowledging its difficulties in recruiting members of racial and ethnic minority groups, AARP began a Minority Affairs Initiative. In 1996, the spokeswoman for this initiative, Margaret Dixon, became AARP's first African American president (AARP 2003, 2017).

People grow old in many different ways. Not all the elderly face the same challenges or enjoy the same resources. Whereas AARP lobbies to protect older adults in general, other groups work in more specific ways. Large special-interest groups represent retired federal employees, retired teachers, and retired union workers.

Older adults in the United States are better off today financially and physically than ever before. Many of them have strong financial assets and medical care packages that will take care of almost any need. But, as we have seen, a significant segment is impoverished and faces the prospect of declining health and mounting medical bills. Older people of color may have to add being aged to a lifetime of discrimination.

Although organizations such as AARP are undoubtedly valuable, the diversity of the nation's older population necessitates many different responses to the problems of older adults. For example, older African Americans and Hispanics tend to rely more on family members, friends, and informal social networks than on organizational support systems. Because of their lower incomes and greater incapacity resulting from poor health, older Blacks and Hispanics are more likely to need substantial assistance from family members than are older Whites. In recent years, older people of color have emerged as a distinct political force, independent of the larger elderly population, in some urban centers and in the Southwest. Low-income elderly are often the least represented among advocacy groups for the aged.

A significant stigma is attached to having a major visible disability. Not wishing to present an image of a "disabled" president, Franklin Roosevelt enlisted the cooperation of the press corps to avoid being shown in a wheelchair or using crutches. This picture shows the president leaving a New York City townhouse in 1933, with a rare view of the president's leg braces.

People with Disabilities: Moving On

17.2 Summarize the experience of people with disabilities.

John Grant, 50 years old, has had a difficult time finding work after his career as a computer programmer and instructor came to a sudden end. He was let go when his position was eliminated, and the response to his job seeking has been, to use his word, "ruthless." Brown has had a hearing impairment since birth and, like a lot of people with disabilities, he has found it difficult to find a job in the wake of the recent economic recession. If a company calls to speak with Grant and he is having difficulty hearing, he asks if he can call back using a third-party transcription service. The service provides real-time captions of what the caller is saying so that people like Grant can more easily follow the conversation. Often, his request to use this service causes the job search to end; sometimes the potential employer just hangs up (Murray 2010).

Throughout history, people have been socially disadvantaged not because of the limits of their own skills and abilities but because assumptions are made about them based on some group characteristics. People with disabilities are one such group. The very term *disability* suggests lack of ability in some area, but as we shall see, society often

New York Daily News Archive/Getty Images

assumes that a person with a disability is far less capable than she or he really is. Furthermore, society limits the life chances of people with disabilities in ways that are unnecessary and unrelated to any physical infirmity.

Disability in Contemporary Society

Societies have always had members with disabilities. Rarely have people with disabilities been treated as equals. According to the Bureau of the Census, an estimated 38 million people had a disability in 2011. A **disability** is a reduced ability to perform tasks one would normally do at a given stage in life. The category "people with disabilities" therefore includes everyone from those who have difficulty carrying 10 pounds to people who use wheelchairs, crutches, or walkers (Brault 2012).

We often marginalize people with disabilities, but many individuals with disabilities have accomplished much in their lives. As Table 17.1 shows, some people's disabilities are well known, whereas others' go largely unnoticed.

Disabilities are found in all segments of the population, but racial and ethnic minorities are disproportionately more likely to experience them and also to have less access to assistance. African Americans and Latinos report higher rates of disability. Fewer African Americans and Hispanic people with disabilities are graduating from college compared

Table 17.1 Famous People with Disabilities

Can you match the person with the disability? All the famous people listed in this table have at least one disability. Match each person with one or more disabilities, then check your answers below.
Match the letters in Column A with the names in Column B.

Column A	Column B
A. Blind	____Napoleon Bonaparte
B. Learning disability	____Beethoven
C. Polio	____Tom Cruise
D. Epilepsy	____Michael J. Fox
E. Dwarfism	____Homer
F. Parkinson's disease	____James Earl Jones
G. Quadriplegic	____Frida Kahlo
H. Deaf	____Keira Knightley
I. Stutter	____John Lennon
J. HIV–AIDS	____Jay Leno
K. Multiple sclerosis	____John Mellencamp
L. Attention-deficit hyperactivity disorder	____"Mini-me" Verne Troyer
M. Bipolar disorder	____Richard Pryor
N. Spina bifida	____Christopher Reeve
O. Dyslexia	____Franklin Delano Roosevelt
	____Axl Rose
	____Charles Schwab
	____Steven Spielberg
	____Sting
	____Montel Williams
	____Stevie Wonder

Answers: Bonaparte N; Beethoven HL; Cruise BO; Fox F; Homer A; Jones I; Kahlo CN; Knightley O; Lennon L; Leno IO; Mellencamp B; Pryor K; Reeve G; Roosevelt C; Rose BL; Schwab O; Spielberg O; Sting BL; Troyer E; Williams K; Wonder AL.

SOURCE: Prepared by author.
SOURCE: Prepared by author.

with White people with disabilities. They also have incomes consistently lower than their White counterparts (Brault 2012; Steinmetz 2006).

Although disability knows no social class, about two-thirds of working-age people with a disability in the United States are unemployed. African Americans and Hispanics with disabilities are even more likely to be jobless. Most of them believe that they would be able to work if they were offered the opportunity or if some reasonable accommodation could be made to address the disability (Kirkpatrick 1994; Noble 1995; Shapiro 1993).

Labeling People with Disabilities

Labeling theorists, drawing on the work of sociologist Erving Goffman (1963), suggest that society attaches a stigma to many forms of disability and that this stigma leads to prejudicial treatment. Indeed, people with disabilities often observe that people without disabilities see them only as blind, deaf, wheelchair users, and so forth, rather than as complex human beings with individual strengths and weaknesses whose blindness or deafness is merely one aspect of their lives.

In the Speaking Out feature, we hear sociologist Erik Olin Wright, the 2012 president of the American Sociological Association, describing his visit to Gallaudet University. The college, founded in 1864 to serve deaf students, is located in Washington, DC. Wright very clearly acknowledges that when entering this campus of a school that was created to serve the deaf, he is entering a different culture that he seeks to understand and appreciate.

Speaking Out

My Journey into the Deaf World

Erik Olin Wright

The first image of Gallaudet: Two students in animated conversation strolling along a walk next to classic liberal arts type buildings—an ordinary, everyday thing to see on campus, only they are talking with their hands. I have, of course, seen people signing before, and once, at a performance of a play in Madison [Wisconsin] by the National Theater of Deaf, I had been at an event with many people signing, but this was the first time I had visited a place in the Deaf world and spoken, with the help of an interpreter, for an extended period with Deaf people. The day was extraordinary....

In preparation for the visit I decided to learn some ASL [American Sign Language] so I could give a greeting at the beginning of my talk....

At first doing this sequence of signs was really hard—I had to constantly look at my notes, and everything was stilted and jerky. By my third lesson the ASL teacher said that I was making a lot of progress, but needed to pay a little attention to phrasing—otherwise it would be like speaking in a monotone with equal emphasis on every word. She also said not to worry about little mistakes. They would just seem like someone saying "wabbit" instead of "rabbit."....

The lecture was in a beautiful space designed with the specific objective of being congenial to the Deaf. This meant having lots of light and good sight lines for visual communication.

Erik Olin Wright

The room was a kind of atrium-like space with a circular balcony on the second floor overlooking the lecture space below and with clear glass panels perhaps four feet high instead of a guard rail. You could sit behind these panels and still communicate with people below—communicating through walls, I was told. The elevators that went up from the bottom of the atrium-space also had glass sides so people in the elevator could talk to people outside with ASL.

I was introduced at the talk by Thomas Horejes, a young, energetic, very appealing Deaf sociologist on the Gallaudet faculty. Then I did my signed greeting—quite smoothly, without hesitation, I thought. Later one person said that although everyone understood what I meant, my "thrilled" look a little like "pasta," so the greeting was: "Hello, I'm pasta and honored to be here...." Other people reassured me that my sign looked pretty close to "thrilled." Anyway, wabbit or pasta, everyone seemed very appreciative of my effort.

After I did my signed introduction, I added a few comments about my experience signing....

After I was finished speaking there was a lively question and answer discussion. A number of students and professors came up and asked me questions in ASL....

A young African-American woman: "I wanted to ask you about utopia. Do you think that this ignores individualism or individual expectations because it focuses so much on the group? Especially in such a highly individualistic society I think it would be hard in America to combine both a group and individuals goals as well." I responded by talking about the utopian aspiration being to create the conditions for individual persons to flourish. The issue is really about the relationship between institutions and individuals more than between groups and individuals. (I also realized when I was listening to this young woman's question that I was looking at the interpreter who was speaking rather than at the person who was signing the question. I guess this is a natural mistake by someone not used to interacting with Deaf people—making eye contact with the speaking interpreter rather than the silent signing person. But from then on I looked at the person asking the question.)

....

When the lecture was done, we went to lunch with a number of faculty members from the sociology department. At lunch there was a really interesting discussion of the complex issue of cochlear implants between one person who had been Deaf from birth and the other who became Deaf as an adult. Both had actually learned ASL as adults. The person who was Deaf since birth had been mainstreamed as a child, learning lip-reading, and only learned ASL as a young adult. Many issues were in play in the discussion:

- At what age was it appropriate to have cochlear implants [which allow some deaf people to hear]? If a young child is to have this procedure done, then it means that the parents would have the power to impose it on a child. One position is that this should not be done until around age 9 when the child could decide. But, the contrary argument goes, the benefits of the procedure are greatest if done very early, since then the brain can adapt more easily to the cochlear implant signals. Also, if done earlier, this can have a bigger impact on language acquisition and cognitive development.

- A deaf child born to a deaf parent is a very different situation from a deaf child born to a hearing parent.

- All this raised the issue of what is "normal" and what needs to be "fixed." The deaf/hearing spectrum is a natural form of variation, and so being deaf is not "abnormal," it is just one form in which human lives take place.

- There was also an interesting disagreement over whether a person could in fact be fully part of both worlds. Why can't a child with a cochlear implant which results in some hearing also become fully conversant in sign language and thus be in both worlds? The person who was opposed to early childhood implants felt that this is in practice very unlikely. This led to a very interesting discussion of ways in which the long-term trajectory of medical solutions to deafness is likely to undermine the support for signing and deaf culture. The disappearance of those supports would mean that in the future ASL would become less of an available option for parents. One of the hearing people at lunch who was fluent in ASL said that she would be happy with a deaf child, but if the supports disappeared she would definitely do an implant because the task of providing those supports would be overwhelming.

- There was a time when most deafness was the result of medical conditions, not genes, but now medical interventions have greatly reduced deafness as a consequence of disease. Eventually most deafness will be because of genes, rather than disease, and since the genetic conditions are rare this means that being Deaf will become very rare. As Deafness becomes rarer it will be harder to become proficient in sign since there will be no one to sign with. There is also a decline in Deaf schools with more mainstreaming, which also results in decreased proficiency of signing.

- The next controversy will be over aborting fetuses with the deaf gene, just like there is controversy over aborting fetuses with Down syndrome.

After lunch we had a brief tour of the campus. It is a lovely environment—some old, charming late 19th century buildings along with new, well designed modern ones. The University was chartered by Abraham Lincoln in 1864 and clearly has become an anchor for Deaf culture and education....

At 4 pm I met with a group of undergraduates for a freewheeling discussion. A few of the questions seemed a bit naïve to me, or at least not well informed. Later Margaret explained that many of the students at Gallaudet have large challenges to overcome because they haven't had access to the kind of diffuse general knowledge while growing up that most undergraduates have. Much of this knowledge is picked up serendipitously in overhearing conversations, casually watching the news and listening to the radio, all things which are much less likely for a Deaf child, especially if their parents are hearing. A child Deaf from birth also has a much bigger challenge learning to read, since the English words are all purely marks on a page with no sounds connected to them. This is more like learning to read Chinese or some other system of symbols that have no sounds connected to them. Each word has to be learned as a separate entity. As a result many students read at a pretty low level, but are still trying to do college work. These are really very stiff challenges.

The day ended with relaxing, laughter-filled dinner at a Sushi restaurant with a number of sociology faculty and two interpreters. The interpreters had to work really hard, and their professional code meant that they weren't supposed to eat while on the job. It really is a full translation issue, because the grammar of ASL and spoken English are not the same. As it was explained to me, ASL does not have a fixed word order the way spoken English does. And of course, there is not a direct sign for every word in English, so sometimes the interpreter has to spell out the word with hand spelling. They seemed to do a really good job, because the conversation flowed very smoothly and easily. In one way this was a bit easier than if they were translating from English to a foreign language: in ordinary translation, the translation needs to be sequential at a dinner table, because the interpreter cannot speak at the same time as one is talking. But in signed interpretation, they can do the signing as a simultaneous translation, since there are no sounds.

Source: Wright, Erik Olin. 2012: 12, 13. My Journey Into the Deaf World: A Visit to Gallaudet University. Footnotes (March): 11–12. Used with permission.

As they have with other subordinate statuses, the mass media have contributed to the stereotyping of people with disabilities. Too often, they are treated with a mixture of pity and fear. Nationwide charity telethons promote a negative image of people with disabilities as being childlike and nonproductive, suggesting that until they are "cured," they cannot contribute to society like other people. At the very least, the poster-child image proclaims that it is not okay to have a disability. By contrast, in literature and film, evil characters with disabilities—from Captain Hook to Dr. Strangelove to Freddy Krueger—reinforce the view that disability is a punishment for being evil. Efforts to encourage sober driving or safety in the workplace use images of people with disabilities to frighten people into the appropriate behavior.

There has been some evidence of positive portrayal of people with disabilities on television series such as *Ironside* (1967–1975, again in 2013), *Life Goes On* (1989–1993), *Breaking Bad* (2008–2013), *Secret Life of the American Teenager* (2008–2013), *Lie to Me* (2009–2013), *The Michael J. Fox Show* (2013), and *Glee* (2009–2015), but there is a lot of ground to make up in the image department. An analysis of the 2016–2017 television season shows 15 regular characters with a disability, or about 1.7 percent of all roles (GLAAD 2016).

Negative attitudes are not the only challenge facing people with disabilities. Among men and women age 16–64 with any kind of disability, 35 percent are employed, compared to 72 percent without a disability. People with disabilities are also 1.5 times more likely to be victims of both violent and nonviolent crimes. In about one in five incidents, the victim felt that his or her disability was the reason for his or her victimization (Brault 2012; Rand and Harrell 2009).

In Chapter 3, we introduced **institutional discrimination**, which is the denial of opportunities and equal rights to individuals or groups resulting from the normal operations of a society. People with disabilities certainly experience institutional discrimination. For example, society is sometimes organized in a way that limits people with disabilities. Architectural barriers and transportation difficulties often add to the problems of people with disabilities when they seek and obtain employment. Simply getting around city streets can be quite difficult for people with mobility challenges. Many streets are not properly equipped with curb cuts for wheelchair users. A genuinely barrier-free building needs more than a ramp; it should also include automatic doors, raised letters and Braille on signs, and toilets that are accessible to people with disabilities. Even if a person with disabilities finds a job, and even if the job is in a barrier-free building, he or she still faces the problem of getting to work in a society in which many rail stations and most buses remain inaccessible to wheelchair users and others with disabilities.

Advocacy for Disability Rights

Until recently, people with disabilities as a group have scarcely been thought of in any terms except perhaps pity. Often history has forgotten how deep the mistreatment has been. There has been a steadily growing effort to ensure not only the survival of people with disabilities but also the same rights enjoyed by others. In the early 1960s, Ed Roberts and some other young adults with disabilities wanted to attend the University of California at Berkeley. Though reluctant at first, the university was eventually persuaded to admit them and agreed to reserve space in the university infirmary as living quarters for students with disabilities. These students and others established their own student center and became known as the Rolling Quads. They eventually turned their attention to the surrounding community and established the Berkeley Center for Independent Living, which became a model for hundreds of independent living centers (Brannon 1995).

By the early 1970s, following the example of the Rolling Quads, a strong social movement for disability rights had emerged across the United States, which drew on the experiences of the Black civil rights movement and the feminist movement. This movement now includes a variety of organizations; some work on behalf of people with a single disability (such as the National Federation of the Blind), and others represent people with any of many disabilities (such as New York City's Disabled in Action). The large number of Vietnam veterans with disabilities who joined the effort gave a boost to advocacy efforts and a growing legitimacy in larger society.

Many of these organizations worked for the 1990 passage of the Americans with Disabilities Act (ADA). In many respects, this law is the most sweeping antidiscrimination legislation since the 1964 Civil Rights Act. The ADA went into effect in 1992, covering people with a disability, defined as a condition that "substantially limits" a "major life activity" such as walking or seeing. It prohibits bias against people with disabilities in employment, transportation, public accommodations, and telecommunication. Businesses with more than 15 employees cannot refuse to hire a qualified applicant with a disability; these companies are expected to make a "reasonable accommodation" to permit such a worker to do the job. Commercial establishments such as office buildings, hotels, theaters, supermarkets, and dry cleaners are barred from denying service to people with disabilities (Burgdorf 2005).

The ADA represents a significant framing of the issues of people with disabilities. Basically, we can see it taking a civil-rights view of disabilities that seeks to humanize the way society sees and treats people with disabilities. The ADA does not take the perspective adopted in other nations, such as Great Britain, of seeing disability as totally an entitlement issue; that is, because you have a disability, you automatically receive certain benefits. Rather, its perspective is that people with disabilities are being denied certain rights. As disability rights activist Mark Johnson said, "Black people fought for the right to ride in the front of the bus. We're fighting for the right to get on the bus" (Shapiro 1993:128; see also Albrecht 2005; Burgdorf 2005).

A more specific concern relevant to people with disabilities has arisen at Gallaudet University (see the Speaking Out feature). Gallaudet has been the scene of unrest during the past 30 years concerning the selection of its president. Many students and sympathetic supporters believe that the president of this institution must not only be deaf but also embrace the primacy of American Sign Language (ASL). First in 1988 and then again in 2006, students mounted "Deaf President Now" campaigns after presidents were proposed who were not "deaf enough" because they relied too much on reading lips or spoke without using ASL. The disability rights movement has caused people both with and without disabilities to rethink what constitutes fairness and equity (Basken 2007).

Some businesses are pioneers in expanding opportunities to people with disabilities. The National Governors Association has worked with Walgreens to expand the retailer's talent pool with those with disabilities, ranging from autism or developmental disabilities to those who are visually or hearing impaired. Walgreens' own research shows that workers with disabilities are often more efficient and loyal, and have lower absenteeism. Any cost of accommodating such workers with new technologies and education has been shown to be minimal (National Governors Association 2013; Walgreens 2013).

Rethinking the rights of people with disabilities began with the ADA but has now extended to the call for visitability. **Visitability** refers to building private homes so that they are accessible for visitors with disabilities. In the mid-1990s, cities such as Atlanta, Georgia, and Austin, Texas, passed ordinances encouraging new homes to have at least one no-step entrance, wider doorways, grab bars in bathrooms, and other accommodations. This new idea suggests that *all* environments should be accessible—not just public places, such as courtrooms or token handicapped-accessible accommodations in hotels, but *all* living spaces.

Visitability refers to a living environment able to accommodate people with mobility issues, so it would have no steps, at least one bathroom on a main floor, and doors with 32 inches of clear passage space.

Many people oppose such a move as unnecessary government interference; others see it as a long-overdue recognition that people with disabilities should be able to move freely throughout the country (Buchholz 2003; Visitability 2013).

Activists remain encouraged since the passage of the ADA. Those working on behalf of the veterans of the Iraq and Afghanistan wars who have returned with significant disabilities have joined longtime activists in their continuing efforts for disability rights. The ADA has now been in effect for almost three decades, and studies reveal that people with disabilities feel empowered and perceive increased access to employment opportunities. However, one must remember that civil rights activists felt a measure of optimism after passage of the major civil rights legislation more than 50 years ago (Albrecht 2005; Meyer 2008).

breadmaker/123RF

Roman Samborskyi/
Shutterstock

The LGBT Community: Coming Out for Equality

17.3   Identify the equality issues facing the LGBT community.

When and how did you first realize you were a heterosexual?
What do you think caused your heterosexuality?
Is it possible that your heterosexuality is just a phase you may grow out of?
Why are heterosexuals so promiscuous?

These are not questions heterosexuals are likely to be asked, because these queries assume something is wrong with being attracted to members of the opposite sex. In contrast, many of us are accustomed to hearing homosexuals and other members of the LGBT community questioned about their orientation.

We live at a time when heterosexuality is considered healthy and taken for granted. Homosexuality is, therefore, seen as a social issue. Yet, at certain times in many societies, it was possible to acknowledge same-sex and bisexual love and act on it without necessarily encountering open hostility.

In the United States, and to a varying degree in all contemporary societies, heterosexuality is privileged and labeled as "normal." Young children are often presented with the idea that romantic relationships occur only between a man and a woman. Heterosexuality is taken for granted without need for explanation. Gay male and lesbian relationships are often invisible and, in some households, are openly scorned. While presenting heterosexuality as the norm is not necessarily motivated by homophobia, it still serves to raise heterosexuality to the standard of what children should expect of others and, most importantly, of themselves. Well before dating, much less mate selection, terms like "boyfriends" and "girlfriends" are used in a way that reinforces opposite-sex relationships (Fischer 2013; Martin 2009; Martin and Luke 2010).

Many preschool educators now talk of the value of such books as *My Two Mommies, It's OK to Be Different, My Princess Boy, William's Doll*, and *Daddy, Papa, and Me* to broaden toddlers' realization that there are many household types. However, these books exist in a social environment where homosexuality is not the norm.

The focus in this chapter is on differential treatment because one is gay or lesbian—recognizing that human sexuality and sexual identity are very diverse. Yet typically in the United States, sexual orientation is constructed as either homosexual or heterosexual and ignores *bisexuals*—that is, individuals who are sexually attracted to both sexes. Included in this discussion about gays, lesbians, and bisexuals are *transgender persons*—people whose gender identity does not match their physical identity at birth; transgender individuals, for example, may see themselves as both male and female. *Transsexuals* are people who see themselves as the sex opposite of their birth identity and may take surgical measures to bring their physical being closer to their gender identity. Sometimes confused with these issues of gender identity and sexual orientation is the older term *transvestites*, which today usually refers to cross-dressers who wear clothing of the opposite sex. These are typically men choosing to wear women's clothing, and their orientation may be either gay or heterosexual.

Being Gay, Lesbian, Bisexual, or Transgender in the United States

There are anecdotal accounts of public recognition of homosexuality throughout U.S. history, but it was not until the 1920s and 1930s that it became visible. By that time, clubs for gays and lesbians were growing in number, typically in urban areas. Plays, books, and organizations were created to meet the social needs of gays and lesbians. As homosexuality has become more visible, efforts to suppress it have been institutionalized. At about the same time, the U.S. Army hired psychiatrists to screen recruits for evidence of homosexuality and dismissed volunteers who were gay (Schwartz 1992).

Figure 17.4 Same-Sex Couple Households as a Percent of All Households

About 594,000 same-sex couples lived in the United States in 2010.

SOURCE: 2010 American Community Survey data in Lofquist 2011: 4.

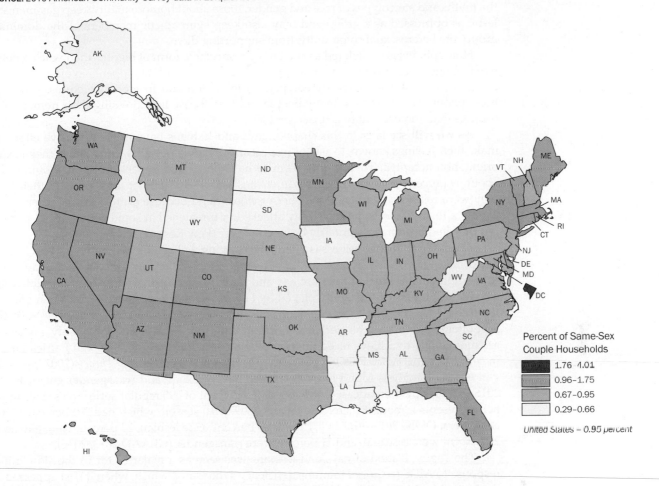

Percent of Same-Sex
Couple Households

■	1.76–4.01
▨	0.96–1.75
▩	0.67–0.95
□	0.29–0.66

United States – 0.95 percent

Given that gay men and lesbians are severely stigmatized, accurate data are hard to obtain. Researchers for the National Health and Life Survey and the Voter News Service in their election exit polls estimate that 2 percent to 5 percent of U.S. adults identify themselves as gay or lesbian. An analysis of the 2010 Census shows the numbers of gay and lesbian adult population approaching 10 million (Laumann et al. 1994; Lofquist 2011).

In Figure 17.4, we see the national pattern of same-sex households. The highest proportion is found in the Northeast, parts of the Midwest, and the Far West. Typically, relatively high levels are found in states that have a history of laws that prohibit discrimination based on sexual orientation (Gates and Newport 2013).

Growing recognition of a sizable gay population has not led to a consistent effort to promote understanding over the past 60 years. The general focus was to explore ways to prevent and control homosexuality as a disease, which is what psychiatrists thought it was. Well into the 1960s, discrimination against gays and lesbians was common and legal. Police raided bars frequented by people seeking same-sex partners, and patrons were jailed, their names often published in local newspapers. Although not surprising, it was disappointing to hear that the county board in Rhea County, Tennessee, unanimously passed a measure in 2004 that allowed the county to prosecute someone for being gay or lesbian as a "crime against nature." A few days later, after recognizing the losing court battle they would face, the county commissioners rescinded the antigay motion, but clearly they did not take back their view of gays and lesbians. Little wonder, then, that public health officials have detected increased risk for a variety of risky behaviors as well as mental health disorders, including depression, among adolescent lesbian and gay youth (Barry 2004; Coker, Austin, and Shuster 2010).

Prejudice and Discrimination

Homophobia, the fear of and prejudice against homosexuality, is present in every facet of life: the family, organized religion, the workplace, official policies, and the mass media. Like the myths and stereotypes of race and gender, those about homosexuality keep gay men and lesbians oppressed as a group and may also keep sympathetic members of the dominant group, the heterosexual community, from supporting them.

Homophobia is considered a much more respectable form of bigotry than voicing negative feelings and ideas against other oppressed groups. People still openly avoid homosexuals, and group members are stereotyped on television and in motion pictures. Although homophobia has decreased, many people still feel at ease in expressing their homophobic feelings that homosexuality is unacceptable.

As we will see later in this chapter, gays and lesbians have made extensive efforts to make their feelings known, to ask for respect and a variety of rights, and to have their sexual orientation accepted. Their efforts seem to have had some impact on public opinion, yet about 39 percent of gay and lesbian Americans said in 2013 that at some point in their lives they were rejected by a family member or close friend because of their sexual orientation. Nearly a third report being physically attacked or threatened at some point, and 21 percent felt they had been treated unfairly by an employer (Pew Research Center 2013).

The entertainment business is often seen as being welcoming to openly gay and lesbian performers. The reality appears to be different. Although openly gay actors and actresses find employment, starring roles are few and far between. Furthermore, highly visible roles of gay individuals are generally played by heterosexual actors, such as Sean Penn playing the title role in the 2008 motion picture *Milk,* which chronicles the life of Harvey Milk, the first openly gay man to be elected to office in California. And ironically, openly gay actors are more likely to achieve recognition in playing straight roles, such as Neil Patrick Harris in *How I Met Your Mother* (2005–2014) and Jim Parsons in *The Big Bang Theory* (2007–present).

A recent analysis found only 43 lesbian, gay, bisexual, and transgender characters in 2016–2017 scripted broadcast television, or 4.8 percent of 895 regular series roles. This number represents a modest increase over the 2009–2010 season, which had 3.0 percent LGBT characters. Of the 2016–2017 LGBT roles, 43 percent were lesbian, 23 percent were gay men, 26 percent were bisexual, and 11 percent were transgender (GLAAD 2013, 2016).

The stigmatization of gays and lesbians was seen as a major factor in the slow initial response to AIDS (acquired immune deficiency syndrome), which, when it first appeared in the United States, overwhelmingly claimed gay men as its victims. The inattention and the reluctance to develop a national policy forced gay communities in major cities to establish self-help groups to care for the sick, educate the healthy, and lobby for more responsive public policies. The most outspoken AIDS activist group has been the AIDS Coalition to Unleash Power (ACT-UP), which has conducted controversial protests and sit-ins in the halls of government and at scientific conferences. Although initially such efforts may have siphoned away participants from the broader gay rights effort, ultimately new constituencies of gay men and lesbians were created, along with alliances with sympathetic supporters from the heterosexual community (Adam 1995; Shilts 1982).

In 1998, the nation was shocked by the unprovoked, brutal murder of Matthew Shepard, a University of Wyoming student, by two men. Subsequent investigation showed simply because he was gay, the attackers murdered Shepard rather than leaving him alone after robbing him. This tragic event galvanized a move to include sexual orientation as a basis of hate crimes in many states. Gays and lesbians began to actively resist their mistreatment, sometimes working with local law enforcement agencies and prosecutors to end antigay violence. Many activists bemoan the fact that there is still no memorial and no antigay violence law in Wyoming. Yet Congress did pass the Matthew Shepard Act, which extends hate-crime protection to gay men and lesbians.

On an everyday level, studies point to the price people pay for being gay, lesbian, bisexual, or transgender. While some entrepreneurial people may create successful gay-oriented businesses in entertainment or travel, most of society proceeds against a backdrop that normalizes heterosexuality. Still, progress has been made. Finally, beginning in 2013, gay couples no longer had to file separate tax forms, which generally deprived them of some significant tax savings experienced by heterosexual married people. Even more significant changes are likely as federal courts in 2017 ruled that the 1964 Civil Rights Act, which prohibits sex discrimination, extends to issues of sexual orientation, potentially leading to a major workplace victory for the LGBT community (Mize 2016; Wolf 2017).

The quest for transgender equality has generally been a part of seeking an end to discrimination against gays and lesbians, though transgender advocacy has been much less visible. Current controversies include the opposition to allowing transgender persons to use their gender identity rather than the one assigned to them at birth. This battle has surfaced in obtaining driver's licenses, ability to compete in sports, voter ID laws, Social Security registrations, and the use of public restrooms. For the nearly 1.4 million transgender people in the United States, these struggles mirror similar efforts of African Americans 60 years ago to be able to vote freely, compete in athletics, or use the restroom of their choice (Herman et al. 2017; Jonsson 2016b).

Advocacy for LGBT Rights

The first homosexual organization in the United States was founded in Chicago in 1924. Such groups grew steadily over the next 50 years, but they were primarily local and were more likely to be self-help and social rather than confrontational groups. The social movements of the 1950s and 1960s on behalf of African Americans and women caused lesbians and gay men also to reflect more directly on the oppression their sexual orientation caused.

The contemporary gay and lesbian movement marks its beginning in New York City on June 28, 1969. Police raided the Stonewall Inn, an after-hours gay bar, and forced patrons into the street. Instead of meekly dispersing and accepting the disruption, the patrons locked police inside the bar and rioted until police reinforcements arrived. For the next three nights, lesbians and gay men marched through the streets of New York, protesting police raids and other forms of discrimination. Within months, gay liberation groups appeared in cities and on campuses throughout the United States.

Despite the efforts of the lesbian and gay rights movement, in 1986 the Supreme Court in *Bowers v. Hardwick* ruled by a 5–4 vote that the Constitution does not protect homosexual relations between consenting adults, even in the privacy of their own homes. The decision sent a clear message endorsing the normality of heterosexuality. This position held until the Court reversed itself in 2003 by a 6–3 vote in *Lawrence v. Texas*. The divisiveness of the issue nationally was reflected among the justices. Justice Anthony Kennedy declared in *Lawrence* that gays are "entitled to respect for their private lives" while Justice Antonin Scalia complained that the decision indicated that the Court had "largely signed on to the so-called homosexual agenda" (Faderman 2015).

In 2000, the Supreme Court hurt the gay rights movement when it ruled 5–4 that the Boy Scouts organization had a constitutional right to exclude gay members because opposition to homosexuality was part of the organization's message. The Court clearly stated in its ruling that it was not endorsing this view but rather supporting the organization's right to hold this position and to limit participation based on it. Despite its court victory, the Boy Scouts eventually rescinded the ban in 2013 and began welcoming transgender boys in 2017.

Issues involving gays and lesbians have always been present, but because of advocacy efforts, political leaders and the courts are advancing the concerns. In 1993, President Bill Clinton, under pressure from the gay community, reviewed the prohibition on homosexuals serving in the military. However, he encountered even greater pressure from opponents and eventually compromised in 1994 with the "Don't Ask, Don't Tell" policy. The policy allowed lesbians and gay men to continue to serve in the military as long as they kept their homosexuality secret. Finally, in the face of court action likely to overturn the policy, "Don't Ask, Don't Tell" officially ended in 2011, allowing openly gay and lesbians to serve in the military for the first time.

The most vocal recent debate was over whether gay and lesbian couples should be able to get married. Finally in 2013, by a 5–4 vote in *United States v. Windsor*, the Supreme Court in effect declared that the federal government must recognize gay marriage in the 12 states where it was legal at the time. An analysis of Social Security records revealed that by 2014, there were at least 183,0000 legal same-sex marriages (Bui 2016).

The change in acceptance of different gender and sexual identities has been striking over the past two generations. In 1970 only one in ten people in a national survey were prepared to say that same-sex relations were "not wrong at all." Now, over 80 percent say that members of the LGBT community should have equal job rights. Still, in 2016, about a quarter of non-LGBT people felt uncomfortable having LGBT people at their place of worship, as family members, or as their child's teacher (Fetner 2016; GLAAD 2017)

We have used assimilation throughout this book to describe the process by which individuals forsake their own heritage to become a part of a different culture. Assimilation has emerged as an issue in the gay community. Some argue that promoting marriage equality is merely trying to assimilate or to become like the oppressors by adopting their social conventions. In addition, some argue that these efforts siphon energy away from those already marginalized in the LGBT community, such as people of color, transgender people, and those who prefer other forms of intimacy over marriage (Bernstein and Taylor 2013).

In the book's final Spectrum of Intergroup Relations (Figure 17.5) we summarize how aspects of these relationships, like assimilation, have been utilized throughout this textbook. Efforts to downplay overt expressions of homosexuality are yet another example of assimilation. Critics of assimilation argue that equal treatment is the real issue and should not be the result of conforming to the ways of the heterosexual-dominant society. The debate is unlikely to be resolved soon because full acceptance of LGBT people is far removed from today's social and political agenda. But this discussion repeats a pattern found with every subordinate group—how to maintain one's unique identity and become part of a multicultural society (Hartocullis 2006; Hequembourg and Arditi 1999).

Figure 17.5 Spectrum of Intergroup Relations

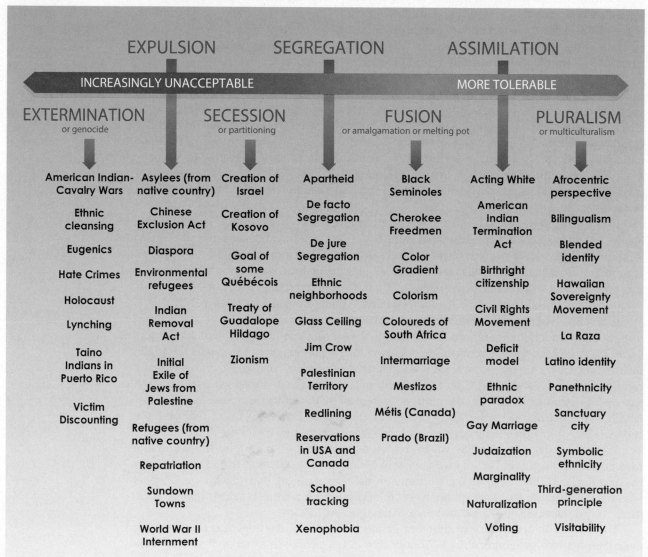

Conclusion

As the United States promotes racial, ethnic, and religious diversity, it also strives to impose universal criteria on employers, educators, and realtors so that subordinate racial and ethnic groups can participate fully in the larger society. In some instances, to bring about equality of results—not just equality of opportunity—programs have been developed to give competitive advantages to women and minority men. Only more recently have similar strides been made on behalf of people with disabilities. These latest answers to social inequality have provoked much controversy over how to achieve the admirable goal of a multiracial, multiethnic society, undifferentiated in opportunity and rewards.

The huge quantity of information gathered by the census documents the racial and ethnic diversity of the entire nation. As we see in Figure 17.6, driving the growth of the diverse population is the growing proportion of schoolchildren who are Latino, African American, Asian Pacific American, or Native American.

Relations among racial, ethnic, or religious groups take two broad forms, as situations characterized by either consensus or conflict. Consensus prevails where assimilation or fusion of groups has been completed. Consensus also prevails in a pluralistic society in the sense that members have agreed to respect differences between groups. By eliminating the contending group, extermination and expulsion also lead to a consensus society. In the study of intergroup relations, it is often easy to ignore conflict where there is a high degree of consensus because it is assumed that an orderly society has no problems. In some instances, however, this assumption is misleading. Through long periods of history, misery inflicted on a racial, ethnic, or religious group was judged to be appropriate, if not actually divinely inspired.

In recent history, harmonious relations among all racial, ethnic, and religious groups have been more accepted as a worthy goal. The struggle against oppression and inequality is not new. It dates back at least to the revolutions in England, France, and the American colonies in the seventeenth and eighteenth centuries. The twentieth century was unique in the extension of equality to the less-privileged groups, many members of which are racial and ethnic minorities. Nonetheless, conflict along racial and ethnic lines is especially bitter now because it evokes memories of slavery, colonial oppression, and overt discrimination. Today's African Americans are much more aware of slavery than contemporary poor people are of seventeenth-century debtors' prisons.

Unquestionably, the struggle for justice among racial and ethnic groups has not completely met its goals. While the election of Barack Obama as president was historic and worthy of the global celebration it received a decade ago, it does not reflect the broad movement of members of racial and ethnic groups into positions of power in the private and public sectors.

Figure 17.6 Changes in Minority School Population, 1995 and 2022

NOTE: Data for public elementary and secondary schools. Race categories exclude Hispanics.

SOURCE: Hussar and Bailey 2014:33; National Center for Education Statistics 2013: Table 44.

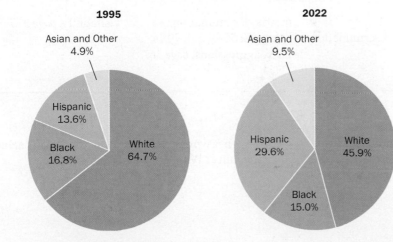

Even gender equality seems to have stalled. Many noted and were puzzled by the fact that the number of female CEOs among Fortune 500 companies actually declined in 2016. As evidenced by very public racist and sexist remarks, many people are still committed to oppression. Such oppression leads to the dehumanization of both the subordinated individual and the oppressor.

Growth in equal rights movements and self-determination for developing countries largely populated by non-White people has moved the world onto a course to confront social inequality that seems irreversible. The old ethnic battle lines now renewed in the Darfur region of Sudan, Kenya, the Kurdish areas of Turkey and Iraq, the Georgia Republic, and Chechnya in Russia have only added to the tensions.

Self-determination, whether for groups or individuals, often is impossible in societies as they are currently structured. Bringing about social equality, therefore, will entail significant changes in existing institutions. Because such changes are not likely to come about with everyone's willing cooperation, the social costs will be high. However, if there is a trend in racial and ethnic relations in the world today, it is the growing belief that the social costs, however high, must be paid to achieve self-determination.

It is naive to foresee a world of societies in which one person equals one vote and all are accepted without regard to race, ethnicity, religion, gender, age, disability status, or sexual orientation. It is equally unlikely to expect a society, let alone a world, that is without a privileged class or prestigious jobholders. Contact between different peoples, as we have seen numerous times, precedes conflict. Contact also may initiate mutual understanding, appreciation, and respect.

Summary of Learning Objectives

17.1 Explain how the aged are a social minority.

1. The elderly in the United States are growing in numbers and proportions, with a growing proportion being people of color. Although many gains have been made in ensuring the health and safety of older Americans, those who choose to continue to work often face ageism. The Age Discrimination in Employment Act is intended to prevent discrimination against older employees.

17.2 Summarize the experience of people with disabilities.

2. Advocacy efforts by people with disabilities and others on their behalf have a long history.

A major milestone was achieved in 1990 with the passage of the Americans with Disabilities Act.

17.3 Identify the equality issues facing the LGBT community.

3. Members of the LGBT community have been working to achieve equality, and some progress has been made. Issues such as gay marriage dominate newspaper coverage, but day-to-day concerns such as discrimination in employment often remain unaddressed.

Key Terms

ageism, *page 366*
disability, *page 371*
homophobia, *page 378*

intersectionality, *page 365*
institutional discrimination, *page 374*

matrix of domination, *page 365*
microaggressions, *page 367*

visitability, *page 375*

Review Questions

1. In what ways are the aged stereotyped, and how do these stereotypes affect their quality of life?

2. What common challenges face people with disabilities?

3. In what ways have gay men and lesbians achieved equality? What challenges remain?

Critical Thinking

1. Sociologists use the term *master status* to describe a status that dominates all other statuses and thereby determines a person's general position in society. To what degree can that term be applied to the three groups considered in this chapter?

2. The media—in advertisements, dramas, and situation comedies—portray life in society. What are some examples, both positive and negative, of how older adults, people with disabilities, and gays and lesbians are presented in the media that you have seen? In what ways are these groups stereotyped?

3. How might advances in technology, including innovations for the home and electronic technologies, have a unique effect on each of the groups discussed in this chapter trying to overcome exclusion?

4. How do policymakers trying to bring about change use the model of "half full" and "half empty"—either to argue for change on behalf of minorities or to use the same concepts to maintain that the status quo is adequate for addressing issues of social inequality?

Glossary

abolitionists Whites and free Blacks who favored the end of slavery. (163)

absolute deprivation The minimum level of subsistence below which families or individuals should not be expected to exist. (56)

acting White Taking school seriously and accepting the authority of teachers and administrators. (184)

affirmative action Positive efforts to recruit subordinate group members, including women, for jobs, promotions, and educational opportunities. (68)

Afrocentric perspective An emphasis on the customs of African cultures and how they have pervaded the history, culture, and behavior of Blacks in the United States and around the world. (26)

ageism Prejudice and discrimination against the elderly. (366)

amalgamation The process by which a dominant group and a subordinate group combine through intermarriage to form a new group. (23)

anti-Semitism Anti-Jewish prejudice or discrimination. (37)

apartheid The policy of the South African government intended to maintain separation of Blacks, Coloureds, and Asians from the dominant Whites. (358)

apartheid schools All-Black schools. (183)

arranged marriage When one's marital partner is chosen by others and the relationship is not based on any preexisting mutual attraction. (268)

assimilation The process by which a subordinate individual or group takes on the characteristics of the dominant group. (24)

asylees Foreigners who have already entered the United States and now seek protection because of persecution or a well-founded fear of persecution. (98)

authoritarian personality A psychological construct of a personality type likely to be prejudiced and to use others as scapegoats. (37)

bamboo ceiling The barrier that talented Asian Pacific Americans face because of resentment and intolerance directed toward them. (266)

bilingual education A program designed to allow students to learn academic concepts in their native language while they learn a second language. (90)

bilingualism The use of two or more languages in places of work or education and the treatment of each language as legitimate. (90)

biological race The mistaken notion of a genetically isolated human group. (8)

blaming the victim Portraying the problems of racial and ethnic minorities as their fault rather than recognizing society's responsibilities. (15)

blended identity Self-image and worldview that is a combination of religious faith, cultural background based on nationality, and current residency. (243)

blood quantum A standard of ancestry based on the degree of American Indian or Alaska Native blood from a federally recognized tribe. (147)

Bogardus scale Technique to measure social distance toward different racial and ethnic groups. (47)

borderlands The area of a common culture along the border between Mexico and the United States. (225)

bracero Contracted Mexican laborers brought to the United States during World War II. (222)

brain drain Immigration to the United States of skilled workers, professionals, and technicians who are desperately needed in their home countries. (86)

casual Islamophobia Anti-Islam statements previously regarded as extreme but now becoming accepted by large portions of the general public. (249)

chain immigration Immigrants sponsor several other immigrants who, on their arrival, may sponsor still more. (79)

civil disobedience A tactic promoted by Martin Luther King, Jr., based on the belief that people have the right to disobey unjust laws under certain circumstances. (172)

civil religion The religious dimension in American life that merges the state with sacred beliefs. (123)

class As defined by Max Weber, people who share similar levels of wealth. (13)

colonialism A foreign power's maintenance of political, social, economic, and cultural dominance over people for an extended period. (18)

color-blind racism Use of race-neutral principles to defend the racially unequal status quo. (41)

colorism The ranking or judging of individuals based on skin tone. (6)

color gradient The placement of people on a continuum from light to dark skin color rather than in distinct racial groupings by skin color. (204)

conflict perspective A sociological approach that assumes that the social structure is best understood in terms of conflict or tension between competing groups. (15)

contact hypothesis An interactionist perspective stating that intergroup contact between people of equal status in noncompetitive circumstances will reduce prejudice. (48)

creationists People who support a literal interpretation of the biblical book of Genesis on the origins of the universe and argue that evolution should not be presented as established scientific thought. (128)

curanderismo Hispanic folk medicine. (227)

daughter effect Phenomenon in which fathers who have daughters are more likely to support women's equality. (327)

de facto segregation Segregation that is the result of residential patterns. (183)

deficit model of ethnic identity One's ethnicity is viewed by others as a factor of subtracting away the characteristics corresponding to some ideal ethnic type. (242)

de jure segregation Children assigned to schools specifically to maintain racially separated schools. (171)

denomination A large, organized religion not officially linked with the state or government. (120)

Diaspora The exile of Jews from Palestine. (354)

differential justice Whites being dealt with more leniently than Blacks, whether at the time of arrest, indictment, conviction, sentencing, or parole. (193)

disability Reduced ability to perform tasks one would normally do at a given stage in life. (371)

discrimination The denial of opportunities and equal rights to individuals and groups because of prejudice or for other arbitrary reasons. (34)

dysfunction An element of society that may disrupt a social system or decrease its stability. (14)

emigration Leaving a country to settle in another. (17)

environmental justice Efforts to ensure that hazardous substances are controlled so that all communities receive protection regardless of race or socioeconomic circumstances. (67)

environmental refugees People forced to leave their communities because of natural disasters or the effects of climate change and global warming. (100)

ethnic cleansing Forced deportation of people accompanied by systematic violence. (20)

ethnic group A group set apart from others because of its members' national origin or distinctive cultural patterns. (6)

ethnic paradox The maintenance of one's ethnic ties in a way that can assist with assimilation in larger society. (107)

ethnocentrism The tendency to assume that one's culture and way of life are superior to all others. (32)

ethnonational conflicts Conflicts between ethnic, racial, religious, and linguistic groups within nations, which replace conflicts between nations. (345)

ethnophaulisms Ethnic or racial slurs, including derisive nicknames. (33)

eugenics The belief that human genetic quality can be improved through selective breeding. (9)

Eurocentrism Emphasizing the customs and traditions of European culture. (26)

evacuees Japanese Americans interned in camps for the duration of World War II. (291)

exploitation theory A Marxist theory that views racial subordination in the United States as a manifestation of the class system inherent in capitalism. (37)

familism Pride and closeness in the family that result in placing family obligation and loyalty before individual needs. (288)

feminine mystique Society's view of a woman as only her children's mother and her husband's wife. (327)

feminism An ideology establishing equal rights for women. (328)

feminization of poverty The trend since 1970 in which women account for a growing proportion of those who live below the poverty line. (335)

fish-ins Native American tribes' protests over government interference with their traditional rights to fish as they like. (143)

fringe-of-values theory Behavior that is on the border of conduct that a society regards as proper and is often carried out by subordinate groups, subjecting those groups to negative sanctions. (306)

functionalist perspective A sociological approach emphasizing how parts of a society are structured to maintain its stability. (14)

fusion A minority and a majority group combining to form a new group. (23)

gender identity How people see themselves as male, female, or something else. (324)

gender roles Expectations regarding the proper behavior, attitudes, and activities of males and females. (324)

genocide The deliberate, systematic killing of an entire people or nation. (19)

glass ceiling The barrier that blocks the promotion of a qualified worker because of gender or minority membership. (334)

glass escalator The male advantage experienced in occupations dominated by women. (75)

glass wall A barrier to moving laterally in a business to positions that are more likely to lead to upward mobility. (75)

globalization Worldwide integration of government policies, cultures, social movements, and financial markets through trade, movements of people, and the exchange of ideas. (17)

gook syndrome David Riesman's phrase describing Americans' tendency to stereotype Asians and to regard them as all alike and undesirable. (274)

hajj Pilgrimage to Mecca to be completed at least once in a Muslim's lifetime. (245)

halakha Jewish laws covering obligations and duties. (317)

Haoles Native Hawaiians' term for Caucasians. (276)

hate crime Criminal offense committed because of the offender's bias against a race, religion, ethnic or national origin group, or sexual orientation group. (58)

hijab A variety of garments that allow Muslim women to follow the guidelines of modest dress. (252)

Holocaust The state-sponsored systematic persecution and annihilation of European Jewry by Nazi Germany and its collaborators. (20)

Holocaust revisionists People who deny the Nazi effort to exterminate the Jews or who minimize the numbers killed. (307)

hometown associations Nonprofit organizations that maintain close ties to immigrants' hometowns in Mexico and other Latin American countries. (226)

homophobia The fear of and prejudice toward homosexuals. (39)

hui kuan Chinese American benevolent associations organized on the basis of the district of the immigrant's origin in China. (285)

ilchomose The 1.5 generation of Korean Americans—those who immigrated into the United States as children. (271)

immigration Coming into a new country as a permanent resident. (17)

income Salaries, wages, and other money received. (61)

in-group virtues Proper behaviors by one's own group; these behaviors become unacceptable when practiced by outsiders (out-group vices). (307)

institutional discrimination A denial of opportunities and equal rights to individuals or groups resulting from the normal operations of a society. (59)

intelligence quotient (IQ) The ratio of a person's mental age (as computed by an IQ test) to his or her chronological age, multiplied by 100. (9)

intelligent design View that life is so complex that it must have been created by a higher intelligence. (128)

intersectionality The overlapping and interdependent system of advantage and disadvantage that positions people in society on the basis of race, class, gender, and other characteristics. (27)

Intifada The Palestinian uprising against Israeli authorities in the occupied territories. (356)

Islamophobia A range of negative feelings toward Muslims and their religion that ranges from generalized intolerance to hatred. (249)

Issei First-generation immigrants from Japan to the United States. (290)

jihad Struggle against the enemies of Allah, usually taken to mean one's own internal struggle. (245)

Jim Crow Southern laws passed in the late nineteenth century that kept Blacks in a subordinate position. (164)

Judaization The lessening importance of Judaism as a religion and the substitution of cultural traditions as the tie that binds Jews. (304)

kanaka maoli The "real" or "true people" of Hawai'i, that is, the Native Hawaiians. (276)

kashrut Laws pertaining to permissible (kosher) and forbidden foods and their preparation. (314)

Kibei Japanese Americans of the Nisei generation sent back to Japan for schooling and to have marriages arranged. (290)

kye Rotating credit system used by Korean Americans to subsidize the start-up costs of businesses. (272)

labeling theory A sociological approach introduced by Howard Becker that attempts to explain why certain people are viewed as deviants but others engaging in the same behavior are not. (15)

La Raza Literally meaning "the people," the term refers to the rich heritage of Mexican Americans; it is therefore used to denote a sense of pride among Mexican Americans today. (222)

life chances People's opportunities to provide themselves with material goods, positive living conditions, and favorable life experiences. (227)

maquiladoras Foreign-owned companies on the Mexican side of the border with the United States. (225)

marginality The status of being between two cultures at the same time, such as the status of Jewish immigrants in the United States. (13)

Marielitos People who arrived from Cuba in the third wave of Cuban immigration, most specifically those forcibly deported by way of Mariel Harbor. The term is generally reserved for refugees seen as especially undesirable. (211)

matrix of domination Cumulative impact of oppression because of race, gender, and class, as well as sexual orientation, religion, disability status, and age. (365)

medical apartheid The separate and unequal healthcare system in the United States that often has and continues to characterize healthcare for African Americans as well as Latinos. (195)

melting pot Diverse racial or ethnic groups or both, forming a new cultural entity. (23)

mestizo People in the Americas of mixed European (usually Spanish) and local indigenous ancestry. (345)

microaggressions Commonplace verbal indignities experienced daily by members of a minority group. (33)

migration A general term that describes any transfer of population. (17)

minority group A subordinate group whose members have significantly less control or power over their own lives than do the members of a dominant or majority group. (4)

mixed status Families in which one or more members are citizens and one or more members are noncitizens. (88)

model minority A group that, despite past prejudice and discrimination, succeeds economically, socially, and educationally without resorting to political or violent confrontations with Whites. (264)

mojados "Wetbacks"; derisive slang for Mexicans who enter illegally, supposedly by swimming across the Rio Grande. (222)

mommy tax Lower salaries women receive over their lifetime because they have children. (339)

mommy track An unofficial corporate career track for women who want to divide their attention between work and family. (334)

mulatto escape hatch Notion that Brazilians of mixed ancestry can move into high-status positions. (352)

nativism Beliefs and policies favoring native-born citizens over immigrants. (82)

naturalization Conferring of citizenship on a person after birth. (95)

neocolonialism Continuing dependence of former colonies on foreign countries. (230)

Neoricans Puerto Ricans who return to the island to settle after living on the U.S. mainland (also called Nuyoricans). (235)

Nisei Children born of immigrants from Japan. (290)

normative approach The view that prejudice is influenced by societal norms and situations that encourage or discourage the tolerance of minorities. (38)

occupational segregation The tendency for racial, ethnic, or gender groups to be employed in different occupations from one another. (92)

orientalism The simplistic view of the people and history of the Orient, with no recognition of change over time or the diversity within its many cultures. (239)

out-group vices In-group virtues that become unacceptable when practiced by outsiders. (307)

panethnicity The development of solidarity between ethnic subgroups as reflected in the terms *Hispanic* and *Asian American*. (11)

pan-Indianism Intertribal social movements in which several tribes, joined by political goals but not by kinship, unite in a common identity. (143)

pass laws Laws that controlled internal movement by non-Whites in South Africa. (358)

pay equity The same wages for different types of work that are judged to be comparable by such measures as employee knowledge, skills, effort, responsibility, and working conditions; also called comparable worth. (334)

Pentecostalism A religion similar in many respects to evangelical faiths that believes in the infusion of the Holy Spirit into services and in religious experiences such as faith healing. (210)

peoplehood Milton Gordon's term for a group with a shared feeling. (319)

pluralism Mutual respect for one another's culture, a respect that allows minorities to express their own culture without suffering prejudice or discrimination. (25)

powwows Native American gatherings of dancing, singing, music playing, and visiting, accompanied by competitions. (145)

prejudice A negative attitude toward an entire category of people, such as a racial or ethnic minority. (33)

principle of third-generation interest Marcus Hansen's contention that ethnic interest and awareness increase in the third generation, among the grandchildren of immigrants. (145)

Québécois The French-speaking people of the province of Quebec in Canada. (33)

racial formation A sociohistorical process by which racial categories are created, inhibited, transformed, and destroyed. (10)

racial group A group that is socially set apart because of obvious physical differences. (6)

racial profiling Any arbitrary police-initiated action based on race, ethnicity, or national origin rather than a person's behavior. (255)

racism A doctrine that one race is superior. (10)

redlining   The pattern of discrimination against people trying to buy homes in minority and racially changing neighborhoods. (64)

refugees   People living outside their country of citizenship for fear of political or religious persecution. (98)

relative deprivation   The conscious experience of a negative discrepancy between legitimate expectations and present actualities. (56)

religion   A unified system of sacred beliefs and practices that encompass elements beyond everyday life that inspire awe, respect, and even fear. (120)

remittances   The monies that immigrants return to their countries of origin. (93)

repatriation   The 1930s program of deporting Mexicans. (222)

resegregation   The physical separation of racial and ethnic groups reappearing after a period of relative integration. (21)

respectable bigotry   Attitudes linking a minority group with crime and characterizing its members as criminals. (115)

restrictive covenant   A private contract or agreement that discourages or prevents minority-group members from purchasing housing in a neighborhood. (170)

reverse discrimination   Actions that cause better-qualified White men to be passed over for women and minority men. (71)

riff-raff theory   Also called the rotten-apple theory; the belief that the riots of the 1960s were caused by discontented youths rather than by social and economic problems facing all African Americans. (175)

rising expectations   The increasing sense of frustration that legitimate needs are being blocked. (175)

sanctuary cities   Areas in which local law-enforcement officers do not actively hand over illegal immigrants to federal enforcement agents. (95)

Sansei   The children of the Nisei—that is, the grandchildren of the original immigrants from Japan. (290)

scapegoating theory   A person or group blamed irrationally for another person's or group's problems or difficulties. (306)

secessionist minority   Groups that reject assimilation and promote coexistence and pluralism. (127)

second shift   The double burden—work outside the home followed by childcare and housework—that is faced by many women and that few men share equitably. (338)

segmented assimilation   The outcome of immigrants and their descendants moving into different classes of the host society. (24)

segregation   The physical separation of two groups, often imposed on a subordinate group by the dominant group. (21)

self-fulfilling prophecy   The tendency to respond to and act on the basis of stereotypes, a predisposition that can lead one to validate false definitions. (16)

sexism   The ideology that one sex is superior to the other. (39)

sexual identity   Self-awareness of being romantically or sexually attracted to a defined group of people; also called *sexual orientation*. (324)

sexual harassment   Any unwanted and unwelcome sexual advances that interfere with a person's ability to perform a job and enjoy the benefits of a job. (335)

sharing economy   Online economic transactions that place buyers and sellers in direct peer-to-peer contact with no change in the ownership of goods and services; purchases can range from car rides to short-term accommodations. (65)

sinophobes   People with a fear of anything associated with China. (82)

slave codes   Laws that defined the low position held by slaves in the United States. (162)

slavery reparations   Act of making amends for the injustices of slavery. (166)

social distance   Tendency to approach or withdraw from a racial group. (47)

sociology   The systematic study of social behavior and human groups. (13)

sovereignty   Tribal self-rule. (146)

sovereignty movement   Effort by the indigenous peoples of Hawai'i to secure a measure of self-government and restoration of their lands. (277)

stereotypes   Unreliable, exaggerated generalizations about all members of a group that do not take individual differences into account. (16)

stratification   A structured ranking of entire groups of people that perpetuates unequal rewards and power in a society. (13)

suffragists   Women and men who worked successfully to gain women the right to vote. (326)

sundown towns   Communities in which non-Whites were systematically excluded from living. (161)

symbolic ethnicity   Herbert Gans's term that describes emphasis on ethnic food and ethnically associated political issues rather than deeper ties to one's heritage. (107)

tiger mother   A demanding mother who pushes her children to high levels of achievement following practices common in China and other parts of Asia. (288)

tongs   Chinese American secret associations. (285)

tracking   The practice of placing students in specific curriculum groups on the basis of test scores and other criteria. (184)

transnationals   Immigrants who sustain multiple social relationships that link their societies of origin and settlement. (97)

tsu   Clans established along family lines and forming a basis for social organization by Chinese Americans. (285)

two-state solution   An Israel and Palestine living side by side and recognized by the entire world community. (356)

underemployment   Working at a job for which the worker is overqualified, involuntary working part time instead of full time, or being intermittently employed. (189)

victim discounting   Tendency to view crime as less socially significant if the victim is viewed as less worthy. (194)

victimization surveys   Annual attempts to measure crime rates by interviewing ordinary citizens who may or may not have been crime victims. (193)

Viet Kieu   Vietnamese living abroad, such as in the United States. (274)

visible minorities   In Canada, persons other than Aboriginal or First Nation people who are non-White in racial background. (350)

visitability   Building private homes to be accessible for visitors with disabilities. (375)

wealth   An inclusive term encompassing all of a person's material assets, including land and other types of property. (61)

White primary   Legal provisions forbidding Black voting in election primaries; in one-party areas of the South, these laws effectively denied Blacks their right to select elected officials. (165)

White privilege   Rights or immunities granted as a particular benefit or favor for being White. (35)

world systems theory   A view of the global economic system as divided between nations that control wealth and those that provide natural resources and labor. (19)

xenophobia   The fear or hatred of strangers or foreigners. (82)

yellow peril   A term denoting a generalized prejudice toward Asian people and their customs. (265)

Yiddishkait   Jewishness. (316)

Yonsei   The fourth generation of Japanese Americans in the United States; the children of the Sansei. (290)

Zionism   Traditional Jewish religious yearning to return to the biblical homeland, now used to refer to support for the state of Israel. (310)

zoning laws   Legal provisions stipulating land use and the architectural design of housing, often used to keep racial minorities and low-income people out of suburban areas. (192)

References

Cyan color type denotes reference citations new to this fifteenth edition.

AARP. 2003. *AARP Home*. Accessed May 12, 2003, at http://www.aarp.org.

———. 2017. Letter on the American Health Care Act. March 17. Accessible at www.aarp.org.

Abbott, Andrew, and Ranier Egloff. 2008. The Polish Peasant in Oberlin and Chicago. The Intellectual Trajectory of W. I. Thomas. *American Sociologist*, 39: 217–258.

ABC Television. 2013. Arkansas Schools to Start Moment of Silence When Classes Begin. August 2. Accessed September 8, 2013, at http://www.4029tv.com.

Abdo, Geneive. 2004b. New Generation Lifting Muslims. *Chicago Tribune* (September 3): 1, 8.

Abdulrahim, Raja. 2009. UC Urged to Expand Ethnic Labels. *Los Angeles Times* (March 31): A4.

Abe, Yukiko. 2011. The Equal Employment Opportunity Law and Labor Force Behavior of Women in Japan. *Journal of the Japanese and International Economies*, 25 (March): 39–55.

Abel, Jaison R., and Richard Deitz. 2014. The Causes and Consequences of Puerto Rico's Declining Population. *Current Issues in Economics and Finance*, 20 (4).

Abrahamson, Alan, and Judy Pasternak. 1998. For U.S. Jews, Era of Plenty Takes Many Far from Roots. *Los Angeles Times* (April 20): A1, A10–11.

Abrahamson, Mark. 1996. *Urban Enclaves: Identity and Place in America*. New York: St. Martin's Press. Accessible at http://www.msnbc.msn.com/id/23690567/print/1/displaymode/1098.

Abu Dhabi Gallup. 2011. *Muslim Americans: Faith, Freedom, and the Future*. Accessible at http://www.gallup.com.

Acosta, Aidé. 2015. La Raza. In David J. Leonard and Carmen R. Lugo-Lugo (Eds.), *Latino History and Culture: An Encyclopedia*, pp. 279–280. New York: Routledge.

Adam, Barry D. 1995. *The Rise of a Gay and Lesbian Movement*, rev. ed. New York: Twayne.

Adler, Patricia A., Steven J. Kess, and Peter Adler. 1992. Socialization to Gender Role: Popularity Among Elementary School Boys and Girls. *Sociology of Education* (July), 65: 169–187.

Adorno, T. W., Else Frenkel-Brunswik, Daniel J. Levinson, and R. Nevitt Sanford. 1950. *The Authoritarian Personality*. New York: Wiley.

Aguirre, DeAnne, Leila Hoteit, Christine Rupp, and Karim Sabbagh. 2012. *Empowering the Third Billion: Women and the World of Work in 2012*. New York: Booz & Co.

Ajrouch, Kristine J. 2011. Correspondence with author. June 12.

Ajrouch, Kristine J., and Amancy Jamal. 2007. Assimilating to a White Identity: The Case of Arab Americans. *International Migration Review* (Winter): 860–879.

Akaka, Daniel. 2011. *Native Hawaiian Federal Recognition*. Accessed June 1, 2011, at http://Akaka.senate.gov/public/index.cfm?FuseAction=Issues.Home&issues=Akaka%20Bill&content_id=24#Akaka%20Bill.

Albrecht, Gary L. (ed.). 2005. *Encyclopedia of Disability*. Thousand Oaks, CA: Sage Publications.

Alexander, Michelle. 2012. *The New Jim Crow: Mass Incarceration in the Age of Colorblindness*, rev. ed. New York: The New Press.

Allport, Gordon W. 1979. *The Nature of Prejudice*, 25th anniversary ed. Reading, MA: Addison-Wesley.

Alvord, Valerie. 2000. Refugees' Success Breeds Pressure, Discrimination. *USA Today* (May 1): 74.

American Community Survey. 2009. *American Community Survey 2008*. Data released August 2009 and accessible at http://www.census.gov.

———. 2015b. 2010–2014 American Community Survey 5-Year Estimates. Accessible at www.census.gov.

———. 2016a. 2015 ACS 1-Year Estimates. Accessible at www.census.gov.

———. 2016b. 2015 American Community Survey 5-Year Estimates. Accessible at www.census.gov.

American Indian Higher Education Consortium. 2017. Home page. Accessible at www.aihec.org.

American Jewish Committee. 1965. *Mutual Savings Banks of New York City*. New York: American Jewish Committee.

———. 1966a. *Mutual Savings Banks: A Follow-Up Report*. New York: American Jewish Committee.

———. 1966b. *Patterns of Exclusion from the Executive Suite: Corporate Banking*. New York: American Jewish Committee.

———. 2005. *2005 Annual Survey of American-Jewish Opinion*. New York: American Jewish Committee.

———. 2010a. *2010 Annual Survey of American Jewish Opinion*. April 7. Accessible at http://www.ajc.org.

———. 2010b. *Fall 2010 Survey of American Jewish Opinion*. October 11. Accessible at http://www.ajc.org.

American Social and Economic Supplement. 2016. Current Population Survey (CPS) 2015 Annual Social and Economic (ASEC) Supplement. Accessible at www.census.gov.

Anderson, Elijah. 2011. *The Cosmopolitan Canopy: Race and Civility in Everyday Life*. New York: W. W. Norton and Company.

Anderson, Monica. 2015. 6 Key Findings about Black Immigration to the U.S. April 9. Accessible at www.pewresearch.org.

Anderson, Warwick. 2003. *The Cultivation of Whiteness: Science, Health and Racial Destiny in Australia*. New York: Perseus Books.

Angwin, Julia, and Terry Parris, Jr. 2016. Facebook Lets Advertisers Exclude Users by Race. *ProPublica* (October 28). Accessible at www.propublica.org.

Ansell, Amy E. 2008. Color Blindness. Pp. 320–322 in vol. 1, *Encyclopedia of Race, Ethnicity, and Society*, Richard T. Schaefer, ed. Thousand Oaks, CA: Sage.

Anti-Defamation League. 2015a. New ADL Poll Finds Dramatic Decline in Anti-Semitic Attitudes in France; Significant Drops in Germany and Belgium. June 30. Accessible at www.adl.org.

———. 2015b. What Is the Nation of Islam? November 1. Accessible at www.adl.org.

———. 2016. *Audit of Anti-Semitic Incidents, 2015*. Accessible at www.adl.org.

Applebome, Peter. 1996. 70 Years After Scopes Trial, Creation Debate Lives. *New York Times* (March 10): 1, 22.

Aptekar, Sofya. 2016. Celebrating New Citizens, Defining the Nation. *Contexts* 15 (Spring): 47-51.

Apuzzo, Matt, and Joseph Goldstein. 2014. New York Drops Unit That Spied Among Muslims. *New York Times* (April 16): A1, A3.

Aran, Kenneth, Herman Arthur, Ramon Colon, and Harvey Goldenberg. 1973. *Puerto Rican History and Culture: A Study Guide and Curriculum Outline*. New York: United Federation of Teachers.

Archibold, Randal C. 2007. A City's Violence Feeds on Black-Hispanic Rivalry. *New York Times* (January 17): A1, A15.

Archibold, Randal C., and Julia Preston. 2008. Homeland Security Stands by Its Fence. *New York Times* (May 21).

Arden, Harvey. 1975. The Pious Ones. *National Geographic* (August), 168: 276–298.

Arias, Elizabeth. 2015. United States Life Tables. 2011. *National Vital Statistics Reports*, 64 (September 22).

Arizona Republic, The. 2013. Cultures Blend Over Time. (March 6): B6.

Asante, Molefi Kete. 2007. *An Afrocentric Manifesto: Toward an African Renaissance*. Cambridge, UK: Polity.

———. 2008. Afrocentricity. Pp. 41–42 in vol. 1, *Encyclopedia of Race, Ethnicity, and Society*, Richard T. Schaefer, ed. Thousand Oaks, CA: Sage.

———. 2015. Book Review of *The Afrocentric Praxis of Teaching for Freedom: Connecting Culture to Learning. Journal of Black Studies*, 47 (1): 88–89.

Asi, Maryam, and Daniel Beaulieu. 2013. *Arab Households in the United States 2006–2010*. ACSBR/10-20. Accessible at http://www.census.gov.

Asian-American Coalition for Education. 2017. Homepage. Accessible at www.asianamericanforeducation.org.

Asian American Federation. 2008. *Revitalizing Chinatown Businesses: Challenges and Opportunities*. New York: Asian American Federation.

Asian American Foundation. 2016. *NYC's Economic Engine: Contributions and Challenges of Asian Small Businesses*. Accessible at www.aafny.org.

Aust, Scott. 2016. No. 1: Community Comes Together Following Foiled Attack Plot. *The Garden City Telegram* (December 30). Accessible at www.gctelegram.com.

Attwood, Bain. 2003. *Rights for Aborigines*. Crows Nest, Australia: Allen and Unwin.

Australian Bureau of Statistics. 2012a. *The Health and Welfare of Australia's Aboriginal and Torres Strait Islander Peoples*. December 19. Accessed September 2013, at http://www.abs.gov.au/ausstats/abs@nsf/mf/4704.0.

———. 2012b. *Experimental Estimates and Projections, Aboriginal and Torres Strait Islander Australians*. Accessed September 2013, at http://www.abs.gov.au/ausstats.

Avila, Oscar. 2003. Muslim Holiday Testing Schools. *Chicago Tribune* (November 24): 1, 16.

Awad, Nihad. 2015. May America Be True to Her Dream. July 4. Accessible at www.cair.com.

Bachelder, Kate. 2015. Harvard's Chinese Exclusion Act. *Wall Street Journal* (June 6): A9.

Bada, Xóchitl. 2014. *Mexican Hometown Associations in Chicagacán: From Local to Transnational Civic Engagement*. New Brunswick, NJ: Rutgers University Press.

———. 2016. Collective Remittances and Development in Rural Mexico: A View from Chicago's Mexican Hometown Associations. *Population, Space, and Place*, 22 (May): 343–355.

Badgett, M. V. Lee, and Heidi I. Hartmann. 1995. The Effectiveness of Equal Employment Opportunity Policies. Pp. 55–83 in *Economic Perspectives in Affirmative Action*, Margaret C. Simms, ed. Washington, DC: Joint Center for Political and Economic Studies.

Bagby, Ihsan. 2012. *The American Mosque 2011*. Washington, DC: Council on American-Islamic Relations.

Bahr, Howard M. 1972. An End to Invisibility. Pp. 404–412 in *Native Americans Today: Sociological Perspectives*, Howard M. Bahr, Bruce A. Chadwick, and Robert C. Day, eds. New York: Harper & Row.

Bailey, Stanley R. 2004. Group Dominance and the Myth of Racial Democracy: Antiracism Attitudes in Brazil. *American Sociological Review*, 69 (October): 728–747.

———. 2009a. Public Opinion on Nonwhite Underrepresentation and Racial Identity Politics in Brazil. *Latin American Politics and Society*, 51 (4): 69–99.

———. 2009b. *Legacies of Race: Identities, Attitudes, and Politics in Brazil*. Stanford, CA: Stanford University Press.

Bailey, Stanley R., and Michelle Péria. 2010. Racial Quotas and the Culture War in Brazilian Academia. *Sociology Compass*, 4 (8): 592–604.

Baker, Bryan C. 2009. *Trends in Naturalization Rates: 2008 Update*. Washington, DC: Department of Homeland Security.

Balderrama, Francisco E., and Raymond Rodriguez. 2006. *Decade of Betrayal: Mexican Repatriation in the 1930s*. Revised. Albuquerque: University of New Mexico Press.

Baldwin, Neil. 2001. *Henry Ford and the Jews: The Mass Production of Hate*. New York: Public Affairs.

Baltzell, E. Digby. 1964. *The Protestant Establishment: Aristocracy and Caste in America*. New York: Vintage Books.

Bamshad, Michael J., and Steve E. Olson. 2003. Does Race Exist? *Scientific American* (December): 78–85.

Banton, Michael. 2008. The Sociology of Ethnic Relations. *Ethnic and Racial Studies* (May): 1–19.

———. 2012. The Colour Line and the Colour Scale in the Twentieth century. *Ethnic and Racial Studies*, 35 (July): 1109–1131.

Barclay, William, Krishna Kumar, and Ruth P. Simms. 1976. *Racial Conflict, Discrimination, and Power: Historical and Contemporary Studies*. New York: AMS Press.

Barbery, Marcos. 2013. Slave Descendants Seek Equal Rights from Cherokee Nation. May 21. Accessible at www.salon.com.

Barnes, Jessica S., and Claudette L. Bennett. 2002. *The Asian Population: 2000*. Census Brief C2KBR/01-16. Washington, DC: U.S. Government Printing Office.

Barnett, Jessica C., and Marina S. Vornovitsky. 2016. Health Insurance Coverage in the United States: 2015. *Current Population Reports* P60-257(RV). Accessible at www.census.gov.

Barrett, James. 2016. "Yes, Obama's Really a Muslim," Claim Muslims …? *Daily Wire* (January 21). Accessible at www.dailywire.com.

Barron, Milton L. 1953. Minority Group Characteristics of the Aged in American Society. *Journal of Gerontology* (October), 8: 477–482.

Barry, Ellen. 2004. County Rescinds Vote. *Los Angeles Times* (March 19): A16.

Barry, Ellen, and Nida Najar. 2017. After the Shootings of Two Engineers, Indians Are Wary of Moving to the U.S. *New York Times* (February 27): A11.

Bash, Harry M. 2001. *If I'm So White, Why Ain't I Right? Some Methodological Misgivings on Taking Identity Ascriptions at Face Value*. Paper presented at the annual meeting of the Midwest Sociological Society, St. Louis.

Basken, Paul. 2007. A Year After Turmoil, Gallaudet Sees Progress and Problems. *Chronicle of Higher Education* (October 20), 54: A27.

Bates, Karen Grigsby. 2017. Race and Feminism: Women's March Recalls the Touchy History. January 21. Accessible at www.npr.org.

Baum, Geraldine. 1998. New Power of Women Recasts Judaism. *Los Angeles Times* (April 21): A1, A14, A15.

Ba-Yunus, Ilyas, and Kassim Kone. 2004. Muslim Americans: A Demographic Report. Pp. 299–322 in *Muslims' Place in the American Public Square*, Zahid H. Bukhari et al., eds. Walnut Creek, CA: Altamira Press.

Beaman, Jean. 2015. From Ferguson to France. *Contexts* (Winter): 65–67.

Bean, Frank D., and G. Stevens. 2003. *America's Newcomers and the Dynamics of Diversity*. New York: Russell Sage Foundation.

Beardstown CUSD 15. 2017. Illinois Report Card 2015–2016. Accessible at www.illinoisreportcard.com.

Bélanger, Alain, and Éric Caron Malenfant. 2005. Ethnocultural Diversity in Canada: Prospects for 2017. *Canadian Social Trends* (Winter).

Bell, Derrick. 1994. The Freedom of Employment Act. *The Nation* (May 23), 258: 708, 710–714.

Bell, Wendell. 1991. Colonialism and Internal Colonialism. Pp. 52–53 in *The Encyclopedic Dictionary of Sociology*, 4th ed., Richard Lachmann, ed. Guilford, CT: Dushkin Publishing Group.

Bellafante, Ginia. 2005. Young South Asians in America Embrace "Assisted" Marriages. *New York Times* (August 23): A1, A15.

Bellah, Robert. 1967. Civil Religion in America. *Daedalus* 96 (Winter): 1–21.

Belliard, Juan Carlos, and Johnny Ramirez-Johnson. 2005. Medical Pluralism in the Life of a Mexican Immigrant Woman. *Hispanic Journal of Behavioral Sciences* (August), 27: 267–285.

Belluck, Pam. 2009. New Hopes for Reform in Indian Health Care. *New York Times* (December 2): A1, A28.

Belson, Ken. 2013. Redskins' Name Change Remains Activist's Unfinished Business. *New York Times* (October 10): A1, B16.

Belt, Don. 2002. The World of Islam. *National Geographic* (January): 76–85.

Bem, Sandra L., and Daryl J. Bem. 1970. Case Study of a Nonconscious Ideology: Training the Woman to Know Her Place. Pp. 89–99 in *Beliefs, Attitudes, and Human Affairs*, Daryl J. Bem, ed. Belmont, CA: Brooks/Cole.

Bennett, Vivienne S. 1995. Gender, Class, and Water: Women and the Politics of Water Service in Monterrey, Mexico. *Latin American Perspective* (September), 22: 76–99.

Bennett, Vivienne S. Dávila-Poblete, and M. N. Rico, eds. 2005. *Opposing Currents: The Politics of Water and Gender in Latin America.* Pittsburgh: University of Pittsburgh Press.

Berger, Joseph. 2008. Salvadorans, Building Their Own Cultural Bridge. *New York Times* (May 4).

———. 2015. Settlement over Anti-Semitic Bullying at Pine Bush Central Schools Is Approved. *New York Times* (July 9). Accessible at www.nytimes.com.

Berger, Ronald J. 2010 Jewish Americans and the Holocaust. *Contexts* (Winter): 40–45.

Bergman Institute. 2011. *FAQs on American Jews: Intermarriage Data.* May 11. Accessible at http://www.jewishdatabank.org.

Berlin, Ira. 2010. *The Making of African America: The Four Great Migrations.* New York: Viking Press.

Bernard, Tara Siegel. 2015. How to Help in a Global Refugee Crisis. *New York Times* (December 25). Accessible at www.nytimes.com.

———. 2017. How You Can Help Refugees Around the World. *New York Times* (February 17). Accessible at www.nytimes.com.

Bernstein, Mary, and Verta Taylor, eds. 2013. *The Marrying Kind?* Minneapolis: University of Minnesota Press.

Biagas, Jr., David E., and Alison J. Bianchi. 2015. The Latin Americanization Thesis: An Exception States Approach. *Social Forces,* 94 (March): 1335–1358.

Bialik, Kristen. 2017. Key Facts About Race and Marriage, 50 Years After Loving v. Virginia. June 12. Accessible at www.pewresearch. org.

Bigelow, Rebecca. 1992. Certain Inalienable Rights. *Friends Journal* (November), 38: 6–8.

Bilefsky, Dan. 2013. Roma Say Inquiries on Children Fan a Backlash. *International New York Times* (October 26): 1–2.

Bilker, Molly. 2016. New Poll by Cronkite News, Univision News, and The Dallas Morning News Shows Strong Sense of Community on Both Sides of the U.S.-Mexico Border. July 17. NPR News [Phoenix]. Accessible at https://cronkitenews.azpbs.org/2016/07/17/border-poll-overview.

Bjerk, David. 2008. Glass Ceilings or Sticky Floors? Statistical Discrimination in a Dynamic Model of Hiring and Promotion. *The Economic Journal,* 118 (530): 961–982.

Blackfeet Reservation Development Fund. 2006. *The Facts v. the Brochure.* Blackfeet Restoration.

Blackstock, Nelson. 1976. *COINTELPRO: The FBI's Secret War on Political Freedom.* New York: Vintage Press.

Blas, Lorena. 2016. Niche Cable Networks Target Diverse Audiences. *USA Today* (November 2): 3D.

Blazak, Randy. 2011. Isn't Every Crime a Hate Crime? The Case for Hate Crime Laws. *Sociology Compass,* 5 (4): 244–255.

Blee, Kathleen. 2015. Manufacturing Fear: Muslim Americans and the Politics of Terrorism. *Contemporary Sociology,* 45 (1): 6–9.

Bloom, Leonard. 1971. *The Social Psychology of Race Relations.* Cambridge, MA: Schenkman Publishing.

Blow, Charles M. 2010. Abortion's New Battle Lines. *New York Times* (May 1), A19.

Bobo, Lawrence. 2013. The Antinomes of Racial Change. *DuBois Review,* 10 (1): 1–5.

Bobo, Lawrence, and Mia Tuan. 2006. *Prejudices in Politics: Group Position, Public Opinion, and the Wisconsin Treaty Rights Dispute.* Cambridge, MA: Harvard University Press.

Bogardus, Emory. 1968. Comparing Racial Distance in Ethiopia, South Africa, and the United States. *Sociology and Social Research,* 52 (January): 149–156.

Bohmer, Susanne, and Kayleen V. Oka. 2007. Teaching Affirmative Action: An Opportunity to Apply, Segregate, and Reinforce Sociological Concepts. *Teaching Sociology* (October), 35: 334–349.

Bonilla-Silva, Eduardo. 1996. Rethinking Racism: Toward a Structural Interpretation. *American Sociological Review* (June), 62: 465–480.

———. 2002. The Linguistics of Color Blind Racism: How to Talk Nasty About Blacks Without Sounding Racist. *Critical Sociology,* 28 (1–2): 41–64.

———. 2006. *Racism Without Racists.* 2nd ed. Lanham, MD: Rowman & Littlefield.

———. 2012. The Invisible Weight of Whiteness: The Racial Grammar of Everyday Life in Contemporary America. *Ethnic and Racial Studies* (February), 35: 173–194.

Bonilla-Silva, Eduardo, and David Dietrich. 2011. The Sweet Enchantment of Color-Blind Racism in Obamerica. *The ANNALS of the American Academy of Political and Social Science* (March), 634: 190–206.

Bonilla-Silva, Eduardo, and David G. Embrick. 2007. "Every Place Has a Ghetto…" The Significance of Whites' Social and Residential Segregation. *Symbolic Interaction,* 30 (3): 323–345.

Bonilla-Silva, Eduardo, and David G. Embrick, with Louise Seamster. 2011. The Sweet Enchantment of Color Blindness in Black Face: Explaining the "Miracle," Debating the Politics, and Suggesting a Way for Hope to be "For Real" in America. *Political Power and Social Theory* (22): 139–175.

Bonus, Rick. 2000. *Locating Filipino Americans: Ethnicity and the Cultural Politics of Space.* Philadelphia, PA: Temple University Press.

Bork, Robert H. 1995. What to Do About the First Amendment. *Commentary* (February), 99: 23–29.

Bositis, David A. 1996. The Farrakhan Factor. *Washington Post National Weekly Edition* (December 16), 14: 24.

Bourcier, Nicolas. 2012. Brazil Tries to Face Its "Cordial" Racism. *The Guardian Weekly* (October 26): 28.

Bourmont, Martin de. 2017. For Roma in France, Education Is an Elusive Path to Integration. *New York Times* (February 10). Accessible at www.nytimes.com/2017/02/09/world/europe/for-roma-in-france-education-is-an-elusive-path-to-integration.html.

Bowman, Tom. 1998. Evangelicals Allege Bias in U.S. Navy, Marine Chaplain Corps. *Baltimore Sun,* 23 (August): A12.

Bowser, Benjamin, and Raymond G. Hunt, eds. 1996. *Impacts of Racism on White Americans.* Beverly Hills, CA: Sage Publications.

Brannon, Ruth. 1995. The Use of the Concept of Disability Culture: A Historian's View. *Disability Studies Quarterly* (Fall), 15: 3–15.

Brault, Matthew W. 2012. Americans with Disabilities: 2010. *Household Economic Studies* (July). Accessible at http://www.census.gov.

Brennan Center. 2006. *Citizens Without Proof.* November. New York: Brennan Center for Justice at NYU School of Law.

———. 2013. *Election 2012 Laws Roundup.* Accessed January 13, 2013, at http://www.brennancenter.org.

Brennan, Christopher. 2017. Black 15-Year-Old Wins Essay Contest on White Privilege in Affluent Connecticut Town. *New York Daily News* (April 6). Accessible at www.nydailynews.com.

Brittingham, Angela, and G. Patricia de la Cruz. 2005. We the People of Arab Ancestry in the United States. CENSR-21. Washington, DC: U.S. Government Printing Office.

Bromwich, Jonah Engel. 2016. Muslims Denounce Talk of Japanese Internment as "Precedent" for Registry. *New York Times* (November 10): A18.

Brown, Hana, and Jennifer A. Jones. 2015. Rethinking Panethnicity and the Race-Immigration Divide: An Ethnoracialization Model of Group Formation. *Sociology of Race and Ethnicity,* 1 (1): 181–191.

Browne, Juliet. 2013. *Spirit of Black Paris.* Accessible at http://-spiritof-blackparis.blogspot.com.

Brown, Patricia Leigh. 2009. Invisible Immigrants, Old and Left with "Nobody to Talk To." *New York Times* (April 3): A1, A10.

Brown, Ryan Lenora. 2015. Nigeria's Export—Fervent Christianity. *Christian Science Monitor* (September 28): 21–23.

Browne, Mark. 2017. Experts Explore Feasibility of Using Remittances to Fund U.S.-Mexico Border Wall. January 19. Accessible at www.cnsnews.com.

Browning, Christopher R., Catherine A. Calder, John L. Ford, Bethany Boettner, Anna L. Smith, and Dana Hayne. 2017. Understanding Racial Differences in Exposure to Violent Areas: Integrating Survey,

Smartphone, and Administrative Data Resources. *Annals of the American Academy of Political and Social Sciences,* 669 (January): 41–62.

Brulliard, Karin. 2006. A Proper Goodbye: Funeral Homes Learn Immigrants' Traditions. *Washington Post National Weekly Edition* (May 7): 31.

Bruinius, Harry. 2016. Asian-Americans Rush to Cop's Aid. *Christian Science Monitor Weekly* (March 7): 10–11.

———. 2017. What's the Same, What's Different. *Christian Science Monitor Weekly* (February 27): 10–11.

Buchanan, Angela B., Nora G. Albert, and Daniel Beaulieu. 2010. *The Population with Haitian Ancestry in the United States: 2009.* ACSR/09-18. Accessible at http://www.census.gov.

Buchholz, Barbara Ballinger. 2003. Expanded Access. *Chicago Tribune* (January 26): sect. 16, 1R, 5R.

Buck, Stuart. 2011. *Acting White: The Ironic Legacy of Desegregation.* New Haven: Yale University Press.

Budig, Michelle J. 2002. Male Advantage and the Gender Composition of Jobs: Who Rides the Glass Escalator? *Social Problems,* 49 (2): 258–277.

Budig, Michelle J., and Joya Misra. 2010. How Care-Work Employment Shapes Earnings in Cross-National Perspective. *International Labour Review,* 149: 441–460.

Bui, Quoctrung. 2016. The Most Detailed Map of Gay Marriage in America. *New York Times* (September 15): A3.

Bukowczyk, John J. 2007. *A History of Polish Americans.* New Brunswick, NJ: Transaction Books.

Bureau of the Census. 1951. *Statistical Abstract of the United States 1951.* Accessible at http://www2.census.gov/prod2/statcomp/documents/1951-01.pdf.

———. 1981. *Statistical Abstract of the United States 1981.* Accessible at http://www2.census.gov/prod2/statcomp/documents.

———. 1984. *Statistical Abstract of the United States 1984.* Accessible at http://www2.census.gov/prod2/statcomp/documents.

———. 1996. *Statistical Abstract of the United States 1996.* Accessible at http://www2.census.gov/prod2/statcomp/documents.

———. 2007a. *The American Community Survey—Asians: 2004.* ACS-05. Washington, DC: U.S. Government Printing Office.

———. 2007b. *The American Community—Pacific Islanders: 2004.* ACS-06. Washington, DC: U.S. Government Printing Office.

———. 2008. *National Population Projections.* Accessible at http://www.census.gov/population/www/projections/summarytables.html.

———. 2009a. *Asian and Hispanic Children More Likely to Dine with Their Parents.* March 4. Accessed March 10, 2009, at http://www.census.gov/Press-Release/www/releases/archives/children/013383.html.

———. 2009b. *Irish-American Heritage Month (March) and St. Patrick's Day (March 17th): 2009.* Washington, DC: U.S. Census Bureau.

———. 2010a. *Statistical Abstract of the United States, 2011.* Washington, DC: U.S. Government Printing Office.

———. 2011a. *Statistical Abstract of the United States: 2012.* Accessible at http://www.census.gov.

———. 2011b. *Irish-American Heritage Month (March) and St. Patrick's Day (March 17): 2011.* Census Brief CB11-FF, 03, January 13.

———. 2011d. *Educational Attainment in the United States: 2010.* Accessible at http://www.census.gov/hhes/socdemo/education/data/cps/2010/tables.html.

———. 2011e. *2010 Center of Population.* Accessible at http://2010.census.gov/news/pdf/03242011_pressbrf_slides230pm.pdf.

———. 2012c. *U.S. Census Bureau Projections Show a Slower Growing, Older, More Diverse Nation a Half Century from Now.* News Release December 12. Accessible at http://www.census.gov.

———. 2012d. *Most Children Younger Than Age 1 Are Minorities, Census Bureau Reports.* May 17. Accessible at http://www.census.gov/newsroom/releases/archives/population/cb12-90.html.

———. 2014a. Ten of the Largest Native North American Languages by Number of Speakers Age 5 and Older in the U.S. Accessible at www.census.gov.

———. 2015a. Detailed Languages Spoken at Home and Ability to Speak English for the Population 5 Years and Over: 2009-2013. October 2015. Accessible at www.census.gov.

———. 2016c. Hello, My Name Is. December 15. Accessible at www.census.gov.

———. 2016f. *America's Family and Living Arrangements, 2016.* Accessible at www.census.gov.

———. 2016i. CPS Income Tables. Accessible at www.census.gov.

———. 2016n. American Indian and Alaska Native Heritage Month: November 2016. November 2. Accessible at www.census.gov.

———. 2016r. *2015 American Community Survey 1-Year Estimates.* Accessible at www.census.gov.

———. 2016v. Electorate Profiles: Selected Characteristics of the Citizen. 18 and Older Populations. October 28. Accessible at www.census.gov.

———. 2017b. Quick Facts: United States and Puerto Rico. February 3. Accessible at www.census.govquickfacts/tablePST045216/00 and /72.

———. 2017c. Educational Attainment in the United States: 2016. March 2017. Accessible at www.census.gov.

Bureau of Indian Affairs. 1986. *American Indians Today: Answers to Your Questions.* Washington, DC: U.S. Government Printing Office.

———. 2005. *American Indian Population and Labor Force Report.* Washington, DC: BIA, Office of Indian Services.

———. 2017. Certificate of Degree of Indian or Alaska Native Blood Instructions. Expiration Date December 31, 2017. Accessible at www.bia.gov.

Bureau of Labor Statistics. 2004. *Time-Use Survey—First Results Announced by BLS.* News September 14. Accessible at http://www.bls.gov/tus/.

———. 2016a. Labor Force Statistics from the Current Population Reports. Accessible at www.bls.gov.

———. 2016b. American Time Use Survey—2015 Results. June 24. Accessible at www.bls.gov.

———. 2017a. Employment Status of the Civilian Population by Race, Sex, and Age. Accessible at www.bls.gov.

———. 2017b. Household Data, Annual Averages, Table 39. February 18. Accessible at www.bls.gov.

Burgess, Melinda, Karen E. Dill, S. Paul Stermer, Stephen R. Burgess, and Brian P. Brown. 2011. Playing with Prejudice: The Prevalence and Consequences of Racial Stereotypes in Video Games. *Media Psychology,* 14: 289–311.

Burgdorf, Robert L., Jr. 2005. Americans with Disabilities Act of 1990 (United States). Pp. 93–101 in Gary Albrecht, ed., *Encyclopedia of Disability.* Thousand Oaks, CA: Sage.

Butler, Robert N. 1990. A Disease Called Ageism. *Journal of the American Geriatrics Society* (February), 38: 178–180.

Byker, Tanya. 2016. The Opt-Out Continuation: Education, Work, and Motherhood from 1984 to 2012. *The Russell Sage Foundation Journal of the Social Sciences,* 2 (4): 24–70.

Cainkar, Louise. 2006. Immigrants from the Arab World. Pp. 182–196 in *The New Chicago,* John P. Koval et al., eds. Philadelphia: Temple University Press.

Cal, Weiyl, and Scott Clement. 2016. What Americans Think About Feminism Today. *Washington Post* (January 26). Accessible at www.washingtonpost.com.

Calavita, Kitty. 2007. Immigration Law, Race, and Identity. *Annual Reviews of Law and Social Sciences,* 3: 1–20.

Callahan, Rebecca M., and Patricia C. Gándara (eds.). The Bilingual Advantage: Language, Literacy, and the U.S. Labor Market. September 17. Los Angeles: UCLA Civil Rights Project. Accessible at www.civilrightsproject.ucla.edu.

Camarillo, Albert. 1993. Latin Americans: Mexican Americans and Central Americans. Pp. 855–872 in *Encyclopedia of American Social History,* Mary Koplec Coyton, Elliot J. Gorn, and Peter W. Williams, eds. New York: Charles Scribner.

Camarota, Steven A. 2007a. *Immigrants in the United States, 2007: A Profile of America's Foreign-Born Population.* Washington, DC: Center for Immigrant Statistics.

Cameron, Darla. 2017. How Sanctuary Cities Work, and How Trump's Executive Order Might Affect Them. *Washington Post* (January 25). Accessible at www.washingtonpost.com.

Campbell, Alexia Fernández. 2016. The Truth about Undocumented Immigrants and Taxes. *The Atlantic* (September 12). Accessible at www.theatlantic.com.

Campion, Siah. 2013. Interview. September. Montello WI.

Campoy, Ana. 2014. Migrant Death Toll Declines. *Wall Street Journal* (September 9): 14.

Canak, William, and Laura Swanson. 1998. *Modern Mexico*. New York: McGraw-Hill.

Cañas, Jesus, Roberto Coronado, and Robert W. Gilmer. 2006. U.S., Mexico Deepen Economic Ties. *Southwest Economy*, 1 (January/February). Accessible at http://www.dallasfed.org.

Capps, Randy, Ku Leighton, and Michael Fix. 2002. *How Are Immigrants Faring after Welfare Reform? Preliminary Evidence from Los Angeles and New York City*. Washington, DC: Urban Institute.

Capriccioso, Rob. 2011b. The Donor Party. *Indian Country Today* (March 23): 43–49.

Carlson, Dawn S., K. Michele Kacmar, and Dwayne Whitten. 2006. What Men Think They Know About Executive Women. *Harvard Business Review* (September), 84: 28.

Carmichael, Stokely, with Ekwueme Michael Thelwell. 2003. *The Life and Struggles of Stokely Carmichael (Kwame Ture)*. New York: Scribner.

Carrigan, William D., and Clive Webb. 2013. *Forgotten Dead: Mob Violence in the United States, 1848–1928*. New York: Oxford University Press.

———. 2015. When Americans Lynched Mexicans. *New York Times* (February 20): A27.

Carroll, Joseph. 2006. Public National Anthem Should Be Sung in English. *The Gallup Poll* (May): 3.

Casey, Nicholas. 2015. Buyers' Rule in L.I. Town Is Relic of Nazi Past. *New York Times* (October 20): A1, A23.

Carson, E. Ann, and Elizabeth Anderson. 2016. *Prisoners in 2015*. December. Accessible at www.bjs.gov.

Carter, Jimmy. 1978. *Public Papers of the President of the United States. Book Two: June 30, to December 31, 1978*. Washington, DC: National Archives and Records Service.

Catalyst. 2001. *Women Satisfied with Current Job in Financial Industry but Barriers Still Exist*. Press release July 25, 2001. Accessed January 31, 2002, at http://www.catalystwomen.org.

———. 2016. *2015 Catalyst Census: Women and Men Board Directors*. June 14. Accessible at www.catalyst.org.

———. 2017a. *Pyramid Women in S&P 500 Companies*. March 1. New York: Catalyst.

———. 2017b. *Women CEOs of the S&P 500*. March 1. New York: Catalyst.

Center for Constitutional Rights. 2011. *Stop-and-Frisks of New Yorkers in 2010 Hit All-Time High at 600, 601; 87 percent of Those Stopped Black and Latino*. Accessed March 2, 2011, at http://ccrjustice.org.

Center for Work-Life Policy. 2011. *Asian-Americans Still Feel Like Outsiders in Corporate America, New Study from the Center for Work-Life Policy Finds*. July 20. New York: Center for Work-Life Policy.

Centers for Disease Control and Prevention. 2013. CDC Health Disparities and Inequities Report–United States, 2013. *MMWR Supplements*, 62 (Past Volume). Accessible at www.cdc.gov.

Central Intelligence Agency. 2011. *The World Factbook*. Accessed June 18, 2011, at http://www.cia.gov/library/publications/the-world-factbook/geos/is.html.

Chacko, Elizabeth, and Rajiv Menon. 2013. Longings and Belongings: Indian American Youth Identity, Folk Dance Competitions, and the Construction of "Tradition." *Ethnic and Racial Studies*, 36 (1): 97–116.

Chakravorty, Sanjoy, Deuesh Kapur, and Niruikar Singh. 2017. *The Other One Percent: Indians in America*. New York: Oxford University Press.

Chambers Book of Facts. 2005. Edinburgh: Chambers Harrap Publishers.

Champagne, Duane. 1994. *Native America. Portrait of the Peoples*. Detroit: Visible Ink.

Chanes, Jerome A. 2007. Anti-Semitism. Pp. 90–110 in *American Jewish Yearbook 2007*, David Singer and Lawrence Grossman, eds. New York: American Jewish Committee.

———. 2008. *A Primer in the American Jewish Community*. 3rd ed. New York: American Jewish Committee.

Chaney, Kathy. 2009. Are there too few Black criminal court judges? *Chicago Defender* (March 11). Accessible at http://www.chicago-defender.com/article3442-are-there-too-few-black-criminal-court-judges.html.

Chang, Cindy. 2007. Asians Flex Muscles in California Politics. *New York Times* (February 27): A11.

Chase-Dunn, Christopher, and Thomas D. Hall. 1998. World-Systems in North America: Networks, Rise and Fall and Pulsations of Trade in Stateless Systems. *American Indian Culture and Research Journal*, 22 (1): 23–72.

Chazan, Guy, and Ainsley Thomson. 2011. Tough Irish Economy Turns Migration Influx to Exodus. *Wall Street Journal* (January 21): A8.

Cheah, Charissa S. L., Christy Y. L. Leung, and Nan Zhou. 2013. Understanding "Tiger Parenting" Through the Perceptions of Chinese Immigrant Mothers: Can Chinese and U.S. Parenting Coexist? *Asian American Journal of Psychology*, 4 (1): 30–40.

Chen, Carolyn. 2012. Asians: Too Smart for Their Own Good? *New York Times* (December 20): A35.

Chertok, Fern, Benjamin Phillips, and Leonard Saxe. 2008. *It's Not Just Who Stands Under the Chuppah: Intermarriage and Engagement*. Waltham, MA: Marilyn Cohen Center for Modern Jewish Studies, Brandeis University.

Chin, Ko-lin. 1996. *Chinatown Gangs: Extortion, Enterprise, and Ethnicity*. New York: Oxford University Press.

Chin, Margaret M. 2016. Asian Americans, Bamboo Ceilings, and Affirmative Action. *Contexts* (Winter): 70–73.

Chirot, Daniel, and Jennifer Edwards. 2003. Making Sense of the Senseless: Understanding Genocide. *Contexts*, 2 (Spring): 12–19.

Chiswick, Carmel U. 2009. *Occupation and Gender: American Jews at the Millennium*. Accessed June 14, 2011, at http://www.thearda.com/workingpapers/

Chou, Roslaind S., and Joe R. Feagin. 2008. *The Myth of the Model Minority: Asian Americans Facing Racism*. Boulder: Paradigm Publishers.

Chrisafis, Angelique. 2011. Muslim Women Protest on First Day of France's Face Veil Ban. *Guardian* (April 11). Accessible at http://www.guardian.co.uk.

Christensen, Kim. 2012. Interview. Wisconsin School District. November 8.

Christopher, Gail. 2013. The Conversation We're *Not* Having About Affirmative Action. *The Huffington Post*. (June 6). Accessible at http://www.huffingtonpost.com/dr-gail-christopher/the-conversation-were-not-having_b_3398540.html.

Christopulos, Diana. 1974. Puerto Rico in the Twentieth Century: A Historical Survey. Pp. 123–163 in *Puerto Rico and Puerto Ricans: Studies in History and Society*, Adalberto Lopez and James Petras, eds. New York: Wiley.

Chua, Amy. 2011. *Battle Hymn of the Tiger Mother*. New York: Penguin Press.

———. 2016. The "Tiger Mother" Has a Contract for Her Cubs. *Wall Street Journal* (June 11): C3.

Citrin, Jack, Amy Lerman, Michael Murakami, and Kathryn Pearson. 2007. Testing Huntington: Is Hispanic Immigration a Threat to American Identity? *Perspectives on Politics* (March), 5: 31–48.

Clemmitt, Marcia. 2005. Intelligent Design. *CQ Researcher* (July 29), 95: 637–660.

Coates, Ta-Nehisi. 2015. The Black Family in the Age of Mass Incarceration. *The Atlantic* (December): 60–84.

Cockburn, Andrew. 2003. True Colors: Divided Loyalty in Puerto Rico. *National Geographic Magazine* (March), 203: 34–55.

Coddou, Marion. 2016. An Institutional Approach to Collective Action: Evidence from Faith-Based Latino Mobilization in the 2006 Immigrant Rights Protests. *Social Problems*, 623: 127–150.

Cognard-Black, Andrew J. 2004. Will They Stay, or Will They Go? Sex—Atypical Among Token Men Who Teach. *Sociological Quarterly*, 45 (1): 113–139.

Cohen, Adam. 2016. *Imbeciles: The Supreme Court, American Eugenics, and the Sterilization of Carrie Buck.* New York: Penguin Press.

Cohen, Steven M. 1988. *American Assimilation or Jewish Revival?* Bloomington: Indiana University Press.

Cohn, D'Vera. 2015. Future Immigration Will Change the Face of America by 2065. October 5. Accessible at www.pewresearch.org.

Coker, Tumaini, et al. 2009. Perceived Racial/Ethnic Discrimination Among Fifth-Grade Students and Its Association with Mental Health. *American Journal of Public Health*, 99 (5): 878–884.

Coker, Tumaini., S. Bryan Austin, and Mark A. Shuster. 2010. The Health and Health Care of Lesbian, Gay, and Bisexual Adolescents. *Annual Review of Public Health*, 31: 456–477.

Colby, Sandra L., and Jennifer M. Ortman. 2015. Projections of the Size and Composition of the U.S. Population: 2014 to 2060. March. *Current Population Reports P25-1143*. Washington, DC: U.S. Government Printing Office.

Collier, Paul. 2013. How Migration Hurts Poor Countries. *New York Times* (December 1), sect. SR, p. 3.

Collins, Eliza. 2017. Obamacare Repeal Could Put Native American Health Care at risk. *USA Today* (January 24). Accessible at www.usatoday.com.

Collins, Patricia Hill. 2000. *Black Feminist Thought: Knowledge, Consciousness, and the Politics of Empowerment*, 2nd ed. New York: Routledge.

———. 2013. *On Intellectual Activism.* Philadelphia: Temple University Press.

———. 2015. Intersectionality's Definitional Dilemmas. *Annual Review of Sociology*, 41: 1–20.

Collins, Patricia Hill, and Sirma Bilge. 2016. *Intersectionality.* Cambridge, MA: Polity Press.

Comas-Díaz, Lillian, M. Brinton Lykes, and Renato D. Alarcón. 1998. Ethnic Conflict and the Psychology of Liberation in Guatemala, Peru, and Puerto Rico. *American Psychologist* (July) 53: 778–792.

Comeau, Joseph A. 2012. Race/Ethnicity and Family Contact: Toward a Behavioral Measure of Familism. *Hispanic Journal of Behavioral Sciences*, 34 (2): 251–268.

Commission on Civil Rights. 1976. *Fulfilling the Letter and Spirit of the Law: Desegregation of the Nation's Public Schools.* Washington, DC: U.S. Government Printing Office.

———. 1981. *Affirmative Action in the 1980s: Dismantling the Process of Discrimination.* Washington, DC: U.S. Government Printing Office.

Commission on Wartime Relocation and Internment of Civilians. 1982a. *Recommendations.* Washington, DC: U.S. Government Printing Office.

———. 1982b. *Report.* Washington, DC: U.S. Government Printing Office.

Committee of 100. 2001. *American Attitudes Towards Chinese Americans and Asian Immigrants.* New York: Committee of 100.

Connelly, Marjorie. 2008. Dissecting the Changing Electorate. *New York Times* (November 8): sect. WK.

Connor, Phillip. 2016. Migrant Remittances Worldwide Drop in 2015 for First Time since Great Recession. August 31. Accessible at www.pewresearch.org.

———. 2016a. U.S. Admits Record Number of Muslim Refugees in 2016. October 5. Accessible at www.pewresearch.com.

Connor, Walter. 1994. *Ethnonationalism: The Quest for Understanding.* Princeton, NJ: Princeton University Press.

Costantini, Cristina. 2011. Beardstown, Small Midwestern Meatpacking Town, Wrestles with Immigration Issue. *Huffington Post* (December). Accessible at http://www.huffingtonpost.com/2011/12/07/beardstown-illinois-small-town-wrestles-with-immigration-issues_n_1134797.html.

Conver, Bill. 1976. Group Chairman Lists Problems Endangering Jewish Family. *Peoria Journal Star* (December 4): A2.

Conyers, James L., Jr. 2004. The Evolution of Africology: An Afrocentric Appraisal. *Journal of Black Studies* (May), 34: 640–652.

Conyers, John. 2013. *Issues: Reparations.* Accessed September 20, 2013, at http://conyers.house.gov/index.cfm/reparations.

Coogan, Michael D. 2003. *The Illustrated Guide to World Religions.* Oxford University Press.

Coontz, Stephanie. 2010. *A Strange Stirring: "The Feminine Mystique" and American Women at the Dawn of the 1960s.* New York: Basic Books.

———. 2013. Progress at Work, But Mothers Still Pay a Price. *New York Times* (June 9): Week in Review section, p. 5.

Cooper, Richard S., Charles N. Rotimi, and Ryk Ward. 1999. The Puzzle of Hypertension in African Americans. *Scientific American* (February): 56–63.

Cooperman, Alan. 2005. One Way to Pray? *Washington Post National Weekly Edition* (September 5), 22: 10–11.

Copeland, Larry. 2011. Asian Farmers Crop Up in Southeast. *USA Today* (February 9): 3A.

Corbet, Sylvie. 2013. French Lawmaker on Defensive After Recorded Saying "Maybe Hitler Didn't Kill Enough." *Associated Press* (April 6). Accessible at http://www.neurope.eu.

Cordova, Carlos. 2005. *The Salvadoran Americans.* Westport, CT: Greenwood Press.

Cornacchia, Eugene J., and Dale C. Nelson. 1992. Historical Differences in the Political Experiences of American Blacks and White Ethnics: Revisiting an Unresolved Controversy. *Ethnic and Racial Studies* (January 15): 102–124.

Cornell, Stephen. 1984. Crisis and Response in Indian–White Relations: 1960–1984. *Social Problems* (October), 32: 44–59.

———. 1996. The Variable Ties That Bind: Content and Circumstance in Ethnic Processes. *Ethnic and Racial Studies* (April), 19: 265–289.

Cose, Ellis. 1993. *The Rage of a Privileged Class.* New York: HarperCollins.

———. 2008. So What If He Were Muslim? *Newsweek* (September 1): 37.

Coser, Lewis A. 1956. *The Functions of Social Conflict.* New York: Free Press.

Coser, Lewis A., and Rose Laub Coser. 1974. *Greedy Institutions.* New York: Free Press.

Council on American-Islamic Relations. 2016. For the Record: CAIR Releases Results of Presidential Election Exit Poll. November 22. Accessible at www.cair.com.

Covay, Elizabeth. 2013. Book Review Essay. *Social Forces*, 92 (September): 407–411.

Cox, Oliver C. 1942. The Modern Caste School of Social Relations. *Social Forces* (December), 21: 218–226.

Craemer, Thomas. 2015. Estimating Slavery Reparations: Present Value Comparisons of Historical Multigenerational Reparations Policies. *Social Science Quarterly* 96 (June): 639–65.

Creighton, Mathew J., David Post, and Hyunjoon Park. 2016. Ethnic Inequality in Mexican Education. *Social Forces* 94 (3): 1187–1220.

Crenshaw, Kimberlé. 1989. Demarginalizing the Intersection of Race and Sex: A Black Feminist Critique of Antidiscrimination Doctrine, Feminist Theory, and Antiracist Politics. Chicago, IL: University of Chicago Legal Foundation.

———. 2015. Why Intersectionality Can't Wait. *The Washington Post* (December 24). Accessible at www.washingtonpost.com.

Cultural Survival Quarterly. 1988. An Historical Overview of the Navajo Relocation. *Cultural Survival Quarterly Magazine* (September). Accessible at www.culturalsurvival.org.

DaCosta, Kimberly McClain. 2007. *Making Multiracials: State, Family, and Market in the Redrawing of the Color Line.* Stanford, CA: Stanford University Press.

Dade, Corey. 2012a. *Census Bureau Rethinks the Best Way to Measure Race.* Accessible at http://www.wbur.org.

———. 2012b. *The Fight Over Voter ID Laws Goes to the United Nations.* March 9. Accessible at http://www.npr.org.

Dallo, Florence J., Kristine J. Ajrouch, and Soham Al-Snih. 2008. The Ancestry Question and Ethnic Heterogeneity: The Case of Arab Americans. *International Migration Review* (Summer): 505–517.

Dally, Chad. 2011. Hmong Heritage Month Refocuses on Health. *Wausau Daily Herald* (April 3): A3.

D'Angelo, Chris. 2015. Historic Native Hawaiian Election Called Off by Organizers. *Huffington Post* (December 15). Accessible at www.huffingtonpost.com.

Daniel, G. Reginald. 2006. *Race Multiraciality in Brazil and the United States: Converging Paths?* University Park: Pennsylvania State University Press.

Dansie, Roberto. 2004. Curanderismo. *Indian Country Today* (December 8): C5.

David, Gary C. 2003. Rethinking Who's an Arab American: Arab-American Studies in the New Millennium. *Al-Jadid* (Fall): 9.

———. 2007. The Creation of "Arab American": Political Activism and Ethnic (Dis)Unity. *Critical Sociology*, 32: 833–862.

———. 2008. Arab Americans. Pp. 84–87 in vol. 2, *Encyclopedia of Race, Ethnicity, and Society*, Richard T. Schaefer, ed. Thousand Oaks, CA: Sage.

David, Gary C., and Kenneth Kahtan Ayouby. 2004. Perpetual Suspects and Permanent Others: Arab Americans and the War and Terrorism. Pp. 30–71 in *Guerras e Imigracioes*, Marco Aurélio Machado de Oliveira, ed. Campo Grande, Brazil: Universidade Federal de Mato Grosso do Sul.

David, Gary C., and Paul L. Jalbert. 2008. Undoing Degradation: The Attempted "Rehumanization" of Arab and Muslim Americans. *Ethnographic Studies* 10: 23-47.

Davis, David. 2008. Olympic Athletes Who Took a Stand. *Smithsonian* (August). Accessible at http://www.smithsonianmag.com/articles/olympic-athletes-who-took-a-stand-593920.

Davis, James A., Tom W. Smith, and Peter V. Marsden. 2007. *General Social Surveys, 1972–2006: Cumulative Codebook*. Chicago: NORC.

Davis, Julie Hirschfeld. 2017. Hispanic Political Fund Sets Meeting on Strategy. *New York Times* (February 23): p. A15.

Davis, Michelle R. 2008. Checking Sources: Evaluating Web Sites Requires Careful Eye. (Released by *Education Week*, March 6.) Accessed June 20, 2008, at http://www.edweek.org.

Day, Alan, Ashley Gomez, and Aamer Madhani. 2015. In Puerto Rico, a Mass Exodus from the Island. *USA Today* (August 26): 8A.

Degler, Carl N. 1971. *Neither Black nor White: Slavery and Race Relations in Brazil and the United States*. New York: Macmillan.

Dell'Angela, Tracy. 2005. Dakota Indians Say Kids Trapped in "School-to-Prison" Pipeline. *Chicago Tribune* (November 29): 1, 12.

DellaPergola, Sergio. 2007. World Jewish Population, 2007. Pp. 551–600 in *American Jewish Yearbook 2007*, David Singer and Lawrence Grossman, eds. New York: American Jewish Committee.

———. 2015. World Jewish Population, 2015. *Current Jewish Population Reports* (Number 14). Berman Jewish Databank. Accessible at www.jewishdatabank.org.

Deloria, Vine, Jr. 1969. *Custer Died for Your Sins: An Indian Manifesto*. New York: Avon.

———. 1971. *Of Utmost Good Faith*. New York: Bantam.

———. 1992. Secularism, Civil Religion, and the Religious Freedom of American Indians. *American Indian Culture and Research Journal*, 16 (2): 9–20.

———. 1995. *Red Earth, White Lies*. New York: Scribner's.

———. 2004. Promises Made, Promises Broken. Pp. 143–159 in *Native Universe: Voices of Indian America*, Gerald McMaster and Clifford E. Trofzer, eds. Washington, DC: National Geographic.

Deloria, Vine, Jr. and Clifford M. Lytle. 1983. *American Indians, American Justice*. Austin: University of Texas Press.

Demick, Barbara. 2017. How Trump's Policies and Rhetoric Are Forging Alliances Between U.S. Jews and Muslims. *Los Angeles Times* (February 5). Accessible at www.latimes.com.

DeNavas-Walt, Carman, Bernadette D. Proctor, and Jessica C. Smith. 2013. *Income, Poverty, and Health Insurance Coverage in the United States: 2012*. Washington, DC: U.S. Government Printing Office.

Denton, Nancy A., and Jacqueline Villarrubia. 2007. Residential Segregation on the Island: The Role of Race and Class in Puerto Rican Neighborhoods. *Sociological Forum* (March), 22: 1573–1586.

Department of Agriculture. 2010. *2007 Census Publications: Wisconsin*. Accessed August 13, 2010, at http://www.agcensus.usda.gov/Publications/2007/Full_Report/Census_by_State/Wisconsin.

Department of Diné Education 2012. *Navaho Nation Department of Diné Education*. Accessed December 10, 2010, at http://www.navajonationdode.org.

Department of Energy. 2000. *Final Report: Task Force Against Racial Profiling*. Washington, DC: U.S. Government Printing Office.

Department of Homeland Security. 2017. Welcome to the Civics Practice Test! Accessible at www.dhs.gov.

Department of Justice. 2000. *The Civil Liberties Act of 1988: Redress for Japanese Americans*. Accessed June 29, 2000, at http://www.usdoj.gov/crt/ora/main.html.

———. 2001. *Report to the Congress of the United States: A Review of Restrictions on Persons of Italian Ancestry During World War II*. Accessed February 1, 2002, at http://www.house.gov/judiciary/Italians.pdf.

Department of Labor. 1965. *The Negro Family: The Case for National Action*. Washington, DC: U.S. Government Printing Office.

———. 1995. *Good for Business: Making Full Use of the Nation's Capital*. Washington, DC: U.S. Government Printing Office.

———. 2011. *Women at Work*. March 2011. Accessible at http://www.bls.gov/spotlight/2011/women/.

———. 2013c. *International Comparisons of Annual Labor Force Statistics, 1970–2012*. June 7. Accessible at http://www.bls.gov.

———. 2016. *The Economic Status of Asian Americans and Pacific Islanders*. Accessible at www.dol.gov.

Department of State. 2008. *Immigrant Visas Issued to Orphans Coming to U.S.* Accessed September 3, 2008, at http://www.travel.state.gov/family/adoption/stats/stats_451.html.

———. 2013. *US State Department Services Dual Nationality*. Accessed August 7, 2013, at http://travel.state.gov/travel/cis_pa_tw/cis/cis_1753.html.

———. 2017. *Summary of Refugee Admissions as of 31 January 2017*. Accessible at www.ds.gov.

DeSante, Christopher D. 2013. Working Twice as Hard to Get Half as Far: Race, Work Ethic, and America's Deserving Poor. *American Journal of Political Science*, 57 (April): 342–356.

DeSilver, Drew. 2013. More Than 3.4M Americans Trace Their Ancestry to the Philippines. (November 13.) Accessible at www.pewresearch.org.

Desmond, Matthew, Andrew V. Papachristos, and David S. Kirk. 2016. Police Violence and Citizen Crime Reporting in the Black Community. *American Sociological Review*, 81 (5): 857–876.

Desmond, Scott A., and Charise E. Kubrin. 2009. The Power of Place: Immigrant Communities and Adolescent Violence. *Sociological Quarterly*, 50: 581–607.

DeVoe, Jill Fleury, Kristen E. Darling-Church, and Thomas D. Snyde. 2008. *Status and Trends in the Education of American Indians and Alaska Natives: 2008*. Washington, DC: National Center for Education Statistics.

Dhingra, Pawan. 2012. *Life Behind the Lobby: Indian American Motel Owners and the American Dream*. Stanford, CA: Stanford University Press.

Dhingra, Pawan, and Robyn Magalit Rodriguez. 2014. *Asian America: Sociological and Interdisciplinary Perspectives*. Cambridge, UK: Polity Press.

Diamond, Jared. 2003. Globalization, Then. *Los Angeles Times* (September 14): M1, M3.

Dickerson, Caitlin. 2017. A Town Divided Still Stands. *New York Times* (January 16): A1, A14.

Dickson, Lisa M. 2006. Book Review: Italians Then, Mexicans Now. *Industrial and Labor Relations Review*, 60 (2): 293–295.

Dinnerstein, Leonard. 1994. *Anti-Semitism in America*. New York: Oxford University Press.

DiTomaso, Nancy, Corinne Post, and Rochelle Parks-Yancy. 2007. Workforce Diversity and Inequality: Power, Status, and Numbers. *Annual Review of Sociology*, 33: 473–501.

Divine, Robert A., T. H. Breen, R. Hal Williams, Ariela Gross, and H.W. Brands. 2013. *America: Past and Present*, 10th edition. Upper Saddle River, NJ: Pearson.

Dixon, Robyn. 2007. Running for Their Lives. *Los Angeles Times* (September 9): A1, A10.

Dobbin, Frank, and Alexandra Kalev. 2013. The Origins and Effects of Corporate Diversity Programs. Pp. 253–281 in *Oxford Handbook of Diversity and Work*, Quintetta M. Roberson, ed. New York: Oxford University Press.

Dobbin, Frank, Alexandra Kalev, and Erin Kelly. 2007. Diversity Management in Corporate America. *Contexts*, 6 (4): 21–27.

Dobbin, Frank, Soohan Kim, and Alexandra Kalev. 2011. You Can't Always Get What You Need: Organizational Determinants of Diversity Programs. *American Sociological Review*, 76 (3): 386.

Dolan, Sean, and Sandra Stotsky. 1997. *The Polish Americans.* New York: Chelsea House.

Dolan, Timothy. 2013. Immigration and the Welcome Church. *Wall Street Journal* (October 18): A11.

Dolnick, Sam. 2011. Many Korean Grocers, a New York Staple, Are Closing Down. *New York Times* (June 2): A19.

Dolnick, Sam, and Kirk Semple. 2011. Scattered Across New York, with Disaster at Home. *New York Times* (March 16): A25-26.

Domino, John C. 1995. *Sexual Harassment and the Courts.* New York: HarperCollins.

Dorris, Michael. 1988. For the Indians, No Thanksgiving. *New York Times* (November 24): A23.

Dorschner, Cheryl. 2013. *The New Face of Vermont Dairy Farming.* Accessed August 13, 2013, at http://www.uvm.edu/~cals/?Page=news&storyID=15296&category=calshome.

Downey, Douglas B. 2008. Black/White Differences in School Performance: The Oppositional Culture Explanation. *Annual Review of Sociology*, 34: 107–126.

Du Bois, W. E. B. 1903. *The Souls of Black Folks: Essays and Sketches* (reprint). New York: Facade Publications, 1961.

———. 1935. Does the Negro Need Separate Schools? *Journal of Negro Education* (July), 1: 328–335.

———. 1952. *Battle for Peace: The Story of My 83rd Birthday.* New York: Masses and Mainstream.

———. 1968. *Dusk of Dawn.* New York: Schocken.

———. 1969a. *An ABC of Color* [1900]. New York: International Publications.

———. 1969b. *The Suppression of the African Slave-Trade to the United States of America, 1638–1870.* New York: Schocken.

———. 1970. *The Negro American Family.* Cambridge, MA: MIT Press.

———. 1996. *The Philadelphia Negro: A Social Study* [1899]. Philadelphia: University of Pennsylvania Press.

———. 2003. *The Negro Church* [1903]. Walnut Creek: Alta Mira Press.

———. The Social Significance of Booker T. Washington. Reprinted from 1935 in *Du Bois Review*, 8 (2): 367–376.

Dugger, Celia W. 2010. South Africa Redoubles Efforts Against AIDS. *New York Times* (April 26): A1, A3.

Dunaway, Wilma. 2003. *The African-American Family in Slavery and Emancipation.* New York: Cambridge University Press.

Duquette-Rury, Lauren. 2016. Migrant Transnational Participation: How Citizen Inclusion and Government Engagement Matter for Local Democratic Development in Mexico. *American Sociological Review*, 61(4): 771–799.

Durkheim, Émile. 2001. *The Elementary Forms of Religious Life* [1912]. New translation by Carol Cosman. New York: Oxford University Press.

———. 2008 [1899]. Anti-Semitism and Social Crisis. *Sociological Theory*, 26: 321–323.

Duszak, Thomas. 1997. Lattimer Massacre Centennial Commemoration. *Polish American Journal* (August). Accessed June 4, 2008, at http://www.polamjournal.com/Library/APHistory/Lattimer/lattimer.html.

Dyson, Michael Eric. 1995. *Making Malcolm: The Myth and Meaning of Malcolm X.* New York: Oxford University Press.

Eckholm, Erik. 2010. In Drug War, Tribe Feels Invaded by Both Sides. *New York Times* (January 25): A1, A10.

Eckstrom, Kevin. 2001. New, Diverse Take Spot on Catholic Altars. *Chicago Tribune* (August 31): 8.

The Economist. 2014. Not Black and White. (March 22): 33.

———. 2015a. The Diaspora: The Worldwide Web. (May 23): 15.

———. 2015b. The Model Minority Is Losing Patience. (October 3): 23–25.

———. 2015c. Indigenous Canadians: Truth and Consequences. (June 6): 28.

———. 2016. Slavery's Legacies. (September 10): 51.

———. 2017a. Indigenous Australians: Ministering to His Own (January 28): 34.

———. 2017b. The Ultimate Fantasy. (February 11): 41–43.

———. 2017c. El Salvador: Unhappy Anniversary. (January 21): 25-26.

Edelman, Benjamin, Michael Luca, and Dan Svirsky. 2017. Racial Discrimination in the Sharing Economy: Evidence from a Field Experiment. *American Economic Journal: Applied Economics.* Forthcoming.

Ehara, Yumiko. 2005. Feminism in the Grips of a Pincher Attack—Traditionalism, Liberalism, and Globalism. *International Journal of Japanese Sociology*, 14 (November): 6–14.

El-Haj, Nadia Abu. 2007. The Genetic Reinscription of Race. *Annual Review of Anthropology*, 16: 283–300.

Eligon, John. 2013. Down-Home American, Korean Style. *New York Times* (January 6): 17, 21.

———. 2016. A Question of Environmental Racism in Flint. *New York Times* (January 21). Accessible at www.nytimes.com.

Elkins, Stanley. 1959. *Slavery: A Problem in American Institutional and Intellectual Life.* Chicago: University of Chicago Press.

Elliott, Andrea. 2006. Muslim Voters Detect a Snub from Obama. *New York Times* (June 24): A1, A20.

———. 2011. Generation 9/11. *New York Times* (September 11): 25.

Ellis, Mark R. 2004. Denver's Anti-Chinese Riot. Pp. 142–143 in *Encyclopedia of the Great Plains*, David J. Wishart, ed. Lincoln: University of Nebraska Press.

Ellis, Renee R., and Tavia Simmons. 2014. Coresident Grandparents and Their Grandchildren: 2012. *Current Population Report*, P20-576. Accessible at www.census.gov.

Equal Employment Opportunity Commission. 2001. *Age Discrimination in Employment Act (ADEA), Changes FY 1992–FY 2000.* Accessed December 10, 2001, at http://www.eeoc.gov/stats/adea.html.

Equal Justice Initiative. 2015. *Lynching in America: Confronting the Legacy of Racial Terror.* 2nd ed. Montgomery, AL: EJI.

Erdmans, Mary Patrice. 1998. *Opposite Poles: Immigrants and Ethnics in Polish Chicago, 1976–1990.* University Park: Pennsylvania State University.

———. 2006. New Chicago Polonia: Urban and Suburban. Pp. 115–127 in *The New Chicago*, John Koval et al., eds. Philadelphia: Temple University Press.

Erlanger, Steven, and Elvire Camus. 2012. In a Ban, a Measure of European Tolerance. *New York Times* (September 2): 6, 8.

Eschbach, Karl, and Kalman Applebaum. 2000. Who Goes to Powwows? Evidence from the Survey of American Indians and Alaskan Natives. *American Indian Culture and Research Journal*, 24(2): 65–83.

Espiritu, Yen Le. 1992. *Asian American Panethnicity: Bridging Institutions and Identities.* Philadelphia: Temple University Press.

Euless Historical Preservation Committee. 2011. Halatono Netane with Chris Jones. Accessible at http://www.eulesstx.gov/history/narratives/HalatonoNetane.htm.

European Union Agency for Fundamental Rights. 2013. *Discrimination and Hate Crime Against Jews in EU Member States: Experiences and Perceptions of Anti-Semitism.* Vienna: European Union.

European Roma Rights Centre. 2008. *Ostravis Case: D. H. and Others v. The Czech Republic.* Accessed June 29, 2008, at http://www.errc.org.

———. 2012. *Czech Republic: A Report by the European Roma Rights Centre.* Accessible at http://www.errc.org.

Faderman, Lillian. 2015. *The Gay Revolution: The Story of the Struggle.* New York: Simon and Schuster.

Fallows, Marjorie R. 1979. *Irish Americans: Identity and Assimilation.* Englewood Cliffs, NJ: Prentice Hall.

Farkas, Steve. 2003. *What Immigrants Say About Life in the United States.* Washington, DC: Migration Policy Institute.

Farley, Maggie. 2008. Canada to Apologize for Abuse of Native Students. *Los Angeles Times* (June 10): A4.

Fathi, Nazila. 2006. Iran Opens Conference on Holocaust. *New York Times* (December 12).

Feagin, Joe R., and José A. Cobas. 2008. Latinos/as and White Racial Frame: The Procrustean Bed of Assimilation. *Sociological Inquiry* (February), 78: 39–53.

———. 2014. *Latinos Facing Racism: Discrimination, Resistance and Endurance.* Boulder: Paradigm Books.

Feagin, Joe R., and Karyn D. McKinney. 2003. *The Many Costs of Racism.* Lanham, MD: Rowan and Littlefield.

Feagin, Joe R., and Eileen O'Brien. 2003. *White Men on Race, Power, Privilege, and the Shaping of Cultural Consciousness.* Boston: Beacon Press.

Feagin, Joe R., Hernán Vera, and Pinar Batur. 2000. *White Racism,* 2nd ed. New York: Routledge.

Federal Bureau of Investigation. 2016a. *2015 Hate Crime Statistics.* Accessible at www.ucr.fbi.gov.

———. 2016b. *2015 Crime in the United States.* Accessible at www.ucr.fbi.gov.

Feldman, Marcus W. 2010. The Biology of Race. Pp. 136–159 in *Doing Race,* Hazel Rose Markus and Paula M. L. Moya, eds. New York: W. W. Norton.

Ferber, Abby L. 2008. Privilege. Pp. 1073–1074 in vol. 3, *Encyclopedia of Race, Ethnicity, and Society,* Richard T. Schaefer, ed. Thousand Oaks, CA: Sage.

Fetner, Tina. 2016. U.S. Attitudes Toward Lesbian and Gay People Are Better Than Ever. *Contexts* (Spring): 20–27.

Fihel, Agnieszka, and Izabela Grabowski-Lusinska. 2014. Labour Market Behaviours of Back-and-Forth Migrants from Poland. *International Migration,* 52 (1): 22–35.

File, Thom. 2013. *The Diversifying Electorate-Voting Rates by Race and Hispanic Origin in 2012 (and Other Recent Elections). Current Population Survey P20-568.* Accessible at http://www.census.gov.

———. 2017. Voting in America: A Look at the 2016 Presidential Election. May 10. Accessible at www.census.gov.

Finder, Alan. 1994. Muslim Gave Racist Speech, Jackson Says. *New York Times* (January 23): 21.

Finestein, Israel. 1988. The Future of American Jewry. *The Jewish Journal of Sociology,* 30 (December): 121–125.

Fing, Jing, Shantha Madhavan, and Michael H. Alderman. 1996. The Association Between Birthplace and Mortality from Cardiovascular Causes Among Black and White Residents of New York City. *New England Journal of Medicine* (November 21), 335: 1545–1551.

Fischer, Nancy L. 2013. Seeing "Straight," Contemporary Critical Heterosexuality Studies and Sociology: An Introduction. *Sociological Quarterly,* 54: 501–510.

Fitzgerald, Kathleen J. 2008. Native American Identity. Pp. 954–956 in vol. 2, *Encyclopedia of Race, Ethnicity, and Society,* Richard T. Schaefer, ed. Thousand Oaks, CA: Sage.

Flexner, Eleanor. 1959. *Century of Struggle: The Women's Rights Movement in the United States.* Cambridge, MA: Harvard University Press.

Flores, René, and Edward Telles. 2010. Social Stratification in Mexico: Disentangling Color, Ethnicity, and Class. *American Sociological Review* 77 (3): 486–494.

Foner, Eric. 2006. *Forever Free: The Story of Emancipation and Reconstruction.* New York: Knopf.

———. 2015. *Gateway to Freedom: The Hidden History of the Underground Railroad.* New York: W. W. Norton.

Forced Migration Studies Programme. 2010. *Population Movements In and To South Africa.* Witwatersrand, South Africa: FMSP.

Fordham, Signithia, and John U. Ogbu. 1986. Black Students' School Success: Coping with the Burden of "Acting White." *Urban Review,* 18 (3): 176–206.

Fox, Stephen. 1990. *The Unknown Internment.* Boston: Twayne.

Fox, Susannah, and Gretchen Livingston. 2007. *Hispanics with Lower Levels of Education and English Proficiency Remain Largely Disconnected from the Internet.* Washington, DC: Pew Hispanic Center.

Frankel, Bruce. 1995. N.Y.'s "Jewish Rosa Parks" Wins Bus Battle. *USA Today* (March 17): 4A.

Franklin, John Hope, and Evelyn Brooks Higginbotham. 2011. *From Slavery to Freedom: A History of African Americans,* 9th ed. New York: McGraw-Hill.

Freedman, Samuel G. 2003. *Sex and the City* Celebrates Judaism. *USA Today* (July 17): 13A.

Freeman, Jo. 1973. The Origins of the Women's Liberation Movement. *American Journal of Sociology* (January), 78: 792–811.

———. 1975. *The Politics of Women's Liberation.* New York: David McKay.

French, Howard W. 2003. Japan's Neglected Resource: Female Workers. *New York Times* (July 25).

Frey, William H. 2016. Analysis of 2000 Census and 2011–2015 American Community Survey (Released December 8, 2016). Table 2: Segregation Measured by Dissimilarity Index: Metropolitan Areas over One Million Population, 2000 and 2011–2015. Accessible at https://www.brookings.edu/wp-content/.../2016/12/freywhit-eneighborhoods_table2.xls.

Friedan, Betty. 1963. *The Feminine Mystique.* New York: Dell.

———. 1981. *The Second Stage.* New York: Summit Books.

———. 1991. Back to *The Feminine Mystique? The Humanist* (January–February), 51: 26–27.

Friedman, Georges. 1967. *The End of the Jewish People?* Garden City, NY: Doubleday.

Frosch, Dan. 2008. Its Native Tongue Facing Extinction, Arapaho Tribe Teaches the Young. *New York Times* (October 17): A14.

Frosch, Dan, and Alan Zibel. 2014. Tribes' Economic Lifeline Faces Squeeze. *Wall Street Journal* (July 24): A3.

Fryer, Roland G., Lisa Kahn, Steven D. Levitt, and Jörg L. Spenkuch. 2012. The Plight of Mixed Race Adolescents. *Review of Economics and Statistics* (August), 94: 6231–6234.

Fuller, Bruce, Sara McElmurry, and John Koval. 2011. *Latino Workers Hitting a Blue-Collar Ceiling.* Berkeley CA: Institute of Human Development.

Galewitz, Phil. 2012. Many Migrants Get Care in Field. *USA Today* (June 7): 3A.

Gallup, George H. 1972. *The Gallup Poll, Public Opinion, 1935–1971.* New York: Random House.

Gans, Herbert J. 1956. American Jewry: Present and Future. *Commentary* (May), 21: 424–425.

———. 1979. Symbolic Ethnicity: The Future of Ethnic Groups and Cultures in America. *Ethnic and Racial Studies* 2 (January): 1–20.

———. 2014. The Coming Darkness of Late-Generation European American Ethnicity. *Ethnic and Racial Studies,* 37 (5): 757–765.

Garfinkel, Herbert. 1959. *When Negroes March.* New York: Atheneum.

Garner, Roberta. 1996. *Contemporary Movements and Ideologies.* New York: McGraw-Hill.

Garroutte, Era M. 2009. Religiosity and Spiritual Engagement in Two American Indian Populations. *Journal for the Scientific Study of Religion,* 48 (3): 480–500.

Gates, Gary J. 2017. U.S. Satisfaction with Immigration Levels Reaches New High. January 18. Accessible at www.gallup.com.

Gates, Gary J., and Frank Newport. 2013. *Gallup Special Report: New Estimates of the LGBT Population in the United States.* February. Accessed September 23, 2013, at http:williansinstutute.law.ucla.edu/research/census-lgbt-demographics-studies/gallup-lgbt-pop-feb-2013/.

Geddes, Diana. 2010. The Price of Freedom: A Special Report on South Africa. *The Economist* (June 5): 1–16.

Gelles, David. 2016. For Standing Up, Scorn. *New York Times* (November 1): B1–B2.

Gerson, Kathleen. 2007. What Do Women and Men Want? *The American Prospect* (March): A8–A11.

Gerth, H. H., and C. Wright Mills. 1958. *From Max Weber: Essays in Sociology.* New York: Galaxy Books.

Gibbs, Nancy. 2001. A Whole New World. *Time* (June 11): 36–45.

Gibson, James L., and Christopher Classen. 2010. Racial Reconciliation in South Africa: Interracial Contact and Changes over Time. *Journal of Social Issues*, 66 (2): 255–272.

Gibson, William E. 2014. Borinqueneers' Gold Medal Honor a Shining Moment. *South Florida Sun Sentinel* (June 11): 1A, 9A.

Girardelli, Davide. 2004. Commodified Identities: The Myth of Italian Food in the United States. *Journal of Communication Inquiry* (October), 28: 307–324.

Giroux, Henry A. 1997. Rewriting the Discourse of Racial Identity: Towards a Pedagogy and Politics of Whiteness. *Harvard Educational Review* (Summer) 67: 285–320.

Gittler, Joseph B., ed. 1981. *Jewish Life in the United States: Perspectives from the Social Sciences*. New York: New York University Press.

GLAAD. 2013. *Where We are on TV 2013*. Accessible at http://www.glaad.org/whereweareontv13.

———. 2016. *Where We Are on TV: 16-17*. Accessible at www.glaad.org.

———. 2017. Accelerating Acceptance 2017. Accessible at www.glaad.org.

Gladstone, Benjamin. 2016. Anti-Semitism at My University. *New York Times* (October 2): SR2.

Glazer, Nathan. 1990. American Jewry or American Judaism? *Society* (November–December), 28: 14–20.

Gleason, Philip. 1980. American Identity and Americanization. Pp. 31–58 in *Harvard Encyclopedia of American Ethnic Groups*, Stephen Therstromm, ed. Cambridge, MA: Belknap Press of Harvard University Press.

Glenn, Evelyn Nakano. 2015. Settler Colonialism as Structure: A Framework for Comparative Studies of U.S. Race and Gender Formation. *Sociology of Race and Ethnicity*, 1 (1): 54–74.

Global Forum in Migration and Development. 2017. *Tres por Uno (Three for One) Program*. Accessible at www.gfmd.org.

Glusac, Elaine. 2016. My House Is Your House. Or Is It? *New York Times* (June 26): sect. TR, 8.

Gobodo-Madikizela, Pumla. 2003. *A Human Being Died That Night*. New York: Houghton Mifflin.

Goering, John M. 1971. The Emergence of Ethnic Interests: A Case of Serendipity. *Social Forces* (March), 48: 379–384.

Goffman, Erving. 1963. *Stigma: Notes on Management of Spoiled Identity*. Englewood Cliffs, NJ: Prentice Hall.

Gold, Matea, and Joseph Tanfani. 2012. Tribal Leaders Bet on Obama. *Chicago Tribune* (September 27): 19.

Gold, Michael. 1965. *Jews Without Money*. New York: Avon.

Goldberg, Jeffrey. 2013. New Chapter, Old Story. *New York Times* (October 13): Book Review section, p. 28.

Goldhagen, Daniel Jonah. 2013. *The Devil That Never Dies: The Rise and Threat of Global Anti-Semitism*. New York: Little, Brown.

Goldscheider, Calvin. 2003. Are American Jews Vanishing Again? *Contexts* (Winter): 18–24.

Goldstein, Evan R. 2010. Not Everybody Is Ready for an Orthodox Rabbi. *New York Times* (April 23): W11.

Goldstein, Joseph. 2013. Judge Rejects New York Stop-and-Frisk Policy. *New York Times* (August 12): A1, A16.

Goldstein, Laurie. 2016. Both Feeling Threatened, American Muslims and Jews Join Hands. *New York Times* (December 6): A19.

Goldstein, Sidney, and Calvin Goldscheider. 1968. *Jewish Americans: Three Generations in a Jewish Community*. Englewood Cliffs, NJ: Prentice Hall.

Gomez, Alan. 2014. Obama Could Reshape a Rural Landscape. *USA Today* (December 9): 1A, 5A.

———. 2015. Central Americans Flee Mayhem Back Home. *USA Today* (November 20): 15A.

Gomez, David F. 1971. Chicanos: Strangers in Their Own Land. *America* 124 (June 26), 649–652.

Gonzales, Roberto G. 2011. Learning to Be Illegal: Undocumented Youth and Shifting Legal Contexts in the Transition to Adulthood. *American Sociological Review*, 76 (45): 602–619.

Gonzalez, David. 2009. A Family Divided by 2 Worlds, Legal and Illegal. *New York Times* (April 26): 1, 20–21.

González, Jennifer. 2012. Tribal Colleges Offer Basic Education to Students "Not Prepared for College." *Chronicle of Higher Education* (April 13): A25.

Goodstein, Laurie. 2005. Issuing Rebuke: Judge Rejects Teaching of Intelligent Design. *New York Times* (December 21): A1, A21.

———. 2010. American Muslims Ask, Will We Ever Belong? *New York Times* (September 6): A1, A3.

———. 2011. Report Offers Surprises on Muslims' Growth. *New York Times* (January 27): A8.

———. 2013a. Bar Mitzvahs Get New Look to Build Faith. *New York Times* (September 4): A1, A13.

Goodstein, Laurie, and Jennifer Steinhauer. 2010. Pope Picks Latino to Lead Los Angeles Archdiocese. *New York Times* (April 7): A17.

Gordon, Milton M. 1964. *Assimilation in American Life: The Role of Race, Religion, and National Origins*. New York: Oxford University Press.

Gorski, Phillip S. 2010. *Civil Religion Today* (ARDA Guiding Paper Series). State College, PA: Association of Religion Data Archives at the Pennyslvania State University. Accessible at http://www.thearda.com/rrh/papers/guidingpapers.asp.

Gose, Ben. 2013. Diversity Offices Aren't What They Used to Be. *Chronicle of Higher Education* (June 14): A14–A15, A17.

Government Accountability Office. 2015. *Indian Gaming: Regulation and Oversight by the Federal Government, States, and Tribes*. June. Washington, DC: Government Printing Office.

Gradín, Carlos. 2014. Race and Income Distributions: Evidence from the USA, Brazil, and South Africa. *Review of Development Economics* 18 (1): 73–92.

Grall, Timothy. 2016. Custodial Mothers and Fathers and Their Child Support: 2013. January. *Current Population Reports P60-255*. Accessible at www.census.gov.

Gray-Little, Bernadette, and Hafdahl, Adam R. 2000. Factors Influencing Racial Comparisons of Self-Esteem: A Qualitative Review. *Psychological Bulletin*, 126 (1): 26–54.

Greeley, Andrew M. 1981. *The Irish Americans: The Rise to Money and Power*. New York: Harper & Row.

Green, Alexander R., et al. 2007. Implicit Bias Among Physicians and Its Prediction of Thrombolysis Decisions for Black and White Patients. *Journal of General Internal Medicine* (September), 22: 1231–1238.

Greene, Leonard. 2014. Dominicans Now Outnumber Puerto Ricans in NYC. *New York Post* (November 13). Accessible at www.nypost.com.

Greenhouse, Linda. 1996. Court Accepts Case Tied to Separation Powers. *New York Times* (October 16). Accessed November 20, 2013, at http://www.nytimes.com/1996/10/16/us/court-accepts-case-tied-to-separation-of-powers.html?pagewanted=all&src=pm.

———. 2008. Justices, in Bias Case, Rule for Older Workers. *New York Times* (June 20): A15.

Greenhouse, Steven. 2012. Equal Opportunity Panel Updates Hiring Policy. *New York Times* (April 26): B3.

———. 2015. Protests and Progress on Farmworker Wages. *New York Times* (July 4): B1, B3.

Greer, Christina M. 2013. *Black Ethnics: Race, Immigration, and the Pursuit of the American Dream*. Cambridge, MA: Oxford University Press.

Grimshaw, Allen D. 1969. *Racial Violence in the United States*. Chicago: Aldine.

Grinspan, Jon. 2013. When the Civil War Came to New York. *New York Times* (July 14): Week in Review, p. 8.

Grossman, Cathy Lynn. 2008. Muslim Census a Difficult Count. *USA Today* (August 6): 5D.

Guerin-Gonzales, Camille. 1994. *Mexican Workers and American Dreams*. New Brunswick, NJ: Rutgers University Press.

Guerrero, Diane. 2014. "Orange is the New Black" Actress: My Parents Were Deported. *Los Angeles Times*. November 15. Accessible at www.latimes.com.

Guest, Kenneth J. 2003. *God in Chinatown: Religion and Survival in New York's Evolving Immigrant Community*. New York: University Press.

Guglielmo, Jennifer, and Salvatore Salerno, eds. 2003. *Are Italians White?* New York: Routledge.

Guillermo, Emil. 2015. Model Minority? In St. Paul, Asian-American Test Scores Lag. (May 5.) Accessible at www.nbcnews.com.

Guly, Christopher, and Maggie Farley. 2008. Canada Natives Get Apology. *Los Angeles Times* (June 12): A3.

Guo, Jeff. 2016. The Sharing Economy Has a Serious Racism Problem—But There May Be a Way to Fix It. Wonkblog. November 2. Accessible at www.washingtonpost.com.

Gutierrez, Luis. 2011. *Rep. Gutierrez Returns to House Floor to Address Civil Rights Crisis in Puerto Rico Speech to House of Representatives Underscores Congressman's Commitment to Free Speech, Asserts Puerto Ricans Cannot Be Silenced.* Accessed September 10, 2011, at http://www.gutierrez.house.gov/index.php?option=com_content&task=view&id=647&Itemid=71.

Guttmacher Institute. 2015. State Policies in Brief as of November 1, 2015. An Overview of Abortion Laws. Accessible www.guttmacher.org.

Guynn, Jessica. 2014. High-Tech Pay Gap: Minorities Earn Less. *USA Today* (October 12): A1.

———. 2016. Airbnb Seeks Help from Civil Rights Leaders. *USA Today* (June 23): 3B.

———. 2017. Jackson to Uber: Release Diversity Data. *USA Today* (January 6): 1B–2B.

Guzmán, Betsy. 2001. *The Hispanic Population.* Census 2000 Brief Series C2kBR/01-3. Washington, DC: U.S. Government Printing Office.

Haak, Gerald O. 1970. Co-Opting the Oppressors: The Case of the Japanese-Americans. *Society* (October), 7: 23–31.

Hacek, Miro. 2008. Roma. Pp. 1168–1170 in vol. 3, *Encyclopedia of Race, Ethnicity, and Society*, Richard T. Schaefer, ed. Thousand Oaks, CA: Sage.

Hacker, Helen Mayer. 1951. Women as a Minority Group. *Social Forces* (October), 30: 60–69.

———. 1974. Women as a Minority Group: Twenty Years Later. Pp. 124–134 in *Who Discriminates Against Women*, Florence Denmark, ed., Beverly Hills, CA: Sage Publications.

Haeri, Shaykh Fadhilalla. 2004. *The Thoughtful Guide to Islam.* Alresford, UK: O Books.

Hakimzadeh, Shirin, and D'Vera Cohn. 2007. *English Usage Among Hispanics in the United States.* Washington, DC: Pew Hispanic Center.

Haller, William, Alejandro Portes, and Scott M. Lynch. 2011. Dreams Fulfilled, Dreams Shattered: Determinants of Segmented Assimilation in the Second Generation. *Social Forces*, 89 (3): 733–762.

Halpern, Sue, and Bill McKibben. 2014. Manchester's Melting Pot. *Smithsonian* (April): 25–30.

Halstead, Mark L. 2008. Islamophobia. Pp. 762–764 in vol. 2, *Encyclopedia of Race, Ethnicity, and Society*, Richard T. Schaefer, ed. Thousand Oaks, CA: Sage.

Hampson, Rick. 2017. Confederate Monuments Reopen Old Racial Wounds. *USA Today* (May 23): 1A, 5A.

Handlin, Oscar. 1951. *The Uprooted: The Epic Story of the Great Migrations That Made the American People.* New York: Grossett and Dunlap.

Hansen, Marcus Lee. 1952. The Third Generation in America. *Commentary* (November 14): 493–500.

Harlow, Caroline Wolf. 2005. *Hate Crime Reported by Victims and Police.* Bureau of Justice Statistics Special Report (November). Accessed May 8, 2008, at http://www.ojp.usdoj.gov/bjs/pub/pdf/hcrvp.pdf.

Harrison, Jill Lindsay, and Sarah E. Lloyd. 2012. Illegality at Work: Deportability and the Productive New Era of Immigration Enforcements. *Antipode*, 44 (2): 365–385.

Harrison, Jill Lindsay, Sarah E. Lloyd, and Trish O'Kane. 2009. *Overview of Immigrant Workers on Wisconsin Dairy Farmers.* Briefing No. 1. Madison WI: Program on Agricultural Technology Studies.

Hartocullis, Anemona. 2006. For Some Gays, a Right They Can Forsake. *New York Times* (July 30): sect. ST, 2.

Harzig, Christine. 2008. German Americans. Pp. 540–544 in vol. 1, *Encyclopedia of Race, Ethnicity, and Society*, Richard T. Schaefer, ed. Thousand Oaks, CA: Sage.

Hassrick, Elizabeth McGhee. 2007. *The Transnational Production of White Ethnic Symbolic Identities.* Paper presented at the Annual Meeting of the American Sociological Association.

Hawaiian State Data Center. 2016. *Statistical Report: Detailed Languages Spoken at Home in the State of Hawaii.* March. Accessible at www.hawaii.gov.

Haxton, Charrisse, and Kristen Harknett. 2009. Racial and Gender Differences in Kin Support. *Journal of Family Issues* (August), 30: 1019–1040.

Haynes, V. Dio. 2009. Blacks Hit Hard by Economy's Punch. *Washington Post* (November 24). Accessed July 27, 2011, at http://www.washingtonpost.com/wp-dyn/content/article/2009/11/23/AR2009112304092.html.

He, Wan, Manisha Sengupta, Victoria A. Velkoff, and Kimberly A. DeBarros. 2005. 651 in the United States: 2005. *Current Population Reports.* Ser. P23. No. 209. Washington, DC: U.S. Government Printing Office.

Heilman, Madeline E. 2001. Description and Prescription: How Gender Stereotypes Present Women's Ascent Up the Organizational Ladder. *Journal of Social Issues*, 57 (4): 657–674.

Henry, William A., III. 1994. Pride and Prejudice. *Time* (February 28), 143: 21–27.

Hentoff, Nicholas. 1984. Dennis Banks and the Road Block to Indian Ground. *Village Voice* (October), 29: 19–23.

Hequembourg, Amy, and Jorge Arditi. 1999. Fractured Resistances: The Debate over Assimilationism Among Gays and Lesbians in the United States. *Sociological Quarterly*, 40 (4): 663–680.

Herbert, Bob. 2010. Jim Crow Policy. *New York Times* (February 2): A27.

Herman, Jody L., Andrew R. Flores, Taylor N. T. Brown, Bianca D. M. Wilson, and Keith J. Conron. 2017. *Age of Individuals Who Identify as Transgender in the United States.* Los Angeles: The Williams Institute, UCLA School of Law.

Hernández-Arias, P. Rafael. 2008. Salvadoran Americans. Pp. 1185–1187 in vol. 3, *Encyclopedia of Race, Ethnicity, and Society*, Richard T. Schaefer, ed. Thousand Oaks, CA: Sage.

Herrnstein, Richard J., and Charles Murray. 1994. *The Bell Curve: Intelligence and Class Structure in American Life.* New York: Free Press.

Herschthal, Eric. 2004. Indian Students Discuss Pros, Cons of Arranged Marriages. *Daily Princetonian* (October 20).

Herzig-Yoshinaga, Aiko, and Marjorie Lee (eds.). 2011. *Speaking Out for Personal Justice (Site Summaries of Testimonies and Witnesses Registry).* Los Angeles, CA: UCLA Asian American Studies.

Hevesi, Dennis. 2011. Elouise Cobell, 65, Sued for Indian Funds. *New York Times* (October 18): A19.

Higham, John. 1966. American Anti-Semitism Historically Reconsidered. Pp. 237–258 in *Jews in the Mind of America*, Charles Herbert Stember, ed. New York: Basic Books.

Hill, Robert B. 2003. *The Strengths of Black Families.* 2nd ed. Lanham, MD: Rowman & Littlefield.

Hill, Margari, Daniel Kowalski, Meral Kocak, Hakeem Muhammad, Sherouk Ahmed, and Namira Islam. 2015. *Muslim Anti-Racism Collaborative Study of Intra-Muslim Ethnic Relations: Muslim American Views on Race Relations.* Muslim Anti-Racism Collaborative. Accessible at www.muslimarc.org.

Himmelfarb, Harold S. 1982. Research on American Jewish Identity and Identification: Progress, Pitfalls, and Prospects. Pp. 56–95 in *Understanding American Jewry*, Marshall Sklare, ed. New Brunswick, NJ: Transaction Books.

Hirsch, Mark. 2009. Thomas Jefferson: Founding Father of Indian Removal. *Smithsonian Institution* (Summer): 54–58.

Hirsh, Michael. 2016. The FBI's Secret Muslim Network. *This Week* (April): 36–37.

Hirsley, Michael. 1991. Religious Display Needs Firm Count. *Chicago Tribune* (December 20), section 2: 10.

Hisnanick, John J., and Katherine G. Giefer. 2011. *Dynamics of Economic Well-Being: Fluctuations in the U.S. Income Distribution 2004–2007.* Washington, DC: U.S. Government Printing Office.

Hispanic Association on Corporate Responsibility. 2013. *2013 HACR Corporate Governance Study.* Accessible at www.hacr.org.

Hixson, Lindsay, Bradford B. Hepler, and Myoung Ouk Kim. 2012. *Islander Population: 2010.* May 2012. C2010BR-12. Washington, DC: U.S. Government Printing Office.

Hjelmgaard, Kim. 2015. Violence Against Jews Surges. *USA Today* (April 16): 3A.

Hmong Studies Journal. 2017. 2015 Hmong Census. Accessible at www. hmongstudies.org.

Hochschild, Arlie Russell. 1990. The Second Shift: Employed Women Are Putting in Another Day of Work at Home. *Utne Reader* (March–April), 38: 66–73.

———. 2016. The Right vs. the Family. *Dissent,* 63 (1): 42–47.

Hoeffel, Elizabeth M., Sonya Rastogi, Myoung Ouk Kim, and Hasan Shahid. 2012. *The Asian Population: 2010.* C2010BR-11. Accessible at http://www.census.gov.

Hogan, Bernie, and Brent Berry. 2011. Racial and Ethnic Biases in Rental Housing: An Audit Study of Online Apartment Listings. *City and Community,* 10 (4): 351–372.

Holson, Laura M., and Nick Bilton. 2012. Facebook's Royal Wedding. *New York Times* (May 25).

Honda, Mike. 2014, Who I Am. Accessed May 31, 2014, at http:// honda.house.gov/meet-mike/who-i-am.

Hoover, Eric. 2013. Colleges Contemplate a "Race Neutral" Future. *Chronicle of Higher Education* (October 18): 30, 32–33.

Hopi Tribe. 2016. Two Nations, One Voice Discussions Between Navajo and Hopi Continue Press Release. May 18. Accessible at www.hopi-nsn.gov.

Hosokawa, Bill. 1969. *Nisei: The Quiet Americans.* New York: Morrow.

Hout, Michael. 2016. Saint Peter's Leaky Boat: Falling Intergenerational Persistence among U.S.-Born Catholics since 1974. *Sociology of Religion,* 77 (1): 1–17.

Howden, Lindsay, and Julie A. Meyer. 2011. *Age and Sex Composition: 2010.* May. C2010BR-03. Accessible at http://www.census.gov.

Hu, Winnie. 2012. To Revive Communities in U.S., Jewish Groups Try Relocation Bonuses. *New York Times* (September 19): A23–A24.

Hubbard, Amy S. 1993. *U.S. Jewish Community Responses to the Changing Strategy of the Palestinian Nationalist Movement: A Pilot Study.* Paper presented at annual meeting of the Eastern Sociological Society, Boston.

Hudgins, John L. 1992. The Strengths of Black Families Revisited. *The Urban League Review* (Winter), 15: 9–20.

Hughley, Matthew W., and Jessie Daniels. 2013. Racist Comments at Online News Sites: A Methodological Dilemma for Discourse Analysis. *Media, Culture & Society,* 35 (3): 332–347.

Huhndorf, Roy M., and Shari M. Huhndorf. 2011. Alaska Native Policies Since the Alaska Native Claims Settlement Act. *The South Atlantic Quarterly,* 111 (2): 385–401.

Humes, Karen R., Nicholas A. Jones, and Roberto R. Ramirez. 2011. Overview of Race and Hispanic Organization. *2010 Census Briefs.* C2010 BR-02.

Hung, Minh. 2015. It's Still Hard for Foreigners, Viet Kieu to Buy Houses in Vietnam. September 15. Accessible at www.thanhniennews.com.

Hunter, Lori M., Jessie K. Luna, and Rachel M. Norton. 2015. Environmental Dimensions of Migration. *Annual Review of Sociology* 41: 377–397.

Huntington, Samuel P. 1993. The Clash of Civilizations? *Foreign Affairs,* 73 (3), (Summer): 22–49.

———. 1996. *The Clash of Civilizations and the Remaking of World Order.* New York: Simon & Schuster.

Hurh, Won Moo. 1994. Majority Americans' Perception of Koreans in the United States: Implications of Ethnic Images and Stereotypes. Pp. 3–21 in *Korean Americans: Conflict and Harmony,* H. Kwon, ed. Chicago: Center for Korean Studies.

Hurh, Won Moo. 1998. *The Korean Americans.* Westport, CT: Greenwood Press.

Hurh, Won Moo, and Kwang Chung Kim. 1984. *Korean Immigrants in America: A Structural Analysis of Ethnic Confinement and Adhesive Adaptation.* Cranbury, NJ: Farleigh Dickinson University Press.

Hussar, William J., and Tabitha M. Bailey. 2014. *Projection of Education Statistics to 2022,* 41st ed. February. Accessible at www. nces.gov.

Huteson, Pamela Rae. 2008. Canada, First Nations. Pp. 230–233 in vol. 1, *Encyclopedia of Race, Ethnicity, and Society,* Richard T. Schaefer, ed. Thousand Oaks, CA: Sage.

Hyun, Jane. 2006. *Breaking the Bamboo Ceiling: Career Strategies for Asians.* New York: Harper Business.

———. 2009. Better Luck Tomorrow: Breaking the Bamboo Ceiling. Interview with Peter Nguyen. (October 14.) Accessed July 30, 2012, at http://diversitymbamagazine.com.

IAAMS. 2009. *Italian-Americans Against Media Stereotypes.* Accessed January 4, 2011, at http://iaams.blogspot.com.

IBGE. 2006. *PME–Color and Race.* (November 17.) Instituto Brasiliro de Geografia e Estatistica. Accessed June 8, 2011, at http://www. ibge.gov.br/english/presidencia/noticias/noticia_impressao. php?id_noticia=737.

Ignatiev, Noel. 1994. Treason to Whiteness Is Loyalty to Humanity. Interview with Noel Ignatiev. *Utne Reader* (November–December): 83–86.

———. 1995. *How the Irish Became White.* New York: Routledge.

Indian and Northern Affairs Canada and Canadian Polar Commission. 2000. *2000–2001 Estimates.* Ottawa: Canadian Government Publishing.

Indian Arts and Crafts Board. 2017. Home page. Accessible at www. doi.gov.

Innis, Michelle. 2016. An Heir to a Tribe's Culture Ensures Its Language Is Not Forgotten. *New York Times* (April 9): A7.

Inoue, Miyako. 1989. Japanese Americans in St. Louis: From Internees to Professionals. *City and Society* (December), 3: 142–152.

Institute for Jewish and Community Research. 2008. *How Many Jews Are in World Today.* Accessed September 7, 2008, at http://bechol-lashon.org/population/today.php.

Intelligence Report. 2004. Wal-Mart Drops Protocols, but Controversy Lives On (Winter): 3.

International Herald Tribune. 2007. Black Residents of France Say They Are Discriminated Against. *International Herald Tribune* (January 31). Accessible at http://www.nytimes.com.

International Labour Organization. 2016. Labor Force Participation Rate, Female (% of Female Population Ages 15+). Accessible at www.data.worldbank.org.

Inter-Parliamentary Union. 2017. Women in National Parliaments. Situation as of January 1. Accessible at www.ipu.org.

Isaac, Mike, 2017. Uber Chief, Facing Worker Ire, Quits Team of Trump Advisers. *New York Times* (February 3): 1, 13.

Iwamasa, Gayle Y. 2008a. Internment Camps. Pp. 745–747 in vol. 2, *Encyclopedia of Race, Ethnicity, and Society,* Richard T. Schaefer, ed. Thousand Oaks, CA: Sage.

———. 2008b. Japanese American Citizens League. Pp. 781–782 in vol. 2, *Encyclopedia of Race, Ethnicity, and Society,* Richard T. Schaefer, ed. Thousand Oaks, CA: Sage.

Iwasaki, Michiko, and Alexander Brown. 2013. Qualitative Application of the Acculturation Model by Schwartz et al.: A Sample of Japanese American Women. *Asian American Journal of Psychology,* 4 (1): 325–334.

Izadi, Elahe. 2017. Airbrushing Civil Rights History. *Washington Post.* Reprinted in *The Week* (January 27): 12.

Jacobson, Cardell, J. Lynn England, and Robyn J. Barrus. 2008. Familism. Pp. 477–478 in vol. 1, *Encyclopedia of Race, Ethnicity, and Society,* Richard T. Schaefer, ed. Thousand Oaks, CA: Sage.

Jaher, Frederic Caple. 1994. *A Scapegoat in the New Wilderness.* Cambridge, MA: Harvard University Press.

Janisch, Roy F. 2008. Wounded Knee 1890 and 1973. Pp. 1415–1417 in vol. 3, *Encyclopedia of Race, Ethnicity, and Society,* Richard T. Schaefer, ed. Thousand Oaks, CA: Sage.

Japanese American Citizens League (JACL). 2013. *Goals of the JACL Anti-Hate Program.* Accessed September 13, 2013, at http://www. jacl.org/public_policy/goals.htm.

——. 2016. JACL Statement on Liang Decision. February 25. Accessible at www.jacl.org.

Jardina, Ashley, and Nancy Burns. 2016. Advances and Ambivalence: The Consequences of Women's Educational and Workforce Changes for Women's Political Participation in the United States, 1952 to 2012. *The Russell Sage Foundation Journal of the Social Sciences,* 2 (4): 272–301.

Jaroszyn'ska-Kirchmann, A. 2004. *The Exile Mission: The Polish Political Diaspora and Polish Americans, 1939–1956.* Athens: Ohio University Press.

Jefferies, Sierra M. 2007. Environmental Justice and the Skull Valley Goshute Indians' Proposal to Store Nuclear Waste. *Journal of Land, Resources, and Environmental Law,* 27 (2): 409–429.

Jefferys, Kelly. 2006. *Refugees and Asylees: 2005.* June. Washington, DC: Department of Homeland Security. Accessible at www.dhs.gov.

Jiménez, Tomás R. 2007. The Next Americans. *Los Angeles Times* (May 27): M1, M7.

Johnson, David. 2005. Uncertain Progress 25 Years After Defying State. *News from Indian County* (June 27), 19: 1, 5.

Johnson, David R., and Lauren K. Bachan. 2013. What Can We Learn from Studies Based on Small Sample Sizes? Comment on Regan, Lakhanpal, and Anguiano. *Psychological Reports: Relationships & Communications,* 113 (1): 221–224.

Johnson, Jenna, and David Weigel. 2015. Donald Trump Calls for "Total" Ban on Muslims Entering the United States. *Washington Post* (December 8). Accessible at www.washingtonpost.com.

Johnson, Tallese D., Merarys Rios, Malcolm P. Drewery, Sharon R. Ennis, and Myoung Ouk Kim. 2010. People Who Spoke a Language Other Than English at Home by Hispanic Origin and Race: 2009. *American Community Survey Brief* ACSBR/09-19. Accessible at http://www.census.gov.

Johnston, Tim. 2008. Australia to Apologize to Aborigines for Past Mistreatment. *New York Times* (January 31).

Joint Center for Political and Economic Studies. 2011. *National Roster of Black Elected Officials: Fact Sheet.* Washington, DC: JCPES.

Jolivette, Andrew. 2008. Pan-Indianism. Pp. 1022–1028 in vol. 2, *Encyclopedia of Race, Ethnicity, and Society,* Richard T. Schaefer, ed. Thousand Oaks, CA: Sage.

Jones, Nicholas. 2012. *Who Is "Black" in America?* (July 6.) Accessible at http://www.census.gov/newsroom/cspan/black/.

Jones, Rachel K., Mia R. S. Zolna, Stanley K. Henshaw, and Laurence B. Finer. 2008. Abortion in the United States: Incidence and Access to Services, 2005. *Perspectives on Sexual and Reproductive Health* (March), 40: 6–16.

Jones-Puthoff, Alexa. 2013. *Is the U.S. Population Getting Older and More Diverse?* (June 14.) Accessible at http://www.census.gov/newsroom/cspan/pop_diverse/.

Jonsson, Patrik. 2005. Noncitizen Soldiers: The Quandaries of Foreign-Born Troops. *Christian Science Monitor* (July 5): 1.

——. 2016a. Ellis Island of the South. *Christian Science Monitor* (January 18): 26-32.

——. 2016b. Transgender Issues Get Wider Airing. *Christian Science Monitor Weekly* (June 6): 17.

Jordan, Miriam. 2009. Got Workers? Dairy Farmers Run Low on Labor. *Wall Street Journal* (July 30). Accessible at http://online.wsj.com.

——. 2012. Heartland Draws Hispanics to Help Revive Small Towns. *New York Times* (November 9): A1, A8.

Joseph, Dan. 2010. *America's 10 Poorest Counties Are in Gulf Coast States, Kentucky and on Indian Reservations.* (December 17.) Accessed April 27, 2011, at http://www.cnsnews.com.

Jung, Linda P., Desiree Baolin Qin, and Irene J. K. Park. 2013. Deconstructing the Myth of the "Tiger Mother": An Introduction to the Special Issue on Tiger Parenting, Asian-Heritage Families, and Child/Adolescent Well-Being. *Asian American Journal of Psychology,* 4 (1): 1–6.

Kahlenberg, Richard D. 2010. 10 Myths About Legacy Preference in College Admissions. *Chronicle of Higher Education* (October 1): A23–A25.

Kalev, Alexandria, Frank Dobbin, and Erin Kelly. 2006. Best Practices or Best Guesses? Diversity Management and the Remediation of Inequality. *American Sociological Review,* 71: 589–617.

Kalita, S. Mitra. 2003. *Suburban Sahibs: Three Immigrant Families and Their Passage from India to America.* New Brunswick, NJ: Rutgers University Press.

Kambayashi, Takegiko. 2013. Kyoko Okutani Helps Women Start Their Own Businesses, So They Can Skirt Japan's Gender Gap in the Workplace. *Christian Science Monitor Weekly Edition* (September 9): 44–45.

Kana'iaupuni, Shawn Malia. 2008. Hawaiians. Pp. 599–602 in vol. 1, *Encyclopedia of Race, Ethnicity, and Society,* Richard T. Schaefer, ed. Thousand Oaks, CA: Sage.

Kana'iolowalu. 2016. *Rebuilding the Hawaiian Nation.* April 21. Accessible at www.kanaiolowalu.org.

Kaneda, Toshiko, and Kristin Bietsch. 2016. *2016 World Population Data Sheet.* Accessible at www.prb.org.

Kang, Jerry, and Kristen Lane. 2010. Seeing Through Colorblindness: Implicit Bias and the Law. *UCLA Law Review,* 58: 465–520.

Kang, K. Connie. 1996. Filipinos Happy with Life in U.S. but Lack United Voice. *Los Angeles Times* (January 26): A1, A20.

Kashima, Tetsuden. 2003. *Judgment Without Trial: Japanese Americans Imprisonment During World War II.* Seattle: University of Washington Press.

Katz, Jeffrey. 2012. Google's Monopoly and Internet Freedom. *Wall Street Journal* (June 8): A15.

Katz, Michael B., Mark J. Stern, and Jamie J. Fader. 2007. The Mexican Immigration Debate. *Social Science History,* 3 (Summer): 157–189.

Keane, Colleen. 2015. 2015—A Look Back at a Year of Native Youth Activism. *Navajo Times* (December 30): 1, 7.

Kearns, Rick. 2011. On the Rise. *Indian County Today* (May 18): 10.

Keaton, Trica Danielle, T. Dean Sharpley-Whiting, and Tyler Stoval, eds. 2012. *Black France/France Noire: The History and Politics of Blackness.* Durham, NC: Duke University Press.

Keister, Lisa, Judy Agius Vallejo, and E. Paige Borelli. 2014. Mexican American Mobility: Early Life Processes and Adult Wealth Ownership. *Social Forces* (March): 1015–1046.

Kelly, Cara. 2016. *The Bachelor's Chance to Break the Diversity Stalemate.* *USA Today* (March 7).

Kenji America. 2013. *Cheerios Parody "Just Checking" Response to Haters.* Accessed August 5, 2013, at http://www.youtube.com/user/kenjiamerica.

——. 2010. *Large Wealth Gap Among U.S. Racial and Ethnic Groups.* Accessed September 9, 2010, at http://www.prb.org/Articles/2010/usnetworth.aspx?p=1.

Keveney, Bill. 2016. Opportunity Still Lags Behind the Scenes. *USA Today* (November 2): 2D.

Khadour, Ghaith. 2016. Islam in Higher Education: Exploring the Intra-Religious Interactions Between Shia & Sunni Students. December 30. Wilfred Laurier University. Accessible at www.schol-ars.wiu.ca.

Kieh, George Klay, Jr. 1995. Malcolm X and Pan-Africanism. *Western Journal of Black Studies,* 19 (4): 293–299.

Killian, Lewis M. 1975. *The Impossible Revolution, Phase 2: Black Power and the American Dream.* New York: Random House.

Kim, Barbara, and Grace J. Yoo. 2008. Korean Americans. Pp. 811–814 in vol. 2, *Encyclopedia of Race, Ethnicity, and Society,* Richard T. Schaefer, ed. Thousand Oaks, CA: Sage.

Kim, Chang Hwan, and Arthur Sakamoto. 2010. Have Asian American Men Achieved Labor Market Parity with White Men? *American Sociological Review,* 73 (6): 934–957.

Kim, Joon K. 2008. Wetbacks. Pp. 1393–1395 in vol. 3, *Encyclopedia of Race, Ethnicity, and Society,* Richard T. Schaefer, ed. Thousand Oaks, CA: Sage.

Kim, Kiljoong. 2006. The Korean Presence in Chicago. In *The New Chicago,* John Koval et al., eds. Philadelphia: Temple University Press.

Kim, Nadia U. 2008. *Imperial Citizens: Koreans and Race from Seoul to LA.* Stanford, CA: Stanford University Press.

Kim, Su Yeong, Yijie Wang, Diana Orozco-Lapray, Yishan Shen, and Mohammed Murtuza, 2013. Does "Tiger Parenting" Exist? Parenting Profiles of Chinese Americans and Adolescent Development Outcomes. *Asian American Journal of Psychology*, 4 (1): 7–18.

Kimura, Yukiko. 1988. *Issei: Japanese Immigrants in Hawaii*. Honolulu: University of Hawaii Press.

King, J. E., and E. E. Swartz. 2015. *The Afrocentric Praxis of Teaching for Freedom: Connecting Culture to Learning*. New York: Routledge.

King, Martin Luther, Jr. 1958. *Stride Towards Freedom: The Montgomery Story*. New York: Harper.

———. 1963. *Why We Can't Wait*. New York: Mentor.

———. 1967. *Where Do We Go from Here: Chaos or Community?* New York: Harper & Row.

———. 1971. I Have a Dream. Pp. 346–351 in *Black Protest Thought in the Twentieth Century*, August Meier, Elliott Rudwick, and Francis L. Broderick, eds. Indianapolis, IN: Bobbs-Merrill.

King, Peter. 2004. Private Moments in the Public Eye. *Los Angeles Times* (August 5): A1, A16, A17.

King, Thomas. 2012. *The Inconvenient Indian: A Curious Account of Native People in North America*. Minneapolis: University of Minnesota Press.

Kinloch, Graham C. 1974. *The Dynamics of Race Relations: A Sociological Analysis*. New York: McGraw-Hill.

Kinzer, Stephen. 2000. Museums and Tribes: A Tricky Truce. *New York Times* (December 24), sec. 2: 1, 39.

Kirkpatrick, P. 1994. Triple Jeopardy: Disability, Race and Poverty in America. *Poverty and Race*, 3: 1–8.

Kitagawa, Evelyn. 1972. Socioeconomic Differences in the United States and Some Implications for Population Policy. Pp. 87–110 in *Demographic and Social Aspects of Population Growth*, Charles F. Westoff and Robert Parke, Jr., eds. Washington, DC: U.S. Government Printing Office.

Kitano, Harry H. L. 1976. *Japanese Americans: The Evolution of a Subculture*, 2nd ed. Englewood Cliffs, NJ: Prentice Hall.

Kitano, Harry H. L. 1980. Japanese. In *Harvard Encyclopedia of American Ethnic Groups*, Stephen Thernstrom, ed. Cambridge, MA: Belknap Press of Harvard University Press.

Klas, Patricia. 2016. Hispanic Growth in Florida: Will It Determine the Election? *Miami Herald* (July 2). Accessible at www.miamiherald.com.

Klausner, Samuel Z. 1988. Anti-Semitism in the Executive Suite: Yesterday, Today, and Tomorrow. *Moment* (September), 13: 32–39, 55.

Klinkenborg, Verlyn. 2013. Notebook: A Striking Absence of Women. *New York Times* (October 13): 10.

Koch, Wendy. 2006. Push for "Official" English Heats Up. *USA Today* (October 9): 1A.

Kochhar, Rakesh. 2006. *Growth in the Foreign-Born Workforce and Employment of the Native Born*. Washington, DC: Pew Hispanic Center.

Kochhar, Rakesh, and Richard Fry. 2014. Wealth Inequality Has Widened Along Racial, Ethnic Lines Since End of Great Recession. December 12. Accessible at www.pewresearch.org/fact-tank/2014/12/12/racial-wealthgaps-great-recession/.

Kohli, Martin. 2013. Correspondence with author. Chief Regional Economist, Bureau of Labor Statistics.

Kolowich, Steve. 2015. Diversity Training Is in Demand. Does It Work? *Chronicle of Higher Education* (November 27): A6.

Kopacz, Maria A., and Bessie Lee Lawton. 2013. Talking About the YouTube Indians: Images of Native Americans and Viewer Comments on a Viral Video Site. *Howard Journal of Communications*, 24: 17–37.

Koser, Khalid. 2008. *Protecting Displaced Migrants in South Africa*. Brookings Institution (June 23). Accessible at http://www.brookings.edu.

Kosmin, Barry A. 2009. *The Changing Population Profile of American Jews 1990–2008*. Paper presented at the Fifteenth World Congress of Jewish Studies, Jerusalem, Israel, August.

Krase, Jerome. 2006. Seeing Ethnic Succession in Little Italy: Change Despite Resistance. *Modern Italy*, 11 (February): 79–95.

Krauss, Clifford. 2006. Seven Years into Self-Rule, Inuit Are Struggling. *New York Times* (June 18): 4.

Krausz, Ernest. 1973. Israel's New Citizens. Pp. 385–387 in *1973 Britannica Book of the Year*. Chicago: Encyclopedia Britannica.

Kreiter, Marcy. 2016. Who Voted for Trump? 2016 Exit Polls Compared to 2012 Voter Turnout. *International Business Times* (November 9). Accessible at www.ibtimes.com.

Kroeger, Brooke. 2004. When a Dissertation Makes a Difference. *New York Times* (March 20). Accessed January 15, 2005, at http://www.racematters.org/devahpager.htm.

Krogstad, Jens Manuel. 2015. In a Shift Away from New York, More Puerto Ricans Head to Florida. October 30. Accessible at www.pewresearch.org.

———. 2016. 5 facts About Illegal Immigration in the U.S. September 3. Accessible at www.pewresearch.org.

———. 2016a. Rise in English Proficiency Among U.S. Hispanics Is Driven by the Young. April 20. Accessible at www.pewresearch.org.

Krogstad, Jens Manuel, and Mark Hugo Lopez. 2016. Hillary Clinton Won Latino Vote But Fell Below 2012 Support for Obama. November 29. Accessible at www.pewresearch.org.

Krysan, Maria, Reynolds Farley, and Mick P. Couper. 2008. In the Eye of the Beholder. *DuBois Review*, 5 (1): 5–26.

Kurien, Prena. 2004. Multiculturalism, Immigrant Religion, and Diasporic Nationalism: The Development of an American Hinduism. *Social Problems*, 51 (3): 362–385.

Kurien, Prena. 2007. Who Speaks for Indian Americans? Religion, Ethnicity, and Political Formation. *American Quarterly* 59 (September): 759–783.

Kurzman, Charles. 2016. Islamophobia and the Trump Campaign. *Footnotes*, 44 (December): 6.

Kutner, Jeremy, and Ann Hermes. 2013. Erasing Apartheid's Legacy. *Christian Science Monitor Weekly* (November 11): 21–23.

Kwong, Peter. 1994. The Wages of Fear. *Village Voice* (April 26), 39: 25–29.

Kyodo News. 2010. *Japanese Women Stand Low on Corporate Ladder 25 Years After Law Change*. (August 30.) Accessed June 14, 2011, at http://www.japantoday.com.

La Crosse Office of the Mayor. 2016. Official Proclamation from Mayors Kabat and Medinger. December 8. Accessible at sundown.tougaloo.edu/sundowntowns.php.

LaFraniere, Sharon, and Andrew W. Lehren. 2015. The Disproportionate Risk of Driving While Black. *New York Times* (October 25): A1, A22–23.

Lai, K. K. Rebecca, and Jasmine C. Lee. 2016. 10 Percent of Florida Adults Are Ineligible to Vote. Why? *New York Times* (October 7): A13.

Lakota People's Law Project. 2015. *Native Lives Matter*. February. Accessible at www.lakota.org.

Lal, Barbara Ballis. 1995. Symbolic Interaction Theories. *American Behavioral Scientist* (January), 38: 421–441.

Lamborn, Susie D., Jacqueline Nguyen, and Joel O. Bocanegra. 2013. Hmong American Adolescents' Perceptions of Mothers' Parenting Practices: Support, Authority, and Intergenerational Agreement. *Asian American Journal of Psychology*, 4 (1): 50–60.

Landale, Nancy S., and R. S. Oropesa. 2002. White, Black, or Puerto Rican? Racial Self-Identification Among Mainland and Island Puerto Ricans. *Social Forces*, 81 (1): 231–254.

———. 2007. Hispanic Families: Stability and Change. *Annual Review of Sociology*, 33: 381–405.

Landry, Alysa. 2016. John McCain Visits Navajo Country to Discuss "Critical Issues." Indian Country Media Network (September 19). Accessible at www.indiancountrymedianetwork.com.

Lara, Marielena, Cristina Gamboa, M. Iya Kahramanian, Leo S. Morales, and David E. Hayes Bautista. 2005. Acculturation and Latino Health in the United States: A Review of the Literature and Its Sociopolitical Context. Pp. 367–397 in *Annual Review of Public Health 2005*. Palo Alto, CA: Annual Reviews.

Lau, Yvonne M. 2006. Re-Envisioning Filipino American Communities: Evolving Identities, Issues, and Organizations. Pp. 141–153 in

The New Chicago, John Koval et al., eds. Philadelphia: Temple University Press.

Laumann, Edward O., John H. Gagnon, Robert T. Michael, and Stuart Michaels. 1994. *The Social Organization of Sexuality: Sexual Practices in the United States.* Chicago: University of Chicago Press.

Lavender, Abraham D., ed. 1977. *A Coat of Many Colors: Jewish Subcommunities in the United States.* Westport, CT: Greenwood Press.

Lawrence, Lee. 2014. American Way. *Christian Science Monitor* (February 17): 27–32.

Laxson, Joan D. 1991. "We" See "Them": Tourism and Native Americans. *Annals of Tourism Research,* 18 (3): 365–391.

Lazar, Louie. 2013. Delivering News from the Homeland. *Wall Street Journal* (September 6): A16, A17.

Leavitt, Paul. 2002. Bush Calls Agent Kicked Off Flight "Honorable Fellow." *USA Today* (January 8).

Ledward, Brandon C. 2008. Haole. Pp. 579–581 in vol. 2, *Encyclopedia of Race, Ethnicity, and Society,* Richard T. Schaefer, ed. Thousand Oaks, CA: Sage.

Lee, J. J., and Marion R. Casey. 2006. *Making the Irish American.* New York: New York University Press.

Lee, James. 2011. *U.S. Naturalizations: 2010.* Washington, DC: Office of Immigration Statistics.

Lee, Jennifer. 2001. Manhattan's Chinatown Reeling from the Effects of September 11. *New York Times* (November 21): B1, B9.

Lee, Jennifer, and Frank D. Bean. 2007. Redrawing the Color Line. *City and Community* (March), 6: 49–62.

Lee, Jennifer, and Min Zhou. 2014a. The Success Frame and Achievement Paradox: The Costs and Consequences for Asian Americans. *Racial and Social Problems,* 6: 38–55.

————. 2014b. From Unassimilable to Exceptional: The Rise of Asian Americans and "Stereotype Promise." *New Diversities,* 16 (1): 7–22.

Lee, Sou. 2013. Asian Gangs in the United States: A Meta-Synthesis. M.A. Thesis, University of Wisconsin – Eau Claire. May. Accessible at www.opensiuc.lib.siu.edu.

Lee, Wen Ho, with Helen Zia. 2006. *My Country Versus Me: The First-Hand Account by the Los Alamos Scientist Who Was Falsely Accused of Being a Spy.* New York: Hyperion.

Lee, Yueh-Ting, Sandy Vue, Richard Seklecki, and Yue Ma. 2007. How Did Asian Americans Respond to Negative Stereotypes and Hate Crimes? *American Behavioral Scientist* (October), 51: 271–293.

Leehotz, Robert. 1995. Is Concept of Race a Relic? *Los Angeles Times* (April 15): A1, A14.

Lem, Kim. 1976. Asian American Employment. *Civil Rights Digest* (Fall), 9: 12–21.

Leonard, Karen Isaksen. 2003. *Muslims in the United States: The State of Research.* New York: Russell Sage Foundation.

Leonhardt, Leon. 2013. Hispanics, the New Italians. *New York Times* (April 20).

Let Puerto Rico Decide. 2005. *Status Choices.* Accessed October 7, 2006, at http://www.letpuertoricodecide.com (Citizens' Educated Foundation 2005).

Levin, Dan. 2016. Black Lives Matter Here, Too, Say Canadians Angered by Police Shootings. *New York Times* (June 16): A4.

Levin, Jack, and Jim Nolan. 2011. *The Violence of Hate: Confronting Racism, Anti-Semitism, and Other Forms of Bigotry,* 3rd ed. Upper Saddle River, NJ: Pearson.

Levine, Naomi, and Martin Hochbaum, eds. 1974. *Poor Jews: An American Awakening.* New Brunswick, NJ: Transaction Books.

Levitt, Peggy, and B. Nadya Jaworsky. 2007. Transnational Migration Studies: Past Developments and Future Trends. *Annual Review of Sociology,* 33: 129–156.

Lewin, Tamar. 2006. Campaign to End Race Preferences Splits Michigan. *New York Times* (October 31): A1, A19.

Lewinson, Paul. 1965. *Race, Class, and Party: A History of Negro Suffrage and White Politics in the South.* New York: Universal Library.

Lewis, Amanda E. 2004. "What Group?" Studying Whites and Whiteness in the Era of "Color-Blindness." *Sociological Theory* (December), 22: 623–646.

————. 2013. The "Nine Lives" of Oppositional Culture? *DuBois Review,* 10 (1): 279–289.

Lewis, Neil A. 2003. Secrecy Is Backed on 9/11 Detainees. *New York Times* (June 18): A1, A16.

Lewis, Shawn D. 2008. Pressuring Culture: Japanese-Style Private School Thrives with U.S. Transplants. *Detroit News* (July 17).

Lieber, Ron. 2017. Refugees Need Help Here. But How? *New York Times* (February 8): B1, B2.

Liebman, Charles S. 1973. *The Ambivalent American Jew.* Philadelphia: Jewish Publication Society of America.

Light, Ivan H., Georges Sabagh, Mendi Bozorgmehr, and Claudia Der-Martirosian. 1994. Beyond the Ethnic Enclave Economy. *Social Problems* (February), 41: 65–80.

Light, Steven Andrew, and Kathryn R. L. Rand. 2007. *Indian Gaming and Tribal Sovereignty: The Casino Compromise.* Lawrence: University of Kansas Press.

Lin, Sam Chu. 1996. Painful Memories. *AsianWeek* (July 12), 17: 10.

Lincoln, C. Eric. 1994. *The Black Muslims in America,* 3rd ed. Grand Rapids, MI: William B. Eerdmans.

Lind, Andrew W. 1946. *Hawaii's Japanese: An Experiment in Democracy.* Princeton, NJ: Princeton University Press.

Lindner, Eileen. 2012. *Yearbook of American and Canadian Churches 2011.* Nashville, TN: Abingdon Press.

Lindsey, Brink. 2013. Why People Keep Misunderstanding the "Connection" Between Race and IQ. *The Atlantic* (May 15). Accessible at www.theatlantic.com.

Linthicum, Kate. 2011. Pain Propels a Quest for the Truth. *Chicago Tribune* (July 26): 13.

Lipka, Michael. 2013. *Abercrombie Hijab Firing Highlights Muslim Concern About Discrimination.* (September 11.) Accessed September 24, 2013, at http://www.researchcenter.org.

————. 2016. Muslims and Islam: Key Findings in the U.S. and Around the World. July 25. Accessible at www.pewresearch.org.

Liptak, Adam. 2014. Supreme Court Rejects Contraceptives Mandate for Some Corporations. *New York Times* (June 30). Accessible at www.nytimes.com.

————. 2014a. A Discredited Supreme Court Ruling That Still, Technically, Stands. *New York Times* (January 28): N A15.

Liu, Michael, and Kim Geron. 2008. Changing Neighborhood: Ethnic Enclaves and the Struggle for Social Justice. *Social Justice* 35 (2): 18–35.

Llana, Sara Miller. 2013. Brazil's Affirmative Action Law Offers a Huge Hand Up. *Christian Science Monitor* (February 13). Accessible at http://www.csmonitor.com.

————. 2015. A New Era for Muslims in France? *Christian Science Monitor* (January 26): 13.

Llosa, Alvaro Vargas. 2013. *Global Crossings: Immigration, Civilization, and America.* Oakland, CA: The Independent Institute.

Loewen, James. 2005. *Sundown Towns: A Hidden Dimension of American Racism.* New York: Free Press.

————. 2017. Sundown Towns. Accessible at sundown.tougaloo.edu/sundowntowns.php.

Loewen, James, and Richard Schaefer. 2008. Sundown Towns. Pp. 301–304 in vol. 2, *Encyclopedia of Race, Ethnicity, and Society,* Richard T. Schaefer, ed. Thousand Oaks, CA: Sage.

Lofquist, Daphne. 2011. Same-Sex Couple Households. *American Community Survey Briefs.* ACSBR/10-03. (September.) Accessible at http://www.ccnsu.gov.

Lofquist, Daphne, Terry Lugaila, Martin O'Connell, and Sarah Feliz. 2012. *Households and Families: 2010.* C2012BR-14. Accessible at http://www.census.gov/newsroom/releases/archives/2012_census/cb12-68.html.

Logan, John R., and Brian J. Stults. 2011. *The Persistence of Segregation in the Metropolis: New Findings from the 2010 Census.* Providence RI: US 2010 Project.

Logan, John R., and Richard N. Turner. 2013. *Hispanics in the United States: Not Only Mexicans.* Brown University: US 2010 Project.

Lomax, Louis E. 1971. *The Negro Revolt,* rev. ed. New York: Harper & Row.

Longman, Jeré. 2008. Polynesian Pipeline Feeds a Football Titan. *New York Times* (October 8): A1, A20.

Lopata, Helena Znaniecki. 1994. *Polish Americans,* 2nd ed. New Brunswick, NJ: Transaction Books.

López, Gustavo, and Ana Gonzalez-Barrera. 2016. Afro-Latino: A Deeply Rooted Identity Among U.S. Hispanics. March 1. Accessible at www.pewresearch.org.

Lopez, Julie Amparano. 1992. Women Face Glass Walls as Well as Ceilings. *Wall Street Journal* (March 3).

Lopez, Mark Hugo, and Ana Gonzalez-Barrera. 2013. If They Could, How Many Unauthorized Immigrants Would Become U.S. Citizens? (June 27). Accessible at http://www.pewresearch.org.

Lopez, Mark Hugo, Gretchen Livingston, and Rakesh Kochhar. 2009. *Hispanics and the Economic Downturn: Housing Woes and Remittance Cuts.* Washington, DC: Pew Hispanic Center.

Lopez, Mark Hugo, Jeffrey Passel, and Molly Rohal. 2015. Modern Immigration Wave Brings 59 Million to U.S., Driving Population Growth and Change Through 2065. September 28. Accessible at www.pewresearch.org.

Lopez, Mark Hugo, and Gabriel Velasco. 2011. *A Demographic of Puerto Ricans, 2009.* Washington, DC: Pew Hispanic Center.

Lorber, Judith. 2005. *Breaking the Bounds: Degendering and Feminist Change.* New York: W. W. Norton.

Los Angeles Times Poll. 1998. American and Israeli Jews. Los Angeles: Los Angeles Times and Yedioth Ahronoth.

LoSasso, Anthony T., Michael R. Richards, Chiu-Fang Chou, and Susan E. Gerber. 2011. The $16,819 Pay Gap for Newly Trained Physicians: The Unexplained Trend of Men Earning More Than Women. *Health Affairs,* 30 (2): 193–201.

Louie, Andrea. 2004. *Chineseness Across Borders: Renegotiation Chinese Identities in China and the United States.* Durham, NC: Duke University Press.

Loury, Glenn C. 1996. Joy and Doubt on the Mall. *Utne Reader* (January–February), 73: 70–73.

Loveless, Tom. 2017. *How Well Are American Students Learning?* Washington, DC: Brown Center on Education Policy at Brookings.

Loveman, Mora, and Jeronimo O. Muniz. 2007. How Puerto Rico Became White: Boundary Dynamics and Intercensus Racial Reclassification. *American Sociological Review* (December), 72: 915–939.

Luce, Clare Boothe. 1975. Refugees and Guilt. *New York Times* (May 11): E19.

Luconi, Stefano. 2001. *From Peasant to White Ethnics: The Italian Experience in Philadelphia.* Albany: State University Press of New York.

Lugo, Luis, Alan Cooperman, James Bell, Erin O'Connell, and Sandra Stencel. 2013. *The World's Muslims: Religion, Politics and Society.* Washington, DC: Pew Research Center.

Lugo, Luis, Alan Cooperman, Gregory A. Smith, Erin O'Connell, and Sandra Stencel. 2013a. *A Portrait of Jewish Americans: Findings from a Pew Research Center Survey of U.S. Jews.* (October 1.) Accessible at http://www.pewforum.org/files/2013/10/jewish-american-full-report-for-web.pdf.

Luker, Kristin. 1984. *Abortion and the Politics of Motherhood.* Berkeley: University of California Press.

Luo, Michael. 2006b. An Orthodox Jewish Woman and Soon, a Spiritual Leader. *New York Times* (August 21): B1, B4.

Lustick, Ian S. 2013. Two-State Illusion. *New York Times* (September 6), Sunday Review section, pp. 1,6.

Lytle, Ashley, and Sharon R. Levy. 2015. Reducing Heterosexuals' Prejudice Toward Gay Men and Lesbian Women via an Induced Cross-Orientation Friendship. *Psychology of Sexual Orientation and Gender Diversity,* 2 (4): 447–455.

Macartney, Suzanne, Alemayehu Bishaw, and Kayla Fontenot. 2013. Poverty Rates for Selected Detailed Race and Hispanic Groups by State and Place: 2007–2011. (February.) *American Community Survey Briefs.* ACSBR/11-17. Accessible at http://www.census.gov.

MacDonald, Alistair, and Paul Viera. Canada's Own Pipeline Problem. *Wall Street Journal* (April 20): A1, A10.

MacFarlane, Marco. 2006. Demographics. Pp. 1–50 in *South African Survey 2004/2005.* Johannesburg: South African Institute of Race Relations.

———. 2008. South Africa in Brief. *Fast Facts,* 10 (October): 1–15.

MacFarquhar, Neil. 2008. Resolute or Fearful, Many Muslims Turn to Home Schooling. *New York Times* (March 26).

Mack, Raymond W. 1996. Whose Affirmative Action? *Society* 33 (March–April): 41–43.

Macmillan, Leslie. 2012. Uranium Mines Dot Navajo Land, Neglected and Still Perilous. *New York Times* (April 1): 16.

Magin, Janis L. 2008. Occupation of Royal Palace Invigorates Native Hawaiian Movement. *New York Times* (May 3): A14.

Maheshwari, Sapna, and Mike Isaac. 2016. Facebook Limits Ads Targeted by Race. *New York Times* (November 12): B1.

Mahler, Jonathan. 2016. Report Cites Rise in Anti-Semitic Posts on Twitter, Many by Trump Backers. *New York Times* (October 16): A14.

Malhotra, Nei, and Yotam Margalit. 2009. State of the Nation: Anti-Semitism and the Economic Crisis. *Boston Review* (May/June). Accessible at http://bostonreview.net/BR34.3/malhotra_margalit.php.

Malkin, Michelle. 2004. *In Defense of the Internment: The Case for Racial Profiling in World War II and the War on Terror.* Regency Books.

Malone, Nolan, Kaari F. Baruja, Joseph M. Costanzo, and Cynthia J. Davis. 2003. *The Foreign-Born Population: 2000.* C2KBR-34. Accessible at http://www.census.gov/prod/2003pubs/c2kbr-34.pdf.

Mandela, Nelson. 1990. Africa, It Is Ours. *New York Times* (February 12): A10.

Mann, Keith A. 2008. France. Pp. 506–508 in vol. 1, *Encyclopedia of Race, Ethnicity, and Society,* Richard T. Schaefer, ed. Thousand Oaks, CA: Sage.

Manning, Robert D. 1995. Multiculturalism in the United States: Clashing Concepts, Changing Demographics, and Competing Cultures. *International Journal of Group Tensions* (Summer): 117–168.

Marist Poll. 2015. PBS NewsHour/Marist Poll. Summary of National Findings. September 2015. Accessible at www.pbs-newshour-marist-poll-sep2015.pdf.

Marosi, Richard. 2007. The Nation: A Once-Porous Border Is a Turning-Back Point. *Los Angeles Times* (March 21): A1, A20.

Marshall, Patrick. 2001. Religion in Schools. *CQ Researcher* (July 12), 11: 1–24.

Martin, Daniel C., and James E. Yankay. 2013. *Refugees and Asylees: 2012.* Washington, DC: Office of Immigration Statistics.

Martin, Joel W. 2001. *The Land Looks After Us: A History of Native American Religion.* New York: Oxford University Press.

Martin, Karin A. 2009. Normalizing Heterosexuality: Mothers' Assumptions, Talk, and Strategies with Young Children. *American Sociological Review,* 24 (April): 190–207.

Martin, Karin A., and Katherine P. Luke. 2010. Gender Differences in the ABC's of the Birds and the Bees: What Mothers Teach Young Children About Sexuality and Reproduction. *Sex Roles,* 62 (3–4): 151–291.

Marx, Anthony. 1998. *Making Race and Nation: A Companion of the United States, South Africa, and Brazil.* Cambridge, UK: Cambridge University Press.

Marx, Karl, and Frederick Engels. 1955. *Selected Works in Two Volumes.* Moscow: Foreign Languages Publishing House.

Masayesva, Vernon. 1994. The Problem of American Indian Religious Freedom: A Hopi Perspective. *American Indian Religions: An Interdisciplinary Journal,* 1 (Winter), pp. 93–96.

Masci, David. 2014. Why Has Pentecostalism Grown So Dramatically in Latin America? November 14. Accessible at www.pewresearch.org.

Mason, Christopher. 2007. Immigrants Reject Quebec's Separatists. *New York Times* (May 20): 6.

Massey, Douglas S. 2016. Residential Segregation Is the Linchpin of Racial Stratification. *City & Community,* 15 (March): 4–7.

———. 2011. The Past and Future of American Civil Rights. *Daedalus*, 140 (Spring): 37–54.

———. 2012. Reflections on the Dimensions of Segregation. *Social Forces*, 91 (1): 39–43.

Massey, Douglas S., and Nancy A. Denton. 1993. *American Apartheid: Segregation and the Making of the Underclass*. Cambridge, MA: Harvard University Press.

Massey, Douglas S., and Margarita Mooney. 2007. The Effects of America's Three Affirmative Action Programs on Academic Performance. *Social Problems*, 54 (1): 99–117.

Mastony, Colleen. 2013. Poland Calling Them Home. *Chicago Tribune* (January 13): 1, 12.

Masud-Piloto, Felix. 2008b. Marielitos. Pp. 872–874 in vol. 2, *Encyclopedia of Race, Ethnicity, and Society*, Richard T. Schaefer, ed. Thousand Oaks, CA: Sage.

Matar, Shadi. 2015. Arab Portrayal in Film: A History of Stereotypes. March 20. Blog at Arab American Anti-Discrimination Committee. Accessible at www.aaadc.org.

Mather, Mark, and Kelvin Pollard. 2007. Hispanic Gains Minimize Population Losses in Rural and Small-Town America. *Population Reference Bureau*. Accessible at http://www.prb.org/Articles/2007/HispanicGains.aspx.

Mathias, Christopher. 2017. You Can Help Rebuild a Mosque That Was Burned Down in America. *The Huffington Post* (January 16). Accessible at http://www.huffingtonpost.com/entry/mosque-arson-fire-bellevue-washington_us_587cfcfce4b09281d0ebc346.

Matthiessen, Peter. 1991. *In the Spirit of Crazy Horse*. New York: Peking.

———. 2014. *Sal Si Puedes (Escape If You Can): César Chávez and the New American Revolution*. With a New Forward by Marc Grossman. Berkeley: University of California Press.

Mauro, Tony. 1995. Ruling Helps Communities Set Guidelines. *USA Today* (December 21): A1, A2.

Mazzei, Patricia. 2016. Ugly Rift Opens Among Once-United Cuban Americans over Push to Partner with Castro Regime. *Miami Herald* (December 6). Accessible at www.miamiherald.com.

Mazzocco, Philip J., Timothy C. Brock, Gregory J. Brock, Kristen R. Olson, and Mahzarin R. Banaji. 2006. The Cost of Being Black: White Americans' Perceptions and the Question of Reparations. *DuBois Review*, 3 (2): 261–297.

McCabe, Kristen. 2012. *Foreign-Born Health Care Workers in the United States*. (June.) Accessible at http://www.migrationinformation.org/USfocus/display.cfm?id=898.

McCauley, Mary Beth. 2015. Why Religion Still Matters. *Christian Science Monitor* (October 12): 26–32.

McCloud, Aminah Beverly. 1995. *African American Islam*. New York: Routledge.

McCormick, John. 2015. Bloomberg Politics Poll, December 9. Accessible at www.bloomberg.com.

McGee, Celia. 2010. The Open Road Wasn't Quite Open to All. *New York Times* (August 23), pp. C1, C2.

McGurn, William. 2009. New Jersey's "Italian" Problem. *Wall Street Journal* (July 28): A15.

McIntosh, Peggy. 1988. *White Privilege: Unpacking the Invisible Knapsack*. Wellesley, MA: Wellesley College Center for Research on Women.

McKinley, James C., Jr. 2005. Mexican Pride and Death in U.S. Service. *New York Times* (March 22): A6.

McKinney, Karyn D. 2003. I Feel "Whiteness" When I Hear People Blaming Whites: Whiteness as Cultural Victimization. *Race and Society*, 6: 39–55.

McNamara, Keith, and Jeanne Batalova. 2015. *Filipino Immigrants in the United States*. (July 21). Accessible at www.migrationpolicy.org.

McNickle, D'Arcy. 1973. *Native American Tribalism: Indian Survivals and Renewals*. New York: Oxford University Press.

Meagher, Timothy J. 2005. *The Columbia Guide to Irish American History*. New York: Columbia University Press.

Meier, Allison. 2015. The Freedmen Fight for Tribal Citizenship in a New Documentary. June 18. Accessible at http://hyperallergic.com.

Meister, Alan. 2013. *Indian Gaming Industry Report 2013*. Newton, MA: Casino City Press.

———. 2016. *Casino City's Indian Gaming Industry Report*. Newton, MA: Casino City Press.

Melia, Michael. 2017. White Privilege Essay Contest Stirs Passions in Upscale Town. January 31. Associated Press. Accessible at www.staging.hosted.ap.org.

Menchaca, Charles. 2008. Scholars Learn Hmong Basics. *Wausau Daily Herald* (August 14).

Meraji, Shereen Marisol. 2014. Before "Brown v. Board," Mendez Fought California's Segregated Schools. May 16. NPR. Accessible at www.wbur.org.

Merton, Robert K. 1949. Discrimination and the American Creed. Pp. 99–126 in *Discrimination and National Welfare*, Robert M. MacIver, ed. New York: Harper & Row.

———. 1968. *Social Theory and Social Structure*. New York: Free Press.

———. 1976. *Sociological Ambivalence and Other Essays*. New York: Free Press.

Messner, Michael A. 1997. *Politics of Masculinities: Men in Movements*. Thousand Oaks, CA: Sage.

Meyer, Karen. 2008. Americans with Disabilities Act. In *Encyclopedia of Race, Ethnicity, and Society*, Richard T. Schaefer, ed. Thousand Oaks, CA: Sage.

Meyers, Gustavus. 1943. *History of Bigotry in the United States* (rev. by Henry M. Christman, 1960). New York: Capricorn Books.

Michigan Civil Rights Commission. 2017. *The Flint Water Crisis: Systemic Racism Through the Lens of Flint*. February 17. Lansing, MI: Michigan Department of Civil Rights.

Migration Policy Institute. 2015. *The Salvadoran Diaspora in the United States*. Washington, DC: Migration Policy Institute.

Mihesuah, Devon A., ed. 2000. *Reparation Reader: Who Owns American Indian Remains?* Lincoln: University of Nebraska Press.

Miles, Tiya Alicia. 2009. "One of the Longest Unwritten Chapters": The Interrelated Histories of African and Native America. *Symposium on Indivisible: African-Native American Lives in the Americas*. Accessible as a video on www.nmau.si.edu.

Miller, Claire Cain. 2017a. Why Men Don't Want the Jobs Done Mostly by Women. *New York Times* (January 4). Accessible at www.nytimes.com.

———. 2017b. Race and Class Define Men Who Take "Women's Jobs." *New York Times* (March 10): B1, B6.

Miller, David L. 2014. *Introduction to Collective Behavior and Collective Action*, 3rd. ed. Long Grove, IL: Waveland Press.

———. (ed.). 2013. *Koreans in North America: Their Twenty-First Century Experiences*. Lanham, MD: Lexington Books.

Miller, Leila. 2014. A History of Jews in Argentina. July 16. Accessible at www.jewishjournal.com.

Minority Rights Group. 2017. Mexico—Indigenous Peoples. March 30. Accessible at www.indigenousgroups.org.

Mir, Shabana. 2014. *Muslim American Women on Campus: Undergraduate Social Life and Identity*. Chapel Hill: University of North Carolina Press.

Mitra, Diditi. 2008. Pan-Asian Identity. Pp. 1016–1019 in vol. 2, *Encyclopedia of Race, Ethnicity, and Society*, Richard T. Schaefer, ed. Thousand Oaks, CA: Sage.

Mize, Trenton. 2016. Sexual Orientation in the Labor Market. *American Sociological Review* 81 (6): 1132–1160.

Mocha, Frank, ed. 1998. *American "Polonia" and Poland*. New York: Columbia University Press.

Molinary, Rosie. 2007. *Hijas Americanas*. Emeryville, CA: Seal Press.

———. 2017. About Rosie Molinary. Accessible at www.rosiemolinary.com.

Montagu, Ashley. 1972. *Statement on Race*. New York: Oxford University Press.

Monk, Jr., Ellis P. 2016. The Consequence of "Race and Color" in Brazil. *Social Problems* 63: 413–430.

Mora, G. Cristina. 2014. Cross-Field Effects and Ethnic Classification: The Institutionalization of Hispanic Panethnicity, 1965 to 1990. *American Sociological Review*, 79 (2): 183–210.

Morris, Aldon D. 2015. *The Scholar Denied: W. E. B. Du Bois and the Birth of Modern Sociology*. Berkeley: University of California Press.

Morris, Edward W. 2005. From "Middle Class" to "Trailer Trash": Teachers' Perceptions of White Students in a Predominantly Minority School. *Sociology of Education,* 78 (April): 99–121.

Moskos, Charles C., and John Sibley Butler, eds. 1996. *All That We Can Be: Black Leadership and Racial Integration the Army Way.* New York: Basic Books.

Mossaad, Nadwa. 2016. *Refugees and Asylees: 2015.* November. Washington, DC: Department of Homeland Security. Accessible at www.dhs.gov.

Motel, Seth, and Eileen Patten. 2012. *The 10 Largest Hispanic Origin Groups: Characteristics, Rankings, Top Counties.* Washington, DC: Pew Hispanic Center.

Moulder, Frances V. 1996. *Teaching About Race and Ethnicity: A Message of Despair or a Message of Hope?* Paper presented at annual meeting of the American Sociological Association, New York.

Mueller, Jennifer C. 2017. Producing Colorblindness: Everyday Mechanisms of White Ignorance. *Social Problems,* 64: 219-236.

Mujcic, Redzo, and Paul Frijters. 2013. Still Not Allowed on the Bus: It Matters If You're Black or White! March. Working paper (The Institute for the Study of Labor in Bonn, Germany). Accessible at ftp.iza.org.

Mun, Eunmi. 2010. Sex Typing of Jobs in Hiring: Evidence from Japan. *Social Forces,* 88 (5): 1999–2026.

Murray, Sara. 2010. Disabled Face Sharply Higher Jobless Rate. *Wall Street Journal* (August 26): A5.

Muslim Jewish Advisory Council. 2017. What We Stand For. Accessible at www.muslimjewishadvocacy.org.

Myers, Dowell, John Pitkin, and Julie Park. 2004. *California's Immigrants Turn the Corner. Urban Initiative Policy Relief.* Los Angeles: University of Southern California.

Myrdal, Gunnar. 1944. *An American Dilemma: The Negro Problem and Modern Democracy.* New York: Harper & Row.

NaFFAA. 2016. President Obama Signs Bill Granting Recognition to Filipino World War II Veterans. National Federation of Filipino American Associations *National Newsletter,* 5 (December): 1–3.

Nagel, Joane. 1988. *The Roots of Red Power: Demographic and Organizational Bases of American Indian Activism 1950–1990.* Paper presented at annual meeting of the American Sociological Association, Atlanta, GA.

———. 1996. *American Indian Ethnic Renewal: Red Power and the Resurgence of Identity and Culture.* New York: Oxford University Press.

Nahm, H. Y. 2012. *23 Big Milestones in Asian American History.* Accessed November 9, 2013, at http://goldsea.com/AAD/Milestones/milestones.html.

Naimark, Norman M. 2004. Ethnic Cleaning, History of. Pp. 4799–4802 in *International Encyclopedia of Social and Behavioral Sciences,* N. J. Smelser and P. B. Baltes, eds. New York: Elsevier.

Nash, Manning. 1962. Race and the Ideology of Race. *Current Anthropology* (June), 3: 285–288.

National Advisory Commission on Civil Disorders. 1968. *Report.* New York: Bantam.

National Asian Pacific American Legal Consortium. 2002. *Backlash: When America Turned on Its Own.* Washington, DC: NAPALC.

National CAPACD. 2012. *Data Points: Asian American and Pacific Islander Poverty.* (May 1, 2012.) Accessible at http://www.national-capacd.org/.

National Center for Education Statistics. 2013. *Digest of Education Statistics.* Accessible at http://nces.ed.gov/programs/digest/2012menu_tables.asp.

———. 2016. *Digest of Education Statistics 2015.* Accessible at www.nces.ed.gov.

National Committee on Pay Equity. 2017. New Pay Equity Bill Introduced. January 17. Accessible at www.pay-equity.org.

National Conference of State Legislatures. 2017. Voter Identification Requirements/Voter ID Laws. June 5. Accessible at www.ncsl.org.

National Congress of American Indians. 2012. *Toward a New Era. Annual Report 2010–2011.* Washington, DC: NCAI.

National Federation of State High School Associations. 2016. *Participation Statistics 2015–2016.* September 12. Accessible at www.nfhs.org.

National Governors Association. 2013. A Better Bottom Line: Employing People with Disabilities. Accessed September 23, 2013, at http://ci.nga.org/cms/home/1213/index.

National Italian American Foundation. 2006. Stop Ethnic Bashing. *New York Times* (January). Accessed June 4, 2008, at http://www.niaf.org/news/index.asp?id.

National Museum of the American Indian. 2017. *Indivisible: African-Native American Lives in the Americas.* Accessible at www.nmai.si.edu.

National Organization for Men Against Sexism. 2017. 42 Years of NOMAS. Accessible at www.nomas.org.

National Park Service. 2009. *Chinatown and Little Italy Historic District.* Accessible at http://www.nps.gov.

———. 2012. *The War Relocation Camps of World War II: When Fear Was Stronger Than Justice—Supplementary Resources.* Accessed July 16, 2012, at http://www.nps.gov/history/nr/twhp/wwwlps/lessons/89nanzanar/89lrnmore.htm.

Native Federation. 2013. *Native Rights.* Accessed September 10, 2013, at http://www.natiefederation.org/publications/native-rights/.

Navarrete, Federico. 2016. *México Racista: Una Denucia.* Mexico City: Penguin Random House Grupo Editorial.

Navarro, Mireya. 2004. Young Japanese-Americans Honor Ethnic Roots. *New York Times* (August 2): A1, A15.

Navarro-Rivera, Juhem, Marry A. Kosmin, and Ariela Keysar. 2010. *U.S. Latino Religious Identification 1990–2008 Growth, Diversity & Transformation.* Hartford, CT: American Religious Identification Project, Trinity College. Accessible at http://www.americanreligionsurvey-aris.org/latinos2008.pdf.

Nawa, Fariba. 2011. Struggling to Stay Bilingual. *Christian Science Monitor* (October 17): 38–39.

Nelsen, Frank C. 1973. The German-American Immigrants Struggle. *International Review of History and Political Science,* 10 (2): 37–49.

Neugarten, Bernice L. 1996. *The Meanings of Age. Selected Papers of Bernice L. Neugarten.* Ed. with a forward by Dail A. Neugarten. Chicago: University of Chicago Press.

Nevin, Tom. 2008. S. Africa's "Open Door" Initiative Under Fire. *African Business* (July): 54.

New America Media. 2007. *Deep Divisions, Shared Destiny.* San Francisco: New America Media.

Newman, Jon O. 2016. End Racial Bias in Jury Selection. *New York Times* (May 28).

Newman, William M. 1973. *American Pluralism: A Study of Minority Groups and Social Theory.* New York: Harper & Row.

Newport, Frank. 2016. Most Americans Still Believe in God. June 29. Accessible at www.gallup.com.

———. 2017. About Half of Americans Say Trump Moving Too Fast. February 2. Accessible on www.gallup.com.

New York Times. 1991. For Two, an Answer to Years of Doubt on Use of Peyote in Religious Rite (July 9): A14.

———. 1992. Group to Improve Black-Korean Relations Disbands in Los Angeles. (December 26). Accessible at www.nytimes.com.

———. 2005. Warnings Raised About Exodus of Philippine Doctors and Nurses (November 27): 13.

Nicholas, Peter, and Neil King, Jr. 2013. Uneven Election Success for Black Politicians. *Wall Street Journal* (August 28): A4.

Nicholson, David. 2013. First Slaves First Hope. *American History* (June): 68–71.

Niebuhr, Gustav. 1998. Southern Baptists Declare Wife Should "Submit" to Her Husband. *New York Times.*

Nielsen, Joyce McCarl, Glenda Walden, and Charlotte A. Kunkel. 2000. Gendered Heteronormality: Empirical Illusions in Everyday Life. *Sociological Quarterly,* 41 (2): 283–296.

Nishi, Setsuko Matsunga. 1995. Japanese Americans. Pp. 95–133 in *Asian Americans: Contemporary Trends and Issues,* Pyong Gap Min, ed. Thousand Oaks, CA: Sage Publications.

Noah, Trevor. 2016. *Born a Crime: Stories from a South African Childhood.* New York: Random House.

Noble, Barbara Presley. 1995. A Level Playing Field, for Just $121. *New York Times* (March 5): F21.

Noel, Donald L. 1972. *The Origins of American Slavery and Racism.* Columbus, OH: Charles Merrill.

Norrell, Robert J. 2009. *Up from History: The Life of Booker T. Washington.* Cambridge, MA: Harvard University Press.

Norris, Tina, Paula L. Vines, and Elizabeth M. Hoeffel. 2012. *The American Indian and Alaska Native Population: 2010.* C2010BR-10. Accessible at http://www.census.gov.

North, Michael S., and Susan T. Fiske. 2013a. Act Your (Old) Age: Prescriptive, Ageist Biases over Succession, Consumption, and Identity. *Personality and Social Psychological Bulletin,* 39 (6): 720–734.

———. 2013b. A Prescriptive Intergenerational Tension: Ageism Scale: Succession, Identity, and Consumption. *Psychological Assessment Advance* online publication. Doi:10.1037/a0032367.

———. 2013c. Subtyping Ageism: Policy Issues in Succession and Consumption. *Social Issues and Policy Review,* 7(1): 36–57.

Norton, Michael I., and Samuel R. Sommers. 2011. Whites See Racism as a Zero-Sum Game That They Are Now Losing. *Perspectives on Psychological Science,* 6 (3): 215.

Norwood, Kimberly Jade. 2014. *Color Matters: Skin Tone Bias and the Myth of a Post-Racial America.* New York: Routledge.

Novelli, William D. 2004. Common Sense: The Case for Age Discrimination Law. Pp. 4, 7 in *Global Report on Aging.* Washington, DC: AARP.

Nudd, Tim. 2013. It's 2013, and People Are Still Getting Worked Up About Interracial Couples in Ads. *Adweek* (May 30). Accessible at http://www.adweek.com.

Obama, Barack. 2017. Remarks by the President in Final Press Conference. January 18. Accessible at www.whitehouse.gov/thepressoffice.

Oberschall, Anthony. 1968. The Los Angeles Riot of August 1965. *Social Problems* (Winter), 15: 322–341.

Ochoa, Guda L. 2013. *Academic Profiling: Latinos, Asian Americans, and the Achievement Gap.* Minneapolis: University of Minnesota Press.

Office of Immigration Statistics. 2009. *Yearbook of Immigration Statistics: 2008.* Accessible at www.dhs.gov.

———. 2016. *Yearbook of Immigration Statistics 2015 and Data Tables.* Accessible at www.dhs.gov.

Ogbu, John U. 2004. Collective Identity and the Burden of "Acting White" in Black History, Community, and Education. *Urban Review* (March), 36: 1–35.

Ohnuma, Keiko. 1991. Study Finds Asians Unhappy at CSU. *AsianWeek* (August 8), 12: 5.

Okamoto, Dina, and Melanie Jones Gast. 2013. Racial Inclusion or Accommodation? Expanding Community Boundaries Among Asian American Organizations. *DuBois Review,* 10 (1): 131–153.

Okamura, Jonathan Y. 2008. *Ethnicity and Inequality in Hawaii.* Philadelphia, PA: Temple University Press.

Olemetson, Lynette. 2005. Adopted in China, Seeking Identity in America. *New York Times* (March 23): A1.

Oliver, Melvin L., and Thomas M. Shapiro. 1996. *Black Wealth/White Wealth: New Perspective on Racial Inequality.* New York: Routledge.

Olzak, Susan. 1998. Ethnic Protest in Core and Periphery States. *Ethnic and Racial Studies* (March), 21: 187–217.

Omi, Michael, and Howard Winant. 1994. *Racial Formation in the United States,* 2nd ed. New York: Routledge.

———. 2015. *Racial Formation in the United States,* 3rd ed. New York: Routledge.

O'Neill, Maggie. 2008. Authoritarian Personality. Pp. 119–121 in vol. 1, *Encyclopedia of Race, Ethnicity, and Society,* Richard T. Schaefer, ed. Thousand Oaks, CA: Sage.

Onishi, Morimitsu. 2012. At Internment Camp, Pilgrims Explore Choices of the Past. *New York Times* (July 6): A8.

Ontario Human Rights Commission. 2013. *Room for Everyone: Human Rights and Rental Housing Licensing.* Accessed September 19, 2013, at http://www.ohrc.on.ca/en/.

Orenstein, Peggy. 2011. Did I Know You at Camp? *New York Times Sunday Magazine* (September 26): 18.

Orfield, Gary, Jongyeon Ee, Erica Frankenberg, and Genevieve Siegel-Hawley. 2016. *Brown at 62: School Segregation by Race, Poverty and State.* May 16. Los Angeles: Civil Rights Project/*Proyecto Derechos Civiles,* UCLA.

Orfield, Gary, and Erica Frankenberg. 2014. Brown at 60: Great Progress, a Long Retreat, and an Uncertain Future. May 15. Accessible at www.civilrightsproject.ucla.edu.

Organisation for Economic Co-operation and Development. 2016. *OECD Labour Force Statistics 2015.* Paris: OECD.

Orsagh, Matt. 2016. The Current Status of Women on Boards in 2016: A Roundup. *Market Integrity Insights* (October 7). Accessible at blogs.cfainstitute.org.

Orozco, Anthony. 2016. Bridge Name Would Recognize Puerto Rican Veterans. *Reading Eagle* (February 7). Accessible at www.readingeagle.com.

Orlov, Ann, and Reed Ueda. 1980. Central and South Americans. Pp. 210–217 in *Harvard Encyclopedia of American Ethnic Groups,* Stephan Thernstrom, ed. Cambridge, MA: Belknap Press of Harvard University Press.

Ortman, Jennifer, Victoria A. Velkoff, and Howard Hogan. *An Aging Nation: The Older Population in the United States. Current Population Reports 1140.* Accessible at www.census.gov.

Ottaway, David S., and Paul Taylor. 1992. A Minority Decides to Stand Aside for Majority Rule. *Washington Post National Weekly Edition* (April 5), 9: 17.

Padget, Martin. 2004. *Indian Country: Travels in the American Southwest, 1840–1935.* Albuquerque: University of New Mexico Press.

Padilla, Efren N. 2008a. Filipino Americans. Pp. 493–497 in vol. 1, *Encyclopedia of Race, Ethnicity, and Society,* Richard T. Schaefer, ed. Thousand Oaks, CA: Sage.

Pager, Devah. 2003. The Mark of a Criminal. *American Journal of Sociology,* 108: 937–975.

Pager, Devah, and Bruce Western. 2012. Identifying Discrimination at Work: The Use of Field Experiments. *Journal of Social Issues,* 68 (2): 221–237.

Pager, Devah, Bruce Western, and Bart Bonikowski. 2009. Discrimination in a Low-Wage Labor Market: A Field Experiment. *American Sociological Review,* 74 (October): 777–799.

Pais, Jeremy, Kyle Crowder, and Liam Downey. 2014. Unequal Trajectories: Racial and Class Differences in Residential Exposure to Industrial Hazard. *Social Forces* (March): 1189–1215.

Pariser, Eli. 2011a. *The Filter Bubble: What the Internet Is Hiding from You.* New York: Penguin Press.

———. 2011b. In Our Own Little Internet Bubbles. *The Guardian Weekly* (June 24): 32–33.

Park, Robert E. 1928. Human Migration and the Marginal Man. *American Journal of Sociology* (May), 33: 881–893.

———. 1950. *Race and Culture: Essays in the Sociology of Contemporary Man.* New York: Free Press.

Park, Robert E., and Ernest W. Burgess. 1921. *Introduction to the Science of Sociology.* Chicago: University of Chicago Press.

Parks, Sarah J., and Hyung Choi Yoo. 2016. Does Endorsement of the Model Minority Myth Relate to Anti-Asian Sentiments Among White College Students? The Role of a Color-Blind Racial Attitude. *Asian American Journal of Psychology,* 7 (4): 287–294.

Parrillo, Vincent. 2008. Italian Americans. Pp. 766–771 in vol. 2, *Encyclopedia of Race, Ethnicity, and Society,* Richard T. Schaefer, ed. Thousand Oaks, CA: Sage.

Parrillo, Vincent, and Christopher Donoghue. 2013. The National Social Distance Study: Ten Years Later. *Sociological Forum,* 28 (3): 597–614.

Parsons, Talcott, and Robert Bales. 1955. *Family, Socialization and Interaction Process.* Glencoe, IL: Free Press.

Passel, Jeffrey S., and D'Vera Cohn. 2009. *A Portrait of Unauthorized Immigrants in the United States.* Washington, DC: Pew Hispanic Center.

Passel, Jeffrey S., Wendy Wang, and Paul S. Taylor. 2010. *Marrying Out: One-in-Seven New U.S. Marriages Is Interracial or Interethnic.* Washington, DC: Pew Research Center. Accessible at http://www.pewsocialtrends.org/files/2010/10/755-marrying-out.pdf.

Pasternak, Judy. 2010. *Yellow Dirt: An American Story of a Poisoned Land a People Betrayed.* New York: Simon and Schuster.

Pattillo, Mary E. 2013. *Black Picket Fences: Privilege and Peril Among the Black Middle Class.* 2nd ed. Chicago: University of Chicago Press.

Paul, Annie Murphy. 2011. The Roar of the Tiger Mother. *Time* (January 31): 34–40.

Peckham, Pat. 2002. Hmong's Resettlement Changes Agency's Focus. *Wausau Daily Herald* (February 10): 1A, 2A.

Peréz, Linsandro. 2001. Growing Up in Cuban Miami: Immigrants, the Enclave, and New Generations. Pp. 91–125 in *Ethnicities*, Ruben G. Rumbaut and Alejandro Portes, eds. Berkeley: University of California Press.

Peri, Giovanni. 2014. Does Immigration Hurt the Poor? *Pathways* (Summer): 15-18.

Perlmann, Joel. 2005. *Italians Then, Mexicans Now: Immigrant Origins and Second-Generation Progress, 1890–2000.* New York: Russell Sage Foundation.

Perry, Barbara, ed. 2003. *Hate and Bias Crime: A Reader.* New York: Routledge.

Perry, Tony, and Richard Simon. 2009. Filipino Veterans of WWII to Get Long-Overdue Funds. *Los Angeles Times* (February 18): B1, B7.

Peters, Jeremy W. 2016. Asian-Americans' Drift Left Is Cause for Republican Worry. *New York Times* (October 2): 1, 21.

Peterson, Ruth D. 2012. The Central Place of Race in Crime and Justice. *Criminology*, 50 (2): 303–327.

Pettigrew, Thomas F. 2010. Commentary: South African Contributions to the Study of Intergroup Relations. *Journal of Social Issues* 66 (2): 417–430.

———. 2011. Did Brown Fail? *Du Bois Review*, 8 (2): 511–516.

Pew Charitable Trust. 2000. *Jews and the American Public Square Data.* Accessed May 23, 2001, at http://www.pewtrusts.org.

Pew Forum on Religion and Public Life. 2008a. *U.S. Religious Landscape Survey.* Washington, DC: Pew Forum. Accessible at http://religions.pewforum.org/pdf/report2-religious-landscape-study-full.pdf.

———. 2008b. *U.S. Religious Landscape Survey: Religious Beliefs and Practices: Diverse and Politically Relevant.* Washington, DC: Pew Forum on Religion and Public Life.

———. 2011. *The Future of the Global Muslim Population.* Washington, DC: Pew Forum.

———. 2012. *Asian Americans: A Mosaic of Faiths.* (July 19.) Accessed November 1, 2013, at http://www.pewforum.org/2012/07/19/asian-americans-a-mosaic-of-faiths-overview/.

Pew Hispanic Center. 2009. *Between Two Worlds: How Young Latinos Come of Age in America.* Washington, DC: Pew Hispanic Center.

———. 2011a. Mapping the Latino Electorate. Accessible at http://pewhispanic.org/docs/?DocID=26.

———. 2011b. *Unauthorized Immigrants: Length of Residency, Patterns of Parenthood.* (December 1.) Washington, DC: Pew Hispanic Center.

———. 2012a *When Labels Don't Fit: Hispanics and Their Views of Identity.* (April 4.) Washington, DC: Pew Hispanic Center.

Pew Research Center. 2004. *Beliefs That Jews Were Responsible for Christ's Death Increase.* Washington, DC: Pew Research Center.

———. 2013. *A Survey of LGBT Americans: Attitudes, Experiences and Values in Changing Times.* (June 13.) Accessible at http://www.pewresearch.org.

———. 2015. *Multiracial in America: Proud, Diverse, and Growing in Numbers.* June 11. Accessible at www.pewresearch.org.

———. 2015a. *U.S. Public Becoming Less Religious.* November 3. Accessible at www.pewresearch.org.

———. 2015b. *America's Changing Religious Landscape.* May 12. Accessible at www.pewresearch.org.

———. 2015c. Jews. April 2. Accessible at www.pewforum.org.

———. 2016. *On Views of Race and Inequality, Blacks and Whites Are Worlds Apart.* June 27. Accessible at www.pewresearchcenter.org.

———. 2016a. Israel's Religiously Divided Society. March 8. Accessible at www.pewresearchcenter.org.

Pew Research Center for the People and the Press. 2013. *Big Racial Divide over Zimmerman Verdict.* July 22. Accessible at www.people-press.org.

Pew Research Global Attitudes Project. 2013. *Mexicans and Salvadorans Have Positive Picture of Life in U.S.* (October 24.) Accessible at http://www.poewglobal.org.

Pew Research Center Religion and Public Life. 2014. The Shifting Religious Identity of Latinos in the United States. May 7. Accessible at www.pewresearch.org.

Pew Research Center U.S. Politics and Policy. 2014. Growing Concern About Rise of Islamic Extremism at Home and Abroad. September 10. Accessible at www.pewresearch.org.

Pew Social and Demographic Trends. 2012. *The Rise of Asian Americans.* Washington, DC: Pew Social and Demographic Trends.

Pew Templeton. 2015. *The Future of World Religions: Population Growth Projections, 2010–2050.* April 2. Washington, DC: Pew-Templeton Global Religious Futures. Accessible at www.pewresearch.org.

Pewewardy, Cornel. 1998. Our Children Can't Wait: Recapturing the Essence of Indigenous Schools in the United States. *Cultural Survival Quarterly* (Spring): 29–34.

Pfaelzer, Jean. 2007. *Driven Out: The Forgotten War Against Chinese Americans.* New York: Random House.

Pfeifer, Mark. 2008a. Hmong Americans. Pp. 633–636 in vol. 2, *Encyclopedia of Race, Ethnicity, and Society*, Richard T. Schaefer, ed. Thousand Oaks, CA: Sage.

Pido, Antonio J. A. 1986. *The Filipinos in America.* New York: Center for Migration Studies.

Pincus, Fred L. 2003. *Reverse Discrimination: Dismantling the Myth.* Boulder, CO: Lynne Rienner.

———. 2008. *Reverse Discrimination.* Pp. 1159–1161 in vol. 3, *Encyclopedia of Race, Ethnicity, and Society*, Richard T. Schaefer, ed. Thousand Oaks, CA: Sage.

Pineo, Christopher, and Bill Donovan. 2015. 2015 One of the Most Chaotic. *Navajo Times* (December 30): A1, A3.

Pinkney, Alphonso. 1975. *Black Americans*, 2nd ed. Englewood Cliffs, NJ: Prentice Hall.

Pitt, Nicola Ann. 2013. *The Cultural and Political Significance of Tiger Mothering.* Doctorate. Monash University.

Polzin, Theresita. 1973. *The Polish Americans: Whence and Whither.* Pulaski, WI: Franciscan Publishers.

Porter, Catherine. 2017a. Canadian Immigration Is More Complex Than It Looks. *New York Times* (March 3): A20.

———. 2017b. College Built for Canadian Settlers Envisions an Indigenous Future. *New York Times* (June 21): A6.

Porter, Catherine, Dan Levin, and Ian Austen. 2017. Losing Hope in U.S., Refugees Make Icy Trek to Canada. *New York Times* (February 12): 6.

Porter, Eduardo. 2015. For Immigrants, America Is Still More Welcoming Than Europe. *New York Times* (December 8). Accessible at www.nytimes.com.

Portes, Alejandro. 2006. Paths of Assimilation in the Second Generation. *Sociological Forum* (September), 21: 499–503.

Portes, Alejandro, Cristina Escobar, and Alexandria Walton Radford. 2007. Immigrant Transitional Organizations and Development: A Comparative Study. *International Migration Review* 41 (Spring): 242–281.

Portes, Alejandro, and Rubén G. Rumbaut. 2006. *Immigrant America*, 3rd ed. Berkeley: University of California Press.

Posadas, Barbara M. 1999. *The Filipino Americans.* Westport, CT: Greenwood Press.

Poston, Jr., Dudley, and Demetrea Nichole Farris. 2012. Which States Lose House Seats If Puerto Rico Becomes a State? *The Social Contract*, 22 (2).

Potok, Mark. 2016. The Year in Hate and Extremism. *Intelligence Report* (Spring): 35–42.

Powell-Hopson, Darlene, and Derek Hopson. 1988. Implications of Doll Color Preferences Among Black Preschool Children and White Preschool Children. *Journal of Black Psychology* (February): 14: 57–63.

Power, John. 2016. How One Australian State Is Rethinking Its Relationship with Aboriginals. *Christian Science Monitor* (May 12). Accessible at www.csmonitor.com.

Pratt, Timothy. 2012. More Asian Immigrants Find Options on Ballots. *New York Times* (October 19): A14.

President's Task Force on Puerto Rico's Status. 2005. *Report by the President's Task Force on Puerto Rico's Status.* Washington, DC: U.S. Government Printing Office.

Preston, Julia. 2007. Polls Surveys Ethnic Views Among Chief Minorities. *New York Times* (December 13).

———. 2010. On Gangs, Asylum Law Offers Little. *New York Times* (June 30): A15, A19.

Prime, Jeanine. 2011. The Daughter Effect? May 27. Blog at www.catalyst.org.

Prison Policy. 2017. States of Incarceration: The Global Context. Accessible at www.prisonpolicy.org.

Proctor, Bernadette D., Jessica L. Semega, and Melissa A. Kollar. 2016. *Income and Poverty in the United States: 2015. Current Population Reports* P60-256(RV). Accessible at www.census.gov.

Purnell, Newley. 2017. Indian Workers Fear H-1B Curbs. *Wall Street Journal* (February 28): B1–B2.

Quadagno, Jill. 2014. *Aging and the Life Course: An Introduction to Social Gerontology,* 6th ed. New York: McGraw-Hill.

Quillian, Lincoln. 2006. New Approaches to Understanding Racial Prejudice and Discrimination. Pp. 299–328 in *Annual Reviews of Sociology 2006,* Karen S. Cook, ed. Palo Alto, CA: Annual Reviews Inc.

Quirk, Matthew. 2008. How to Grow a Gang. *The Atlantic* (May), 301: 24–25.

Rabinovitch, Simon. 2011. China Labour Costs Soar as Wages Rise 22%. *Financial Times* (October 25). Accessed March 2, 2012, at http://www.ft.com/intl/cms/s/0/25f1c500-ff14-11e0-9b2f-00144feabdc0.html#axzz1nziV8URS.

Railton, Ben. 2016. The Real Precedents Set by Japanese American Internment. *The Huffington Post* (November 17). Accessible at www.huffingtonpost.com.

Ramakrishnan, Karthick. 2016. *Asian American Voices in the 2016 Election.* October 5. Accessible at www.naassurvey.com.

Ramirez, Roberto. 2015. Census Bureau's Working Classification of Middle Eastern or North African for the 2015 National Content Test. May 29. Accessible at www.census.gov.

Rand, Michael R., and Erika Harrell. 2009. Crime Against People with Disabilities. *2007 Bureau of Justice Statistics Special Report* (October).

Raymo, James M., and So-jung Lim. 2011. A New Look at Married Women's Labor Force Transitions in Japan. *Social Science Research,* 40: 460–472.

Read, Jen'nan Ghazal. 2007. More of a Bridge Than a Gap: Gender Differences in Arab-American Political Engagement. *Social Science Quarterly* (December), 88: 1072–1091.

Reardon, Sean F., Lindsay Fox, and Joseph Townsend. 2015. Neighborhood Income Composition by Household Race and Income, 1990–2009. *Annals of the American Academy of Political and Social Sciences,* 660 (Issue 1, July 2015): 78–97.

Reardon, Sean F., and Ann Owens. 2014. 60 Years After *Brown* Trends and Consequences of School Segregation. *Annual Review of Sociology,* 40: 199–218.

Reckard, E. Scott. 2007. A Power Shift in Koreatown. *Los Angeles Times* (May 25): C1, C4.

Regan, Pamela C., Saloni Lakhanpal, and Carlos Anguiano. 2012. Relationship Outcomes in Indian-American Love-Based and Arranged Marriages. *Psychological Reports,* 110 (3): 915–924.

Reid, Catherine K., Debbie Bocian, We Li, and Roberto G. Quercia. 2017. Revisiting the Subprime Crisis: The Dual Mortgage Market and Mortgage Defaults by Race and Ethnicity. *Journal of Urban Affairs,* 39: forthcoming.

Reskin, Barbara F. 2012. The Race Discrimination System. *Annual Review of Sociology:* 38.

Reskin, Barbara F., and Patricia A. Roos. 2009. *Job Queues, Gender Queues.* Philadelphia, PA: Temple University Press.

Rhee, Nissa 2016. Segregation Nation. *Christian Science Monitor* (September 17): 25–32.

Ribas-Mateos, Natalia. 2015. A Border Laboratory? The Mexican-U.S. Border as a Reference. In Natalia Ribas-Mateos (Ed.), *Border Shifts: New Mobilities in Europe and Beyond,* pp. 56–91. New York, NY: Springer.

Rich, Motoko. 2013. Creationists on Texas Panel for Biology Textbooks. *New York Times* (September 29): 16, 20.

Richey, Warren. 2016. A Florist Caught Between Faith and Discrimination. *Christian Science Monitor* (August 15): 26–32.

Richmond, Anthony H. 2002. Globalization: Implications for Immigrants and Refugees. *Ethnic and Racial Studies* (September), 25: 707–727.

Ríos, Kristopher. 2011. After Long Fight, Farmworkers in Florida Win an Increase in Pay. *New York Times* (January 19): A11.

Riosmena, Fernando, Elisabeth Root, Jamie Humphrey, Emily Steiner, and Rebecca Stubbs. 2015. The Waning Hispanic Health Paradox. *Pathways* (Spring): 24-29.

Robbins, Liz. 2015. With an Influx of Newcomers, Little Chinatowns Face a Changing Brooklyn. *New York Times* (April 16): A21–A22.

Roberts, Sam. 2011. Little Italy, Littler by the Year. *New York Times* (February 22): A19.

Robertson, Dwanna L. 2012. Myth of Indian Casino Riches. *This Week from Indian Country Today* (September 12): 9.

Robinson, Greg. 2001. *By Order of the President: FDR and the Internment of Japanese Americans.* Cambridge: Harvard University Press.

———. 2009. *A Tragedy of Democracy: Japanese Confinement in North America.* New York: Columbia University Press.

———. 2012. *After Camp: Portraits in Midcentury Japanese Americans Life and Politics.* Berkeley: University of California Press.

Robles, Frances. 2017. 23% of Puerto Ricans Vote in Referendum, 97% of Them for Statehood. *New York Times* (June 11). Accessible at www.nytimes.com.

Robnett, Belinda, and Cynthia Feliciano. 2011. Patterns of Racial-Ethnic Exclusion by Internet Daters. *Social Forces,* 80 (No. 3, March): 807, 828.

Roediger, David R. 1994. *Towards the Abolition of Whiteness: Essays on Race, Politics, and Working Class History (Haymarket).* New York: Verso Books.

———. 2006. Whiteness and Its Complications. *Chronicle of Higher Education* (July 14), 52: B6–B8.

———. 2009. To Be Continued? The "Problem of the Color-Line" in the Twenty-First Century. Pp 281-286 in *Twenty-First Century Color Lines,* Andrew Grant-Thomas and Gary Orfield, eds. Philadelphia: Temple University Press.

Roodt, Marius. 2008. Xenophobic Violence: Simmering Volcano or Nasty Surprise? *Fast Facts* (August): 4–7.

Roof, Wade Clark. 2007. Introduction. *The Annals* (July), 612: 6–12.

Roscigno, Vincent J., and Theresa Schmidt. 2007. How Sexual Harassment Happens. Pp. 73–88 in *The Face of Discrimination,* Vincent J. Roscigno. Lanham, MD: Rowman & Littlefield.

Rose, Arnold. 1951. *The Roots of Prejudice.* Paris: UNESCO.

Rosenberg, Tom. 2000. Changing My Name After 60 Years. *Newsweek* (July 17), 136: 10.

Rosenbloom, Raquel. 2014. Being Jewish in Buenos Aires. Berkley Center for Religion, Peace, and World Affairs. Accessible at https://berkleycenter.georgetown.edu/posts/being-jewish-in-buenos-aires.

Rosenstiel, Thomas B. 1990. Paper's Editorial Sparks Racial Uproar In Philadelphia: Media: *The Inquirer* Advocated That Poor Black Women Be Encouraged to Use New Long-Term Birth Control Implants. *New York Times* (December 20). Accessible at www.nytimes.com.

Roth, Wendy D. 2012. *Race Migrations: Latinos and the Cultural Transformation of Race.* Stanford: Stanford University Press.

Roth, Wendy D., and Nadia Y. Kim. 2013. Relocating Prejudice: A Transnational Approach to Understanding Immigrants' Racial Attitudes. *International Migration Review* 47 (Summer): 330–373.

Rothstein, Edward. 2006. The Anti-Semitic Hoax That Refuses to Die. *New York Times* (April 21): B27, B37.

Rouse, Stella M., Betina Cutaia Wilkinson, and James C. Garand. 2010. Divided Loyalties? Understanding Variation in Latino Attitudes Toward Immigration. *Social Science Quarterly*, 91 (September): 856–882.

Rudwick, Elliott. 1957. The Niagara Movement. *Journal of Negro History* (July), 42: 177–200.

Rugh, Jacob S. 2015. Double Jeopardy: Why Latinos Were Hit Hardest by the US Foreclosure Crisis. *Social Forces*, 93 (3): 1139–1184.

Rugh, Jacob S., Len Albright, and Douglas S. Massey. 2015. Race, Space, and Cumulative Disadvantage: A Case Study of the Subprime Lending Collapse. *Social Problems*, 62: 186–218.

Rugh, Jacob S., and Douglas S. Massey. 2014. Segregation in Post–Civil Rights America: Stalled Integration or End of the Segregated Century? *DuBois Review*, 11 (2): 205–232.

Rumbaut, Ruben G., Douglas S. Massey, and Frank D. Bean. 2006. Linguistic Life Expectancies: Immigrant Language Retention in Southern California. *Population and Development Review* (September), 32: 447–460.

Russell, Jan Jarboe. 2015. *The Train to Crystal City*. New York: Scribner.

Russell, Stephen T., Lisa J. Crockett, and Ruth K. Chao. 2010. Asian American Parenting and Parent-Adolescent Relationships. *Journal of Youth and Adolescence*, 40: 245–247.

Russell, Steve. 2011. Of Blood and Citizenship. *Indian County Today* (July 27): 22–29.

Ryan, Camile. 2013. Language Use in the United States: 2011. *American Community Survey Report* (August 2013). Accessible at http://www.census.gov.

Ryan, Patrick. 2016. Streaming, Cable Networks' Diversity Record Is … Diverse. *USA Today* (November 2): 3D.

Ryan, William. 1976. *Blaming the Victim*, rev. ed. New York: Random House.

Saad, Lydia. 2006. Anti-Muslim Sentiments Fairly Commonplace. *The Gallup Poll* (August 10).

———. 2015. Children a Key Factor in Women's Desire to Work Outside the Home. October 7. Accessible at www.gallup.com.

Sabar, Ariel. 2015. The Anti-Redskin. *The Atlantic* (October): 24–26.

Sachs, Susan. 2001. For Newcomers, a Homey New Chinatown. *New York Times* (July 22): A1, A44.

Sadker, David. 2016. *Teachers, Schools, and Society: A Brief Introduction.* 4th ed. New York: McGraw-Hill.

Sahgal, Neha. 2013. *Miss America Pageant Puts Indian Americans in the Spotlight.* (September 16.) Accessible at http://www.pewresearch.org.

Said, Edward. 1978. *Orientalism.* New York: Viking.

Salée, Daniel. 1994. Identity Politics and Multiculturalism in Quebec. *Cultural Survival Quarterly* (Summer–Fall): 89–94.

Sandage, Diane. 2008. Peltier, Leonard. Pp. 1033–1035 in vol. 2, *Encyclopedia of Race, Ethnicity, and Society*, Richard T. Schaefer, ed. Thousand Oaks, CA: Sage.

Santos-Hernández, Jennifer M. 2008. Puerto Rican Armed Forces of National Liberation. Pp. 1084–1085 in vol. 2, *Encyclopedia of Race, Ethnicity, and Society*, Richard T. Schaefer, ed. Thousand Oaks, CA: Sage.

Sanua, Marianne R. 2007. AJC and Intermarriage: The Complexities and Jewish Continuity, 1960–2006. Pp. 3–32 in *American Jewish Yearbook 2007*, David Singer and Lawrence Grossman, eds. New York: American Jewish Committee.

Saperstein, Aliya, and Andrew M. Penner. 2012. Racial Fluidity and Inequality in the United States. *American Journal of Sociology*, 118 (3): 676–727.

Sarkisian, Natalia, Mariana Gerena, and Naomi Gerstel. 2007. Extended Family Integration Among Euro and Mexican Americans: Ethnicity, Gender, and Class. *Journal of Marriage and Family* (February), 69: 40–54.

Sassler, Sharon L. 2006. School Participation Among Immigrant Youths: The Case of Segmented Assimilation in the Early 20th Century. *Sociology of Education*, 79 (January): 1–24.

Sataline, Suzanne. 2009. Muslims Press for School Holidays in New York City. *Wall Street Journal* (September 15): H10.

Saulny, Susan. 2011. Black? White? Asian? More Young Americans Choose All of the Above. *New York Times* (January 29): A1, A17–A18.

Schachter, Ariela. 2016. From "Different" to "Similar": An Experimental Approach to Understanding Assimilation. *American Sociological Review*, 81 (5): 981–1013.

Schaefer, Richard T. 1971. The Ku Klux Klan: Continuity and Change. *Phylon* (Summer), 32: 143–157.

———. 1976. *The Extent and Content of Racial Prejudice in Great Britain.* San Francisco: R&E Research Associates.

———. 1980. The Management of Secrecy: The Ku Klux Klan's Successful Secret. Pp. 161–177 in *Secrecy: A Cross-Cultural Perspective*, Stanton K. Tefft, ed. New York: Human Sciences Press.

———. 1986. Racial Prejudice in a Capitalist State: What Has Happened to the American Creed? *Phylon*, 47 (September): 192–198.

———. 1992. People of Color: The "Kaleidoscope" May Be a Better Way to Describe America Than "the Melting Pot." *Peoria Journal Star* (January 19): A7.

———. 1996. Education and Prejudice: Unraveling the Relationship. *Sociological Quarterly* (January), 37: 1–16.

———. 2008b. Nativism. Pp. 611–612 in vol. 1, *Encyclopedia of Social Problems*, Vincent N. Parrillo, ed. Thousand Oaks, CA: Sage.

Schaefer, Richard T., and Sandra L. Schaefer. 1975. Reluctant Welcome: U.S. Responses to the South Vietnamese Refugees. *New Community* (Autumn), 4: 366–370.

Schaefer, Richard T., and William Zellner. 2015. *Extraordinary Groups*, 9th ed. Long Grove, IL: Waveland Press.

Schick, Marvin. 2014. *A Census of Jewish Day Schools in the United States 2013–2014.* New York: AVI CHAI Foundation of North America.

Schlossberg, Tatiana. 2014. An Indian Tribe Faces Its Eroding Fortunes. *New York Times* (December 1): A22, A24.

Schulz, Amy J. 1998. Navajo Women and the Politics of Identity. *Social Problems* (August), 45: 336–352.

Schwartz, John. 1994. Preserving Endangered Speeches. *Washington Post National Weekly Edition* (March 21), 11: 38.

Schwartz, Margaret. 2006. A Question in the Shape of Your Body. Pp. 9–14 in *Half/Life: Jewish Tales from Interfaith Homes*, Laurel Synder, ed. Brooklyn, NY: Soft Skull Press.

———. 2008. Argentina. Pp. 87–89 in vol. 1, *Encyclopedia of Race, Ethnicity, and Society*, Richard T. Schaefer, ed. Thousand Oaks, CA: Sage.

Schwartz, Pepper. 1992. Sex as a Social Problem. Pp. 794–819 in *Social Problems*, Craig Calhoun and George Ritzer, eds. New York: McGraw-Hill.

Schweimler, Daniel. 2007. Argentina's Last Jewish Cowboys (February 12). Accessed September 5, 2008, at http://www.bbc.com.

Scigliana, Eric. 2013. Bellevue Mosque: The Only Mosque in Town. *Crosscut: News of Great Nearby* (March 30). Accessible at www.crosscut.com.

Scott, Mark, and Melissa Eddy. 2016. Hate Speech Laws Test Facebook. *New York Times* (November 29): B1, B3.

Scully, Marc. 2012. Whose Day Is It Anyway? St. Patrick's Day as a Contested Performance of National and Diasporic Irishness. *Studies in Ethnicity and Nationalism*, 12 (1): 118–135.

Sears, David O., and J. B. McConahay. 1969. Participation in the Los Angeles Riot. *Social Problems* (Summer), 17: 3–20.

———. 1970. Racial Socialization, Comparison Levels, and the Watts Riot. *Journal of Social Issues* (Winter), 26: 121–140.

———. 1973. *The Politics of Violence: The New Urban Blacks and the Watts Riots.* Boston: Houghton-Mifflin.

Selod, Saher. 2013. The Politics of Islamophobia: Race, Power, and Fantasy. *Sociology of Race and Ethnicity*, 2 (1): 120–124.

Selod, Saher, and David G. Embrick. 2013. Racialization and Muslims: Situating the Muslim Experience in Race Scholarship. *Sociology Compass*, 7/8: 644–655.

Selzer, Michael. 1972. *"Kike": Anti-Semitism in America.* New York: Meridian.

Semple, Kirk. 2016. U.S., Shifting Policy, Will Step Up Deportations of Haitians. *New York Times* (September 23): A4.

Shah, Priyank G. 2012. *Asian Americans' Achievement Advantage: When and Why Does It Emerge?* Dissertation. The Ohio State University.

Shanklin, Eugenia. 1994. *Anthropology and Race.* Belmont, CA: Wadsworth.

Shapiro, Joseph P. 1993. *No Pity: People with Disabilities Forging a New Civil Rights Movement.* New York: Times Books.

Sharkey, Patrick. 2014. Spatial Segmentation and the Black Middle Class. *American Journal of Sociology,* 119 (January): 903–954.

Sherman, C. Bezalel. 1974. Immigration and Emigration: The Jewish Case. Pp. 51–55 in *The Jew in American Society,* Marshall Sklare, ed. New York: Behrman House.

Sheskin, Ira, and Arnold Dashefsky. 2015. Jewish Population in the United States, 2015. *Current Jewish Population Reports* (Number 13). Berman Jewish Databank. Accessible at www.jewishdatabank.org.

Shilts, Randy. 1982. *The Mayor of Castro Street: The Life and Times of Harvey Milk.* New York: St. Martin's.

Shin, Hyon B., and Robert A. Kominski. 2010. Language Use in the United States 2007. *Census Brief ACS-12.* Washington, DC: U.S. Government Printing Office.

Shufro, Cathy. 2008. The Daughter Effect: Legislators with Daughters Are More Liberal. *Yale Alumni Magazine* (July/August). Accessible at www.yalealumnimagazine.com.

Sigelman, Lee, and Steven A. Tuch. 1997. Metastereotypes: Blacks' Perception of Whites' Stereotypes of Blacks. *Public Opinion Quarterly,* 61 (Spring): 87–101.

Silberman, Charles E. 1971. *Crisis in the Classroom: The Remaking of American Education.* New York: Random House.

Simon Wiesenthal Center. 2008. *iReport: Online Terror + Hate: The First Decade.* Los Angeles: Simon Wiesenthal Center.

Simpson, Jacqueline C. 1995. Pluralism: The Evolution of a Nebulous Concept. *American Behavioral Scientist* (January), 38: 459–477.

Skrentny, John D. 2008. Culture and Race/Ethnicity: Bolder, Deeper, and Broader. *Annals* 619 (September): 59–77.

Slavin, Robert E., and Alan Cheung. 2003. *Effective Reading Programs for English Language Learners.* Baltimore: Johns Hopkins University, Center for Research on the Education of Students Placed at Risk.

Small, Cathy A. 2011. *Voyages: From Tongan Villages to American Suburbs,* 2nd ed. Ithaca, NY: Cornell University Press.

Smith, Bryan. 2015. Spike Lee Sounds Off on Chi-Raq, Gun Violence, and Rahm. *Chicago* (October 22).

Smith, Gregory A., and Jessica Martínez. 2016. How the Faithful Voted: A Preliminary 2016 Analysis. November 9. Accessible at www.pewresearch.org.

Smith, Julian. 2011. Insider: Who Owns the Dead? *Archaeology,* 64 (January/February).

Smith, Mitch. 2014. Decades of Neglect Show Starkly As Indian Schools Cry Out for Repairs. *New York Times* (November 14): A12, A16.

Smith, Stacy L., Marc Choueiti, and Katherine Pieper. 2016. *Media, Diversity, and Social Change Initiative.* Los Angeles: USC Annenberg School for Communication and Journalism.

Smith, Tom W. 2006. *Taking America's Pulse III. Intergroup Relations in Contemporary America.* Chicago: National Opinion Research Center, University of Chicago.

Snipp, C. Matthew. 1989. *American Indians: The First of This Land.* New York: Sage.

Social Security Administration. 2017. *Asian Americans and Pacific Islanders.* Accessible at www.ssa.gov/people/aapi.

Society for Human Resource Management. 2010. *Workplace Diversity Practices: How Has Diversity and Inclusion Changed over Time?* Alexandria, VA: SHRM.

———. 2011. *SHRM Survey Findings: An Examination of Organizational Commitment to Diversity and Inclusion.* Alexandria, VA: SHRM.

Soltas, Evan, and Seth Stephens-Davidowitz. 2015. Are All Muslims Terrorists? *New York Times* (December 13), sect. WK, 1, 6.

Soltero, Sonia White. 2008. Bilingual Education. Pp. 142–146 in vol. 1, *Encyclopedia of Race, Ethnicity, and Society,* Richard T. Schaefer, ed. Thousand Oaks, CA: Sage.

Somerville, Will, Jamie Durama, and Aaron Matteo Terrazas. 2008. Hometown Associations: An Untapped Resource for Immigrant Integration? *MPI Insight* (July).

Song, Tae-Hyon. 1991. *Social Contact and Ethnic Distance Between Koreans and the U.S. Whites in the United States.* M.A. thesis, Western Illinois University, Macomb.

Sorkin, Andrew Ross. 2017. Frantic Phoning Among CEOs: How to Address Trump Ban? *New York Times* (January 31): 1, 2.

South African Institute of Race Relations. 2007. *South Africa Survey 2006/2007.* Johannesburg: SAIRR.

———. 2010. *South Africa Survey 2009–2010.* Johannesburg: SAIRR.

———. 2011. *South Africa Survey 2010/2011.* Johannesburg: SAIRR.

Southern Poverty Law Center. 2010. *Ten Ways to Fight Hate: A Community Response Guide.* Montgomery, AL: SPLC.

———. (2015, 2017). *Speak Up: Responding to Everyday Bigotry.* January 25. Accessible at www.splcenter.org under Publications.

Stahler-Sholk, Richard. 2008. Zapatista Rebellion. Pp. 301–304 in vol. 2, *Encyclopedia of Race, Ethnicity, and Society,* Richard T. Schaefer, ed. Thousand Oaks, CA: Sage.

Stampp, Kenneth M. 1956. *The Peculiar Institution: Slavery in the Ante-Bellum South.* New York: Random House.

Stand with Standing Rock. 2017. Letter to President Trump. January 26. Accessible at www.standwithstandingrock.net.

Stansell, Christine. 2010. *The Feminist Promise: 1792 to the Present.* New York: The Modern Library.

Stark, Rodney, and Charles Glock. 1968. *American Piety: The Nature of Religious Commitment.* Berkeley, CA: University of California Press.

Statistics Canada. 2012. *Aboriginal Peoples.* (Modified December 24.) Accessed September 19, 2013, at http://www.statcan.gc.ca/pub/11-402-x/2012000pdf-eng.htm.

———. 2007. *Race Relations: A Critique.* Stanford, CT: Stanford University Press.

Statistics South Africa. 2016. Mid-Year Estimates 2016. August 25. Accessible at www.statsaa.gov.za.

Statista. 2017. The 20 Countries with the Highest Population Decline Rate in 2016 (Compared to the Previous Year). Accessible at www.statista.com.

Steinberg, Stephen. 2007. *Race Relations: A Critique.* Stanford, CA: Stanford University Press.

Steinhardt Social Research Institute. 2016. American Jewish Population Project. Accessible at http://ajpp.brandeis.edu/publications.php#section3.

Steinmetz, Erica. 2006. Americans with Disabilities: 2002. *Current Population Reports.* Ser. P70, No. 107. Washington, DC: U.S. Government Printing Office.

Stockman, Farah. 2017. Women's March on Washington Opens Contentious Dialogues About Race. *New York Times* (January 9). Accessible at www.nytimes.com.

Stone, Emily. 2006. Hearing the Call—In Polish. *Chicago Tribune* (October 13): 15.

Stonequist, Everett V. 1937. *The Marginal Man: A Study in Personality and Culture Conflict.* New York: Scribner's.

Stout, David. 2000. At Indian Bureau, a Milestone and an Apology. *New York Times* (September 9): A47.

Strong, John A. 1998. *"We Are Still Here!" The Algonquian Peoples of Long Island Today,* 2nd ed. Interlaken, NY: Empire State Books.

Sturtevant, William C., and Jessica R. Cattelino. 2004. Florida Seminole and Miccosukee. Pp. 429–449 in *Handbook of North American Indians (Southeast),* Vol. 14, R. D. Fogelson, ed. Washington, DC: Smithsonian Institution Press.

Sue, Christina A. 2013. *Land of the Cosmic Race: Race Mixture, Racism, and Blackness in Mexico.* New York: Oxford University Press.

Sue, Derald Wing. 2010. *Microaggressions in Everyday Life: Race, Gender, and Sexual Orientation.* New York: John Wiley.

Sulzberger, A. G. 2011. Hispanics Reviving Faded Towns on the Plains. *New York Times* (November 14): A1, A20.

Supreme Court. 1923. *United States v. Bhagat Singh Thind.* Decided February 19. *United States Reprints,* v. 261, October Term, 1922, 204–215.

Swagerty, William R. 1983. Native Peoples and Early European Contacts. Pp. 15–16 in *Encyclopedia of American Social History,* Mary Kupiec Clayton, Elliot J. Gorn, and Peter W. Williams, eds. New York: Scribner's.

Swarns, Rachel L. 2015. Long Banned, Mortgage Bias Is Back as Issue. *New York Times* (October 21): A1, A3.

Takaki, Ronald. 1998. *Strangers from a Different Shore: A History of Asian Americans.* Updated and revised. Boston, MA: Little, Brown, Back Bay edition.

Takezawa, Yasuko I. 1991. Children of Inmates: The Effects of the Redress Movement Among Third Generation Japanese Americans. *Qualitative Sociology* (Spring), 14: 39–56.

Talbot, Steve. 2015. *Native Nations of North America: An Indigenous Perspective.* New York: Pearson.

Tannenbaum, Frank. 1946. *Slave and Citizen.* New York: Random House.

Tavory, Iddo. 2016. *Summoned.* Chicago, IL: University of Chicago Press.

Taylor, Keeanga-Yamahtta. 2016. *From #BlackLivesMatter to Black Liberation.* Chicago: Haymarket Books.

Taylor, Paul (Ed.). 2013. *The Rise of Asian Americans,* updated edition. Accessible at www.pewresearch.com.

Taylor, Stuart, Jr. 1987. High Court Backs Basing Promotion on a Racial Quota. *New York Times* (February 26): 1, 14.

Taylor, Verta, Leila J. Rupp, and Nancy Whittier. 2009. *Feminist Frontiers,* 8th ed. New York: McGraw-Hill.

Telles, Edward E. 1992. Residential Segregation by Skin Color in Brazil. *American Sociological Review* (April), 57: 186–197.

———. 2004. *Race in Another America: The Significance of Skin Color in Brazil.* Princeton, NJ: Princeton University Press.

Telles, Edward E., and Vilma Ortiz. 2008. *Generations of Exclusion: Mexican Americans, Assimilation, and Race.* New York: Russell Sage Foundation.

Telles, Edward, and Tianna Paschel. 2014. Who Is Black, White, or Mixed Race? How Skin Color, Status, and Nation Shape Racial Classification in Latin America. *American Journal of Sociology,* 120 (November): 864–907.

Telsch, Kathleen. 1991. New Study of Older Workers Finds They Can Become Good Investments. *New York Times* (May 21): A16.

ten Broek, Jacobus, Edward N. Barnhart, and Floyd W. Matson. 1954. *Prejudice, War and the Constitution.* Berkeley: University of California Press.

Teranishi, Robert T. 2010. *Asians in the Ivory Tower: Dilemmas of Racial Inequity in American Higher Education.* New York: Teachers College Press.

Thakore, Bhoomi C. 2014. Must-See TV: South Asian Characterizations in American Popular Media. *Sociology Compass,* 8 (2): 149–156.

Tharoor, Ishaan. 2015. What Americans Thought of Jewish Refugees on the Eve of World War II. *The Washington Post* (November 17). Accessible at www.washingtonpost.com.

Third World Institute. 2007. *The World Guide,* 11th ed. Oxford: New Internationalist.

Thomás Rivera Policy Institute. 2009. *Majority/Near-Majority of First Graders in Top Ten U.S. Cities Are Latino.* Released March 5.

Thomas, Curlew O., and Barbara Boston Thomas. 1984. Blacks' Socioeconomic Status and the Civil Rights Movement's Decline, 1970–1979: An Examination of Some Hypotheses. *Phylon* (March), 45: 40–51.

Thomas, Dorothy S., and Richard S. Nishimoto. 1946. *The Spoilage: Japanese-American Evacuation and Resettlement.* Berkeley: University of California Press.

Thomas, Oliver. 2007. So What Does the Constitution Say About Religion? *USA Today* (October 15): 15A.

Thomas, William Isaac. 1923. *The Unadjusted Girl.* Boston: Little, Brown.

Thomas, William Isaac, and Florian Znaniecki. 1996. *The Polish Peasant in Europe and America* (5 vols.), Eli Zaretsky, ed. Urbana: University of Illinois Press.

Thomason, Andy. 2015. The Long Strange Demise of North Dakota's "Fighting Sioux" Nickname. *The Chronicle of Higher Education* (October 30): A14.

Thompson, Ginger. 2005. Uneasily, a Latin Land Looks at Its Own Complexion. *New York Times* (May 19): A5.

Thompson, Ginger, and Sarah Cohen. 2014. More Deportations Follow Minor Crimes, Data Shows. *New York Times* (April 7): A1, A12.

Thurgood Marshall College Fund. 2017. Historically Black Colleges and Universities. Accessible at www.tmcf.org.

Time. 1974. Are You a Jew? (September 2), 104: 56, 59.

Timerman, Jacob. 2002. *Prisoner Without a Name, Cell Without a Number.* Madison: University of Wisconsin Press.

Timiraos, Nick. 2016. Exodus Worsens Puerto Rico's Crisis. *Wall Street Journal* (June 30): A1, A8.

Tizon, Thomas Alex. 2004. Internment Lesson Plan Is Under Attack. *Los Angeles Times* (September 12): A21.

Toensing, Gale Courey. 2011. Recession-Proof Is in the Pudding. *Indian Country Today* (April 13): 28–31.

Tomaskovic-Devey, Donald, and Patricia Warren. 2009. Explaining and Eliminating Racial Profiling. *Contexts,* 8 (Spring): 34–39.

Tomlinson, T. M. 1969. The Development of a Riot Ideology Among Urban Negroes. Pp. 226–235 in *Racial Violence in the United States,* Allen D. Grimshaw, ed. Chicago: Aldine.

Tonelli, Bill. 2004. *Arrivederci, Little Italy.* (September 27.) Accessed August 28, 2013, at http://nymag.com/nymetro/urban/features/9904/.

Tong, Benson. 2000. *The Chinese Americans.* Westport, CT: Greenwood Press.

Toppo, Greg, and Paul Overberg. 2014. Second Immigration Wave Reshapes Nation. *USA Today* (October 22): 1A, 5A.

Torkelson, Jason and Douglas Hartmann. 2010. White Ethnicity in Twenty-First-Century America: Findings from a New National Survey. *Ethnic and Racial Studies,* 33 (8): 1310–1331.

Townsend, Sarah S. M., Hazel R. Markos, and Hilary Bergsieker. 2009. My Choice, Your Categories: The Denial of Multiracial Identities. *Journal of Social Issues,* 65 (1): 185–204.

Tran, My-Thuan. 2008. Their Nation Lives On. *Los Angeles Times* (April 30): B1, B8–B9.

Tredoux, Colin, and Gillian Finchilescu. 2010. Mediators of the Contact-Prejudice Relation Among South African Students on Four University Campuses. *Journal of Social Issues,* 66 (2): 289–308.

Truman, Jennifer L., and Rachel E. Morgan. 2016. *Criminal Victimization, 2015.* October. Accessible at www.bjs.gov.

Truth and Reconciliation Commission of Canada. 2015. *Final Report of Truth and Reconciliation Commission of Canada. Volume One: Summary.* Ottawa: Truth and Reconciliation Commission of Canada.

Tsuda, Takeyuki. 2014. "I'm American, Not Japanese!": The Struggle for Racial Citizenship Among Later-Generation Japanese Americans. *Ethnic and Racial Studies,* 37 (3): 405–424.

———. 2016. *Japanese American Ethnicity: In Search of Heritage and Homeland Across Generations.* New York: New York University Press.

Tsui, Bonnie. 2011. The End of Chinatown. *The Atlantic* (December): 17–18.

Ture, Kwame, and Charles Hamilton. 1992. *Black Power: The Politics of Liberation.* New York: Vintage Books.

Turkewitz, Julie. 2015. Revisiting a World War II Internment Camp, As Others Try to Keep Its Story from Fading. *New York Times* (May 19): A9, A12.

Turner, Ralph H. 1994. Race Riots Past and Present: A Cultural-Collective Approach. *Symbolic Interaction,* 17 (3): 309–324.

Turner, Richard Brent. 2003. *Islam in the African-American Experience,* 2nd ed. Bloomington: Indiana University Press.

Two Bridges. 2017. Two Bridges Neighborhood Council. Accessible at www.twobridges.org.

Twohey, Megan. 2007. Outside, It's Suburban; Inside, It's Japan. *Chicago Tribune* (December 29): 1, 2.

Tyson, Alec, and Shiva Maniam. 2016. Behind Trump's Victory: Divisions by Race, Gender, Education. November 9. Accessible at www.pewresearch.org.

Tyson, Ann Scott. 1996. Alabama Ferry to Bridge Racial Divide. *USA Today* (February 13), Sect. 4: 4.

Tyson, Karolyn. 2011. *Integration Interrupted: Tracking, Black Students, & Acting White After Brown.* New York: Oxford University Press.

———. 2013. Tracking, Segregation, and the Opportunity Gap: What We Know and Why It Matters. Chapter 12 in *Closing the Opportunity Gap: What America Must Do to Give Every Child an Even Chance*. Edited by Prudence L. Carter and Kevin G. Welner. New York: Oxford University Press.

Uchitelle, L. 2003. Older Workers Are Thriving Despite Recent Hard Times. *New York Times* (September 8): A1, A15.

Uhlig, Keith. 2015. Gang Accusations, Racial Taunts Spark Concern. *Wausau Daily Herald* (March 15): A01.

Ulrich, Roberta. 2010. *American Indian Nations from Termination to Restoration, 1953–2006*. Corvallis, OR: Oregon State University Press.

United Jewish Communities. 2003. *The National Jewish Population Survey 2000–01*. New York: United Jewish Community.

United Nations High Commission on Refugees. 2015. Figures at a Glance. Accessible at www.unchr.org.

———. 2016. Indicators of host country capacity and contributions, mid-2015. Accessible at www.unchr.org.

USA Today. 2017. A Look at the 115th Congress (February 15): 9A.

U.S. Conference of Catholic Bishops. Hispanic/Latino Affairs. Accessible at www.usccb.org.

U.S. English. 2017. Official English. Accessible at www.usenglish.org/official-english/.

van den Berghe, Pierre L. 1965. *South Africa: A Study in Conflict*. Middletown, CT: Wesleyan University.

———. 1978. *Race and Racism: A Comparative Perspective*, 2nd ed. New York: Wiley.

Vanetik, Yuri, and Thomas Tucker. 2015. Many Hispanics Agree with Donald Trump on Enforcing the Border. *Chicago Tribune* (October 8). Accessible at www.chicagotribune.com.

Van Landingham, Mark J. 2015. Post-Katrina, Vietnamese Success. *New York Times* (August 16): 10.

Vang, Chia Youyee. 2010. *Hmong America: Reconstructing Community in America*. Champaign: University of Illinois Press.

Vega, Irene I. 2014. Conservative Rationales, Racial Boundaries: A Case Study of Restrictionist Mexican Americans. *American Behavioral Scientist*, 58 (13): 1764–1783.

Vian, Jourdan. 2016. La Crosse Mayors, Community Pledge to Work Toward Equality. *La Crosse Tribune* (December 9). Accessible at www.lacrossetribune.com.

Victor, Daniel. 2017. "White Privilege" Essay Contest for Students Stirs Up Connecticut Town. *New York Times* (February 4): A18.

Viera, Paul. 2014. Liberals Beat Separatists in Quebec Election. *Wall Street Journal* (April 8): A16.

Vincent, Louise. 2008. The Limitations of "Inter-racial Contact" Stories from Young South Africa. *Ethnic and Racial Studies*, 31 (November): 1426–1451.

Visitability. 2013. *Visitability*. Accessed November 10, 2013, at http://www.visitability.org.

Vonderlack-Navarro, Rebecca, and William Sites. 2015. The Bi-National Road to Immigrant Rights Mobilization: States, Social Movements, and Chicago's Mexican Hometown Associations. *Ethnic and Racial Studies*, 38 (1): 141–157.

Wacquant, Loïc. 2007. *Urban Outcasts: A Comparative Sociology of Advanced Marginality*. New York: Polity.

Wagley, Charles, and Marvin Harris. 1958. *Minorities in the New World: Six Case Studies*. New York: Columbia University Press.

Wagmiller, Jr., Robert L., and Kristen Schulz Lee. 2014. Are Contemporary Patterns of Black Male Joblessness Unique? Cohort Replacement, Intracohort Change, and White Men's Employment. *Social Problems*, 61 (2): 305–327.

Waitzkin, Howard. 1986. *The Second Sickness: Contradictions of Capitalistic Health Care*, rev. ed. New York: Free Press.

Waldinger, Roger. 2007. *Between Here and There: How Attached Are Latino Immigrants to Their Native Country?* Washington, DC: Pew Hispanic Center.

———. 2015. *The Cross-Border Connection: Immigrants and Their Homelands*. Cambridge, MA: Harvard University Press.

Waldman, Carl. 1985. *Atlas of North American Indians*. New York: Facts on File.

Walgreens. 2013. *Recognizing Talent: Facing Stereotypes*. Accessed September 23, 2013, at http://www.walgreens.com/topic/sr/recognizing_talent.jsp.

Wall Street Journal. 2011. Tiger Mom's Long-Distance Cub. (December 24).

Wallace, Jean E., and Fiona M. Kay. 2012. Tokenism, Organizational Segregation, and Coworker Relations in Law Firms. *Social Problems*, 59 (3): 389–410.

Waller, David. 1996. Friendly Fire: When Environmentalists Dehumanize American Indians. *American Indian Culture and Research Journal*, 20 (2): 107–126.

Wallerstein, Immanuel. 1974. *The Modern World System*. New York: Academic Press.

———. 2004. *World-Systems Analysis: An Introduction*. Durham, NC: Duke University Press.

Waln, Vi. 2016. Kinship in Modern Times. *Lakota Country Times* (September 29). Accessible at http://www.lakotacountrytimes.com/news/2016-09-29/Voices/Kinship_In_Modern_Times.html.

Walzer, Susan. 1996. Thinking About the Baby. Gender and Divisions of Infant Care. *Social Problems* (May), 43: 219–234.

Wang, L. Ling-Chi. 1991. Roots and Changing Identity of the Chinese in the United States. *Daedalus* (Spring), 120: 181–206.

Wark, Colin, and John F. Galliher. 2007. Emory Bogardus and the Origins of the Social Distance Scale. *American Sociologist*, 38: 383–395.

Warner, W. Lloyd, and Leo Srole. 1945. *The Social Systems of American Ethnic Groups*. New Haven, CT: Yale University.

Warry, Wayne. 2007. *Ending Denial: Understanding Aboriginal Issues*. Orchard Park, NY: Broadview Press.

Washburn, Wilcomb E. 1984. A Fifty-Year Perspective on the Indian Reorganization Act. *American Anthropologist* (June), 86: 279–289.

Washington, Booker T. 1900. *Up from Slavery: An Autobiography*. New York: A. L. Burt.

Washington, Harriet. 2007. *Medical Apartheid: The Dark History of Medical Experimentation on Black Americans from Colonial Times to Present*. New York: Doubleday.

Watanabe, Teresa. 2007. Reclaiming Cultural Ties. *Los Angeles Times* (May 13): B1, B13.

Waters, Mary. 1990. *Ethnic Options. Choosing Identities in America*. Berkeley: University of California Press.

Waters, Mary C., Philip Kasinitz, and Asad L. Asad. 2014. Immigration and African Americans. *Annual Review of Sociology*, 40: 369–390.

Wausau School District. 2016. *Student Demographics 2016–2017*. October 24. Accessible at www.wausauschools.org.

Wax, Murray L. 1971. *Indian Americans: Unity and Diversity*. Englewood Cliffs, NJ: Prentice Hall.

Wax, Murray L., and Robert W. Buchanan. 1975. *Solving "the Indian Problem": The White Man's Burdensome Business*. New York: New York Times Book Company.

Weber, Rebecca L. 2014. "Born Frees" Show Little Interest in S. Africa Election. *USA Today* (May 7): 7A.

Weber, Max. 1947. *The Theory of Social and Economic Organization* [1913–1922], trans. by Henderson and T. Parsons. New York: Free Press.

The Week. 2016. The Tiger Mom's Children. (February 19): 12.

Weinberg, Daniel H. 2004. Evidence from Census 2000 About Earnings by Detailed Occupation for Men and Women. *CENSR-15*. Washington, DC: U.S. Government Printing Office.

Weiner, Rebecca. 2008. *The Virtual Jewish History Tour*. Accessed September 8, 2008, at http://www.jewishvirtuallibrary.org/jsource/vjw/Argentina.html.

Weiner, Tim. 2004. Of Gringos and Old Grudges: This Land Is Their Land. *New York Times* (January 9): A4.

Weiser, Benjamin. 2013a. Swastikas, Slurs and Torment in Town's Schools. *New York Times* (November 8): A1, A20.

———. 2013b. Cuomo Orders Investigation into Claims of Anti-Semitic Acts in a School District. *New York Times* (November 8). Accessible at http://www.nytimes.com.

Welch, William M. 2011. More Hawaii Resident Identify as Mixed Race. *USA Today* (February 28).

Whitman, David. 1987. For Latinos, a Growing Divide. *U.S. News and World Report* (August 10), 103: 47–49.

Wickham, De Wayne. 1993. Subtle Racism Thrives. *USA Today* (October 25): 2A.

Wiesel, Elie. 2006. *Night* (trans. from French by Marion Wiesel). New York: Hill and Wang.

Wijeyesinghe, Charmaine L., and Bailey W. Jackson III. 2012. *New Perspectives on Racial Identity Development: Integrating Emerging Frameworks,* 2nd ed. New York: New York University Press.

Wilder, Craig Steven. 2013. *Ebony & Ivory: Race, Slavery, and the Troubled History of America's Universities.* New York: Bloomsbury.

Willeto, Angela A. 1999. Navajo Culture and Female Influences on Academic Success: Traditional Is Not a Significant Predictor of Achievement Among Young Navajos. *Journal of American Indian Education* (Winter), 38: 1–24.

———. 2007. Native American Kids: American Indian Children's Well-Being Indicators for the Nation and Two States. *Social Indicators Research* (August), 83: 149–176.

Williams, Carol J. 2006. Puerto Rico Could Soon Get Real Vote on Status. *Los Angeles Times* (February 17): A15.

Williams, Carol J. 2007. Emotions Run High in Puerto Rican Debate. *Los Angeles Times* (April 26): A27.

Williams, Kim M. 2005. Multiculturalism and the Civil Rights Future. *Daedalus,* 134 (1): 53–60.

Williams, Timothy. 2012a. U.S. Will Pay a Settlement of $1 Billion to 41 Tribes. *New York Times* (April 14): A10.

———. 2012b. Sioux Racing to Find Billions to Buy Sacred Land in Black Hills. *New York Times* (October 4): A1, A20.

———. 2012c. $1 Million Each Year for All, Until Tribe's Luck Runs Out. *New York Times* (August 9): A1, A4.

———. 2013. Quietly, Indians Reshape Cities and Reservations. *New York Times* (April 14): 14.

Willoughby, Brian. 2004. *10 Ways to Fight Hate on Campus.* Montgomery, AL: Southern Poverty Law Center.

Wilson, William Julius. 1973. *Power, Racism and Privilege: Race Relations in Theoretical and Sociohistorical Perspectives.* New York: Macmillan.

———. 2011. The Declining Significance of Race: Revisited and Revised. *Annals of the American Academy of Arts and Sciences,* 140 (Spring): 55–69.

Winant, Howard. 1994. *Racial Conditions: Politics, Theory, Comparisons.* Minneapolis: University of Minnesota Press.

———. 2001. *The World Is a Ghetto: Race and Democracy Since World War II.* New York: Basic Books.

———. 2004. *The New Politics of Race: Globalism, Difference, Justice.* Minneapolis: University of Minnesota Press.

Winerip, Michael. 2011. New Influx of Haitians, But Not Who Was Expected. *New York Times* (January 16): 15, 22.

———. 2013. Three Men, Three Ages. Which Do You Like? *New York Times* (July 23): B1,B5.

Wines, Michael, and Stephanie Saul. 2015. Supremacists Extend Reach Through Web. *New York Times* (July 6): A1, A3.

Wingfield, Nick. 2014. Microsoft Chief Sets Off a Furor on Women's Pay. *New York Times* (October 10): 1, 7.

Winks, Robin W. 1971. *The Blacks in Canada: A History.* Montreal: McGill-Queen's University Press.

Winseman, Albert L. 2004. *U.S. Churches Looking for a Few White Men.* Accessed July 27, 2004, at http://www.gallup.com.

Winter, S. Alan. 2008. *Symbolic Ethnicity.* Pp. 1288–1290 in vol. 3, *Encyclopedia of Race, Ethnicity, and Society,* Richard T. Schaefer, ed. Thousand Oaks, CA: Sage.

Wisniewski, Mary. 2012. Transformed by Immigration, an Illinois Farm Town Thrives. *Chicago Tribune* (July 15). Accessible at http://www.chicagotribune.com.

Witt, Bernard. 2007. What Is a Hate Crime? *Chicago Tribune* (June 10): 1, 18.

Woesthoff, Julia M. 2008. Muslims in Europe. Pp. 925–928 in vol. 2, *Encyclopedia of Race, Ethnicity, and Society,* Richard T. Schaefer, ed. Thousand Oaks, CA: Sage.

Wolf, Richard. 2017. Court: Civil Rights Laws Cover LGBT Bias. *USA Today* (April 5): 1A, 3A.

Wolfe, Ann G. 1972. The Invisible Jewish Poor. *Journal of Jewish Communal Services,* 48 (3): 259–265.

Wong, Janelle, S. Karthick Ramakrishnan, Taeku Lee, and Jane Junn. 2011. *Asian American Political Participation: Emerging Constituents and Their Political Identities.* New York: Russell Sage Foundation.

Woodward, C. Vann. 1974. *The Strange Career of Jim Crow,* 3rd ed. New York: Oxford University Press.

Working, Russell. 2007. Illegal Abroad, Hate Web Sites Thrive Here. *Chicago Tribune* (November 13): A1, A15.

World Bank Group. 2016. *Migration and Remittance Factbook 2016.* Third Edition. Washington, DC: World Bank Group.

World DataBank. 2017. World Development Indicators. Accessible at www.worldbank.org.

Wozniacka, Gosia. 2011. United Farm Workers Fight Dwindling Membership. *Press Democrat* (Santa Rosa, CA) (April 20).

Wright II, Earl. 2006. W. E. B. Du Bois and the Atlantic University Studies on the Negro Revisited. *Journal of African American Studies,* 9 (4): 3–17.

Wright, Erik Olin. 2012. My Journey into the Deaf World: A Visit to Gallaudet University. *Footnotes* (March): 11–12.

Wu, Frank M. 2002. *Yellow: Race in America beyond Black and White.* New York: Basic Books.

Wyman, Mark. 1993. *Round-Trip to America. The Immigrants Return to Europe, 1830–1930.* Ithaca, NY: Cornell University Press.

Xu, Jun, and Jennifer C. Lee. 2013. The Marginalized "Model" Minority: An Empirical Examination of the Racial Triangulation of Asian Americans. *Social Forces,* 91 (4): 1363–1397.

Yamato, Jen. 2017. "Look what happens when we don't talk to each other": Korean American Filmmakers' L.A. Riots Stories. *Los Angeles Times* (April 2). Accessible at www.latimes.com.

Yancey, George. 2003. *Who Is White? Latinos, Asians, and the New Black–Nonblack Divide.* Boulder, CO: Lynne Rienner.

Yemma, John. 2013. Teaching the Freedom to Believe. 2013. *Christian Science Monitor* (June 17): 5.

Young, Jeffrey R. 2003. Researchers Charge Racial Bias on the SAT. *Chronicle of Higher Education* (October 10): A34–A35.

Zafar, Sadia, and Erin C. Ross. 2015. Interreligious Contact, Attitudes, and Stereotypes: A Study of Five Religious Groups in Canada. *Canadian Journal of Behavioural Science,* 47 (January): 37–46.

Zambrana, Ruth Enid. 2011. *Latinos in American Society: Families and Communities in Transition.* Ithaca: Cornell University Press.

Zarembro, Alan. 2004. Physician, Remake Thyself: Lured by Higher Pay and Heavy Recruiting, Philippine Doctors Are Getting Additional Degrees and Starting Over in the U.S. as Nurses. *Los Angeles Times* (January 10): A1, A10.

Zempi, Irene. 2016. "It's a Part of Me, I Feel Naked Without It": Choice, Agency, and Identity for Muslim Women Who Wear the Niqab. *Ethnic and Racial Studies,* 39 (10): 1738–1754.

Zeng, Zhen, and Yu Xie. 2004. Asian-Americans' Earnings Disadvantage Reexamined: The Role of Place of Education. *American Journal of Sociology* (March), 109: 1075–1108.

Zhao, Yilu. 2002. Chinatown Gentrifies, and Evicts. *New York Times* (August 23): A13.

Zhou, Min. 2009. *Contemporary Chinese America.* Philadelphia: Temple University Press.

Zimmerman, Seth. 2008. *Immigration and Economic Mobility.* Washington, DC: Economic Mobility Project.

Zittrain, Jonathan. 2008. *The Future of the Internet and How to Stop It. With a New Forward by Lawrence Lessig and New Preface by the Author.* New Haven: Yale University Press.

———. 2010. *51% Expect Major Terror Attack This Year and 25% Plan to Fly Less.* (February 4.) Accessed March 2, 2011, at http://www.zogby.com.

Zogby, James. *National Survey: American Teen-Agers and Stereotyping.* Submitted to National Italian American Foundation by Zogby International. Accessible at http://www.naif.org/research/report_zogby.asp?print=1&.

Zong, Jie, and Jeanne Batalova. 2014. *Korean Immigrants in the United States.* December 3. Accessible at www.migrationpolicy.org.

Index